Perspectives in Pragmatics, Philosophy & Psychology

Volume 10

More information about this series at http://www.springer.com/series/11797

Francesca Poggi • Alessandro Capone
Editors

Pragmatics and Law

Practical and Theoretical Perspectives

Springer

Editors
Francesca Poggi
Department of "Cesare Beccaria"
Section of Philosophy of Law
University of Milan
Milan, Italy

Alessandro Capone
Department of Humanities
University of Messina
Messina, Italy

ISSN 2214-3807 ISSN 2214-3815 (electronic)
Perspectives in Pragmatics, Philosophy & Psychology
ISBN 978-3-319-44599-1 ISBN 978-3-319-44601-1 (eBook)
DOI 10.1007/978-3-319-44601-1

Library of Congress Control Number: 2016959461

Printed on acid-free paper

This Springer imprint is published by Springer Nature
The registered company is Springer International Publishing AG
The registered company address is: Gewerbestrasse 11, 6330 Cham, Switzerland

Preface

This volume is the second part of a project which aims at exploring the last boundaries of the interdisciplinary studies concerning both legal theory and philosophy of language. The first part of the same project is represented by the book *Pragmatics and Law: Philosophical Perspective* (Springer, 2016). Here, using the most sophisticated tools available in the international debate, a group of experts in pragmatics, sociolinguistics, cognitive sciences, artificial intelligence and legal theory engage problems concerning the relationship between language and law to highlight the salient features of both phenomena.

Law is a linguistic phenomenon. Legal provisions of all levels (i.e. pertaining to constitutions, statutes, contracts, and so on) are written in natural language (even if with the addition of technical terms and in a peculiar style), and this language is supposed to guide citizens' everyday life and to ground the courts' decisions. Not surprising, some legal philosophers have claimed that law is language – it's the language of the sovereign (Bentham 2010, 45ff.) or the legislator (Bobbio 1950). Now everybody recognizes that picture as too simplistic. The law is not merely a set of signs carrying a meaning; it is a more complex phenomenon and a practice, but, as outlined by Hart (1961), a practice which presents peculiar linguistic features or which emerges at a linguistic level. Therefore, both legal experts and legal theorists engage with linguistic issues to solve practical legal problems (e.g. to interpret legal texts or to value the reliability of a testimony), to grasp the salient features of legal practice and/or to clarify the nature of law. It then is clear that the theories and concepts elaborated within the philosophy of language (in a broad sense) can help legal scholars in their tasks. A first issue that this book deals with is precisely how to employ tools pertaining to pragmatics, sociolinguistics, cognitive sciences and, more in general, philosophy of language to solve debated legal problems concerning the practice, the theory (i.e. the conceptualization of the practice) and the nature of law.

Not only can the philosophy of language improve our legal knowledge, but legal knowledge can improve the philosophy of language. In fact, the law represents a new field of investigation for linguistic experts – a field in which they can test their theories, explore their limits and enhance the knowledge of ordinary conversation by comparing it with legal language. In this comparison, legal philosophy is an essential speaker; its theories, conceptual instruments and problems are unavoidable coordinates for any discussion on law.

While the previous volume mainly faces problems related to the similarity and divergence between legal texts and ordinary conversations (and, therefore, between legal theory and philosophy of language), this book focuses on single relevant legal problems. It aims to solve these problems as well as to refine the conceptual tools elaborated within pragmatics, sociolinguistics, cognitive sciences and philosophy of language, testing their explicative power within the legal field.

In particular, this volume is divided into three parts. The first part, which includes seven chapters, is devoted to the problems of legal interpretation, i.e. the problems concerning the identification and understanding of the meaning of legal texts. The authors face questions such as what should count as the meaning of a legislative act, what is the role of the speaker's communicative intentions, and, especially, whether those intentions are decisive, must be limited by other factors (such as contextual elements and/or some kinds of rules) or do not play any salient role by themselves. These topics are inquired both in general (see Chaps. 1, 5, and 6) and in particular (see Chaps. 2, 3, 4, and 7).

General enquiries are conducted through reconstructions of the salient features of legal interpretation and proposals of a theoretical framework of legal meaning and/or of processes of grasping it while others focus in regard to more particular (although sometimes pervasive) aspects of legal interpretation such as legal implicit meanings, the phenomenon of legal vagueness, the possibility of non-literal legislative speech and the phenomenon of semantic battles. The authors do not all share the same theoretical background. To explain the aforementioned phenomena, they employ theoretical tools elaborated by different pragmatic/semantic approaches, from Brandom's inferentialism to Gricean and post-Gricean theories to (various forms of) contextualism. This enables the reader to get an idea of the different perspectives and to compare their explanatory force respect to legal interpretation.

More specifically, the content of the first part, *Pragmatics and Legal Interpretation*, is as follows. In Chap. 1, Kasia Jaszczolt addresses a very fundamental metasemantic question, namely what should count as meaning of expressions for the purpose of theoretical inquiry, and in particular what should count as the intended message of a legislative act. She claims that semantic theory ought to deal with intuitive meaning, that is, with the meaning intended by the speaker and recovered by the addressee, with the proviso that all goes well in assuming at one hand, and recovering at the other, the background that enables the interlocutors to leave some aspects of the message unsaid. This is called primary meaning. The core question, however, remains and concerns the kinds of contributions that context makes to this richly, contextually construed, truth-conditional representation. Jaszczolt demonstrates through selected examples that any attempt to regiment meaning by using the explicit/implicit distinction, directly referential/contextually referential, or indexical/non-indexical distinction do not yield the primary meaning intended and recovered in linguistic interaction. As a result, the question of accountability arises; if the primary meaning can be implicit, context-driven and multidimensional, then is it this meaning for which the speaker should be accountable? To ask this question, the author proposes a sophisticated version of salience-based contextualism and shows how it applies to represent the (legal) primary meaning in a famous court case.

In Chap. 2, Marina Sbisà claims that full comprehension of a text includes the grasping of its presuppositions (content the truth of which is taken for granted) and implicatures (content made available to the recipient in addition to what is said), insofar as these can be worked out by the receiver on the basis of linguistic triggers included in the text and under the assumption of Grice's Cooperative Principle (see Grice 1989, 22ff.) and therefore normatively determined. What she calls the 'normativity of implicitness' is thus a limit to arbitrariness in legal interpretation and enables the recipients of normative texts to exploit presuppositions and implicatures to get a more complete grasp of the normative background surrounding a norm, the motivations of the norm, its content and possible applications. Such an understanding, according to Sbisà, constitutes a premise both to one's capacity to conform to the norm and to one's ability to take a critical stance with respect to it. Sbisà exemplifies her approach to the practices of explicitation and their results by discussing two examples, one from the regulations of a condominium and another from a law proposal of the Italian Parliament.

Chapter 3 deals with the fundamental problems of the representation of meaning, or the role of the speaker's intention and context in legal interpretation, but it does so from a different perspective and employing different theoretical apparatus. Damiano Canale challenges the traditional picture according to which the full linguistic content of an authoritative legal sentence is what the author intended to communicate by uttering it in a given context, and, therefore, in the case of vague legal sentences, intentional content would be the only suitable means to determine whether a borderline case falls under the regulation in question. Canale argues that this picture does not provide a convincing explanation of how legal language works because it does not consider the peculiar characteristics of institutional legal contexts. Therefore he outlines an alternative account of linguistic content and vagueness in law based on Brandom's inferentialist approach to semantics and pragmatics (Brandon 1994, 2000, 2008). On this account vagueness is a feature of language which depends on a specific form of disagreement between the participants in an exchange of reasons. By looking at the linguistic interplay among the parties and the judge in a legal dispute, the chapter shows how vagueness arises and how it is reduced by courts to settle the case at issue.

Chapter 4 again faces the problem of the relevance of a legislator's intention in grasping legal meaning but through the peculiar perspective of non-literal speech. Hrafn Asgeirsson enquires whether non-literal legislative speech can occur in law. He claims that, due to the fact that legislative contexts generally contain little unequivocal information about legislative intent, interpreters typically are not warranted in taking the legislature to have intended to communicate something non-literal. The author says that this argument has some significant consequences for the extent to which we should take the content of the law to be determinate. The basic idea is that in the relevant scenarios the audience ought to withhold belief regarding the speaker's communicative intentions, in which case the primary content of the relevant utterance is indeterminate between the literal content of the sentence uttered and some pragmatic enrichment thereof. This has strong implications for the analysis of a number of important but controversial legal cases, which Asgeirsson discusses in detail.

In Chap. 5, Pierluigi Chiassoni reaches conclusions opposite to those in the previous chapter as regards the possibility of a genuine knowledge of the literal meaning and its identification with the speaker's meaning. Chiassoni engages in the perennial debate about the proper account of judicial interpretation. Briefly, this dispute turns on the following alternative: Is judicial interpretation necessarily (i.e. as a matter of empirical necessity) an evaluative, practical, judgment-dependent, decision-making activity, or, at least sometimes, is it rather just a matter of knowledge, a pure 'grasping' of the content of law? The thesis called *skepticism* (or *non-cognitivism*) supports the first alternative, while the view named *formalism* (or *cognitivism*) supports the latter. Here Chiassoni defends interpretive legal skepticism as the proper account of judicial interpretation through pragmatic arguments. He shows that philosophy of language and pragmatics as a substantive part thereof, far from providing support for some form of cognitivism, suggest contrariwise that it should be abandoned.

Chapter 6 deals with the same topic as Chap. 5 but Nicola Muffato focuses on the philosophical and rhetorical contact points between general communicational skepticism and interpretive legal skepticism. He explores how interpretive legal skepticism can be grounded on Quine's and Davidson's indeterminist conclusions (see Davidson 1973; Quine 1987) and on deconstructionism (Derrida 1988), and then he enquires as to the possibility of employing against interpretive legal skepticism a criticism of these conceptions, based on Wittgensteinian arguments (Wittgenstein 1958) and developable along various lines by 'practice-based' conceptions of meaning.

In Chap. 7, Ekkehard Felder deals with the fascinating topic of the "semantic battles" approach: The attempt to implement certain linguistic forms as expressions of specific interest-led action and thought patterns in a domain of knowledge. Through this approach, he shows that dominance and power are exercised through semantics! The semantic battle is differentiated as an implicit or explicit conflict about the fittingness of linguistic expression with regard to three perspectives: the level of designation and definition (a number of expressions give prominence to different aspects of a fact), the level of meaning (one and the same expression has different connotations and accentuations) and the level of facts and reference objects (seemingly identical or actually identical reference objects are differently constituted). The author offers clear examples of semantic battles at all three levels. In particular, Felder characterizes the speech acts performed by legal workers in the battle over the applicability of verbal formulations and the accompanying perspectives.

The second part of the book, *Pragmatics and Legal Theory*, includes five chapters that appeal to the most sophisticated pragmatic tools to deal with debated issues of legal theory. Problems like the normativity of legal norms (Chap. 8), the strength of legal positivism (Chap. 9), the theoretical structures of imperatives (Chap. 10), the aims of the law (Chap. 11) and, the institutional design of new field of experiences and systems of knowledge (Chap. 12) are discussed, employing theories and concepts developed within pragmatics, socio-linguistic and philosophy of language – concepts and theories such as presuppositions, metalinguistic negotiations, illocutionary force and web-semantics.

In Chap. 8, Michael Green faces a traditional, highly problematic topic of legal philosophy: a commonly assumed requirement for an adequate theory of law (the *requirement*, for short) is that it must explain the unique role of legal norms in practical reasoning. It must explain why participants in legal practices should justify their decisions by appeal to legal norms rather than pointing solely to how practice-independent norms, such as morality and prudence, are triggered by the existence of legal practices as social facts. He critically analyses how the most important theories of law (Kelsen's, Hart's, Dworkin's, Shapiro's and legal realistics' theories) faces the requirement. In particular, he argues that Hart's response to the requirement is centred on the notion of internal legal statements (ILSs) and that it is deceptive (see Hart 1961). According to Green, Hart provides no account of why officials should justify their decisions through ILSs rather than solely on moral and prudential grounds. This casts doubt on Hart's theory of law as a whole. Hart fails to explain why law vanishes when officials stop making ILSs and begin justifying their decisions by reference to morality and prudence. In particular, Green critically analyses the Hartian claim according to which someone making an ILS presupposes the rule of recognition, showing how this presupposition links with Hart's failure in satisfying the requirement.

In Chap. 9, Teresa Marques discusses arguments advanced by Plunkett and Sundell (Plunkett and Sundell 2013), who have made an original use of resources from linguistics and philosophy of language to reply to arguments for legal anti-positivism, the thesis according to which moral or value facts are part of what determines what the law is in a given jurisdiction at a given time. Plunkett and Sundell's strategy for resisting anti-positivism appeals to the notion of a metalinguistic negotiation, which incorporates the notion of a metalinguistic or context disagreement. A further notion deployed is that of conceptual ethics, an essential component of metalinguistic negotiations. Marques asks about the strength of both notions against disagreement-based arguments for legal anti-positivism. She argues that metalinguistic negotiations displace disagreements from the semantic to the metalinguistic level but do not eliminate the appeal to moral or other normative reasons from legal disagreements. In fact, according to Marques, on a broad understanding of legal reasoning and practice, metalinguistic negotiations and conceptual ethics are an integral part of it and hence are consistent with evaluative and normative facts being essential to, and constitutive of, the law.

In Chap. 10, Alessio Sardo deals with one of the central issues in normative language: the relation between semantic meaning and illocutionary force. The main question is whether or not we should consider the two features as neatly separated. Those authors who give a positive answer to this question maintain that every speech act expresses the same type of semantic content (a proposition) and confine all those elements that belong to illocutionary force in the domain of pragmatics.

Those who give a negative answer to the question maintain that illocutionary force also has a semantic dimension: What we do *in* saying something is determined also by certain features that are encoded in the deep logical structure a statement, or utterance, by convention. This problem was present in Frege and always has been the object of a lively discussion, at least in philosophy of language. Sardo offers a general and broad survey of the main solutions offered to this quandary both in philosophy of language and in legal theory. His analysis also takes into account some of the most recent theories and suggests that an integrated approach would be the best.

In Chap. 11, Leticia Barrera leads a sociolinguistic study on legal technicalities (e.g. legal instrumentalism, managerialism, procedures), exploring the means to end a relationship enclosed in legal techniques. In particular, she engages a context-based analysis of the technical knowledge embedded in the constitution of legal and financial instruments in the context of sovereign debt agreements. The study draws on a concrete case of sovereign debt litigation in US courts: *NML Capital, Ltd. v. Republic of Argentina* that came out of this country's foreign debt default in 2001 (following a larger economic crisis) and debt restructurings in 2005 and 2010. The US court's ruling, however, is not analysed in its legal, economic and political effects; the study moves beyond the question of judicial interpretation of contractual terms to look at the function that those legal devices are thought to perform in the contexts in which they are placed, represented, appropriated, negotiated and even anticipated by the agents. In this vein, Barrera assesses the political spin of legal technicalities by looking into their constitution as mere vehicles of pragmatism while serving a disputable ideological agenda, and thus, they are means to multiple ends.

In Chap. 12, Pompeu Casanovas, Víctor Rodríguez-Doncel and Jorge González-Conejero explore the new boundaries of the intersection between pragmatics and artificial intelligence, focusing on the concepts Semantic Web, Web of Data and regulatory models, and inquiring about their relations with the law. Firstly, they describe the languages of the Semantic Web and show how the perspective of the Web of Services and Linked Data is related to the conditions under which services can be offered, managed and used. Secondly, they show that the nature of law is experiencing a deep transformation in the cloud. What links the information flow, social intelligence, rights management and modelling in the Web of Data is the pragmatic approach – what we call the pragmatic turn – the representation of users' needs and contexts to facilitate the automated interactive and collective management of knowledge. The Web of Data brings about new challenges in agency, knowledge, communication and the coordination of actions; it calls for a new regulatory and institutional design.

Finally, the third part of this volume, *Pragmatics and Legal Adjudication*, embraces six essays devoted to various aspects of legal adjudication and its pragmatic analysis. The first (Chap. 13) is about the role of legal adjudication within legal practice. It deals with the relationship between legislative and judicial law-making and how both are grounded on judicial customs. The other five essays analyse more specific problems of legal adjudications – both original issues such as the weight of pragmatic disorders within the prisons' population and how they can hinder the wide range of interactions that take place from arrest to conviction and imprisonment (Chap. 14) – and more traditional epistemic problems such as the role of stereotypes in judicial decisions (Chap. 15), and testimony (Chaps. 16 and 17).

In Chap. 13, Mauro Barberis challenges some common views about legal sources (in particular the relationship between legislation and adjudication). He lays the foundations of a realistic, pragmatic and inferentialist theory of law in which Anglo-American precedents and European-continental jurisprudence play an important role as self-restraining devices emerging from the working of adjudication itself. Historically, legislation was designed to remedy arbitrariness in adjudication; after two centuries, however, the cure proved to be worse than the disease. Today, statutes are less a restraint than a tool for judicial interpretation, and the latter, paradoxically enough, is converted into the last remedy to the darkness of legislation.

In Chap. 14, Louise Cummings bring us into the dark world of mental illness. First, she shows that there is a sizeable burden of pragmatic disorder in the prison population. Second, she enquires as to what implications, if any, this has for those pragmatically impaired individuals who are in the criminal justice system. From the point of arrest to conviction and imprisonment, incarcerated individuals must negotiate a range of verbally mediated interactions. Through a careful analysis of some of these interactions (police interviews, courtroom examinations and prison rehabilitation programs), Cummings demonstrates that they exceed the pragmatic language capacities of incarcerated individuals. Some of the specific pragmatic features of these interactions pose significant and, in some cases, insurmountable difficulties for clients with pragmatic disorder. Finally, it is argued that a much greater level of priority must be afforded to the assessment and treatment of pragmatic disorders in forensic settings than has been the case to date.

In Chap. 15, Federico José Arena develops a deep analysis of stereotypes and their function in legal decision-making. Stereotypes are a kind of social categorization that plays a fundamental role in social interactions as a mechanism to form expectations about people's behaviours and attitudes. Their use, however, is not free of controversy; social categories are closely related to sensible issues such as individual auto perception, identity construction and discriminations. Therefore, in legal domain, it often is claimed that judges should avoid or contrast the negative effects of social categorizations. It is not easy to determine, however, if all stereotypes should be avoided or if, instead, some of them are inevitable or valuable and therefore acceptable or mandatory uses of stereotypes. Arena shows that some of these difficulties arise because the term *stereotype* has heterogenic uses. Therefore through accurate analytical distinctions, he highlights different roles of different stereotypes in judicial reasoning.

In Chap. 16, Sune Sønderberg Mortensen and Janus Mortensen undertake a refined analysis of courtroom interactions. This sort of analysis pertains to a well-established scientific genre which has seen contributions from a range of disciplines, including conversational analysis, interactional sociolinguistics, pragmatics, corpus linguistics, semantics and rhetorical studies. The authors focus on epistemic issues. After a deep discussion of the linguistic expressions of certainty and uncertainty, the so-called epistemic stance markers and their features and roles in communicative interactions, the authors enquire how they are used by participants during examinations in a recent Danish criminal trial (which was audio recorded). Although the investigation concerns Danish linguistic expressions (always translated in the text), its results are of interest for the innovative theoretical and methodological approach and seem generalizable to a wide range of other languages, thus marking an important step in the progress of forensic linguistics.

Last but not least, in Chap. 17, Florencia Rimoldi and Hernan Bouvier address some platitudes surrounding the epistemology of testimony in legal domain by taking into account how epistemology explains the different but related phenomenon of forming beliefs based on the words of others. Although there is no agreement between epistemologists about how does testimony obtain its epistemic import in the case of human cognisans, the authors propose that some accounts fit better to explain theoretically the legal practice. For that purpose they explore sophisticated discussions belonging to the philosophy of testimony, among them, reductionism, universalism and interpersonal views of testimony. Resorting to what it is called a doxastic approach, they aim to demonstrate that epistemological assumptions in the legal field regarding testimony cannot be held together especially because of some pragmatic implications involved in the way jurists treat that kind of evidence. The authors focused on the considerations regarding the case of three types of witnesses: single, expert and eyewitnesses.

Milan, Italy Francesca Poggi
Messina, Italy Alessandro Capone

References

Bentham, J. (2010). *Of the limits of the Penal Branch of Jurisprudence* (P. Schofield, Ed.). Oxford: Clarendon Press.

Bobbio, N. (1950). Scienza del diritto e analisi del linguaggio. *Rivista trimestrale di diritto e procedura civile, 4*(2), 342–367.

Brandom, R. B. (1994). *Making it explicit. Reasoning, representing, and discursive commitment.* Harvard/London: Harvard University Press.

Brandom, R. B. (2000). *Articulating reasons. An introduction to inferentialism.* Cambridge, MA/London: Harvard University Press.

Brandom, R. B. (2008). *Between saying and doing. Towards an analytic pragmatism.* Oxford/New York: Cambridge University Press.

Davidson, D. (1973). Radical Interpretation. *Dialectica, 27*, 313–328.

Derrida, J. (1988). *Limited Inc.* Evanston: Northwestern University Press.

Grice, P. H. (1989). *Studies in the way of word.* Cambridge/London: Harvard University Press.

Hart, H. L. A. (1961). *The concept of law.* Oxford: Claredon Press.

Plunkett, D., & Sundell, T. (2013). Disagreement and the semantics of normative and evaluative terms. *Philosophers' Imprint, 13*(23), 1–37.

Quine, W. V. O. (1987). Indeterminacy of translation again. *The Journal of Philosophy, 84*(1), 5–10.

Wittgenstein, L. (1958). *Philosophical investigations.* Oxford: Blackwell.

Contents

The original version of this book was revised. An erratum to this book can be found at DOI 10.1007/978-3-319-44601-1_18

Part I
Pragmatics and Legal Interpretation

Slippery Meaning and Accountability

Kasia M. Jaszczolt

Abstract In his 'Fishy business', Mark Sainsbury (Analysis 74:3–5, 2014) presents a puzzle: in order to have a *substantive disagreement*, one has to first agree on the meaning of a proposition that is the object of this disagreement. Now, since before Linnaeus' classification the criteria for counting as 'fish' were such that they allowed for the inclusion of whales, while the new classification (1758) excludes them, a substantive disagreement ought not to arise across these two. And yet, in a court case from 1818 he refers to, the judges did not dismiss the disagreement on semantic grounds. They proclaimed whales to count as fish, and, according to Sainsbury, we, the readers, are equally able to reach a verdict in that we would proclaim the jury to be wrong. The question I address in this paper is a metasemantic one, namely what should count as meaning of expressions for the purpose of theoretical inquiry. I point out that truth-conditional analysis of meaning increasingly makes use of pragmatically derived interpretations in radical versions of contextualism and that this pragmatization of meaning is supported by the increasingly common philosophical stance on reference according to which reference is to be pursued on the level of cognitive mechanisms rather than types of noun phrases. It is in this milieu that I analyse the cognitive construct of the primary meaning of an utterance that corresponds to the intended and recovered meaning in a model situation, derived here by employing the sources of information and processes identified in Default Semantics. I demonstrate through selected examples that any attempts to regiment meaning by using the explicit/implicit distinction, directly-referential/contextually-referential, or indexical/nonindexical distinction do not yield the primary meaning intended and recovered in linguistic interaction. As a result, the question of accountability arises: if the primary meaning can be implicit, context-driven and multidimensional, then is it this meaning that the speaker should be accountable for? If so, we need a normative theory that would predict such meanings. If not, then we would have to make the speaker accountable for some content that is not intended. I propose that a normative, radical contextualist account that places meaning on the level of a conceptual structure, while at the same time preserving the truth-conditional method of analysis, acts in favour of this accountability on the grounds of primary,

K.M. Jaszczolt (✉)
Department of Theoretical and Applied Linguistics, University of Cambridge, Cambridge, UK
e-mail: kmj21@cam.ac.uk

F. Poggi, A. Capone (eds.), *Pragmatics and Law*, Perspectives in Pragmatics, Philosophy & Psychology 10, DOI 10.1007/978-3-319-44601-1_1

intended meaning, irrespective of its explicit or implicit status. I tentatively conclude by pointing out one obvious corollary, namely that this pragmatization of meaning affects both sides of language in the courtroom but not to the same degree: the relevant law cannot have a *communicative* rather than *textual* content beyond certain limitations imposed on the generalizations over admissible contexts, while the primary content of the plaintiff's and the defendant's contributions, firmly situated in the co-constructed context, can easily cross the explicit/implicit boundary.

Keywords Accountability • Contextualism • Default Semantics • Maurice v Judd case • Merger representation • Metasemantics • Primary meaning • Salience-based contextualism • Salient meanings • Substantive disagreement

1 Fish Oil and Metasemantics

In his 'Fishy business', Mark Sainsbury (2014) discusses a court case that took place in New York in 1818 and concerned the meaning of the term 'fish oil'.[1] A fee was requested for 'gauging, inspecting and branding' caskets of fish oil – refused by the defendant on the grounds that the oil in question came from spermaceti whales and as such does not qualify as 'fish oil'. The verdict presents a theoretical puzzle concerning the so-called *substantive disagreement*: in order to have a substantive disagreement, the parties have to first agree on the meaning of a proposition that is the object of this disagreement. Since before Linnaeus' new classification (1758) the criteria for counting as 'fish' were such that they allowed for the inclusion of whales, while the new classification excludes them, a substantive disagreement ought not to have arisen across these two. And yet, in the court case Sainsbury refers to, the judges did not dismiss the disagreement on semantic grounds. They proclaimed whales to count as fish. Moreover, according to Sainsbury, we, the readers, are equally able to reach a verdict in that we would proclaim the jury to be wrong – a claim which I inspect more carefully in the course of the discussion.

Sainsbury (2014: 5) concludes with a tongue-in-cheek but at the same time perspicacious comment:

> There is something paradoxical about fish. An adequate resolution will require carefully formulated metasemantic principles

The question I address in this paper is precisely a metasemantic one, but my objectives are considerably different from those of Sainsbury's. Instead of focusing on knowledge attributions, I ask a more general question, namely what should count as meaning of expressions for the purpose of theoretical inquiry. Perhaps predictably, I shall take on board semantic contextualism, as distinguished from, say, contextualism about knowledge attributions (e.g. Blome-Tillmann 2013, 2014; Lutz 2014),

[1] 'Maurice v Judd', see Historical Society of the New York Courts, http://www.nycourts.gov/history/legal-history-new-york/legal-history-eras-02/history-new-york-legal-eras-maurice-judd.html

and in particular the question of the extent to which pragmatics can shape the primary intended message that becomes the object of such courtroom judgements. Are there clear principles that can/ought to be discerned and implemented for judging such difficult cases? More generally, what principles, if any, do interlocutors adopt in order to establish the primary message on the basis of which the truth or falsity of the statement ought to be assessed? Do indirect forms of communicating information that are so frequent in our everyday discourse qualify as providers of such primary, truth-evaluable meanings to be assessed as true or false and, on the above scenario, to constitute the basis for courtroom verdicts?

There are different ways of approaching this set of questions, and these ways come with their different methods of inquiry. First, one could go empirical and compile a database of pertinent court cases, investigate the extent to which what the defendants and the witnesses 'said' was modified as compared with the minimal content of the sentence as it is understood in semantic minimalism, preferably of the propositional variety (Borg 2004, 2012; Cappelen and Lepore 2005), and produce a generalization over what the parties involved in the case judge to be the content of the speech act that plays a role in reaching the verdict. But this method is not very reliable in that there is no doubt that a variety of meanings is bound to be conveyed. Next, we can go empirical and try to establish how interlocutors understand the concept of the main conveyed message, utilising a questionnaire method. This has already been attempted, with the suitable attention paid to the instructions that variously do, or do not, mention the term 'what is said' as opposed to, say, 'the main communicated message'.[2] The result of these studies clearly indicates that addressees discern the main message, what the speaker mainly said, conveyed, intentionally communicated, and so forth, equally well, independently of the association of the content with the logical form of the uttered sentence. In other words, the main message can be communicated (i) directly in virtue of the sentence content alone; (ii) directly in virtue of the sentence, enriched with the effect of pragmatic processing or some default inferences; or (iii) indirectly. All three formats are equally accessible to the addressees. In other words again, what is psychologically real is not the distinction between the meaning communicated via the sentence structure and the meaning communicated pragmatically, but rather the primary as opposed to the secondary meaning – the first being either explicit or implicit.

I have written at length on the primary/secondary meaning distinction being orthogonal to the explicit/implicit one elsewhere and will not be concerned with these arguments directly in what follows.[3] Instead, let us continue with the list of available methods of enquiry. One can go empirical again, embark on a project in the neuroscience of language, and test brain activation pertaining to (i–iii) above. But this would be premature: finding brain correlates of linguistic processes in patterns of neuronal activation, or correlates of representations we form in response to acts of linguistic communication in neuronal structures is not what we are able to

[2] See e.g. Nicolle and Clark 1999; Pitts 2005; Schneider 2009.

[3] See e.g. Jaszczolt 2005, 2010, and 2016, and in particular the argument from cancellability in Jaszczolt 2009a.

reliably do. Neuronal structures and patterns of neuronal activation remain a long shot from an explanatorily adequate theory of meaning.[4]

Leaving empirical methods aside, let us consider conceptual analysis. As Sainsbury rightly observes, we have a metasemantic problem here and the most obvious method to tackle it in the first place is theoretical argumentation that takes on board the semantics/pragmatics boundary, and in particular the suitability of semantic minimalism vis-à-vis contextualism about meaning for handling the question as to *what kind of meaning* ought to count. Now, 'what kind of meaning ought to count' is still too vague as the object of enquiry. After all, the meaning that counts in courtroom verdicts need not be the same as the meaning that ought to be regarded as the object of semantic analysis. Whether it is or not largely depends on the strength and quality of argumentation on the semantics/pragmatics divide, and thus on the selected assumptions. Moreover, the meaning that ought to be agreed on as the object of semantics need not necessarily be the same beast and the meaning that undergoes the truth-conditional analysis. After all, semantics may be considered minimal, founded on the structure of the sentence, and not even falling prey to propositionalism in that not all complete sentences express complete propositions (Bach, e.g. 2004, 2006); or contextualism about meaning can be so construed that truth-conditional analysis takes as its object the meaning that exceeds the scope of semantics: pragmatic modifications ('enrichments', 'modulations', and so forth) are not structure-driven and as such fall outside the domain of semantics while having their rightful place in the proposition expressed (Recanati, e.g. 2010, 2012a, b).[5] So, in order to proceed with our question we have to make one methodological assumption. We have to assume that semantic theory ought to deal with intuitive meanings, that is, with the meanings that are intended by the speakers, and, if all goes well, also recovered by addressees,[6] as the *main intended message*. We also have to make a choice of the method for semantic analysis (not to be confused with the method for our current *metasemantic* analysis). Our choice is to adopt the truth-conditional method in that truth conditions offer the most successful tool to date for providing a formalizable, explanatorily adequate theory of meaning. While traditionally, in Montagovian semantics, they tended to go together with the sentence-based object of enquiry and formal models, since the late 1980s approaches within dynamic semantics have opened up the possibility of incorporating more and more pragmatically derived meaning into the proposition to which truth conditions are applied.[7] Model theory and possible worlds follow suit as essential aspects of this analysis. The theory we will end up adopting here constitutes a further, arguably the most radical, step in this history of pragmatization of truth-conditional semantics – the

[4] For a discussion of the aims of the neuroscience of language see Pulvermüller 2010.

[5] Cf.: "On this issue I am happy to part company with the most radical contextualists – the 'sceptics' who would go for the holistic guesswork answer (…). Like Stanley and the formal semanticists, I maintain that semantic interpretation is grammar-driven." Recanati (2012a: 148).

[6] As I argue at length elsewhere (Jaszczolt 2005, 2010, 2016), miscommunication is not the topic for semantic theory but rather for applied linguistics.

[7] See e.g. Kamp and Reyle 1993; Groenendijk and Stokhof 1991; van der Sandt 1992, 2012.

most radical in that it marries the methods of formal semantic analysis with the object of study that may have a very loose connection with the syntactic structure of the uttered sentence. This object of study is the speech act that conveys the main intended message – be it directly or indirectly, as long as it is conveyed sufficiently strongly and unambiguously to be grasped without doubt as what was intended.

2 On Types of Semantic Content: A Sketch

We have answered one of our initial questions by a stipulation: the meaning that our semantic theory takes as its object is the meaning intended by the speaker and recovered by the addressee, with the proviso that all goes well in assuming at one end, and recovering at the other, the background that allows the interlocutors to leave some aspects of the message unsaid. In Default Semantics that we will end up adopting for this purpose (Jaszczolt 2005, 2010), this is called a Model Speaker/Model Addressee meaning. This construal also allows us to overcome a rather unproductive discussion that keeps appearing in the post-Gricean literature addressing the question as to whether speaker's meaning or addressee's meaning ought to be *the* meaning that is represented by the theory. To repeat, we leave such questions to psychological studies within applied linguistics.

The core question, however, remains and cannot be set by methodological or theoretical stipulations. It concerns the kinds of contributions that context makes to this richly, contextually construed truth-conditional representation. At first blush, we have three qualitatively different 'levels' of meaning that are all good candidates for primary meanings. These are (a) minimal sentence meaning; (b) expanded/modulated sentence meaning; and (c) implicatures. The first two have been well discussed in the post-Gricean tradition, where, arguably, the dominant view is that context always has to be consulted in construing the truth-conditional representation, and as such the expanded meaning is the standard case, with the minimal sentence meaning being a special one in that it is only an accidental feature of a given discourse that no enrichment or other modifications were needed. In other words, Recanati's (e.g. 1989, 2012c) *what is said* or the relevance-theoretic *explicature* (e.g. Sperber and Wilson 1995, 2012; Carston 1988, 2002) that constitute the developments of the logical form of the sentence have become the focus of attention and the locus from which the enquiry into the types of modifications that produce them sprang out. But it has also been extensively argued, mostly in the late-Wittgensteinian speech-act tradition, that the correct object of study for a theory of meaning is not some in-between construct that cannot be analysed by appealing to the study of the language system alone (lexicon and syntax) or, on the other hand, may not pertain to the main, strongly communicated message either. For example, in (1), it is not the extended sentence meaning in (1a) that is predominantly communicated but rather the implicature that can be formulated as in (1b) or (1c).

(1) A little boy to his mother:
Everybody has an iPhone 6. (minimal proposition)

(1a) Everybody in the boy's class has an iPhone 6. (enriched proposition)
(1b) The boy is asking his mother to buy him an iPhone 6. (implicature)
(1c) Please buy me an iPhone 6. (implicature)

It is this primary meaning that will be subjected to the truth-conditional analysis, following our initial stipulation that the objective is to model the main intended message.

In short, we admit (a) sentence meaning, (b) the pragmatically modified sentence meaning, and (c) the indirect meaning that the uttered sentence produces in the given context as equally legitimate objects of the truth-conditional analysis. Naturally, this radically pragmatic approach comes with a radical reanalysis of the level at which compositionality is to be sought, the way in which this compositionality of meaning is achieved (again, on the assumption that a semantic theory requires compositionality as its fundamental methodological assumption). These issues have been dealt with at length elsewhere throughout the development of Default Semantics (henceforth DS, Jaszczolt, e.g. 2005, 2009b, 2010, 2016). For our purpose at this point in the argument we shall simply adopt the DS-theoretic tenet that the representation of intended meaning draws on various linguistic and extralinguistic sources of information and all these sources are treated on an equal footing, producing as a result a compositional representation where compositionality is predicated of the level at which the outputs of these sources merge (the so-called *merger representation*). These sources come with corresponding processes that contribute to the construction (and reconstruction) of the intended meaning – to repeat, assuming our Model Speaker – Model Addressee communication. A more detailed discussion of the sources and processes identified in DS will become pertinent in Sect. 5 when we provide a merger representation for the 'fish oil' example.

What remains unresolved in DS is how exactly lexical meaning fares in this multidimensional,[8] radically context-driven semantics. This is the question that will permeate the current discussion. So, having adopted the primary meanings that are free from the constraints of the logical form of the sentence, as exemplified in (1), we will now focus on this additional problem of what exactly, in the case of word meaning, can be attributed to those various sources and processes, and what remains the core of the lexical meaning. Compounds such as 'fish oil' from our earlier courtroom example are relatively unproblematic. On the one hand, standard definitions are anatomy-based: "Fish oil is oil derived from the tissues of oily fish" and "Fatty predatory fish like sharks, swordfish, tilefish, and albacore tuna may be high in

[8] The term 'multidimensional' has been used in many different ways in semantics. In the current approach we are using it to mean the variety of sources and processes that contribute to the final representation.

omega-3 fatty acids".[9] However, looked at from the perspective of language change, there is no reason to assume that Linnaeus' reclassification of whales as mammals carries across to compounds with an immediate effect; compounds have a life of their own in the history of the language. This observation is worth mentioning at this juncture because it would be too simplistic to assume that the jury's verdict in favour of the plaintiff (namely, that payment for inspecting three casks of 'fish oil' is due) can be traced merely to the considerations to do with the context, purpose or function, or, in other words, with putting the merchants' perspective above the anatomists' one. Compounds do have a life of their own, a 'blackboard' did not become a 'greenboard' (when the colour started varying within the range on which white chalk could still be used) before being replaced by 'whiteboard'; the replacement was instead driven by the more distinctive properties of the new piece of classroom equipment. After all, compounding means "combining two (or more) existing words into a new word" (Trask 1996: 30) and a new word can lead a life independent of the history of word-formation; internal compositionality is compromised at this point to some, smaller or greater, degree.[10]

In short, cases such as our 'fish oil' debate can occur for different reasons. They can occur because (i) there is a discrepancy between various considerations that have an impact on the meaning, such as, say, (i.a) a merchant's vs. an anatomist's perspective, or to give another example, (i.b) a functional vs. a perception-based one. The latter is evident when we refer to, say, an artistically designed functional object – for example an armchair in the shape of a large soft toy, a teapot in the shape of a pear, and so forth. The second reason can pertain to (ii) the compromised compositionality of a compound and the different diachronic path it adopts as compared with its constituent words, as discussed earlier in this section. Both considerations can be instrumental in the ascription of the primary communicated meaning to the speaker. *Nota bene*, only (i.a) and (i.b) require a contextualist perspective in that (ii) incorporates the non-compositional meaning of 'fish oil' in the minimal lexical content.

We have discussed so far three qualitatively different cases of the departure of the semantic content, as it is understood in radical contextualism of DS, from the minimal meaning of the uttered sentence: [1] enrichment/modulation of the minimal proposition; [2] replacement of the uttered proposition with the indirectly but strongly communicated primary meaning (an implicature), and [3] context-driven interpretation of an utterance that does not require enrichment but would, without this context or adopted perspective, remain either ambiguous, or underdetermined, or taken to mean what was not intended. Case [3] is instantiated by our 'fish oil' example on the (i.a) scenario (to repeat, the reason (ii) above does not necessitate a departure from the minimal content). Without adopting a contextualist outlook, the 'fish oil' scenario would be likely to produce the minimal meaning that is not

[9] Wikipedia, https://www.google.co.uk/?gws_rd=ssl#q=fish+oil

[10] It is generally acknowledged that the written form as one word (hyphenated or not) or two words is semantically irrelevant in English as long as the construct counts as a compound for morphological and semantic purposes.

intended – the meaning that was given in our earlier definition, "fish oil is oil derived from the tissues of oily fish". However, other examples falling into this category may produce instead semantic underdetermination or ambiguity. For example, the often discussed case of referent shift in (2) or (3) yield, so to speak, 'the wrong meaning' when viewed in the minimalist perspective.[11]

(2) Putnam is on the top shelf.
(3) The chicken burger left you a tip.

Needless to say, in contextualist perspective, they become (2a) and (3a).

(2a) The book(s) by Putnam are on the top shelf.
(3a) The person who ordered a chicken burger left you a tip.

We have presented here some examples of the scenarios that produce 'wrong meanings' and underdetermination as sub-categories of [3]. The final sub-category is that of an ambiguity.[12] Examples are equally easy to attest in that they constitute simple cases of lexical (4) or structural (5) ambiguity which, without the help of context, remain such.

(4) I want to design a pen.
(5) An intelligent student's essay was the topic of discussion at lunch.

Syntactic and lexical ambiguities are normally easy to resolve – we can agree with Kaplan (1989a, b) that they are pre-semantic, in that disambiguation is mandatory in order to proceed with any truth-conditional analysis. Moreover, they do not arise as ambiguities in processing: they only arise when the speaker's assumptions are not well adjusted to match the addressee's background information. Underdetermination and 'wrong meaning', however, are likely to lead to debates concerning the literal/nonliteral distinction and, as a moral corollary, also to discussions concerning speaker's accountability. Do speakers take responsibility for the strongly communicated meaning where the latter can have different provenance and display different degrees of reliance on the literal? Or are they accountable for the literal content?

Here we can register help from a supplementary argument: a yes/no answer to the latter question would have to presuppose that, on the metasemantic level, the literal/nonliteral distinction can be discerned.[13] But can it? Firstly, there are different

[11] See also Recanati, e.g. 2004, 2005 and 2012b on the literal/nonliteral distinction.

[12] 'Wrong meaning', 'underdetermination' and 'ambiguity' are labels that can be assigned when we ask the question as to what the addressee would obtain in principle if no context were given. As such, they are quite loosely attached labels and it has to be remembered that from the point of view of a formal semantic analysis all three can be placed in the same category – computational linguists would prefer the 'ambiguity' label here (see e.g. Lepore and Stone 2015), while relevance theorists who adopt and liberally apply psychologism, opt for underdetermination.

[13] This question is particularly pertinent with reference to language that causes offence, such as the use of slurs. See Sileo 2015.

ways of defining literality: with respect to departures from the minimal content, with respect to departures that are felt and consciously accepted as departures (at least *post hoc*, in a reflective process), to mention the basic two.[14] Cognitive linguistics certainly gives us strong reasons for classifying metaphorical expressions that pertain to standard metaphorical schemas as literal: they are not *felt* as non-literal and they are productive. Having a 'full life', an 'empty life', 'getting the most out of life', or 'living one's life to the fullest' are all said to exemplify the conceptual schema LIFE IS A CONTAINER (Lakoff and Johnson 1980: 51). Regardless of the cognitive status we wish to afford such schemas (and this will depend either on theoretical assumptions or on the assessment of evidence), the feeling of literalness of such expressions is a strong one, and, arguably, becomes even stronger in the cases of clear embodiment ('I am feeling up') or further progressing standardisation ('Don't waste my time').[15] All in all, the case for accountability for literal meaning looks feeble indeed. We can now intentionally misquote Sainsbury (2014: 5): "we think the jury gave the *correct* verdict".

3 Accountability Again

Arguably, the state of the art in modelling meaning is this. In addition to the progressing pragmatization of truth-conditional semantics discussed in Sect. 1, dynamic approaches to word meaning currently seem to dominate in semantic literature (see e.g. Asher 2011; Ludlow 2014). This pragmatization of meaning on all fronts, reflected in our types [1–3] above, is also supported by the increasingly common philosophical stance on reference according to which reference is to be pursued on the level of cognitive mechanisms rather than types of noun phrases.[16] It is in this milieu that we are analysing the cognitive construct that we call in DS the primary meaning of an utterance. We have also demonstrated that any attempts to regiment meaning by using the explicit/implicit distinction or the literal/nonliteral distinction do not yield the primary meaning intended and recovered in linguistic interaction. As a result, the question of accountability arises with a new force: if the primary meaning can be implicit, context-driven and multidimensional, then is it this meaning that the speaker should be accountable for? If so, we need a normative theory that would predict such meanings. If not, then we would have to make the speaker accountable for some content that is not intended and that, as Sect. 2 clearly indicated, cannot be discerned – or even *assumed* to be discernible. In this context, I suggest that we need a normative, radical contextualist account that places meaning on the level of a conceptual structure, while at the same time preserving the truth-conditional method of analysis. Evidence from what counts in everyday conversation acts in favour of this accountability on the grounds of primary, intended

[14] See for example Recanati (2004: 78) for an elaborate classification.

[15] See also e.g. Lakoff and Johnson 1999.

[16] See e.g. Hawthorne and Manley 2012; also Soames 2014 on cognitive propositions.

meaning, irrespective of the explicit or implicit status of the latter. DS provides such a radically contextualist framework. But before we turn to an analysis of the 'fish oil' example in DS, it is necessary to address the question of salient interpretations.

4 Salience-Based Contextualism

One need not conduct experiments to know that some meanings are recovered fast, others more slowly; some meanings require conscious processing, others do not. We will call the latter *automatic meanings* or *conversational defaults*, following the definition of default meanings adopted in DS according to which they are meanings that arise automatically, without involving a process of pragmatic inference. They are defined for the Model Speaker-Model Addressee pair (or other relevant set of interlocutors) and for the particular situation rather than for a type of linguistic expression. In other words, the definitional characteristic of defaults in DS is their automatic nature rather than a relation to items from the language system – lexical items or structures. A DS-theoretic default is thus a categorically different concept from, say, Levinson's (2000) presumptive meanings that are identified precisely for elements of the language: for Levinson, it is a word or part of the sentence structure that triggers a presumptive meaning – a generalised conversational implicature. Presumptive meanings capture at most strong tendencies in how language (or sometimes *a* language) is used but they come at a cost: they have to be defeasible, and they have to be so quite often. They also come with a speculative principle for their identification: what is it in language use or in the language system that makes us classify the understanding of 'a nanny' as 'a female nanny'? What evidence do we need to postulate a presumptive meaning in the first place, and what evidence does it take to, say, acknowledge that an alleged presumptive meaning no longer holds because society and culture have moved on? Equally, what does it take to demonstrate that exclusive disjunction ('*p* or *q* but not both') is the presumptive meaning of 'or'? These, and many other, foundational as well as descriptive questions remain unanswered there.

Instead, DS emphasises the importance of *salient meanings*. Salient meanings are interesting and not easy to analyse because, as ample experimental evidence convincingly suggests, they can be intended by the speaker or not intended (as long as they, *per se*, are salient to the interlocutors), and they can be literal or nonliteral. There is experimental evidence that meanings that do not constitute the intended content but yet are salient to the interlocutors are in fact activated.[17] As Giora (2003: 33) notes, "[t]he criterion or threshold a meaning has to reach to be considered salient is related only to its accessibility in memory due to such factors as frequency of use or experiential familiarity." Taking this evidence on board, we are justified in proposing that the concept of literalness as it is presented in the current state of

[17] See Giora, e.g. 2003, 2012, Peleg and Giora 2011.

semantics is of a more limited use for a theory of meaning than that of salience: first, as we have argued, there is no single clear literal/nonliteral distinction to rely on, and second, salient meanings easily cross even the most intuitive literal/nonliteral divide. Metaphorical meanings can be more salient than literal as long as they pertain to strongly activated, usually frequently utilised, concepts.

This gives us an option of redefining literality: a meaning is 'literal' *not* because it is not 'figurative' but rather because it is salient and as such activated automatically. This activation can reach a higher or a lower level according to Giora's (2003) Graded Salience Hypothesis but it is intuitively plausible to treat such automatic meanings as literal, in the most natural sense of the term: they do not require conscious processing, they are common, and appear basic.[18] What we gain is a gradable concept of salience that helps explain the non-gradable concept of literalness, pre-empting the need to choose between a plethora of criteria for the literal/nonliteral distinction.[19] Salience and automaticity will play an important role in our analysis of the 'fish oil' example, as it is an example of meaning that has to be resolved not only with reference to standard contextual parameters[20] but also with reference to function and purpose with which the expression was used.

Salience has an important provenance. It can come from the fact that language is a socio-cultural phenomenon, and as such a dynamic one, constantly created in the process of its use. Or it can come from the fact that language is a cognitive phenomenon and so is dependent on – and as such benefiting from, as well as being restricted by – the structure and operations of the brain. These two sources of salience are formalised in DS as two different types of processes: *cognitive defaults* and *socio-cultural and world-knowledge defaults* respectively. A brief introduction to sources and processes identified in DS is the topic to which we turn in Sect. 5, with an objective in view to provide a merger representation of the jury's verdict in the 'fish oil' case, namely a semantic representation of the meaning that was deemed to be relevant – a representation that will also give some insight (as far as semantic theory requires it) into the processing that produced it.

---

[18] This view goes beyond Recanati's (2004) definitions of 'literal', where metaphors that do not require conscious processing are regarded as '*p*-literal' and non-figurative, while consciously processed metaphorical expressions are '*p*-literal' and figurative, where '*p*-literal' classifies them as primary meanings.

[19] I discuss this issue in much more detail in Chapter 1 of Jaszczolt 2016, where I dub this form of contextualism *Salience-Based Contextualism*.

[20] According to Kaplan's (1989a) two-dimensional semantics, context is to be defined as a set of all the parameters that are necessary for semantics, such as agent, time, location, and world, with the proviso that more parameters can be added when required.

5 Representing Primary Meanings: An Example

Theories of meaning define their object of study in different ways. It goes without saying that when our object of analysis is the main, primary intended meaning of the speaker's utterance, we need to either resort to pragmatics when our semantics was assumed to be minimal, or construe semantic theory in such a way that it can accommodate this object of study independently of how difficult it is to represent – that, is independently of its degree of resemblance to the logical form of the uttered sentence. In the preceding sections I have argued for the latter option, and in particular for the theory that is most radical in this respect, that is DS. In what follows, we will implement it by providing an example of a DS-theoretic merger representation, representing the meaning of an example of utterance that is likely to be encountered in connection with the 'fish oil' court case. In order to do so, it is necessary to start by a brief overview of the sources of information and processes identified in DS that result in the compositional merger representation.

First, merger representation is *assumed* to be compositional, in virtue of a methodological as well as an epistemological assumption: language is systematic and productive and this systematicity and productivity suggest that compositionality of meaning has to be found on some level of analysis of human communication. Attempts in formal semantics to find compositionality in sentence structure have all failed: to make language fully compositional requires bringing in theoretical devices that testify against compositionality in the first place. On the other hand, non-compositional semantics is unthinkable; compositionality of meaning at some level or other is an empirical fact and as such an epistemological assumption about possible human languages. At the very least, it is plausible to assume that compositionality of language – or, better, of communication – supervenes on compositional reality (see e.g. Schiffer 1991; Szabó 2000). Be that as it may, the methodological assumption of a compositional structure at the level of conceptual representations follows as a corollary.

Merger representations, symbolised as Σ for the summation of information coming from different sources, are such compositional conceptual structures, combining information about meaning that comes from (i) world knowledge (WK); (ii) word meaning and sentence structure (WS); (iii) situation of discourse (SD); (iv) properties of the human inferential system (IS); and (v) stereotypes and presumptions about society and culture (SC).[21] While in traditional formal semantic accounts compositionality was sought at the level of the output of WS, in DS, following the adopted radical contextualist orientation, compositionality is predicated of the output to which any of these five sources can contribute. All the sources have equal status, in the sense that they do not simply modify the logical form, that is the output of WS. To repeat, the resulting representation may not be isomorphic to the output

[21] The sources as they are presented here come from the revised version of DS first proposed in Jaszczolt 2009b. The reader is referred there, or Jaszczolt 2010 and 2016, for a detailed account of the sources and processes.

of WS and, in the case of indirectly communicated primary meaning, may not even resemble it structurally; it may exemplify any of the three categories (a–c) distinguished in Sect. 2.[22]

Next, the sources map onto processes that jointly produce a merger representation. It is not always a one-to-one mapping but stable correlations are discernible. WK and SC can give rise to automatic, default interpretations called social, cultural, and world-knowledge defaults (SCWD)[23] or to a conscious process of pragmatic inference (CPI). CPI can also be triggered by SD, and this is where the role of SD is exhausted: it triggers a one-to-one mapping. WS is assumed to require processing that is specialised for language and hence maps onto 'processing of word meaning and sentence structure', also abbreviated as WS.[24] Next, IS results in cognitive defaults (CD) – automatic, default interpretations that rely on the structure and operations of the brain. In Σs, the processes that are responsible for specific contributions to the overall meaning are marked as an index following the closing of a square bracket that contains the relevant unit of conceptual structure. The length of the material in square brackets is not fixed once and for all for a given sentence: just as expressions can adopt different meanings in different contexts, so the processes can operate on different units in different circumstances. For example, in one context a determiner 'some' will lead to an automatic enrichment to 'some but not all' (N.B., to repeat, 'automatic' for the speaker and the context), while in another it will not. In yet another it may lead to a conceptual structure for the primary meaning that does not contain a quantifier at all.[25] The DS-theoretic terminology for this fact is

[22] It has to be borne in mind that some philosophers of language use the term 'logical form' very broadly, in such a way that it is also likely to encompass our merger representation. For example, Stainton (2006: 186) extends the term to non-linguistic means of communication. Since merger representations draw on linguistic as well as non-linguistic sources of information, DS makes a clear distinction between the representation of the meaning of the sentence of the natural language (logical form) and the representation of the primary meaning of an act of communication (merger representation).

[23] The need to incorporate sociocultural considerations in pragmatic theory is now widely recognised, not only in accounts of Generalized Conversational Implicatures (GCIs) and linguistic politeness. See e.g. Ariel (2010: xiv, 212–213).

[24] DS is still a theory in progress and in its current form it is compatible both with modular accounts on which language processing proceeds through specialised, dedicated mechanisms (here captured as WS) and with connectionist models where WS process can be understood as simply reading information from the lexicon and structure, not necessarily using dedicated processing. It has to be remembered in this context that WS reflects the incremental nature of discourse processing and therefore in the process of comprehension the construction of the logical form can be, so to speak, 'interrupted' at various points by the output of other processes that together lead to the merger representation. But details of this process lie beyond the remit of a semantic theory – even a radically contextualist one – and belong with psycholinguistics and neurolinguistics. While it is hoped that the latter will shed light on the construction of merger representations in discourse, the incremental process itself is of no utility to the semantic theory assuming it. In Jaszczolt (2005) I called this idea 'methodological globalism'.

[25] See e.g. 'some people are neurotic' clearly used to mean 'You appear neurotic', or 'Some say he killed his wife and threw her body into a lake' when said to mean 'Rumour has it that he killed his wife and threw her body into a lake'.

that inferential bases and bases for automatic meanings are *flexible* and they correspond to linguistic meanings that are equally flexible – or, using Kaplan's (1989a) content/character distinction, *fluid characters* (Jaszczolt 2012 and 2016).

We are now in a position to employ DS to the analysis of our courtroom scenario from Sect. 1. Let us first stipulate that the offending event can be summarised, from our and from Judd's perspective, in the sentence in (6), quoted form 'Maurice v Judd', after the website of the Historical Society of the New York Courts.[26]

(6) Samuel Judd purchased three barrels of whale oil that had not been inspected.

Let us next stipulate that James Maurice, the tax collector, presents the case as in (7).

(7) Samuel Judd purchased three barrels of fish oil that had not been inspected.

The ensuing verdict supports (7) in a recommendation that can be formulated for our purposes as (8) and is based on the law in (9).

(8) The Court sentences Samuel Judd to paying $75 for failing to have three barrels of fish oil inspected.
(9) Fish oil sold in New York must be gauged, inspected and branded.

Partial merger representations for (6–9) are given in Figs. 1, 2, 3, and 4 respectively.[27]

The language of merger representations uses amended and extended language of Discourse Representation Theory (Kamp and Reyle 1993), adapted for the purpose of a radical contextualist account to handle primary meanings that, to repeat, can substantially depart from the logical form of the sentence. The variables in the first row stand for discourse referents; capital 'Y' marks a plural referent. The following rows contain discourse conditions. The referent pertaining to the proper name is given by processing the name itself (WS) and by the cognitive default associated with the standard referential and presuppositional processing of names – a CD in that it has been extensively argued in DS that this standard reading pertains to the high degree of informativeness and high intentionality that is assumed of human communication and of human mental states respectively. Next, in the second condition, Y is given by WS and CD in that information comes from the description (WS, 'barrels of whale oil') but the collective reading is derived from the tendency to read plural referents collectively (CD). The next row specifies the cardinality of Y given in the sentence, and thus by WS. The fourth condition relies on the theory of tem-

[26] http://www.nycourts.gov/history/legal-history-new-york/legal-history-eras-02/history-new-york-legal-eras-maurice-judd.html

[27] 'Partial' in that the detailed representation of the aspects of the conceptual structure that are not directly relevant to the presented issue are omitted.

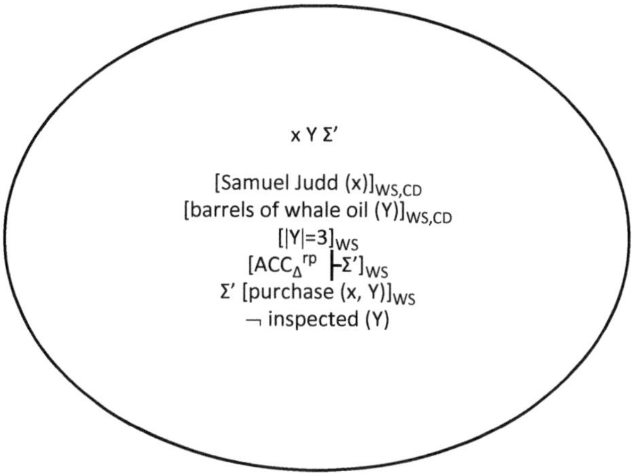

Fig. 1 Partial Σ for example (6): 'Samuel Judd purchased three barrels of whale oil that had not been inspected'

poral reference developed in DS (Jaszczolt 2009b) whereby temporality is supervenient on epistemic modality and represented by a uniform operator of acceptability: '$ACC_{\Delta}^{rp} \vdash \Sigma$' reads 'it is acceptable to the degree pertaining to regular past that it is the case that Σ'. Here the symbol '$\vdash$' stands for epistemic modality. The following two conditions are self-explanatory.

Now, (7), the conceptual representation of the tax collector's perspective, substitutes the description of Y as in Fig. 2.

The condition of interest to us is the second one, namely [barrels of fish oil $(Y)]_{WS, CD, SCWD}$. Since, after Sainsbury (2014), we claim that the court case involves a substantive rather than a faultless disagreement, we must identify the culprit in this disagreement. Contextualist semantics such as DS allows us to do precisely this: the plaintiff uses the term 'fish oil' following WS (the description itself) and SCWD, the default meaning – a default for this speaker and this context. We must remember that the relevant scenario is a merchant's scenario, trading in oil extracted from sea-creatures as opposed to, say, a discussion on the anatomy of whales. So, the speaker's use of the term 'fish oil', and for the purpose of the truth-conditional analysis, the context together with the circumstances of evaluation,[28] are the culprit we need – a culprit that in a suitably context-friendly semantics can be represented and explained without difficulty as in Fig. 2. In Σ, this culprit is represented as SCWD.

It has to be noted that a condition [barrels of fish oil $(Y)]_{WS, CD, CPI}$ would work just as well, and corresponds to an equally plausible scenario where functional considerations lead two opposite parties in two different directions. I have opted for SCWD to represent the case of a genuine disagreement that is not staged and not founded on pretence. On the scenario where the plaintiff deliberately makes a choice between the two labels in order to claim taxes, CPI is the correct process to represent. To

[28] On the need for circumstances of evaluation in truth-conditional semantics and a solution as to how to integrate them see e.g. Predelli 2005a, b.

Fig. 2 Σ for example (7): 'Samuel Judd purchased three barrels of fish oil that had not been inspected'

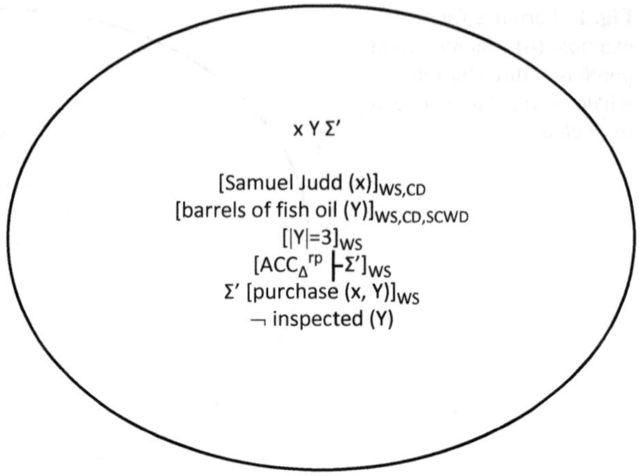

compare, the accused merchant is likely to use the description 'fish oil' as [fish oil]$_{WS}$, or, without assuming the shared background of the new taxonomy but rather the fluctuating state of the term instead, [fish oil]$_{WS, CPI}$, overriding for the purpose of the court case the functionally appropriate [fish oil]$_{WS, SCWD}$.

In the examples relevant for the case, 'fish oil' constitutes part of the expression 'barrel of fish oil'. And 'barrel of fish oil' is itself a character on this occasion of use, following the idea of fluid characters summarised earlier in this section, and as such is amenable to influences, called by Recanati (2012b) 'lateral influences', that yield the functional rather than the anatomical reading. 'Purchasing' and 'inspecting' are the sources of such lateral influences and create the relevant 'merchants' scenario'. In addition, as we have observed earlier, the expression 'fish oil' is a compound and as such is governed by its own, internal rules of compositionality in that the internal compositionality of compounds is less transparent as compared with expressions that do not have this status – say, 'whale oil'. All in all, there are multiple grammatical as well as pragmatic reasons for the non-anatomical reading, all well captured in a contextualist DS-theoretic representation.

Next, we are moving to the use of the term 'fish oil' by the jury and to example (8), with its merger representation given in Fig. 3.

The subscript CPI on [barrels of fish oil (Y)]$_{WS, CD,CPI}$ represents the fact that the jury had to make a conscious decision on the meaning of the term. In the sixth condition, the symbol '!' stands for the deontic necessity operator, loosely following Grice's (2001) unified account of modality.[29] The symbol '<' in the final condition stands for temporal precedence, derived from the structure of the sentence and thus via WS. Now, CPI is a conscious inferential process but it has firm foundations in the law:

> The New York State Legislature had enacted legislation to protect the public from contaminated oil by requiring that all fish oil sold in New York be gauged, inspected and branded.

[29] Note that Grice used ! to represent practical modality: 'let it be the case that *p*'.

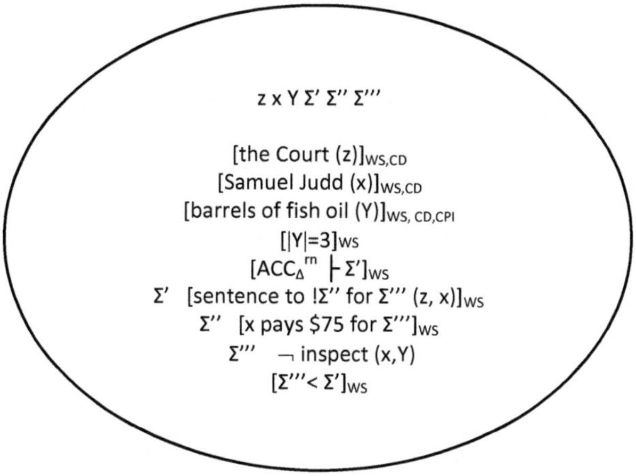

Fig. 3 Σ for example (8): 'The Court sentences Samuel Judd to paying $75 for failing to have three barrels of fish oil inspected'

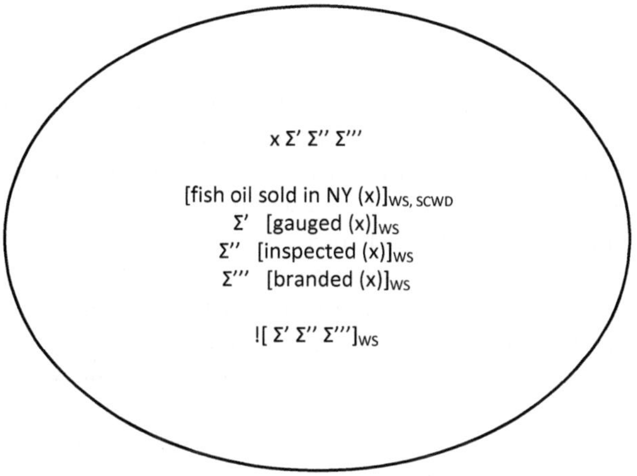

Fig. 4 Σ for example (9): 'Fish oil sold in New York must be gauged, inspected and branded'

> The law allowed the fish oil inspectors to impose a penalty of $25 per barrel on those who failed to comply. (Maurice v Judd, *ibid.*)[30]

Legal documents must not be open to contradictory interpretations, neither can they be founded on semantic underspecification that can lead to contradictory interpretations. The term 'fish oil' can only be used unambiguously as given by the lexicon of the language (WS), or by defaults that stem out of human universal principles governing mental operations (CD), or finally by default, standard meanings that are shared by those who are supposed to comply with this law (SCWD). This brings us to the formulation of the law we have given in (9) and the representation in Fig. 4.

The referent for the compound 'fish oil' will again be provided by grammatical as well as functional considerations (WS and SCWD), which this contextualist, truth-conditional semantic representation is capable of capturing.

[30] See fn 26.

6 Conclusion

Meanings that are relevant for the situation at hand can be derived from a variety of sources and through a variety of processes. A theory of meaning that aspires to the level of generalization that would give it suitable predictive power has to be able to represent them. We have proposed here that DS is such a theory. At the same time, a disclaimer is due in that this analysis is not intended to reflect the actual reasoning that the jury adopted – neither is it likely to have achieved such an objective. The semantic representations are just that: *semantic* representations and as such can show how a disagreement can be substantial and at the same time yielding to a semantic explanation. Sainsbury (2014: 4–5) concludes:

> Substantive disagreement requires agreement in meaning. There needs to be some proposition that one party affirms and the other denies. If the ancient meaning differed from the modern one, no proposition expressed by 'Whales are fish', or its negation, meets this condition. That is certainly not how things seemed to the protagonists in *Maurice vs. Judd*, and nor is it how it strikes us today: we think the jury gave the wrong verdict.

There is indeed substantive disagreement but here is where *our* agreement with Sainsbury ends: when viewed from the perspective of a radical contextualist semantics, we need not end up with a conclusion that "the jury gave a wrong verdict": we have devices at our disposal, notably the interactive, pragmatic compositionality of merger representations, and within it the circumstances of evaluation, the 'lateral influences', the fluid character, as well as the simple fact of the compromised compositionality of a compound in this fluid character, that perform all the tasks we want the constructs and principles of an explanatorily adequate theory to perform, and leave us no sense of a puzzle at all.

All in all, to sum up, in our court scenario, the verdict of the jury is a predictable one when analysed from the perspective of DS: (i) substantive disagreement is the default option, but also (ii) the use of the expression 'fish oil' is justified when the cognitive/functional approach to meaning is adopted. I tentatively conclude by pointing out one obvious corollary, namely that this pragmatization of meaning affects both sides of language in the courtroom but not to the same degree. On the one hand, the content of the relevant law cannot be taken to be the *communicative* rather than *textual* content (see Marmor and Soames 2011) beyond certain limitations imposed on the generalizations over admissible contexts: the law cannot be open to contradictory interpretations. On the other hand, the primary content of the plaintiff's and the defendant's contributions, firmly situated in the co-constructed context, can easily involve constituents form outside the language system (lexicon and structure) and as such can only be represented by a radical contextualist account such as DS. That said, it appears that we have given the semantics, as well as the metasemantic foundations, that Sainsbury deems wanting.

References

Ariel, M. (2010). *Defining pragmatics*. Cambridge: Cambridge University Press.

Asher, N. (2011). *Lexical meaning in context: A web of words*. Cambridge: Cambridge University Press.

Bach, K. (2004). Minding the gap. In C. Bianchi (Ed.), *The semantics/pragmatics distinction* (pp. 27–43). Stanford: CSLI Publications.

Bach, K. (2006). The excluded middle: Semantic minimalism without minimal propositions. *Philosophy and Phenomenological Research, 73*, 435–442.

Blome-Tillmann, M. (2013). Knowledge and implicatures. *Synthese, 190*, 4293–4319.

Blome-Tillmann, M. (2014). *Knowledge and presuppositions*. Oxford: Oxford University Press.

Borg, E. (2004). *Minimal semantics*. Oxford: Clarendon.

Borg, E. (2012). *Pursuing meaning*. Oxford: Oxford University Press.

Cappelen, H., & Lepore, E. (2005). *Insensitive semantics: A defense of semantic minimalism and speech act pluralism*. Oxford: Blackwell.

Carston, R. (1988). Implicature, explicature, and truth-theoretic semantics. In R. M. Kempson (Ed.), *Mental representations: The interface between language and reality* (pp. 155–181). Cambridge: Cambridge University Press.

Carston, R. (2002). *Thoughts and utterances: The pragmatics of explicit communication*. Oxford: Blackwell.

Giora, R. (2003). *On our mind: Salience, context, and figurative language*. Oxford: Oxford University Press.

Giora, R. (2012). The psychology of utterance processing: Context vs salience. In K. Allan & K. M. Jaszczolt (Eds.), *The Cambridge handbook of pragmatics* (pp. 151–167). Cambridge: Cambridge University Press.

Grice, P. (2001). *Aspects of reason*. Oxford: Clarendon.

Groenendijk, J., & Stokhof, M. (1991). Dynamic predicate logic. *Linguistics and Philosophy, 14*, 39–100.

Hawthorne, J., & Manley, D. (2012). *The reference book*. Oxford: Oxford University Press.

Jaszczolt, K. M. (2005). *Default semantics: Foundations of a compositional theory of acts of communication*. Oxford: Oxford University Press.

Jaszczolt, K. M. (2009a). Cancellability and the primary/secondary meaning distinction. *Intercultural Pragmatics, 6*, 259–289.

Jaszczolt, K. M. (2009b). *Representing time: An essay on temporality as modality*. Oxford: Oxford University Press.

Jaszczolt, K. M. (2010). Default semantics. In B. Heine & H. Narrog (Eds.), *The Oxford handbook of linguistic analysis* (pp. 215–246). Oxford: Oxford University Press.

Jaszczolt, K. M. (2012). "Pragmaticising" Kaplan: Flexible inferential bases and fluid characters. *Australian Journal of Linguistics, 32*, 209–237.

Jaszczolt, K. M. (2016). *Meaning in linguistic interaction: Semantics, Metasemantics, Philosophy of Language*. Oxford: Oxford University Press.

Kamp, H., & Reyle, U. (1993). *From discourse to logic: Introduction to modeltheoretic semantics of natural language, formal logic and discourse representation theory*. Dordrecht: Kluwer.

Kaplan, D. (1989a). Demonstratives: An essay on the semantics, logic, metaphysics, and epistemology of demonstratives and other indexicals. In J. Almog, J. Perry, & H. Wettstein (Eds.), *Themes from Kaplan* (pp. 481–563). New York: Oxford University Press.

Kaplan, D. (1989b). Afterthoughts. In J. Almog, J. Perry, & H. Wettstein (Eds.), *Themes from Kaplan* (pp. 565–614). New York: Oxford University Press.

Lakoff, G., & Johnson, M. (1980). *Metaphors we live by*. Chicago: University of Chicago Press.

Lakoff, G., & Johnson, M. (1999). *Philosophy in the flesh: The embodied mind and its challenge to Western thought*. New York: Basic Books.

Lepore, E., & Stone, M. (2015). *Imagination and convention: Distinguishing grammar and inference in language*. Oxford: Oxford University Press.

Levinson, S. C. (2000). *Presumptive meanings: The theory of generalized conversational implicature*. Cambridge, MA: MIT Press.

Ludlow, P. (2014). *Living words: Meaning underdetermination and the dynamic lexicon*. Oxford: Oxford University Press.
Lutz, M. (2014). The pragmatics of pragmatic encroachment. *Synthese, 191*, 1717–1740.
Marmor, A., & Soames, S. (Eds.). (2011). *Philosophical foundations of language in the law*. Oxford: Oxford University Press.
Nicolle, S., & Clark, B. (1999). Experimental pragmatics and what is said: A response to Gibbs and Moise. *Cognition, 69*, 337–354.
Peleg, O., & Giora, R. (2011). *Salient meanings: The whens and wheres*. In K. M. Jaszczolt & K. Allan (Eds.), *Salience and defaults in utterance processing* (pp. 35–51). Berlin: De Gruyter Mouton.
Pitts, A. (2005). *Assessing the evidence for intuitions about* what is said (Ms). University of Cambridge.
Predelli, S. (2005a). *Contexts: Meaning, truth, and the use of language*. Oxford: Clarendon.
Predelli, S. (2005b). Painted leaves, context, and semantic analysis. *Linguistics and Philosophy, 28*, 351–374.
Pulvermüller, F. (2010). Brain-language research: Where is the progress? *Biolinguistics, 4*, 255–288.
Recanati, F. (1989). The pragmatics of what is said. *Mind and Language, 4*. Reprinted in: S. Davis (Ed.). (1991). *Pragmatics: A reader* (pp. 97–120). Oxford: Oxford University Press.
Recanati, F. (2004). *Literal meaning*. Cambridge: Cambridge University Press.
Recanati, F. (2005). Literalism and contextualism: Some varieties. In G. Preyer & G. Peter (Eds.), *Contextualism in philosophy: Knowledge, meaning, and truth* (pp. 171–196). Oxford: Clarendon.
Recanati, F. (2010). *Truth-conditional pragmatics*. Oxford: Clarendon.
Recanati, F. (2012a). Contextualism: Some varieties. In K. Allan & K. M. Jaszczolt (Eds.), *The Cambridge handbook of pragmatics* (pp. 135–149). Cambridge: Cambridge University Press.
Recanati, F. (2012b). Compositionality, flexibility, and context dependence. In M. Werning, W. Hinzen, & E. Machery (Eds.), *The Oxford handbook of compositionality* (pp. 175–191). Oxford: Oxford University Press.
Recanati, F. (2012c). Pragmatic enrichment. In G. Russell & D. Graff Fara (Eds.), *The Routledge companion to philosophy of language* (pp. 67–78). New York: Routledge.
Sainsbury, M. (2014). Fishy business. *Analysis, 74*, 3–5.
Schiffer, S. (1991). Does Mentalese have a compositional semantics? In B. Loewer & G. Rey (Eds.), *Meaning in mind: Fodor and his critics* (pp. 181–199). Oxford: Blackwell.
Schneider, A. (2009). *Understanding primary meaning: A study with reference to requests in Russian and British English*. PhD dissertation, University of Cambridge.
Sileo, R. (2015). *Expressives taken to court: The conventionality v. context case* (Ms). University of Cambridge.
Soames, S. (2014). Cognitive propositions. In J. C. King, S. Soames, & J. Speaks (Eds.), *New thinking about propositions* (pp. 91–124). Oxford: Oxford University Press.
Sperber, D., & Wilson, D. (1995). *Relevance: Communication and cognition* (2nd ed.). Oxford: Blackwell.
Sperber, D., & Wilson, D. (Eds.). (2012). *Meaning and relevance*. Cambridge: Cambridge University Press.
Stainton, R. (2006). *Words and thoughts: Subsentences, ellipsis, and the philosophy of language*. Oxford: Clarendon.
Szabó, Z. G. (2000). Compositionality as supervenience. *Linguistics and Philosophy, 23*, 475.
Trask, R. L. (1996). *Historical linguistics*. London: Arnold.
van der Sandt, R. (1992). Presupposition projection as anaphora resolution. *Journal of Semantics, 9*, 333–377.
van der Sandt, R. (2012). Presupposition and accommodation in discourse. In K. Allan & K. M. Jaszczolt (Eds.), *The Cambridge handbook of pragmatics* (pp. 329–350). Cambridge: Cambridge University Press.

Implicitness in Normative Texts

Marina Sbisà

Abstract The paper deals with implicitness in normative texts. Assuming a definition of normative text and considering as implicit meaning whatever is presupposed or implicated by a text, it is argued that the retrieval of implicit meaning is indispensable to the understanding of normative texts as well as of informative ones. The reliability of explicitation practices relies, however, upon the normativity of implicitness, without which we could not distinguish between correct understanding and failure to understand. The implications of the claim that implicitness is normative are examined and the explicitation of presuppositions and implicatures of normative texts is exemplified by reference to passages drawn from the regulations of a condominium and a draft law presented to Italian parliament. Explicitation practices are shown to yield information about the normative background and the motivations of the norm at issue, and to contribute to the content of the norm and to its possible applications.

Keywords Implicitness • Legal interpretation • Presupposition • Implicature

1 Premise

In this paper I deal with implicitness in normative texts.[1] Like those texts whose aims are mainly informative, texts having normative function, too, usually have presuppositions and implicate assumptions that they do not specify explicitly. I will refer to what is presupposed or implicated by a text as its "implicit meaning", thereby also intending to refer to possible kinds of meaning not explicitly specified in a text, which might not fit the definitions of either presupposition (Strawson 1950; Stalnaker 1973, 1999; Sbisà 1999, 2007; Simons 2013) or implicature (Grice

---

[1] This paper develops a theme already discussed in my contribution entitled "Normatività e comunicazione" to the volume *Questioni di genere nel diritto: impliciti e crittotipi*, edited by Lucia Morra and Barbara Pasa, Torino: Giappichelli. I thank Lucia Morra and Francesca Poggi for insightful exchanges.

M. Sbisà (✉)
Department of Humanities, Università degli Studi di Trieste, Trieste, Italy
e-mail: sbisama@units.it

F. Poggi, A. Capone (eds.), *Pragmatics and Law*, Perspectives in Pragmatics, Philosophy & Psychology 10, DOI 10.1007/978-3-319-44601-1_2

1989; Sperber and Wilson 1995; Sbisà 2007; Bianchi 2013). I will explore what functions such implicit meaning serves within the overall meaning of a normative text, and what role is played by explicitation practices in our understanding of texts of this kind.

By "normative texts" I mean those linguistic productions (oral or written) that display the following properties:

(i) they attribute to target agents one or more deontic modal predicates, so that, in the deontic sense of these verbs, they can or cannot do something or abstain from something, or have to or have not to do something or to abstain from something, and the like (the dominant illocutionary force of normative texts may be called "exercitive", see Austin 1962, p. 151–157);
(ii) they do not prescribe specific acts or kinds of acts unconditionally to their addressees, as commands do;
(iii) they address groups: it is a task of the addressees to recognize that certain deontic modal attributions hold, but the agents targeted by these attributions do not need to coincide with the whole set of the addressees;
(iv) their addresser or enunciator is often not an individual agent endowed with a mind, but a collective or an institutional agent, without a mind of its own, but recognized nonetheless as possessing competence, authority, capacities, and responsibilities.

Notwithstanding the objections raised by Poggi (2011), the collective or institutional character of the enunciator of a normative text does not hinder its being an enunciator, since, in my perspective, this notion is concerned with a figure correlated to the text, which the text itself presupposes and constitutes, and not with the physical and psychological individual who speaks or writes. Following Goffman (1981), I distinguish three functions related to text production (and linguistic action, but also, to action in general): animator, author and principal. In the case of many normative texts, the animator is the person or persons who actually utter or write the words, the author is a collective agent including whoever contributed to deciding what to say or write, and the principal is the agent, often an institution, who issues the norm. It is the principal who is attributed the meaning intention projected by the text and the responsibility for its illocutionary effects, and who, therefore, can be identified as its enunciator.

2 Normative Texts and Implicit Meaning

It is perhaps trivial to recall that to be complied with at all, a norm must be understood by its addressees. Behavior conforming to norms in absence of an understanding of the norms appears to be merely accidental. It is not sanctioned, because it does not amount to violation either, but we would not recognize it as behavior determined or guided by the norms. This gives to the understanding of norms a salient role in their way of operating. The relevant understanding is not a matter of grasping information: a normative text may provide information to its addressees, but since this is not its specific function, there are usually also other sources from which the same information is obtained, often more fully and more explicitly. Rather, it is a matter of understanding what that text imposes on its targets, and what kinds of behavior are counted as complying with it. Thus, also in order to understand a normative text, we need to elaborate at least some of its presuppositions and implicatures. There might be cases in which knowledge of the situational context in which the norm was issued is indispensable to understand what counts as the norm's application, but is not obtainable by the recipient by acquaintance and is not made available by the text itself either (for example, by means of description). In these cases, the retrieval of implicit meaning would help the recipient to grasp at least some salient aspects of the situational context. Moreover, explicitation of implicit meaning is helpful (albeit not always decisive) when, in order to understand what behavior counts as conforming to a norm and what does not, recipients feel they should consider the "intention" with which the norm was issued, intention which (because of the particular nature of the agent issuing the norm) cannot be equivalent to a mental state of an individual, but is to be derived from the aims and reasons that guided the decisional process by which the collective or institutional agent responsible for issuing the norm has come to establish it. In identifying this "intention", a central role is played by the intentions that can be ascribed to the author of the text on the basis of the text itself and the rules and reasons that support our understanding of what is presupposed and implicated. So, we might say that anything in a normative text which helps the recipient to retrieve the relevant aspects of the situational context in which a norm was issued, or to elaborate the intentions that can be reasonably attributed to the legislator on the basis of the produced text, contributes substantively to its comprehension. These activities are, or are sustained by, explicitation practices.

It could be objected that by including content that is not explicitly said in the content of a norm, or allowing implicit meaning to determine what counts as the application of a norm, we lay ourselves open to free interpretations which, in this field, can only be dangerous and should be avoided. Indeed, when a norm is addressed to us, we need to be certain about what is permitted or mandated or forbidden by it, while implicit meaning is often not completely determined: implicatures, for example, have been described as consisting of open disjunctions (Grice 1989) or as entertained with various degrees of strength or weakness (Sperber and Wilson 1995). Moreover, implicit meaning is typically context-dependent and this makes it variable. Norms are typically given written form in order to make them stable, but (ironically enough) written texts are particularly exposed to the contextual variation of implicit meaning, precisely because the stability of their form makes it possible for them to be received by different readers at different places, times, and kinds of situations. While authors such as Marmor (2008) and Höfler (2014) accept presuppositions, insofar as they are activated by linguistic triggers, as a kind of implicit meaning that contributes to the overall meaning of a normative text, serious doubts have been raised with respect to implicature, particularly conversational implicature, in consideration of its relying upon the assumption of the

Cooperative Principle (Grice 1989) as a guideline for interpretation. Marmor (2008) and Poggi (2011) exclude conversational implicature from contributing to the meaning of normative texts, especially when the interaction in which these are contextualized is conflictual, while Morra (2011, 2015) finds it wholly acceptable and Bianchi (2016), albeit not defending the assumption of the Cooperative Principle, accepts implicature as an interpretive tool governed by the innate, cognitive Relevance Principle (Sperber and Wilson 1995).

My defence of implicit meaning of all kinds as contributing to the overall meaning of normative texts as well as texts of any other kind rests upon the claim, for which I have argued elsewhere (2007: 193–194), that implicitness (in texts of any kind) is normative. This claim is in contrast with the widespread inclination to deal with implicit meaning as always relative to a communicative situation, an addresser, a recipient, and their cognitive states, and therefore always *ad hoc*. My reason for opposing this inclination is that it is only by admitting that the implicit meaning of a text is not merely what it happens to be, but what it *should* be, that we can distinguish between correct and incorrect understanding, legitimate and illegitimate interpretations. If there are no normative constraints on implicit meaning or normative guidelines to it, one interpretation of a text is worth another and we can distinguish at most, on completely extra-textual grounds, between reliable and less reliable intepreters. This, however, requires criteria for the reliability of interpreters, which must necessarily include some indirect or concealed reference to their capability to provide good interpretations, and therefore to some assessment of the interpretations themselves. Of course, if in order to avoid this difficulty we consider implicitness as endowed with some kind of normativity, we need also specify in what sense and to what extent.

The claim that implicitness is normative should not be taken to mean that there is an obligation for the recipient to actually work out the implicit meaning of the utterances he receives and spell it out explicitly (see Bianchi 2013, 126). Indeed, it would be counter-intuitive if explicitation practices were mandatory. They take time and effort and participants in a conversation can hardly ever pause to go through them. Readers have the advantage of having the whole text at their disposal, so that they can pause and reflect; however, with written texts too, not all the presuppositions or implicatures which they may be said to trigger or invite need to be given explicit form on every occasion, for every possible aim, in order to be helpful. Indeed, the status of most implicit meanings in our everyday conversation as well as in the fruition of written texts is enduring implicitness.

Attributing normativity to implicitness involves claiming that the implicit meaning of a text does not comprise anything which *cannot* be attributed to that text as part of its meaning, and that it *must* be retrievable from the text on the basis of some rule or reason. An alleged presupposition or implicature cannot be attributed to a text as part of its implicit meaning when, for example, the text clearly makes statements incompatible with it. In fact, explicitly formulated meaning takes priority over implicit meaning. If this simple principle is sometimes difficult to apply, it is due to the unstable and partly fuzzy border between what is (explicitly) said and what is (implicitly) meant. Indeed, there are cases, especially cases of flouting of the maxim of Quality "Try to say something true", in which (as has often been suggested) what is actually *said* is not the literal meaning of the uttered sentence, but what (in the Gricean framework) is its re-elaboration conforming to the Cooperative Principle (for example, its metaphorical or other figurative meaning). In these cases, the metaphorical or figurative meaning of the utterance will take priority over other possible presuppositions or implicatures, whenever some incompatibility arises (Grice 1989; Sbisà 2007, 99–100; Carston 2002; Bianchi 2009). Another case in which we refrain from attributing a certain implicit meaning is when it turns out that for some reason, the enunciator of the text *could not* mean that (for example because at that moment, she did not possess the relevant knowledge or because, soon after text production, she reformulates what she means in an incompatible way. These are circumstances that cancel or annul a possible attribution, but they should not be confused with those in which the question of whether there is or is not a certain implicit meaning does not even arise (because the text does not provide any indication that there should be that implicit meaning). As to the principle according to which what a text presupposes or implicates must be retrievable from it on the basis of some rule or reason, this has diverse applications depending on the kind of implicit meaning at issue. According to my perspective, which keeps presuppositions distinct from both conventional and conversational implicatures (Sbisà 1999, 2007), implicit meaning can be retrieved from a text in the following ways:

(i) as the presupposition of an utterance, triggered by some linguistic feature of it:

(1)(a) John has stopped smoking.
→ John used to smoke (presupposition of the lexical item *stop*)

(1)(b) Peter's son is asleep.
→Peter has got a son (existential presupposition triggered by a definite description)

(1)(c) It was John who shouted.
→Someone shouted (presupposition triggered by the syntactic form of the sentence)

(ii) as the conventional implicature of a linguistic expression used in the text, for example:

(2) He is rich but honest.
→ A rich man may have gathered his richness in dishonest ways (implicature associated with the use of "but" in the place of "and")

(iii) as a conversational implicature, retrieved by inference and (in a Gricean framework at least) on some argumentative grounds, for example:

(3)(a) A: I am out of petrol.

B: There is a garage round the corner.
→The petrol can be bought at the garage round the corner
(implicature according to the first maxim of Quantity)

(3)(b) A: Where is John?
B: His car is parked in front of Ann's house.
→John is likely to be at Ann's
(implicature according to the maxim of Relation)

(3)(c) A: Is the party going on?
B: Some guests have gone.
→Not all of the guests have gone
(generalized implicature according to the first maxim of Quantity)

(3)(d) John made the car stop.
→John did not do so by using the regular brakes of that very same car
(generalized implicature according to the maxim of Manner)

(3)(e) You are the salt of Earth.
→You give taste/meaning/value [...] to the world/to human life
(metaphor: flouting of the maxim of Quality)

The borders between the categories of presupposition, conventional implicature, and conversational implicature are not always self-evident (for example, is the implicated assumption in (3)(c) a generalized conversational implicature or a conventional one?), and the resulting partition of the field of implicit meaning is not without residues (for example, how do evaluative connotations, such as those of slurs, exactly work?). Moreover, these categories are likely not to exhaust the field of implicit meaning (does backgrounded content work as presupposed? Do "free enrichments" or "implicitures" contributing to the utterance's truth-conditions count as implicit or explicit?). Here, I will propose some sketchy characterizations of them, as a selective synthesis of decades of debates. We will then see in what sense each of these ways of conveying and retrieving implicit meaning is normative.

I characterize presupposition in the following way:

> A sentence *s* presupposes a sentence *p* (or: has the presupposition that *p*) when the truth of *p* has to be taken for granted by whoever accepts the utterance of *s* as appropriate.

Thus, the normative feature of presupposition depends on the truth of the presupposed sentence being a requirement for the appropriateness of the speech act performed by uttering the sentence that triggers the presupposition. There is a rule that requires that, in order for the speech act to be appropriate, the situation should display certain features and therefore the sentence specifying these should be true. As an alternative, if an internalist framework is adopted, the same rule may be formulated as requiring that, in order for the speech act to be held to be appropriate by the participants in the conversation, participants should believe that the utterance's appropriateness conditions hold (for the point made here, the contrast between an externalist and an internalist view is not really relevant: I am not raising the question of whether a certain speech act is, or is not, actually felicitous and appropriate). However, the externalist version of the requirement is stronger in that it gives a stronger motivation to presupposition accommodation: we take for granted that the presupposed sentence is true because if it were not, the utterance presupposing it would be an inappropriate speech act, possibly infelicitous up to being null and void at the illocutionary level. This also explains why an utterance triggers a presupposition even if the recipient does not trust the speaker and does not take the truth of the presupposed sentence as granted. Likewise, the utterance of sentence *s* has presupposition *p* also when the user (speaker or recipient) of sentence *s* does not pay any attention at all to *s*'s presuppositions: but she might, indeed, find herself entangled, at other times and contexts, by the presuppositional commitment she has undertaken without reflection.

As to implicature, its general characterization is problematic, given the differences between conversational and conventional implicature. I propose the following:

> An utterance of sentence *s* implicates *i* if sentence *i* can be inferred, as an addition or a correction to what sentence *s* says, from the fact that a certain speaker has uttered sentence *s*.

This allows us to further distinguish between:

- conventional implicature: inference activated by the conventional meaning of a word or phrase in sentence *s*;
- conversational implicature: inference based upon reasoning from the assumption of the observance of the Cooperative Principle (for generalized implicatures) together with possible other contextual assumptions (for particularized implicatures).

In the case of conventional implicature, normativity resides again in a rule: a rule activating an inference with a particular kind of content is associated with one of the expressions that compose sentence *s*. In the case of conversational implicature, the retrieval of implicit meaning is supported by reasons, namely, it occurs in conformity with (though not necessarily by means of) a possible argumentative route (which comprises the assumption that the Cooperative Principle holds, one or more of its maxims and, possibly, further contextual information). While normativity is apparent enough when the implicit meaning depends on a rule, – if there is a rule, there is also conformity to or difformity from the rule, and therefore one can (or rather must) distinguish between right and wrong –, with conversational implicatures the situation is more complicated: normativity, and the consequent possibility to distinguish between right and wrong, have to do with the reasons upon which the retrieval of implicit meaning depends, which have to be good reasons and contribute to forming good arguments.

I would like to underscore that the claim that implicitness is normative does not mean that the participants in the conversation actually have to be cooperative. There are implicatures that it is correct or acceptable to attribute to a text, and alleged implicatures that do not pertain to it: which ones are actually retrieved or made explicit in further utterances is a matter of fact and not of norm. The implicatures that it is correct or acceptable to attribute to the text remain the same, whether the recipient actually retrieves them or not. Therefore, if a recipient takes an uncooperative attitude and refuses to recognize a speaker as cooperative, this will have consequences on his understanding of the speaker's text and on the subsequent development of the encounter, but does not affect the implicit meaning to be retrieved.

3 Implications of the Normativity of Implicitness

The claim that implicitness is normative has certain implications. It makes it possible (or, rather, makes it necessary) to distinguish between what is presupposed or implicated and what is not said, and between what is presupposed or implicated and the psychological associations and encyclopaedic assumptions made by the recipient. A more puzzling consequence of it is that some implicit meaning might be retrievable, or even actually retrieved, according to rules or reasons, even when the speaker denies having so meant. When it is beyond doubt that the retrieval of the implicit meaning in question is legitimate, the solution of the puzzle lies in recognizing the text itself as the target of meaning attributions and, therefore, as the locus of some (derived) agency.

Let us consider these implications in more detail.

3.1 What Is Presupposed or Implicated vs. What Is Not Said

The distinction between what is presupposed or implicated and what is not said limits implicit meaning to those contents that can be retrieved from the text according to rules or reasons. As I have already said, if there are no such rules or reasons it becomes impossible to distinguish between implicit meaning correctly attributable to the text (and possibly to the speaker too) and implicit meaning that should not be so attributed. The field of implicit meaning thereby loses those "pragmatic presuppositions" which consist of assumptions that are shared by speaker and addressees (and believed to be shared) (Stalnaker 1973, 1999), but which are not indicated in the text in such a way as to make them retrievable. I do not intend to deny the existence of these assumptions and their importance for the efficiency of communication, but they should be kept distinct (as assumptions that the participants entertain independently of the ongoing conversation) from implicit meaning, namely, those assumptions that the text makes available to the participants, so that they can work them out as a part of their understanding of the text. The function of assumptions that are shared and believed to be shared is to provide premises (not retrievable from the text alone) which enter as such into the comprehension processes, making contextualization possible. For example, they may be used in the retrieval of particularized conversational implicatures. The distinction between what is presupposed, or implicated, and what is not said, aims to distinguish the implicit meaning that can be retrieved from the text from those assumptions which, whether useful or not for understanding the text, have to be searched for from other sources if they are to become part of the common ground.

The distinction between what is presupposed or implicated and what is not said is relevant to communication in educational contexts: assumptions of the two kinds are often equally necessary for the aims of learning, but different strategies are required for their retrieval. Using extra-textual strategies to search for what is presupposed or implicated will not do, while attempting to argue from the text to the assumptions that the speaker supposes to be shared (but neglects to specify) may be a waste of time. The distinction is also relevant to the interpretation of normative texts, since it makes a lot of difference whether the text is to be held merely to say nothing about a certain topic, or to implicate something about it, for example that it should *not* be dealt with in the same way as those dealt with in the text.

3.2 *What Is Presupposed or Implicated vs. Psychological or Encyclopaedic Associations*

The distinction between what is presupposed or implicated and psychological or encyclopaedic associations separates what is presupposed or implicated (as part of the overall meaning of the text) from the inferences that the interlocutor makes on the basis of his own psychological dispositions or the information he possesses thanks to past experience or previous communications. The recipient's state may be known to the speaker and may therefore be exploited by her in the process of choosing the form of her message, but the strategic calculations that this knowledge makes possible are in no way part of her communicative intentions. In general, it does not make much sense to imagine that what the speaker intends, in all such cases, comprises communicating to the recipient that she has knowledge of his psychological or epistemic state.

A slightly different kind of case is that in which a recipient infers from the speaker's utterance (or in general from the text produced by the speaker) that the speaker entertains a certain psychological or epistemic state, but this is not – and cannot be – the reception of something that the speaker has meant. Imagine a speaker who talks in a hurry or with insistence, who comes back to the same point again and again. She does not mean "I am anxious": even if her behavior manifests anxiety or worry, even if the recipient may identify the object or the cause of her psychological state, her behavior is merely a symptom of that state and the recipient's inferences do not commit him to attribute to her the intention, intended to be recognized, to make him form certain beliefs about her psychological state. Indeed, when we want to deal with such manifestations of anxiety as communication, we often take it that the addresser is not the speaker herself but her "unconscious", an agent within the agent, to whom (as an enunciator) we attribute the communicative intention corresponding to "X is anxious".

3.3 Textual Agency

If implicitness is normative, a speaker may be mistaken about what she means, particularly as regards to what she presupposes or implicates. This is puzzling, because it does not fit Grice's original theory (Bianchi 2013, 126; see also Saul 2002). The puzzle can be solved/explained if we introduce textual agency.

Suppose that a speaker claims she did not actually mean what she was understood as presupposing or implicating. Since no intention can be attributed to a person who explicitly disowns it, we can no longer attribute to her the communicative intention corresponding to that implicit meaning. But if our retrieval of the implicit meaning is sound enough (because is it correctly based on a rule or supported by good reasons), at the normative level that implicit meaning is still there. What we can do is to recognize the text itself as "meaning" something. Indeed, we often speak of what an utterance or a text "mean" and Grice himself (1957, 1989: 165–189) admits of such a use of *to mean*, albeit as deriving from the more basic use concerning speaker's meaning. In the case we are considering, what the speaker may have wanted to mean is completely distinct from what her text turns out to mean, and one way to describe this situation is to say that the text as an artifact is itself endowed with agency. In this perspective, the speaker turns out to be wrong about the meaning of her text, but only to the extent to which the text she has produced invites the attribution of communicative intentions other than those she actually entertains: she is wrong about the properties of her text, not about her intentions. To allow for this case, therefore, we need not claim that there are circumstances in which a speaker does not control her intentions. The distinction proposed can, however, be made more plausible by recognizing that sometimes the communicative intention of a speaker may not be wholly transparent to the speaker herself, either because of lack of conscious reflection upon it, or because of some emotional conflict that leads her, so to say, to misunderstand herself.

This consequence of the normativity of implicitness, namely the attribution of agency to the text itself, is more controversial than the other two which I have illustrated above, particularly in consideration of Grice's original definition of implicating (1989), according to which implicating is a kind of speaker's meaning. But I am focusing here on the text's property to permit and elicit the attribution of a certain communicative intention to the speaker: recognizing this property does not amount to stating that the speaker actually has that intention in mind (perhaps consciously). We might know nothing about the speaker, or the speaker might disconfirm the attribution that has quite reasonably been made to her (by claiming, for example, that she did not mean or intend so and so) and there might follow some interactional negotiation directed at restoring an intersubjectively acceptable understanding of the communicative event. I think that the safest policy is to attribute to the text as an artifact that which can reasonably be attributed to the speaker, taking it that to allege that the speaker (that is, the speaking individual) actually entertains a certain intention in her mind and is even aware of this intention, requires a further step.

This proposal is not completely incompatible with the original Gricean picture of speaker's meaning. As I have already mentioned, Grice himself grants that meaning attributions can also be expressed in terms of utterance-tokens. He considers this form of attribution as derivative with respect to the corresponding attributions of meaning to the speaker herself ("speaker's meaning" proper). But what he thus establishes is essentially the logical priority of speaker's meaning with respect to any other form in which meaning may be articulated or reported or represented. This does not require recipients to attribute meaning, on each concrete occasion, first to the speaker, and then derivatively to her text. Indeed, in text comprehension, we would appear to proceed in the opposite direction. We "know" the speaker's communicative intention from her text; if we knew it "directly" from the speaker, this would (quite paradoxically) require the production and reception of another text, of a metalinguistic character, such as a declaration of intention or a meaning explanation.

The notion of textual agency appears all the more indispensable, the more the text under consideration (as a written, recorded, printed, or electronic text) can make the speaker's voice reach contexts completely separated from those in which her physical presence is located (on this, and on non-human agency in general, see Cooren 2010). Finally, it is also indispensable to talk about meaning as communicative intention in the case of texts whose enunciator does not coincide with an individual speaker, but with a collective or institutional agent. For obvious reasons, this latter case comprises many kinds of normative texts, such as regulations, codes, and laws.

To admit of textual agency, however, does not solve the problem of how one should determine the meaning of different occurrences of the same text in different contexts. It remains open whether the meaning of a text (novel, poem, law, sacred book) is, or is not, a function of each new context in which it is received. While in the case of a novel or a poem, the reply to this question is essentially a matter of aesthetics and literary criticism, for legal texts (and likewise, but more intriguingly, for sacred books), it has important social repercussions. In the perspective developed in this paper, the new context allows whoever receives the text to reinterpret it, but only to the extent to which the original formulation of the text has left room to do so. Nearly all texts allow for some such room, but this room is never without constraints: reinterpretations must keep on accounting for the text's surface and must not add anything that cannot be motivated by reference to it.

4 Explicitation Practices and Their Functions

I will now consider some examples of explicitation of implicit meaning from normative texts. By their discussion I intend to characterize the functions served by what is presupposed or implicated with respect to the overall meaning of the text, and the uses to which explicitation practices may be put with respect to the process of understanding and applying a norm. A first group of examples comes from a normative text belonging to ordinary life: the regulations of a condominium. From these regulations and their attachments, I have extracted some passages, to the overall meaning of which what is presupposed or implicated substantially contributes.[2]

(4)(a) *Condominio "Camilla"- Regolamento di condominio*
[…]
Art. 2 – Quote dei partecipanti:
[…]
Nessun condomino può rinunciare ***ai suoi diritti di comproprietà sulle parti comuni, né a quelle di particolare sua proprietà, né all'uso dei servizi comuni, allo scopo di essere esonerato dal pagamento dei relativi contributi*** *a suo carico, in virtù del presente regolamento e per legge (art. 1118 del C.c.).*

'Condominium "Camilla" – Regulations of the condominium
[…]
Quotas owed by participants:
[…]
No co-owner may relinquish **his/her rights to joint ownership of the common areas**, nor **to those of his own property**, nor **to the use of common facilities, with the aim of being absolved of payment of the relative sums** owed by him by virtue of these regulations and by law.'

By presupposition, it is here conveyed that: co-owners have rights to joint ownership of the common areas; common areas exist in the condominium; the co-owners have a right to use common facilities; there exist common facilities of the condominium; each co-owner owes the payment of sums relative to rights to joint ownership of the common areas, areas of his own property, and use of common facilities. Moreover the adjunct *allo scopo di essere esonerato...* ('with the aim of being absolved…') implicates according to the maxim of Relation that some co-owner may not wish to pay the quotas owed by him and may attempt to achieve this aim by giving up his corresponding rights.

The contents thus made available to the recipient are mainly informative in nature, at two different levels. The presuppositions have informative value for recipients who are not familiar with norms and regulations about condominiums. They make available to the recipient the complex setting of rights and obligations concerning common areas and use of common facilities.

[2] I cite my examples in their original language (Italian, which is my mother tongue), followed by the English translation. In so doing, I assume that the characteristics of the textual genre at issue, which are relevant here, are not language-specific.

The implicature we have noticed amounts to the insinuation that some participants might have dishonest attitudes and plans and reveals (should the recipient have cause to reflect upon it) the reasons behind this particular rule – what that particular rule is meant to be for.

(4) (b) *Regolamento interno – Allegato C*
Art. 1 – Tutti i condomini e/o inquilini sono tenuti a comportarsi da ***persone educate e civili****, osservando* ***le norme di buon vicinato*** *con reciproca tolleranza e rispetto, evitando ogni motivo di molestia e disturbo agli altri.*

'Internal regulations – Attachment C
Art. 1 – All co-owners and/or tenants are required to behave like **courteous, civilised people**, adhering to **the norms of good neighbourliness** with mutual tolerance and respect, avoiding causing any nuisance and bother to others.'

We notice here the presupposition that there exist *norme di buon vicinato* ('norms of good neighbourliness'), which however are not further specified (perhaps because their existence is taken for granted and should therefore be common ground: it is thus implicated – by the first maxim of Quantity – that what their content is, is common ground too). This presupposition is, however, hardly informative (it would be such only with respect to a recipient who has never heard of norms of good neighbourliness). There is also an implicature from cohesion, which I explain as following from the maxim of Relation (Sbisà 2007, 147–150). Textual cohesion is indeed a matter of the relations holding between the component expressions of a text. This implicature arises from the connection between the main sentence and the gerund phrases *osservando*... ('adhering to...'), *evitando*... ('avoiding...') and yields a sort of definition of what it is for persons to be *educate e civili* ('courteous and civilised'). Courteous and civilised people are those who observe the norms of good neighbourliness and avoid causing any nuisance and bother to others. This implicature too fails to provide the reader with precise indications about the behavior admitted or required, but as a cumulative effect, the presuppositions and implicatures of this passage create a framework in which anybody who feels they are being annoyed or bothered is entitled to protest. This is, incidentally, most probably the aim of the rule.

(4) (c) *Regolamento interno – Allegato C*
Art. 3 – Per il rispetto del riposo altrui è vietato ***qualsiasi rumore*** *dalle ore 13.00 alle 16.00 e dalle ore 23.00 alle ore 8.00.*

'Internal regulations – Attachment C
Art. 3 – Out of respect for other people's rest, it is forbidden to make **any noise** from 1.00 pm to 4.00 pm and from 11 pm to 8.00 pm.'

Here one may wonder what it means that "any noise" is forbidden. From which volume up does the prohibition apply? Possible further details concerning the upper limit of that natural noise production which escapes prohibition must exploit the so-called "free enrichments" of the norm's content (Recanati 2004, 23–25). If the added detail depends on pragmatic processes of language understanding, this confirms once again that the strategy already observed in our remarks to example (4)(b) is at work, namely, that (without saying it explicitly) the norm legitimates any complaint on the part of any resident who feels annoyed or bothered. The solution of controversies is thus deferred from the domain of explicit regulations to that of interpersonal negotiations.

I take another example from a draft law approved by the Italian Chamber of Deputies on September 19, 2013 entitled *Disposizioni in materia di contrasto dell'omofobia e della transfobia* ('Measures designed to contrast homophobia and transphobia'). This draft law basically consists of extending certain sections of a pre-existing law (Law n.654 of October 13, 1975) and of a decree (n.122 of 26 April 1993) to apply them to discriminatory discourse and behaviour of a homophobic and transphobic nature, simply by adding the words *o fondati sull'omofobia o la transfobia* ('or based on homophobia or transphobia') in those places where they are needed. However, while there are no exceptions to the sanctioning of discriminatory behaviour towards people from different ethnic groups or religions, the Chamber of Deputies introduced and approved an additional section (3-bis) with regard to homophobia and transphobia, fixing limitations to the measures introduced by the preceding articles, which reads as follows:

> (5) *3-bis. Ai sensi della presente legge, non costituiscono discriminazione, né istigazione alla discriminazione,* ***la libera espressione e manifestazione di*** *convincimenti od opinioni riconducibili* ***al pluralismo delle idee****, purché non istighino all'odio o alla violenza, né le condotte conformi al diritto vigente ovvero anche se assunte* ***all'interno di organizzazioni che svolgono attività di natura politica, sindacale, culturale, sanitaria, di istruzione ovvero di religione o di culto, relative all'attuazione dei princìpi e dei valori di rilevanza costituzionale che connotano tali organizzazioni.***
>
> 'According to the present law, **the free expression and manifestation of** convictions or opinions attributable to **the pluralism of ideas** does not constitute discrimination, or instigation to discrimination, so long as they do not instigate hatred or violence, nor does conduct assumed within the law or even conduct when occurring **within organizations which carry out activities of a political, trades-union, cultural, health, educational nature, or pertaining to religion and worship, relative to the implementation of the constitutional principles and values which characterize these organizations.'**

The effect of the new section 3-bis upon a normative text designed to contrast homophobia and transphobia is puzzling. Lexical and syntactic complexity and the various disjunctions included in the text make it difficult for readers to make up their minds about what precisely remains forbidden and what is rendered legitimate. Reflecting on implicit meaning helps us to discover this.

The new section presupposes that there is free expression and manifestation of convictions or opinions that can be traced back to the pluralism of ideas and, therefore, also that there is something to be called *il pluralismo delle idee* ('the pluralism of ideas'). It implicates that not always does such free expression and manifestation instigate hatred or violence, but suggests, by so doing, that it might do so. We can very easily observe that presupposing that the pluralism of ideas exists is not the same thing as presupposing the simple and obvious truth that people's opinions may diverge or even be incompatible. Pluralism is an "…ism", that is, a doctrine, rather than a state of affairs. That which Section 3-bis deals with, therefore, is not the mere diversity of opinions, but the expression and manifestation of diverse convictions or opinions made in the persuasion that any idea about the topic at issue is legitimate. But such a belief is not true of convictions and opinions on any possible topic. Where it is relatively easy to reach an agreement based on fact or on shared criteria, how could we maintain that it is legitimate to have different opinions and stop just at that, taking it for granted that those different opinions are irreducible to one another? Indeed, this may happen in domains where no verification is possible (nor, perhaps, required): those of religious belief, moral convictions, and ideologies. We see then that homosexuality and transsexuality are dealt with by Section 3-bis as topics about which one may entertain any opinion, as if there were no fact of the matter, and no fairness to be respected. This amounts to presupposing that there is no truth about homosexuality and transsexuality to be searched for and discovered, no fair attitude to be argued for and recognized. A norm that presupposes this may seem to be very open-minded at first sight: indeed, it uses linguistic expressions such as *libera espressione* ('free expression'), *pluralismo delle idee* ('pluralism of ideas'), and the like. But it runs the risk of legitimating the tolerance of intolerance.

The bundle of implicit assumptions associated with the final lines of the section is also worth consideration. The expression *all'interno di organizzazioni che...* ('within – lit. 'in the inside of' – organizations which…'), followed by a verb in the indicative mood, activates the presupposition that organizations such as those described by the relative clause exist, namely, that there are organizations which carry out activities in various fields but which are characterized by their implementing principles and values relevant to the Constitution of the Italian Republic. It is also suggested (according to the maxim of Relevance) that such organizations, or some of them, might have something to say or do about homosexuality or transsexuality, as a part of their above-characterized activities. By the adoption of Section 3-bis in a norm designed to contrast homophobia and transphobia, these organizations would be allowed to say whatever they like about homosexuality and transsexuality.

It is also presupposed, indeed, that there exists conduct of sorts, apparently relevant to regulations against discrimination (if not, why mention it?), which might not conform to current law (their conformity to law is presented as a member of a disjunction!), but might nevertheless be assumed within organizations implementing, by their activities, principles and values of the Italian Constitution. How this is at all possible, it is not clear. But the existence or however, the possibility of such conduct is presupposed, not asserted (or implicated), and is therefore beyond question for the recipient. If we add to the recognition of what is presupposed some consideration based upon the maxim of Relation, we are lead to reflect upon the bond, which is implicated, between a conduct being assumed within the kind of organization described, and its not amounting to discrimination nor instigation to discrimination. Certainly, there is a causal nexus, in which the determinant role is played by the conformity of the aims of the organization to principles and values belonging to the Constitution of the Italian Republic. Thus, within the presupposed framework, the statute of an organization (its being inspired by constitutional principles and values) turns out to have greater weight than the actual behaviour and claims of the organization when it comes to assessing whether what the organization says and does about homosexuality and transsexuality amounts, or does not amount, to the discrimination, or instigation to the discrimination, of homosexuals and transsexuals.

Here too, I would say, the analysis of what is implicitly meant enables us to determine (insofar as possible) the legal effects of a normative text (in this case, the effects it would have if approved) and the intentions and evaluations which have inspired the norm. As usual, this also enables us to take a stand in favour or against the proposal to adopt such a norm with increased awareness of what is at stake. The analysis of what is presupposed and implicated helps us reply to questions about the (possible) application of the norm, such as, for example, whether the diffusion of booklets in which homosexuality is described as a disease and which invite homosexuals to seek treatment would be legal. Indeed, it would, if made by an organization whose statutory aims are (officially) inspired by constitutional principles and values.

Obviously, the mere analysis of the text cannot yield an assessment of the content of the norm (whether it is fair or unfair, right or wrong…, whether it conforms or not to the principles of the Italian constitution or to human rights regulations) or of the contents of the possible activities and claims that the norm is designed to regulate. But it does show which aspects of the norm would be relevant to an assessment of it, for example, its allowing or forbidding activities and claims on grounds other than their contents.

5 Concluding Remarks

In the examples I have discussed, what is presupposed or implicated contributes to outlining the normative background of a normative text: this background is often not completely familiar to the recipient of the text, who might be a co-owner or a tenant, or a citizen (but also a member of parliament who reads a draft law), so that they have informative value.

Existential presupposition introduces as referents objects of a legal or more generally deontic kind: acts carrying legal value, behavior or attitudes falling under certain legal categories, institutional entities, norms, obligations, rights. This is the ontology upon which the normative text is designed to act.

Sometimes a description of these referents, possibly equivalent to a definition, is also provided (often implicitly, that is, by means of cross-references within the text or implicatures according to the maxim of Relation). The kind of organizations whose existence is presupposed in (5), for example, is characterized in detail and the description implicitly provides the reader with the motivation of the author of Section 3-bis (and therefore the parliamentary Chamber of Deputies which approved it) for granting to members of these organizations whatever conduct they might like to assume with respect to homosexuality and transsexuality, without any normative limitations. A slightly different case, which is also concerned with an implicit definition, is reference made by (4)(b) to courteous and civilised people, where courtesy and civilisation consist in fact of adhering to norms of behavior in line with what is specified in the immediately following gerund phrases.

Implicit definitions are indeed a general phenomenon, occurring in a broad variety of texts and even in conversations. Indeed, this is the way we usually learn the meaning of new lexical items. However, in normative texts they turn out to play a particularly important function. The definitions of the legal terms used in the text belong to the common ground or to what should become common ground to the aims of a correct understanding of the text itself. On the one hand, this seems to qualify them as "pragmatic presuppositions" according to Stalnaker's conception (1973, 1999), while, on the other, the interpreter (especially when he is a citizen lacking the technical knowledge required) must reconstruct them from the text by means of processes that rely upon reference to the maxims of conversation. In this same way, borderline uses or partially innovative uses of a technical term may suggest a new implicit definition of it by constituting a precedent which will contribute to modifying its standard or received meaning.

Vagueness or indeterminacy sometimes affect normative texts too, just like any other. In (4) (c), it is clear that the interpretation of *qualsiasi rumore* ('any noise [whatsoever]') is subject to various possible contextual adjustments, with the risk of allowing for clearly exaggerated applications of the rule. But the authority issuing the regulations runs this risk, partly for practical reasons (applying an objective measure to noise may be difficult), partly perhaps with the aim of implicitly communicating to the residents that during hours of rest any noise may give rise to complaints. In (5), vagueness is part of the strategy that the amendment is serving: the characterization of conduct not amounting to discrimination appears pretty vague. While vagueness in (4) (c) can be exploited to frighten the addressee (the resident or tenant) and help make him compliant, thereby increasing the norm's efficacy, the vagueness of (5) appears at first sight to be aimed at avoiding alarming certain addressees, while further intepretative work is required to establish whether the norm is at risk of legitimating possible discriminating behavior (and, therefore, other addressees should feel alarmed).

In all these uses of what is implicitly meant, the separation between what is said and what is presupposed or implicated is not complete. Indeed, when we are interested in understanding what a normative text prescribes (or permits or prohibits) and what it does not, we must put together the aspects of what is said that are explicitly present in the text's linguistic surface, and the relevant implicitly conveyed contributions, whether affecting what is said such as enrichments, or consisting of presuppositions or implicatures. The result of this work is typically a paraphrase, consisting of a combination of aspects of the former kind with aspects of the latter. In order to distinguish more sharply what is said from what is presupposed or implicated, we need to resort to some theoretical simplification. We could define what is said on the sole basis of Grice's dictiveness (1989: 360–362, cf. Sbisà 2007: 16), that is, for example, by singling out that which would be negated by an interlocutor intending to question the content of the text. What is said, in this case, would amount to that which we deny or question if we want to contradict or belie the speaker. But in so doing, we might find ourselves compelled to neglect the restrictions placed upon what is said by Grice's formality (1989: 360, 362), thereby including in what is said contents that have not been "explicitly" said in the immediate and ordinary sense of this word, and running the risk of moving too far away from the linguistic form of the text.

But if there are these two dimensions, dictiveness and formality, and therefore two conditions or criteria for distinguishing what is said from what is presupposed or implicated, the balancing out of the two criteria is something we already do in order to identify "what is said" in individual cases. In this connection, I would also like to recall the suggestion, made by Saul (2012), to consider the distinction between what is said and what is implicated as context-dependent in itself. The balance between different criteria and in general the question of the separation between what is said and what is presupposed or implicated serve different aims in different contexts and therefore may lead to different solutions. So long as what is of interest is to retrieve and be able to reformulate the complex of "what is said + what is presupposed or implicated" – and for normative texts it is particularly clear that it is so – the incomplete stability of the distinction does not constitute a real problem.

The contextualized character of the distinction between what is said and what is presupposed or implicated might appear to contrast with the claim that implicitness is normative. However, the rules and reasons which I have described as being connected with implicit meaning are also at work in borderline cases. Take explicatures, for example (which according to Relevance Theory are part of what is said, cf. Sperber and Wilson 1995; Carston 2002) and Levinson's generalized implicatures (whose contents in some cases coincide with those of explicatures, but which are considered by neo-Griceans as part of what is implicated, cf. Levinson 2000). Whether the retrieved meaning is taken to be part of what is said, or of what is presupposed or implicated, does not eliminate the distinction between correct and incorrect comprehension and its applicability to the meaning to be retrieved, with all the consequences we have seen.

There are, however, cases in which the normativity of implicitness is not enough to guide the recipient of a normative text towards correct understanding. Possible disjunctive implicatures might have incompatible alternatives among the disjuncts, thus opening the door to ambiguity. Presuppositions activated by subordinate clauses might be subject to cancellation depending on the predicate introducing these clauses, and here too there might be ambiguous cases. A very problematic case, which would be worth further discussion, is connected to the application of Levinson's rule "What is simply expressed, is stereotypically meant", akin (according to Levinson himself) to Grice's second maxims of Quantity. Where the Italian Constitution reads "marriage", without any further specification, does it mean stereotypical marriage (at the time and place at which the Constitution was written) and therefore (if this was the stereotype in Italy in 1948) exclusively heterosexual marriage; or does it simply omit to say anything about the kind of marriage referred to, allowing for variations of admissible referents with time due to the transformations of society (cf. Bairati 2015; Long 2015)? While the normativity of implicitness can establish whether the reasoning applying Levinson's rule is correct, it does not go so far as to decide exactly what stereotype should be attributed to the text as part of its meaning (cf. Poggi 2011: 37). Thus, including this particular kind of conversational implicature in the content of a normative text appears rather unsafe. However, these difficult cases can be isolated and clarified in the light of the normativity of implicitness and, in my opinion, are not enough to counterbalance the above-mentioned advantages of taking into consideration presuppositions and implicatures with the aim of understanding normative texts. The explicitation of implicit meaning remains an indispensable tool for understanding the normative background surrounding a norm, the motivations of the norm, its content and possible applications: an understanding which is one of the premises both to one's really conforming to the norm and to becoming able to take a critical stance with respect to it.

References

Austin, J. L. (1962). *How to do things with words*. Oxford: Oxford University Press. 2nd ed. 1975.

Bairati, L. (2015). La trascrizione del matrimonio omosessuale celebrato all'estero: argomentazioni e strategie interpretative fra implicito e non detto. In L. Morra & B. Pasa (Eds.), *Questioni di genere nel diritto: impliciti e crittotipi* (pp. 111–129). Torino: Giappichelli.

Bianchi, C. (2009). *Pragmatica cognitiva*. Roma-Bari: Laterza.

Bianchi, C. (2013). Implicating. In M. Sbisà & K. Turner (Eds.), *Pragmatics of speech actions* (pp. 107–142). Berlin: de Gruyter Mouton.

Bianchi, C. (2016). What did you (legally) say? Cooperative and strategic interactions. In A. Capone & F. Poggi (Eds.), *Pragmatics and law, philosophical perspectives* (pp. 185–199). Dordrecht: Springer.

Carston, R. (2002). *Thoughts and utterances. The pragmatics of explicit communication*. Oxford: Blackwell.

Cooren, F. (2010). *Action and agency in dialogue*. Amsterdam: John Benjamins.

Goffman, E. (1981). *Forms of talk*. Philadelphia: University of Pennsylvania.

Grice, P. (1957). Meaning. *The Philosophical Review, 64*, 377–388. In Grice: 1989.

Grice, P. (1989). *Studies in the way of words*. Cambridge, MA: Harvard University Press.

Höfler, S. (2014). Between conciseness and transparency: Presuppositions in legislative texts. *International Journal for the Semiotics of Law, 27*, 627–644.

Levinson, S. (2000). *Presumptive meanings*. Cambridge: Cambridge University Press.

Long, J. (2015). Diritto italiano della famiglia e impliciti "normativi". In L. Morra & B. Pasa (Eds.), *Questioni di genere nel diritto: impliciti e crittotipi* (pp. 149–166). Torino: Giappichelli.

Marmor, A. (2008). The pragmatics of legal language. *Ratio Iuris, 21*(4), 423–452.

Morra, L. (2011). Implicature conversazionali nei testi di legge. *Esercizi filosofici, 6*(1), 214–231.

Morra, L. (2015). Conversational implicatures in normative texts. In A. Capone & J. L. Mey (Eds.), *Interdisciplinary studies in pragmatics, culture and society* (pp. 537–562). Dordrecht: Springer.

Poggi, F. (2011). Law and conversational implicatures. *International Journal for the Semiotics of Law, 24*, 21–40.

Recanati, F. (2004). *Literal meaning*. Oxford: Oxford University Press.
Saul, J. (2002). Speaker meaning, what is said, and what is implicated. *Nous, 36*, 228–248.
Saul, J. (2012). *Lying, misleading, and what is said*. Oxford: Oxford University Press.
Sbisà, M. (1999). Presupposition and implicature in text understanding. In P. Bouquet, L. Serafini, P. Brézillon, M. Benerecetti, & F. Castellani (Eds.), *Modeling and using context* (pp. 324–338). Berlin: Springer.
Sbisà, M. (2007). *Detto non detto. Le forme della comunicazione implicita*. Roma-Bari: Laterza.
Simons, M. (2013). Presupposing. In M. Sbisà & K. Turner (Eds.), *Pragmatics of speech actions* (pp. 143–172). Berlin: de Gruyter Mouton.
Sperber, D., & Wilson, D. (1995). *Relevance. Communication and cognition* (2nd ed.). Oxford: Blackwell.
Stalnaker, R. (1973). Presuppositions. *Journal of Philosophical Logic, 2*, 447–457.
Stalnaker, R. (1999). *Context and content*. Oxford: Oxford University Press.
Strawson, P. (1950). On referring. *Mind, 59*, 320–344.

What Inferentialism Tells Us About Combinatory Vagueness in Law

Damiano Canale

Abstract What is the best way to address the problem of combinatory vagueness in legal adjudication? According to a view widely held by philosophers of language, courts must make reference to what the legislature intended to say. Intentional content makes up for the lack of determinacy of meaning and contextual content, and can be used to reduce combinatory vagueness to such an extent that it can be determined whether a combinatory vague norm applies to borderline cases. In this paper I argue that this view does not provide a convincing account of how legal language works since it does not take into consideration the specific characteristics of legislative intention and the institutional dimension of linguistic communication in law. I then put forward a different explanation of combinatory vagueness based on an inferentialist approach to semantics and pragmatics. In this account, combinatory vagueness is a feature of language which depends on a specific form of disagreement between the participants in an exchange of reasons. By looking at the linguistic interplay between parties and judge in a legal dispute, the paper shows how combinatory vagueness arises and how it is reduced by courts in order to settle borderline cases.

Keywords Combinatory vagueness • Inferentialism • Legislative intention

1 Introduction

When philosophers of language examine the characteristics of legal language, they generally look at it as a form of conversational communication. This is not surprising. It is reasonable to believe that through the enactment of statute S the legislature communicates its intentions to law-addressees. If communication is successful, law-addressees understand what the legislature intended to say and become aware of being under the obligation to behave accordingly. However, following Grice, it is often assumed that the linguistic content of S is composed of three elements: the

D. Canale (✉)
Dipartimento di studi giuridici "A. Sraffa", Università Bocconi, Milan, Italy
e-mail: damiano.canale@unibocconi.it

F. Poggi, A. Capone (eds.), *Pragmatics and Law*, Perspectives in Pragmatics, Philosophy & Psychology 10, DOI 10.1007/978-3-319-44601-1_3

conventional meaning encoded in S, the content conveyed by uttering S in a given context, and the intended content of S, i.e. what the legislature intended to communicate. In normal cases – so it is believed – meaning, contextual content and intended content concur to convey the same directive of action, and communication is successful: law-addressees grasp legislative intention by understanding what S says. But, sometimes, legal language falls short in this: the meaning and the contextual content of S may not provide sufficient information, be univocal or truly express legislative intention. In such cases, legal communication fails. In particular, S is combinatory vague when it admits borderline cases of application which have specific characteristics. Take, for instance, Herbert Hart's famous example "No vehicle may be taken into the park" (Hart 1983, 63 ff.; Hart 1994, 126 ff.). Does this statute apply to skateboards? The answer is not straightforward since the term "vehicle" has a variety of conditions of application and we are unable to pinpoint those conditions which are necessary and/or sufficient for the term to apply (Alston 1967; Bueno and Colyvan 2012). Consequently, there will be cases which clearly fall under the statute, cases which do not fall under it, and cases where it will be uncertain whether the statute applies.

Now, it is common knowledge that this uncertainty can be explained in a number of ways depending on the theory of vagueness one subscribes to.[1] Furthermore, it is disputed whether what is referred to as combinatory vagueness is actually a form of ambiguity, generality, contextual dependence, open texture or family resemblances.[2] In this essay I will not go into these issues. What matters here is that the information provided by the statute mentioned above gives rise to borderline cases of norm application. How should a decision be reached by courts in such a situation? The model of conversational communication offers a clear answer to this question: courts must make reference to what the legislature intended to say. Intentional content makes up for the lack of determinacy of meaning and contextual content, and can be used to reduce combinatory vagueness to such an extent that it can be determined whether, in Hart's example, skateboards may be taken into the park.[3]

[1] According to Stewart Shapiro, most theorists of vagueness assume that this phenomenon involves a form of ignorance. See Shapiro 2006, 2. For instance, epistemicists claim that with borderline cases we are ignorant of facts that actually we cannot know (Williamson 1994); a supervaluationist holds that we are ignorant because a vague sentence is neither true nor false (Fine 1975); an incoherentist claims that we do not know whether a vague term apply to a case because our language sometimes is incoherent (Dummett 1975); a contextualist assumes that we are (apparently) ignorant of the conditions of application of vague terms because these conditions shift with context (see Soames 1998 and Raffman 2014). For a discussion of these accounts of vagueness with regard to legal language see Endicott 2000, Jónsson 2009 and Poscher 2012.

[2] Cf. Poscher 2012 and Marmor 2005, 133. It has to be noted that the contemporary philosophical literature on vagueness defines vague preducates in terms of sorites-susceptibility whereas legal theory traditionally considers vagueness as a form of linguistic indeterminacy: a term is vague if there are cases in which there is no definite answer to whether the term applies to something. In this paper I take up the latter approach.

[3] See, for instance, Soames 2012, 100; Marmor 2008, 423; Neale 2007, 253. It is worth recalling that one of Grice's central claims is that human communication essentially consists in the expressions and recognition of intentions. See Grice 1989, essays 1, 7, 14 and 18.

It is worth noting that this standpoint, which is grounded in the traditional account of conversational communication, seems to be consistent with the principles of legality, legal predictability and separation of powers. If a court determined the content of a vague statute independently of legislative intention, this court would not comply with its duty of fidelity to law and would dismiss legislative supremacy (Goldsworthy 2005; Allan 2000). However, one might wonder whether the conversational model provides a convincing account of how legal language works.

In the first part of this essay I will consider two main shortcomings of the conversational model, one which is related to the notion of legislative intention (Sect. 2), the second to the fact that this model does not account for the institutional dimension of linguistic communication in law (Sect. 3). In the second part of the essay I will present an inferentialist picture of combinatory vagueness which might help to overcome these shortcomings and highlight what is special about legal language as opposed to ordinary language. I will firstly outline the basic tenets of the inferentialist approach to semantics and pragmatics (Sect. 4); then I shall put forward a theoretical framework that can be used for a fine-grained analysis of a linguistic exchange of reasons in legal adjudication. With this framework I will explain how combinatory vagueness arises and how it is dealt with by the participants in a legal dispute (Sects. 5 and 6). The explanation I offer is quite schematic and the assumptions it rests on are oversimplified. My aim is to illustrate a new pattern of explanation rather than to defend the semantic and pragmatic theory this pattern is based on. Along these lines, in the last section of this essay (Sect. 7) I will sketch some philosophical concerns that an inferentialist approach to combinatory vagueness gives rise to.

2 What Did the Legislature Intend to Say?

It is reasonable to believe that law is mainly an intentional phenomenon (Gardner 2010, 420). In most cases, laws are made by someone empowered to introduce, change or eliminate them, and it would be puzzling to assume that the content of these laws is not the one intended by the law-maker. As Josep Raz has claimed, “it makes no sense to give any person or body law-making power unless it is assumed that the law they make is the law they intended to make” (Raz 2009, 274). At the same time, however, the notion of legislative intention is highly problematic. It is worth mentioning here some theoretical and practical issues which have been widely discussed by legal scholars over the past few years.

First of all, when we try to track down the intention of the legislature we face an *Ontological Problem*: which entity are we looking for? Many legal scholars claim that, on the one hand, the intention of the legislature as a collective body does not exist, and that, on the other, the intention of the individual legislators is practically undiscoverable and, in any case, irrelevant.[4] It has also been claimed that attributing

---

[4] Cf. e.g. Radin 1930, 870 ff.; Campbell 2001, 292; Boudreau et al. 2007, 972.

an intention to a certain group amounts to the fallacy of composition. Even if it were true that some members of the legislature intend that *p* ought to be the case, it would not follow that the whole legislative body has the same intention.[5] All we know is that the majority intended a legal sentence to be enacted, not that the members of this majority intended to convey the same normative content by enacting it.[6]

Secondly, the notion of legislative intention gives rise to an *Epistemic Problem*: how are we to know legislative intention once we assume that it can be listed in the inventory of the world? Apart from the cases in which it is clearly expressed in legislative texts and provisions, legislative intent is not easily discoverable, in particular when we deal with old statutes and constitutions.[7] Floor debates or the so-called *travaux préparatoires* often provide insufficient evidence to that effect, especially when various documents, subjects and institutional bodies are concerned. It should be also considered that some jurisdictions restrict the use of such documents because it could undermine the principle of the law's publicity: if the law should be knowable in advance the use of such documents to determine its contents should be limited – it is argued – because they are not readily available to law addressees.[8]

Thirdly, if we assume that the intention of the legislature exists and can be known, an *Abstraction Problem* is to be considered: what is the relevant level of abstraction that is needed when we determine legislative intent? Should we seek for the abstract legislative intention or rather for its details?[9] Sometimes the same theoretical issue is addressed in terms of levels of generality: the wording of the relevant legal text might suggest a less general or a more general regulation than the legislature wanted. When problems of this sort arise, how are we to determine the set of things to which the law has to be applied? We need criteria guiding us to more or less abstract, or general, answers.[10]

Fourthly, in those legal systems where legislative decisions are *de facto* in the hands of the executive, we face a *Political Problem*: what is the relevant intent? The legislature's or the executive's (cf. Greenawalt 2000, 645–1646)? Some claim that the notion of proxy agency can be helpful here: legislation can be interpreted in accordance with the intentions of proxies – groups or individuals acting on behalf

[5] Cf. Pettit 2001, 250–251.

[6] The problems just mentioned bears on the notions of "collective intentionality" and "plural subject" that cannot be considered here. See Bratman 1999; Gilbert 2006, 101 ff. It seems plausible to claim that a legislature acts as a body since legislatures are set up by constitutive rules that empower them to enact authoritative legal sentences.

[7] See e.g. Marmor 2005, chaps. 8–9; MacPherson 2010, 2 ff.

[8] This is traditionally the case of Australia and New Zealand: see Goldsworthy 1997, 10–15; Allan 2000, 110–111. Cf. Summers 2000, 251–283, and Ekins 2012, 274.

[9] See Stoljar 1998, 36–37. Cf. Williams 2001, 326–329 and Goldsworthy 1997, 30–31.

[10] Moreso 2005, 136 supports the following solution: if the text is detailed, an interpretive doubt must be solved at the same detailed level, looking for the precise legislative intention; if the text has an abstract formulation (as many constitutional provisions have), a doubt must be solved in the abstract, leaving room for contextual considerations from time to time. Cf. Williams 2001, 337–338.

of the majority party – insofar as "the reasons for interpreting legislation in accordance with the intentions of legislatures are also reasons for interpreting legislation in accordance with proxy groups, when those groups determine the content of the legislation" (MacPherson 2010, 17).

In Grice's spirit, however, one may object that speaker's intention can be inferred from the principles of rational agency and other contextual information (Sperber and Wilson 1995; Recanati 2002). So, attitudes such as intentions can by ascribed to collective bodies on the basis of what is rationally presupposed or implicated by the enactment of a legal sentence in a given context. If we look at legislative intention from this point of view, the ontological, epistemic, abstraction and political problems just mentioned can be easily solved. But even if we accept this standpoint, we face a further issue. As Mark Greenberg has correctly pointed out, there are a number of inferential schemes that are in fact used to discover legislative intention, and each of them potentially leads to a different outcome (Greenberg 2011, 220). If we look at legal practice, it is easy to see that by "legislative intention" courts mean:

1. the content that the legislature intended to communicate at the time the legal sentence was enacted;
2. the content that norm-addressees would have taken the legislature to intend at the time of enactment;
3. the content that the present legislature would have intended to communicate if it had enacted the legal sentence in question;
4. the content that a rational legislature would have intended to communicate;
5. the content that the present norm-addressees would take the legislature to intend;
6. the content that the legislature would have intended to communicate on the basis of other legal sentences or principles belonging to the same legal system;
7. the content expressing the purpose that the legal sentence is designed to serve;
8. the content that the legislature implicated or presupposed but intentionally omitted stating in order to avoid political responsibility.

It is apparent that the expression "legislative intention" refers to different methods of interpretation i.e. rules of inference which govern interpretive and argumentative practice by courts.[11] And the choice of the method to be used to determine what the legislature intended to say depends on the normative theory of legal interpretation judges subscribe to.

It should be added that in most legal systems content ascription by courts is often justified by reasons that are not connected to legislative intention. This occurs when judicial interpretation is seen as an activity which aims not only at identifying the intentional content of legal sentence but also at protecting general principles of law such as coherence, equal treatment, purposiveness. So, either intentional content is consistent with these principles, or it may be considered defective or even irrelevant.

[11] For these reasons, MacCormick claims that "this rather indeterminate element of interpretative argumentation is best considered as one that can range across all the other categories [i.e. interpretive methods] and their types. On that ground, it should be deemed (if rather grandly) a 'transcategorical' type of argument relative to other categories" (MacCormick 2009, 125).

In this sense, legislation and adjudication may be governed "by purposes that transcend, and sometimes conflict with, the conversational ideal of an efficient and cooperative exchange of information" (Soames 2009, 421). Courts often disregard linguistic conventions, consider unambiguous expression as ambiguous, take standard borderline cases as perfectly clear, or determine whether a certain case falls under a combinatory vague legal sentence on the basis of criteria that are independent of legislative intention. When this occurs, courts do not see themselves as a faithful agent of the legislature but as an agent of the law and its overall purposes.[12] Consequently, a judicial decision may be considered legitimate and authoritative even if it does not reflect the lawmaker's intention.

3 The Institutional Dimension of Linguistic Communication in Law

If we look at legal practice, there is another reason why the conversational model seems to be flawed: it does not account for the institutional dimension of linguistic communication in law.

Legal contexts substantially differ from standard conversational contexts. Legal sentences are considered as linguistic inputs that must be inferentially elaborated by legal authorities in order to produce normative outputs. But this can hardly be seen as a contextual process of enrichment, modulation or extension of the semantic content encoded in legal sentences. As we have seen above, legal authorities may be allowed to disregard the conventional meaning of natural language expressions, to reconstruct presuppositions and implicatures independently of the intention of the lawmaker, or even to state that legislative intention is of no importance when determining the content of the law. The inferential elaboration of legal language is typically realized in the context of adjudication, where courts are called upon to apply legal contents. What are the fundamental characteristics of this context? In most contemporary legal systems, the context of adjudication has a triadic, adversarial structure which characterizes legal process; it includes a party which raises a claim, a party which responds to this claim, and an independent court which authoritatively settles the dispute according to the law. Each party inferentially articulates the content of legal sentences in order to achieve its goals. To do this, each party acts strategically: both the claimant and the respondent, or the prosecutor and the defendant, put forward alternative reasons to make their case in accordance with the law. Based

[12] According to William Eskridge, for instance, "judges interpreting statutes (…) are like diplomats acting upon orders from their national foreign service. These diplomats must often apply ambiguous or out-dated communiqués to unforeseen situations, which they do in a creative way, not strictly constrained by their orders. But they are, at bottom, agents in a common enterprise, and their freedom of interpretation is bounded by the mandates of their orders, which are not necessarily consistent or coherent over time, or even at any one time" (Eskridge 1987, 1554). On the idea of courts as "faithful agents of the legislature's intention" see also Manning 2001, 5.

on the reasons provided by the parties, the court then decides who has a right or a duty, who is guilty or liable: courts choose which inferential articulation of the relevant linguistic inputs better fits the case according to the legal system. This basic form of adversarial exchange of reasons may involve other linguistic practitioners (witnesses, experts) and provide a basis for further decisions by other courts, both in common law and civil law countries. In this way, political choices, individual rights, social conflicts and personal interests are incorporated into reasons regarding the content of law. Notice that it is in the context of adjudication that the legal sentences authoritatively display a given content. The first order communication between lawmakers and law-addressees is actually related to (and is partially a result of) the second order, adversarial communication between the parties and the court in a legal process.

It should be emphasized here that the way in which linguistic communication is institutionally framed in legal practice is determined by the law itself. Laws constitute authorities which identify the sources of law, empower individuals or bodies to introduce, change or eliminate legal regulations, determines who is entitled to provide reasons in the legal process, which reasons are relevant in a legal dispute and how a judicial exchange of reasons should take place, empowers courts to determine the content of legal sentences and to settle legal disputes. In short, law regulates the use of language in legal contexts and thereby governs linguistic content.

If all this is true, what about combinatory vagueness in law? This phenomenon assumes peculiar characteristics in judicial practice: it depends on the lexical choices of legislatures, the context of adjudication and the reasons exhibited by parties and court in a legal process. While formulating statutes, legislatures sometimes choose to be vague either to reach political compromises or because this is required by the subject being regulated (cf. Endicott 2011). In the latter case, legislatures assume that courts are in the better position to specify the content of the law in order to achieve a certain social or political goal. The inclusion of a combinatory vague term in a legal sentence has typically the effect of delegating rule-making authority to courts, not in the sense that courts are empowered to create a new law but that they have to specify the content of legal sentences in the light of the circumstances of the case. It should be noted, however, that the formulation of a legal sentence is not sufficient to determine whether this sentence is combinatory vague. Combinatory vagueness depends on context: the content of legal sentence S may admit combinatory borderline cases in the context of adjudication C_1, so that it is not clear whether case x is ruled by S, whereas in context C_2 the content of S appears precise enough to determine whether x falls under S. The lexical choice of the legislature simply identifies the legal domain in which borderline cases may occur and how likely they are. This introduces the second peculiarity of combinatory vagueness in law. Courts authoritatively decide whether the content of a legal sentence admits borderline cases, if the case to be decided is borderline, and how combinatory vagueness is to be reduced in order to reach a legal decision. These choices are based on different criteria: factual evidence, the reconstruction of the facts of the case, and the methods of interpretation used by courts. This does not mean that combinatory vagueness in law depends on an idiosyncratic standpoint of legal authorities; it is determined and administrated by the controversial exchange of reasons that takes place in a legal process. The parties put forward competing reasons relating to the legal sentence that regulates the case, its content, the borderline character of the case, and the interpretive method to be used to reach a decision. Courts are then called upon to identify those reasons which are suitable according to the law.

To conclude, both linguistic communication and combinatory vagueness assume a specific character in law. These phenomena are strongly influenced by the authoritative dimension of legal communication, by the fact that linguistic practitioners play institutional functions ruled by the law, and that content construction in legal adjudication depends on a dialectical exchange of reasons framed by legal proceedings and specific methods of interpretation. Now, the conversational model seems not to be able to account for such characteristics; it rather has a distorting influence on legal theory and practice, an influence which impedes the full understanding of problems such as linguistic indeterminacy in law.[13]

In the following sections I shall outline an alternative strategy of analysis based upon an inferentialist approach to semantics and pragmatics. Such an approach has been chosen here because it does not explain linguistic content from below, offering first an account of the conventional meaning of legal terms, then of the contextual process of enrichment, modulation and extension of meaning, and finally of the inferences that may lead an interpreter to identify legislative intention in order to reduce content indeterminacy. On the contrary, inferentialism adopts a top-down line of explanation (Brandom 2000, 12–16): it starts from the pragmatic exchange of reasons where sentences are used in a given context, and then analyses how such an exchange determines semantic content, i.e. the conditions under which a legal sentence applies to a case. In this sense, inferentialism seems more promising for a reliable account of linguistic exchange in legal adjudication.

4 The Inferentialist Picture: An Overview

An inferentialist approach to semantics and pragmatics is characterized by three theoretical standpoints: (a) conceptual role semantics; (b) normative pragmatics; (c) scorekeeping by linguistic practitioners.

(a) The content of a sentence consists of the conceptual role this sentence plays in linguistic practice. According to Brandom, the conceptual role of a content-bearer is the function it plays in reasoning. This is to say that a sentence has a linguistic content in so far as it serves as an antecedent and a consequence in inferential relations among sentences.[14] These relations *are* the content that sentences bear:

---

[13] As a matter of fact, this model is mainly used by legal scholars to justify a normative standpoint: the idea that that a legal decision is in accordance with the law only if it is the expression of legislative intention. But this standpoint is theoretically troublesome and highly controversial.

[14] The inferential relations we are referring to here are *material* inferences as opposed to *formal* inferences: according to Brandom and Sellars, the validity of a material inference depends on the

they make explicit the rules governing the use of language in a certain discursive context, determine the conditions of application of sentential and sub-sentential expressions and fix their reference. Inferential relations among sentences are of three kinds: *commissive*, *permissive* and *incompatibility* relations (I will consider them at point (b)). So, the inferential role of a sentence is threefold: commissive and permissive relations can be seen, respectively, as sets of inferential antecedents and inferential consequents, whereas incompatibility relations can be thought of as a set of ordered pairs of sentences that are incompatible. As a result, the inferential role of S is articulated as follows: {S's commissive antecedents, S's commissive consequents, S's permissive antecedents, S's permissive consequents, S's incompatibilities}. But how is the inferential role of S determined?

(b) The inferential role of a sentence (how it is used in reasoning) is a function of the normative statuses that speakers assign to one another when performing a speech act in a discursive practice. Brandom's idea is that being a participant in a linguistic practice is to be responsible for the claims one makes, and to be responsible is to be considered responsible by the other participants (Brandom 1994, 161–163). Inferentialism qualifies these normative statuses as *commitments* and *entitlements*: these terms express, respectively, the duty to accept the antecedents and the consequences one is committed to, and the permission to claim the antecedents and to draw the consequences one is entitled to.[15] These normative statuses depend, in turn, on normative attitudes of the participants in linguistic practice. In Brandom's view, there are three basic attitudes in an exchange of reasons: *attributing*, *undertaking* and *acknowledging*. Each participant attributes (takes that another adopts), undertakes (implicitly adopts) and acknowledges (explicitly adopts) commitments and entitlements in a linguistic intercourse. These distinctions shed some light on the nature and source of the inferential roles considered above. According to Brandom, semantics depends on pragmatics: the content (inferential role) of a sentence is a function of how people use that sentence. Commissive, permissive and incompatibility relations account for the status that speakers attribute, acknowledge or undertake to one another on the basis of what they say in an exchange of reasons. More precisely, these inferential relations have the following form:

Commissive relations: if one is committed to *S1*, then she is committed to *S2*.
Permissive relations: if one is entitled to *S1*, then she is *prima facie* entitled to *S2*.[16]
Incompatibility relations: if one is committed to *S1*, then she is not entitled to *S2*.

content of the non logical vocabulary used in reasoning and not on the form of reasoning. See on this Brandom 2000, 52–55; Sellars 1953.

[15] Discursive practices give rise to different kinds of commitments: Brandom distinguishes *doxastic* commitments (which correspond to beliefs) from *inferential* commitments (which correspond to reasons) and *practical* commitments (corresponding to actions). See Brandom 2000, 30–31, 69–79, 93–96.

[16] In the case of permissive inferential relations, if the speaker is entitled to *S1*, she is *prima facie* entitled to *S2* because the latter entitlement is not immune from doubt: in the course of the exchange of reasons, the speaker could prove not to be committed to *S2* and this entitlement would be discarded. See Brandom 1994, 177.

Note that these inferential relations concern the normative status of the participants in a discursive practice (Brandom 2008, 120): the argumentative duty, permission or prohibition – ascribed to each participant by the others – to draw *S2* from *S1* in a given exchange of reasons.

(c) The way in which linguistic content is determined can be explained by considering the participants in a discursive practice as the scorekeepers of each other's commitments and entitlements. In the scorekeeping picture of language use, every time one utters a sentence token, and so undertakes, acknowledges or attributes commitments and entitlements, the score changes in a rule-governed way.[17] At a given moment in an exchange of reasons, the score is just the ordered set of commitments and entitlements associated with each participant by the others. So, content can be seen as a "scoreboard" which registers the linguistic behavior of the practitioners, the antecedents and consequents of each sentence token, and the inferential rules explaining practitioners' behavior.

To give an example of this, imagine the interplay between lawyer Q, lawyer R and judge J in a legal dispute.[18] As Kevin Scharp has pointed out, "we can think of the score at any given moment as a set whose members are sets of commitments and entitlements" (Scharp 2005, 209). Given that Q, R and J may either undertake or acknowledge the commitments and entitlements attributed to the other participants in the legal proceeding, the score kept by each scorekeeper can be represented by a set of twelve sets: {{Q's commitments acknowledged}, {Q's commitments undertaken}, {Q's entitlements acknowledged}, {Q's entitlements undertaken}, {R's commitments acknowledged}, {R's commitments undertaken},{R's entitlements acknowledged}, {R's entitlements undertaken},{J's commitments acknowledged}, {J's commitments undertaken}, {J's entitlements acknowledged}, {J's entitlements undertaken}}.[19]

Now, assume that Q utters the sentence token "*x* is F" (*S1*). Assume also that R and J take *S1* to have the force of an assertion: they attribute to Q a doxastic commitment which is scored under set {Q's commitments acknowledged}. R and J will also keep score of all the commitments that follow from *S1* by commissive inferences. These commitments depend on what R and J take Q to have implicitly claimed by uttering *S1* and go under the set {Q's commitments undertaken}. In doing this, R and J also check whether Q's commitments are compatible with one another. In the case of incompatibility, R and J subtract entitlements from incompatible commitments and Q shall not be entitled to claim *S2* on the basis of *S1*: simply put, if Q claims *S1* then she is not allowed to claim *S2*. The next step of the

[17] Brandom elaborates on this theory first put forward by David Lewis. Lewis claims that the rules specifying the kinematic of the score "can be regarded as constitutive rules akin to definitions", but "what they register depends on the history of the conversation in the way that score should according to the rules" (Lewis 1979, 345–346).

[18] This reconstruction of Brandom's deontic scorekeeping is mainly based, with some variations, on Scharp 2005.

[19] It is obvious that some of these sub-sets will be necessarily empty for each participant. In J's score, for instance, no point can go under {J's entitlements acknowledged} and {J's entitlements undertaken}, since J cannot entitle herself to her own commitments.

scorekeeping process consists in attributing entitlements to Q that follow from permissive inferences. Assume that R and J take Q to be entitled to one of Q's acknowledged commitments; this will be scored under set {Q's entitlements acknowledged}. R and J then figure out which further commitments follow from those already acknowledged on the basis of permissive inferences, and attribute entitlements to these commitments scored under set {Q's entitlements undertaken}. Finally, R and J will assess Q's entitlement to *S1*. Q may be entitled to *S1* if *S1* follows, by commissive or permissive inferences, from other commitments Q is entitled to. This entitlement will also be scored under the set {Q's entitlements acknowledged}. The same process will take place for each speech act performed by Q, R and J.

However, the general picture outlined assumes peculiar characteristics in a judicial exchange of reasons. Firstly, the role played by the three linguistic practitioners is asymmetric. In adversarial legal proceedings, litigation is presented by the parties with the judge serving in a relatively passive role. The parties bear the responsibility of presenting the law and the facts: each party affirms conflicting interests and rights on the basis of doxastic evidence and legal directives, and try to get their opponent and the judge to grant their claims and to disregard the contrary claims. Theoretically, the judge is obliged merely to affirm or reject the parties' contentions from an independent point of view.[20] However, the scorekeeping of the judge authoritatively determines the content of the legal sentences, the facts of the case, and consequently the judicial outcome. Secondly, the entitlements acknowledged by J to Q and R are of different sorts. In judicial decision-making, what finally determines the solution of a legal dispute is the legal qualification of the facts in question. Given legal sentence "F ought to ϕ", and assuming that x is the singular case brought to court, J has to decide whether x is an instance of F. If x is qualified as F by J, then "x ought to ϕ" legally follows. So, in a scorekeeping process the point scored by the party which is *entitled* by the judge to a certain legal qualification of the case is decisive. This point actually determines the content of the law and the judicial outcome with regard to the case in question.

5 Combinatory Vagueness in Legal Adjudication: An Inferentialist Account

Now, what can an inferentialist approach to linguistic content tell us about combinatory vagueness in legal adjudication?

Some critics have pointed out that conceptual role semantics cannot explain linguistic indeterminacy because it cannot admit expressions governed by inconsistent inferential rules (cf. Gupta 1999). It would be impossible for the participants in a

[20] In practice, however, in most adversarial procedural system judges has authority to investigate the facts on the judges' own initiative, and to justify their decision on the basis of reasons not presented by the parties. When this occurs, however, judges' own reasons are strictly related to the positions presented by the parties. See Landsman 1983, 715; Hazard and Taruffo 1993, 86.

linguistic practice to follow different inferential rules and use the same language: either they would not speak the same language or what they say would be meaningless. I do not think that this objection is correct as far as the context of legal adjudication is concerned. An inferentialist explanation of content can actually explain combinatory vagueness in a consistent way and shed some new light on this phenomenon as far as the context of legal adjudication is concerned.

Along the line of the picture presented above, we could say that combinatory vagueness arises in legal adjudication when the parties adopt *alternative* sets of commissive and permissive inferential relations in the interpretation of a legal sentence. Two sets of inferential relations are alternative if, and only if, using a sentence according to the first set constitutes a violation of the second, both sets being consistent with the incompatibility relations governing the use of language in that context. To illustrate this, let us come back to the example discussed by Hart: "No vehicle may be taken into the park". Does this statute apply to skateboards? According to Hart, skateboards are borderline cases: it is not clear whether the sentence applies to them or not. But why is it so?

Imagine a dispute between Q and R, that shall be decided by J, about George riding a skateboard in a public park. Assume that Q says:

(Q1) Since a statute prescribes that no vehicle may be taken into the park, and George entered the park on a skateboard, George ought to be punished thus-and-so.

Through *Q1*, Q explicitly adopts four different commitments (c) from the point of view of R and J:

(c1) A statute prescribes that no vehicle may be taken into the park.
(c2) George entered the park on a skateboard.
(c3) George ought to be punished thus-and-so.

Notice that these commitments are respectively related to the source of legal obligation (*c1*), the fact at issue (*c2*) and the legal consequences of George's conduct (*c3*). Moreover, Q adopts a further, inferential commitment:

(c4*) If *x* is a skateboard, then *x* is a vehicle according to the law.

Commitment *c4** is particularly relevant in this context: it concerns the legal qualification of the facts of the case requested by Q (this special commitment will be marked with *). If Q was entitled by J to *c4**, then Q would defeat R in the legal dispute. J would acknowledge Q's reasons and decide the case at issue accordingly.[21]

Commitments *c1*, *c2*, *c3* and *c4** are included by R and J into the set {Q's commitments acknowledged} in their scoreboard. On the basis of this, R and J shall

[21] This does not means that the other commitments considered in this paper are not relevant from the legal point of view. Each of them may be disputed by Q and R, and different entitlements to these commitments could lead to a different solution of the legal dispute.

attribute further implicit commitments to Q depending on commissive inferential relations. For example, if Q is committed to *c1*, then she is committed to

(c5) That statute is source of law in the legal order in which J has jurisdiction.

If Q is committed to *c2* then she is committed to

(c6) George is a human being,

and

(c7) George was in town that day.

If Q is committed to *c3* then she is committed to

(c8) George's punishment does not admit legal exceptions,

and

(c9) The content of this statute is coherent and consistent with the content of the other statutes belonging to the same legal system.

These commitments are included in R's and J's scoreboards under the set {Q's commitments undertaken}.

Now, in countering *Q1*, imagine that R utters the following sentence:

(R1) It is true that a statute prescribes that no vehicle may be taken into the park and that George entered the park on a skateboard, but since skateboards are not vehicles George ought not to be punished thus-and-so.

Performing speech act *R1*, R acknowledges two entitlements (e) to Q:

(e1) A statute prescribes that no vehicle may be taken into the park.
(e2) George entered the park on a skateboard.

In R's and J's scoreboards these entitlements are scored under {Q's entitlements acknowledged}.[22]

But if this is the case, Q will also be *prima facie* entitled to

(e5) The statute is a source of law in the legal system in which J has jurisdiction.

[22] As a consequence of *R1*, Q and J will obviously attribute to R commitments *c1* and *c2*, which are scored under {R's commitments acknowledged}. Notice that the fact that Q is entitled to *e1* and *e2* by R does not imply that these entitlements are acknowledged by J. On the basis of reasons not yet considered, J might take Q not entitled to *e1* and *e2*. However, we have seen that in an adversarial system judges should decide a case on the basis of the reasons provided by the parties. So, it is plausible to believe that if one party is entitled to a certain claim by the other party, this entitlement will be recognized by the judge if no additional consideration comes into play.

(e6) George is a human being.
(e7) George was in town that day.
(e8) George's punishment does not admit legal exceptions.
(e9) The content of this statute is consistent and coherent with the content of the other statutes belonging to the same legal system.

These implicit entitlements will go into set {Q's entitlements undertaken} according to the permissive inferential relations that characterize the use of language in that context.[23] Entitlements *e3…e9* are *prima facie* attributed to Q because Q did not explicitly acknowledged them. Q could, in a further step of the exchange of reasons, cancel these entitlements by denying that she was actually committed to them.

However, through *R1* three further commitments are explicitly adopted by R, which are incompatible with *c3* and *c4** and are included in {R's commitments acknowledged}:

(c10*) If *x* is a skateboard, then *x* is not a vehicle according to the law.
(c11) George ought not to be punished thus-and-so.

Notice that through *c10** R is committed to an alternative legal qualification of the facts at issue, from which it would follow that George ought not to be punished for his conduct. It is apparent that *c10** is incompatible with *c4**: if one is committed to *c10**, one cannot be entitled to *c4** and vice versa.

At this stage of the exchange of reasons, J's scoreboard can be outlined through the following scheme, where CA is an acronym of "commitments acknowledged", CU of "commitments undertaken", EA of "entitlements acknowledged" and EU of "entitlements undertaken":

Q's CA	Q's CU	Q's EA	Q's EU	R's CA	R's CU	R's EA	R's EU	J's CA	J's CU	J's EA	J's EU
c1		e1		c1							
c2		e2		c2							
c3											
c4*											
	c5		e5		c5						
	c6		e6		c6						
	c7		e7		c7						
	c8		e8		c8						
	c9		e9		c9						
				c10*							
				c11							

[23] These entitlements correspond to commitments *c5…c9* which are also included in {R's commitments undertaken} in Q's and J's scoreboards.

In order to be entitled to *c4** by J, and so to win the trial, Q may provide further reasons to make her case:

(Q2) Since norms of the legal system show that the purpose of this statute is to protect pedestrians, and skateboards are a threat for pedestrians, skateboards are vehicles according to the law.

As a result of *Q2*, three doxastic commitments, scored under {Q's commitments acknowledged}, are attributed to Q by R and J:

(c12) The purpose of the statute is to protect pedestrians.
(c13) Other norms of the legal system show the purpose of the statute.
(c14) Skateboards are a threat for pedestrians.

But the same speech act also gives rise to implicit commitments scored under {Q's commitments undertaken}:

(c15) The statute has to be interpreted according to its purpose.
(c16) Purposive interpretation has to be preferred to other interpretive methods.
(c17) Judges are agents of the law and its overall purposes.

Notice that *c15*, *c13*, *c16* and *c17* are inferentially connected: *c15* makes explicit the interpretive method that should be followed by J, *c13* specifies the content of this method, *c16* puts forward the second-order interpretive rule that should govern the interpretive process, and *c17* synthetically puts forward a normative theory of adjudication, which specifies how J should perceive her institutional role in the legal system and carry it out when interpreting a legal sentence.

At this point of the dispute, R may reply to *Q2* in three different ways:

(a) R may entitle Q to *c12*, *c13*, *c15*, *c16*, and counter *c14*, for instance by claiming that skateboards are not dangerous:

(R2) Given that skateboards are not a danger to pedestrians, skateboards are not vehicles according to the law.

(b) R may entitle Q to *c13*, *c15*, *c16*, *c17*, and claim that the purpose of the law is different from the one identified by Q in *c12*:

(R3) Since the purpose of the law is to reduce pollution and skateboards do not pollute, skateboards are not vehicles according to the law.

(c) Finally, R may not entitle Q to *c15*, *c16* and *c17* by claiming that the purpose of the law is not relevant to the interpretation of the legal sentence, and a different interpretive method should be followed by J:

(R4) On the basis of the statements made in the floor debate, it is apparent that the legislature did not intend to prohibit the use of skateboards, therefore skateboards are not vehicles according to the law.

Apart from the fact that R's reply is *R2*, *R3*, *R4*, or a combination of them, the analysis proposed here shows why the legal sentence "No vehicle may be taken into the park" becomes combinatory vague in this context. The parties ascribe alternative contents to this sentence, so that it is uncertain whether the case brought to court falls under the law. And it is so because each party attributes a different inferential role to the interpreted legal sentence. In our example, George's case becomes a combinatory borderline case if:

(a) R performs speech act *R2*, and disputes whether skateboards have the property of being dangerous;
(b) R's reply to Q is *R3*, thus disputing the purpose of the law and making it doubtful whether prohibiting skateboards in the park complies with this purpose;
(c) R puts forward *R4*, arguing that the interpretive method adopted by Q is not sound and a different method should be followed by J.

To sum up, in Hart's example skateboards may prove to be borderline cases because the participants in the judicial exchange of reasons disagree on the factual properties of the case, on how to use a certain method of interpretation, or which interpretive method should be used. This disagreement is based upon alternative sets of inferences involving the legal sentence in the exchange of reasons.

However, two parties may disagree on the content of a legal sentence only if they share a set of pragmatic and semantic assumptions. In particular, the linguistic behavior of the parties is based on the same *incompatibility relations* between speech acts: these relations can be seen as a set of common background assumptions in the exchange of reasons. According to both Q and R, if one is committed to *c4**, one cannot be entitled to *c10**; if one is committed to *c14*, one cannot be entitled to claim that skateboards are not dangerous; if one is committed to *c12*, one cannot be entitled to claim that the purpose of the legal sentence is to reduce pollution; if one is committed to *c17*, one cannot be entitled to claim that judges are agents of the legislature, and so forth. In this sense, incompatibility relations appear to be the bedrock of pragmatic and semantic content.[24] From this basis, combinatory vagueness may arise as a result of disagreements about the inferential role that a sentence should play in a given exchange of reasons.

[24] Accordingly, Brandom maintains that incompatibility relations can be seen as "semantic primitives" (Brandom 2008, 123–126). As a matter of fact, if the *same* incompatibility relations did not hold for both Q and J, Q's claims could not challenge R's claims and vice versa: an adversarial exchange of reasons could not take place. As Mark Lance has noted, "the semantic relation of incompatibility seems to rest on a pragmatic relation of challenge which holds between an agent and a speech act of another" (Lance 2001, 433).

6 Judicial Scorekeeping

How does the exchange of reasons outlined in the previous section lead to a conclusion? The case will be decided by J, who shall assess the alternative reasons provided by the parties and reduce combinatory vagueness to such an extent that the legal dispute can be settled. In the inferentialist view, J's assessment will be legally justified only if J keeps score of Q's and R's commitments and entitlements. On the basis of her scoreboard, J will then decide which set of inferential relations is to be preferred according to the law. In this sense, J's scorekeeping will determine the content of the legal sentence and whether the skateboard case is covered by it.

Let us assume, for the sake of simplicity, that R's reply to *Q2* is *R4*. If this is the case, Q and J attribute the following doxastic commitments to R, that are scored under {R's commitments acknowledged}:

(c18) The legislature did not intend to prohibit the use of skateboards in the park.
(c19) Floor debates show that *c18* is the case.

On the basis of the commissive inferential relations governing the use of language, Q and J will also attribute some implicit commitments to R scored under {R's commitments undertaken}.

(c20) The statute has to be interpreted according to legislative intention.
(c21) Legislative intention has to be preferred to other interpretive methods.
(c22) Judges are agents of the legislature.

In this exchange of reasons, it is apparent that *c20*, *c21* and *c22* are incompatible, respectively, with *c15*, *c16* and *c17*. If one is committed to the former claims, one cannot be entitled to the latter and vice versa. In fact, R puts forward through *R4* an alternative method of interpretation based upon a different normative theory of adjudication, that J should subscribe to.

At this second stage of the exchange of reasons between the parties, the score registered in J's scoreboard evolves this way:

Q's CA	**Q's CU**	**Q's EA**	**Q's EU**	**R's CA**	**R's CU**	**R's EA**	**R's EU**	**J's CA**	**J's CU**	**J's EA**	**J's EU**
c1		e1		c1		e1					
c2		e2		c2		e2					
c3											
c4*											
	c5		e5		c5		e5				
	c6		e6		c6		e6				
	c7		e7		c7		e7				
	c8		e8		c8		e8				
	c9		e9		c9		e9				

				c10*							
				c11							
c12											
c13											
c14											
	c15										
	c16										
	c17										
				c18							
				c19							
					c20						
					c21						
					c22						

Now, assume that J decides the case as follows:

(J1) Given that George entered the public park by skateboard, that a statute prescribes that no vehicle may be taken into the park, that this statute has to be interpreted according to its purpose, that the purpose of the law is to protect pedestrians and that skateboards are a threat for them, it follows that skateboards are vehicles according to the law, and therefore George has violated the statute and ought to be punished thus-and-so.

By means of *J1*, on the one hand, J acknowledges the following entitlements to Q and R, which correspond to the commitments attributed to J by the parties:

(e1) A statute prescribes that no vehicle may be taken into the park.
(e2) George entered the park on a skateboard.

J also implicitly attributes a set of entitlements to Q and R:

(e5) The statute is a source of law in the legal system in which J has jurisdiction.
(e6) George is a human being.
(e7) George was in town that day.
(e8) George's punishment does not admit legal exceptions.
(e9) The content of this statute is consistent and coherent with the content of the other statutes belonging to the same legal system.

Through the same speech act, J then acknowledges the following entitlements to Q, scored under {Q's entitlements acknowledged}:

(e15) The statute has to be interpreted according to its purpose.
(e12) The purpose of the statute is to protect pedestrians.
(e14) Skateboards are a threat for pedestrians.

J also implicitly undertakes a set of entitlements scored under {Q's entitlements undertaken}:

(e16) Purposive interpretation has to be preferred to other interpretive methods.
(e17) Judges are agents of the law and its overall purposes.

However, the most important inferential move in J's reasoning is related to the legal qualification of the case.[25] In fact, by means of *J1* J entitles Q to a key commitment in this exchange of reasons, which is included in {Q's entitlements acknowledged}:

(e4*) If *x* is a skateboard, then *x* is a vehicle according to the law.

So, if *e4** is the case, then Q is entitled by J to

(e3) George ought to be punished thus-and-so.

In the calculation of the points scored by Q and R during the exchange of reasons, Q scores the best result from J's viewpoint and wins the trial. At the same time, J's interpretive scorekeeping fixes the content of the legal sentence acknowledging the qualification of the case put forward by Q and rejecting the qualification proposed by R. Obviously, R's counter reasons are not cancelled: combinatory vagueness is authoritatively reduced to such an extent to settle the singular case.

So, J's scoreboard registers the following score at the final stage of the exchange of reasons:

Q's CA	**Q's CU**	**Q's EA**	**Q's EU**	**R's CA**	**R's CU**	**R's EA**	**R's EU**	**J's CA**	**J's CU**	**J's EA**	**J's EU**
c1		e1		c1		e1		c1			
c2		e2		c2		e2		c2			
c3		e3						c3			
c4*		**e4***						c4*			
	c5		e5		c5		e5		c5		
	c6		e6		c6		e6		c6		
	c7		e7		c7		e7		c7		
	c8		e8		c8		e8		c8		
	c9		e9		c9		e9		c9		
				c10*							
				c11							
c12		e12						c12			
c13											
c14		e14						c14			
	c15	e15							c15		

[25] It is worth underlying that the legal dispute between Q and R could be focused on a different issue, such as fact finding, procedural requirements or the determination of punishment. This would change the way in which the legal dispute and J's scoreboard evolve over time on the basis of the reasons provided by Q and R.

	c16		e16						c16		
	c17		e17						c17		
				c18							
				c19							
					c20						
					c21						
					c22						

J's scoreboard shows how the legal sentence "No vehicle may be taken into the park" becomes combinatory vague in the course of an exchange of reasons between the parties and the judge, and the way in which a borderline case has been settled. Note that J's decision is still disputable in our example and J's score might change over time. For instance, R could challenge *e3* and *e4* and *e5*, treating them as commitments the judge cannot be entitled to. This is the case when R appeals J's decision. In the appeal, a new exchange of reasons will start and the parties will discuss whether J is entitled to her decision from a legal point of view. If the appellate court does not entitle J to *c4**, and to the other commitments attributed to her in the new exchange of reasons, J's decision will be reversed and the skateboard case could be ruled differently. These points will be scored under sets {J's entitlements acknowledged} and {J's entitlements undertaken} in the scoreboard of the appellate court.

7 Final Remarks

We can now turn back to the main question addressed in this essay: what does inferentialism tell us about combinatory vagueness in law? According to an inferentialist approach to content, combinatory vagueness is a sort of linguistic indeterminacy which depends on the pragmatic interaction between the participants in an exchange of reasons. A statute is combinatory vague when legal practitioners disagree on its content in a specific way, and this disagreement gives rise to borderline cases of norm application. Consequently, the practice of giving and asking for reasons is both the source of combinatory vagueness in law, and the way in which this sort of linguistic indeterminacy can be reduced on the basis of reasons. A legal case is borderline under two conditions: (a) if linguistic practitioners use the *same* statute according to *different* sets of commissive and permissive inferential relations, so that it becomes uncertain whether the case is ruled by the statute, and (b) if the linguistic behavior of these practitioners is consistent with the *same* set of incompatibility inferential relations, which make disagreement possible.

The analysis proposed in this essay leads us to an additional consideration. An inferentialist approach to content does not describe communication in law as the transmission of information from lawmakers to law-addressees through the use of a meaningful code. Content is not a mental entity linguistically conveyed to other minds; it is rather a set of inferential relations in which a content bearer plays the role of premise or conclusion. These relations depend on the normative status that linguistic practitioners attribute to one another, and change over time in a rule-governed way.[26] This picture accounts for the institutional dimension of linguistic communication in law and shows that legislative intention is simply one of the reasons that may justify content ascription in legal adjudication.

The inferentialist picture, however, is not immune from criticism. First, one might wonder whether we need to adopt a completely different strategy of philosophical explanation in order to elucidate how legal language works. As a matter of fact, the standard approach to semantics and pragmatics seems to have the resources to do this: the institutional framework in which legal communication takes place, the specific features of legislative intention, and the authoritative character of legal sentences can be explained in terms of the presuppositions and implicatures which enrich, narrow or modulate meaning in the legal context. So, why should we overturn the fundamental axioms of the traditional picture? One possible answer is that different approaches to semantics and pragmatics highlight different aspects of language and communication; therefore, each approach is more or less compelling depending on the linguistic domain under examination and the purpose of the philosophical inquiry. The inferentialist strategy has the advantage that it primarily focuses on some aspects of linguistic communication which are of paramount importance in law, whereas the standard picture tends to overlook these features or to regard them as peripheral to other phenomena. Thus, inferentialism might allow legal theory to emphasize what is special about legal language as opposed to ordinary language.

Secondly, in the inferentialist picture combinatory vagueness appears as the result of a specific form of disagreement between the participants in an exchange of reasons. In ordinary linguistic exchange, however, Q and R disagreeing on the content of a term does not lead us to the conclusion that that term is combinatory vague. Suppose that Q and R disagree on the content of the term "vehicle": Q claims that kangaroos count as vehicles, whereas R does not. Would this be a good reason for us to think that the term "vehicle" is indeterminate in the statute? Of course not. Rather, what seems to matter is that there is sufficiently widespread disagreement as to what counts as a member of the set of things picked out by the term "vehicle". A possible reply to this objection is the following: the inferentialist approach assumes that vagueness is not due to the current state of our knowledge. The semantic indeterminacy of vague terms is rather conceived as a defective feature of a language game. Therefore, skateboards are borderline cases of "vehicle", completely independent from whatever we might come to know about skateboards. More challenging is the problem related to the scope of linguistic disagreement. Does the disagreement between Q and R suffice to make the content of a term indeterminate? It is worth noting in this respect that commissive, permissive and incompatibility relations capture a number of background assumptions that are shared in a linguistic

[26] See Canale and Tuzet (2007). As stated by Brandom, "for information (…) to be communicated is for the claims undertaken by one interlocutor to become available to others (who attribute them) as premise for inference. Communication is the social production and consumption of reasons" (Brandom 1994, 474).

community: the exchange of reasons between Q and R simply makes these assumptions (partially) explicit. On the basis of this background, it is reasonable to treat skateboards as borderline cases whereas kangaroos do plainly fall outside the extension of the term "vehicle", at least in the considered context. However, it is not clear how inferentialism can discriminate between the background assumptions of a linguistic community and the idiosyncratic assumptions of the participants in an exchange of reasons. With regard to this, the inferentialist framework needs to be further elaborated.

Thirdly, an inferentialist explanation of combinatory vagueness faces the threat of high-order vagueness. We have seen that a term is vague when the participants in an exchange of reasons disagree on the commissive and permissive relations the term is involved in, whereas they recognize the same incompatibility relations. But what about the situation in which the incompatibilities between deontic statuses are combinatory vague, that is, the participants disagree on whether being committed to *S1* is compatible with being entitled to *S2*? To solve this issue, the inferentialist approach should specify what sort of high-order disagreements are admissible in an exchange of reasons. Furthermore, it is unclear how inferentialism might elucidate other forms of vagueness such as sorites susceptibility, which is at the centre of philosophical literature on vagueness today.[27] Does this approach have the theoretical resources for a logical analysis of sorites paradoxes? At first glance, it is difficult to see how inferentialism could carry out this task.

To conclude, the inferentialist approach to semantics and pragmatics provides an innovative explanation of combinatory vagueness in law, an explanation which highlights certain features of legal language that are usually neglected in philosophical literature. Yet this picture still gives rise to theoretical concerns and, thus, needs further clarification and development.[28]

References

Alston, W. P. (1967). Vagueness. In P. Edwards (Ed.), *The encyclopedia of philosophy* (Vol. 8, pp. 218–221). New York/London: Macmillan & Free Press.

Allan, J. (2000). Constitutional interpretation v. statutory interpretation. Understanding the attractions of "original intent". *Legal Theory, 6*, 109–126.

Boudreau, C., Lupia, A., McCubbins, M. D., & Rodriguez, D. B. (2007). What statutes mean: Interpretive lessons from positive theories of communication and legislation. *San Diego Law Review, 44*, 957–992.

Brandom, R. B. (1994). *Making it explicit. Reasoning, representing, and discursive commitment.* Harvard/London: Harvard University Press.

Brandom, R. B. (2000). *Articulating reasons. An introduction to inferentialism.* Cambridge, MA/London: Harvard University Press.

[27] See e.g. Hyde 2011; Weber and Colyvan 2010; Williamson 1994.

[28] An early version of this essay was presented at the conference "Pragmatist and Contextualist Approaches to Vagueness in Legal Theory and in Philosophy", University of Freiburg, 1–3 July 2011. I am grateful to Scott Soames for his critical comments during the conference.

Brandom, R. B. (2008). *Between saying and doing. Towards an analytic pragmatism*. Oxford/New York: Cambridge University Press.

Bratman, M. E. (1999). *Faces of intention. Selected essay on intention and agency*. Cambridge: Cambridge University Press.

Bueno, O., & Colyvan, M. (2012). Just what is vagueness? *Ratio, 25*, 19–33.

Campbell, T. (2001). Legislative intent and democratic decision making. In N. Naffine, R. J. Owens, & J. Williams (Eds.), *Intention in law and philosophy* (pp. 291–319). Aldershot: Ashgate.

Canale, D., & Tuzet, G. (2007). On legal inferentialism. Towards a pragmatics of semantic content in legal adjudication? *Ratio Juris, 20*, 32–44.

Dummett, M. (1975). Wang's paradox. *Synthese, 30*, 301–324.

Ekins, R. (2012). *The nature of legislative intent*. Oxford: Oxford University Press.

Endicott, T. (2000). *Vagueness in law*. Oxford: Oxford University Press.

Endicott, T. (2011). The value of vagueness. In A. Marmor & S. Soames (Eds.), *Philosophical foundations of language in the law* (pp. 14–30). Oxford: Oxford University Press.

Eskridge, W. N. (1987). Dynamic statutory interpretation. *University of Pennsylvania Law Review, 135*, 1479–1555.

Fine, K. (1975). Vagueness, truth and logic. *Synthese, 30*, 265–300.

Gardner, J. (2010). Ethics and law. In J. Skorupski (Ed.), *The Routledge companion to ethics* (pp. 420–430). London: Routledge.

Gilbert, M. (2006). *A theory of political obligation. Membership, commitment, and the bonds of society*. Oxford: Oxford University Press.

Goldsworthy, J. (1997). Originalism in constitutional interpretation. *Federal Law Review, 25*, 1–50.

Goldsworthy, J. (2005). Legislative intentions, legislative supremacy, and legal positivism. *San Diego Law Review, 42*, 493–518.

Greenawalt, K. (2000). Are mental states relevant for statutory and constitutional interpretation? *Cornell Law Review, 85*, 1609–1672.

Greenberg, M. (2011). Legislation as communication? Legal interpretation and the study of linguistic communication. In A. Marmor & S. Soames (Eds.), *Philosophical foundations of language in the law* (pp. 217–264). Oxford: Oxford University Press.

Grice, H. P. (1989). *Studies in the way of words*. Cambirdge, MA: Harvard University Press.

Gupta, A. (1999). Meaning and misconceptions. In R. Jackendoff, P. Bloom, & K. Wynn (Eds.), *Language, logic, and concepts* (pp. 15–41). Cambridge, MA: MIT Press.

Hart, H. L. A. (1983). Positivism and the separation of law and morals. In H. L. A. Hart (Ed.), *Essays in jurisprudence and philosophy* (pp. 49–87). Oxford: Clarendon.

Hart, H. L. A. (1994). *The concept of law* (2nd ed.). Oxford: Clarendon.

Hazard, G. C., & Taruffo, M. (1993). *American civil procedure*. New Haven: Yale University Press.

Hyde, D. (2011). The sorites paradox. In G. Ronzitti (Ed.), *Vagueness: A guide* (pp. 1–18). Dordrecht/New York: Springer.

Jónsson, O. P. (2009). Vagueness, interpretation and the law. *Legal Theory, 15*, 193–214.

Lance, M. (2001). The logical structure of linguistic commitment III: Brandomian scorekeeping and incompatibility. *Journal of Philosophical Logic, 30*, 439–464.

Landsman, S. (1983). A brief survey of the development of the adversary system. *Ohio State Law Journal, 44*, 713–740.

Lewis, D. (1979). Scorekeeping in a language game. *Journal of Philosophical Logic, 8*, 339–359.

MacCormick, N. (2009). *Rhetoric and the rule of law. A theory of legal reasoning*. Oxford: Oxford University Press.

MacPherson, J. A. E. (2010). Legislative intentionalism and proxy agency. *Law and Philosophy, 29*, 1–29.

Manning, J. F. (2001). Textualism and the equity of the statute. *Columbia Law Review, 101*, 1–127.

Marmor, A. (2005). *Interpretation and legal theory* (2nd ed.). Oxford/Portland: Hart Publishing.

Marmor, A. (2008). The pragmatics of legal language. *Ratio Juris, 21*, 423–452.
Moreso, J. J. (2005). *Lógica, argumentación e interpretación en el derecho*. Barcelona: Editorial UOC.
Neale, S. (2007). On location. In M. O'Rourke & C. Washington (Eds.), *Situating semantics. Essays on the philosophy of John Perry* (pp. 253–293). Cambridge, MA/London: MIT Press.
Pettit, P. (2001). Collective intentions. In N. Naffine, R. J. Owens, & J. Williams (Eds.), *Intention in law and philosophy* (pp. 241–254). Aldershot: Ashgate.
Poscher, R. (2012). Ambiguity and vagueness in legal interpretation. In L. Solan & P. Tiersma (Eds.), *Oxford handbook on language and law*. Oxford: Oxford University Press.
Radin, M. (1930). Statutory interpretation. *Harvard Law Review, 43*, 863–885.
Raffman, D. (2014). *Unruly words. A study of vague language*. Oxford/New York: Oxford University Press.
Raz, J. (2009). *Between authority and interpretation. On the theory of law and practical reason*. Oxford: Oxford University Press.
Recanati, F. (2002). Does linguistic communication rest on inference? *Mind & Language, 17*, 105–126.
Scharp, K. (2005). Scorekeeping in a defective language game. *Pragmatics and Cognition, 13*, 203–226.
Sellars, W. (1953). Inference and meaning. *Mind, 62*, 313–338.
Shapiro, S. (2006). *Vagueness in context*. Oxford: Oxford University Press.
Soames, S. (1998). *Understanding truth*. Oxford: Oxford University Press.
Soames, S. (2009). Interpreting legal texts: What is, and what is not, special about the law. In S. Soames (Ed.), *Philosophical essays. Vol. 1. Natural language: What it means and how we use it* (pp. 403–423). Princeton/Oxford: Princeton University Press.
Soames, S. (2012). Vagueness and the law. In A. Marmor (Ed.), *The Routledge companion to philosophy of law* (pp. 95–108). New York: Routledge.
Sperber, D., & Wilson, D. (1995). *Relevance: Communication and cognition* (2nd ed.). Oxford: Blackwell.
Stoljar, N. (1998). Counterfactuals in interpretation: The case against intentionalism. *Adelaide Law Review, 20*, 29–59.
Summers, R. S. (2000). *Essays in legal theory*. Dordrecht: Kluwer.
Weber, Z., & Colyvan, M. (2010). A topological sorites. *The Journal of Philosophy, 107*, 311–325.
Williams, J. (2001). Constitutional intention: The limits of originalism. In N. Naffine, R. J. Owens, & J. Williams (Eds.), *Intention in law and philosophy* (pp. 321–341). Aldershot: Ashgate.
Williamson, T. (1994). *Vagueness*. London: Routledge.

On the Possibility of Non-literal Legislative Speech

Hrafn Asgeirsson

Abstract The existing literature on indeterminacy in the law focuses mostly on the use of vague terms in legislation – terms the use of which makes the content of the relevant utterance to some extent indeterminate. As I aim to show, however, not only is the content of a legislative utterance often indeterminate, it is often indeterminate what the content of such an utterance is. In the second and third section of the chapter, I discuss in some detail the conditions for successful non-literal speech and address the question whether these conditions are satisfied in the legal context. I argue that due to the fact that legislative contexts generally contain little unequivocal information about legislative intent, interpreters are typically not warranted in taking the legislature to have intended to communicate something non-literal. In the fourth section, I consider what I take to be the strongest case against my argument: the wealth of actual cases in which the courts have taken the content of the law to be something other than its literal content, seemingly based on relatively straightforward inferences about the legislature's communicative intentions. As I hope to show, however, very few of these cases are as straightforward as they appear to be. In the fifth, and final section, I argue that the argument from sections two and three has important consequences for the extent to which we should take the content of the law to be determinate. This has significant implications for the analysis of a number of important but controversial legal cases, which I discuss in some detail.

Keywords Linguistic communication • Non-literal speech • Pragmatics • Legal directives • Legal interpretation • Legislative intent • Linguistic indeterminacy • Legal indeterminacy

H. Asgeirsson (✉)
School of Law, University of Surrey, Guildford, UK
e-mail: h.asgeirsson@surrey.ac.uk

F. Poggi, A. Capone (eds.), *Pragmatics and Law*, Perspectives in Pragmatics, Philosophy & Psychology 10, DOI 10.1007/978-3-319-44601-1_4

1 Introduction

The existing literature on indeterminacy in the law focuses mostly on the use of vague terms in legislation – terms the use of which makes the content of the relevant utterance to some extent indeterminate.[1] There is another form of indeterminacy, however, that appears to have been somewhat neglected.[2] As I aim to show, not only is the content of a legislative utterance often indeterminate, it is often indeterminate what the content of such an utterance is. The reason, I'll argue, is that because legislative contexts generally contain little unequivocal information about legislative intent, it is often indeterminate whether the content of a law is its literal content or some pragmatic enrichment thereof.

In Sects. 2 and 3 of the chapter, using a recent argument by Andrei Marmor as my starting point, I discuss in some detail the conditions for successful non-literal speech and address the question whether these conditions are satisfied in the legal context.[3] I argue that – generally, albeit with certain qualifications – due to the fact that legislative contexts generally contain little unequivocal information about legislative intent, interpreters are typically not warranted in taking the legislature to have intended to communicate something non-literal.

In Sect. 4, I consider what I take to be the strongest case against my argument. Ekins (2012) offers a wealth of actual cases in which the courts have taken the content of the law to be something other than its literal content, seemingly based on relatively straightforward inferences about the legislature's communicative intentions. As I hope to show, however, only one of Ekins's examples is as straightforward as he suggests. If that is correct, his accumulative empirical argument from examples does not go through.

In the final section, Sect. 5, I argue that the revised argument has important consequences for the extent to which we should take the content of the law to be determinate. The basic idea is that sometimes the audience of a speaker's remark ought to withhold belief regarding her communicative intentions, in which case the primary content of the relevant utterance is indeterminate between the literal content of the sentence uttered and some pragmatic enrichment thereof.[4] This has signifi-

[1] See e.g. Hart (1958), Waldron (1994), Endicott (2000), Endicott (2011), Waldron (2011), Soames (2011).

[2] With some recent exceptions, see e.g. Poscher (2012), Marmor (2014), chapter 4, and Marmor (2016). Endicott (2000) also dedicates a few pages to this type of indeterminacy; see pp. 50–55.

[3] Marmor (2008).

[4] The primary content of an utterance is the content that a speaker counts as having primarily communicated, as opposed to secondarily (such as by implicature). This may be the literal content of the speaker's remark, but may also be – or may even have to be – some non-literal enrichment of that content. For a discussion, see Jaszczolt (chapter "Slippery meaning and accountability" this volume); see also Recanati (2012).

cant implications for the analysis of a number of important but controversial legal cases, which I discuss in some detail.[5]

2 The Conditions for Non-literal Speech and the Legislative Context

In ordinary conversation, it frequently happens that speakers assert something other than what they literally say. When I utter the words 'I haven't had breakfast' to the waiter at the airport café, for example, it is obvious that I don't intend to assert that I haven't had breakfast *ever*. Rather, I am asserting that I haven't had breakfast *today*, perhaps in the hope that he tells me they are still serving. Given the ubiquity of this phenomenon, it makes sense to ask whether it also frequently happens that *legislatures* assert something other than what they literally say.[6]

Consider for example the *Federal Tort Claims Act*, which guarantees the government immunity from "[a]ny claim arising in respect of [...] the detention of any goods, merchandize, or other property by any officer of customs or excise or any other law enforcement officer."[7] On a literal reading of the Act, it guarantees immunity from claims arising in respect of certain actions on behalf of law enforcement officers of *any kind*. But it is reasonable – given the context of the Act – to wonder whether the legislature intended to communicate something slightly different,

[5] I should note that throughout the paper, I assume that the legal content of a statute *directly corresponds* to its linguistic content and thereby presuppose a version of of what Mark Greenberg calls the *communicative-content theory of law*; see Greenberg (2011). For those who hold that there is more to the legal content of a statute than what is provided by way of legislative communication, it is worth pointing out – as Greenberg does – that it is still "uncontroversial that, on any plausible view, the meaning of a statute's text is highly relevant to the statute's contribution to the content of the law;" see Greenberg (2011), 219. Nevertheless, those who do not subscribe to some version of the communicative-content theory probably won't be inclined to accept everything I say in the last section of the paper, in which I argue that, due to the fact that legislative contexts generally contain little unequivocal information about legislative intent, the legal content of statutes is often to some extent indeterminate. The reason, of course, is that this is true only if some version of the communicative-content theory is correct.

[6] In this paper, I will be concerned only with statutory law. For a valuable discussion about the way in which different areas of law might be affected differently by the kinds of considerations discussed here, see Solum (2013). "For interpretation of a legal text to succeed," Solum says, "the interpreter must ... understand the distinct constraints on successful communication associated with the type of legal text" (507). He then goes on to argue that the role communicative content plays in determining legal content differs between areas of law, due crucially to these systematic differences in the various contexts of legal speech.

[7] 28 U.S.C. 2680(c).

namely that immunity is guaranteed in respect of certain actions on behalf of law enforcement officers *working in customs or related domains*. The difference in content is significant. Abdus-Shahid M.S. Ali, for example, wanted to sue the government because prison officers lost property belonging to him, but this would require a non-literal reading of the Act. The Supreme Court held that a literal reading was appropriate and Ali was not allowed to sue.[8]

Or consider the US Criminal Code, 18 U.S.C. § 922(g)(1), which makes it "unlawful for any person … who has been convicted in any court, of a crime punishable by imprisonment for a term exceeding 1 year … to … possess … any firearm."[9] Read literally, there is no restriction on the location of the conviction – a conviction in *any* court will do. But, again, it makes sense to ask whether the legislature intended to communicate something slightly different from the literal content of the statute, namely that possession of a firearm is unlawful if one has been convicted in a *US* court. As before, the difference in content is significant. Gary Small, for example, had been convicted of violating 18 U.S.C. § 922(g)(1), but the Supreme Court reversed the decision on appeal, on the basis of a non-literal reading of the Code.[10]

These cases are by no means unique – there is a wealth of cases the outcome of which turns on whether the legislature can reasonably be said to have asserted something other than what it literally said. Thus, questions about the existence and extent of non-literal assertion in the law have considerable practical, in addition to theoretical, significance.

2.1 Marmor's Skepticism About Non-literal Legislative Speech

Marmor (2008) argues that it *rarely* happens that the law asserts something other than what it literally says.[11] (As I understand him, what he means by 'rare' is not so much that it almost never occurs – although a few passages in the text suggest this – but rather that non-literal legislative speech is infrequent in comparison to non-literality in ordinary conversation.[12]) He substantiates his skepticism by first contrasting successful cases of pragmatic enrichment with unsuccessful ones, in an

---

[8] *Ali v. Federal Bureau of Prisons*; 552 U.S. 214 (2008). I discuss this case in more detail below.

[9] 18 U.S.C. § 922(g)(1).

[10] *Small v. United States*; 544 U.S. 385 (2005). I also discuss this case in more detail below.

[11] Marmor (2008), 424–429. For an interesting – and relatively early – discussion of non-literal legislative speech and epistemic constraints, see Goldsworthy (1994), esp. 168–70.

[12] Thanks to Jeffrey Goldsworthy and Lawrence Solum for pressing me to clarify this.

effort to identify the feature that the former cases have and the latter cases lack, and by then showing that – typically – this feature is absent in the context of legislative utterances. The distinguishing feature, Marmor thinks, is *obviousness*: typically, in cases in which a speaker successfully asserts something other than what she literally says, it is – due to a sufficiently rich conversational background – just obvious that she couldn't be intending to assert the literal content of her remark. It is *this* feature that Marmor thinks is – for the most part – absent in the context of legislation.

Marmor begins by noting that in ordinary conversation, we often come across examples like the following, in which the assertive content clearly goes beyond what is literally said[13]:

(1) A doctor examining a gunshot wound tells the patient: "Don't worry, you are not going to die." Clearly, the doctor did not assert that the patient is never going to die, but only that he is not going to die from this particular wound.
(2) When I get home in the evening and my wife asks me "Have you eaten?" it is quite clear that she is asking me if I have already eaten dinner tonight, not whether I have ever engaged in the activity of eating.[14]

What makes these cases obvious is in large part that certain information is taken for granted by the participants in the conversation, including information about the purpose of the exchange, and partly that other interpretations would make the respective utterances less than fully cooperative (given the purpose of the relevant conversation). (Generally, I will refer to this information either as *background assumptions*, *conversational background*, *common ground*, or just *context*.) For our purposes, the general lesson to take away from these examples is the following, according to Marmor: "A speaker would *normally* succeed in conveying assertive content that differs from what he says, *when it would be obvious to the hearer, in the particular context of the conversation, that it just cannot be the case that the speaker asserts exactly what he says*."[15]

Obviousness of this sort, then, is – according to Marmor – a *sufficient* condition for non-literal speech (on the assumption that certain other background conditions are satisfied). It is clear, however, that Marmor thinks that, in normal circumstances, the obviousness criterion is also a *necessary* condition for such speech. To borrow

[13] Note that the following examples and their analyses assume that the literal content of the relevant utterances are complete propositions. This assumption is controversial, and some would be inclined to argue that the literal content is incomplete (i.e. not truth-evaluable). For a discussion, see e.g. Soames (2010), 155–156. Here, however, I will – for the sake of argument – assume that the literal content of the utterances in examples (1) and (2) *are* complete propositions.

[14] Marmor (2008), 426. As Marmor notes, these examples are slight variations of examples discussed by Bach (1994) and Soames (2008).

[15] Marmor (2008), 428; my emphasis.

his example, it is quite possible that in uttering 'Have you had blackberries?', a speaker can be meaning to ask whether or not the hearer has *ever* had blackberries or can be meaning to ask whether or not the hearer has had blackberries *that day*. If the contextual background is not sufficiently rich to make it obvious which question is intended, Marmor says, and it would consequently make sense for the hearer to ask for clarification, then "this would be a clear indication that [the speaker has] not succeeded in asserting some content that differs from what [she] said."[16] Obviousness, then, is supposed to be central in explaining our intuitions regarding successful cases of asserting something other than what is literally said – like (1) and (2) above – as well as our intuitions about unsuccessful cases – like the "blackberry scenario". The focus here, however, will be on obviousness as a necessary condition for successfully asserting something other than what one literally said.

In order to illustrate his general claim that legislatures rarely succeed in asserting something other than what they literally say, due to the fact that very little can jointly be taken for granted by the legislature and its audience(s), Marmor discusses the famous case of *Church of the Holy Trinity v. US*.[17] In *Holy Trinity*, the relevant question was whether the *Alien Contract Labor Act* of 1885,[18] which prohibited the importation of "labor or service of any kind" except "professional actors, artists, lecturers or singers" and "persons employed strictly as personal or domestic servants," prohibited the importation of people intended to serve as rectors or clergymen. The circuit court for the southern district of New York held that it did, while the Supreme Court held that it did not. As Justice Brewer put it, in delivering the opinion of the court: "It is a familiar rule that a thing may be within the letter of the statute and yet not within the statute, because not within its spirit nor within the intention of its makers."

Marmor asks whether it is plausible to argue – in the spirit of Justice Brewer's remark – that in enacting the *Alien Contract Labor Act*, the legislature asserted something different from what it said. That is, can we argue that although the importation of rectors and clergymen was prohibited according to what the law literally said, the *assertive* content of the legislative utterance was different, in that it did not

[16] Marmor (2008), 428.

[17] 143 U.S. 457 (1892).

[18] 23 Stat. 332 (codified as amended at 29 U.S.C. §2164 (1901)), *superceded by* Act of Mar. 3, 1903, Pub. L. No. 162, 32 Stat. 1213.

apply to such conduct? Marmor thinks that for a couple of reasons it would be a stretch to argue this, and I think he is quite right. Given Marmor's obviousness requirement, we can say that the primary reason for this is that the context in which the *Alien Contract Labor Act* was enacted has a number of features in virtue of which it makes sense to ask whether Congress could have had in mind to prohibit the importation of foreign clergymen.[19] And if that is so, then it cannot be *obvious* that it did not mean to assert what it literally said. So in case Congress really did intend to assert something different from what it literally said, it did not succeed. Or so Marmor argues.

Now, as Marmor recognizes, it is perhaps not entirely fair to pick *Holy Trinity* as the only case study. And I think that is correct. He believes, however, that we get the same results with simpler examples (assuming they are sufficiently realistic, of course[20]). For our purposes, it is not important how these examples go. Marmor's explanation for why the law – in these cases – does not succeed in asserting something different from what it literally says is the same: "the context is not rich enough to make it obvious and transparent that the legislature could not have meant/asserted what it said."[21]

2.2 *Assertion, Warrant for Belief, and the Obviousness Requirement*

On the picture under scrutiny, then, reinterpreting a speaker to be asserting something other than what she literally said is warranted only if it is obvious to a rational and informed hearer that the speaker could not be intending to assert what she literally said, conditional on the assumption that she is being cooperative[22]:

[19] For more detailed discussion of *Holy Trinity*, see Sect. 5.1 below.

[20] It is quite possible, I think, to invent cases in which lawmakers and their audience(s) share a wealth of beliefs/knowledge and that – consequently – the law has no problem asserting something other than what it says. But this does not affect Marmor's argument, since he is only committed to the claim that, *given the way the law tends to work*, such cases will be relatively rare.

[21] Marmor (2008), 429.

[22] I should note that Marmor is not alone in positing comparably strict pragmatic requirements – we have something rather similar, for example, in Paul Grice's pragmatic framework. Assuming that Grice would have classified the examples we are concerned with as examples of conversational implicature (rather than assertion), it follows from Grice's (1989) definition thereof that the relevant speech acts are successful only if the hearer *must* reinterpret the speaker's remark in order to make it consistent with the Cooperative Principle (see Grice (1989), 30–31)). See also Bach and Harnish (1979), 12, 61.

OBVIOUSNESS Normally, a speaker asserts something other than what she literally says only if it is obvious to her that the speaker cannot be intending to assert what she literally says.

To be sure, this requirement seems to be satisfied in many cases in ordinary conversation. The question, however, is whether it is true of *all* normal cases in which a speaker asserts something other than what she literally says that it is *impossible* – relative to the body of information available to the hearer – that she could be intending to assert what she says. It seems to me that it isn't. As I will explain below, I think that there is a distinctive set of cases of successful non-literal assertion in which it is clearly not obvious – albeit *significantly more likely than not* – that the speaker is not intending to assert what she literally says. These cases, I will argue, give us good reason to reject OBVIOUSNESS in favor of a weaker, more flexible, requirement.

In order to get at what I take to be the heart of the matter, we need to dissect OBVIOUSNESS a little further. First, Marmor and I both accept an account of assertion on which the following principle is true:

ASSERTION A speaker asserts p only if a rational hearer, knowing the relevant conversational background and context, is warranted in taking her to be intending to assert p.[23]

On this account, the epistemic position of the hearer plays a central role in determining the content of the speaker's assertion.[24] That is, it is partly *in virtue of* facts about epistemic justification that a speaker counts as having asserted a particular proposition.[25]

In the case of non-literal assertion, the above requirement takes the following form:

ASSERTION* Normally, a speaker asserts something other than what she literally says only if a rational hearer, knowing the relevant conversational background and context, is warranted in taking her not to be intending to assert what she literally says.

Marmor's obviousness requirement is produced when we combine ASSERTION* with the following principle:

---

[23] See e.g. Marmor (2013), 55.

[24] Several authors – many of whom accept the basic tenets of Grice's framework – embrace this partly objective account of assertive/communicative content; see e.g. Goldsworthy (2005), Soames (2011), and Marmor (2013). Many devout Griceans, however, favor a subjective account, on which a speaker means, says, asserts, etc. what he intends to mean, say, assert, etc; see e.g. Schiffer (1972), Neale (2005), and Bach (2006).

[25] Note that, although this is one sense in which the relevant account of assertion is properly said to be normative, this is different from the normativity associated with the so-called *norms of assertion*. While the norms of assertions are partly constitutive of an utterance's being an assertion, the normative considerations I am discussing in this section concern what it takes for an utterance not just to be an assertion but to be an assertion of p. That is, it concerns the content of a given utterance.

STRICT WARRANT Normally, a rational hearer, knowing the relevant conversational background and context, is warranted in taking a speaker not to be intending to assert what she literally says only if it is obvious to her that the speaker cannot be intending to assert what she literally says.

It is *this* principle which brings out what I believe is really at issue here. Contra Marmor, I think that there *are* in fact perfectly normal instances of successful non-literal assertion in which it is less than obvious to a rational and informed hearer that the speaker could not be intending to assert the literal content of her remark. If I am able to find counterexamples to STRICT WARRANT, I will by the same token have found counterexamples to OBVIOUSNESS. I turn to this task next.

2.3 Low-Stakes Loose Talk Scenarios as Systematic Counterexamples to Warrant?

I should begin by explaining what sort of cases I believe make for the most plausible counterexamples to the principle STRICT WARRANT, and consequently to Marmor's obviousness requirement. In the first instance, these have to be cases in which it is not obvious that the speaker just cannot be intending to assert the literal content of the sentence she utters, yet in which nothing appears to be amiss, pragmatically speaking. That is, they must be cases in which the communicative act can reasonably be said to have gone well.

A case like this goes reasonably well – I submit – if (but not necessarily only if) (i) the speaker intends to assert something other than what she literally says, (ii) it is, relative to the epistemic position of a rational hearer, knowing the relevant conversational background and context, significantly more likely than not that the speaker is so intending, and (iii) the hearer in fact takes the speaker to be so intending. In many cases of this sort – as I will illustrate below – the hearer may not have any significant reason to ask for clarification, although it may perhaps not be outright silly to ask for it either. In such cases, it would seem that things have gone well and so I see no reason to say that the speaker did not succeed in asserting something other than what she literally said. It seems to me that the speaker succeeded in doing what she intended to do.[26]

Let us fix the relevant ideas by trying out an example in which the speaker is speaking "loosely". Imagine that my friend Kory tells me that he can only stay for

[26] I should note that if I am right about these cases, then Marmor's "clarification-test" for successful non-literal assertion is too strict: a speaker successfully asserts something other than what she literally said only if it would be silly of the hearer to ask for clarification about what the speaker meant. Sometimes, as I hope to show, non-literal assertion is successful despite the fact that it would not be outright silly to ask for clarification. These are cases in which the hearer has a reason to ask the speaker for clarification *only if* that reason comes from the hearer's own desire to know for certain what the speaker intended to communicate.

20 min or so for the premiere of my wife's new orchestra piece and that he asks me how long the piece is. Imagine also that in response I utter the following: 'It's 12 min long.' In this context, it is surely *possible* that I am intending to speak literally, i.e. it is not obvious that I just cannot be intending to communicate that the piece is *exactly* 12 min long. Yet, it is – given what is "required by the accepted purpose of the conversation" – significantly more likely than not that I am intending to communicate that the work is *approximately* 12 min long. Thus, it is true both that (1) in uttering the relevant sentence in the relevant context, I have given Kory significantly more reason than not to believe that I intended to communicate that the piece is approximately 12 min long and that (2) it doesn't matter much, for the purposes of the conversation, if I in fact intended to communicate that the piece is exactly 12 min long; since Kory is able to stay for the entire piece, nothing hangs on it.

It seems to me that there is no reason here to claim that Kory is not warranted in taking the speaker (i.e. me) to be intending to assert something other than the literal content of the sentence uttered. In case Kory infers that I intended to communicate that the piece is approximately 12 min long, nothing appears to be amiss – and nothing appears to be amiss because nothing *is* amiss. Further, if Kory has any reason to ask me to clarify what I meant to communicate, this reason will be grounded exclusively in his desire to know for certain what I meant. If all this is correct, then STRICT WARRANT is false – the bar for successful assertion is sometimes lower than postulated by OBVIOUSNESS.

The scenario I have just described is not out of the ordinary – it is a perfectly normal case of successful non-literal assertion. The same reasoning, I maintain, can be applied to many, if not all, low-stakes loose-talk scenarios – and such situations appear to occur quite frequently, at least frequently enough to make them non-exceptional.[27] It seems, therefore, that we have a robust and systematic set of counterexamples to OBVIOUSNESS, in which case Marmor's argument for the conclusion that non-literal legislative speech is rare is unsound.

[27] For a second example, imagine that someone asks an artist how her show went and that in response she utters the following: 'Nobody came to my show!' In most situations, a rational hearer would infer that the artist intended to communicate that *almost* nobody came to her show. But it's not outright *impossible* that the artist is intending to assert that zero people showed up. However, given that it is rare that absolutely nobody shows up for a show, the artist has given her interlocutor good reason to believe that she is intending to communicate that *almost* nobody came to the show – it is significantly more likely than not that she is so intending. Moreover, it does not matter – vis-à-vis this particular context – which proposition the artist in fact intended to communicate; either way, the artist has conveyed that the show didn't go well, which suffices for the purposes of the conversation. As before, it may not be outright silly to ask the artist whether she meant that *absolutely* nobody or *almost* nobody showed up, but in the stipulated scenario there is – given what is "required by the accepted purpose of the conversation" – no reason to ask for clarification that is independent of the interlocutor's desire to know for certain. This further indicates that *strict warrant* is false, and that successful non-literal assertion does not require obviousness – at least not across the board.

As a matter of general theorizing about language, the most natural way to proceed, I think, is to opt for a weaker, more flexible, requirement, one that can accommodate both the examples that *prima facie* motivate OBVIOUSNESS and the examples that I take to constitute counterexamples to it:

FLEX A speaker asserts something other than what she literally says only if it is *significantly more likely than not* that she is intending to do so.

It is a virtue of the resulting account that it is able to explain our intuitions both about the cases in which the hearer is, despite uncertainty, warranted in drawing conclusions about the speaker's intention to assert something other than what she literally says and about the cases in which the hearer is warranted in doing so only if it is obvious that the speaker is so intending. Rather than to postulate a strict invariant requirement for all types of cases, this account allows some flexibility in what it takes to be warranted in drawing conclusions about a speaker's communicative intentions, a flexibility determined by what is at stake in each case.

Before I go on to discuss whether lowering the epistemic bar in this way is fatal to Marmor's line of thought or the revised requirement can be used to reconstruct something akin to his argument, I want to consider a possible reply to my argument against OBVIOUSNESS – one that seeks to show that, in my loose-talk scenarios, the hearer is warranted only in believing to a certain degree that the speaker intends to assert something other than what she literally says, but not in believing it outright. If that's true, then these scenarios are not counterexamples to STRICT WARRANT, on the assumption that this allows the objector to deny that they constitute examples of successful assertion.

2.4 Degree of Belief vs. Outright Belief: Pragmatic Encroachment on Utterance Content

In my loose-talk example, I reasoned in the following way about the hearer's warranted belief about speaker intention. Given that the relevant sentence was uttered in the relevant context, it is significantly more likely than not – relative to Kory's epistemic position – that I am intending to assert that my wife's new piece is approximately 12 min long (rather than intending to assert that it is exactly 12 min long). That is, I provided Kory with good evidence of my non-literal communicative intention – good enough so that he was warranted in taking me not to be intending to assert what I literally said on the basis of that evidence.

This line of reasoning, however, invites the following question. If the evidence supports the conclusion that it is significantly more likely than not that I am intending to assert something other than what I literally say, why do I say that Kory is warranted in outright believing that I so intend? That is, why is Kory's epistemic warrant in this case not confined just to the appropriate degree of belief? The problem for me is that if it is, then my loose-talk example isn't a genuine counterexample to Strict Warrant, because it would no longer be safe to assume – as the principle does – that something has been successfully asserted.

One attractive way to respond to this objection originates in theories that attempt to explain what has come to be known in epistemology as *pragmatic encroachment*. For my purposes here, *any* theory that manages to explain how pragmatic factors – what is at stake in a context – can affect an agent's warrant for outright belief without affecting her warrant for degrees of belief will do, but on this occasion I will make use of an account of belief proposed by Ross and Schroeder (2012): the *Reasoning Disposition Account*. This account attempts to explain pragmatic encroachment by arguing that, because of the function that outright belief serves for human beings, such belief is warranted as long as the relevant proposition is significantly more probable than its negation and the cost of being wrong is not too great.[28]

The *Reasoning Disposition Account* is motivated by the intuitive normative difference between low-stakes cases and high-stakes cases of the following sort[29]:

> Low: Five minutes ago, Hannah made three sandwiches and placed them in the refrigerator. She told Sarah that she placed the peanut butter sandwich on the left, the tuna sandwich in the middle, and the almond butter sandwich on the right. Hannah then departed just as Sarah's friend Almira arrived for lunch. Sarah knows that Almira has no allergies. Almira says: "I'd love an almond butter sandwich." And so Sarah opens the refrigerator door, points to the sandwich on the right, and says: "The sandwich on the right is an almond butter sandwich. You can have it."

> High: This case is just like Low, except here it is Sarah's nephew Algernon who is visiting for lunch, and he has a severe peanut allergy. He asks Sarah for a sandwich. Sarah knows that the peanut butter sandwich would be fatal to Algernon, but that the almond butter sandwich would be harmless. She also knows that he would slightly prefer the almond butter sandwich to the tuna sandwich. When Sarah goes to the fridge, she can tell, by visual inspection, which is the tuna sandwich, but she cannot tell, by visual inspection, which is the peanut butter sandwich and which is the almond butter sandwich. So she gives him the tuna sandwich.

As Ross and Schroeder note, one of the most natural explanations for the difference between the two cases seems to be that in Low Sarah knows that the sandwich on the right is the almond butter sandwich, while in High she doesn't. The explanation for this difference in knowledge is taken to be that in Low Sarah is warranted in believing that the sandwich on the right is the almond butter sandwich, while in High she is not. Without going into detail, the *Reasoning Disposition Account* grounds this explanation by claiming that in both scenarios the evidence warrants a dispositional belief, but that only in Low does it also warrant an occurrent belief – in High, the warrant for outright belief is overridden because the cost of being wrong is particularly salient.[30]

[28] See Ross and Schroeder (2012).

[29] These cases are described in Ross and Schroeder (2012), 261.

[30] See Ross and Schroeder (2012), 271–3.

On the *Reasoning Disposition Account*, outright beliefs have a distinct functional role, due to the competing ends that they serve for human beings. Belief, on this account, serves two competing ends: to allow the believer to arrive at good deliberative conclusions and to prevent the cognitive overload that would result from reasoning in an ideal Bayesian manner on the basis of degrees of belief alone. The optimal balance seems to be struck by something like the following principle: an agent is permitted to treat a proposition *p* as true in her reasoning if the evidence significantly favors *p* over its negation and the cost of being wrong isn't too great. Treating these uncertain propositions as true in our reasoning (i.e. believing them), then, is a sort of optimal heuristic, justified by its benefit over the long run.[31]

The *Reasoning Disposition Account* allows me to argue that – in my loose-talk scenarios – the hearer has, given the evidence available in the context and the low stakes, a warranted non-overridden disposition to believe the speaker intended to assert something other than what she literally said, from which it follows that she (the hearer) is warranted in occurrently believing it.[32] We can call this *pragmatic encroachment on utterance interpretation*, which – if we assume that the epistemic position of the hearer plays a central role in determining the *content* of the speaker's assertion (as per Assertion) – entails *pragmatic encroachment on utterance content*. This will prove particularly significant in the fifth and last section of the paper, where I discuss the implication of what I say for how determinate we should expect the content of legislative utterances to be.

3 Revising the Argument: Restrict, Reconstruct, or Both?

There are, I believe, two rather straightforward ways in which to respond to my objection to Marmor's argument for the claim that the law rarely asserts something other than what it literally says. One is to *restrict* the argument to the legal context and claim that, *in law*, the stakes are high enough so that obviousness is indeed required for successful non-literal assertion, and the other is to *reconstruct* the argument using another, related requirement instead of Obviousness.

Both options provide significant departures from Marmor's line of argument and are worth examining in some detail. Doing so will allow us see more clearly exactly what features of the legislative context make it difficult for lawmakers to issue determinate non-literal legal directives. I will argue that neither strategy is sufficient on its own, but that conjoining them will provide a plausible argument for the claim that successful non-literal legislative speech is rare. It is quite plausible that, *in law*,

[31] Ross and Schroeder (2012), 273–5.

[32] I should emphasize that nothing hangs on the adequacy of the *Reasoning Disposition Account*; for my purposes, any account that allows for pragmatic encroachment will do.

a speaker succeeds in asserting something other than what she literally says only if she shares a great deal of *relevant* common ground with her intended audience – more specifically, sufficiently unequivocal information regarding the "all-things-considered" purpose of the legislative utterance. And that – I agree – is rarely the case in law.

3.1 Restricting the Argument: Is Obviousness Required in Law?

In the previous section of the paper, I spent a great deal of effort casting doubt on Obviousness and – at least as a matter of general theorizing about language – proposed to replace it with Flex, a somewhat weaker, more flexible requirement. The basic idea was that a speaker succeeds in asserting something other than what she literally says only if it is *significantly more likely than not* that she is intending to do so. What counts as significantly more likely than not, I argued, depends on the practical context – on what is at stake. If nothing much is at stake, the epistemic constraint is relatively low, but if *enough* is at stake, then obviousness may indeed be required for successful non-literal assertion. It makes sense, then, to ask whether, *in law*, the practical context is such that obviousness is required. If it is, then it is possible to simply restrict Flex to the legal context, and the argument will be sound.

On the face of it, this amendment is quite plausible. In fact, it seems to be in the nature of law that it deals only with practically significant matters. It is very natural to assume, for example, that legislative utterances are made for good normative reasons and that something significant is at stake in all cases in which legal interpretation is called for. Despite the strong *prima facie* plausibility of this suggestion, however, I think we have reason to believe that the obviousness requirement fails here, too. Typically, a legal system will contain a considerable amount of relatively insignificant run-of-the-mill legislation, such as littering laws and pet identification regulations, to name some examples. While there is of course generally good reason to have laws of this sort, the stakes associated with their interpretation are in most cases not very high – certainly not high enough to provide sufficient support for the claim that, in law generally, successful non-literal assertion requires obviousness.[33] (It is important to keep in mind that the need for legal interpretation is not confined to court cases; officials often have to interpret the law in situations with little or no danger of evolving into full-fledged legal disputes. In many cases, the absence of such danger is exactly due to the relatively low stakes, or so I submit.)

Granted, this kind of regulation is most common in civil law and it therefore makes sense to ask whether we could just put a further restriction on the require-

[33] Thanks to Dale Smith for emphasizing this point in conversation.

ment and limit the argument to criminal law. However, legal systems typically also have a number of relatively insignificant criminal laws; laws with low fine-only options provide a good case in point. We have good reason, then, to conclude that simply restricting the linguistic premise of Marmor's argument – whether to law in general or specifically to criminal law – does not make for a sufficient revision.

Of course, if it were somehow settled by legal practice that non-literal legislative speech requires obviousness, then that would be sufficient to ground a restricted obviousness requirement, given that law – as Kelsen put it – regulates its own creation and content. However, I do not know of any jurisdiction in which legal practitioners robustly treat legislative speech in such a way as to genuinely establish such a requirement. As a matter of fact, the issue of epistemic constraints on legislative speech is distinctly under-addressed, both in judicial opinions and in scholarly literature. And the few authors that have discussed the issue all have more or less different opinions about what it is, or should be.[34]

3.2 *Reconstructing the Argument: The Richness Requirement*

On Marmor's view, OBVIOUSNESS produces a further requirement on the success of non-literal assertion when combined with the principle that it is obvious to a competent hearer that a speaker is intending to assert something other than what she literally says only if the speaker and hearer share a great deal of (relatively) specific background assumptions:

> RICHNESS Normally, a speaker asserts something other than what she literally says only if the speaker and hearer share a great deal of (relatively) specific background assumptions.

Now, if OBVIOUSNESS does not obtain, then RICHNESS is not derivable in the way proposed by Marmor. One way, however, to reply to my critique is to say that although this requirement cannot be *derived* from OBVIOUSNESS in the intended way, it is still *independently* plausible. It might even be argued that *whatever the epistemic constraint on non-literal assertion turns out to be*, that constraint is satisfied only if the conversational background is relatively rich. If that is correct, then RICHNESS – in place of OBVIOUSNESS – can be used to construct something akin to Marmor's original argument. The revised argument then states that legislatures rarely assert something other than what they literally say because they rarely share a great deal of (relatively) specific background assumptions with their audience.

---

[34] Barak (2005), for example, thinks that the standard of proof for propositions of law is the preponderance of evidence, while Greenawalt (2010) believes that the standard is higher in cases of purported non-literality. And while Lawson (1992) argues that it ought – for political reasons – to be as high as obviousness, Alexander (1992) argues that there is no good reason that the standard of proof of law should mirror the standard of proof of fact, and that even in criminal law obviousness may be too strict a requirement.

For the sake of argument, I will provisionally accept it as true that legislatures rarely share a great deal of (relatively) specific background assumptions with their audience, although it may vary across the different legal contexts – and, indeed, systems – how much information is shared between speaker and audience. Presumably, the legislature shares more common ground, for example, with administrative agencies and courts than it does with ordinary citizens. And, quite plausibly, the British Parliament shares more common ground with administrative agencies and courts than the United States Congress does.

That, then, leaves the question whether successful non-literal assertion always requires speaker and audience to share a great deal of information. I will argue that it does not. I will make my case in two steps, which is intended to highlight the two analytically distinct roles that shared information plays in non-literal assertion: the role it plays in determining *that* the speaker intends to assert something other than what she says and the role it plays in determining *what* the speaker intends to assert (instead).

Let us start with the first role. In order for it to be significantly more likely than not that a speaker isn't intending to assert what she literally says, all the speaker has to do – assuming certain background conditions obtain – is to utter a sentence the semantic content of which is incompatible in *some* way with *some* part of the conversational background (things presupposed, purpose of the conversation etc.). *Strictly speaking*, then, all that is required – vis-à-vis the common ground – is that the speaker and hearer knowingly share *one* bit of information. They may, of course, normally share all sorts of information – both knowingly and unknowingly – but what is *required* for the conversational background to play this first role in non-literal assertion is very minimal.

The most basic examples presumably involve quantification (both universal and existential). Consider, for example, universal quantification restricted – on the semantic level – only to humans, e.g. of the form *Everyone is F*. There are very few predicates that apply to absolutely *everyone* and so if a speaker utters the words, say, 'Everyone is coming to the party!' it will be obvious to any competent hearer that she does not intend to assert the literal content of her remark (on the assumption that the speaker is observing the maxims governing cooperative conversation). And in order for this to be obvious, all that is required is that the speaker and hearer knowingly share the information *that no party is such that everyone is coming to it*.

This very ordinary example shows that it is not generally true that the conversational background has to be fairly rich in order for it to play its first role in non-literal assertion. In many normal cases, only minimal common ground is required for determining *that* the speaker intends to assert something other than what she says.

Next, let us turn to the second role, the role that the conversational background plays in determining *what* the speaker intends to assert. Consider again the case in which a speaker utters the words 'Everyone is coming to the party!' Assuming it is significantly more likely than not that the speaker does not intend to assert the literal content of her remark, we can proceed to ask how much it takes – vis-à-vis shared information – to determine what the speaker intended to assert instead. Now, depending on what the speaker in fact intends to assert, it presumably varies hugely how much common ground is required in order for the hearer to recognize the speaker's communicative intention. In many cases, a rich conversational background is certainly necessary, but in other – perfectly normal – cases, the speaker and hearer have to share very little information.

Say, for example, that – in addition to knowingly share the information *that no party is such that everyone is coming to it* – the speaker and hearer share the information *that the speaker has recently sent out party invitations*. In tandem with the fact that the speaker uttered the words 'Everyone is coming to the party!' these two bits of shared information give the hearer good reason to believe that the speaker intended to assert that *everyone who was invited is coming to the party*. Nothing more is strictly required.[35]

Now, although a rich conversational background is not – as a general matter – *required* for successful non-literal assertion, the conversational background will still *limit* the possibility of such assertion, by limiting the ways in which the conversational maxims can be violated and by limiting the range of plausible candidates for intended assertive content. This suggests that a rich conversational background is presumably required for *rich* pragmatic enrichment; in other words, the content of an assertion can only be as rich as the conversational background allows.

We should note, however, that there are at least two types of pragmatic enrichment for which a rich background is needed. On the one hand, there are cases in which *the material that gets added to the semantic content is relatively rich*. On the other hand, there are cases in which *material gets added to relatively rich semantic content*. In the next sub-section, I will argue that in the *legislative context*, questions about pragmatic enrichment are typically questions about enrichment of rich semantic content. If that is correct, then that will allow us to (i) replace Marmor's obviousness requirement with the richness requirement and, further, (ii) restrict that requirement to the legislative context.

3.3 Pragmatic Enrichment in the Legislative Context

Legislative texts are usually pretty complex, and even the least complex ones do not come anywhere close to the brevity of sentences like 'Everyone is coming to the party'. We should therefore, as a general matter, expect that successful non-literality

[35] No doubt, in real-world situations similar to the one described, people frequently do share a great deal of related information (what kind of party, date and time, etc.), but the fact that people often assert something other than what they literally say in circumstances in which the conversational background is relatively rich does not entail that such a rich background is *required* for such assertion. I should also note that in many real-world cases in which the conversational background is relatively rich, the hearer's warrant for concluding that the speaker is intending to assert that p is *overdetermined*, meaning that the context provides the hearer with multiple sufficient reasons to draw the relevant conclusion. Only one such reason, of course, is strictly required.

in legislation – if it occurs – consists in the enrichment of already rich semantic content. If that is correct, then successful non-literality in the context of legislation will require a relatively rich conversational background.

The cases of *Holy Trinity* and *Ali*, which I described earlier in the paper, provide good cases in point.[36] In *Holy Trinity*, as we recall, the question was whether the *Alien Contract Labor Act* of 1885,[37] which prohibited the importation of "labor or service of any kind" except "professional actors, artists, lecturers or singers" and "persons employed strictly as personal or domestic servants," also prohibited the importation of people intended to serve as rectors or clergymen. According to many commentators, the Act only prohibited the importation of *manual* labor or service, and it is therefore natural to ask whether an argument can be made that the legislature asserted something other than what it literally said. (It is important to note that, at this point, I make no claims about whether or not the proposed requirements are met in the examples under discussion.)

Although the issue concerns the addition of very limited material – i.e. the content of the term 'manual' – the addition was allegedly made to content that is already very rich. As a result, the common ground has to be very rich in order for it to be significantly more likely than not that the legislature did not intend to assert the literal content of the text. And it has to be even richer in order for it to be significantly more likely than not that the legislature intended to assert that the prohibition concerned only manual labor.

Recall also *Ali*, in which the Supreme Court ruled that Abdus-Shahid M.S. Ali could not sue the government for having lost property belonging to him. The reason, the court said, was that the *Federal Tort Claims Act* preserves immunity for *all* federal law enforcement officers, since it guarantees immunity for "[a]ny claim arising in respect of […] the detention of any goods, merchandize, or other property by any officer of customs or excise *or any other law enforcement officer*."[38] Ali, of course, argued, and the dissent agreed, that the clause did not guarantee immunity for the government in relation to the actions of *prison* officers, but only of officers *working in customs or related domains*.

The relevant section of the Act is – like the *Alien Contract Labor Act* – very rich in content. As a result, if the proposed non-literal assertion is to be considered successful, the common ground must be rich as well, in order for the hearer both to determine that it is significantly more likely than not that the legislature was not intending to assert what it literally said and to determine what it was that it intended to assert instead.

---

36 143 U.S. 457 (1892) and 552 U.S. 214 (2008), respectively.

37 23 Stat. 332 (codified as amended at 29 U.S.C. §2164 (1901)), *superceded by* Act of Mar. 3, 1903, Pub. L. No. 162, 32 Stat. 1213.

38 28 U.S.C. 2680(c); my emphasis.

On the assumption that neither the *Alien Contract Labor Act* nor the *Federal Tort Claims Act* are exceptional in any way, it seems safe to say that non-literal assertion in the legislative context requires that the legislature and its audience share a great deal of relevant information. In other words, if we restrict our attention to *legislative utterances*, we have a very plausible richness requirement:

RICHNESS-IN-LAW Normally, in legislation, a speaker asserts something other than what she literally says only if the speaker and hearer share a great deal of (relatively) specific background assumptions.

Now, it will vary between areas of law – and perhaps also within them – how well the restricted richness requirement is satisfied, depending on the intended audience. Criminal law, for example, is arguably to a large extent addressed to the general public, in which case the common ground between speaker and audience is relatively thin. In addition, the stakes are generally – albeit not always, as we have seen – fairly high. Overall, then, the conditions for non-literal speech do not seem to be very favorable in the area of criminal law.

In civil law, the stakes are perhaps generally lower, but – at least in the US – only a limited amount of such law comes from legislative enactment. In addition, a great deal of civil law is arguably also addressed to the general public, which makes for a rather thin common ground. I should note, though, that there is an important part of US civil law that *is* largely statute-based – namely *administrative law* – and, here, a considerable amount of relevant information is arguably shared by speaker and audience (administrative agencies and, arguably, courts). Thus, we have good reason to expect that *if* the legislature ever successfully asserts something other than what it literally says, it will primarily be in the area of administrative law, and perhaps in the area of criminal law addressed to officials.

However, even if the lawmakers do share substantial common ground with both judges and administrative officials, there is reason to believe that the relevant background is often not quite rich enough to *determinately* satisfy the relevant requirements. As I will argue in the next sub-section, there is a relevant difference in what the common ground must be like when we compare non-literal (descriptive) assertion and non-literal directives. And although there is no *structural* difference between the two types of context as far as the pragmatic reasoning goes, it is still the case that, *as a matter of fact*, people tend to have less access to the relevant facts when it comes to non-literal directives – including, and especially, *legal* directives. Thus, although it is indeed natural to think that the conditions for non-literal assertion are most favorable in administrative law and least favorable in criminal law addressed to the general public, with criminal law addressed to courts somewhere in between, we should nevertheless considerably temper our expectations concerning the existence of *actual, determinate* cases of such assertion.

3.4 *The Pragmatics of Directives and the Context of Legislation*

Let us, following Bach and Harnish (1979), define directives as utterances that "express the speaker's attitude toward some prospective action by the hearer and his intention that his utterance, or the attitude it expresses, be taken as a reason for the hearer's action."[39] Familiar pragmatic reasoning applies in the case of directives, too, and so we need some plausible reformulations of at least some of the maxims governing cooperative conversation for that particular context. In order to get at some such reformulations, let us look at a few examples.

Say that a speaker instructs a hearer to 'invite everyone to the party' and that the attitude expressed is that of desire. Clearly, it would be obvious to any competent hearer that the speaker doesn't desire that *absolutely everyone* be invited to the party. Or, to borrow and adapt an example from Manning (2003) (who borrowed and adapted it from MacCallum (1966)), say that your boss tells you to 'gather all the ashtrays you can find and bring them to the conference room'. It is obvious to you that your boss does not want you to bring *all* the ashtrays you can possibly find. Rather, she wants you to bring all the ashtrays you can find *in the building*, perhaps also assuming they belong to the company, that they are not bolted down, etc.

To take a legal example, consider the case of *Small v. United States*,[40] in which the majority argued that the relevant legal directive could not – if interpreted literally – reasonably be regarded as the legislature's view of how the addressees ought to behave. In *Small*, the question was whether petitioner Gary Small, who had been convicted for smuggling in a Japanese court in 1994, had – by owning a firearm – violated the US Criminal Code, 18 U.S.C. § 922(g)(1), which makes it "unlawful for any person … who has been *convicted in any court,* of a crime punishable by imprisonment for a term exceeding 1 year … to … possess … any firearm."[41] The question before the court was whether the phrase 'convicted in any court' applied "only to convictions entered in any *domestic* court or to *foreign* convictions as well."[42] The Court held that it applied only to domestic convictions and reversed the prior court's judgment.

The majority claimed that – *as a matter of common sense* – "Congress generally legislates with domestic concerns in mind."[43] For our purposes here, we can characterize this "legal presumption" as a fact about the concerns of the legislature that is – via its commonsensical nature – part of the common ground between the legis-

[39] Bach and Harnish (1979), 41.

[40] 544 U.S. 385 (2005).

[41] 18 U.S.C. § 922(g)(1).

[42] 18 U.S.C. § 922(g)(1).

[43] Here, the Court is referring to *Smith* v. *United States*, 507 U.S. 197, 204, n. 5 (1993).

lature and officials (and perhaps even between the legislature and the general public, although that claim is more difficult to defend). Read literally, then, the relevant part of the Code clashes with the common ground, prompting a non-literal interpretation. On the assumption that Congress generally legislates with domestic concerns in mind, a reasonable hearer cannot attribute to Congress the view that officials ought to convict a person for owning a firearm if she has been sentenced in a court *just anywhere*. Thus, read literally, the directive cannot be authoritatively binding. Or so the reasoning goes.

In the examples above, the hearer is prompted to reinterpret the speaker's directive because she cannot reasonably attribute to the speaker the attitude associated with the literal interpretation of the utterance. Thus, in the context of directives, the so-called *maxim of Quality* – which is normally the operative maxim in non-literal assertion – is perhaps best taken to be something like the following: *Do not direct a person to do that which you do not desire/intend/etc.*[44]

In the context of non-literal directives, then, the common ground has to contain information about the speaker's relevant *attitudes*, i.e. about her desires/ends/values/preferences. However, the common ground has to not only contain information about particular attitudes but also – crucially – information about their *interrelationship*. In this sense, then, the pragmatics of directives is different from – and more complex than – the pragmatics of constatives. And in many types of speech contexts, it is rarely the case that information about the interrelation between the speaker's desires/ends/values/preferences can be taken for granted. This includes law, or so I argue. If what I say below is correct, the context of legislation rarely determinately contains facts about the appropriate weight to be given to law's various ends, vis-à-vis the relevant legislative utterance. As a result, the common ground *relevant* for generating non-literal directives is not sufficiently rich, even if the total information knowingly shared is often substantial.

The reason that the relevant information is scarce in the legislative context, I maintain, is that law's ends compete with each other in extremely complex ways – generally, so complex that the structure of "law's preferences", i.e. the relationship that holds between law's various ends, is too complex to be part of what is genuinely taken for granted in legislative speech contexts. In order, however, for a non-literal legal directive to succeed, it is not sufficient simply that a literal reading be at odds with just *some* end that is taken for granted in the context. It is not necessarily irrational for a speaker to express a wish or intention that is in conflict with a particular hope or a desire that she has, *even if knowledge of that hope or desire is part of the common ground between speaker and hearer*. Rather, the wish associated with the literal content of the directive has to be at odds with the *proper balance* of the relevant hopes or desires. In the case of a legal directive, then, the desire associated with its literal content has to be at odds with the proper balance of those ends of the law that can be said to be part of the common ground.[45] And it seems to me that – due in

[44] See Grice (1989), 27.

[45] Of course, there may be some obvious facts about "the law's preferences" that *are* part of the common ground, at least between the legislature and officials. In some legal systems, for example, *Lex Posterior*, *Lex Superior*, and *Lex Specialis* arguably each embody such a preference.

large part to the general defeasibility of aims and desires – *very* few facts about such balances can genuinely be taken for granted, although it is of course not uncommon for individual interpreters to surmise that they possess such information. If this is correct, then the common ground between the legislature and its audience rarely determinately contains facts of exactly the kind required for (successfully) issuing non-literal directives.

To fix this idea, let us revisit the case of *Small v. United States*. In brief summary, the majority's reasoning was that, due to a legal presumption that "Congress generally legislates with domestic concerns in mind", the Court was invited to infer that the phrase 'any court' should be construed non-literally, its proper content being *any domestic court*. The dissent, however, argued that "the context of [the relevant section of the federal criminal code] … suggests that there is no geographic limit on the scope of [the phrase]." One of the central concerns of the dissent was that although it is true that that legislation of Congress is generally meant to "apply only within the territorial jurisdiction of the United States," the specific purposes of the relevant section of the Code would be fully promoted by a literal interpretation of the phrase, i.e. by taking 'any courts' to include foreign courts. Thus, a literal interpretation of the legislature's utterance was perhaps in conflict with one of law's very general aims, but not with other, more specific aims. The implication of this for my argument here is that unless the common ground between legislature and courts contains unequivocal information regarding the proper balance of legislative purpose – general and specific – the legislature cannot be said to have successfully communicated something other than what it literally said. In *Small*, it seems a plain fact that such information is not available – at least not in the sense of being taken for granted. But it also seems to me that *Small* is non-exceptional, and that we can therefore generalize to say that the kind of information required for successful non-literal legislative speech is rarely available. Even if interpreters may have access to all sorts of information – including information about law's many purposes, general and specific – they are rarely warranted in taking for granted information about the proper balance of these aims. I discuss further examples in the last section of the paper, but the idea is that – as a general matter – this lack of unequivocal information about legislative intent adversely affects the possibility of successful non-literal legislative speech.

These considerations suggest what I take to be a sound reconstruction of something akin to Marmor's original argument, albeit with significant departures from his line of thought. The requirement that is claimed to be rarely satisfied in the legislative context is now much more specific to that particular context:

RICHNESS-IN-LAW* Non-literal legislative speech is successful only if the legislature and its audience share a great deal of (relatively) specific background assumptions regarding the interrelationship between the legislature's desires/ends/values/preferences.

Thus, although it does not suffice simply to restrict Marmor's argument to the legislative context or to reconstruct it using RICHNESS, we can combine these strategies to produce a significant, but plausible, revision of the main premise. The bottom line is that despite the fact that the conversational background between lawmakers and officials often contains quite a bit of information, it rarely contains very much of exactly the kind of information required for lawmakers to issue non-literal directives.

I do not mean to suggest that lawmakers never intend to communicate something non-literal in issuing legislative directives, nor do I want to claim that they are never successful when they do. If what I have said is correct, all that has been established is that it is rarely the case that interpreters have information unequivocal enough to warrant the conclusion that the legislature intended to communicate something non-literal, or – if it does – then to warrant a unique conclusion about what non-literal content the legislature intended to communicate.[46]

4 Testing the Argument Against Experience: Ekins's Argument from Examples

Ideally, we should be able to test the kind of argument I have put forward against experience. Far from being an abstract exercise, the argument delivers – in a robust enough sense – predictions about linguistic behavior in the legal context (broadly understood). So it is important to consider how the conclusion holds up against what we can glean from our experience of the law as it actually is.

Ekins (2012) provides a laudably thorough case against the claim that successful non-literal legislative speech is rare, offering a wealth of actual cases in which the courts have taken the content of the law to be something other than its literal content, seemingly based on relatively straightforward inferences about the legislature's communicative intentions.[47] Ekins takes this to falsify conclusions of the sort I reached in the last sub-section *tout court*, and identifies the second premise as the culprit; in contrast to what I argued above, Ekins holds that "the context in which [the legislative] agent acts is not thin or opaque, but rich and complex."[48]

First, Ekins's examples. For brevity's sake, I will only present a handful and generalize from those[49]:

A. Witnesses who attest 'any will or codicil {of real estate}' under which they are beneficiaries shall be treated as good witnesses, but the gifts made to them shall be void.[50]

[46] Keep in mind that – as Neale (2005) points out – in order to form communicative intentions speakers do not need to believe that their audience will be likely to correctly identify them, only that it is not impossible for them to do so. See e.g. Neale (2005), 181.

[47] See generally Ch. 7 of Ekins (2012). Most of the examples are offered originally in Bennion (1990).

[48] Ekins (2012), 256.

[49] See Ekins (2012), 200–1, and Bennion (1990), 233–4.

[50] *Brett v. Brett* (1826).

B. All drug shops 'shall be closed … at 10 pm on each and every day of the week {and shall stay closed until morning}'.[51]
C. It is an offence to 'stab, cut or wound' any person {with a weapon or instrument}.[52]
D. Every person who fraudulently harbours uncustomed goods shall forfeit a specified sum, 'and the offender {or apparent offender} may either be detained or proceeded against by summons'.

In each of these examples, the parenthetical content was unexpressed, but inferred by the court to be part of what the legislature meant to convey in using the respective sentence, on Ekins's analysis. Ekins rightly says that such examples are not out of the ordinary – rather, they constitute a large class of examples, all of which put direct pressure on my conclusion that successful non-literal legislative speech is rare. At the very least, they constitute a significant *prima facie* problem for the argument I have presented.

As Ekins presents them, these examples are all cases in which the court appropriately inferred that the legislature had clearly intended to communicate something non-literal. I take it that, on Ekins's account, this is evidenced in part by his own verdict about the quality of the court's inferences – vis-à-vis the legislature's communicative intentions – and in part by the fact that the decisions were unanimous. This, together with his assumption that such examples are pretty standard, constitutes what we can call *Ekins's argument from examples*, against the claim that successful non-literal legislative speech is rare. As I hope to show, on closer inspection, only one of the examples, case (B), is as straightforward as Ekins suggests. In the other cases, there is so much else going on that it is difficult to draw any firm conclusions about the role of language and pragmatic inference in the court's decisions. In any case, I will argue that cases (A), (C), and (D) are cases in which the legislative communication is not entirely successful. If that is correct, Ekins's argument from examples does not go through.

First, a brief general remark on drawing conclusions about genuine agreement from the fact that a decision is unanimous. Perhaps, in systems in which dissent within the higher courts is rife – such as the US and Australian systems – the fact that a decision is unanimous is some indication that the matter is fairly clear (setting aside the issue of separate, concurring opinions). In the UK, however, dissent is (and generally has been) the exception, with an extremely high rate of unanimous decisions – which is arguably just as much explained by the internal structure of the appeals process and a culture generally skeptical about the value of dissent at the appellate level, as by actual agreement about the proper legal outcome and its basis.[53] This should give us some pause in taking – as a general matter – unanimous decisions to indicate actual agreement. It seems that in systems such as the UK one, it is, at best, highly defeasible indication thereof.

---

[51] *Rex v. Liggetts-Findlay Drug Stores Ltd.* (1919).

[52] *Rex v. Harris* (1836).

[53] For an interesting discussion, see e.g. Kerr (2012).

Now on to the actual examples. As I indicated above, the most straightforward case is case (B), the Canadian case of *Rex v. Liggetts-Findlay Drug Stores Ltd.*, in which the issue was whether closing a drug store at 10 pm and opening it a little later constituted a violation of a law requiring drug stores to close at 10 pm (without further explicit specification). In this case, I simply agree with Ekins (and other commentators) that something like 'and shall stay closed until morning' is implicated conversationally.[54] Marmor (2008), commenting on his own hypothetical example, also plainly accepts that implicatures can be successful in cases of this sort:

> Suppose that a municipal regulation requires cafés and restaurants to have "clean and well kept indoor restrooms." Given the context of such a requirement, surely it would be implicated by this regulation that the restrooms must be actually open for the patrons to use.

Indeed, some cases of legislative speech do seem to be so clear that interpreters can straightforwardly infer that the intention is to communicate something non-literal, and can infer pretty well what that content is.

So far, of course, this does not pose a problem. All I have argued for is the qualified claim that successful non-literal legislative speech is infrequent in comparison to successful non-literality in ordinary conversation, not that it never occurs. The pressure that Ekins's examples put on my argument is "accumulative", and so is generated only if the rest of them go much the same way. I will argue that once we examine them closely enough, we see that they do not. In contrast to the *Liggetts-Findlay* case, examples (A), (C), and (D) merely exhibit the appearance of being straightforward.

Consider case (A), the case of *Brett v. Brett*, in which the issue was whether the phrase 'any will or codicil' – occurring in the Wills Act 1752 – was being used literally by the legislature or to mean 'any will or codicil {of real estate}'; if the former, the phrase included reference to personal property.[55] The judgment in the case was provided by Sir John Nicholl, who held that the phrase, viewed in "connexion with its whole context in the statute, is not even difficult of interpretation," and that it was clearly being used to convey the more limited meaning.[56] The judgment was affirmed on appeal, by a court of nine judges, after hearing Counsel for the Appellant only. This all counts in favor of Ekins's argument from examples.

However, despite the fact that Sir Nicholl in certain places presents the case as a fairly obvious one and that his judgment was affirmed on appeal, the same phrase had received the other interpretation 15 years prior. In *Lees v. Summersgill*, Sir William Grant held – claiming also to interpret the phrase "in context" – that the phrase should be interpreted generally, to apply to *any* will or codicil, whether of real estate or not.[57] Sir Nicholl even acknowledges this in his judgment in *Brett*. So

---

[54] See also Goldsworthy (2010), 234–5.

[55] 25 Geo. 2. c. 6.

[56] *Brett v. Brett* (1826), 162 E.R. 459.

[57] *Lees v. Summersgill* (1811).

even though, historically, the statute in question was for a short while treated as fairly straightforward (in practice and in the courts), in line with Nicholl's judgment in *Brett*, things are – at least philosophically – not so simple.[58] As *Lees* attests to, there is plenty room for disagreement among competent, well-informed interpreters about what the legislature's communicative intention was in enacting the statute.

Next, case (C). In *Rex v. Harris*, the issue was whether biting off the tip of someone's nose constituted 'wounding' them, for the purposes of the Offences Against the Person Act 1828.[59] As Ekins presents the case, Sir John Patteson straightforwardly held that it did not, because attending to the context revealed that use of a weapon or instrument was implied.[60] Again, this counts in favor of Ekins's argument.

In fact, however, the "straightforwardness" of *Harris* is owed to the fact that Sir Patteson instructed the jury that the matter had been decided in an entirely comparable case – *Rex v. Stevens* – just a couple of years prior. In *Stevens*, John Stevens was held not to have wounded a policeman by biting off the end of his finger because no instrument was used. The matter, however, was controversial, and Stevens was first convicted by jury but with the sentence respited by the presiding judge, with the intention that all the judges could take up the matter and vote on it. 13 out of 15 judges were present for the meeting and the verdict was close – seven held that use of a weapon or instrument was implied, six did not. The matter, therefore, is nowhere near as straightforward as the *Harris* case suggests.

Finally, let's consider case (D), which – in view of the opinions – may seem no less straightforward than *Liggetts-Findlay*, i.e. case (B). In *Barnard v. Gorman*, the issue was whether officials had the authority to detain merely suspected offenders in virtue of the Customs Consolidation Act 1875, which provides that an "offender may either be detained or proceeded against by summons."[61] If not, then persons who are detained but turn out to be innocent are able to recover damages for false imprisonment. It was unanimously held that the only way to make sense of the Act was to read it to include reference to apparent offenders.

In his opinion, Lord Wright said that reading the Act so as to apply only to actual offenders would involve a manifest absurdity, as it would require a conclusive determination of guilt before action could be taken – "[t]he provision," he said, "is clearly intended for the purpose of bringing the charge to investigation."[62] Accordingly, he

[58] Sir Nicholl's judgment in *Brett* was followed in 1827 and 1829 in the cases of *Emanuel v. Constable* and *Foster v. Banbury*, respectively. But that was about it – less than a decade later, the Wills Act 1752 was re-enacted in amended form as section 15 of the Wills Act 1837 so as to include reference to *any* will (and 'will' was defined so as to include codicils). As a further note, it is of course very hard to say what light, if any, the 1837 Act sheds on how to understand the original Act, but it seems within reason to argue that this undermines Sir Nicholl's reasoning to the extent that he based his interpretation on what he took to be the aims reasonably attributable to the legislature.

[59] *Rex v. Harris* (1836); 9 Geo. 4. c31. s12.

[60] Ekins more or less follows Bennion (1990) in presenting these examples.

[61] *Barnard v. Gorman* (1941).

[62] *Barnard v. Gorman* (1941), A.C. 391.

concluded that 'offender' here meant 'One who is suspected of or charged with the offence'."[63] Viscount Simon argued that it was the duty of the court "to take the words as they stand to give them their true construction, having regard to the language of the whole section, and as far as relevant, of the whole Act always preferring the natural meaning of the word involved, but none the less always giving the word its appropriate construction according to the context."[64] And Lord Romer based his decision in part on the claim that "the context in which a word is found may be, and very often is, strong enough to show that it is intended to bear other than its ordinary meaning."[65] As before, this all counts in favor of Ekins's argument.[66]

Barnard, however, is not quite as straightforward as it seems, despite the unanimous decision. As Bennion (1990) points out, although the opinions in *Barnard* can be construed as pragmatic reasoning in response to legislative ellipsis,[67] it seems equally reasonable to analyze the case as one in which the legislative project is "misconceived through some mistake of fact" on behalf of the drafter.[68] On Bennion's analysis, *Barnard* properly belongs to a class of cases "where the draftsman has failed to get into his head the true nature of the factual situations with which the Act will in future have to deal."[69] The relevant section of the Customs Consolidation Act 1876, he says, "clearly operates upon a misunderstanding of the

[63] *Barnard v. Gorman* (1941), A.C. 391.

[64] *Barnard v. Gorman* (1941), A.C. 384.

[65] *Barnard v. Gorman* (1941), A.C. 396.

[66] On this analysis, *Barnard* is analogous to the US case of *Green v. Bock Laundry Machine Co.* (490 U.S. 504 (1989)), a civil product liability case in which Justice Scalia argued that the term 'defendant' – as it occurred in Rule 609(a) of the Federal Rules of Evidence – was clearly being used to mean 'criminal defendant', and that therefore the trial court had not erred in denying Green's pretrial motion of impeaching evidence. (The rule has since been amended to address the issue.)

[67] Although it should be noted that none of the judges wanted to read the relevant power to detain apparent offenders into the statute by implication, as Ekins's presentation suggests. Rather, they reasoned that the term 'offender' ought to be taken to mean 'apparent offender' in the relevant context.

[68] Bennion (1990), 256.

[69] Bennion (1990), 273. Bennion classifies *Wiltshire v. Barrett* (1966), which relies crucially upon *Barnard*, the same way. In *Wiltshire*, the issue – like in *Barnard* – was whether officials had the authority to detain merely suspected drunk drivers in virtue of the Road Traffic Act 1960, which provides that officials may arrest "a person committing an offence under this section." And as in *Barnard*, the court unanimously held that the statute ought to be considered as applying to persons 'apparently committing an offense'.

factual situation."[70] If that is correct, then *Barnard* does not – after all – count in favor of Ekins's argument from examples, at least not strongly so.[71]

I hope to have shown that – contra Ekins – the examples he provides (following Bennion) do not, after all, amount to an accumulative empirical argument against the claim that successful non-literal legislative speech is infrequent in comparison to successful non-literality in ordinary conversation. Now, I do agree with Ekins that *as a general matter* the legislative context is not necessarily thin or opaque, and that it arguably varies both between areas of law and between legal systems how much information is shared between the legislature and its audience. However, as I have tried to show (in particular in Sect. 3.4), the problem is that the common ground *relevant* for generating non-literal directives is not sufficiently rich, even if the total information knowingly shared is often substantial. The reason, I argued, is that law's ends compete with each other in extremely complex ways – generally, so complex that the relationship that holds between law's various ends is too complex to be part of what is genuinely taken for granted in legislative speech contexts. To put the point in Ekins's terms, although the total information knowingly shared may be substantial, the context typically does not contain unequivocal enough information about the "complex means-end package on which the legislature acts."[72] It is *this* part of the legislative context which is generally relatively thin or opaque.

Before I go on to discuss what happens, on my account, when non-literal legislative speech is unsuccessful – vis-à-vis the content of the relevant law – I should note that there is a potentially significant difference between the frameworks that Ekins and I employ, which could help to explain to some extent our differing judgments about the cases discussed above. As I have tried to show, despite the fact that these cases may seem straightforward, there is in most of them plenty room for disagreement among competent and well-informed judges about the communicative intentions of the legislature. On the framework adopted in this paper, assertive content is – as we have seen – partly determined by the inferences that the hearer is warranted in making about the speaker's communicative intention and so this kind of peer disagreement has implications for how successful we ought to count the relevant legislative speech act to have been (whether the intention was to communicate something literal or non-literal).

---

[70] Ibid.

[71] On this analysis, *Barnard* is analogous to the US case of *United States v. Marshall* (908 F.2d 1312 (7th Cir. 1990)), in which the question was whether or not Mr. Marshall, who had sold around 12,000 doses of LSD, should be taken to fall under a statute triggering a mandatory minimum punishment if the sold items contain "a mixture or substance containing a detectable amount" of the relevant drug (21 U.S.C. §960). The statute has the unintended consequence that it obligates judges to impose disproportionate sentences on people who sell LSD, due to the fact that the lawmakers did not realize how the drug is sold (LSD requires a particularly heavy carrier). Because the most likely explanation of the problematic result is that it was simply not foreseen, the statute does not warrant a non-literal interpretation. As a result, the main question in *Marshall* is about how to appropriately react to a problematic result that follows from the content of the legislative utterance. Same goes for *Barnard*, on Bennion's analysis.

[72] Ekins (2012), 258.

On Ekins's view, however, "[a] successful instance of communication occurs when the hearer identifies the intended meaning by recognising the speaker's intention to this effect," and failure "where the hearer fails to identify the speaker's intention."[73] On this framework, the quality of the interpreter's inference does not matter – as long as she arrives at the right conclusion, success is guaranteed. Consequently, assuming – as Ekins must – that the courts correctly identified the legislature's communicative intentions in the above examples, nothing more is needed for success. Perhaps, then, the argument ultimately boils down to what the right linguistic framework is – i.e. to what conditions of success in communication we should adopt?

I don't think it does. The reason is that, in discussing Ekins's examples, I hope to have shown that – by and large – for each case of what on Ekins's account constitutes successful non-literal communication, there is an unsuccessful case. It is perhaps not easy math to figure out exactly how – on Ekins's framework – success and failure stack up against each other, but if we can generalize at all from my discussion of the examples above, it seems that the successful cases of non-literal legislative speech do not outnumber the unsuccessful cases by much.

5 Indeterminacy About Utterance Content

After the discussion in the previous sections, it is natural to ask what exactly happens – vis-à-vis the content of a legislative utterance – when the conversational background isn't rich enough to warrant a reinterpretation. And it may seem equally natural to infer that in such cases, the primary content of the relevant statutory text just is its literal content. If that is correct and if the conversational background is generally not rich enough to warrant a reinterpretation, then the primary content of a statutory text normally just is its literal content. In this section, however, I aim to show that this would be a significant overstatement. Such a result follows only if we assume a very strong version of what is often called the *presumption of literalness*, which I – along with many others – wish to deny.

On a strong version of the presumption of literalness, failure to make it sufficiently clear that one intends to communicate something non-literal entails that one is justifiably taken to have intended to communicate the literal content of one's remark. On a weaker, more plausible, version, however, there is no such entailment – rather, the priority of the literal just amounts to an assumption (of varying strength) that the speaker is intending to communicate the literal content of her remark, which can be treated like something akin to a variably high prior probability assigned to that hypothesis.[74]

---

[73] Ekins (2012), 210.

[74] This reading is subscribed to, for example, by Bach and Harnish (1979).

I do recognize that the my argument may, like Marmor's, give the impression that in case the relevant requirement isn't satisfied, then the content of the law is – by default – its literal content. There is, however, plenty room for indeterminacy about utterance content on the framework I have adopted, assuming the weaker reading of the literalness presumption. The underlying notion is that – as a general epistemological matter – the fact that one is not warranted in inferring that *p* does not entail that one is warranted in inferring that *not-p*; sometimes, one should simply withhold belief. When this happens in communication (with respect to the speaker's communicative intention), then the primary content of the relevant utterance will be indeterminate between the literal content of the sentence uttered and some non-literal enrichment thereof. That is, if it is – all things considered – neither significantly more nor significantly less likely than not that the speaker is intending to assert what she literally said, then the hearer is justified only in withholding belief about the speaker's communicative intention. Consequently, since – on the view expounded here – assertive content is partly determined by the inferences that the hearer is warranted in making about the speaker's communicative intention, the assertive content in such cases is to some extent indeterminate.[75]

5.1 Indeterminacy and Levels of Pragmatic Reasoning

It is important to note that indeterminacy can enter into the picture at two different levels, given the two roles that the common ground plays in pragmatic reasoning: it can either be indeterminate *that* the speaker asserted something other than what she literally said or indeterminate *what* pragmatically enriched proposition the speaker asserted. As discussed in Sect. 3, these notions are – although closely related – analytically distinct.

[75] I want to explain briefly why I take the indeterminacy discussed in this paper to be a type of vagueness, since – on the face of it – indeterminacy about utterance content seems rather removed from, say, borderline cases of 'blue', 'crowd', 'vehicle', etc. I think it can be shown that it comes from the vagueness of speech act terms like 'say', 'assert', 'command', etc. To see this, recall that assertion was partly defined in terms of epistemic warrant: A speaker asserts *p* only if a rational hearer, knowing the conversational background and context, is warranted in taking her to be intending to assert *p*. And epistemic warrant, in this context, was defined partly in terms of a vague probabilistic concept: A rational hearer, knowing the conversational background and context, is warranted in taking a speaker to be intending to assert *p* only if it is *significantly more likely than not* that the speaker is intending to assert *p*. The phrase 'it is significantly more likely than not that' is obviously vague – it both admits of borderline cases and is Sorites-susceptible. Imagine, for example, a case in which it is clearly significantly more likely than not that *S* intended to assert *p* and let's then say that there is a small change in the context with the result that it is now trivially less likely that S intended to assert *p*. Such a small change doesn't make a difference for whether it is appropriate to say that it is significantly more likely than not that *S* intended to assert *p*. If we introduce enough minute changes into the context, however, we end up with a full-fledged Sorites-series.

Let's first revisit two significant legal cases that I believe are best analyzed as cases in which it is indeterminate that the legislature asserted something other than what it literally said: *Church of the Holy Trinity v. US* and *Ali v. Federal Bureau of Prisons*. In the context of *Holy Trinity* and the *Alien Contract Labor Act*, it was presumably pretty clear to all parties that what Congress wished to accomplish was to prevent the importation of cheap unskilled labor. Further, as Vermeule (1998) notes, the Court later argued that "in no event could [the Act] be construed as applying to a contract for the services of a rector or a pastor of a religious corporation,"[76] suggesting that it took it to be common knowledge that Congress did not wish to "prohibit the immigration under contract of a Christian minister."[77] This is all significant evidence that Congress did not intend to enact the literal content of the Act. Still, the Act did include a number of specific exceptions that cannot count as exceptions on a pragmatically enriched reading of the Act. An exception for professional artists, for example, cannot be an exception to a law that prohibits the importation of manual labor or service. This significantly undercuts the evidence mentioned so far (at this point, I wish to remain silent about whether or not the explicit exceptions provide evidence that Congress did intend the relevant part of the Act to be taken literally).[78]

In this case, it seems to me reasonable to say that the common ground between Congress and the courts was neither rich enough to make it significantly more likely than not that Congress did not intend to prohibit the importation of all types of labor or service, including those of rectors and clergymen, nor rich enough to make it significantly more likely than not that they positively did intend to do so. Taking everything into account, the evidence seems to favor neither claim over the other. If that is correct, the content of the *Alien Contract Labor Act* was to some extent indeterminate. There is simply no answer to the question 'Does the Act apply to people intended to serve as pastors?'

Similar reasoning applies in *Ali*, I believe. It seems safe to say that it was part of what was (reasonably) taken for granted both by Congress and the Supreme Court that, in enacting the *Federal Tort Claims Act*, Congress wished – as Justice Kennedy of the dissent put it – to "[allow] those who allege injury from governmental actions over a vast sphere to seek damages for tortious conduct."[79] Citing the case of *Kosak v. United States*, Justice Kennedy also pointed out – rightly, I think – that "unduly generous interpretations of the exceptions [established by the *Federal Tort Claims Act*] run the risk of defeating the central purpose of the statute."[80] The majority, however, further pointed out that since the exception relevant to *Ali* concerned the

---

[76] *US v. Laws*, 163 U.S. 258, 264. Cited by Vermeule (1998), 1842, footn. 41.

[77] Vermeule (1998), 1842.

[78] As it turns out, there was also significant debate about the issue in Congress, but since the legislative history was not part of the common ground, it did not – on my view – play a part in determining the content of the law.

[79] 552 U.S. 214 (2008).

[80] 465 U.S. 848, 854 (1984).

detention of property, it was far from obvious that interpreting the exception to apply to absolutely all law enforcement officers would go against the wishes of Congress. Thus, given the fact that Congress uttered the relevant text in the relevant context, it is arguably neither significantly more likely than not that Congress intended federal immunity from the relevant type of tort claims to extend only to officers working in customs or related domains nor that it intended such immunity to extend to officers of all kinds. If that is correct, then the *Federal Torts Claim Act* is indeterminate *in that respect*.[81]

In addition to cases in which it is indeterminate whether or not the speaker asserts something other than what she literally says, there are also cases in which it is significantly more likely than not that the speaker did not intend to assert what she literally said but indeterminate what enriched proposition she asserted instead. Consider for example a case in which a speaker utters the following: 'Everyone is coming to the party!' And let us say that the hearer is in charge of supplying chips and salsa for said party. Now, let us further stipulate that – given the context – it is indeterminate whether the speaker intended to assert that *everyone in the department* is coming to the party or that *everyone in the group of students* is coming to the party. In this case, what the speaker asserted is indeterminate, but it is still determinate that she did not assert the literal content of her remark.

To take an analogous legal example, consider the case of *United States v. Gonzales*.[82] In *Gonzales*, the question was whether or not the Court could order that a federal prison sentence could run concurrently with a state imposed sentence, despite the fact that a section of 18 U. S. C. §924 states that a sentence imposed under it "shall [not]…run concurrently with any other term of imprisonment." The majority held that it could, but Justice Stevens of the dissent argued that the statute could not "reasonably be interpreted as containing any command to state sentencing judges or as requiring the suspension of any federal sentences when concurrent state sentences are later imposed."[83] "[C]ommon sense," he said, "requires us to reject a purely literal reading of the text."[84] I take this to indicate that Justice Stevens thought that it was obvious that – taken literally – the code has certain legal consequences and that it was obvious that these consequences clashed with Congress's wishes.

If – for the sake of argument – we concede that Justice Stevens is correct, then it is indeed significantly more likely than not that Congress did not intend the statute to be understood literally. However, as he rightly notes, it still remains to be determined what non-literal content was intended, and this may well make a difference to the outcome of the case. According to Justice Stevens, there were two plausible

[81] There were of course a number of other issues that were relevant to *deciding* the case, but since questions about non-literal statutory content turn just on the language used and the common ground, these issues concerned the proper *development* of the Act, given that it was indeterminate what the exact content of it was.

[82] 520 U.S. 1 (1997).

[83] 520 U.S. 1 (1997).

[84] 520 U.S. 1 (1997).

candidates. Either Congress intended to use the phrase 'any other term of imprisonment' to mean *any other term of imprisonment {that has already been imposed}* or to mean *any other {federal} term of imprisonment*. Only the latter was in favor of the respondent.

Justice Stevens cited three reasons why he thought that it was more likely than not that Congress intended to use the phrase to mean *any other {federal} term of imprisonment*. However, he did not go so far as to claim that it was obvious that Congress could not have intended to use the phrase in the former way. Since *Gonzales* was a criminal case, and the epistemic constraint is therefore arguably high, this arguably means that it was *not* significantly more likely than not that Congress intended to say that a sentence imposed under the relevant code "shall [not]...run concurrently with any other {federal} term of imprisonment." But it certainly does not mean that it was *significantly* more likely than not that Congress intended to say that a sentence imposed under the relevant code "shall [not]...run concurrently with any other federal term of imprisonment {that has already been imposed}." As a result, it is determinate that the content of the statute is not its literal content but indeterminate what exactly the content of the statute is (on the assumption that Justice Stevens is right).

5.2 Indeterminacy About Content and the Notion of a Well-Functioning Legal System

There is a prima facie worry here. Neither the *Alien Contract Labor Act*, the *Federal Torts Claim Act*, nor 18 U. S. C. §924 seem like unique – or exceptional – cases. If that is correct, then indeterminacy about the content of the law appears to be rampant. If such indeterminacy is seen as a failure – e.g. as a failure on behalf of lawmakers to communicate to subjects what their legal rights and obligations are – then this would indicate a widespread failure in the legal system. Hasn't something gone seriously wrong if it is the normal state of affairs that the persons to whom the law is addressed are not able to fully determine what the lawmakers intended to communicate?

The answer, I think, is no. Scenarios like the ones we have been considering do not necessarily indicate a general pragmatic failure – neither in ordinary conversation nor in law. In the "salsa case", for example, the reason for the speaker's assertion – the knowledge of which we stipulate to be shared by speaker and hearer – is that she wants the hearer to be able to bring enough chips and salsa to the party. In case the difference between the two sets of people is immaterial, vis-à-vis the relevant purpose, nothing has really gone wrong. And although the speaker presumably had in mind one of the two candidate propositions, the student-to-faculty ratio in the department may be high enough so that it does not matter that the hearer has insufficient evidence about which enriched proposition the speaker intended to communicate.[85]

[85] I'm assuming in this case – safely, I think – that it has no non-instrumental value for the speaker to have her communicative intention fully recognized.

Similarly, despite being indeterminate to some extent, the *Alien Contract Labor Act* still determinately applies to manual labor. And the immunity established by the *Federal Torts Claim Act* still determinately extends to officers working in customs or related domains. Finally, the section of the 18 U.S.C. §924 that states that a sentence imposed under it "shall [not]...run concurrently with any other term of imprisonment" still determinate prohibits that a sentence imposed under it run concurrently with any other federal term of imprisonment that has already been imposed. The general principle here is that even if it may be indeterminate what the content of a particular statute is, the statute still determinately applies to those cases to which it applies *on any reasonable enrichment.*

Ultimately, then, it is the practical context that determines if, and to what extent, something has gone wrong, and cases like the salsa case appear to be a regular – and relatively unproblematic – feature of successful human communication. Similarly, partially indeterminate legal directives like the *Alien Contract Labor Act*, the *Federal Torts Claim Act*, and 18 U.S.C. §924 are regular features of any legal system. Insofar as the number of actual cases of indeterminacy resulting from such directives is manageable, such indeterminacy is also relatively unproblematic. Although the law is often to some extent indeterminate, due to the fact the common ground between the legislature and its audience rarely contains sufficiently specific information about legislative intent, this will not necessarily prevent it from functioning reasonably well. As a general principle applying both to the case of ordinary conversation and to the legislative context, we can perhaps say that as long as a rational hearer, knowing the conversational background and context, is able to extract sufficient information from the speaker's utterance, relative to the purpose(s) of the conversation, the relevant speech act counts as reasonably successful.[86]

References

Alexander, L. (1992). Proving the law: Not proven. *Northwestern University Law Review, 86*, 905.

Bach, K. (1994). Conversational impliciture. *Mind and Language, 9*, 124–162.

Bach, K. (2006). The top 10 misconceptions about implicature. In B. J. Birner & G. Ward (Eds.), *Drawing the boundaries of meaning*. Amsterdam: John Benjamins.

Bach, K., & Harnish, R. M. (1979). *Linguistic communication and speech acts*. Cambridge, MA: MIT Press.

Barak, A. (2005). *Purposive interpretation in law*. Princeton: Princeton University Press.

[86] This research was supported in part by research grants from the Australian Research Council (DP1092523) and the Icelandic Research Fund. I am grateful to Andrei Marmor, Gideon Yaffe, Jeffrey Goldsworthy, Dale Smith, Patrick Emerton, Lawrence Solum, and Nicholas Allott for valuable comments on prior versions of this paper. Also to audiences at the Center for Study of Mind in Nature (CSMN) in Oslo, the University of Antwerpen Centre for Law and Cosmopolitan Values, and the Monash Law and Language Workshop.

Bennion, F. (1990). *Bennion on statute law* (IIIth ed.). Harlow: Longman.
Ekins, R. (2012). *The nature of legislative intent*. Oxford: Oxford University Press.
Endicott, T. (2000). *Vagueness in law*. Oxford: Oxford University Press.
Endicott, T. (2011). The value of vagueness. In A. Marmor & S. Soames (Eds.), *The philosophical foundations of language in the law* (pp. 14–30). New York: Oxford University Press.
Goldsworthy, J. (1994). Implications in language, law, and the constitution. In G. Lindell (Ed.), *Future directions in Australian constitutional law* (pp. 150–184). Sydney: Federation Press.
Goldsworthy, J. (2005). Moderate and strong intentionalism: Knapp and Michaels revisited. *San Diego Law Review, 42*, 669.
Goldsworthy, J. (2010). *Parliamentary sovereignty: Contemporary debates*. Cambridge: Cambridge University Press.
Greenawalt, K. (2010). *Legal interpretation: Perspectives from other disciplines and private texts*. Oxford: Oxford University Press.
Greenberg, M. (2011). Legislation as communication? Legal interpretation and the study of linguistic communication. In A. Marmor & S. Soames (Eds.), *The philosophical foundations of language in the law* (pp. 217–256). New York: Oxford University Press.
Grice, H. P. (1989). *Studies in the way of words*. Cambridge, MA: Harvard University Press.
Hart, H. L. A. (1958). Positivism and the separation of law and morals. *Harvard Law Review, 71*, 593–629.
Kerr, B. (2012). *Dissenting judgments – Self-indulgence or self-sacrifice?* https://www.supremecourt.uk/docs/speech-121008.pdf
Lawson, G. (1992). Proving the law. *Northwestern University Law Review, 86*, 859.
MacCallum, G. (1966). Legislative intent. *The Yale Law Journal, 75*(5), 754–787.
Manning, J. F. (2003). The absurdity doctrine. *Harvard Law Review, 116*(8), 2387–2486.
Marmor, A. (2008). The pragmatics of legal language. *Ratio Juris, 21*, 423–452.
Marmor, A. (2013). Truth in law. In M. Freeman & F. Smith (Eds.), *Current legal issues: Law and language* (pp. 45–61). Oxford: Oxford University Press.
Marmor, A. (2014). *The language of law*. Oxford: Oxford University Press.
Marmor, A. (2016). Defeasibility and pragmatic indeterminacy in law. In A. Capone & F. Poggi (Eds.), *Pragmatics and law: Philosophical perspectives* (pp. 15–32). Dordrecht: Springer.
Neale, S. (2005). Pragmatism and binding. In Z. Szabó (Ed.), *Semantics versus Pragmatics* (pp. 165–285). Oxford: Oxford University Press.
Poscher, R. (2012). Ambiguity and vagueness in legal interpretation. In L. Solan & P. Tiersma (Eds.), *The Oxford handbook of language and law* (pp. 128–144). Oxford: Oxford University Press.
Recanati, F. (2012). Pragmatic enrichment and conversational implicature. In D. Graff Fara & G. Russell (Eds.), *The Routledge companion to philosophy of language* (pp. 67–78). London: Routledge.
Ross, J., & Schroeder, M. (2012). Belief, credence, and pragmatic encroachment. *Philosophy and Phenomenological Research, 88*, 259–288.
Schiffer, S. (1972). *Meaning*. Oxford: Oxford University Press.
Soames, S. (2008). Drawing the line between meaning and implicature—and relating both to assertion. *Nous, 42*(3), 529–554.
Soames, S. (2010). *Philosophy of language*. Princeton: Princeton University Press.
Soames, S. (2011). What vagueness and inconsistency tell us about interpretation. In A. Marmor & S. Soames (Eds.), *Philosophical foundations of language in the law* (pp. 31–57). Oxford: Oxford University Press.
Solum, L. (2013). Communicative content and legal content. *Notre Dame Law Review, 89*, 479–520.
Vermeuly, A. (1998). Legislative history and the limits of judicial competence: The untold story of holy Trinity Church. *Stanford Law Review, 50*, 1833–96.
Waldron, J. (1994). Vagueness in law and language: Some philosophical issues. *California Law Review, 82*, 509–540.
Waldron, J. (2011). Vagueness and the guidance of action. In A. Marmor & S. Soames (Eds.), *Philosophical foundations of language in the law* (pp. 58–82). Oxford: Oxford University Press.

The Pragmatics of Scepticism

Pierluigi Chiassoni

Abstract My aim in this paper is arguing for interpretive scepticism from a pragmatics point of view. The argument will develop in four steps. In the first step, I will lay down the conceptual framework I am going to use. In the second step, I will make clear what I consider scepticism and formalism to be. Here, I will contrast scepticism (non-cognitivism) with two varieties of formalism (integral and restricted cognitivism, respectively), and set forth a few criticisms of them. In the third step, I will consider a sophisticated version of restricted cognitivism: the one defended by Andrei Marmor in a series of valuable essays. Marmor makes his case by resorting to philosophy of language. I will argue, however, that philosophy of language, and pragmatics as a substantive part thereof, far from providing support for the restricted form of cognitivism Marmor advocates, suggest contrariwise that it should be abandoned. In the fourth, and last, step, I will lay down the outline of a pragmatic interpretivist theory of judicial interpretation.

Keywords Legal interpretation • Formalism • Scepticism • Philosophy of language • Pragmatics

1 Foreword

Legal theorists still debate about the proper account of judicial interpretation. The dispute turns on the following alternative: Is judicial interpretation necessarily (i.e., as a matter of empirical necessity) an evaluative, practical judgment-dependent, decision-making activity, or, at least sometimes, is it rather just a matter of knowledge, a pure "grasping" of the content of law? "Scepticism" (non-cognitivism) sides with the first alternative, while "formalism" (cognitivism) sides with the latter.

My aim in this paper is arguing for interpretive scepticism from a pragmatics point of view. The argument will have a four-steps development. In the first step, I

P. Chiassoni (✉)
TILPH – Tarello Institute for Legal Philosophy, Department of Law, Università degli Studi di Genova, Genova, Italy
e-mail: Pierluigi.Chiassoni@unige.it

F. Poggi, A. Capone (eds.), *Pragmatics and Law*, Perspectives in Pragmatics, Philosophy & Psychology 10, DOI 10.1007/978-3-319-44601-1_5

will lay down the conceptual framework I am going to use. In the second step, I will make clear what I consider scepticism and formalism to be. Here, I will contrast scepticism (non-cognitivism) with two varieties of formalism (integral and restricted cognitivism, respectively), and set forth a few criticisms of them. In the third step, I will consider a sophisticated version of restricted cognitivism: the one defended by Andrei Marmor in a series of valuable essays. Marmor makes his case by resorting to philosophy of language. I will argue, however, that philosophy of language, and pragmatics as a substantive part thereof, far from providing support for the restricted form of cognitivism Marmor advocates, suggest contrariwise that it should be abandoned. In the fourth, and last, step, I will lay down the outline of a pragmatic interpretivist theory of judicial interpretation.

2 Judicial Interpretation: A Conceptual Framework

Scepticism and cognitivism purport to provide true accounts of judicial interpretation.[1] Unfortunately, the accounts they provide are at odds. Which, if any, is right? To the purpose of making clear what I mean by them, and also in order to prevent confusion, which is a plentiful commodity in this field, I will indulge in the definition of a few key-terms. These are 'interpretation', 'integration', 'interpretive discretion', 'integration discretion', and 'situation of interpretive discretion'.

By *interpretation* I mean the activity, performed by a judge in order to decide a lawsuit, which consists in translating a source-sentence into one or more explicit norms. These norms are 'explicit' since the judge presents and, if necessary, defends them as the legally correct meaning-content of the source-sentence at hand. A source-sentence is any sentence belonging to the authoritative discourse of the sources of a positive legal order: it is, in other words, an authoritative rule-formulation; what we also call a legal "clause" or a legal "provision", like, for instance, any sentence in the U.S. Constitution, in the French Civil code, in the European Human Rights Convention, etc.[2]

---

[1] Barberis 2014: 196–204, claims that scepticism and the so-called mixed theory – in my view, a variety of cognitivism which I will consider in a moment – would *both* provide correct answers, since they would aim at different questions. The mixed theory would provide a true answer to the question: "How is law being in fact applied by judges?" It would be concerned, accordingly, with so-called "concrete interpretation". Contrariwise, scepticism would provide a true answer to the different question: "How is law being in fact interpreted by jurists and judges?" It would be concerned, consequently, with the interpretation of legal texts apart from their application to individual cases, i.e., with so-called "abstract interpretation". I suspect that the presumed way out suggested by Barberis depends on a confusion about the notion of "concrete interpretation", as I shall suggest in the following footnote.

[2] Some authors – Guastini 2011: 138–140; Barberis 2014–draw a distinction between *abstract interpretation* (interpretation *in abstracto*, "text-oriented interpretation") and *concrete interpretation* ("interpretation *in concreto*", "fact-oriented interpretation"). Abstract interpretation amounts to translating a source-sentence into an explicit general norm, without paying attention to the application of the norm to individual cases, while paying attention, instead, to overcoming ambiguity

By *integration* I mean the activity, performed by a judge in order to decide a lawsuit, which consists in identifying the implicit components of a positive legal order. In a very broad and generic sense of the term, these implicit components are norms – principles, rules, criteria for conflict resolution, definitions, etc. – that, by hypothesis, are not explicit, since they cannot be presented and defended as the legally correct meaning-contents, as the legally correct translations, of any definite source-sentence whatsoever, but depend on some integration process and technique.

By *interpretive discretion* I mean, for any judge whatsoever, in relation to the interpretation of a previously identified set of source-sentences, the power, that is assumed to have been explicitly or tacitly conferred by the law, of choosing between two or more reasonable alternatives concerning the legally correct way of translating the source-sentences at hand, and using the selected alternative as a correct premise of the judicial reasoning. It is necessary to define interpretive discretion in terms of reasonable alternatives, if we wish to account for a basic aspect of judicial interpretation in our legal culture: that is to say, its being an argumentative game, belonging to the realm of rhetoric.[3] Reasonable alternatives, accordingly, are those alternatives that, though they may be strongly disputable (even to the point of being considered as utterly "outrageous" by some sector of society or public opinion), are

---

problems: that is to say, problems arising from the capability of source-sentences to be translated into a set of alternative (abstract) explicit norms. Concrete interpretation is concerned, contrariwise, with the qualification of individual cases according to previously identified abstract general norms; it focuses on the reference (*Bedeutung*) of the descriptive expressions featuring in the general norms; it is meant to overcome problems of vagueness or open texture, if any, of the concepts to be used for qualifying cases. I think the notion of concrete interpretation, as it is usually defined, suffers from an ambiguity that must be brought to the fore, in order to get a clearer conceptual apparatus. Indeed it seems worthwhile distinguishing two notions of concrete interpretation. On the first notion, concrete interpretation is a part of the activity of translating a source-sentence into a general norm. This I shall call *concrete-interpretation-as-translation*. On the second notion, contrariwise, concrete interpretation amounts to qualifying a certain individual fact in terms of a previously identified general norm. This I shall call *concrete-interpretation-as-qualification*. The output of concrete-interpretation-as-qualification is a qualification sentence: like, for instance, "John Smith's entering the park on roller-skates is – has the value of, amounts to, counts as – entering the park with a vehicle". On the contrary, the outcome of concrete-interpretation-as-translation is a norm, the formulation of which incorporates a parenthetic, denotative, definition of the relevant qualifying expression: like, for instance, "No vehicles (automobiles, motorcycles, bicycles, roller-skates, etc.) are allowed into the park". In a well-designed judicial opinion, the outcome of concrete-interpretation-as-qualification logically depends on the outcome of a corresponding concrete-interpretation-as-translation. To be sure, the judicial process of interpretation-as-translation, broadly conceived, usually has its starting point in the description of an individual case ("John Smith entered the city park on roller-skates") and in a legal issue arising in its connection ("Did John Smith's behaviour violate the Mayor's ordinance 'No vehicles into the city park'?"). The two notions of concrete-interpretation are precisely useful to emphasize this central aspect of adjudication.

[3] From the standpoint of judicial interpretation and integration, the law can in fact be considered as a rhetorical normative system. As a system, to wit, that consists, at any given time, of the totality of the rhetorical consequences of a given set of source-sentences. I have offered a short presentation of this view in Chiassoni 2014.

not, nonetheless, wholly "preposterous". Ultimately, they are supported by some set of ethical principles – concerning justice, democracy, the constitution, the rule of law, the proper role of the judiciary in the institutional context, the proper interpretive method, etc. – judges adopt as paramount on the basis of a fundamental ethical option that is not itself liable to any conclusive justification.[4] Due to such argumentation requirement, interpretive discretion is not absolute power to choose interpretive outputs. It is, rather, a power the exercise thereof is constrained by a burden of reasoning that involves ultimate practical commitments.

By *integration discretion* I mean, for any judge whatsoever, in relation to the identification of the implicit components of a previously identified set made of source-sentences, explicit norms and implicit norms, the power of choosing among two or more reasonable alternatives concerning the legally correct enrichment of that set – for instance, by adding some implicit background principle or implicit norm of detail.

To the present purpose, I will leave integration discretion aside and focus, instead, on interpretive discretion. Now, if we pay attention to the kinds of alternatives among which there may be room for choice, it seems worthwhile distinguishing two

---

[4] Interpretive discretion as power is the legal power, for a judge, to make interpretive decisions, aimed at the resolution of an individual case at hand. The content of such interpretive decisions depends on the exercise of interpretive discretion as a fact, namely, of a liberty of choice that arises as a de facto feature of adjudication. It is apparently with discretion as fact that Herbert Hart deals in a posthumous, recently published essay. There, after claiming that «discretion occupies an intermediate place between choices dictated by purely personal and momentary whim and those which are made to give effect to clear methods of reaching clear aims or to conform to rules whose application in the particular case is obvious», Hart emphasizes that every discretional decision always consists in the making of a "leap", for it can never be supported by conclusive reasons: «phrases often used to describe the exercise of discretion, such as "intuition" [and] "recognition of an implicit guiding purpose," may encourage the illusion that we never reach the point where we have to reconcile conflicting values or choose between them without some more ultimate principle to guide us. I think the suggestion that we never reach the "leap" is just as wrong as a description of discretion as a mere arbitrary choice would be. It seems to me clear that just because there is a point at which we can no longer be guided by principles and at the best can only ask for the confirmation of our judgment by persons who have submitted themselves to a similar discipline before deciding, that we have in discretion the sphere where arguments in favour of one decision or another may be rational without being conclusive» (Hart 1956, 658, 665; see also Hart 1961: 273–276). As it is well known, Ronald Dworkin singles out "weak" from "strong" discretion. The former obtains whenever an official's decision depends on a «use of judgment» that is «controlled by a standard furnished» by a particular authority: for instance, a sergeant is ordered by the lieutenant to "take his five most experienced men on patrol". The latter obtains whenever an official's decision is *not* «controlled by a standard furnished» by a particular authority, but must nonetheless keep within the limits set by the general standards of «rationality, fairness, and effectiveness»: for instance, a sergeant is simply ordered to "take five men on patrol" (Dworkin 1977: 31–33). Clearly, weak discretion and strong discretion are different not by quality, but by quantity: strong discretion obtains whenever the decision-maker has weaker constraints to abide by. Both notions can be captured by Hart's notion. On discretion in law, see also: Lifante Vidal 1989; Ruiz Manero 1990: 181–198; Iglesias Vila 1999; Laporta 2007: 207–208 («When the law is indeterminate, when its sentences are defeasible, when cases are hard cases, it shows up in front of us the riddle of judicial discretion»).

varieties of interpretive discretion. I shall call them selective discretion and application discretion.

Selective discretion consists, for any judge whatsoever, in relation to the interpretation of a previously identified set of source-sentences, in the power – limited, of course, by the aforementioned burden of argumentation – of determining which, between two or more alternative interpretive codes, is "the legally correct one". An interpretive code is a discrete set of directives concerning the proper way of interpreting a certain (kind of) source-sentence. It consists, in common talk, in a discrete set of interpretive "methods", "techniques", "canons", "rules", or "arguments". Usually, the interpretive code that judges use in their opinions is a definite sub-set of the larger, and usually open, set of interpretive methods, canons, rules, etc. available to them on the basis of the present culture, tradition and positive law.

Application discretion consists, contrariwise, for any judge whatsoever, in relation to the interpretation of a previously identified source-sentence, in the (limited) power of choosing between two or more reasonably alternative translations of that source-sentence which are made possible by uncertainties showing up in the application of the directives of the previously selected interpretive code.[5]

To complete the framework, one more notion is needed. This is the notion of 'situation of interpretive discretion'. By *situation of interpretive discretion* I mean, for any judge whatsoever, in relation to the interpretation of a previously identified set of source-sentences, the situation that consists in the necessity for the judge of exercising her powers of interpretive discretion: be it the power of selective discretion (discretion as to the choice of the interpretive code), the power of application discretion (discretion in applying the directives of a previously selected interpretive code), or both.[6]

3 Three Views About the Nature of Judicial Interpretation

Legal philosophers often make a distinction between three alternative views about the "nature" of judicial interpretation. *Formalism* ("the noble dream theory") considers judicial interpretation to be an activity of knowing the legally correct

[5] Suppose, for instance, that the following situation obtains: (i) the interpretive code prescribes to interpret "according to the original legislative intent"; but (ii) competing interpretations are available of what the original legislative intent was, each one pointing to a different way of translating the source-sentence at hand. In that case, the judge will enjoy application discretion in relation of selecting what, all-things-considered, is to be taken as the governing legislative intent. To be sure, application discretion is something that can also be conferred explicitly by some directive of the selected code. Suppose, for instance, an interpretive code contains a default directive like, e.g.: "Whenever no (clear) legislative intent is available, interpret in such a way as to realize justice for the individual case".

[6] Are situations of interpretive discretion judge-dependent or judge-independent? For the reasons that will appear in the following, I am inclined to think that they depend on context, which, in turn, is neither always, nor wholly, waterproof to judicial beliefs, preferences, attitudes and expectations.

meaning of source-sentences ("grasping the true meaning of a law in view of its application to an individual case at hand"). *Scepticism* ("realism", "the nightmare theory"), contrariwise, considers judicial interpretation to be an activity that always, and necessarily, involves some practical evaluation and decision about the legally correct meaning of source-sentences.[7] Finally, so-called *mixed* or *intermediate theory* ("eclecticism", "the vigil theory") considers judicial interpretation to be something of a hybrid nature: sometimes it is just knowledge ("law-finding"), sometimes it is practical evaluation and decision ("law-creation").[8]

The notions of interpretive discretion I have just defined suggest drawing a somewhat different, perhaps a little bit more precise, picture of the competing theories about the nature of judicial interpretation. Here, the featuring items are integral cognitivism, restricted cognitivism, and non-cognitivism.

3.1 Cognitivism: Integral and Restricted

Integral cognitivism claims that, in relation to the interpretation of any set whatsoever of source-sentences, judges can never find themselves in situations of interpretive discretion: neither in situations of selective discretion, nor in situations of application discretion. In other words, judges can never enjoy the possibility of exercising a (limited) power of interpretive choice: either in order to select the interpretive code, or in order to apply it.[9]

It is worthwhile considering the state of affair that must obtain for the claims of integral cognitivism to be true. Upon consideration, such a state of affair must amount to the existence of an objective interpretive code, endowed with strict normativity, and characterized by the joint properties of completeness, exclusivity, and efficiency. Such a code is *objective*, since it is an evident datum to every judge and jurist: something "out there", which can just be known by any competent lawyer. It is *endowed with strict normativity*, since, to any competent lawyer, it is undefeasibly binding on interpretation. It is *complete*, since it exhausts the set of interpretive

[7] Sometimes two varieties of scepticism are singled out, according to the role they ascribe to interpretation in the determination of the meaning of source-sentences. Radical scepticism claims that there is really no meaning before interpretation: interpretation creates the meaning of source-sentences. Contrariwise, moderate scepticism claims that source-sentences are always open to a plurality of meanings. There are meanings before interpretation; interpretation, however, necessarily consists in deciding, for any case at hand, which is the (all-things-considered) correct one. See Guastini 2011: 150, 156–159.

[8] See, for instance, Carrió 1965: part II; Hart 1977; Diciotti 2003: 5 fn 2; Guastini 2010: 121ss.; Chiassoni 2011: ch. II.

[9] A staunch representative of integral cognitivism is the German jurist Carl Friedrich von Savigny, the founder of the Historical School. For a recent account of his theory of legal interpretation, see, e.g., Chiassoni 2009: ch. IV, § 4.

directives available for correctly interpreting the source-sentences. It is *exclusive*, since no alternative objective code exists. It is, finally, *efficient*, since the directives of the objective code, combined with the relevant interpretive resources (the data that are necessary to apply them), always point to (just) one definite translation for any source-sentence whatsoever. Such a code is, accordingly, something any judge can simply know and follow.

Restricted cognitivism claims that, in relation to the interpretation of any set whatsoever of source-sentences, judges cannot ever find themselves in situations of selective discretion. This is so because interpreters face an objective, strictly normative, complete and exclusive interpretive code. It may happen, however, that the code proves inefficient. It may occur that its directives, together with the interpretive resources available, do not point to one definite translation for some source-sentence at hand. In such cases, the interpreter finds herself in a situation of application discretion. There is a guidance failure in the directives of the objective code, and such failure must be fixed up in order to decide the case at hand. As a consequence, in those cases where the objective code has run out, interpretation cannot amount just to "finding" the legally correct meaning of source-sentences. It must amount, rather, to making ("creating") what is to count as their legally correct meaning.

3.2 *Integral and Restricted Cognitivism: A Few Perplexities*

Both varieties of cognitivism – as general theories of judicial interpretation – depend on the idea of there being, in every legal order, an objective, strictly normative, complete, and exclusive interpretive code, though they disagree upon one of its virtues (efficiency). Indeed, if my account of the conditions which are necessary to make cognitivism work is correct, there must be a code like that, endowed with those properties, if judicial interpretation is to be considered as a knowing-activity (as an "act of knowledge"): as a whole or, at least, in a large part.

Let us leave the efficiency property aside, since it is put down even by the restricted variety of cognitivism, and pause to consider the other ones. Here, a few perplexities immediately arise. First, the very idea of there being an objective, strictly normative, complete, and exclusive interpretive code in *every* legal system is in itself, to say the least, open to reasonable doubt. Second, even if we admit, for the sake of argument, that such an objective, strictly normative, complete, and exclusive code does in fact exist, it seems nonetheless doubtful that it would turn judicial interpretation into a piece of knowledge. Let's have a closer look at these perplexing issues.

3.3 Are There Objective, Strictly Normative, Complete, and Exclusive Interpretive Codes?

In which sense, if any, there may be an objective, strictly normative, complete, and exclusive interpretive code in every legal system? To my mind, only two possibilities are available.[10]

To begin with, an interpretive code may be objective, strictly normative, complete and exclusive as a matter of social fact: as a cultural and institutional datum. In that case, however, the existence of such a code would be a purely contingent social phenomenon: it would be a matter of how a legal and political culture, in a certain age, happens to be.

It must be noticed however that, if that were the case, cognitivism would be a false account of judicial interpretation for most, if not all, of the legal cultures we know. In our legal cultures there is, to be sure, an objective set of interpretive directives that is handed down by tradition and, sometimes, is also sanctioned by positive laws. Unfortunately, however, such a set of objective directives does not make a code: it is interpreters that make codes out of them, according to their passing or stable interests. Furthermore, jurists are used to think that new directives can be added, as time goes by, to the objective set handed down by tradition, and that each of them is (tacitly) accompanied by an "unless" clause.[11] So that, from the standpoint of history and culture, we must conclude that the set of objective directives is neither complete, nor exclusive, nor made of indefeasible prescriptions. Finally, objective directives are usually very broad interpretive instructions, which always call for selective (specification) and application discretion.[12]

A second possibility must be considered, hoping for a better chance. This is the hypothesis according to which the claim that there is, in every legal order, an objective, strictly normative, complete and exclusive interpretive code, making of judicial interpretation really a matter of knowledge, is a piece of methodological naturalism. I call 'methodological naturalism' the view according to which legal texts, in virtue of their essential properties, dictate the complete and exclusive set of rules for their own correct interpretation. Consequently, the problem of the correct interpretive method would become an issue of knowing the code and faithfully following it, as we follow the rules of grammar and arithmetic.

---

[10] A more complicated version of the argument would take into account the possibility of there being, in any legal system, a (different) objective code like that for each sector of positive law (constitutional law, private law, administrative law, criminal law, etc.). This complication would not alter the gist of the argument.

[11] See e.g. Wróblewski 1985: 35 ff.; Wróblewski 1992: 87 ff.

[12] Consider, for instance, the literal meaning directive as it is usually found in juristic textbooks and judicial opinions ("Interpret the source-sentences according to their literal meaning"). Does it instruct to take into account the literal meaning at the time the source-sentence was enacted, or, rather, the literal meaning at the time of its application? This is something the directive, as usually understood in our legal cultures, leaves to the interpreters to decide.

If we pause for a moment, however, we cannot avoid feeling how queer, from the standpoint of institutional ontology, the idea of methodological naturalism is. After all, texts are but strings of words. They cannot "dictate" anything at all. They do have properties, of course; but which out of these are "essential properties" they cannot "tell". It is interpreters that, fatally, will pick up essential properties and draw interpretive instructions out of them.

Apparently, our reflexions upon the idea of an objective, strictly normative, complete and exclusive interpretive code have led us to a disenchanting conclusion: cognitivism – in both varieties – seems to be doomed either to plain falsity, or to plain queerness.

3.4 Would an Objective Code Turn Judicial Interpretation into a Piece of Knowledge?

Let us now consider the second perplexity I mentioned before. Suppose for the sake of the argument that an objective, strictly normative, complete, and exclusive code exists in every legal system. Would that fact turn judicial interpretation (always or at least in many occasions) into an act of knowledge, as cognitivists claim?

The question seems to command a negative answer.

To begin with, that would be the case if, and only if, interpretive directives worked as self-applying instructions. Unfortunately, that is not the case. Interpretive directives – "our" interpretive directives – needs to be selected, interpreted and specified in order to be put to the task of interpretation guidelines.

Furthermore, the objective directives of our methodological tradition are not endowed with anything like the strict normativity cognitivists (tacitly) assume. In our methodological tradition, the degree of strict normativity of interpretive directives, if any, always involves a special practical commitment on the part of each interpreter: it depends on a basic (reflexive or un-reflexive) act of acceptance on the part of the judge, engaging her practical responsibility as a law-official.

Such practical commitment on the part of interpreters, which appears to be a necessary feature of our interpretive landscape, suggests a final point. A given piece of judicial interpretation may not involve, properly speaking, any "law-creation". For instance, judge *A* interprets a law in a hard case exactly in the same way as another judge, *B*, in a previous decision, has already interpreted it. Besides, in easy cases, she just follows what everybody has always done. Nonetheless, this does not turn interpretation into a pure act of "law-finding", that is to say, into a pure act of knowing, nor is evidence of the directives' strict normativity. Here too interpreting involves taking side: it is not lawmaking proper, but neither it is just a neutral piece of law-description. Indeed, easy cases are easy always for pragmatic reasons. All these aspects of the phenomenon of judicial interpretation as it is in fact in our legal cultures appear to be obscured by the pictures cognitivists purport to provide.

3.5 Non-cognitivism

Non-cognitivism claims that, in relation to the interpretation of any set whatsoever of source-sentences, judges necessarily find themselves in situations of selective discretion. Furthermore, depending on the interpretive code they have selected, they also can find themselves in situations of application discretion. The necessary presence of situation of selective discretion is a consequence of the trivial fact I have just mentioned: legal texts are not self-interpreting items, nor they do "dictate" any interpretive directive at all for their own correct interpretation. Accordingly, any interpretive venture – the venture between text and interpreter – always depends on methodological and substantive options by the interpreters. These options, in turn, mirror the endorsement of some ideology of legal interpretation: the acceptance of some set of claims about how interpretation ought to be.

It may happen of course that, in a given legal culture, with regard to a certain kind of source-sentences, a certain interpretive code comes to be widely regarded by judges and jurists as the "correct" interpretive code, and acquires in that way the sort of contingent social objectivity I mentioned before. Also in those situations, however, interpreters will have occasions for exercising selective discretion. They will fatally be called to making reasoned choices about precisifying, putting into hierarchical order, and enriching the directives of the "objective" code.[13] To sum up, the point of non-cognitivism is this: in any legal culture, selective discretion may have, in fact, different scopes for different judges and different kinds of source-sentences at different times. Because of structural features of legal interpretation, however, it is never a non-existent phenomenon, as integral and restricted cognitivism (must) claim.

The case for non-cognitivism will become stronger – or so I hope – by going into the details of a powerful version of restricted cognitivism and showing its many shortcomings.

---

[13] An example from history may perhaps help. The French jurists of the so-called Exegetical School apparently shared the same principles, which they regarded as evident, about the proper way of interpreting the *Civil Code*. These were the principle of "respect for the legislature" and the principle of "primacy of the text". These principles represented the core of the "objective" interpretive code considered as absolutely binding in French XIXth century legal culture. Nonetheless, the two principles, due to their eminent indeterminacy, formed the basis for different, more specific, codes, adopted by individual interpreters. On this point, see e.g. Chiassoni 2009: ch. IV, § 3. Similar considerations hold for those cultures where principles like "literal interpretation and legislative intent", "systemic interpretation", "constitution-oriented interpretation", "respect for the Constitution", etc. are paramount.

4 Pragmatic Cognitivism: A Critique

In my attempt at providing an account of the properties that, to my mind, identify restricted cognitivism, I took inspiration from a set of theories the archetype of which is usually thought to stay with Herbert Hart's defence of a middle-ground between formalism ("the noble dream") and rule-scepticism ("the nightmare").[14]

To be sure, somebody might feel shocked, or perhaps even horrified, by the claim that Hart, while setting forth his view concerning legal interpretation, might have been committed – though tacitly, or by way of presupposition – to the idea of an objective, strictly normative, complete, and exclusive interpretive code. Perhaps, however, the sense of horror will wane, at least a bit, if we look at what may be considered as the more sophisticated version of the Hartian theory now afoot. I mean the theory defended by Andrei Marmor.[15]

One feature makes of Marmor's theory of judicial interpretation something particularly worth of attention from the standpoint of my present concern. This is Marmor's methodical resort to philosophy of language and pragmatics. In the following, I will briefly rehearse Marmor's "pragmatic cognitivism", as I shall call it, in view of suggesting two points. First, the objective code hypothesis, so far as Marmor's theory is concerned, seems to be endowed with explanatory power. Second, Marmor's pragmatic cognitivism is objectionable as a viable – i.e., a coherent and explanatory – theory about the nature of judicial interpretation.

4.1 Marmor's Pragmatic Cognitivism

Marmor deals with judicial interpretation while dealing with legal interpretation. In a nutshell, Marmor's theory of legal interpretation characterizes for four basic claims: the communication model claim, the reasonable hearer claim, the exception claim, and, finally, the no-interpretivism claim.

4.1.1 The Communication Model Claim

In Marmor's view, written law – and legislation as the foremost piece thereof – is evidently to be accounted for by resorting to a communication model: it is, in fact, a communication enterprise, where the legislature intends to convey to judges, officials, and, above all, people at large, the communication content of its enactments.[16]

[14] See Hart 1983: 62–72, 84–87; Hart 1961: ch. VII; Hart 1977: 124–144; a revised view is suggested in Id., *Problems of the Philosophy of Law*, 1967, and Id., *Introduction*, 1983, both in Hart 1983: 105–106, 6–8.

[15] See Marmor 2005, esp. chaps. 2 and 6; Marmor 2011, chaps. 4 and 6; Marmor 2014.

[16] Marmor 2014: 1 ff.

As a consequence, any theoretically sound account of the complex phenomenon that jurists often identify by the phrase "legal interpretation" must turn on the distinction between «understanding» («reasonable uptake») of «what the law says», on the one hand, and «interpretation» proper («interpreting it»), on the other hand.[17]

4.1.2 The Reasonable Hearer Claim

Speakers (legislatures) can «fail to communicate all that they had intended to». As a consequence, understanding must be conceived as reasonable uptake: as the understanding of the communicative content of any piece of legislation by a reasonable hearer.[18] Though Marmor does not put it in these terms, what he regards as "understanding" or "reasonable uptake", and opposes to "interpretation", apparently encompasses two distinct operations, which correspond to the two components of the explicit communicative content of a piece of legislation. I will dub such operations semantic understanding and pragmatic understanding, respectively.

Semantic understanding is a matter of grasping the «semantic content» of source-sentences on the basis of the syntactical and semantic rules of the relevant natural language. It depends on linguistic skills. It is a necessary, un-reflexive, rule-determined, original and independent cognition process.[19] In the plentiful situations of easy cases, Marmor argues, judges simply understand the semantic content of a source-sentence. In those cases, the semantic content is, by hypothesis, tantamount to the «assertive content» (or «prescriptive content») of source-sentences («what the law says»). Accordingly, by getting to know the semantic content of legislative

[17] Marmor 2011: 10, 97–108, 136–145; Marmor 2014: 19 ff., 107–109.

[18] Marmor explains the idea of "reasonable uptake", which corresponds roughly to what in previous essays qualified as "understanding", in the following terms: «the subjective intentions of the speaker are only partly constitutive of assertive content; speakers can sometimes fail to communicate all that they had intended to. Therefore, the content that is said or asserted by a speech act partly depends on its reasonable uptake. Assertive content, on this view (that I share), must be defined objectively as the kind of content that a reasonable hearer, with full knowledge of the contextual background of the speech, would understand the speaker to have intended to convey, given what the speaker expressed, the relevant contextual knowledge, and the relevant conversational norms that apply» (Marmor 2014: 19).

[19] Marmor 2011: 142 «Our ability to understand each other in a communicative context depends on a shared, at least tacit, understanding about the kind of conversation we are engaged in, and the norms governing it. Understandings of this kind are, of course, subject to occasional misunderstandings or deviations of various kinds, in which case, typically some aspect of the communication fails. None of this, however, is a matter of interpretation. From the fact that there is some normative framework governing the kind of conversation one is engaged in, it does not follow that a hearer's grasp of the communicative content hangs in the air, as it were, until she comes up with an interpretation of the relevant maxims. Maxims are typically common knowledge between speaker and hearer, in no need of interpretation»; pp. 144–145: «Mostly, just like in an ordinary conversation, we hear (or read, actually) what the legal directive says and thereby understand what it requires. In some cases, it is unclear what the law says, and interpretation is called for».

utterances (source-sentences), judges get to know the law as it is (or, in other terms, what is the law for the question at hand), and give voice to it in their decisions.[20]

Pragmatic understanding is not always, and indeed quite rarely, necessary.[21] It becomes necessary whenever the semantic content of source-sentences needs to be pragmatically enriched. That is the case whenever source-sentences contain context-sensitive expressions like, e.g., personal pronouns, possessive ascriptions, domain quantifiers, contextual anaphora. In these situations, the assertive content of source-sentences, what the law says, is the output of a «defeasible inference» from (i) the semantic content «of the expression used», (ii) context («the contextual background that is common knowledge between speaker and hearer»), and (iii) conversational maxims («the relevant normative framework governing the conversation in question»).[22]

4.1.3 The Exception Claim

Interpretation proper becomes necessary whenever understanding, or reasonable uptake, does not lead to a determinate outcome. This can happen because of such factors of law indeterminacy like vagueness, ambiguity, gaps, normative conflicts, uncertainty about the correspondence between the semantic content and the assertive content of a source-sentence, uncertainty about the legal implicatures of a source-sentence at hand.[23] Interpretation is a contingent, reflexive, not rule-determined, but, at most, paradigm-guided, parasitic, evaluative activity.[24] In virtue of its contingent character, interpretation is – as Marmor emphasizes – «only the *exception* to understanding what the law says, not the standard way of grasping its content».[25] The exception amounts, furthermore, to a dramatic change in the nature of the judicial performance. Indeed, whenever a judge finds herself in need of

[20] Marmor 2005: 10 ff.; I have offered a synoptic table of the differences between understanding and interpretation in Chiassoni 2008: 257. See also Endicott 1994: 451–479; Endicott 2014: §.2.2.

[21] Marmor 2014: 27, 28 ff., 33: «in the context of statutory law, the gap between semantic and assertive content is much more limited and infrequent compared with ordinary conversation».

[22] Marmor 2014: 22 ff., 28 ff., 33–34, 108. In other parts of the book, pragmatic understanding, as part of the reasonable uptake of the full communicative content of a speech act, also concerns the identification of the implicated content of the communication, beyond the assertive content. See, e.g., Marmor 2014: 49 ff. Marmor (2011: 141) makes clear that: «every communicative interaction is guided by some norms that govern the kind of contribution to the conversation that speakers are supposed to make. Without such a normative framework, typically shared by the relevant conversational parties, communication would not be possible».

[23] Marmor 2011: 145–159; Marmor 2014: 118–129 and ch. 3.

[24] Marmor 2005: ch. 2, 10 ff.; Chiassoni 2008: 257.

[25] Marmor 2011: 137; see also pp. 9–10: against «Dworkin's argument that we can never grasp what the law says without interpretation», so that, given the partly evaluative nature of it, «understanding what the law requires is necessarily dependent on some evaluative considerations», Marmor wishes to argue that Dworkin's conception «of what it takes to understand a legal directive is based on a misunderstanding of language and linguistic communication […] when linguistic considerations are taken into account in the appropriate ways, we will realize that interpretation

interpreting a source-sentence, she finds herself in need of performing a law-creation activity. Interpretation modifies – «completes» – the law: if only temporarily, by closing up the law's loose ends as to the individual case to be adjudicated.[26]

4.1.4 The No-Interpretivism Claim

Some scholars – and notably, Ronald Dworkin – adopt an interpretivist account of law: they claim that interpretation, as an evaluative and constructive (purpose-imposing, point-imposing, sense-imposing and meaning-determining) activity, is ubiquitous in law. But, Marmor says, they are wrong.

On the one hand, the ubiquity claim is at odds with («flies in the face of») everyday experience. Both outside of law, and also inside of it; there are in fact plenty of cases where judges just understand the meaning of the source-sentences relevant to deciding the cases at hand.[27]

On the other hand, philosophy of language – which is obviously relevant in dealing with theoretical legal problems, due to the linguistic, communicative, dimension of law[28] – shows that interpretation is a marginal phenomenon as regards to linguistic communication: both in general, and as regards to legal "conversations", i.e., to the linguistic transactions in law, like those among legislators, between legislatures and people at large, or between legislatures and judges or other officials. This is the case, Marmor argues, for three different reasons. First, the contextual dependence of utterance meaning is, in general, an intermittent property, depending on the presence of context-sensitive expressions; and, when it does show up, it does not necessarily require interpretation. Second, the normative framework represented by the conversational maxims that rule over linguistic transactions cannot always be «open for grabs»; this is so because, if that were the case, communication would not be possible (the «parties to a conversation could not possibly engage in a communicative interaction»).[29] Third, there is nothing in legal conversations that makes them so

becomes the exception, not the standard form of understanding what the law says»; Marmor 2014: 107–109.

[26] See, e.g., Marmor 2014: 74.

[27] Marmor 2011: 107–108, 138: «When we conduct an ordinary conversation, it is not our experience that every utterance by a speaker is somehow followed by a pause, when the hearer thinks about ways to interpret what has been said. Under the normal circumstance of a conversation, we just hear the utterances and thereby understand what has been said». See also Marmor 2014: 107–109.

[28] Marmor 2011: 136: «Philosophy of language is central to an understanding of law for a different reason. Law, as we have seen in previous chapters, consists of authoritative directives. The content of the law is tantamount to the content that is communicated by various legal authorities. Authorities communicate, of course, in a natural language. Therefore, an understanding of how linguistic communication works and, in particular, how much is actually determined by various semantic and pragmatic aspects of language, is central to an understanding of what law is»; Marmor 2014: 1: «Language is to lawyers what a piano is to the pianist: the tool of trade».

[29] Marmor 2011: 141.

unlike ordinary conversations, as to make of interpretation in law not just the exception, but, rather, the rule.[30]

The four claims I have just recalled should make clear why Marmor's general theory of legal interpretation, in so far as it is also a theory of judicial interpretation (which is my concern here), features as an instance of restricted, pragmatic, cognitivism.

To begin with, and this is the first point I think worthwhile emphasizing, it maintains that judicial interpretation – broadly conceived as the process leading to the identification of the meaning of a given source-sentence – sometimes is just a matter of pure knowledge, sometimes is, instead, a matter of evaluation and law-creation. The former situation occurs whenever it simply amounts to the understanding, or reasonable uptake, of the relevant legal texts. The latter situation occurs instead whenever, due either to the semantic indeterminacy of the source-sentence (because of vagueness or ambiguity), or to other problems like the presence of normative conflicts and uncertainties about pragmatic implicatures, legal interpretation proper must be performed.

Furthermore, and this is the second point I think worthwhile emphasizing, in so maintaining, Marmor's theory exhibits a tacit commitment to the view according to which, in the terminology I have introduced before:

(a) there is an objective interpretive code, endowed with strict normativity, which is tantamount to the syntactical and semantic rules of the natural language to which the source-sentences belong;
(b) such a code may be complemented, at the level of pragmatic understanding, by a likewise objective normative framework of conversational maxims;
(c) such an integrated semantic-pragmatic code, however, may prove inefficient as a guide to the assertive (and implicated) content of the source-sentences;
(d) whenever that happens, interpreters who put up with such inefficiencies really do not resort to the interpretive rules of some different normative framework; so that, in the terms I have introduced before, the interpretive discretion they enjoy does actually amount to application discretion: it is an interpretive discretion that is exercised in applying the directives of the integrated semantic-pragmatic code.

4.2 *The Failures of Pragmatic Cognitivism*

Marmor claims his theory of judicial interpretation – which, as we have seen, represents a sophisticated version of restricted cognitivism – to be supported by philosophy of language and, as a substantive part thereof, pragmatics. It is worthwhile considering whether Marmor's claim really is right, as he pretends. The following arguments seem to suggest a negative answer.

[30] Marmor 2011: 9–10, 97–108, 136–145; Marmor 2014: 107 ff.

4.2.1 What Does Pragmatics Suggest?

Pragmatics is the theory of language from the standpoint of language users: speakers/hearers, writers/readers, authors/interpreters, senders/addressees, etc. In its Gricean cast, pragmatics studies linguistic transactions ("conversations") in view of identifying the rules ("conversational maxims") that characterize the several kinds of conversation afoot, singling out each kind as a different variety of language game.

By the same token, legal pragmatics may be defined as the theory of legal language from the standpoint of its users: legislators, legislatures, judges and other officials, jurists, lawyers, people at large. In a Gricean cast, legal pragmatics studies legal conversations in view of identifying the conversational maxims that single out several kinds of language games in law, marking each kind as a different sort.

What does legal pragmatics suggest about the nature of the "conversation" between judges and legislature (though, clearly, speaking of "conversation" here is talking metaphor)?

Marmor presents the judges-legislature conversation (hereafter: JLC) as a special case of ordinary, cooperative, information-exchange, conversation (hereafter: OC). Like in any OC, context (shared contextual knowledge) and (shared) conversational maxims intervene in JLC to help putting up with two problems: (i) in order to perform the pragmatic enrichment of the semantic content of source-sentences, in the rare cases where this may be needed; (ii) in order to identify legal implicatures, that is to say, the implicated content of the legislative or constitutional communication. Marmor assumes that, in both situations, the relevant conversational maxims are the maxims of OC, though they may be defeated in virtue of the special property of JLC, which is represented by the strategic (non-cooperative) purposes and behaviours of the players.

One point must be emphasized. Viewing the JLC as a special case of OC is functional to defending three related claims of special importance to Marmor's mind, namely: (i) the no-ubiquity of interpretation claim, or the idea that interpretation is an exception also within the law; (ii) the idea that the content of the law – what the law is, what the law says, what the law dictates – is tantamount to the linguistic meaning (semantic content) of legal provisions; (iii) the idea that such content is something that, ordinarily, can simply be grasped by linguistic understanding or reasonable uptake, unless some crisis in communication occurs. These three claims represent the cornerstone of Marmor's positivist theory of law. For this reason, if Marmor succeeds in showing that they find support in philosophy of language and pragmatics, this would make the case for Marmor's positivist legal theory stronger.

At this point, however, a few remarks are in order. First, as Marmor concedes, there is not just one philosophy of language, not just one pragmatics, out there, telling good legal theories from bad ones; there are, instead, several and contrasting philosophies of language and pragmatics.[31] Second, the business of the several philosophies of language and pragmatics is providing true and explanatory accounts of (ordinary) language and discourse. Can they really provide any support to

[31] Marmor 2014: 19, 20.

questionable theories of law like Marmor's positivism? Third, suppose we accept the philosophy of language and pragmatics Marmor has opted for in his essays. Does such a philosophical-linguistic outlook really support the three claims about law I have listed above? Does it support, in particular, the no-ubiquity of interpretation claim, which is the pillar of Marmor's restricted cognitivism?

To the present purpose, I will consider the last question only. Now, I think that question commands a negative answer. I think, more precisely, that the following conclusion must be entertained: from the standpoint of the very pragmatics adopted by Marmor, the JLC is to be regarded as *a constructive interpretation game* (though not necessarily of the Dworkinian sort), *which judges* (together with lawyers and jurists) *play with the dummy* (that is to say, the legislature), *by means of a shared set of authoritative materials* (source-sentences) *and interpretive tools*, which they may select, combine, arrange, modify, revise, integrate, etc., according to the pursued interests. Indeed, not even Marmor, who strongly opposes "interpretivism", as we have seen, cannot avoid it. In the following, I will bring to the fore a few pieces of incoherence and self-defeating points in Marmor's case. These, in turn, will appear like as many concessions to the ubiquity of interpretation and non-cognitivism claims.

4.2.2 Necessity of Constructive Interpretation: Establishing the Interpretive Relevance of Linguistic Meaning in Legal Interpretation

A first incoherence that, to my mind, casts a sinister light on Marmor's theory of judicial interpretation shows up in the way Marmor deals with the interpretive relevance of linguistic meaning (semantic content), on the one hand, and the interpretive relevance of lawgiver's intent, on the other.

Marmor presents the interpretive relevance to law of the semantic content of source-sentences as a matter of course. That would be so, apparently, because source-sentences are expressed in a natural language and, as a consequence, they cannot but share in the fate of any natural language expression.[32]

Contrariwise, so far as legislative or framers' intent is concerned, Marmor agrees that Dworkin is right; that is to say, that the interpretive relevance of legislative or framers' intent, namely, its importance in view of a legally correct reading of the law, depends on evaluative considerations:

> A very similar line of reasoning applies to the possible roles of intention of legislatures in the interpretation of statutes and the possible role of the framers' intentions in the context

[32] See, e.g., Marmor 2011: 138–139: «It is a very familiar aspect of natural language that the content communicated by a speaker is often partly determined by certain contextual and normative factors. These contextual and normative determinates of linguistic contents are called the *pragmatic* aspects of language. In other words, it is a well-recognized fact that semantics and syntax (meaning) are essential vehicles for conveying communicative content, but the content that is actually communicated is often partly determined by various pragmatic factors».

> of constitutional interpretation. Whether it makes sense to defer to such intentions must also depend on a theoretical argument about where value lies in the relevant genre, namely, the authority of legislation or the authority and legitimacy of a constitution.
>
> Thus the conclusion so far is that the author's-intention model of interpretation only makes sense as an instance or application of the constructive [interpretation] model.[33]

Now, such asymmetric treatment seems unjustified. If deference to legislative or framers' intent necessarily depends on some evaluative, theoretical argument about authority and legitimacy, why deference to semantic content should, instead, be something evaluation-free, something, so to speak, *before* and *above* of any evaluation? Indeed, one may query, the very claim according to which the interpretive value of the semantic content of source-sentences would be "above" and "outside" of the province of evaluative, theoretical argument, is not in itself an evaluative claim, depending on some theoretical argument? How can we establish the legal relevance of some interpretive resource (be it literal meaning, legislative intent, the purpose of the law, consistency with the constitution, etc.) without engaging in an evaluative "theoretical" argument, without taking side and selecting the proper canons and resources for reading the law properly?

4.2.3 Necessity of Constructive Interpretation: Establishing the Similarity and Differences Between Art, Law, and Ordinary Conversation

The preceding argument – the first meant to bring to the fore the incoherence besetting Marmor's theory – ended with a few rhetorical questions. To these questions there is, in Marmor's theory, a reply: the law (and JLC) is closer to ordinary conversation, than, say, to art, where constructive interpretation and evaluations are ubiquitous.

> A work of art is not intended to convey a determinate communicative content that can simply be understood (or misunderstood); it is created with an intention to be somewhat indeterminate in content, or ambiguous in various ways, open to various interpretations. None of this, however, applies to law. In fact, art and law could not be less similar in this respect. Legal instructions are meant to generate concrete results, providing people with particular reasons for action, thus aiming to affect our conduct in some specified ways. The level of specification may vary, of course; some laws are very specific, instructing specific modes of conduct or avoidance of them, while others are much more general. And then, the more general the legal norm is, the more likely it is that circumstances will arise where interpretation is called for. But, generally speaking, it is not in the nature of law, as it is in the nature of art, to become a cultural object that is detached from the specific communicative content it is meant to convey. Art is there to be interpreted; law is there to be acted upon.
>
> Are there some other features unique to law that would make it the case that interpretation is always called for?[34]

---

[33] Marmor 2011: 105.

[34] Marmor 2011: 143.

Is there any reply available? I think there are. There is in fact something of a paradox here: in Marmor's defence of the idea of an evaluation-free zone concerning the identification of law, the need for making interpretive evaluations appears in even a stronger light. Let us see.

First, in the passage just quoted, where Marmor establishes the essential character (the point, the purpose) of (the practice of) law, and contrasts it with the essential character of art, Marmor is clearly performing an act that, in Dworkinian and Marmor's own terms, qualifies as a piece of constructive interpretation.

Second, suppose Marmor retorts that such presumed "constructive interpretation" of the point (purpose, essence) of law is really no interpretation at all, being rather the ascertainment of something that is altogether "evident" to everybody. Who would dare claiming that the laws are made to the purpose of being open to interpretations? Who would deny that the laws are done to the purpose of "generating concrete results", of "guiding behaviours", of "being acted upon"? Perhaps, Marmor is right; nobody could deny such platitudes. Unfortunately, however, they are perfectly empty; and that explains why they are so "evident". As a consequence, once we have accepted this platitudinous view about the law (about its essence, purpose, point), we still have to solve momentous problems: what does it mean that the law's purpose is "generating concrete results"? How the "guiding behaviours" purpose is to be understood and carried out? How the "acting upon" purpose is, again, to be understood and, if I may say so, acted upon? All these questions are not open for evaluation-free, practical-commitment-free, answers. Marmor tries to throw constructive interpretation out of the window. But it does come back: this happens, unavoidably, as soon as the empty platitudes, which would make of law a very different enterprise from art, must be set to work.

4.2.4 Necessity of Constructive Interpretation: Establishing the Easiness of an Easy Case

Another weak point in Marmor's defence of the understanding/interpretation divide, and the related variety of restricted cognitivism, has to do, to my mind, with Marmor's theory of easy cases. Marmor cites easy cases, an evident phenomenon in everyday legal reality, as witnesses on behalf of his view:

> the truth is that both the laymen's picture of how determinate the law is, and the law students' impression of how indeterminate it is, are distorted. The law is much less clear than people tend to think, but it is much more clear than law students are led to believe, because they spend most of their studies focusing on the difficult or problematic cases that tend to reach the appellate courts[35]

When the law is clear, so the argument goes, there is no need for interpretation. This, in turn, shows: (i) that interpretation – and the evaluations it brings along with

[35] Marmor 2011: 138.

it – is not ubiquitous; (ii) that there are cases where judges simply find the law, by means of understanding or reasonable uptake, and do not need to make it.

The argument seems invincible; and so has appeared to many scholars. Unfortunately, the impression is wrong. This is so because the notion of easy case Marmor employs is questionable.

Marmor characterizes an "easy case" as follows:

> An "easy case" [...] means that the relevant legal norm can simply be understood, and applied to the particular case without the mediation of the interpretation of the norm; we just understand what the law says, and know that it applies, or not, to the case at hand[36]

By way of a tentative analysis, Marmor's concept of an easy case is open to different readings. In fact, a source-sentence (in Marmor's terms: a "legal norm") "can" simply "be understood and applied" in no less than three different ways.

Linguistic Possibility The relevant source-sentence is capable, by means of a simple linguistic understanding or reasonable uptake, to provide the judge with a legal norm under which the case at hand clearly may, or may not, be subsumed.

Methodological Possibility If a judge (i) provides a linguistic reading of the relevant source-sentence, and (ii) applies its semantic content to the case at hand, her way of proceeding is fully justified according to the interpretive code that the judge may invoke as the "proper" or "correct" code. Notice that from the perspective of this notion of an easy case, stopping at the linguistic understanding of a source-sentence is not only a linguistic possibility (linguistic-can); it is also a methodological possibility, that is allowed for, and justified by, the directives of the interpretive code the judge deems proper to use. One point must be emphasized. The outcome of the judicial activity in a methodological easy case is, by hypothesis, tantamount to the semantic content of the relevant source-sentence. Such an outcome, however, does not depend on linguistic understanding only: it also depends on a reflexive activity, by means of which the judge considers whether staying with the semantic content of a source-sentence is methodologically justified. This reflexive activity, which goes beyond linguistic understanding, is part of what, in legal discourse, usually goes under the name of "interpretation".

Shared Social Axiology Possibility If a judge (i) provides a linguistic reading of the relevant source-sentence, and (ii) applies its semantic content to the case at hand, her way of proceeding will be praised as reasonable, good, proper, fully justified, etc., by fellow judges, and/or competent jurists, and/or society-at-large, etc. Notice that, from the perspective of this notion of an easy case, stopping at the linguistic understanding of a source-sentence is not only a linguistic possibility (linguistic-can), nor only a methodological possibility (methodological-can); it is also a course of action that is in tune with (allowed, approved, justified by) the methodological

[36] Marmor 2005: 97.

and normative attitudes of the generality of the relevant interpretive community, the public opinion, etc. (social axiology-can). Here again, the judge who applies a source-sentence according to its semantic content does not only perform the un-reflexive activity of linguistic understanding. She also performs the reflexive activity concerning the methodological and axiological viability of that semantic content as the legally correct meaning of that source-sentence. This reflexive activity is, again, what in legal discourse is usually captured by the term "interpretation".

The different notions of easy case suggest a few considerations.

1. Marmor's notion of an easy case apparently mirrors the first view; it makes the easiness of a case to be a purely linguistic property, fully independent from interpretive directives, ideologies, and social attitudes.
2. These latter ingredients, however, are part of the stock-in-trade of the judicial interpretation business, at least in our present legal cultures. As Frederick Schauer points out, according to juristic commonsense an easy case is not simply a linguistically clear case; it is, rather, a *linguistically clear and sensible* case: that is to say, it is a case where the linguistically clear meaning of the relevant source-sentence is, at the same time, not at odds with purpose, not at odds with superior legal principles, not at odds with morality, justice and convenience.[37]
3. As a consequence, Marmor's notion of an easy case flies in the face of juristic commonsense. What is more, contrary to Marmor's opinion, juristic commonsense suggests judicial interpretation to be at work *also* when an easy case is being decided. So far as judges are concerned, the identification of the general norm to be applied to a case at hand never is just the outcome of an un-reflexive process of linguistic understanding.[38] Marmor's conceptual framework however, due to its peculiar understanding/interpretation dualism, is not even equipped to capture this aspect of adjudication: in fact, it rules that out altogether.
4. Marmor, as I have said in passing, considers normative conflicts as situations of law's indeterminacy calling for interpretation (see Sect. 4.1 above). Would not this aspect of Marmor's theory be suitable to overcome the objections I have just set forth concerning the notion of an easy case? I think the answer must be, again, in the negative. In fact, Marmor's theory of the several factors that produce indeterminacy, and make legal interpretation necessary, is self-defeating: it represents, so to speak, the reef on which his whole theory of judicial interpretation sinks. This outcome is particularly clear, in my view, in the case of normative conflicts and pragmatic indeterminacies.

[37] See Schauer 1984: 399, 414–423, 430–31; see also Dascal and Wroblewski 1988: 203–224.

[38] Perhaps, that may be the case with ordinary people, but that's another story, to be carefully considered.

4.2.5 A Self-Defeating Theory of Legal Indeterminacies: The Sting of Normative Conflicts

Marmor uses "interpretation" broadly, to refer to the activity that is needed to deal with any sort of indeterminacy in the law.[39] Normative conflicts (antinomies), as I have said, are singled out among the situations calling for interpretation, together with gaps, vagueness, ambiguity, and pragmatic uncertainties.

Marmor's theory of normative conflicts presents a few questionable points.[40]

First, Marmor claims interpretation is needed to cope with antinomies, without noticing that, as he conceives of them, they are cases of gap. Indeed he maintains that, whenever there is a fixed criterion to solve the conflict, there is really no conflict (there cannot be holes in the trousers, provided there are tailors capable of putting up with them!).

Second, Marmor overlooks that normative conflicts are interpretation-dependent (in the common juristic sense of "interpretation"). In fact, they cannot be *identified* unless on the basis of some previously selected interpretive code, be it even the "simple linguistic understanding" code that Marmor endorses.

Third, as it already appeared while dealing with easy cases, Marmor overlooks that the judges' preoccupation with normative conflicts, which Marmor correctly takes into account, suggests that there is always something more than simple linguistic understanding behind the judicial application of law. It suggests, more precisely, that judicial interpretation, in the common juristic sense, is at work even when the relevant source-sentence has a clear semantic content that is identifiable by means of linguistic understanding. This is so because, once the semantic content has been identified, before applying it to the case at hand it must be evaluated against other relevant norms of the system, to "see" whether any normative conflict is afoot. This point shows that Marmor's understanding/interpretation structural model of the judicial identification of the normative premise of judicial reasoning must be abandoned, and replaced by a model where interpretation is general. Let us see.

The judicial application of a legal norm to an individual case at hand presupposes that the norm to be applied has been previously identified. If the norm is a statutory norm, the starting point for its identification consists in identifying the text of the norm: the statutory clause, the source-sentence of which the norm is, generally speaking, the meaning. This is something Marmor does not pay attention to, taking this preliminary activity for granted. His understanding/interpretation model encompasses three stages: the semantic understanding stage, the pragmatic understanding stage, and, finally, the interpretation stage. The first stage, devoted to the semantic understanding of the source sentence, represents, as we have seen, a necessary step. If the outcome is a clear semantic content, which is immediately applicable to the case at hand, the identification process is over. It may happen, however, that the semantic content needs to be pragmatically enriched. The judge moves then to the second stage. Here a process of pragmatic understanding is performed, which,

[39] Marmor 2011: 145; Marmor 2014: 107–109.

[40] Marmor 2011: 145–146; Marmor 2014: 107–109, 118–120.

by the way, may also cast light upon the implicated side of the full communicative content of the legislative speech act. It may happen, however, that reasonable (semantic and pragmatic) uptake does not lead to a determinate result, both in itself and in relation to the case at hand. In that case, a third stage is needed. This is the stage of interpretation proper, where, fatally, judicial interpretation must be guided by some normative view about the proper allocation of power between judiciary and legislature.[41]

Now, it should be clear why Marmor's theory of normative conflicts is at odds with the understanding/interpretation structural model above. Indeed, we may query, *how* do judges come to "know" that a certain semantic content is at odds with some other, superior, norms of the system? How do they get to identify normative conflicts, calling for interpretation (in Marmor's sense)? Clearly, that would be altogether impossible if the judges just stayed with the simple linguistic understanding of isolated source-sentences. The identification of normative conflicts necessarily calls for a systemic consideration of law. This, in turn, makes the idea of simple linguistic understanding a sheer and misleading illusion.

4.2.6 A Self-Defeating Theory of Legal Indeterminacies: The Sting of Pragmatic Indeterminacies

Pragmatic indeterminacies are situations of uncertainty about the full communication content of a legislative or constitutional speech act, which depend on context. Marmor pays particular attention to two varieties of pragmatic indeterminacy: the mismatch problem (as I will call it) and the legal implicatures problem. I will argue that, while dealing with both problems, Marmor in fact endorses an interpretivist stance, which flies in the face of the rigorous understanding/interpretation model he stays for.

A *mismatch problem* arises any time that what is said apparently does not correspond to what is communicated. It is a problem of mismatch between the semantic content (sentence-meaning) and the assertive content (author's meaning) of a source-sentence. Marmor provides his way out to such problems in a passage that is worthwhile quoting:

> Does it happen in the legal context that the law asserts something different from what it says? It could happen, but not very frequently. First, lawmakers would certainly try to avoid this since it would be too easy to misunderstand what they meant. Second, in the legal context, we would normally lack sufficiently rich contextual background to enable the conclusion that what the law asserts is obviously not what it says. Consider, once again, the "no vehicles are allowed in the park" rule. Suppose, for example, that the legislature of this rule had taken it for granted that only motor vehicles are meant here and that is the content it intended to assert. One can imagine some circumstances in which it would be obvious that this is the case, but those would have to be pretty special circumstances, knowledge of which is shared by all parties concerned. We can imagine, for example, that the "no vehicles in the park" is enacted as a response to specific complaints about pollution, that this is

[41] Marmor 2014: 107–109.

known to be the case, and maybe forms part of a larger legislative measure that curbs motor vehicle pollution—then, yes, perhaps it is obvious that the ordinance is confined to motor vehicles. Otherwise, it is likely to remain an open question[42]

The passage, to my view, provides further evidence for concluding that a purely linguistic notion of easy case and the understanding/interpretation structural model of judicial identification of the normative premise are wrong, since they provide theoretically bad devices to cope with the reality of judicial interpretation and application. In fact, though we may find the conversational metaphor appealing, a judge is *not* engaged in a conversation with the legislature: they are not together in the same place, chatting about the law to be applied, nor are they in touch by phone or any other long-distance communication device; they cannot talk to each other; they do not even know each other. As a consequence, how can a judge even think at a mismatch between the semantic content and the assertive content of an act, unless she goes beyond both linguistic understanding, and the OC notion of a conversational context (which amounts strictly to shared knowledge), to venture into the province of juristic context and interpretation? Once she has passed that border, she will find herself into another – centuries old – world. Here, the mismatch problem is usually to be considered under the aegis of the twin juristic maxims presiding on corrective interpretation (*interpretatio correctiva*): *lex magis dixit quam voluit, lex minus dixit quam voluit*. And, in doing so, the judge, *pace* Marmor, will be performing interpretation at its purest.

A problem of *legal implicature* arises whenever there is uncertainty about the implicated content of a legislative or constitutional speech act. Suppose the legislature enacts a law saying "All X ought to *f*, unless F, G, or H". According to Marmor, from the standpoint of the maxims of OC, such a piece of legislation has a clear conversational implicature: it implies, conversationally, that *only if* F, G, or H the X have not the duty to *f*. It does often happen, however, that courts do not read legal implicatures that way; that, contrariwise, they do not (want to) see the implicature, and read instead a source-sentence like that as providing an incomplete, open list of exceptions.

The judicial decision in *Holy Trinity* is a case in point. To be sure, the fact that judges tend to ignore these kind of implicatures does not mean that the implicature is not there; judges tend to ignore them because they are skeptical, and perhaps rightly so, of a legislature's ability to determine in advance all the possible justified exceptions to the general norm enacted. But again, this testifies to the fact that the discourse between the legislature and the courts is not necessarily a cooperative business, and that the division of labour between legislatures and courts is a morally-politically contentious issue[43]

This is a very telling passage. Marmor admits, apparently, that the JLC is a very different sort of "conversation" from OC. He seems to think, however, that the province of "morally-politically contentious issues" about the division of labour between courts and legislature only concerns the cases of indeterminacy. But why should that be so? Marmor does not see, apparently, that his admission is tantamount to

[42] Marmor 2011: 150–151.

[43] Marmor 2008: 30.

admitting that, after all, interpretivism is right. That, all things considered, interpretivism, though not necessarily of Dworkin's variety, provides a true account of judicial interpretation.[44]

5 Outline of a Pragmatic Interpretivist Theory of Judicial Interpretation

The failure of pragmatic cognitivism is the failure of a theory of judicial interpretation, which, as we have seen, has been worked out by combining (certain) philosophy of language and pragmatics with a communication model of legislation bound to the understanding/interpretation divide.[45]

It is time to learn from such a (very instructive) failure for exploring the viability of a different theory of judicial interpretation. This is the output, instead, of the combination of pragmatics with interpretivism. To be sure, it is not here the place for presenting such a theory in a full-fledged form. I will limit myself to laying down a few scattered fragments.

5.1 Two Views About the Judge-Interpreter

In the background of non-cognitivism and pragmatic cognitivism, respectively, there are two alternative views of the judge-interpreter.

According to pragmatic cognitivism, the judge-interpreter proceeds in the ordinary conversation way through linguistic "understanding" ("reasonable uptake") of legal texts; and only if something goes wrong, only if some drawback shows up, she turns to the reflexive, speculative attitude inherent to "interpretation". The judge-interpreter, here, is an intermittent speculator.

According to non-cognitivism, on the contrary, every activity concerning the determination of the meaning of a legal text to be applied to a case at hand, be it understanding or interpretation proper, is performed in the shadow of a reflexive, speculative, background attitude. The judge-interpreter, here, is a continuous speculator. Linguistic understanding, so far as it goes, is never a purely spontaneous undertaking; it is instead, so to speak, always by design. A judge never simply understands, but always also decides to stay with her understanding, if sufficient systemic reasons grant that course of action. This design dimension of understanding, which in hermeneutical theory is captured by the idea of the "postulate of reflexivity", totally escapes from Marmor's view.

[44] This conclusion finds support in many passages by Marmor: see, e.g., Marmor 2011: 151, 154, 157; Marmor 2014: chaps. 5–6. In chap. 6, Marmor deals with constitutional interpretation in a thoroughly interpretivist way.

[45] Marmor 2014: 11–12.

5.2 Three Levels of "Meaning" of the Source-Sentences

From the standpoint of a pragmatic interpretivist theory of judicial interpretation, the proper way of accounting for the several levels of meaning of any given source-sentence requires to single out the following three items: (i) sentence meaning, (ii) explicit systemic meaning, and, with regards to the full communication content of an institutional (legislative or constitutional) speech act, (iii) implicit (or implicated) systemic meaning. *Sentence meaning* is the literal, conventional, a-contextual meaning, or semantic content, of the legal provision. *Explicit systemic meaning* is the meaning (assertive content, prescriptive content) of the source-sentence, from the standpoint of the legal system and the proper way of interpreting its provisions. Explicit systemic meaning may be different from sentence meaning. *Implicated systemic meaning*, finally, is the meaning or communication content that is implicated by the explicit systemic meaning of the legal provision on the basis of integration maxims, or integration directives. These maxims, so far as law is concerned, typically include the directives of analogical reasoning, *a fortiori* reasoning, *a contrario* or *e silentio* reasoning, and naturalistic reasoning.

5.3 The Shared Maxims of the Judges-Legislature Conversation

Legal pragmatics looks for the shared maxims of legal conversations. So far as the JLC is concerned, such an inquiry must, first of all, get rid of the conversational metaphor. As I said in passing, two properties makes of JLC a very far cry from OC. First, the JLC is a "conversation" with a dummy (the legislature) that cannot reply, at least not immediately: indeed, a new law is needed to cancel any "wrong" judicial interpretation, and such law needs being interpreted in turn. The JLC really is a game that judges play with authoritative texts. Second, if there is something that judges (lawyers, jurists, and, in a presumptive sense, the legislature and the legislators) do share in the game, this is a set of legal materials, provided by legislatures, and, most important to the present purpose, a toolbox, which is made of a set of interpretive directives, maxims, canons, etc.

Now, if we cast a Gricean glance inside the toolbox, we will see that the toolbox contains interpretive maxims of two different kinds: first-order maxims and second-order maxims.

First-order maxims correspond to the interpretive canons, techniques, methods, etc. circulating in the legal culture, handed down by tradition, and, sometimes, even sanctioned by positive law. They form a contingent set, to be identified for any given legal culture and legal order. First-order maxims identify *prima facie* correct ways of interpreting source-sentences. Usually, such a set includes such maxims like the literal meaning maxim, the original intention of the historical legislature maxim, the teleological maxim, the coherence maxim, the completeness maxim, the comparative law maxim, the *per absurdum* maxim, the equity maxim, the naturalistic maxim, the analogical (interpretive) maxim, the *a fortiori* (interpretive) maxim, the *a contrario* (interpretive) maxim, etc..[46]

Second-order maxims are, roughly speaking, what Gricean conversational maxims are to OC. They establish interpreters' duties and entitlements in the use of first-order maxims. At a very general and abstract level, the second-order maxims that rule upon judicial interpretation in our legal cultures seem to be, roughly, the following five: (i) the No-Preposterousness Maxim; (ii) the Combination Maxim; (iii) the Precisification Maxim; (iv) the Resource Selection Maxim; (v) the Integration Maxim.

The No-Preposterousness Maxim, or, as we may also say, the Principle of Prudent Interpretation, runs as follows: judges are empowered with the maximum interpretive discretion, compatible with the need to present their interpretive outcomes as imposed by, or at any rate drawn from, legal materials, according to the principle *Iudex iudicare debet secundum ius* ("The judge ought to adjudicate according to the law"). By the way, this is, apparently, a very different maxim from the Gricean "principle of interpretive co-operation". Indeed, it allows for a wide range of interpretive attitudes and goals, some of which – at least from certain perspectives – would seem no "co-operative" at all. For instance, Italian judges in the late 1960s interpreted statutory law according to a principle of cooperation not with the actual legislature, but, rather, with the "good legislature", that is to say, with a legislature that was presumed to make laws that were respectful of formal justice, logical consistency, instrumental rationality, non-redundancy, linguistic rigor, systemic arrangement, and completeness.[47]

Like in the Gricean framework, the other four maxims of judicial interpretation are as many maxims of detail: they entitle judges to specific courses of action, within the (loose) limits set by the principle of prudent interpretation.[48]

The Combination Maxim allows each judge to combine first-order maxims to form the interpretive code that, in the light of the case at hand, the maxim of prudent interpretation, and relevant social axiologies, she thinks to be the best in order to present an interpretive output as the legally correct one.

The Precisification Maxim allows each judge to precisify on-going, traditional, first order maxims, in order to adapt them to the decisional needs of the case at hand, always within the limits of the principle of prudent interpretation.

The Resource Selection Maxim allows the judge to select the interpretive resources needed to apply the previously selected first order maxims in such a way

[46] First-order maxims do not stay all on the same plane. A maxim like the literal meaning maxim is endowed with interpretive efficiency: it may be used to translate a source-sentence into some explicit norm; contrariwise, the use of, say, the maxim of coherence is to select the outputs of interpretive efficient maxims. But for the present purpose, this issue may be left aside.

[47] See Bobbio 1971: 243–249.

[48] By way of a thought experiment, I have imagined the maxims of a Gricean code of judicial interpretation in Chiassoni 1999: 95–97.

as to favour the identification of what she considers the legally correct interpretive output, within the usual limits of the principle of prudent interpretation.

The Integration Maxim, finally, allows the judge to add new first-order maxims to the traditional toolbox, provided the principle of prudent interpretation is respected.

5.4 The Context of Source-Sentences

The context, in judicial interpretation of any piece of written law, is not a situation of physical contiguity between speaker and hearer, making available to both a set of shared information, or shared data, as the standard pragmatics of OC maintains. Due to the peculiarity of the JLC, here the context is the set of data that the judge-interpreter herself selects as relevant to the interpretation of the source-sentences at hand. These data, as we have seen from the previous point, are nothing else but interpretive resources. They are identified on the basis of the directives of the code that has been selected. To be sure, among the prominent factors that bear on the determination of the context of any given source-sentence feature the interests to which the interpreter pays allegiance: material or ideal interests, including principles of justice, religious beliefs, ideologies about the proper role of the judiciary according to the constitution, etc.

5.5 The Pragmatic Enrichment of Source-Sentences

From the standpoint of the communication model of legislation adopted by Marmor, as we have seen, there is really almost no room for pragmatic enrichment in JLC. Such a conclusion, however, follows from a Procrustean projection of OC, with its rules of pragmatic enrichment, on the phenomenon of judicial interpretation, where, I claim, an altogether different sort of "conversation" is at stake. From the standpoint of an interpretivist pragmatics, contrariwise, pragmatic enrichment is a function of the contingent first-order interpretation maxims, as selected and played according to second-order maxims.

5.6 Legal Implicatures

Once we get rid of the OC Procrustean prejudice (together, I am afraid, with the communication model as understood by Marmor), once we combine pragmatics with interpretivism, legal implicatures are not anymore a weird phenomenon, something which baffles the neat governance of OC maxims. They are governed, instead, by first-order maxims concerning the identification of "implicit" or "implicated" law, as selected and played by judges according to the second-order maxims.[49]

References

Barberis, M. (2014). *Introduzione allo studio del diritto*. Torino: Giappichelli.
Bobbio, N. (1971). Le bon législateur. *Logique et analyse, 53–54*, 243–249.
Carrió, G. R. (1965). *Notas sobre derecho y lenguaje*. Buenos Aires: Abeledo Perrot.
Chiassoni, P. (1999). Interpretive games: Statutory construction through Gricean eyes. *Analisi e diritto, 1999*, 79–99.
Chiassoni, P. (2008). On the wrong track: Andrei Marmor on legal positivism, interpretation, and easy cases. *Ratio Juris, 21*(2), 248–267.
Chiassoni, P. (2009). *L'indirizzo analítico nella filosofía del diritto. I. Da Bentham a Kelsen*. Torino: Giappichelli.
Chiassoni, P. (2011). *Técnicas de interpretación jurídica. Breviario para juristas*. Madrid/Barcelona/Buenos Aires: Marcial Pons.
Chiassoni, P. (2014). *Legal interpretation without truth*, on file with "Revus", 2016.
Dascal, M., & Wroblewski, J. (1988). Transparency and doubt: Understanding and interpretation in pragmatics and in law. *Law and Philosophy, 7*, 203–224.
Diciotti, E. (2003). *L'ambigua alternativa tra cognitivismo e scetticismo interpretativo*. Siena: Università degli Studi di Siena, Dipartimento di Scienze Storiche, Giuridiche, Politiche e Sociali, Working Paper 45.
Dworkin, R. (1977). The model of rules I. In: Id., *Taking rights seriously*, Cambridge, MA: Harvard University Press.
Endicott, T. (1994). Putting interpretation in its place. *Law and Philosophy, 13*, 451–479.
Endicott, T. (2014). Law and language. In E. N. Zalta (Ed.), *The Stanford encyclopedia of philosophy* (Spring 2014 Edition). URL=http://plato.stanford.edu/archives/spr2014/entries/law-language/
Guastini, R. (2010). *Nuevos estudios sobre la interpretación*. Bogotá: Externado de Colombia.
Guastini, R. (2011). Rule-scepticism restated. In L. Green & B. Leiter (Eds.), *Oxford studies in philosophy of law* (pp. 138–140). Oxford: Oxford University Press.
Hart, H. L. A. (1956). Discretion. *Harvard Law Review, 127*(2013), 652–665.
Hart, H. L. A. (1958). Positivism and the separation of law and morals. In Hart 1983 (pp. 49–87).
Hart, H. L. A. (1961). *The concept of law*. Oxford: Oxford University Press. Third Edition, 2012.
Hart, H. L. A. (1977). *American jurisprudence through English eyes: The nightmare and the noble dream*. In Hart 1983 (pp. 123–144).
Hart, H. L. A. (1983). *Essays in jurisprudence and philosophy*. Oxford: Clarendon.
Iglesias Vila, M. (1999). *El Problema de la discreción judicial. Una aproximación al conocimiento jurídico*. Madrid: Centro de Estudios Políticos y Constitucionales.
Laporta, F. (2007). *El imperio de la ley. Una visión actual*. Madrid: Trotta.
Lifante Vidal, I. (1989). Dos conceptos de discrecionalidad jurídica. *Doxa, 25*, 413–439.
Marmor, A. (2005). *Interpretation and legal theory* (2nd Rev. ed.). Oxford: Hart Publishing.
Marmor, A. (2008). The pragmatics of legal language. *Ratio Juris, 21*, 423–452.
Marmor, A. (2011). *Philosophy of law*. Princeton/Oxford: Princeton University Press.
Marmor, A. (2014). *The language of law*. Oxford: Oxford University Press.

[49] A first version of the present paper was presented at the "Oxford-Girona-Genoa Seminar in Jurisprudence", Oxford, April 10, 2015. I wish to thank the participants for their queries.

Ruiz Manero, J. (1990). *Jurisdicción y normas. Dos estudios sobre función jurisdiccional y teoría del derecho*. Madrid: Centro de Estudios Constitucionales.
Schauer, F. (1984). Easy cases. *Southern California Law Review, 58*, 399–440.
Wróblewski, J. (1985). *Constitución y teoría general de la interpretación jurídica*. Madrid: Civitas.
Wróblewski, J. (1992). In Z. Bankowski & N. MacCormick (Eds.), *The judicial application of law*. Dordrecht: Kluwer Academic Publishers.

Doubting Legal Language: Interpretive Skepticism and Legal Practice

Nicola Muffato

Abstract The present paper revisits and critically reconstructs one central tenet of interpretive legal skepticism, which I will label the "equivocity thesis". According to this thesis, each statutory provision and judicial opinion can be constructed or interpreted in many ways, due to the plurality of the admissible hermeneutic techniques, methods, doctrines, and normative theories ("plurality thesis") and their equal legal value ("parity thesis"): this leaves the interpreter with the discretional power to choose the legal solution he deems more correct ("normative unbindingness thesis"). The main purpose of this essay is an investigation of the scope of these theses and their philosophical and rhetorical/strategic relations with a more general semiotic skepticism, according to which the belief that communication requires both mutual understanding and shared linguistic meanings is unjustified. More precisely, I will first explore how interpretive legal skepticism can be grounded on Quine's and Davidson's indeterminist arguments (Sect. 3) and on deconstructionism (Sect. 4), and then test the possibility of employing a criticism of these conceptions against interpretive legal skepticism, based on Wittgensteinian arguments and developed along various lines by "practice-based" conceptions of meaning (Sect. 5).

Keywords Meaning-skepticism • Legal realism • Critical legal studies • Interpretation • Practice-based conceptions

1 Introduction

Skepticism is a philosophical attitude that consists in doubting the possibility of justifying theoretical or practical commitments. It can be global or local, lead to a denial of beliefs and practical attitudes, to a suspension of judgment (ἐποχή) or to

N. Muffato (✉)
IUSLIT Department, University of Trieste, Trieste, Italy
e-mail: nmuffato@units.it

F. Poggi, A. Capone (eds.), *Pragmatics and Law*, Perspectives in Pragmatics, Philosophy & Psychology 10, DOI 10.1007/978-3-319-44601-1_6

non-deductive reasoning[1]. Communicational (or semiotic) skepticism treats the belief that communication requires both *mutual understanding* and *shared linguistic meanings* as unjustified. Yet, if there are no independent foundations/justifications for this claim, there are not even foundations/justifications for our linguistic uses: meanings turn out to be necessarily indeterminate, while understanding a piece of oral or written communication would be a solipsistic act (or status) which depends entirely on the particularistic operant conditioning, psycho-physic predispositions, and intentionality (beliefs and preferences) of each individual immersed in a social environment.

In this essay I will focus on the relations between this general "external" skepticism about communication and one of its local "internal" varieties[2]: interpretive legal skepticism. The latter conception transplants the doubt about mutual understanding and meaning sharing into the analysis of legal language, denying the determinacy of legal norms and the objectivity of legal interpretation. The skeptic about legal interpretation relaxes the concept of justification and emphasizes the discretion of the individual interpreter/adjudicator, who becomes either the *master* or an *automatism* in the process of signification – depending on one's preference for a free-will or deterministic conception of agency.

Such a view, however, is very rarely pushed to the extremes of an "anything goes" claim: discretion is conceptually linked with justification – even when the latter is intended in a weak sense – so it can never be reduced to pure arbitrariness. But the existence of hermeneutic boundaries obliges the skeptic about legal interpretation to solve a tension between her use of the indeterminacy arguments and the necessity to provide a positive account of these very boundaries. In fact, in order to face this challenge, it is not sufficient for the skeptic to invoke the causal determinacy of the interpretive decisions as opposed to their justificatory indeterminacy: it is necessary either to explain how there can be *unjustified* legal interpretations and solutions or to explain away the very concept of justification without giving up other useful notions (*in primis*, that of "*ratio decidendi*"[3]).

According to Talbot Taylor, the force of skeptical rhetoric rests on a characteristic of the forms of theorizing it serves to criticize: the implicit assumption that our linguistic intuitions, what we consider commonsensical platitudes about language and express through practical/pre-theoretical meta-discourses (discourses about other discourses, meaning, understanding, etc.), can be treated as general (albeit folk) *empirical* hypotheses – justifiably affirmable only if and when certain underlying "facts of language" obtain[4] – which the theories of language should test, fix,

[1] For an interesting criticism of skepticism about practical reason in ethics, literature and law, see Nussbaum 1994.

[2] I take the distinction between internal and external skepticism from Dworkin 1986, 78–80.

[3] Note, however, that in many legal systems there is no a general obligation to give reasons for a judicial decision. For a survey, see Dyzenhaus and Taggart 2008.

[4] For example: the communicational and cognitive "relevance principle"; the homogeneous, "negative" meaning holism of an abstract *langue* internalized in the minds of language users; the existence of objective mind-independent thoughts that language users can grasp learning language (see

improve and make systematic at the level of theoretical/intellectual meta-discourse[5]. As the author correctly remarks, «there is an *internal relation* between treating [such] locution[s] as [...] empirical hypothes[e]s and the rhetorical opposition between believing and doubting [their] justification»[6]. The main target of doubt is the idea of the determinacy of meaning and interpretation, where «Determinate [...] means settled, complete in and of itself, and therefore in no need of further elaboration or addition. Determinate rules perform as barriers or walls on which is written "beyond this point interpretation cannot go"»[7].

Were Taylor's diagnosis correct, interpretive legal skepticism could be seen as a reaction against the claim that there are some recognizable, underlying facts about legal language (which we can grasp through our common sense and express through practical meta-discourses) that fix and determine the meanings of constitutional or statutory provisions and judicial opinions. Both the "internal" and the "external" skeptic bring into question the theoretical admissibility of such a view. But note the difference: the external skeptic tries to exploit the similarities between ordinary language and legal language in order to export her indeterminacy arguments from the philosophical analysis of the former to that of the latter; the "internal" skeptic, on the contrary, argues that since language in legal contexts is pragmatically very different from natural languages as used in conversations and written communications[8] (see *infra* §4), we'd better give up our intuitions (and practical meta-discourses) or observations about the latter and replace them with empirically testable claims about the former[9].

In the following sections, I will focus on the philosophical and rhetorical contact points between general communicational skepticism and interpretive legal skepticism. I will try to highlight the main theses defended by these positions, their similarities and the relations they entertain with the idea that legal interpretation and application face limits that transcend theorizing about the language of constitutions, statutes and judicial opinions, and finally depend on the education of future legal professionals.

---

the next sections) or of a transcendent canonical text that constraints interpretation. See *infra*, §§ 3–4.

[5] See Taylor 1992, 14–15.

[6] Taylor 1992, 17. See also Quine 1975, 67: «[The skeptic] is quite within his rights in assuming science in order to refute science; this, if carried out, would be a straightforward argument by *reductio ad absurdum*. I am only making the point that skeptical doubts are scientific doubts».

[7] Fish 1988, 885.

[8] See Jori 1993, 2119–2121. Jori, however, rejects any kind of skeptical conclusion.

[9] What the skeptic must avoid is replacing intuitions about ordinary language with intuitions about legal language and treating the latter as empirical hypotheses: for this would give rise to a second-order skepticism about the grounds of first-order skeptical conclusions.

2 Humpty Dumpty in Robes? On the Scope of Interpretive Legal Skepticism

I shall begin by trying to characterize some of the kinds of skepticism haunting jurisprudence and legal practice. To be fair, this task was already faced by Herbert L.A. Hart in chapter VII of his seminal work, *The Concept of Law*. There, he distinguished five main varieties of "rule-scepticism"[10]: (1) the idea that talk about legal rules is a myth created to hidden the truth that law consists solely of judicial decisions and the prediction of them; (2) the thesis according to which there are not duty imposing legal rules but – once again – just judicial decisions and jurisprudential predictions of those decisions; (3) the contention that it is impossible to circumscribe the area of open texture of legal concepts and rules; (4) the assertion that in many cases judges decide in an intuitive way and only after deciding they pretend they acted on a rule; (5) the idea that final judicial decisions are infallible.

However, one need not be a legal realist to remark that Hart's reconstruction of legal skepticism is at least incomplete (if not to say uncharitable), and its subsequent dismissal too quick. Leaving aside Hart's option for not taking into account what Jerome Frank called "fact-skepticism", legal realists (followed by critical legal theorists) developed at least a sixth skeptical thesis – call it the "equivocity thesis"[11]. The equivocity thesis results from combining three ideas. First, *each* legal text (constitutional and statutory provisions, international treaties, administrative regulations, written judicial opinions, etc.) *can always* be constructed or interpreted *in several* (at least two) manners, in *each* context of application of the relative norm, by following the ordinary linguistic rules and employing the variety of alternative interpretive methods[12] and techniques[13], legal doctrines[14] and normative theories[15] available to lawyers in their interpretive community. I shall call this premise the "plurality thesis". The plurality thesis doesn't exclude by itself the possibility of elaborating hierarchies of interpretive methods (and outcomes), but it commits to

[10] See Hart 1994, 136–141.

[11] I choose this particular label to avoid using here the more general term "indeterminacy", which covers different phenomena such as vagueness, linguistic ambiguity, contestability. The literature on legal indeterminacy is vast: see Yablon 1985; Kress 1989; D'Amato 1990; Drahos and Parker 1991; Rosenfeld 1992; Bix 1993; Kutz 1993; Coleman and Leiter 1993–1994; Fowler 1995; Perry 1995–1996; Lawson 1996; Tushnet 1996; Solum 1987, 1999; Endicott 2001.

[12] E.g., canons of construction such as the "plain meaning" rule (where the plain meaning is inferred from statutory definitions, case law, administrative regulations, legislative history), the "whole act" rule, the rule to avoid surplusage, the presumption of consistent usage and meaningful variation, the contextual "*noscitur a sociis*", "*eiusdem generis*" and "*expressio unius*".

[13] E.g., distinguishing, overruling, and the creation of legal fictions and presumptions to avoid applying the plain meaning rule (see Gottlieb 1968, 44).

[14] I hereby mention just some potentially conflicting doctrines: "*caveat emptor*" vs. "*caveat venditor*"; "castle doctrine" vs. "duty to retreat"; "*quantum meruit*" vs. "*quantum valebat*"; "spider in the web" vs. "*lex loci*".

[15] E.g., textualism, originalism, instrumentalism, "moral reading" theory, "living tree" doctrine. Of course, each version of these "theories" of interpretation can be articulated in several ways.

the thought that it is always possible to reconstruct many competing hierarchies[16]. Second, all the interpretive outcomes obtained by employing the admitted legal arguments, methods and doctrines are always *equally justified* – call it the "parity thesis". Third: since all interpretive outcomes are equally justified, the judge – more generally: the adjudicator – is, from a legal point of view, normatively free to choose among them the one she prefers to solve the case she's facing. I shall label this third claim the "(legal) normative unbindingness thesis". Note how the unbindingness thesis follows from the parity thesis (and the *non liquet* prohibition).

It is important to remark that the equivocity thesis is intended to avoid a kind of anti-skeptical reply that warms the cockles of the moderate's heart. The objection at stake is the one Hart directed against the third and fifth variety of rule-skepticism: even if legal concepts are unavoidably affected by a more or less extended (actual or potential) vagueness, which allows interpreters to exercise their discretion in applying the rule, there are always "easy" cases that fall under the settled "core" of these concepts. In such easy cases «subsumption and the drawing of a syllogistic conclusion [...] characterize the nerve of the reasoning involved in determining what is the right thing to do»[17]. The application of legal language, concepts, and rules presupposes the logical possibility of error or incorrect application: if the judge could always resort to her discretion and never be wrong in interpreting and applying legal rules, her decisions could never count as correct uses of an already practiced legal language, as correct applications of previously existing legal concepts and rules. Her position would be very similar to that adopted by Humpty Dumpty in Lewis Carroll's tale *Through the Looking Glass*. In sum, a judge, a lawyer, a legal interpreter/adjudicator would become a sort of Humpty Dumpty in robes.

In a skeptical account of legal interpretation, however, the indeterminacy of legal language depends more on equivocity than on open texture[18]. While the latter is a property of concepts, the former is a property of meaningful actions or, for the case, their symbolic traces and marks: written provisions and opinions. A text is equivocal when it can be interpreted in at least two ways, when it carries at least two meanings – which can moreover be gradually or combinatorially, actually or potentially vague. True, the great majority of concepts or combination of concepts (meanings) have a settled core of clear and relevant conditions of application: the problem is that any interpreter can always ascribe more than one meaning to each legal text.

Nonetheless, several readings of the equivocity thesis are possible, depending on the scope of the unbindingness thesis. According to a first, strong reading, the plurality and parity of interpretive techniques, methods, doctrines and normative

---

[16] Just think about Hart's preference for literal meaning (as limited by the common sense and reasonableness assumptions of laymen and lawyers), Lon Fuller's insistence on functional interpretation, and Ronald Dworkin's claims that statutory construction and the interpretation of precedent must respect historical consistency and coherence.

[17] Hart 1994, 127. For a more qualified statement, see Hart 1983b, 105–108.

[18] See Llewellyn 1931a, b, 1230–1231, 1238–1239; Llewellyn 1949–1950, 395–396; Llewellyn 1951, 66–69, 72–75; Gray 1921, 260–261; Ross 1958, §29; Wróblewski 1992, 105–107; Tushnet 1996, 344–349; Chiassoni 2000, 2005; Guastini 2006, 2011. *Contra*, see Hart 1983a, 7–8.

theories allow an interpreter to reach almost whatever hermeneutic outcome she likes, so that she's *de iure* unbound. As we shall see, this view is very similar to some radical skeptical theses about communication. According to a second, moderate reading, the interpreter's freedom is limited and relative to a set of admissible interpretive techniques and outcomes, even when this set is extremely wide: there are always interpretive outcomes – let us call them "easy negative interpretive solutions" – an adjudicator cannot justify resorting to the admitted legal arguments[19].

This distinction can be refined once two other aspects are considered: time and uncertainty about the availability of some interpretive instruments. Both the strong and the moderate readings can indeed be understood synchronically or diachronically, and as taking or not into account the fuzziness of the set of interpretive instruments. A synchronic, radical version of the strong unbindingness thesis affirms that whenever (and wherever) a subject happens to interpret a legal text, she can reach and justify any hermeneutic outcomes she likes. To my knowledge, despite the rhetorical exaggerations of some authors, no one has really ever maintained this conception: nonetheless, it has been the main target of anti-skeptical criticism. A diachronic version of the strong reading – which can be reconciled with a synchronic version of the moderate reading – says instead that even if the interpreter's normative freedom is not absolute, the set of interpretive instruments and contextual constraints is both fuzzy and historically variable[20]: synchronically, there are easy negative interpretive decisions; but diachronically, even these decisions may become hard – that is susceptible to multiple competing justifications.

The equivocity of every legal text is generally defended on the grounds of the following arguments: (1) the identification of the relevant text to be interpreted is not a mechanical operation: it is neither conventional nor customary, but results form an interpretive decision and consists in the reconstruction of the appropriate context (in a broad sense, covering the "co-text", the "inter-text" constituted by other statutes, the constitution and past decisions, and the extra-linguistic context)[21] for textual interpretation; (2) the meaning of the relevant text (thus reconstructed) is neither conventional nor customary: it depends on the decision to apply one (or some) of the relevant interpretive techniques, methods, doctrines and/or theories admitted in a legal community, which are in turn related to the interpretive choices that lead to the selection of the relevant context; (3) both contextual reconstruction and textual interpretation are ultimately based on strategic, political and ethical choices; (4) in the appropriate circumstances, it is possible to enrich the set of

---

[19] I believe that, at least synchronically, negative easy interpretive decisions are very rarely relevant in legal practice, and even less so in judicial decision-making. Advocates and officials form a sort of barrier against the discussion in courtrooms of cases which would be easily dismissed (or sanctioned as *lites temerariae*).

[20] See Tushnet 1996, 345–349.

[21] See Stone 1964, 35–36; Stone 1985, 124–129 (as regards the difficulty of distinguishing between holding and *obiter dicta*); Altman 1986 (as regards the identification of the relevant precedent); Poggi 2013 (as regards the identification of the text to be interpreted in statutory construction).

interpretive options questioning the reasonableness of the exclusion of some hermeneutic techniques and outcomes.

Does this mean that interpretive agreement is impossible? Legal realists and critical legal theorists have an answer to this concern: despite the plurality thesis, lawyers can *converge* on the same interpretive outcomes; but in virtue of the parity and normative unbindingness thesis, this convergence cannot amount to an agreement or a consensus determined by communal interpretive methods and doctrines alone. So they are committed to denying the very existence of (legal) meaning conventions or hierarchies of meaning-rules and interpretive methods shared by lawyers – especially by judges. Moreover, since these theorists also tend to reject the very possibility of an objective (true) morality which determines the proper solutions to practical problems, the kind of convergence in question can only depend on social, cultural, educational, ideological, economical and psychological factors and their dynamics[22].

Two well-known, general ways of making sense of this conclusion are the following. The first one calls for a reduction of the normativity of meaning to factual properties of human behavior: this aim can be pursued by naturalizing legal meaning and jurisprudence[23]. Brian Leiter presents the main consequence of this methodological turn in the following way: «Why not replace […] the "sterile" foundational program of justifying some legal outcomes on the basis of the applicable legal reasons, with a descriptive/explanatory account of what input (that is, what combinations of facts and reasons) produces what output (i.e. what judicial decision)?»[24]. The task of a naturalized jurisprudence – whose epistemological correctness is checked against utility and pragmatic considerations – consists thus in providing an accurate explanation of social and psychological factors which fall into causally determined patterns of behavior in order to allow lawyers (and laymen) to predict judicial decisions. The second way of making sense of meaning indeterminacy calls for a deconstruction of legal texts and talk, a critical enterprise that analyzes and makes explicit the categories, procedures, decisions, power relations and tensions by which these texts are constituted. I shall explore both strategies in the next two sections.

---

[22] Jules Coleman and Brian Leiter (1993–1994, part I, §A) presented this point by distinguishing 1) the determinacy of *reasons* from the determinacy of *causes* and 2) the legal indeterminacy from the extra-legal determinacy. According to the authors, the fact that legal rules and principles are not sufficient to justify or to cause court's decisions doesn't mean that these decisions cannot be predicted by applying a scientific explanation of extra-legal causes. More about indeterminacy in Leiter 2007, 10–12.

[23] See Leiter 2007, especially chapters 1 and 5 and the Postscript to Part II.

[24] Leiter 2007, 41. Leiter explores the vantage points and shortcomings of the analogy between legal realism and the project of a naturalized jurisprudence at 40–46; 54–58.

3 Radical Legal Interpreters? On the Illusion of Sharing Legal Meanings

The project of semantic naturalism developed by Willard v. O. Quine stems from his criticism of the analytic/synthetic distinction and the notion of synonymy, which led him to focus on the interdependence of meaning and belief (conceived in a behaviorist fashion[25]) and pursue a flight from intensions. Given the theoretical necessity of identifying simultaneously the meaning and beliefs expressed by our utterances in order to understand a piece of communication, Quine proposed employing a methodology connected with the thought-experiment of "radical translation"[26]. The task of translating an unknown language must begin with spotting patterns of stimulations that prompt the language users' attitudes of assent or dissent to occasion sentences. However, since not all sentences are directly tied to invariant stimulation patterns, the theorist must rely also on collateral information, dependent on parallel and prior observations, and on "analytical hypotheses" to construct her translation manual. According to Quine, even if the conjectures about the meaning of native utterances ultimately rely on observation sentences, the freedom of the linguist in formulating her tentative translation is enormous. Of course, this freedom will be limited by some methodological constraints: continuity, charity (based on more or less refined psychology and empathy), simplicity. But since the room for a different analytical hypothesis is still substantial, no matter how much evidence fits the translation manual, it will always be possible to elaborate an alternative translation manual that can account equally well for the same evidence. The meaning of a sentence, then, depends on the choice of a translation manual, a choice which is limited only by behavioral evidence and pragmatic considerations (so called "indeterminacy of translation").

Quine extends the results of his theses to all linguistic practices. Radical indeterminacy is thus a necessary feature of our language, but it doesn't lead to nihilism: «Indeterminacy means not that there is no acceptable translation, but that there are many. A good manual of translation fits all checkpoints of verbal behavior, and what does not surface at any checkpoint can do no harm»[27]. Quine's main object of criticism is the idea that communication requires "sameness of meaning". The point of his argument is that in order to understand each other, there's no need for people to share a translation manual or a background theory of meaning: it is sufficient that the same empirical cues be available to language users «under publicly recognizable circumstances»[28]. Quine is also careful to distinguish *underdetermination* from *indeterminacy*, arguing that the latter is not a consequence of the former. The difference is the following: while (in his opinion) every theory of nature is underdetermined

[25] See Quine 1987.

[26] See Quine 1960, ch. II; Quine 1987; Quine 1992, ch. III.

[27] See Quine 1987.

[28] Quine 1992, 27.

because of the relative meagerness of observational data[29], a translation manual (a theory of meaning for a language) «remains indeterminate, even relative to the chosen theory of nature»[30]. In fact, two translators can disagree on the translation of a sentence even when their observations coincide.

Were we to apply these ideas to legal language, we might conclude that statutory construction and the interpretation of precedent are radically indeterminate: two legal interpreters could build different and incompatible doctrines or theories (the jurisprudential equivalent of translation manuals) to ascribe meaning to statutes and written opinions (the jurisprudential equivalent of the unknown language) even if they were to rely on the same behavioral evidence coming from legislators, officials, lawyers, and laymen[31] – an evidence, moreover, which is very meager and presents few "behavioral checkpoints". However, a difference between, say, two judicial reconstructions of the same *ratio decidendi* and, more importantly, the legal solutions they justify, would not prevent legal practice from working: in order to make sense of legal interpretation, legal theory doesn't require to assume a Platonic foundationalist stance – the idea that legal communication consists in the sharing of semantic content between the framers or legislators and the officials (and between the officials and the barristers and/or citizens): insofar as the proposed reconstructions and solutions fit the evidence offered by past behavior, there's no need to worry about meaning skepticism.

Donald Davidson accepts many Quinean insights – *in primis* meaning holism – in elaborating his own methodology and research program. According to this author too, sharing linguistic rules or conventions is neither a necessary nor a sufficient condition for successful communication[32], as is showed by the phenomenon of malapropism[33]. Malapropisms are mistakes about meaning, misuses of words by confusion with others of a similar pronunciation or written form. Since the frequency of linguistic errors and deviations from standard usage doesn't seem to affect the very possibility of understanding, Davidson infers that our interpretive practices do not require conformity to a previously established meaning convention. In order to communicate, language users must be able to construct a theory of interpretation for each idiolect by collecting a finite base of oral or written sentences used by the interpreted subject and formulating hypotheses about her intended meanings in a way that tends to maximize the similarity between the webs of beliefs of the inter-

[29] The underdetermination thesis has been efficaciously criticized in Laudan 1990. Laudan distinguishes several versions of this thesis, showing that «neither logical *compatibility* with the evidence nor logical *derivability* of the evidence is sufficient to establish that a theory exhibiting such empirical compatibility and derivability is rationally acceptable» (276), that is, that the theory is empirically supported by or explains the evidence.

[30] Quine 1987, 10. The same point is made in Davidson 1991, 164.

[31] A behaviorist conception of legal interpretation and adjudication is developed by Underhill Moore and Gilbert Sussman (1931). The authors argue that once it has been discovered a regularity in the behavior of the officials belonging to a specific institution, "measured" the deviations from this regularity and determined at which point the officials intervene to correct the deviation, it is possible to predict which deviations will cause the reactions of the officials.

[32] See Davidson 1985.

[33] See Davidson 1986.

preter and the interpreted subject (such methodological constraint is called "principle of charity")[34]. To individuate the relations between idiolects, Davidson – following Quine – proposes to map the sentences held true by the language users resorting to a Tarskian-style convention T. The application of this recursive device generates T-sentences, which correspond to interpretive hypotheses expressing extensional equivalences between sentences belonging to different idiolects[35]. According to Davidson, then, interpreting another person's speech acts consists in elaborating a "passing theory" of truth for an idiolect.

However, as in the case of radical translation, the ascription of an idiolect to a speaker is always indeterminate: it is always possible to assign different truth-conditions to the speaker's utterances[36]. Davidson maintains that interpreting is a process that links a "first meaning" to the speaker's intended meaning, but he denies the conventionality of the first meaning: from his point of view, the latter can amount to a provisional and independent *ad hoc* assumption, grounded in the general knowledge of the world (encyclopedic knowledge) and some reasonable expectations – governed by the principle of charity – about the communication partner's behavior. This specification, which can be seen as a qualified version of the unbindingness thesis, is made to avoid falling into Humpty Dumpty's extreme subjectivist semantics: even if a sentence were to mean what the interpreted subject intended it to mean, this intention could count as a communicative intention only insofar as it satisfies a reasonableness requirement and manifests itself in providing the interpreter with sufficient linguistic hints related to the context of the utterance. In ordinary conversations, the speaker commits to making the interlocutor adjust her prior theory of meaning (for the speaker's idiolect) until it overlaps with the passing theory she intends the interlocutor to use. What successful communication really needs is the kind of convergence produced by the mutual adjustments of previously independent (in the sense of not being shared) theories of meaning. However, according to Davidson, the ability to interpret, correct, re-interpret a sentence (and so on) doesn't involve the mastery of a linguistic code: it is just – to use a phrase from Quine – a "social art" performed by substantiating very broad principles of rationality in each actual context[37]. In the end, the platitude about the existence of a common (shared) language proves to be a philosophical myth.

Davidson's radical semantic conception of ordinary language interpretation seems to have as its legal counterpart a pragmatic contextualist view about legal interpretation. In fact, a prominent legal scholar such as Alf Ross is very clear in

---

[34] See Davidson 1973.

[35] See Davidson 1967, 1970.

[36] See Davidson 1970, 186: «Quine is right, I think, in holding that an important degree of indeterminacy will remain after all the evidence is in; a number of significantly different theories of truth will fit the evidence equally well». Davidson, however, distances himself from Quine's "proximal" theory of meaning, which led him to radical semiotic skepticism, in a later essay: see Davidson 1990. A clear limit of Davidson's communicational skepticism is his assumption of a massive agreement in beliefs about the world between the interpreter and the interpreted subject.

[37] Davidson, however, does not undervalue the practical (as opposed to the theoretical) importance of other factors, such as time, opportunity, linguistic conditioning, intuition, luck, taste and sympathy (see Davidson 1985, 24–25).

asserting that legal «interpretation has no independent linguistic starting point but [...] from the beginnings it is determined by pragmatic considerations in the form of "common sense"»[38]. This can be translated in Davidson's vocabulary by saying that first meaning depends on the reasonable expectations of the interpreter and the relevant details of the context. Although Ross – unlike Davidson – doesn't deny mutual understanding in ordinary linguistic interactions and explicitly accepts the conventionality of ordinary language syntax and semantics[39], he emphasizes the irrelevance of customary or conventional "literal" meaning for the purposes of statutory construction: «One often comes across the view that statutory interpretation can or must take as its starting point the ordinary meaning of the words as warranted by usage. This view is illusory. No such meaning exists. Only the context and the desire to find "good" or "reasonable" meaning in relation to a given situation determines the meaning of the individual words. But the function of the context is often so taken for granted that it escapes attention»[40]. Note how the author refers to the "contextual determination" of meaning. This thought, however, is further précised in a skeptical fashion – more akin to Quine's and Davidson's indeterminist conclusions.

Ross admits that reasonableness and common sense are limits to judicial discretion[41], but he says that these kinds of considerations are insufficient to bind a court to a certain decision in a certain context. True, interpretive methods and doctrines determine «the area of justifiable solutions»[42]: but since these "maxims" «are unsystematic sets of catch phrases (often couched in proverbial forms) and so imprecise in meaning that they can easily be operated in a way that leads to conflicting results»[43] and since «no objective criteria exist to show when one maxim rather than another should be applied, they offer great scope for the judge to arrive at the result he deems desirable»[44].

Another similarity between Davidson's theory of radical interpretation and Ross' account of pragmatic interpretation concerns the weak, "technical" normativity of interpretive directives ("maxims" or "arguments", in Ross' vocabulary, semantic "rules" or "conventions", in Davidson's language), an idea which stands at the core of the unbindingness thesis. Davidson does not deny that two (or more) people can contingently have conventions and share a language[45]; he denies, instead, that con-

---

[38] Ross 1958, 146. See also Chiassoni 2006, 124.

[39] See Ross 1958, 113.

[40] Ross 1958, 117–118. Compare with Davidson 1986, 446: «there are no rules for arriving at passing theories».

[41] See Ross 1958, 145.

[42] Ross 1958, 153. This "area" may be conceived as delimited by a "frame": see Kelsen 1967, 351: «the law to be applied constitutes only a frame within which several applications are possible, whereby every act is legal that stays within the frame».

[43] Ross 1958, 153.

[44] Ross 1958, 153–154.

[45] See Davidson 1985, 25: «Knowledge of the conventions of language is [...] a practical crutch to interpretation, a crutch we cannot in practice afford to do without – but a crutch which, under

ventions are (and help explain what is) necessary for linguistic communication. It is simply not true that conventions precede and regulate our linguistic skills rather than bending preexisting linguistic habits to public norms: they cannot even «formalize the considerations that lead us to adjust our theory to fit the inflow of new information»[46]. Moreover, even if such meaning conventions were in play, they could only function as rules of thumb or summaries of previous judgments, useful until proven wrong. Ross, in turn, borrows the idea from Max Radin that interpretive maxims «are not actual rules, but implements of a technique which – within certain limits – enables the judge to reach the conclusion he finds desirable in the circumstances, and at the same time to uphold the fiction that he is only adhering to the statute and objective principles of interpretation»[47]. In Ross' opinion, «it would be a mistake to accept the technical arguments as the true reasons [of a legal solution]. The true reasons must be sought in the legal consciousness of the judge or the interests defended by the counsel»[48].

As we've seen, the naturalized and interpretive theories of meaning proposed by Quine and Davidson offer some arguments for not discarding a qualified skeptical view, quite different from the idiosyncratic one adopted by Humpty Dumpty, in a hurry. Moreover, the underlying theoretical commitment of these conceptions has something in common with the strong empiricist methodological approach adopted by legal realists. In fact, both Quine's radical translator and Davidson's radical interpreter – let us call them "radical linguists" – take on the external point of view described by Hart[49]. The radical linguists adopt a third-person detached perspective: they observe people's behavior and formulate hypotheses about the beliefs and intentions of the language users according to the principle of charity. They don't necessarily accept and follow meaning rules nor do they assume critical reflective attitudes (even if they may mimic these reactions for the purposes of communication). Rather, radical linguists elaborate theories of interpretation that allow them to predict the consequences of linguistic interactions and take part in the social linguistic practice (be it a conversation, a literary interpretation, a statutory construction, etc.).

Similarly, Ross' lawyer doesn't follow interpretive conventions, but constructs statutes and interprets precedents by elaborating on more or less rough linguistic materials, trying to predict the social consequences of her arguments and decisions. Ross' theory is an example of the resemblance between an "external" skeptical view about natural language and ordinary interpretation and an "internal" skeptical approach to legal language and interpretation. Both conceptions undermine the pretheoretical commonplaces of the sharing of legal meanings and the mutual under-

optimum conditions for communication, we can in the end throw away, and could in theory have done without from the start». See also Davidson 1994.

[46] Davidson 1985, 25.

[47] Ross 1958, 154. The reference is made to Radin 1945, 219. See also Oliphant 1993, 200; Chiassoni 2006, 117–119; Guastini 2006; 2011, 144–149.

[48] Ross 1958, 153.

[49] Hart 1994, 89, 291.

standing between legal drafters and adjudicators, but the second cannot be seen as a local application of the first because it rests on a statement of the differential traits of legal linguistic practice.

4 A Free Play of Legal Interpretations? On the Openness of Legal Contexts

Now, it is time to turn to deconstructionism. As it is well known, this philosophical movement owes its main guiding lines to Jacques Derrida's critical analysis of Western metaphysic tradition. The polemic targets of Derrida's arguments are "logocentrism" and the "metaphysics of presence", both of which conspire in conceiving communication in terms of the *presence* and crucial importance of three elements: the communicating subject (or her intention), seen as the centering origin of meaning, the object she's referring to in her speech acts, and the addressed audience. On this conception, written language is considered as something derivative and parasitic: understanding a written text is depicted as remounting to its animating authorial intention and originating context (the so called "context of production"), which set the linguistic conventions and necessary and sufficient conditions for a successful communicational exchange.

According to Derrida, on the contrary, the absence of the receiver in writing, the sender in reading, and (potentially) the object referred to in the discourse in both writing and reading contexts, is a typical feature of written communication that cannot be treated nor idealized as a kind of "modification of the presence", as a mere, powerful extension of spoken or gestural communication. More drastically: when the writer addresses her text to a receiver or makes her text public, she cannot be sure that the receiver will read it (or wish to read it); she may change her mind and intentions after sending or publishing the text; when the receiver reads the written text, the sender may have disappeared or already changed her mind; the objects referred to in the text may have been destroyed, and so on.

Derrida contends that the absence of an intentional subjectivity and a convention dominating a complete communication context – the *différance* (difference and deferral at once) – is general and characterizes each "language event". The legibility and intelligibility of a written text depends on the structural iterability of the sign, but this last feature can be projected onto spoken language (and particularly performative speech acts): «this is the possibility on which I want to insist: the possibility of disengagement and citational graft which belongs to the structure of every mark, spoken or written, and which constitutes every mark in writing before and outside of every horizon of semio-linguistic communication; in writing, which is to say in the possibility of its functioning being cut off, at a certain point, from its "original" desire-to-say-what-one-means [*vouloir-dire*] and from its participation in a saturable and constraining context»[50].

[50] Derrida 1988a, 12.

Derrida reverses thus the traditional order of explanation, conceding some sort of philosophical priority to written language and showing how its alleged *differentiae specificae* are indeed extensible to spoken language. The main consequences of this move are linguistic indeterminacy and the loss of a stable normativity of the rules and conventions established in (and for) normal contexts of communication, which cannot bind language users and interpreters. The author insists that «Every sign, linguistic or nonlinguistic, spoken or written (in the current sense of this opposition), in a small or large unit, can be *cited*, put between quotation marks; in so doing it can break with every given context, engendering an infinity of new contexts in a manner which is absolutely illimitable. This does not imply that the mark is valid outside of a context, but on the contrary that there are only contexts without any center or absolute anchoring [*ancrage*]»[51]. If meaning is conventional, and if conventions dress the communicative intentions of the speaker once the context satisfies some "normality" conditions, stressing the iterability of arbitrary signs and the discontinuity between their contexts of use serves to undermine the default presumption of normality and the idea of meaning pre-determinability.

The French philosopher reaches this conclusion also through a criticism of the Saussurean conception of linguistic structure (*la langue*). According to Ferdinand de Saussure, the identity of a sign (the unified duality of a concept – the *signifié* – and an acoustic image – the *signifiant*) is not only arbitrary, but also purely differential and relational, in that it depends on its place in the linguistic system and is negatively defined by its difference from other signs. This makes meaning never immediately present in a (use of a) sign, but disseminated along the whole system of the signifiers: the internal cross-referential structure of dictionaries mirrors the circularity of the process of signification. Saussure, however, maintains that «the statement that everything in language is negative is true only if the signifier and the signified are considered separately; when we consider the sign in its totality, we have something that is positive in its own class»[52]. Derrida contests this assumption, charging the Swiss linguist of surreptitiously assuming the existence of a transcendental signified, a concept independent of language. From a deconstructionist standpoint, when an interpreter ascribes a meaning to a text she gets caught in a never-ending "play": to interpret a sign she must consider those signs to which the former is opposed; but to interpret the latter she must know to what signs they are opposed to, and so on, up to the closure of the circle. This prevents the interpreter from identifying a "real" "positive" meaning of an expression.

Derrida distinguishes then two conceptions of interpretation, advocating for the second: «There are thus two interpretations of interpretation, of structure, of sign, of play. The one seeks to decipher, dreams of deciphering a truth or an origin which

[51] Derrida 1988a, 12. See also Derrida 2001, 365–366. Note the resemblance between Derrida's thesis and what Davidson (1979, 13) calls "the autonomy of linguistic meaning": «Once a feature of language has been given conventional expression, it can be used to serve many extra-linguistic ends; symbolic representation necessarily breaks any close tie with extra-linguistic purpose». An opposite conception about meaning and context is expressed by Frederick Schauer (1991, 55–57).

[52] De Saussure 1966, 121.

escapes play and the order of the sign, and which lives the necessity of interpretation as an exile. The other, which is no longer turned toward the origin, affirms play and tries to pass beyond man and humanism, [where the man is] that being who, throughout [...] his entire history, has dreamed of full presence, the reassuring foundation, the origin and the end of play»[53]. The second conception of interpretation is «a field of infinite substitutions only because [...] there is something missing from it: a center which arrests and grounds the play of substitutions»[54]; it is a Nietzschean hermeneutical view that leads to «the affirmation of a world of signs without fault, without truth, and without origin»[55], that «surrenders itself to *genetic* indetermination»[56].

This apparently strong synchronic version of the equivocity thesis has been subscribed by other deconstruction theorists. Paul de Man, for example, focusing on literary interpretation, translates the notion of free play into that of undecidability of meanings within a text, undertaking both the plurality and the parity thesis: «Two entirely coherent but entirely incompatible readings can be made to hinge on one line, whose grammatical structure is devoid of ambiguity, but whose rhetorical mode turns the mood as well as the mode of the poem upside down [...]. [The reader can't] in any way make a valid decision as to which of the readings can be given priority over the other; none can exist in the other's absence»[57]. In the field of legal interpretation, similar conclusions have been reached by several authors from the "Critical Legal Studies" movement. A good example is the following statement by Charles M. Yablon: «The experienced advocate knows that the doctrinal regime is sufficiently complex that there will always be some set of authoritative materials which, through skillful manipulation of the level of specificity and characterization of the facts, he can declare to be 'controlling' of the case at bar»[58].

In the literature about legal deconstructionism much ink has been spilled to discriminate strong and weak readings of the equivocity thesis[59]. Indeed, its scope depends on the way one understands the unbindingness thesis and the related problem of the normativity of meaning. Derrida points out «The perhaps paradoxical consequence of [...] having recourse to iteration and to code: the disruption, in the last analysis, of the authority of the code as a finite system of rules; at the same time, the radical destruction of any context as the protocol of code»[60]. If one rejects the representation of language as an abstract monolithic system of prefixed meaning rules which govern actual uses inscribing them in typical/normal contexts, then the

[53] Derrida 2001, 369–370.

[54] Derrida 2001, 365.

[55] Derrida 2001, 369.

[56] Derrida 2001, 369.

[57] de Man 1979, 12. *Contra*, see Hirsch 1967

[58] Yablon 1985, 917–918. See also Kairys 1982, 15; Balkin 1987; D'Amato 1990.

[59] See Solum 1987, 470–471. Timothy Endicott (2001, 13–17) shows with abundance of details that many unqualified versions of the equivocity thesis are indeed mere *façons de parler*: in fact, when under attack, critical legal theorists retreat to more moderate thesis.

[60] Derrida 1988a, 8.

abstract normative constraints inherited at each change of (actual) context can be questioned. Moreover, since context and meaning are not separated and independently delimited "entities" (or "areas", a metaphor already employed by Gottlob Frege) to be discovered as final points of arrest for interpretation, the task of ascribing sense to linguistic behaviors and traces is open-ended. Still, the concept of "openness" is ambiguous, in that it can recall an "absolute/unlimited discontinuity of contexts" or a "contextual/limited openness".

Some critics of Derrida equate his deconstructionism to a work of decontextualization that produces an unwarranted interpretive freedom from the historical chain of meanings and contexts. This diagnosis may well be justified by Derrida's frequent obscurities, but, if not further cleared, it results misleading and unfair. It is surely incorrect to charge the French author of invoking unconstrained decontextualization as a crucial aspect of an alternative picture of language. In fact, Derrida explicitly affirms that «one cannot do anything, least of all speak, without *determining* (in a manner that is not only theoretical, but practical and performative) a context»[61] (my emphasis) and that the main aim of deconstruction is «the effort to take this limitless context into account, to pay the sharpest and broadest attention possible to context, and thus to an incessant movement of recontextualization»[62]. Does all this imply a complete freedom from interpretive constraints, a strong synchronic reading of the unbindingness thesis?

Derrida wishes to avoid this conclusion. On one side he states that his way of thinking of the context as indefinite, unsaturated, non-totalized «does not, as such, amount to a relativism, with everything that is sometimes associated with it (skepticism, empiricism, even nihilism)»[63]. In fact, such a conception of context is not maintained as an absolute overview which claims for its independent (transcendent?) criteria of correctness: on the contrary, it is an interpretation rooted in its own context – a discussion about meaning and signification. On the other, he argues that «there is always something political "in the very project of attempting to fix the contexts of utterances". [...] Such an experience is always political because it implies, insofar as it involves determination, a certain type of non-"natural" relation to others [...] In short, [the author does] not believe that any neutrality is possible in this area»[64]. Derrida admits that in some contexts, which are «extremely vast, old, powerfully, stabilized or rooted in a network of conventions (for instance, those of language)»[65] – the paradigmatic case is represented by hard sciences – objectivity and truth impose themselves for several reasons. This is not necessarily the case in other kinds of context, whose shaping may be guided by other kinds of relevance considerations: but even there nothing imposes the absence of local and provisional constraints.

---

[61] Derrida 1988b, 136.

[62] Derrida 1988b, 136.

[63] Derrida 1988b, 137.

[64] Derrida 1988b, 136.

[65] Derrida 1988b, 136. See also Derrida 1981, 133.

Michel Rosenfeld, who tries to extend such conclusions to the legal domain, is more explicit in advocating a moderate reading of the equivocity thesis based on contextual openness: «Conducted at the proper level of abstraction [...] intertextual interpretive practice does not culminate in aimless conflict and hopeless indeterminacy. Whereas it cannot avoid conflict, such interpretive practice can reveal particular conflicts which invite a finite range of possible solutions. Similarly, such interpretive practice unavoidably leads to indeterminacy, but not to the kind of indeterminacy which justifies virtually every conceivable meaning»[66]. Rosenfeld claims that there's a kind of "constrained indeterminacy" which results from the inter-subjective re-contextualization ("rewriting", in a deconstructionist sense of "writing" which includes oral speech acts) of past writings in new cases expecting a legal solution. But, according to this author, the provisional constraints to re-contextualization can only come from the ethical assumptions inscribed in sequences of contexts as parts of processes of historical formation of inter-subjective (social) relations.

To conclude and summarize this sketch presentation, it may be useful to stress that, once again, two strategies are available for the interpretive legal skeptic: she may either assume absolute discontinuity and radical equivocity as features of whatever communicational chain of contexts, or admit that different contexts synchronically present different degrees of openness and indeterminacy, trying to characterize in a pragmatic and contextualist way the central aspects of legal language that avoid falling down to an infinite loop of interpretations.

5 Second-Order Skepticism? From Theorizing to Enculturation

Until now I've offered a tentative picture of some philosophical views that seem to lend support to a qualified version of legal skepticism grounded on the equivocity thesis. The theories elaborated by Quine, Davidson, and deconstructionists have three philosophical features in common: they are interpretive, point out the necessity for a contextualization of meaning-ascriptions, and underscore a commitment to semantic anti-Platonism. Nonetheless, it is important to remark that none of these features – neither separately nor conjunctly taken – are sufficient to justify skepticism. As we've seen (§1), the doubts concerning mutual understanding, sharing a semantic content, and meaning determinacy can arise when their justifications rest on common sense assumptions or pure stipulations. But what if the theorist were to abandon a reifying picture of meaning and a concept of determinacy declined in terms of already given necessary and sufficient conditions? What if a conception of meaning were interpretive, contextualist, anti-Platonic and opted for a replacement of the idea of an absolute, "petrified" determinacy with that of correctness and

[66] Rosenfeld 1992, 159–160.

legitimacy of certain uses and interpretations in specific or particular contexts? Finally, what if the anti-skeptic were to justify her reconstruction not on the basis of its conformity to common sense, but on its interpretive (in the sense of "explanatory") relation with the observable public behavior of language users?

I shall here recall just three conceptions which pursue this strategy.

(i) Meaning contextualism is the view that the content of an utterance – what is said – is context-dependent in ways which go beyond the ordinary processes of saturation (fixation of the reference of indexicals, demonstratives, pronouns, etc.) and disambiguation[67]. The conventional (or encoded) meaning of an utterance is a mere scheme of semantic representation (a logical form), not sufficient to express an explicit proposition with specific truth-conditions. The identification of an ostensive stimulus involves deploying this conceptually articulated scheme that provides an access to encyclopedic entries, plays the role of a hint of what is explicitly and implicitly meant, and stands in need for pragmatic inferential completion, enrichment (so called "explicatures") and reconstruction of the intended contextual assumptions of the speaker that allow reaching the intended information (so called "implicatures")[68]. According to this view, then, (1) the conventional meaning of a linguistic expression is an emergent concept product of many concrete uses in similar contexts; (2) it is better not to classify meaning along the axis "literal-non literal", but in terms of frequency and familiarity of linguistic usages.

The most developed version of semiotic contextualism is relevance theory, according to which the interpretation of the pragmatic unarticulated constituents of a token-sentence is guided by cognitive and communicative relevance principles[69]. The speaker manifestly intends that the utterance be considered by the hearer sufficiently relevant as to deserve an interpretation. To secure this communicational goal, the speaker chooses the utterance she assumes will be interpreted in the most immediate way by the hearer, sparing her the cognitive costs of complex interpretive efforts. On the other hand, the hearer will maximize the relevance of the utterance[70], assuming that the most easily accessible interpretation will be the correct one. The more an interpretive hypothesis is easy to access and satisfies the relevance expectations of the hearer, the more it will plausibly reflect the speaker meaning. Of course, since contextual assumptions are not necessarily shared by speaker and hearer, and pragmatic inferences are non-demonstrative, communication may fail[71]: but it will be always possible to check the correctness of the pragmatic reasoning (explicatures and implicatures) in the subsequent linguistic interactions.

Relevance theory rejects Quinean indeterminacy of translation and assumes that the results of cognitive sciences, which describe more and more accurately our bio-

[67] See Travis 1975; Searle 1978; Sperber and Wilson 1995; Carston 2002; Récanati 2004.

[68] See Sperber and Wilson 1995, §§ 4.2. and 4.3.

[69] See Sperber and Wilson 1995, §§ 3.1. and 3.2.

[70] According to Sperber 2005, the process of "calculating" the relevance of a linguistic stimulus is automatic and subconscious, and depends on a functional property of specific innate modules of our mind that react only to that kind of input.

[71] See Recanati 2004, 54.

logical processes and the epistemic and practical bottlenecks that limit the amount of information we're able to manage at each communicational exchange, allow the theorist to calculate the meaning of a token-sentence in a specific context[72]. The principle of relevance is taken to offer a schematic formulation of these natural constraints and is clearly at odds with the parity thesis: there cannot be more than one (correct?) interpretation of a token-sentence that satisfies the principle.

(ii) Ronald Dworkin's jurisprudence, the "law as integrity" and "as interpretation" approach[73], is moderately contextualist and generally interpretive, in a sense, not so far from that assumed by deconstructionism. In fact, Dworkin also denies that the law is a set of given data "out there", waiting for discovery, and acknowledges that the interpretation of a legal text doesn't take place in a vacuum, but is part of a practice aimed at reconstructing the historical sequence of contexts leading to and justifying the actual one. However, contrary to critical legal theorists, he grants that there are stable constraints binding the development of such an enterprise. To clarify this point, he draws an analogy between the tasks of interpreting the law and writing a chain novel, a literary work in which each chapter is written by a different individual author. According to Dworkin, in both cases the author/interpreter is constrained by the anterior acts (the plot of previous chapters; the relevant line of judicial precedents) of the other members of the collective enterprise and the sense of adequacy and consistency of her contribution with the (aesthetic or moral/politic) values of the practice embedded in those acts. Thus each legal interpretation must fit past ones, but must also do so better than its rivals, justifying its object: it must take into account the central aspects of the practice and illuminate them and the case at hand with the best light to preserve the integrity of the legal process, that is, the values of equal respect and concern.

Dworkin thinks that the concept of "interpretive objectivity" is not a *contraditio in adiecto*. Understanding the law in general, as a practice, and its particular manifestations – a constitutional provision, an enactment, an opinion stated in a past decision – involves engaging in the Herculean task of elaborating a normative (political and moral) theory which links a coherent set of general principles (justice, fairness, equality) and a body of institutionally created provisions[74]: since, according to the author (and against the parity thesis), it is always possible to identify some consistent (formal and substantial) requirements to establish which normative theory is better, adjudication can be a constrained constructive activity too, leading to correct interpretations of legal texts and *univocal* right answers to legal questions.

(iii) Another contextualist conception of meaning has been proposed by the literary critic Stanley Fish. According to this author, Dworkin's metaphor of the chain-novel is seriously misleading: on one hand, the interpretive alternatives do not decrease as the serial novel/line of precedents evolves through time; on the other, it is impossible to separate the interpreter's understanding of the previously established practice and her grasp of the facts of the case. In his words: «It is tempting to

[72] See Sperber and Wilson 2002; Sperber 2005; Wilson 2005.

[73] See Dworkin 1982, 1986.

[74] See Dworkin 1986, 243.

think that the more information one has (the more history) the more directed will be one's interpretation; but information only comes in an interpreted form (it does not announce itself). No matter how much or how little you have, it cannot be a check against interpretation, because even when you first "see it", interpretation has already done its work»[75]. So Dworkin's chain simply doesn't exist: there only are discrete interpretive activities performed by different courts and lawyers.

A consequence of this view is that the search for an a-contextual literal meaning of a text (e.g., a statute) is doomed to failure: «any reading that is plain and obvious in the light of some assumed purpose (and it is impossible not to assume one) is a literal reading; but no reading is *the* literal reading in the sense that it is available apart from any purpose whatsoever [...] It is not that we first read the statute and then know its purpose; we know the purpose first, and only then can the statute be read»[76].

Fish, however, doesn't subscribe to the equivocity thesis. On the contrary, he believes that legal interpreters don't choose between those which, from a-contextual perspective, seem to be real hermeneutic alternatives. He grants that meaning is not text-dependent, but reader-dependent, and that no reading of a text is inherently impossible: if we were playing with logical possibilities, the plurality thesis would in fact hold. But since interpreters are taking part in a cooperative practice, the distinction between ambiguous and unambiguous sentences and the idea of an uninterpreted text are senseless: interpretation is itself a structure of constraints; the correctness of a legal solution to a case will depend on the degree of persuasiveness of the proposed justification within the professional/intellectual interpretive community. As the author writes, «Interpreters are constrained by their tacit awareness of what is possible and not possible to do, and what is and is not a reasonable thing to say, what will and will not be heard as evidence, in a given enterprise; and it is within those same constraints that they see and bring others to see the shape of the documents to whose interpretation they are committed»[77]. Thus, the only "facts" that allow participants to say that certain legal interpretations are admissible are not rules imposed on the interpreters from outside, but the concepts/categories, arguments, styles and standards supplied by the practice itself and internalized through training.

As the reader will have noticed, the above exposed views all deny the parity thesis and conceive the meaning of precedents and statutory provisions as the correct linguistic outcome of a complex, communal, interpretive and argumentative practice. How does then the skeptic react to these alternative reconstructions of legal practice? The "external" communicational skeptic may contend that her opponents' arguments either don't have sufficient empirical basis or deploy too vague and/or contested concepts (e.g., "integrity", "persuasiveness", "relevance") to make them testable (if meaningful at all). The "internal" skeptic, instead, can insist that the anti-skeptic description of the legal practice is inadequate: she then puts on the carpet an

[75] Fish 1983, 274. See also Fish 1988, 891.

[76] Fish 1980, 279.

[77] Fish 1983, 283.

alternative account of the differential pragmatic features of legal language as opposed to ordinary language-games. Here are the main points she may highlight:

(i) even if legal language borrows the great majority of its words from natural languages, (a) the meanings of these words in legal speech acts may well be different, for they don't depend on the semiotic cooperation of all its users (or on rational expectations plus the principle of charity), but on the definitions and interpretive decisions of legal authorities which are given the responsibility of solving semiotic – and, of course, practical – conflicts; (b) there are also many technical linguistic expressions introduced by legal scholarship, legislators and judicial practice, but here again their function doesn't depend on a common aim or a peaceful methodological agreement between language users – as it happens, for example, in mathematics. In fact, it is difficult to extend to legal language a two-phase Carnapian model of analysis inspired by artificial languages, in which one first *institutes* meaning rules by stipulative definitions that fix connections between meanings, expressions and extensions, and then *applies* these rules to formulate theories about the world: «One cannot make sense of the notion of instituting conceptual norms apart from the notion of applying them, and vice versa. *Institution* and *application* are reciprocally dependent conceptions, and reciprocally dependent processes»[78];

(ii) the disparity of semiotic power between kinds of legal language users is much neater than that between the users of natural languages. The speech acts of the different, socially defined participants (framers, legislators, judges, other officials, barristers, jurisprudents, legal scholars, laymen) to the various legal language-games have very different effects on the linguistic and non-linguistic behavior of the participants: some language users are authorities, others are merely influential users; some are elected by citizens and draft canonical texts, others are selected on different grounds and decide controversies applying general rules; etc.[79] Moreover, to identify the "institutional" participants, it is necessary to follow legal rules;

(iii) the law guides people's behavior in some cases by facilitating the emersion of coordinative equilibria (think to the traffic rules) and, in other cases, by interfering through sanctions and invalidities with the expected payoffs of the conducts of citizens in "conflict games", where disagreements and the "fight" for the meaning of certain actions or texts are characteristic features of the global practice. In fact, interpretive legal practice admits that the advocates of the parties of a controversy (a) give opposite descriptions of the facts employing legal language and invoking different interpretations of the legal rules of evidence; (b) affirm the applicability to the case at bar of different provisions or (lines of) precedents; (c) offer conflicting interpretations of the same provision or reconstructions of the rationale of a decision, and so on. On the other hand, according to the same practice, the adjudicators have the last word in establishing

[78] Brandom 2014, 23.

[79] See Chiassoni 2000.

"what the law says", even when no specific rule for the case is available and it is necessary to elaborate it relying on more general principles. When deciding a case, the adjudicators normally mention or make reference to statutory provisions and precedents, and generally try to avoid that their sentences be reversed by superior courts: but they can always use techniques such as distinguishing or invoke some general legal principle to justify a new interpretation;

(iv) it generally makes no sense to look for a specific intention behind legal texts, because (a) they are normally drafted by collegial bodies and institutions, (b) there aren't any reliable procedures for reconstructing the individual intentions of the members of these bodies or isolating a single *ratio iuris* backing a rule, (c) very often the decision to promulgate a specific text is the product of incompletely theorized agreements[80]; (d) very often, to construct a statutory provision, the interpreter resorts to the meaning ascribed to provisions belonging to statutes enacted by different institutional bodies, not to mention common law doctrines, the concepts elaborated and systematized by legal dogmatics, and international, supernational and transnational law. These remarks seem to preclude the extension of the Gricean "Maxims" (Quality, Quantity, Relation, and Manner) – which presuppose an intentionalistic picture of linguistic interactions – to legal interpretation;

(v) according to the plurality thesis, there are much more ways to interpret legal texts than those employed to ascribe meaning to speech acts in ordinary conversation. This is in part due to the writtenness of legal speech acts: in fact, the temporal and spatial distance between the context of production and the context of use of a written text often causes a "presuppositional" distance between the encyclopedic information – which, in legal practice, includes statutes, dogmatic systematizations, doctrines, etc. – of the sender and the receiver. But even when the object of the interpretation is not, strictly speaking, a "text" – think to legal customs, unwritten principles or the rationales of past judicial opinions[81], which merely make explicit, by non-canonical linguistic expressions, norms implicit in the practice – several canons, methods, and normative theories are available to (and are employed by) interpreters and adjudicators. Furthermore, while in the context of literary criticism the plurality of readings and the disagreements between participants are generally seen as a praiseworthy richness of the practice, in legal contexts, which are practical and where interpretive decisions weigh on economic and personal interests and rights, they clash with a powerful push towards univocity.

According to the internal skeptic, all these features point to the conclusion that legal practice is indeterminate in ways ordinary communication is not.

At this stage, the anti-skeptic might pause to evaluate what appears to be a stalemate between opposite reconstructions of the same practice. On one hand, none of the competing views has produced sufficient evidence to dispel a second-order

[80] See Sunstein 1995.

[81] See Moore 1987, 1995, 24–25.

skepticism about their descriptive adequacy: mentioning isolated examples of hard cases is not sufficient to prove interpretive legal skepticism; and the same can be said as regards the anti-skeptic's appeal to negative easy interpretive decisions and easy subsumption cases, which doesn't affect the strong, diachronic reading and the weak synchronic version of the equivocity thesis. On the other hand, it is not clear what would count as a counterexample: the interpretive agreements stemming from conventions (or customs) are accommodated in a skeptical framework by qualifying them as extra-legally caused convergences (or regularities) caused by extra-legal factors, while skeptic's insistence on the parity thesis is rejected replying that plurality does not entail parity, and that *de facto* parity does not entail *de iure* parity – i.e., that skeptic decision-makers may well be wrong in not detecting that, at least in some cases, there's only one admissible solution.

To avoid the impasse, the anti-skeptic could try to apply to legal practice some general arguments against communicational skepticism. Consider a *locus classicus* of anti-realism about meaning, norms, and interpretation: Ludwig Wittgenstein's analysis of rule-following. As Robert Brandom aptly explained[82], Wittgenstein wants us to abandon a picture of (the normativity of) meaning which is presupposed by two opposed reifying conceptions: "regulism" and "regularism". According to the first, actions are liable to normative assessment insofar as they are governed by explicit permissions, prohibitions, and prescriptions. Regulism is a form of Platonism: it assumes that in order to grasp the meaning of a linguistic expression a language user must grasp – through some sort of ostensive definition – an intermediary, an ideal sample (e.g., a sortal) of what the expression is to be correctly applied to. This assumption, however, leads to the infinite regress of interpretations: whatever it is the ideal entity the language user grasps, it can only be something that stands in need of another interpretation – i.e., the postulation of another ideal sample of what the first sample is to be correctly applied to. And so on, *ad infinitum*. The objection applies well to interpretivism and the radical deconstructionist thesis of the absolute openness of contexts to reinterpretation.

According to the second conception, an action is correct if it fits a regularity of behavior or if an agent has a disposition to perform it. Regularism is a kind of naturalism, it presupposes the existence of some fundamental natural/empirical facts which determine certain uses or interpretations of linguistic expressions[83]. Yet, regularism is incapable of accounting for the difference between what *is in fact* regularly done or what some subject has a disposition to do – which may well include systematic mistakes – and what *ought to be* done[84]. Moreover, Wittgenstein points out that every (actual or potential) finite regularity of behavior can be extended in

[82] See Brandom 1994, 18–29.

[83] Quine's view is a dispositional kind of regularism: it aims at replacing inexistent Platonic meanings with natural facts (stimuli).

[84] See also Taylor 1992, 137: «The rhetorical characteristic which is most distinctive of […] this determinist strategy is the "slippage" between the type of necessity governing the *explanans* and that said to be governing the *explanandum*». The first is logical (or, more generally, normative), while the second is natural.

an infinite number of respects (so called "gerrymandering" objection). Since regularities and dispositions are not self-identifying, there's no way of discriminating between them and isolating the relevant ones without using some normative criteria. This problem seems to be fatal for both Quine's semantic naturalism and relevance theory.

The consequence of Wittgenstein's double criticism, however, is not radical communicational skepticism, as many authors have thought[85]. Wittgenstein stressed in several passages of his works[86] that *tertium datur*: there is a way of grasping a rule that does not consist in an interpretation nor in the explicit/propositional knowledge of a natural fact, but in an implicit/practical know-how, constituted by normative attitudes instilled trough conditioning, training, education, and enculturation[87]. In fact, a practice-based account of rule-following and meaning seems to be better equipped to enlighten language learning and linguistic competence than any causal/behavioral and interpretive explanations. The main aspect missed by these conceptions is the transition from stimulation and conditioning to heteronomy and, finally, to autonomy. This gradual shift cannot be explained (*pace* Quine and Davidson) merely in terms of *theorizing*, i.e., of inductive generalizations based on the observation of a connection between words and objects, and procedures of confirmation/falsification which would allow, once integrated with the principle of charity, contextual information, and analytical hypothesis, a radical translation or interpretation. The reason is that these abilities presuppose that the language learner already masters concept use. Moreover, these conceptions can't account for those behaviors that represent "participative attitudes"[88], such as *ascriptions of responsibility* to those subjects who deviate from regular usage, *critical reactions* to these deviations, and for the possibility of reacting to these ascriptions and reactions, that is, of *disagreeing*. In sum: since the beginning, a language user participates in a social practice, so her point of view cannot be external and merely theoretical, as that of a radical linguist.

Wittgenstein's arguments have been applied to the analysis of legal language by several authors, such as Andrei Marmor, Dennis Patterson, Timothy Endicott and Brian Langille[89]. The main point of their analysis is that *understanding* legal rules is something different from and conceptually prior to *interpreting* the provisions or opinions which contribute to make them explicit. Understanding a rule is not a mental act or state, something that could be propositionally expressed: on the contrary, it is the *ability* to specify on request which actions are correct, i.e., in accord with the rule in normal circumstances, and it can only be *exhibited* in action (use, application). Linguistic competence requires a sense of how to preserve the implicit

[85] See Kripke 1982, ch. II; 55–56; Tushnet 1983, 824–827; Stroup 1984, 358; Boyle 1985, 709–710; Brainerd 1985; Radin 1989, 815–816.

[86] See at least Wittgenstein 1958, §§ 201, 208, 238.

[87] For an excellent introduction to these themes, see Medina 2002, ch. 6; Medina 2006, ch. 1.

[88] See Strawson 2008.

[89] See Langille 1988; Endicott 2001, 167–181; Patterson 1996, ch. 5 and 6; Marmor 2005, 112–118.

agreement in judgments and actions (which is quite different from the explicit agreement in opinions and interpretations[90]) and the normative expectations of normalcy of the other participants to the practice[91]. Interpreting a token-sentence, instead, is not an ability: it is an *activity* which consists in choosing between the different ways we have understood that token-sentence, substituting one expression of the rule for another more perspicuous – that is, better understood. According to the above mentioned authors, legal interpretation, even if it is very frequent, is a *parasitic* activity: the necessity of interpretation raises only when understanding is problematic. In conclusion, it is conceptually necessary that there exist easy cases in which the adjudicator understands the rule and needs not to interpret its linguistic expression in order to apply it.

The practice-based conception of meaning can be expanded in several directions. For example, Brandom emphasizes the importance of common law for the articulation of an apparatus of legal concepts that constrains decisions in virtue of the fact that the judges reciprocally acknowledge their authority and rcsponsibility: «each judge is recognized (implicitly) as authoritative both by prior judges (the ones whose decisions are being assessed as precedential or not) and (explicitly) by future judges (the ones who assess the current decision as authoritative, that is precedential, or not). And each judge recognizes the authority both of prior judges (to whose precedential decisions the judge is responsible) and of future judges (on whose assessments of the extent to which the present judge has fulfilled his responsibility to the decisions of prior judges the present judge's authority depends)»[92]. Brandom urges then legal theory to describe the judge as engaged in a progressive social practice that requires her to become responsible to the tradition by appealing to the authority of the past decisions she's rationally reconstructing and integrating in deciding the new cases.

Another anti-skeptical strategy consists in re-shaping and couching Fish's intuitions in non-interpretive-terms. One may stress that the adjudicator's reconstruction of the context for statutory construction and the interpretation of precedent depends on her "sense" of the facts of the case, which is already concept-driven: the concepts she learns to apply as a student and/or beginner in the legal practice constrain her understanding and normative qualification of the facts (as a lawyer, public prosecutor or judge), which in turn lead her to understand the applicable rule without the need of interpreting (or at least to circumscribe the range of possible interpretations).

Finally, José Medina has elaborated a sophisticated normative polyphonic contextualism which aims at dismantling the traditional opposition between individual-

---

[90] See Medina 2006, 35, where a criticism is developed against «the idea that *agreement can fix meaning*. [...] This naïve semantic conventionalism or collectivism would make meaning utterly arbitrary and, therefore, it would be open to a social version of the Humpty Dumpty objection of semantic vacuity [...]. On this view, there is no room for semantic constraints of any kind; linguistic communities [...] are not bound by anything».

[91] See Medina 2006, 39–46.

[92] Brandom 2014, 33.

istic, subject-centered, voluntaristic models and sociological, community-centered, deterministic (or automatistic) accounts of discursive agency. On the first models, «which lure us into the illusion that discursive agency falls fully under the control of speaker»[93], «the powers of intentionality of individual speakers were considered the primary motor of communication; and everything else [...] (intersubjectivity, consensus, linguistic conventions, etc.), were considered secondary and derivative, thus becoming subordinated to the individualistic and intentional domain»[94]. On the second accounts, which also involve an illusion that «portrays speakers and their speech acts as deprived of all subjectivity and spontaneity»[95], «It is only by virtue of some sort of social consensus, of agreed-upon norms and conventions»[96], and of social mechanisms of conditioning that our speech acts do acquire meaning.

According to Medina, these alternatives aren't conjunctly exhaustive and each disjunct presents serious flaws. On one hand, against voluntarism, the positions and perspectives that language users happen to occupy are not always chosen, and their normative attitudes are not always the result of a reasoned process. On the other hand, against the community-centered view, «Through externalization processes subjective elements that are initially idiosyncratic and pertain to the inner workings of individual minds become reflected in speech and behavior [...] [thus] enriching, modifying, and sometimes even radically transforming the social milieu»[97]. Medina warns us against equating discursive agency to the *control* of our words, of the perlocutionary effects of our speech acts: such control is impossible. This is due to some structural aspects of communication: (a) meaning is contextual and interactional; (b) the different contexts of use are never reciprocally independent: each context is part of a historical sequence, and is defined by its relations with other (precedent, subsequent, parallel) contexts; (c) the chain of contexts is incomplete and unfinished, a "totalized speech situation" is an unachievable ideal: this doesn't merely depend on our cognitive limitations, but on the very possibility of new future uses that cannot be predicted, limited, or ruled out in advance. Discursive agency is thus hybrid: it merges freedom and constraint. The meaning of our speech acts depends on citational chains, on a constant process of re-contextualization that repeats and echoes past uses in new circumstances, but in ways that admit the possibility of modifications and eccentric innovations, which can in turn be echoed. Every speech act is thus at the same time linked to and partially constrained by past uses (contexts for use, interpretation, and adjudication are not created *ex nihilo*) and susceptible of innovative re-signification.

These ideas could be deployed to describe the functioning of legal precedent. New judicial decisions are citationally linked to (and echo) past holdings: but every new reconstruction of the norms implicit in the practice is also innovative, even if the degree of innovation may vary (up to reach the limit of overruling).

[93] Medina 2006, 120.

[94] Medina 2006, 118.

[95] Medina 2006, 121.

[96] Medina 2006, 118.

[97] Medina 2006, 122.

6 The Remains of the Interpretation...

Is the interpretive legal skeptic silenced by such philosophical arguments? Perhaps not. In fact, she may contend that the above exposed practice-based conceptions miss the scope and the point of her worries, because they neglect the differential features of legal practice, and this undermines their appeal to understanding and enculturation[98]. The skeptic may argue that one can indeed learn "legal" language-games only after having learned "ordinary" language games. Insistence on the priority of understanding and the exceptionality of interpretation may well be accepted if it is referred to the majority of language-games in extra-legal contexts: but it does not *per se* exclude that legal language could be a constellation of "interpretive games"[99], in which the understood meaning of each custom, opinion, provision is made *problematic* (by lawyers and legal theorists), and stands in need of a justified (or at least justifiable) interpretive (and subsumptive) solution.

According to the skeptic, however, such a justification is only conceptually possible when the adjudicator moves beyond an ordinary understanding of the legal rules and draws interpretive arguments from the arsenal of the admitted competing canons, techniques, doctrines, and normative theories learned through legal enculturation. In other words, it is true that lawyers are trained and educated to frame cases in conformity with the concepts and categories of their legal culture: but they're also trained to bring into question the applicability of each legal concept (or pattern of concepts) and the soundness of each legal justification (of statutory constructions or interpretations of the precedents).

This legal contestability is not, from a synchronic point of view, completely unlimited: on one hand, it must fit what lawyers consider a reasonable "interpretive challenge" (claims that are generally deemed unreasonable are dismissed in negative easy interpretive solutions). Reasonableness, of course, is a vague and essentially contested concept: but its provisional core of clear cases of application may be taken back to the emphasis on understanding of practice-based views. Furthermore, given the conceptual impossibility to sever all citational links to previous contexts of use and the implicit wholesale agreement on the availability of certain hermeneutic instruments, absolute interpretive freedom remains an illusion.

These conclusions, however, are not incompatible with interpretive legal skepticism. The skeptic needs not deny that in the process of resignification and (re)contextualization of legal sentences some aspects of the past uses (interpretations and applications) are preserved; or that judicial decisions tend often to converge on certain interpretive justifications and outcomes; or that interpretive outcomes which are clearly unreasonable cannot be legally justified. Her point is that the legal system never provides a single justification or compel a uniquely warranted outcome in a particular case, because there's always room – given some significant social circumstances – for some reasonable innovations and departures from traditionally estab-

[98] See Arulanantham 1998.

[99] See Chiassoni 2000.

lished hermeneutic lines. The intrinsic openness of each legal interpretation to semiotic alternatives suffices to take the parity thesis and moderate interpretive skepticism seriously.

References

Altman, A. (1986). Legal realism, critical legal studies, and Dworkin. *Philosophy and Public Affairs, 15*(3), 205–235.

Arulanantham, A. T. (1998). Breaking the rules? Wittgenstein and legal realism. *The Yale Law Journal, 107*(6), 1853–1883.

Balkin, J. M. (1987). Deconstructive practice and legal theory. *Yale Law Journal, 96*(4), 743–786.

Bix, B. (1993). *Law, language, and legal determinancy*. Oxford: Clarendon.

Boyle, J. (1985). The politics of reason: Critical legal theory and local social thought. *University of Pennsylvania Law Review, 133*(4), 685–780.

Brainerd, S. (1985). The groundless assault: A Wittgensteinian look at language, structuralism, and critical legal theory. *The American University Law Review, 34*, 1231–1262.

Brandom, R. (1994). *Making it explicit*. Cambridge, MA: Harvard University Press.

Brandom, R. (2014). A Hegelian model of legal concept determination: The normative fine structure of the judges' chain novel. In G. Hubbs & D. Lind (Eds.), *Pragmatism, law, and language* (pp. 19–39). New York: Routledge.

Carston, R. (2002). *Thoughts and utterances: The pragmatics of explicit communication*. Oxford: Blackwell.

Chiassoni, P. (2000). Interpretive games: Statutory construction through Gricean eyes. *Analisi e diritto, 1999*, 79–99.

Chiassoni, P. (2005). Jurisprudence in the snare of vagueness. *Ratio Juris, 18*(2), 258–270.

Chiassoni, P. (2006). A nice derangement of literal meaning freaks: Linguistic contextualism and the theory of legal interpretation. *Analisi e diritto, 2005*, 116–126.

Coleman, J., & Leiter, B. (1993–1994). Determinacy, objectivity, and authority, in Pennsylvania law review, *142*, 549–637; (Reprinted in: A. Marmor (Ed.), *Law and interpretation*, Oxford: Oxford University Press, 1995, 203–278).

D'Amato, A. (1990). Pragmatic indeterminacy. *Northwestern University Law Review, 85*, 148–189.

Davidson, D. (1967). Truth and meaning. *Synthese, 17*(3), 304–323; (Reprinted in: D. Davidson, *Inquiries into truth and interpretation*, Oxford: Clarendon, 1984, 17–36).

Davidson, D. (1970). *Semantics for natural languages*. In O. Camillo (Ed.), *Linguaggi nella società e nella tecnica*, Edizioni di Comunità: Milano, 177–188, (Reprinted in: D. Davidson, *Inquiries into truth and interpretation*, Oxford: Clarendon, 1984, 55–64).

Davidson, D. (1973). Radical interpretation. *Dialectica, 27*, 313–328; (Reprinted in: D. Davidson, *Inquiries into truth and interpretation*, Oxford: Clarendon, 1984, 125–139).

Davidson, D. (1979). *Mood and performances*. In: A. Margalit (Ed.), *Meaning and use* (pp. 9–20). Dordrecht: Reidel; (Reprinted in: D. Davidson, *Inquiries into truth and interpretation*, Oxford: Clarendon, 1984, 109–121).

Davidson, D. (1985). Communication and convention. In M. Dascal (Ed.), *Dialogue: An interdisciplinary approach* (pp. 11–26). Amsterdam: Benjamins.

Davidson, D. (1986). A nice derangement of epitaphs. In R. E. Grandy & R. Warner (Eds.), *Philosophical grounds of rationality* (pp. 156–174). Oxford: Oxford University Press.

Davidson, D. (1990). Meaning, truth and evidence. In R. B. Barrett & R. F. Gibson (Eds.), *Perspectives on Quine* (pp. 68–79). Oxford: Blackwell.

Davidson, D. (1991). Three varieties of knowledge. In A. Phillips Griffiths (Ed.), *A. J. Ayer: Memorial essays* (pp. 153–166). Cambridge: Cambridge University Press.

Davidson, D. (1994). The social aspect of language. In B. McGuinnes & G. Oliveri (Eds.), *The philosophy of Michael Dummett* (pp. 1–16). Dordrecht: Kluwer.

de Saussure, F. (1966 [1916]). *Course in general linguistics.* (English translation by Wade Baskin). New York: McGraw & Hill.

Derrida, J. (1981 [1978]). *Spurs: Nietzsche's Styles. Éperons: les styles de Nietzsche.* English translation by Barbara Harlow. Chicago: University of Chicago Press.

Derrida, J. (1988a [1972]). *Signature event context* (English translation by Samuel Weber and Jeffrey Mehlman), In J. Derrida, *Limited Inc.* (pp. 1–23). Evanston: Northwestern University Press.

Derrida, J. (1988b). Afterword: Toward an ethic of discussion. In J. Derrida, *Limited Inc.* (pp. 111–160). Evanston: Northwestern University Press.

Derrida, J. (2001 [1967]). *Structure, sign, and play in the discourse of the human sciences.* (English translation by Alan Bass). In J. Derrida, *Writing and difference* (pp. 351–370). London/New York: Routledge.

Drahos, P., & Parker, S. (1991) The indeterminacy paradox in law. *Western Australian Law Review, 21*, 305–319.

Dworkin, R. (1982). Law as interpretation. *Critical Inquiry, 9*(1), 179–200.

Dworkin, R. (1986). *Law's empire*. Cambridge, MA: Harvard University Press.

Dyzenhaus, D., & Taggart, M. (2008). Reasoned decisions and legal theory. In D. E. Edlin (Ed.), *Common law theory* (pp. 134–167). Cambridge: Cambridge University Press.

Endicott, T. (2001). *Vagueness in law*. Oxford: Oxford University Press.

Fish, S. (1980). *Is there a text in this class? The authority of interpretive communities*. Cambridge, MA: Harvard University Press.

Fish, S. (1983 [1982]). Working on the chain-gang: Interpretation in law and in literary criticism. In W. J. T. Mitchell (Ed.), *The politics of interpretation* (pp. 271–286). Chicago: University of Chicago Press.

Fish, S. (1988). Force. *Washington and Lee Law Review, 45*(3), 883–902.

Fowler, S. (1995). Indeterminacy in law and legal reasoning. *Stellenbosch Law Review, 6*(3), 324–347.

Gottlieb, G. (1968). *The logic of choice*. London: Allen & Unwin.

Gray, J. C. (1921). *The nature and sources of law*. New York: Columbia University Press.

Guastini, R. (2006). A sceptical view on legal interpretation. *Analisi e diritto, 2005*, 139–144.

Guastini, R. (2011). Rule-skepticism restated. In L. Green & B. Leiter (Eds.), *Oxford studies in philosophy of law* (Vol. 1, pp. 138–161). Oxford: Oxford University Press.

Hart, H. L. A. (1983a). *Introduction.* In H. L. A. Hart (Ed.), *Essays in jurisprudence and philosophy* (pp. 1–18). Oxford: Clarendon.

Hart, H. L. A. (1983b [1967]). Problems of the philosophy of law. In H. L. A. Hart (Ed.), *Essays in jurisprudence and philosophy* (pp. 145–158). Oxford: Clarendon.

Hart, H. L. A. (1994). *The Concept of Law* (2nd ed.). *With a Postscript edited by Penelope A. Bulloch and Joseph Raz*, Oxford: Clarendon.

Hirsch, E. D., Jr. (1967). *Validity in interpretation.* New Haven/London: Yale University Press.

Jori, M. (1993). Legal semiotics. In R. E. Asher & J. M. Y. Simpson (Eds.), *The encyclopedia of language and linguistics* (Vol. IV, pp. 2113–2122). Oxford: Pergamon Press.

Kairys, D. (1982). Legal reasoning. In D. Kairys (Ed.), *The politics of law: A progressive critique* (pp. 11–17). New York: Pantheon Books.

Kelsen, H. (1967 [1960]). *The pure theory of law.* English translation by Max Knight. Berkeley/Los Angeles/London: University of California Press.

Kress, K. (1989). Legal indeterminacy. *California Law Review, 77*(2), 283–337.

Kripke, S. (1982). *Wittgenstein on rules and private language*. Cambridge, MA: Harvard University Press.

Kutz, C. L. (1993). Just disagreement: Indeterminacy and rationality in the rule of law. *Yale Law Review, 103*, 997–1030.
Langille, B. (1988). Revolution without foundation: The grammar of scepticism and law. *McGill Law Journal, 33*(3), 451–505.
Laudan, L. (1990). Demystifying underdetermination. In W. Savage (Ed.), *Scientific theories* (Minnesota studies in the philosophy of science, Vol. 14, pp. 267–297). Minneapolis: University of Minnesota Press.
Lawson, G. (1996). Legal indeterminacy: Its cause and cure. *Harvard Journal of Law and Public Policy, 19*(2), 411–428.
Leiter, B. (2007). *Naturalizing jurisprudence: Essays on American legal realism and naturalism in legal philosophy*. Oxford: Oxford University Press.
Llewellyn, K. (1931a). Law and the modern mind. A symposium: Legal certainty. *Columbia Law Review, 31*, 82–115.
Llewellyn, K. (1931b). Some realism about realism. Responding to Dean Pound. *Harvard Law Review, 44*(8), 1222–1264.
Llewellyn, K. (1949–1950) Remarks on the theory of Appellate decision and the rules or canons about how statutes are to be construed. *Vanderbilt Law Review, 3*(1), 395–406.
Llewellyn, K. (1951). *The bramble bush: On our law and its study* (2nd ed.). New York: Ocean.
De Man, P. (1979). *Allegories of reading: Figural language in Rousseau, Nietzsche, Rilke, and Proust*. New Heaven: Yale University Press.
Marmor, A. (2005). *Interpretation and legal theory*. Oxford: Hart Publishing.
Medina, J. (2002). *The unity of Wittgenstein's philosophy: Necessity, intelligibility, and normativity*. Albany: SUNY Press.
Medina, J. (2006). *Speaking from elsewhere*. Albany: State University of New York Press.
Moore, M. (1987). Precedent, induction, and ethical generalization. In L. Goldstein (Ed.), *Precedent in law* (pp. 183–198). Oxford: Oxford University Press.
Moore, M. (1995). Interpreting interpretation. In A. Marmor (Ed.), *Law and interpretation* (pp. 1–29). Oxford: Oxford University Press.
Moore, U., & Sussman, G. (1931). Legal and institutional methods applied to the debiting of direct discounts. VI. The decisions, the institutions and the degree of deviation. *Yale Law Journal, 40*, 1219–1272.
Nussbaum, M. C. (1994). Skepticism about practical reason in literature and the law. *Harvard Law Review, 107*(3), 714–744.
Oliphant, H. (1993 [1928]). A return to stare decisis. In W. V. III Fisher, M. J. Horwitz, & A. Thomas (Eds.), *American legal realism* (pp. 199–201). New York: Oxford University Press.
Patterson, D. (1996). *Law and truth*. Oxford: Oxford University Press.
Perry, M. J. (1995–1996). Normative indeterminacy and the problem of judicial role. *Harvard Journal of Law and Public Policy, 19*(2), 375–390.
Poggi, F. (2013). The myth of literal meaning in legal interpretation. *Analisi e diritto 2013*, 313–335.
van O Quine, W. (1960). *Word and object*. Cambridge, MA: MIT Press.
van O Quine, W. (1975). The nature of natural knowledge. *Mind and Language, 1*(1), 67–81.
van O Quine, W. (1987). Indeterminacy of translation again. *The Journal of Philosophy, 84*(1), 5–10.
van O Quine, W. (1992). *Pursuit of truth* (2nd ed.). Cambridge, MA: Harvard University Press.
Radin, M. (1945). A case study in statutory interpretation: Western Union Co. vs. Lenroot. *California Law Review, 33*(2), 219.
Radin, M. J. (1989). Reconsidering the rule of law. *Boston University Law Review, 69*(4), 781–819.
Récanati, F. (2004). *Literal meaning*. Cambridge: Cambridge University Press.
Rosenfeld, M. (1992 [1990]). Deconstruction and legal interpretation: Conflict, indeterminacy, and the temptations of the new legal formalism. In D. G. Carlson, D. Cornell, & M. Rosenfeld

(Eds.), *Deconstruction and the possibility of justice* (pp. 152–210). London/New York: Routledge.

Ross, A. (1958). *On law and justice*. London: Steven & Sons.

Schauer, F. (1991). *Playing by the rules*. Oxford: Clarendon.

Searle, J. R. (1978). Literal meaning. *Erkenntnis, 13*(1), 207–224.

Solum, L. B. (1987). On the indeterminacy crisis: Critiquing the critical dogma. *The University of Chicago Law Review, 54*, 462–503.

Solum, L. B. (1999). Indeterminacy. In D. Patterson (Ed.), *A companion to philosophy of law and legal theory* (pp. 488–502). Oxford: Blackwell.

Sperber, D. (2005). Modularity and relevance: How can a massively modular mind be flexible and context-sensitive. In P. Carruthers, S. Laurence, & S. Stich (Eds.), *The innate mind: Structure and content* (pp. 53–68). Oxford: Oxford University Press.

Sperber, D., & Wilson, D. (1995). *Relevance: Communication and cognition* (2nd ed.). Oxford: Blackwell.

Sperber, D., & Wilson, D. (2002). Pragmatics modularity and mind-reading. *Mind and Language, 17*(1), 3–23.

Stone, J. (1964). *Legal system and legal reasoning*. Stanford: Stanford University Press.

Stone, J. (1985). *Precedent and law: Dynamics of common law growth*. Sidney: Butterworths.

Strawson, P. F. (2008 [1962]). Freedom and resentment. In P. F. Strawson (Ed.), *Freedom and resentment and other essays* (pp. 1–27). London/New York: Routledge.

Stroup, D. G. (1984). Law and language: Cardozo's jurisprudence and Wittgenstein's philosophy. *Valparaiso University Law Review, 18*(2), 331–371.

Sunstein, C. R. (1995). Incompletely theorized agreeements. *Harvard Law Review, 108*(7), 1733–1772.

Taylor, T. (1992). *Mutual misunderstanding. Scepticism and the theorizing of language and interpretation*. Durham/London: Duke University Press.

Travis, C. (1975). *Saying and understanding*. Oxford: Blackwell.

Tushnet, M. (1983). Following the rules laid down: A critique of interpretivism and neutral principles. *Harvard Law Review, 96*(4), 781–827.

Tushnet, M. (1996). Defending the indeterminacy thesis. *Quinnipac Law Review, 16*, 339–356.

Wilson, D. (2005). New directions for research on pragmatics and modularity. *Lingua, 115*(8), 1129–1146.

Wittgenstein, L. (1958). *Philosophical investigations* (2nd ed.). (English translation by Gertrude E. M. Anscombe), Oxford: Blackwell.

Wróblewski, J. (1992). *The judicial application of law*. Dordrecht: Kluwer.

Yablon, C. M. (1985). The indeterminacy of the law: Critical legal studies and the problem of legal explanation. *Cardozo Law Review, 6*(4), 917–945.

Legal Text and Pragmatics: Semantic Battles or the Power of the Declarative in Specialized Discourse

Ekkehard Felder

Abstract Legal jargon is rooted in assertions which take on the characteristics of declarative speech acts if they become the basis for a court ruling. Based on this premise this paper develops the paradigm of Semantic Battles and shows: Dominance and power are also exercised through semantics! When viewing language as a means for asserting certain views on controversial topics in intellectual domains (e.g. medicine, economics, natural science, history, law, etc.), quasi disputes arise within debates among professionals with regard to appropriate terminologies and definitions, in other words, "semantic battles" take place. Language directs the constitution of facts within the framework of knowledge; knowledge is developed through language. The contribution examines the forms and functions of the discourse of professionals in various scientific fields. The declarative speech acts of law, therefore, consist of assertive speech acts of scientists from various fields. This form of exercise of power through language must be made transparent if a state of law ("Rechtsstaat") demands loyalty from its citizens.

Keywords Semantic battle • Power • Declarative speech • Legal language

1 Introductory Thoughts

> Consciousness is reflected in the word like the sun is reflected in a droplet of water. The word is a microcosm of consciousness, related to consciousness like a living cell is related to an organism, like an atom is related to the cosmos. The meaningful word is a microcosm of human consciousness. (Vygotsky 1934/1962)

The linguistic surface information of texts and conversations exhibits characteristic indicators of specific ways of thinking. If one sees language use as a means for enforcing certain viewpoints on so-called facts or rather social facts, linguistic approaches instruct the constitution of facts and their affiliated frames of knowledge

E. Felder (✉)
German Department/Europäisches Zentrum für Sprachwissenschaften, University of Heidelberg, D- 69117 Heidelberg, Germany
e-mail: ekkehard.felder@gs.uni-heidelberg.de

F. Poggi, A. Capone (eds.), *Pragmatics and Law*, Perspectives in Pragmatics, Philosophy & Psychology 10, DOI 10.1007/978-3-319-44601-1_7

(for 'frames of knowledge' see also Busse 1991, 1992 and for 'frames in discourse analysis' see Konerding 1993, 2005, 2007, and Ziem 2008).[1] The development and spread of knowledge is directly linked to the respective language usage. This knowledge is linguistically adapted for the purpose of communication. The shaping of viewpoints for the enforcement of interests is thus tied to linguistic signs and their semantics. To be able to establish a certain linguistic access to public discourse means that a specific perspective of linguistically constituted facts is imposed. The perspectivity of linguistic units in the professional constitution of facts is thus understood to be an indispensable prerequisite (see also the explanation of *semiotic captivity* (*semiotische Gefangenschaft*) in Felder 2009b, 32, or Felder 2009a, 29).

In the interest of linguistic investigation, such a wide topic area needs to be stated more precisely with regard to the domains of knowledge (cf. the concept of the research network "Language and Knowledge" in Felder (2008), where linguist specialists work together with professionals of the subject area, who are interested in linguistics, in their respective areas of expertise). The topic may then be roughly demarcated via the following questions: with the help of which linguistic elements is meaning according to a predetermined order intersubjectively constituted, how is it conveyed, and how can such processes of knowledge development be described with the help of linguistics?

During the structural analysis of such processes (i.e. during the conjunction of the objective and subjective sphere through linguistic signs) I assume, that conceptualizations in sign sequences can be made explicit as communicatively learnt and experienced forms of knowledge. Specific sign sequences and sign combinations (Zifonun 2000) can with time be stabilized as linguistic and social patterns of perception and objectification. Such patterns can be delineated in texts through conventionalized signs and sign systems, or rather style traditions (in the meaning of Scherner's (1994) approach of the understanding of texts as "tracking" or "sign-reading"). And these patterns can be understood as linguistically constituted cultural products. Looked at from the point of view of epistemology, these natural linguistic structuring devices order the contents of our mind/imagination and form part of the constitutive parts of perceived meaning. This is why linguistic elements are idiomatic steering devices.

[1] The term *frame of knowledge* is here used as a hypernym for the terms *frame*, *schema*, etc. and includes all the different forms of the knowledge conglomerates that aid understanding and which have been identified by linguistic text analysis up to date (whether isolated or network concepts) (Busse 1992, 37 and Busse 1992, 74 ff.). Frames of knowledge consist of concepts; individual parts of these concepts are called connotations, when they describe an aspect of a greater whole (i.e. a concept) or of a specimen of a category. Concepts are embedded in a network of relationships and thus into a frame. They represent knowledge about facts and thus constitute specialized knowledge. Controversial questions in a domain of knowledge are decided in view of well-known concepts, which are influenced by the frames of knowledge (or rather: through the formation of a certain knowledge conglomerations/dispositions or the filling of so-called slots in schemata). These concepts can in part be made clear through definitions. In this context, the interaction between action (usage), cognition and reference needs to be explained from a semantic point of view ("regulative reference concepts").

By *idiomatic* I understand here the characteristic specificities of language usage in a whole social group – here the professional expert and the institutionalized media communication (cf. Felder 2009a: 24). In the context of the analysis of texts and conversations, the following question is of particular interest: thanks to which qualities language as a system (both in the sense of linguistic knowledge and production) can serve as an orientation of behavior. The idiomatic organization of linguistic knowledge mirrors itself in the specific form of our frames of knowledge and is at the same time the frame for orientation and understanding.[2] Speakers, therefore, use linguistically denoted differentiations in order to articulate experiences and ideas (e.g. the term *nano* (Zimmer 2009) or our linguistic usage of *mobbing* and the world experiences and living conditions associated with it); at the same time, such usage again becomes part of the linguistic knowledge, and this process informs the usage of language in given situations.

In his critique of reason Kant pointed out, that the things we understand are not the things in themselves, but appearances. This changed the point of view from the level of being to the level of expression about being. With his concept of symbolic forms Cassirer (1964) pointed out that a priori moments constitute insight first of all, not only through the structure of reason, but that insights are also informed by the cultural forms of objectification perception of the world. The forms of representation of the facts of life are mainly linguistic signs (i.e. act through linguistic signs). Any perspectivation that comes with linguistic action is an a priori condition of perception. In this way, any cultural formation of signs has an immanent perspectivity (a fundamental semiotic category). This can be understood when we describe, how linguistics signs relate to behavior, i.e. how socially relevant facts are displayed.

The patterns of perception that have been developed by humans and which are culture specific in the form of linguistic signs contain the possibility, to make our processes of perception more diverse and to intentionally make them more perspectival. The semantic vagueness of signs of natural languages in principle assists rather than impedes understanding. That is, the semantic vagueness of the individual signs forces us into linguistic processes of objectification and understanding and to not only understand these signs as patterns, but also as entities, which only achieve their concrete function in the specific context.

Thus, what is of particular interest is the structure of collective knowledge, which manifests in linguistics signs and concatenations of signs, which again co-orient our processes of objectification of concrete ideas (cf. Schmidt 1996: 16): perception is not determined by, but instructed through language.[3] The following elucidations follow the constructivist paradigm only in part, because, if one looks at them critically, the sociological and cognitive-psychological models of communication can be accused of a marginalization of linguistic knowledge. For even though they talk

[2] This corresponds to Feilke's concept of a "common-sense competence", cf. Feilke 1994: 373 ff.

[3] S. J. Schmidt (1996: 16) states in his work with the telling title *The Worlds of the Media*: "Signs and concatenations of signs [can] orient cognitive and communicative processes, but they cannot determine them."

a lot about language, language and linguistic competence is hardly ever seen as (linguistic) product of knowledge of a distinct communicative and cultural community. This is no wonder, for both the analysis of lexical structural patterns and the understanding of the perspectivity of syntactic organizational patterns – from grammatical morphemes over syntactic correlations to fundamental grammatical principles of organization – are difficult. In the attempt to make explicit the mental forces that arise out of the ability to speak in the context of *energeia*, Humboldt described the structural power of linguistic processes of objectification in a both strange and plausible definition of the term: "form can only be understood as a law, a direction and a procedure" (Humboldt 1906: 455). What Humboldt is referring to here are inner-linguistic differences. In the methodological approach taken here, the most important element is to discover the lexical and grammatical patterns of organization as well as the principles of formation that work in them. These different principles of formation are the original entrance for the influence of language on thought – as already pointed out by Humboldt.

This brings me to the first question, i.e. how perspectivity can be established in linguistic forms. For this reason, discourse analyses take text into account, both at the level of the sentence and at the level of lexical and grammatical forms (cf. the program of pragma-semiotic text analysis on the basis of linguistic media analysis in Felder 2009a).

The distinction often used in the media sciences between *actuality* (*Wirklichkeit*) and *reality* (*Realität*) (Schmidt 1996) is helpful here: *Actuality* here means the tangible world that can be experienced and grasped through the senses, *reality* means the medially reproduced and thereby inevitably constructed scenario thereof. In view of this differentiation, we as media recipients of the so-called age of information are to a large degree confronted with reality, i.e. with linguistic products that pretend to be actual. When absorbing socio-politically relevant events we consequently deal with created materials that have transformed actuality into reality. The linguistic and symbolic signs and concatenations of signs of the mass media are, therefore, a selected segment of the world viewed from the specific perspective of an interest-led constitution of reality in the spectrum of diverse actualities.

2 Definition of the Approach "Semantic Battle"[4]

Meanings are also manipulated by power and dominance (Felder 2006, 13). This hypothesis brings the linguistic constitution of technical objects or rather facts to the forefront and thus touches on the linguistic area of semantics. If one furthermore takes the pragmatic assumptions into account, which have made the investigation of linguistic actions their aim, the question arises, how different linguistic strategies of

[4] The explanations are based on introductory article "Semantic battles in domains of knowledge. An introduction to competition between naming, meaning and technical fixation" in *Semantic Battles*, which I edited in 2006.

action (in denoting and signifying) can be described. With such a goal – with respect to socially relevant domains of knowledge or rather sciences – one automatically touches on more or less subtle forms of dissent. These kinds of dissent, however, often take place – not always explicitly but implicitly – in conventionalized technical and communicative discourses. Not all these technical debates can be easily understood by laypersons, because they often also mirror different understandings of technical terms. This brings us to the problem of different meanings (meaning accentuation), which quite obviously contradicts the widely held belief that technical discourses are unambiguous.[5] The difficulty, however, is – and this exacerbates the problem – that such "hidden" differences in meaning can be indicators for certain sciences without this connection becoming clear to the generally interested *zoon politikon*.

This is not unproblematic in so far as such semantic battles are often fought quite vigorously over decades and can become part of the history of science. At the same time, it needs to be made clear that these battles have a hand in constituting the object of research. Thus, they are a necessary prerequisite for the understanding of important research questions, since most of the technical terms belong to a whole school or rather a defined, methodically organized research interest. The implementation of specific technical terminologies and the discussion of facts in the sciences, social sciences and humanities thus are an attempt to structure the world, or rather a part of the world from a central perspective as a systematic space from a particular point of view.

"Semantic battles" or linguistic standardization conflicts take place in most subject areas. "Semantic battle" is here – to first give a general definition – understood as the attempt of a subject area to implement certain linguistic forms as expressions of specific, patterns of thought led by specific interests and actions.

For even though texts and not terms constitute research facts, terms do play a central role. The individual cases will show, how following linguistic rules, terms are formed, stereotyped, confirmed or modified through researchers and sometimes multipliers (lobbyists) who constitute facts through the formation of linguistic terms in their speeches. For it is not the terms themselves that of themselves as entities refer to facts as different entities, but the other way around: the researchers who know the relevant literature are the actors in the process of constitution through their usage of technical terms. For through their usage, they constitute, confirm and change terms in the process of the fixation of facts.

For a terminological explanation, I will differentiate with the help of the well-known semiotic triangle (Ogden and Richards 1923).

[5] Cf. for example Roelcke (1991), Gardt (1998), Felder (2003: 179ff.).

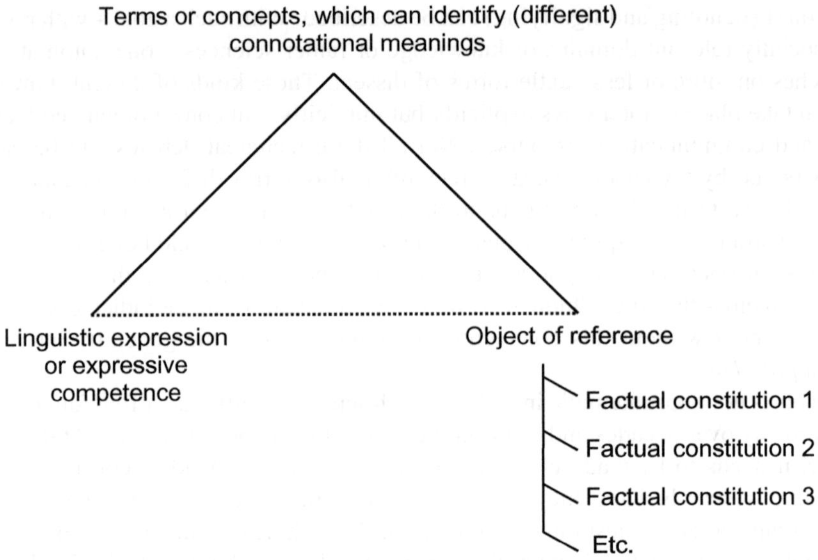

Differentiation of the semiotic tr.iangle (Ogden and Richards 1923)

The formation of a term or a concept[6] (through the specific and repeated usage of a certain linguistic expression) will be termed here an *attempt at meaning fixation* (*Bedeutungsfixierungsversuch*, cf. Wimmer 1979, 1998). Identical expressions can evoke terms or concepts with diverging connotations and thus help the specific factual constitution (here the *process of meaning fixation*, described by Wimmer (1979, 1998) as *Referenzfixierungsakt*, i.e. *referent fixation*). *Guiding principles* or *concepts* are defined as – and I am taking up an investigation on political language use here (Felder 1995) – concepts or terms of linguistic content, which text producers in the constitution and explanation of facts unconsciously make use of or consciously try to implement (Felder 1995, 3 ff., 47 ff.). The described facts vary, depending on the specific concepts and terms. Such differences can be identified via the connotations as aspects of meaning or accentuations. The replication of attempts of semantic and fact fixation of a debated fact is at the heart of the research interest. Meaning should in this context not be understood as an entity, but as a postulation of meaning or rather an interpretative hypothesis that is comprised by the textual and situational interpretations.

[6]Concept here means a cognitive unit or content, which allows characteristics or connotations to be identified (cf. Felder 2003: 43). This still does not touch upon the question, in how far these units are of linguistic nature or not. As Barsalou puts it: "By *concept* I mean the descriptive information that people represent cognitively for a category, including definitional information, prototypical information, functionally important information, and probably other types of information as well"(Barsalou 1992: 31).

By way of the comprehension of the linguistically communicated constitution of facts (the referential action) of the expert (linguistic precedent, reconstruction of the former naming fixation, etc.) other experts not only develop the meaning of an expression, but also possible action patterns, after whose example current denotational fixations can be continued, modified or replaced. This – the assertive positioning of certain connotations of technical terms and/or in the implementation of naming fixation as action patterns – constitutes "semantic battles" in scientific, specialized and general discourses of different domains of knowledge.

3 The Position of the Approach "Semantic Battles" in Discourse Linguistics

The debates to be looked at in discourses (cf. Warnke 2007 and Warnke and Spitzmüller 2008a, b) are the ones in which the protagonists are social actors, who try to shape texts and conversations through their idiomatic usage (cf. e.g. Müller 2007b; Vogel 2009). Such texts and/or conversations (which need to be carefully sorted and complied in a corpus, cf. the Heidelberger Korpus http://www.gs.uni-heidelberg.de/sprache02/hd_korpus/ and Bubenhofer 2009) need to be analyzed for social contextualization from the point of view of discourse linguistics and in view of diverging conceptualizations and action strategies (Busse 2007 and 2008; Konerding 2005, 2007 and 2008). This leads to contentious centers of discourse in the texts that are to be investigated. By contentious centers I understand a competition that is manifested in language games about the controversial acceptance of meaning interpretation, options for action, assertive claims, knowledge guidelines and values in societies. Thus, discourses come to form orientational frames and central variables are always repositioned in the process of meaning formation.

Discourse here is understood, in the sense of Busse and Teubert (1994), as texts that

- deal with an object, a topic, or a concept, that have semantic relations and/or interact on the level of assertion, communication, function or goal orientation,
- stay within the specified borders of the research program with regard to the time, area, social extract, communicative area, text type and other parameters,
- and form an intertextual continuity through implicit or explicit (i.e. realizable through text or context semantics) referencing (Busse and Teubert 1994: 14).

Fraas and Klemm (2005) complete this linguistics inspired by Foucault with the following discourse dimensions, which have also been noted by Warnke (2007) and Warnke and Spitzmüller (2008a, b) in their approach:

(a) Discourses as associations of texts linked by content
(b) Discourses as amalgamations of topics in texts
(c) Discourses as networks of signs, tracks and trails of knowledge segments
(d) Discourses as reference values for individual texts

(e) Discourses as forms of textual dialogues
(f) Discourses as forms of correspondence of systems of thought and arguments
(g) Discourses as interaction in society
(h) Discourses as virtual text corpora

Two of the methods of discourse analysis two will be mentioned here. They take a similar approach but still differ in the specificities. On the one hand, I want to bring up my proposal of a linguistic discourse analysis (Felder 2009a), which I discussed under the paradigm of pragma-semiotic text analysis. Starting from a lexical, syntagmatic and syntactic-semantic analysis from a text semantic point of view, illocutions are systematized in a pragmatically oriented investigation and the speaker attitudes, which are indicated at the text surface, are explained. In addition, certain discourse topics will be analyzed in more detail with regard to topoi and argumentational structures (Wengeler 2003). This will be done at the levels of investigation *lexis – syntagma – syntax – text* (including the intertextual referencing structures), and the text-image-relations, all under the paradigm of pragma-semiotic text analysis. This model is based, amongst others, on the ideas of Polenz (1988), Scherner (2000) and Gardt (2007) and is inductively oriented: departing from the intensive study of the text interpretational hypotheses are offered on the basis of pertinent linguistic criteria – from specific individual instances to overall context.

As a second approach I want to mention Warnke's and Spitzmüller's (2008a, b) multi-level model of discourse analysis, which is structured more deductively. At the heart stand three dimensions: the intratextual level (which is mainly text analytic, i.e. lexeme, proposition and text oriented), secondly, the transtextual (discourse oriented) level and thirdly, the dimension of discourse actors taking into account also the media, the discourse position and the interactional roles of author and addressee. For each level the relevant linguistic methodologies and terminologies are conjoined.

A problem in both models has been pointed out by Konerding: "they still seem rather complimentary-aggregational, less theory-led and systematized or oriented in a convincing way towards an empirically successful research strategy" (Konerding 2009: 90). He correctly points out that the systematic connection between the individual research levels does not become clear and thereby reminds us of the desideratum of linguistic theory, that is that it needs to have a practical operability in actual research projects to develop and prove empirically: "the neglected but central and discourse constitutive concepts of *topic* and *topic discussion* will undoubtedly have to play a central role here" (Konerding 2009, 171).

4 Different Levels of Semantic Battles: Expressive Level (Denotation) – Content Level (Concepts) – Factual Level (Real-World Objects)

"Semantic battles" – as we said above – denotes the attempt to implement certain linguistic forms as expressions of specific interest-led action and thought patterns in a domain of knowledge. This can be achieved in various ways: through definitions or through meaning and fact fixation. Here the semantic battle is differentiated as an implicit or explicit conflict about the fittingness of linguistic expression with regard to three perspectives:

- the level of designation and definition: a number of expressions give prominence to different aspects of a fact;
- the level of meaning: one and the same expression has different connotations and accentuations;
- the level of facts and reference objects: seemingly identical or actually identical reference objects are differently constituted – either in the same expressions or a (supposedly) related (on the level of meaning or factual) manner of expressions.

With the help of attempts at implementation of definitions as action patterns and/or in the assertive positioning of certain connotation of technical terms and/or in the respective idiomatically influenced constitution of facts can semantic battles be fought in individual sciences.

The term *semantic battle* has been used for some time now in critical discourse analysis (e.g. Keller 1977; Klein 1989; Liedtke et al. 1991; Stötzel 1990), but historical and political linguistics that are interested in historical semantics also use this term (e.g. Koselleck 1972 and 1979; Bergsdorf 1979, 1983, 1985, 1988 and 1991), and last but not least, also politics that is oriented towards practical power and interest implementation also makes use of the term (e.g. Biedenkopf 1973 and 1975; Glotz 1985; Hombach 1991).

In most subject areas we find semantic battles or linguistic standardization conflicts that are fought in discourse, and which influence our general thinking and behavior. In this context Foucault introduced the term "dispositive" as a discourse form, in which power, justice and truth are linked and the practices, which satisfy human desires (*désir*) and social hardship (*urgence*), institutionalized (Foucault 1983, 105 f.). According to Foucault, sex is such a dispositive (Foucault 1978, 119 f.). Justice is another one (Foucault 1975; Seibert 2004, 12 ff). *Dispositive* here means a certain acceptance of certain behaviors, discourses, identities and forms of knowledge, etc.

The dispositive constitutes an intervention into the power relations (as e.g. the dispositive power) of certain social hardships. It bundles or functionalizes highly heterogeneous elements such as laws, discourses, (governmental) subsidies, etc. and functions as a means of analysis, with the help of which we try to establish, how a certain pattern could originate and what effects it makes possible. The dispositive allows individuals an appropriation of knowledge, which they need in order to act in a (useful) manner in the world. A fundamental medium of dispositives is language (cf. also Busse et al. 2005; Liebert and Weitze 2006).

5 Examples of Semantic Battles at the Level of Denotation

I want to give two examples for semantic battles on the level of terms and definitions: on the one hand, the debate about cloning (discussed by Zimmer 2006) and, on the other hand, the contraposition of the terms *leading culture* (*Leitkultur*) and *metaculture* (*Metakultur*).

Zimmer (2006) shows with the help of the example of the so-called therapeutic cloning,[7] how scientists try to form or change technical terms and their respective meanings in discourse via semantic battles. He already faces the problem of denoting in the presentation of the research problem, where he is in the difficult position of needing to name a term, whose definition and content, however, are still forming. But since authors already need to designate in order to communicate, Zimmer opted for the term "therapeutic cloning" as the most common one. (He therefore either puts the term in inverted commas or precedes it with "so-called").

Zimmer (2006) analyses the prominent debate between theologians and medical scientists in the German newspaper Frankfurter Allgemeine Zeitung (FAZ) in the years 2000 and 2001. The articles by doctor Oliver Brüstle and Karl Friedrich Sewing, on the one hand, and by the theologian Dietmar Mieth, Ulrich Lüke and Eberhard Schockenhoff, on the other hand, form the heart of the analysis. Here we will only look at the terms *therapeutic cloning* and *research cloning*:

In the texts analyzed for this article the doctors argued for the term *therapeutic cloning* and the theologians rejected the concept. Between these two groups there is dissent both on the level of semantics and on the level of denotation with regard to the linguistic constitution of *therapeutic cloning*.

Both groups used the term in the first phase of the debate. The concepts behind this term, however, are completely different. The advocates of *therapeutic cloning* explicitly situate the technique in the context of healing and therapy. The potential for the development of new treatments is seen as so great, that moral doubts can be put aside. In their eyes, the end justifies the means. The adversaries see *therapeutic cloning* first and foremost as a technique, whose therapeutic potential is still a long way away, but whose ethical consequences are grave. This goes back to the the applicability of the principle that who wants to help may not intervene in the rights of others, especially not in human lives. *Therapeutic cloning* creates human life

[7] "While cloning of whole human beings is – apart from a few exceptions – being rejected by politics, science and the general public, the production of cloned human embryos with the help of core transfer to obtain embryonic stem cells is highly debated. This form of cloning is generally called *therapeutic cloning*. Therapeutic cloning aims to create cells and tissue that may at some point be used for treatment of e.g. neurodegenerative illnesses" (Zimmer 2006: 74).

only to then destroy it again for the extraction of stem cells. For the adversaries, therefore, *therapeutic cloning* belongs to the paradigm of consumptive embryo research (Zimmer 2006, 94).

According to Zimmer these competitions of definition with regard to the usage of the term *cloning* (i.e. *therapeutic cloning* vs. *research cloning*) can be made clear, when the respective connotations, which the respective protagonists try to give prominence to, are deleted. In the context of the supportive usage of the term *therapeutic cloning* these are the connotation of 'promise of healing' and 'acceptance of research in society', whereas the advocates of the term *research cloning* want to implement the connotation of 'open outcome research' and 'assertive positioning of the purpose'. It becomes clear that the advocates of the term *therapeutic cloning* include the concepts of 'healing' and 'therapy' into the approach. The advocates of the term *research cloning*, however, point out that the latter is the more accurate term, since it forms part of consumptive embryo research and this implies that research outcomes cannot be predicted. The term *research cloning* does not – unlike the term *therapeutic cloning* – promise healing.

Zimmer summarizes his research as follows:

If one looks at the relevance the two concepts of meaning have achieved in public opinion, it seems that the battle between the researchers has been decided in favor of the advocates of the paradigm of healing. The view of *therapeutic cloning* as a technique, with the help of which healthy organic tissue that is not rejected by the body's immune system can be produced. In addition, the term *therapeutic cloning* is neither relativized in any way nor replaced by other terms.

A semantic change has, however, taken place the scientific jargon in recent years. The opponents of therapeutic cloning started to replace the term *therapeutic cloning* quite early on with the term *research cloning*. The advocates at first stuck to the term *therapeutic cloning*. Only later did they search for new ways out such as using technical terms, for example, "directed cell reproduction" (gezielte Zellvermehrung). In the end, however, they also adopted the term *research cloning*. The meanings behind the term, however, remain unchanged. Researchers, who support research cloning, continue to see the technique as a step in the development of new therapies, whereas the opprononets continue to see the technique in the context of consumptive embryo research.

The skirmish over the denotation of *therapeutic cloning* was won by the advocates of a strict protection of the embryo, but the concepts behind the word remain very different. Time will tell, whether the new term *research cloning* will be adopted by the general public, which is strongly influenced by the hope for new therapies (Zimmer 2006, 95).

Secondly, I want to point out the semantic competition, which takes place around the public debates about social cultures and their relation between each other with regard to compatibility and dominance.

The question under discussion here, to put it pointedly, is: How implicit or explicit is the semantic battle about the terms *leading culture* and *metaculture*? The expression *leading culture* is already controversial in itself, its significance no less so. Sometimes people, who use this term, are accused of a nationalistic tendencies:

the use of the word itself is seen as a shibboleth of an attitude, where the expression already reveals the political affinity of the user. I will here not deal with the question, how the term *leading culture* is used,[8] but restrict myself to the question, whether alternative termini are already in use in the media. One of the possible replacements is the term *metaculture*. A search in the easily accessible newspaper corpora gives only sparse results. One instance can found in the article by the philosopher Peter Sloterdijk.

Neither more nor less is to be expected of Islam, which will undoubtedly become a leading figure in Europe in the future. What is to be expected in a long-term plan is the Europeanization of Islam and not the Islamization of Europe. This requirement does not express a European arrogation. It forms part of an emerging global project, which expects of all cultures, including the religious ones, a common metaculture, i.e. a globally suitable civilization (Focus Magazin 6.03.2006, 84–86).

Another instance reflects on the question, how diverse cultures can be captured in a city, and whether the term metaculture is helpful in this context (taz 7.01.2002, 14). A third instance regards the author Claudio Magris, who says about his city Trieste: "Trieste only became a great city because of its foreign citizens, who were quickly Italianized and who incorporated the new and the old, the important middle-European element. The metaculture and civilization interested me, which these people created in the face of constant danger of life" (Die Welt, 11.11.2004). A fourth instance seems to be due rather to journalistic creativity, i.e. when an article on the lack of common sense in the stock market is subtitled: "On the mass-psychological metaculture of postmodern finance markets" (Die Welt 14.06.1999, 11). The term is not used in the article itself.

Metaculture has the potential to take up certain connotational aspects of the expression *leading culture*, without needing to distance itself from a conservatively labeled user group. Who uses the expression, of course, also claims new areas, which in time may become ideologically marked (social-communicative fission while taking into account the prototypical social structures, which use the word *leading culture*). A relatively new term (without a history of usage) for a known phenomenon has the potential to become the keyword of certain (different) thought traditions.

6 Examples of Semantic Battles at the Conceptual Level

Semantic battles at the semantic level do not struggle for adequacy of expression, of terms with regard to reference objects – for which the instances cited above on cloning and the social and political situation in social communities with people from different cultural backgrounds serve as examples. Rather, what we are dealing with is an uncontested (because unstated) expression with regard to its connotations, which in themselves may be subject to debate. We are dealing here with the

[8] On this question see for example Fritzsche (2006) or Potthoff et al. (2007).

question, which connotations are to be attributed to the expression and which aspects should be seen as inadequate semantic aspects.

This will be sketched in the following, using the example of *generational justice* and *globalization*. Both concepts differ greatly in one aspect: *Generational justice*, on the one hand, is undisputed, because the idea itself is in itself seen as obvious and appropriate. What is debatable is only, which components (characteristics of living conditions) should be included in the concept and which should not – and of course also how these should be assessed. *Globalisation*, on the other hand, describes a fact in the world, which – despite all its semantic fuzziness – is seen as a given by most discourse agents. The fact itself as a political issue, however, is highly debated.

Generational justice is first and foremost a desired state (an orientational value), not a fact like globalization (although there do exist some, who do not see the world as globalized, most media depicts the world as a globalized one). Therefore, the discussion centers around how close we are (really or apparently) to the orientational value and which components it comprises.

To illustrate the attempts at meaning fixation of *generational justice*, I did a simple search in Lexisnexis (on 24.04.2009) for the following German newspapers: *Der Tagesspiegel, Die Welt, Frankfurter Rundschau, taz*. I wanted to see, which aspects of meaning could be gathered from the usage of the terms in the articles and in how far the status and acceptance of these semantic aspects were implicit or explicit (in the texts).

A first analysis of the newspaper texts with the focus of attempts at meaning fixation, suggested the following connotations:

- 'Factual linkage with other forms of justice such as distributive justice, equal opportunities, with effects on climate change for later generations and with constitutional rights as, for example, human rights'
- 'Generation debt'
- 'The need for a strong or weak state, federal regulation'
- 'Tax and distributive policies'
- 'Double burden: through current contributions for pensioners and reductions for oneself as pensioners of tomorrow; cost-cutting measure: pension augmentation and/or pension contribution augmentation'
- 'Effects of nature and environment conservation'
- 'Inclusion of the aim of generational justice in the constitution (*Grundgesetz*), Art. 20b'
- 'Self-responsibility of the individual versus collective responsibility of the state'.

Summary: Depending on the *weltanschauung* of the discourse protagonists the term *generational justice* is used with differing importance of certain connotational aspects as particularly central components. And this semantic battle (i.e. the attempt to implement certain thought and action patterns) is fought implicitly rather than explicitly. The discursive strategy consists of an assertive illocution, which foregrounds those connotations as indispensable, which serve the plausibility of the own argumentation. It then attempts through an inductive argument a transition so as to convey a particular conclusion as compelling from specific, self-made premises – this is, of course, done via a seemingly logical deduction (Kienpointner 1992).

When discussing the word *globalization* (cf. Liebert 2003 for a linguistic discussion of the term) the question arises, how this term is more useful than *internationalization* or *multinationalization*. This brings in the aspect of whether – in comparison to the age that preceded globalization – we really are living in a qualitatively new condition, which makes a new term advisable or even necessary. Such terms – which come into use in speech communities in quick succession and are sometimes used inflationally – imply that their semantic meaning is both by degree and qualitatively different from the semantic content of similar terms and that the usage of the term instead of already established terms such as, for example, *internationalization* point towards new living conditions.[9]

The assessment in terms of content of the fact of globalization sometimes colors the usage of globalization opponents in such a way that critics only use the word in a marked manner (i.e. in inverted commas or with the distancing attribute *so-called*) und thus pejoratively. The term is to be visibly strategically marked for negativity as a label of disavowal so to speak. The word *globalization* has thus a similar usage dilemma as the word *euthanasia* (cf. Felder 2009c): How am I to act, if I do not want my linguistic usage to automatically decry me as belonging to a certain group of globalization advocates or opponents? Possible solutions – taking into account linguistic strategies – are:

1. Usage of the termini: when terms that are seen as problematic such as e.g. *globalization* are used, it is advised to metalinguistically point this out and mark the individual usage with regard to the usage of known interest groups in the discourse.
2. The usage of a variety of similar terms for reasons of terminological definition and division can achieve a positive estimation of the connotations of cluster 1 and give cluster 2 a pejorative connotation.
3. Avoidance of the terms that are seen as problematic: this strategy works through paraphrasing if applied on its own. The danger of, thereby, being grouped among a certain denomination is thus minimized, but the expenditure of formulating would be much higher with regard to precision, economy and comprehensibility and, in addition, would have to be brought into a form which both the recipient and the speaker would feel to be authentic.

[9] In the context of restrictions of free trade by the first world, for example, it is pointed out that the advocates of globalization, who use the word in an unmarked sense, are strictly speaking not allowed to do so, because they do not fight the restriction of globalization and thus find themselves in the contradiction of proclaiming the advantages of a globalized world, but where its disadvantages impede their interests, they stay silent and accept a non-globalized world, which benefits them. As a linguist I only mention this content-related evaluative problem to be able to give plausible interpretative hypotheses of the different motives for the usages. The physician and biologist Ernst Ulrich v. Weizsäcker summarizes his observations as follows: "All human beings associate both hopes and fears with the term *globalization*. Conspicuous is the following: Who influences the global events, typically speaks positively of globalization. Who feels powerless in the face of them, is overwhelmed by fears. (Source: http://www.globalisierung-online.de/info/text2.php – last accessed 20.10.2015)

7 Examples of Semantic Battles with Regard to the Active Fixation of Facts

The multilayered problem that the fundamental phenomena of our daily lives are not ontological givens, but only develop or are constituted through language, is the basis of the linguistic dimension of attempts at the fixation of facts. I want to illustrate this with an example of the reporting on the economic and cyclical policy, which are based on the publications and statements of so-called leading economic research institutes. Since no one can experience an economic upturn or downturn empirically through the senses, it is a linguistically constituted phenomenon. However, when the present state of the economy is collectively accepted as a prototypical phase of a downturn (a crisis or depression), it is only natural, that we, for example, feel we are seeing more unemployed people during the normal working hours in our urban centers, which we again (causally) connect with the current and collective knowledge about the diagnosed and constituted state of the national and international economy. We thus compare our media constituted models of reality with the empirically and sensually observable.

When we try to retrace how, for example, cyclical estimations are established in the collective knowledge of the memory, we can go back to autumn 2007 when both the media and the economic research institutes declared that Germany was experiencing an economic upturn. This changed, as we know, in the late summer of 2008, when a general worldwide economic depression (financial and world economic crisis) was announced. Experts today all use the model of business cycles and have defined a certain number of characteristics as necessary or sufficient for the classification of the economic phases. The question now is, how the characteristics that underlie the categories can be empirically measured and how many characteristics and with what intensity need to be diagnosed to fulfill the characteristics of a category. These questions are often discussed in the public media by telegenic economic experts (there only seem to be a handful of those available) or economic research institutes, which show with the help of graphics, etc. where we are on the scale of the since our school days deeply ingrained economic phases. In this way facts are constituted and paraphrased as follows: "the German economy is right now in phase X". The business cycle is understood as forming part of general economic processes, which as a rule can be subsumed under (wavelike) fluctuations of the economic situation. The business cycle describes the overall process of the recurrent up- and downturns of economic activities. Four phases are today usually distinguished: expansion, peak (together called upturn), crisis or contraction, depression or trough (together also known as downturn). To clarify this, a few fundamental characteristics of the upturn will be named with the help of an economics dictionary (Gabler Wirtschaftslexikon 2004) improved capacity utilization, rising private investments and wage bill, increasing national income, heightened private consumption. The characteristics of a peak are described as follows: production methods in full time use, growth of actual national income, strong price increases, disruption in the financial markets (Gabler Wirtschaftslexikon 2004).

Now we have reached the central problem of determining how these characteristics can be related to a complex reality. So the question arises, whether these characteristics are empirically present and measurable or not. If some or all characteristics are constituted as empirically diagnosable, the phenomenon can be understood to be a (concrete/material) figure, which can be referred to by the terms *upturn* or *peak*. Or, to put it another way: the phenomenon of an upturn or a peak is only taken to be a given once it has been named. Or to paraphrase again: Such formulations constitute attempts at fact fixation. The current state needs to be determined, labeled and fixed.

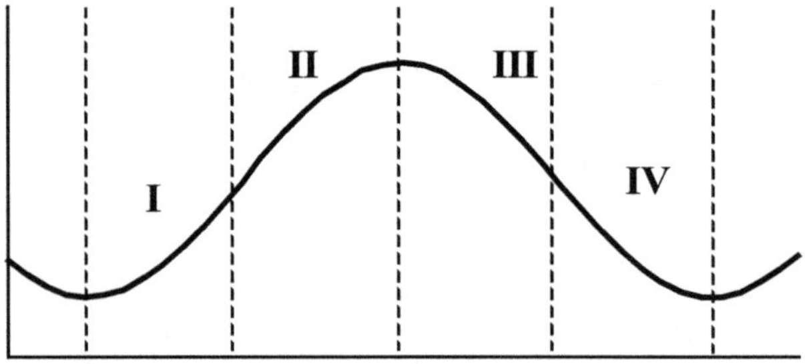

I. Expansion II. Peak III. Crisis/Contraction IV. Trough/Depression

This form of fact fixation becomes especially obvious, when economic research institutes express the current state of the economy in different ways, even though they point more or less at the same location on the above diagram of a prototypical business cycle and base themselves on more or less the same data. As was the case in autumn 2007.

Therefore, I here present extracts of the announcements, which "leading monetary institutes" (their term) publish. First, it pays to take a look at the self-estimation of the institutes, which can be found on the respective webpages. The *Institut der deutschen Wirtschaft* (IW)[10] describes its self-given task as follows:

> The IW is Germany's leading private economic research institute [...] Our task is to promote a better understanding of economic and social processes among politicians, opinion makers and the general public. We analyze facts, reveal trends, explain economic developments and publish our proposals. (Source: http://www.iwkoeln.de)

The "understanding of economic processes", thus is not based on empirically measurable and quantifiable indicators, as the economic layperson might have been inclined to assume, the understanding is rather to be "promoted" (or in the German version "determined and improved"). This admits an implicit semantic battle. The perception of economic processes is to be formed.

Very similarly – even if ideologically differently situated – the Macroeconomic Policy Institute (IMK) in Düsseldorf:

[10]The name is not translated by the institute itself but would be: Institute of the German Economy.

> The IMK was founded in early 2005 to strengthen the macroeconomic perspective both in economic research and in the economic policy debate. The IMK analyses the business cycle on the basis of a coherent macroeconomic modeling framework. In their empirical research the IMK's researchers rely on modern Keynesian economic theory as well as state-of-the-art econometric methods. (Source: http://www.boeckler.de)

This institute admits its consolidation of a particular point of view, which according to them, has so far been neglected. These two self-images show, that economic facts are also not ontologically given and are, thus, just waiting for an empirical recording, but need to be constituted and aspectually perspectivized (according to the individual preconceptions) by experts. This exemplifies the extraordinary relevance of the third level of the approach "semantic battle", on which the different implicitly and explicitly executed attempts at fact fixation by social protagonists are reproduced. At its core, it deals with the determination of who is capable of shaping a current reality that is not perceivable with the senses, and which discursive means are used.

If one thinks about the psychological effect on behavior of economic subjects in dependence of the media reporting on current and business developments of the general economy, the attempts at fact fixation of the economic experts can hardly be said to be innocent pastimes. On the contrary, they are signs of the extraordinarily powerful position of the linguistic structuring of individual discourse agents.[11] The perception of the economic situation is influenced by the medial portrayal (creation of facticity through economic think-tanks). Keeping this in mind, we need to mention with regard to the linguistic access on the general economic situation in the autumn of 2007 some peculiarities. When one looks at the description of the two named institutes in more detail, one cannot help but notice the following:

- Both institutes use the term *upturn*, but try to give it different main connotations. Controversial connotations are the status of the indicators *higher corporate profit* and the meaning of the *distribution of income* taking the question into account, which social groups profit from the upturn.
- The headlines for the current economic situation "a slightly reduced upturn" (IW) versus "Germany threatened by downturn" (IMK) make clear that the seemingly or really identical living conditions are differently arranged – linguistically speaking.
- Both institutes base themselves on similar gross domestic products (GDP), but come to different interpretations with regards to the question, whether the upturn still continues and what effects this will have on the labor market.

A further example for the fact fixations comes from the medical arena. Domasch took the possible introduction of the preimplantation genetic diagnosis in Germany in the years 2000 to 2002 as the subject for her investigation of publicly controversially discussed discourses (cf. the relevant works by Domasch 2006 and 2007). An essential element of this discussion was the struggle for linguistic means of naming new and controversial facts. Embryos are used for the investigations with regard to

[11] For a linguistic research in the context of economic crisis see Wengeler and Ziem (2010).

the genetic disposition in the context of the preimplantation genetic diagnosis (PGD). The facts are first of all ontically constituted, the linguistic terms does not at first seem to play a role. Still, to communicate the results of medical investigations, they need to be linguistically transmitted, so that from the point of view of laypersons facts are only constituted through the linguistic frame. What does it mean for couples, when the potential parents of an embryo are told of a disposition for red-green-blindness? Such facts force people to take decisions. Similarly to the economic reference object of the preceding example, one can at first assume an ontic and linguistically independent fact, that will be formulated in a way to elicit similar concepts in the respective addressees and thus create various aspectual facts. In PGD or prebirth diagnostic embryos are checked for genetic dispositions and get labeled as "healthy" or "fitting", or the embryos do not get "implanted" but "discarded": the are left to "die" (*absterben*, for linguistic aspects see Domasch 2007). The investigation traces the topicalization of language in the programmatic texts of the time and shows, that the systematic search for metalinguistic elements results in a plentitude of linguistically topicalized labels, which in their differentiation with regard to content aim at central controversies of the debate. This points towards the importance of linguistic terminology in public space makes clear that the constitution of knowledge about "progress" in medical technology is linguistically instructed.

Overview of the Levels in the Approach S*emantic Battle*

1. **Specifics of the terminological competition: controversy over the correct term**
   Ex. → *Therapeutic cloning* versus *Research cloning*
   Ex. → *Leading culture* and *Metaculture*: Each term seems to access a seemingly ontic correlate.
2. **Specifics of semantic fixation: Controversy about the fitting semantic aspects of an in itself uncontroversial term (semasiological)**
   → "Generational justice", which needs to be fixated as a value and, therefore, needs to be semasiologically clarified.
   → *Globalization*, of which it seems that we are able to experience it directly or empirically!
3. **Specifics of fact fixation: The fact that is to be shaped (and not to be directly experienced) and that is constantly being referred to does not seem to be aspectually perspectivized through the respective linguistic usage (onomasiological)**
   Ex. → Economic classification within the business cycles
   Ex. → Within the prebirth diagnostic embryos are examined for their genetic dispositions and the discovered characteristics are linguistically constituted and labeled.

8 Semantic Battles – Keyword-Concept – Discourse Analysis

The perception of semantic battles in the current article comprehends mainly the investigation of (controversial) concepts of action, i.e. points of condensation and crystallization in terms of content. The concepts that guide actions are not only to be analyzed as individual lexemes, but also through a complex analysis of the multitude of speech acts of different speakers in diverging conversation and text types. These concepts will however, condense in key words, so that these will automatically be put at the centre of investigations for reasons of practicality. The same is true here, as space will not permit a thorough discussion on various levels (but see Felder (2009a) for a research program). For a in depth analysis of the discourse customs in the context of the current debate about the consequences of the neurobiological research findings for the humanities a thorough investigation is necessary and thus (still) a desideratum.

Out of practical reasons often only keywords are investigated as points of condensation and crystallization in discourse analysis. These are then analyzed from the viewpoint of semantic ascription, which are discursively attributed to the expressions by the individual discourse agents (for a pragmatic semantics of lexemes and a usage oriented lexical semantics cf. Hundsnurscher 1998). If one analyses the central semantic aspects in discourse from a resultative point of view (Hundsnurscher 1991; Gloning 1996), the following becomes clear, which has been mentioned above but will be looked at in more detail here.

1. Synoptically summarized, a dynamic concept is here the basis of the applied understanding of keywords (Liebert 2003): Consequently keywords display the following characteristics,
   - they mirror the self-image of a person or a group in discourse,
   - they are discourse determinative,
   - their contextual meaning is the main one,
   - they display a multitude of meanings,
   - they are sometimes controversial.
2. Words do not exist in isolation in the human mind, but build an interdependent sum of elements with other related words (in a dynamic extension of a rather structuralist viewpoint of *semantic fields*). The starting point for such a semantic field theory is the fact that there do exist usages of expressions that correspond in some semantic aspects (content) and are different in others. This viewpoint correlates with the basic assumptions of semantic field theory, which Gloning (2002, 728) defines as follows: "(i) classification of the lexicon; (ii) mutual determination of meaning of lexical elements (iii) hypothesis of the 'world view' of language; (iv) semantic change as change in the web of semantic fields; (v) usages of words as semantic field members; (vi) process of lexical decomposition" for the explication of semantic similarities and differences.
3. These two aspects of the keyword conception and the semantic field theory can be understood in the paradigm of semantic battles as strategic instruments for the

determination of linguistic access (i.e. specific, interest-led patterns of action and thought) on the level of expressions, meanings and/or the facts constituted in this way (language as power) and to be more than mere meaning explication.

In the light of this theoretical background the following questions pose themselves for the investigation of discourse:

- Which keywords are controversial and how can they be explained in more detail through the paradigm of semantic battles?
- In how far can the approach of semantic battles with its levels of denotation, meaning nuances and attempts at fact fixation lay open these linguistic strategies?

9 Semantic Battles in the Legal Field

Characterizing semantic battles essentially involves investigating the (controversial) concepts that drive actions, that is, those points around which the content condenses and crystalizes. On the expressive side, the action-driving concepts cannot be described merely through an analysis of individual lexemes; rather, what is chiefly needed is a complex analysis of multiple speech acts by different discourse participants in divergent text and conversation types (Felder 2003, 203). Nonetheless, those concepts do crystalize into key words, which for reasons of research practice have taken center stage in academic studies again and again – as can be seen in the paradigm of jurisprudential textual work (Felder 2003; Li 2011; Vogel 2012; Luth 2015).

In this paradigm, working with texts is the central characteristic of a legal functionary's activities (Busse 1992, 1993/2010; Müller et al. 1997; Felder 2003). For this reason, the depiction of legal acts is programmatically referred to as "jurisprudential textual work" (Felder 2003). Legal theoretician Friedrich Müller (2007a) calls this jurisprudential work with texts "legal work," and in his legal methodology the experts who write the laws and those who apply them are called "legal workers." These designations propagate a point of view that emphasizes the role of the jurisprudentially acting subject in concretizing legal prescriptions. I also subscribe to this view, and my aim here is to characterize the speech acts performed by legal workers in the battle over the applicability of verbal formulations and the accompanying perspectives.

When describing jurisprudence, it must be pointed out that working with an interweave of different text types (e.g. aside from legal texts, also expert opinions from other scientific disciplines) stands at the forefront of a legal professional's activities, and that the work of comprehending jurisprudential activities should not be restricted to those professionals' dealings with individual legal texts. Moreover, it should be kept in mind that while legal texts with their potential for directing actions do represent the point of departure for jurisprudence, their importance for determining the course of justice must be viewed in relation to other texts arising from internal communication within the legal field, such as legal commentary, professional jurisprudential literature or supreme court decisions (Müller et al. 1997; Felder 2003).

The focus mentioned above, on the role of the jurisprudentially acting subject in concretizing legal prescriptions, presupposes the following: a legal norm is not an entity given *ante casum* by the texts of laws and constitutions, but rather it is only formed and concretized once a legal functionary becomes involved – in interdependence with the state of affairs being negotiated and the chosen legal text.

The legal norm as a prescription for actions and conduct is only partly contained within legal texts. Even an expert on jurisprudence does not take the norm directly out of a legal clause, in the sense of a container metaphor; rather, he places real-life situations – the so-called "case" – in relation to one or more legal prescriptions, and from this linkage he arrives at an appropriate legal norm for the case at hand. Therefore, this approach centers on the question of how the legal text codified in the law books and the social situation or reality placed in relation to it (the construction of "social facts" (Searle 1995) or "realities") come to be linked with each other in the legal norm (which is more than just the legal text). This question can only be answered at the level of an interweave of jurisprudential texts. As mentioned above, different jurisprudential texts must be considered in the process. A distinction must be made between 1) text types with normative force (with the potential to concretize or shape norms) such as the texts of laws and constitutions; 2) text types that represent legal-text exegesis, such as legal commentary, legal scholars' discussions of court decisions in the professional literature, or head notes from courts; and 3) text types that represent case law (concretization of norms), i.e. court rulings, decisions. Accordingly, while the texts of laws are of central importance, they alone do not contain the actual legal norm in the sense of a storage metaphor; rather, the texts of laws require further elaboration in legal discourse through application and interpretation. They merely contain a partly explicated directive potential with complex implications, presuppositions, and a range of experience in the discursive use of legal texts in relation to prototypical real-life situations.

In accordance with these prerequisites, a semantic-pragmatic analysis based on action theory comes into play at the point where language has an effect on the jurisprudential "processing of reality"; namely, in the "taking of normative positions on a situation," which all too often – in Seibert's formulation – turns into the "construction of reality" (Seibert 1981). Jurisprudence takes hold of the social "reality" (social situation) to be evaluated right at the source: at the categories, which are viewed and described in jurisprudential terms for the elements of a crime. In criminal offenses, theft for example, the descriptive elements (words) used to render the process tangible are themselves suggestive in nature; thus, a labeling has already taken place before the situation can even be construed. Seibert points out that human actions (through their assignment to categories = labeling of actions) have already been socially pre-organized and pre-interpreted. In this way, he elucidates the depiction of the jurisprudential act of "construal of a situation," i.e. the jurisprudentially pre-processed or pre-interpreted selection and preparation of elements of a situation, as the objective of norm application. This preparation, however, cannot simply be juxtaposed with the exegesis of the legal text as another form of interpretation ("understanding"); rather, legal-text interpretation and (jurisprudential) interpretation of social reality are combined in a process of jurisprudential action. In this context, Jeand'Heur (1998) aptly speaks of the "preparatory function," which is intrinsic to the use of specialized legal texts, and through which the "case" is transformed into a legally relevant "state of affairs" in the first place. The concept of "jurisprudential textual work" is used here to illustrate how a legal professional – taking the facts of a case and legal texts as a jurisprudential knowledge framework – "pre-processes" real-life situations from the knowledge framework of the everyday world (Jeand'Heur 1998).

Jurisprudential acts are thus to be understood as the text-aided integration of a situation into jurisprudential schemas for processing reality. The application of laws consists in large part of transforming extralegal states of affairs into legal states of affairs (i.e. institutionally defined and constituted states of affairs) based on various knowledge frameworks. Specific forms of knowledge make it possible to draw inferences and to explore unmentioned or implied states of affairs, and they are adaptable to some extent. In this sense, the concept of "jurisprudential textual work" employed here within the approach to legal theory known as Structuring Legal Theory is not to be understood as a self-contained theory aiming to "deductively derive, using on its own basic concepts, what a legal text is in essence and what should be the nature of the activities of legal functionaries based on that text." Rather, it comes into play in the middle of jurisprudential texts.

> Structuring Legal Theory is to be understood as an accompanying reflection of the practice of law, in which the deciding criteria of jurisprudential rationality are already present in scattered form. It takes as its task the ordering of these elements into a preliminary model, open to new developments. The theoretical assumptions are thus not the prerequisites but the results of an analysis of practice, and the rationality criterion is not one that has been imported from philosophy and retroactively applied to law, but one that is immanent to language games. (Müller et al. 1997, 15)

The postulate of legal fixation has long been criticized in the strongest terms, and not only from within the above-described paradigm. As just one example, we may quote Winfried Hassemer, former Vice President of Germany's Federal Constitutional Court:

> It is obviously preposterous, in the face of the insights gained as to the vagueness and porosity of legal terms or the differences in each judge's prior understanding of them, to insist that a judge must adhere strictly to the law. He cannot do so. The consequence of such a demand, ostensively based on the rule of law, is not that court rulings will adhere more exactly to the legal prescriptions, but rather that they will pretend as if they were only following the law. (Hassemer 1994, 259)

This statement can bear fruit within the context of interest here, through the insight that court proceedings are not "epistemological processes" for investigating the concrete norm that is to be derived from the matter at hand together with the legal text (i.e., the outcome of the case); rather, they are the field where semantic battles are fought, where the parties seek to gain control of the legal text for their own purposes. (Christensen and Kudlich 2008, 207) From this point of view, the judge's role is defined by the fact that on the one hand, his office empowers him to "decide" the conflict between the parties on the level of the designation, the meaning, and the fixation of the state of affairs, and on the other hand he is himself a participant in semantic battles and bears the burden of justifying the decision.

10 Conclusion

The levels of description explained above help us to make clear that such discourses are by no means only determined by the content, but also fundamentally by the historical and area-specific words in use, which can develop a life of their own. Knowledge about attitudes towards such topics as e.g. "neurobiological findings on the consequences of the self-image of humans" form part of a mode of presentation in the specialist publications and the media, and are condensed into describable keywords in the phase of discursive usage formation. Experience has shown that discourse about innovation, for example, in the area of bio- and nano-technology are not simply formed out of the information of the agents in science and economy. Much rather, they are influenced by complex laws, which are based in the functioning of pluralistic democracies, scientific and media systems as well as communicative practices. Last but not least, topics are embedded in the scientific premises and collective stereotypes of the public. The development of a discursive position through the researchers of different scientific cultures, which does not only have to be coherent in the respective science, but must also be accepted by the public, thus requires sufficient knowledge of the specialized discourse of the respective domain of knowledge, as well as in depth knowledge of strategies and practices of transformation in the communication of specialized knowledge in lay circles and, thirdly, experience in the analysis of media discourse, which is shaped by laws difficult to grasp.

When certain linguistic usages become prominent (for example Zimmer's 2006 *therapeutic cloning* or *research cloning*), certain expressions will be used at first sporadically then prototypically and can achieve the role of patterns in general social discourses (the fixation of specific combinations of signs in discourses). We here need to take into account that individual formulations (linking of linguistic signs) as free syntagmata can consolidate themselves in the development of discourse and obtain an increasingly static character. This happens from the development to the usage, i.e. the habitualization and conventionalization, up to the stereotypicality (Beckmann 2001) of schemata-led knowledge usage. This linguistic sedimentation instructs and shapes the social discursively-negotiated knowledge through perspectivized and preferred language patterns.[12]

[12] This paper is a product of my fellowship in South Africa at the "Stellenbosch Institute for Advanced Study" (STIAS). I thank STIAS for the excellent working conditions.

References

Barsalou, L. W. (1992). Frames, concepts, and conceptual fields. In A. Lehrer & E. Feder Kittay (Eds.), *Frames, fields, and contrasts. New essays in semantic und lexical organization* (pp. 21–74). Hillsdale: Erlbaum.

Beckmann, S. (2001). *Die Grammatik der Metapher. Eine gebrauchstheoretische Untersuchung des metaphorischen Sprechens*. Tübingen: Niemeyer.

Bergsdorf, W. (Ed.). (1979). *Wörter als Waffen. Sprache als Mittel der Politik*. Stuttgart: Bonn Aktuell.

Bergsdorf, W. (1983). *Herrschaft und Sprache. Studie zur politischen Terminologie der Bundesrepublik Deutschland*. Pfullingen: Neske.

Bergsdorf, W. (1985). *Über die Schwierigkeiten des politischen Sprechens in der Demokratie*, In R. Wimmer (Ed.), *Sprachkultur. Jahrbuch 1984 des Instituts für deutsche Sprache* (pp. 184–195). Düsseldorf: Pädagogischer Verlag Schwann-Bagel.

Bergsdorf, W. (1988). *Entwicklungslinien der politischen Terminologie in der Bundesrepublik Deutschland*. In T. Goppel, G. V. Lojewski, & H. Eroms (Eds.), *Wirkung und Wandlung der Sprache in der Politik. Symposium an der Universität Passau in Zusammenarbeit mit dem Aktionskreis Wirtschaft, Politik, Wissenschaft e.V. München vom 25. und 26. November 1988*, printed by University of Passau, 22–36.

Bergsdorf, W. (1991). *Zur Entwicklung der Sprache der amtlichen Politik in der Bundesrepublik Deutschland*. In F. Liedtke, M. Wengeler, & K. Böke (Eds.), *Begriffe besetzen. Strategien des Sprachgebrauchs in der Politik* (pp. 19–33). Opladen: Westdeutscher Verlag.

Biedenkopf, K. (1973). *Bericht des Generalsekretärs*. In CDU (Ed.), *22. Bundesparteitag der Christlich Demokratischen Union Deutschlands. Hamburg 18.-20. November 1973*, Bonn: CDU-Bundesgeschäftsstelle, Abteilung Öffentlichkeitsarbeit.

Biedenkopf, K. (1975). *Politik und Sprache*. In H. J. Heringer (Ed.), *Holzfeuer im hölzernen Ofen. Aufsätze zur politischen Sprachkritik* (pp. 189–197, 2nd ed., 1982). Tübingen: Narr.

Bubenhofer, N. (2009). *Sprachgebrauchsmuster. Korpuslinguistik als Methode der Diskurs- und Kulturanalyse*. Berlin/New York: de Gruyter.

Busse, D. (1991). *Textinterpretation. Sprachtheoretische Grundlagen einer explikativen Semantik*. Opladen: Westdeutscher Verlag.

Busse, D. (1992). *Recht als Text. Linguistische Untersuchungen zur Arbeit mit Sprache in einer gesellschaftlichen Institution*. Tübingen: Niemeyer.

Busse, D. (1993/2010). *Juristische Semantik. Grundfragen der juristischen Interpretationstheorie in sprach-wissenschaftlicher Sicht*. Berlin: Duncker & Humblot.

Busse, D. (2007). *Diskurslinguistik als Kontextualisierung – Sprachwissenschaftliche Überlegungen zur Analyse gesellschaftlichen Wissens*. In I. Warnke (Ed.), *Diskurslinguistik nach Foucault. Theorie und Gegenstände* (pp. 81–105). Berlin/New York: de Gruyter.

Busse, D. (2008). *Diskurslinguistik als Epistemologie – Das verstehensrelevante Wissen als Gegenstand linguistischer Forschung*. In I. Warnke & J. Spitzmüller (Eds.), *Methoden der Diskurslinguistik. Sprachwissenschaftliche Zugänge zur transtextuellen Ebene* (pp. 57–87). Berlin/New York: de Gruyter.

Busse, D., & Teubert, W. (1994). *Ist Diskurs ein sprachwissenschaftliches Objekt? Zur Methodenfrage der Historischen Semantik*. In D. Busse, F. Hermanns, & W. Teubert (Eds.), *Begriffsgeschichte und Diskursgeschichte. Methodenfragen und Forschungsergebnisse der historischen Semantik* (pp. 10–28). Opladen: Westdeutscher Verlag.

Busse, D., Niehr, T., & Wengeler, M. (Eds.). (2005). *Brisante Semantik. Neuere Konzepte und Forschungsergebnisse einer kulturwissenschaftlichen Linguistik*. Tübingen: Niemeyer.

Cassirer, E. ([4]1964). *Philosophie der symbolischen Forme*. Darmstadt: Wissenschaftliche Buchgesellschaft.

Christensen, R., & Kudlich, H. (2008). *Gesetzesbindung. Vorm vertikalen und horizontalen Verständnis*. Berlin: Duncker und Humblot.

Domasch, S. (2006). *Zum sprachlichen Umgang mit Embryonen. Semantische Konkurrenzen innerhalb des biomedizinischen Diskurses zur Präimplantationsdiagnostik.* In E. Felder (Ed.), *Semantische Kämpfe. Macht und Sprache in den Wissenschaften* (pp. 99–125). Berlin/New York: de Gruyter.

Domasch, S. (2007). *Biomedizin als sprachliche Kontroverse. Die Thematisierung von Sprache im öffentlichen Diskurs zur Gendiagnostik.* Berlin/New York: de Gruyter.

Feilke, H. (1994). *Common sense-Kompetenz. Überlegungen zu einer Theorie des "sympathischen" und "natürlichen" Meinens und Verstehens.* Frankfurt am Main: Suhrkamp.

Felder, E. (1995). *Kognitive Muster der politischen Sprache – Eine linguistische Untersuchung zur Korrelation zwischen sprachlich gefaßter Wirklichkeit und Denkmustern am Beispiel der Reden von Theodor Heuss und Konrad Adenauer.* Frankfurt am Main: Lang.

Felder, E. (2003). *Juristische Textarbeit im Spiegel der Öffentlichkeit.* Berlin/New York: de Gruyter.

Felder, E. (2006). *Semantische Kämpfe in Wissensdomänen. Eine Einführung in Benennungs-, Bedeutungs- und Sachverhaltsfixierungs-Konkurrenzen.* In E. Felder (Ed.), *Semantische Kämpfe. Macht und Sprache in den Wissenschaften* (pp. 13–46). Berlin/New York: de Gruyter.

Felder, E. (2008). *Das Forschungsnetzwerk » Sprache und Wissen « : Zielsetzung und Inhalte.* In "Zeitschrift für Germanistische Linguistik (ZGL)", 36.2/2008: 270–276.

Felder, E. (2009a). *Sprache – das Tor zur Welt!? Perspektiven und Tendenzen in sprachlichen Äußerungen,* In E. Felder (Ed.), *Sprache. Im Auftrag der Universitätsgesellschaft Heidelberg* (pp. 13–57). Berlin u.a: Springer.

Felder, E. (2009b). *Sprachliche Formationen des Wissens. Sachverhaltskonstitution zwischen Fachwelten, Textwelten und Varietäten.* In E. Felder & M. Müller (Eds.), *Wissen durch Sprache. Theorie, Praxis und Erkenntnisinteresse des Forschungsnetzwerks » Sprache und Wissen«* (pp. 21–77). Berlin/New York: de Gruyter.

Felder, E. (2009c). *Linguistische Sprachkritik im Geiste linguistischer Aufklärung.* In W. Liebert & H. Schwinn (Eds.), *Mit Bezug auf Sprache. Festschrift für Rainer Wimmer* (pp. 163–185). Tübingen: Narr.

Foucault, M. (1975). *Surveiller et Punir. La naissance de la prison.* German translation: Foucault, M. (1976). *Überwachen und Strafen. Die Geburt des Gefängnisses,* Frankfurt am Main: Suhrkamp.

Foucault, M. (1978). *Dispositive der Macht. Über Sexualität, Wahrheit und Wissen,* Berlin: Merve.

Foucault, M. (1983). *Der Wille zum Wissen. Sexualität und Wahrheit I.* Frankfurt am Main: Suhrkamp (Orig. Paris: Gallimard 1976).

Fraas, C., & Klemm, M. (Eds.). (2005). *Mediendiskurse.* Frankfurt am Main: Lang.

Fritzsche, C. (Red.) (2006). *Leitkultur. Vom Schlagwort zur Sache. Stiftung Haus der Geschichte der Bundesrepublik Deutschland.* Bonn: Bouvier.

Gabler Wirtschaftslexikon, ([16]2004). *Die ganze Welt der Wirtschaft: Betriebswirtschaft – Volkswirtschaft – Recht – Steuern.* Wiesbaden: Gabler.

Gardt, A. (1998). *Sprachtheoretische Grundlagen und Tendenzen der Fachsprachenforschung,* in: "Zeitschrift für germanistische Linguistik (ZGL)", 26.1998: 31–66.

Gardt, A. (2007). *Linguistisches Interpretieren. Konstruktivistische Theorie und realistische Praxis.* In F. Hermanns & W. Holly (Eds.), *Linguistische Hermeneutik. Theorie und Praxis des Verstehens und Interpretierens* (pp. 263–280). Tübingen: Niemeyer.

Gloning, T. (1996). *Bedeutung, Gebrauch und sprachliche Handlung. Ansätze und Probleme einer handlungstheoretischen Semantik aus linguistischer Sicht.* Tübingen: Niemeyer.

Gloning, T. (2002). *Ausprägungen der Wortfeldtheorie.* In A. D. Cruse, F. Hundsnurscher, M. Job & P. R. Lutzeier (Eds.), *Lexikologie. Ein internationales Handbuch zur Natur und Struktur von Wörtern und Wortschätzen* (pp. 728–737). Berlin/New York: de Gruyter.

Glotz, P. (1985). *Die Rückkehr der Mythen in die Sprache der Politik.* In G. Stötzel (Ed.), *Germanistik – Forschungsstand und Perspektiven. Vorträge des Deutschen Germanistentages 1984. 1. Teil. Germanistische Sprachwissenschaft, Didaktik der Deutschen Sprache und Literatur* (pp. 231–244). Berlin/New York: de Gruyter.

Hassemer, W. ([6]1994). *Rechtssystem und Kodifikation: Die Bindung des Richters an das Gesetz.* In A. Kaufmann & W. Hassemer (Eds.), *Einführung in Rechtsphilosophie und Rechtstheorie der Gegenwart* (pp. 248–268). Heidelberg: Juristischer Verlag Müller.

Hombach, B. (1991). *Semantik und Politik.* In F. Liedtke, M. Wengeler, & K. Böke (Eds.), *Begriffe besetzen. Strategien des Sprachgebrauchs in der Politik* (pp. 34–43). Opladen: Westdeutscher Verlag.

Humboldt, W. V. (1906). *Grundzüge des allgemeinen Sprachtypus.* In W. V. Humboldt (Ed.), *Gesammelte Schriften*. (Vol. 5, pp. 364–473). Berlin: Behr.

Hundsnurscher, F. (1991). *Über den Zusammenhang von Wortsemantik, Satzsemantik und Textsemantik.* In E. Czucka (Ed.), *"Die in dem alten Haus der Sprache wohnen". Beiträge zum Sprachdenken in der Literaturgeschichte. Helmut Arntzen zum 60. Geburtstag* (pp. 33–44). Münster: Aschendorff.

Hundsnurscher, F. (1998). *Pragmatische Wortsemantik. Zum pragmatischen Hintergrund einer gebrauchstheoretisch orientierten lexikalischen Semantik.* In E. Schmitzdorf, N. Hartl, & B. Meurer (Eds.), *Lingua Germanica. Studien zur deutschen Philologie. Jochen Splett zum 60. Geburtstag* (pp. 128–142). Münster i.a: Waxmann.

Jeand'Heur, B. (1998). *Die neuere Fachsprache der juristischen Wissenschaft seit der Mitte des 19. Jahrhunderts unter besonderer Berücksichtigung von Verfassungsrecht und Rechtsme-thodik'.* In L. Hoffmann, H. Kalverkämper, & H. E. Wiegand (Eds.), *Fachsprachen* (pp. 1286–1295). Berlin/New York: de Gruyter.

Keller, R. (1977). *Kollokutionäre Akte*, "Germanistische Linguistik", 1-2/77: 1–50.

Kienpointner, M. (1992). *Alltagslogik. Struktur und Funktion von Argumentationsmustern.* Stuttgart-Bad Cannstatt: Frommann-Holzboog.

Klein, J. (Ed.). (1989). *Politische Semantik. Beiträge zur politischen Sprachverwendung*. Opladen: Westdeutscher Verlag.

Konerding, K. (1993). *Frames und lexikalisches Bedeutungswissen. Untersuchungen zur linguistischen Grundlegung einer Frametheorie und zu ihrer Anwendung in der Lexikographie.* Tübingen: Niemeyer.

Konerding, K. (2005). *Diskurse, Themen und soziale Topik.* In C. Fraas & M. Klemm (Eds.), *Mediendiskurse* (pp. 9–38). Frankfurt am Main: Lang.

Konerding, K. (2007). *Themen, Rahmen und Diskurse. Zur linguistischen Fundierung des Diskursbegriffes.* In I. Warnke (Ed.), *Diskurslinguistik nach Foucault. Theorie und Gegenstände* (pp. 107–140). Berlin/New York: de Gruyter.

Konerding, K. (2008). *Diskurse, Topik, Deutungsmuster. Zur Komplementarität, Konvergenz und Explikation sprach-, kultur-, und sozialwissenschaftlicher Zugänge zur Diskursanalyse auf der Grundlage kollektiven Wissens.* In I. Warnke & J. Spitzmüller (Eds.), *Methoden der Diskurslinguistik. Sprachwissenschaftliche Zugänge zur transtextuellen Ebene* (pp. 117–150). Berlin/New York: de Gruyter.

Konerding, K. (2009). *Diskurslinguistik – eine neue linguistische Teildisziplin.* In E. Felder (Ed.), *Sprache. Im Auftrag der Universitätsgesellschaft Heidelberg* (pp. 155–177). Berlin i.a: Springer.

Koselleck, R. (1972). *Einleitung.* In O. Brunner, W. Conze, & R. Koselleck (Eds.), *Geschichtliche Grundbegriffe. Historisches Lexikon zur politisch-sozialen Sprache in Deutschland* (pp. XIII-XXVII). Stuttgart: Klett-Cotta.

Koselleck, R. (1979). *Begriffsgeschichte und Sozialgeschichte.* In R. Koselleck (Ed.), *Vergangene Zukunft. Zur Semantik geschichtlicher Zeiten* (pp. 107–129). Frankfurt am Main: Suhrkamp.

Li, J. (2011). *"Recht ist Streit". Eine rechtslinguistische Analyse des Sprachverhaltens in der deutschen Rechtsprechung*. Berlin/Boston: de Gruyter.

Liebert, W. (2003). *Zu einem Dynamischen Konzept von Schlüsselwörtern.* In "Zeitschrift für angewandte Linguistik", *2003*(38), 57–83.

Liebert, W., & Weitze, M. (Eds.). (2006). *Kontroversen als Schlüssel zur Wissenschaft? Wissenskulturen in sprachlicher Interaktion*. Bielefeld: Transcript.

Liedtke, F., Wengeler, M., & Böke, K. (Eds.). (1991). *Begriffe besetzen. Strategien des Sprachgebrauchs in der Politik*. Opladen: Westdeutscher Verlag.

Luth, J. (2015). *Semantische Kämpfe im Recht. Eine rechtslinguistische Analyse zu Konflikten zwischen dem EGMR und nationalen Gerichten*. Heidelberg: Winter.

Müller, F. (2007a). *Juristische Methodik*. Berlin: Duncker & Humblot.

Müller, M. (2007b). *Geschichte, Kunst, Nation. Die sprachliche Konstituierung einer,deutschen' Kunstgeschichte aus diskursanalytischer Sicht*. Berlin/New York: de Gruyter.

Müller, F., Christensen, R., & Sokolowski, M. (1997). *Rechtstext und Textarbeit*. Berlin: Duncker & Humblot.

Ogden, C. K. & Richards I. A. (1923). *The meaning of meaning*. New York: Harcourt, Brace & World. (ger.: *Die Bedeutung der Bedeutung*. Suhrkamp: Frankfurt, 1974).

Polenz, P. V. (1988). *Deutsche Satzsemantik. Grundbegriffe des Zwischen-den-Zeilen-Lesens*. Berlin/New York: de Gruyter.

Potthoff, R., Vogt, A., & Klüting, R. (2007). *Leitkultur? Kultur light! Aphoristisches Wörterbuch zur Kulturkritik*. Bochum: Brockmeyer.

Roelcke, T. (1991). *Das Eineindeutigkeitspostulat der lexikalischen Fachsprachensemantik*. In "Zeitschrift für germanistische Linguistik (ZGL)", 19.1991: 194–208.

Scherner, M. (1994). *Textverstehen als "Spurenlesen" – Zur texttheoretischen Tragweite dieser Metapher*. In P. Canisius, C. Herbemann, & G. Tschauder (Eds.), *Text und Grammatik. Festschrift für Roland Harweg zum 60. Geburtstag* (pp. 317–340). Bochum: Brockmeyer.

Scherner, M. (2000). *Kognitionswissenschaftliche Methoden in der Textanalyse*. In K. Brinker, G. Antos, W. Heinemann, & S. F. Sager (Eds.), *Text- und Gesprächslinguistik. Ein internationales Handbuch zeitgenössischer Forschung* (pp. 183–195). Berlin/New York: de Gruyter.

Schmidt, S. J. (1996). *Die Welten der Medien. Grundlagen und Perspektiven der Medienbeobachtung*. Braunschweig: Vieweg.

Searle, J. R. (1995). *The construction of social reality*. New York: Free Press.

Seibert, T. (1981). *Aktenanalysen. Zur Schriftform juristischer Deutungen*. Tübingen: Narr.

Seibert, T. (2004). *Gerichtsrede. Wirklichkeit und Möglichkeit im forensischen Diskurs*. Berlin: Duncker & Humblot.

Stötzel, G. (1990). *Semantische Kämpfe im öffentlichen Sprachgebrauch*. In G. Stickel (Ed.), *Deutsche Gegenwartssprache. Tendenzen und Perspektiven. Jahrbuch des Instituts für deutsche Sprache 1989*, (pp. 45–65). Berlin/New York: de Gruyter.

Vogel, F. (2009). *"Aufstand" – "Revolte" – "Widerstand". Linguistische Mediendiskursanalyse der Ereignisse in den Pariser Vorstädten 2005*, Frankfurt am Main: Lang.

Vogel, F. (2012). *Linguistik rechtlicher Normgenese. Theorie der Rechtsnormdiskursivität am Beispiel der Online-Durchsuchung*. Berlin/Boston: de Gruyter.

Vygotsky, L. S. (1934/1962). *Thought and language*. Cambridge: MIT Press.

Warnke, I. (ed.). (2007). *Diskurslinguistik nach Foucault. Theorie und Gegenstände*. Berlin/New York: de Gruyter.

Warnke, I., & Spitzmüller J. (2008a). *Methoden und Methodologie der Diskurslinguistik. Grundlagen und Verfahren einer Sprachwissenschaft jenseits textueller Grenzen*. In I. Warnke & J. Spitzmüller (Eds.), *Methoden der Diskurslinguistik. Sprachwissenschaftliche Zugänge zur transtextuellen Ebene*. Berlin/New York: de Gruyter.

Warnke, I., & J. Spitzmüller (Eds.). (2008b). *Methoden der Diskurslinguistik. Sprachwissenschaftliche Zugänge zur transtextuellen Ebene*. Berlin/New York: de Gruyter.

Wengeler, M. (2003). *Topos und Diskurs. Begründung einer argumentationsanalytischen Methode und ihre Anwendung auf den Migrationsdiskurs (1960–1985)*, Tübingen: Niemeyer.

Wengeler, M., & Ziem A. (2010). *Wirtschaftskrisen im Wandel der Zeit. Zur sprachlich-diskursiven Konstitution von "Krisen" in der BRD 1982 und 2003*. In A. Landwehr (Ed.), *Diskursiver Wandel*. Wiesbaden: VS-Verlag für Sozialwissenschaften.

Wimmer, R. (1979). *Referenzsemantik. Untersuchungen zur Festlegung von Bezeichnungsfunktionen sprachlicher Ausdrücke am Beispiel des Deutschen*. Tübingen: Niemeyer.

Wimmer, R. (1998). *Zur juristischen Fachsprache aus linguistischer Sicht.* In "Sprache und Literatur in Wissenschaft und Unterricht", 81/1998: 8–23.

Ziem, A. (2008). *Frame-Semantik. Kognitive Aspekte des Sprachverstehens.* Berlin/New York: de Gruyter.

Zifonun, G. (2000). *Textkonstitutive Funktionen von Tempus, Modus und Genus verbi.* In K. Brinker, G. Antos, W. Heinemann, & S. F. Sager (Eds.), *Text- und Gesprächslinguistik. Ein internationales Handbuch zeitgenössischer Forschung* (pp. 315–330). Berlin/New York: de Gruyter.

Zimmer, R. (2006). *Zwischen Heilungsversprechen und Embryonenschutz – Der semantische Kampf um das therapeutische Klonen.* In E. Felder (Ed.), *Semantische Kämpfe. Macht und Sprache in den Wissenschaften* (73–97). Berlin/New York: de Gruyter.

Zimmer, R. (2009). *Die Rahmung der Zwergenwelt. Argumentationsmuster und Versprachlichungsformen im Nanotechnologiediskurs.* In E. Felder & M. Müller (Eds.), *Wissen durch Sprache. Theorie, Praxis und Erkenntnisinteresse des Forschungsnetzwerks » Sprache und Wissen «* (pp. 279–308). Berlin/New York: de Gruyter.

Part II
Pragmatics and Legal Theory

A Puzzle About Hart's Theory of Internal Legal Statements

Michael S. Green

Abstract In this essay, I describe a puzzle concerning Hart's theory of internal legal statements and the internal point of view from which such statements are made. The puzzle is tied to a commonly assumed requirement for an adequate theory of law (the *Requirement*, for short). According to the Requirement, a theory of law must explain why participants in legal practices should justify their decisions by appeal to legal norms, rather than pointing solely to how practice-independent norms, such as morality and prudence, are triggered by social facts about legal practices. Theories of law that are dissimilar in other respects—such as Scott Shapiro's planning theory, Ronald Dworkin's interpretive theory, and Hans Kelsen's pure theory—all satisfy the Requirement. The American legal realists' prediction theory of law does not.

Hart argues that law cannot exist unless officials justify their decisions through internal legal statements (*ILSs*). In an ILS the existence of legal practices and moral or prudential judgments about the appropriateness of following the standards used in those practices are *presupposed*. An official justifying his decisions solely by examining legal practices in the light of moral or prudential norms is not making an ILS. This is an important reason that Hart rejects prediction theories of law.

But Hart's theory of law fails to satisfy the Requirement. Hart provides no account of why officials *should* justify their decisions through ILSs rather than solely on moral and prudential grounds. As a result, Hart fails to explain why law vanishes when officials stop making ILSs and begin justifying their decisions solely by reference to morality and prudence. I end with a brief discussion of a different, albeit speculative, reading of ILSs, under which Hart's theory of law satisfies the Requirement.

Keywords H.L.A. Hart • Internal legal statements • Internal point of view • Ronald Dworkin • Scott Shapiro • Hans Kelsen • Legal norms

---

M.S. Green (✉)
Marshall-Wythe School of Law, College of William and Mary, Williamsburg, VA, USA
e-mail: msgre2@wm.edu

F. Poggi, A. Capone (eds.), *Pragmatics and Law*, Perspectives in Pragmatics, Philosophy & Psychology 10, DOI 10.1007/978-3-319-44601-1_8

1 The Requirement

1.1 The Challenge of Legal Realism

Consider the model of judicial reasoning that the legal realists Felix Cohen and Walter Wheeler Cook present in their writings, a model which, they believe, will allow judges to both describe and morally assess the law more accurately. Under the model, all statements about the law are exclusively about social facts, in particular, patterns of behavior and attitudes among officials and, in some cases, the population as a whole (Cohen 1935, 839; Cook 1942, 29–33; Green 2011, 393–97, 409–16; Green 2005a, 1967–98). In themselves, these social facts do not give a judge a reason to decide one way rather than another. It is only when these social facts (as well as other relevant descriptive facts) are considered in the light of moral norms that the judge can conclude whether conformity with legal practices is justified. Conformity could be justified, for example, for consequentialist reasons—as a means of satisfying "human expectations based upon past decisions, the stability of economic transactions, and … the maintenance of order and simplicity in our legal system" (Cohen 1935, 840)—or because the oath of judicial office gives the judge a promissory obligation to conform (Cohen 1933, 242).

Cohen and Cook argue that a judge who reasons in this fashion will describe the law more accurately, because he will not confuse the law (that is, patterns of official behavior and attitudes) with how the law morally ought to be (Cohen 1935, 838; Cook 1935). His moral criticism of the law will also be more accurate, because he will not be tempted to assume that the existence of law necessarily entails justified reasons for conformity. Only in the light of moral norms can conformity to legal practices be recommended (Cohen 1935, 828–29, 840).[1]

To get a feel for what a community would look like if all its officials followed the realist model, let us start with a very simple legal system, the Monarchy, in which Rex is king. Rex has issued a number of laws, including: "Drive on the right side of the road" and "Keep your promises or pay the damages that result from your failure to do so." Assume that the Monarchy satisfies the requirements for a legal system under whatever one considers to be the correct theory of law, provided that under this theory officials should generally justify their decisions by reference to legal norms, rather than following the realist model.

Now assume that the Monarchy's officials suddenly change the justification of their decisions to satisfy the realist model.[2] To the extent that an official throws someone in prison or compels someone to pay money, he justifies his decision by pointing to how patterns of official behavior and attitudes, combined with other descriptive facts, morally recommend these results. For example, he might say something like:

> In the past, officials have tended to enforce what Rex says (and the population has tended to obey him as well). For this reason, I predict that in attempting to solve the coordination

[1] For a discussion of a similar argument offered by a current philosopher of law, see Green 2014.

[2] I leave out a description how a lawmaker like Rex would sound if he satisfied the model. For a discussion see Green 2013a.

> problem of which side to drive on, people would find Rex's statement "Drive on the right side of the road" especially salient. I therefore ought to enforce what Rex says, because that decision would help solve the coordination problem and thereby satisfy the moral norm that unnecessary harm to others should be avoided.

or:

> In the past, officials have tended to enforce what Rex says (and the population has tended to obey him as well). For this reason, I predict that people would have their reasonable expectations frustrated if I did not enforce what Rex says. Although his statement "Keep your promises or pay the damages that result from your failure to do so" is an overly inclusive standard for when promises should be enforced, I ought to enforce it nevertheless, because that decision would satisfy the moral norm that people's reasonable expectations ought not be frustrated absent a compelling reason.

These are, of course, only two examples. The moral justification that officials offer could vary greatly. But what is essential is that the only element of the justification that we could call "the law" is a description of social facts and the only element that we could call "a norm" is morality—and the norms of instrumental rationality (or prudence), which govern the means by which aims (in this case the aim of satisfying moral norms) can best be realized. In particular, officials do not justify their decisions by reference to *legal norms*. For example, they do not appeal to laws created under Rex's authority.

Although officials have changed how they justify their decisions, let us assume that as far as the enforcement of what Rex says is concerned things are exactly the same as before. Officials throw the same people in jail, compel the same people to pay money, and so on. Cohen and Cook recognize, after all, that there are very good moral reasons for conformity with legal practices. Thus, it need not follow from their adoption of the realist model that officials conclude that they should stop doing what Rex says.

One might question whether all the officials in the community would continue to enforce what Rex says if all they have to rely upon are their moral obligations. Let us therefore assume the following: After describing social facts about legal practices and identifying any other relevant descriptive facts, officials can justify conformity prudentially as well. For example, a judge might conclude that her decision to enforce what Rex says is the best way of satisfying her desire to get a paycheck. To repeat, officials do not justify their decisions by reference to legal norms.

Let us call the Monarchy with these changes the *Community*. Should a theory of law find the shift from the Monarchy to the Community a problem? Are officials in the Community missing out on an element of practical reason to which they were previously sensitive?

Given the similarities between the Community and the Monarchy, one might think that a theory of law should not find the shift to be a problem. Indeed, the realist model poses a very important challenge in the philosophy of law. The Monarchy and the Community are the same as far as enforcement is concerned: the same people are thrown in jail, the same people compelled to pay money. So why should philosophers of law treat them differently? In short, who needs legal norms?

1.2 Answering the Challenge

The fact remains that many philosophers of law, both positivist and anti-positivist, would conclude that things go wrong when officials in the Monarchy adopt the realist model, because they fail to take into account legal norms. The fact that so many philosophers of law agree on this matter suggests that they all think that there is an essential requirement for an adequate theory of law (which I will call, simply, the *Requirement*) that the realist model violates. A theory of law must account for how legal norms play a role in the practical reasoning of participants in legal practices, a role that cannot be accounted for by reasoning concerning social facts about legal practices (as well as other descriptive facts) and the norms of morality and prudence.

The following is my account of the Requirement. My goal is to describe it at a sufficiently high level of abstraction that it captures a common reason why many philosophers of law, both positivist and anti-positivist, would conclude that the shift by the Monarchy's officials to a realist model is a problem. It is in the light of this requirement for an adequate theory of law that I later criticize Hart's theory of ILSs.

According to the Requirement, a theory of law is adequate only if explains the following:

1. In a legal system, participants in legal practices[3] should generally justify decisions that conform to those practices by reference to legal norms.[4] They should not justify these decisions solely according to the *realist model*—that is, by reference to how social facts about legal practices, combined with other descriptive facts, trigger the practice-independent norms of morality and prudence.
2. Legal norms have normative force for participants. On the basis of a participant's reference to a legal norm, without engaging in reasoning according to the realist model, she should conclude that she has a *pro tanto* reason for her decision.
3. Legal norms, like moral or prudential norms, are non-empirical entities that are not reducible to social facts.[5]

[3] In many theories of law, these participants are officials only (or, more narrowly, judges), but it is possible for a theory of law to cast the net more broadly to include the general population.

[4] I keep the identity of the legal norms to which participants must justify their decisions vague here, to account for the different types of legal norm at issue in the theories of law that satisfy the Requirement. Legal norms might consist of statutes, constitutional provisions, and the like—and I will often use these as examples. But under a particular theory of law (for example, Dworkin's) the relevant legal norms might be different.

[5] To say that legal norms are non-empirical means that they cannot be identified with any empirical entities and that they have no spatial location. In that sense they are like moral norms. The moral duty not to upset reasonable expectations is not located in any particular place and cannot be identified with anything empirical, such as a physical object, a social practice, or a psychological state. By the same token, the Securities Exchange Act, understood as a legal norm, is not equivalent to anything empirical, whether it is the piece of paper signed by President Roosevelt, the social practice of enforcing that piece of paper, or the mental states of those engaging in enforcement. At least some legal norms might be understood as having clear temporal parameters, however. The Securities Exchange Act might be understood to have been created at a particular time (when it was

4. Legal norms, unlike moral or prudential norms, are practice-dependent, in the sense that they have normative force only for participants.

A number of clarifications of the Requirement are in order. First, it is not a problem under the Requirement that participants in legal practices justify decisions *in part* by reference to social facts about their legal practices, since legal norms can make such social facts legally relevant. For example, American officials might justify their decisions by reference to the social fact that a certain percentage of the members of Congress raised their hands, because the United States Constitution tells them to look to that social fact.[6]

Second, the idea that legal norms have *normative force* captures the notion that they play a role in the practical reasoning of participants. One reason this might be the case is that the existence of the legal norm is itself a *pro tanto* reason for a decision, the way the existence of a moral norm can be a *pro tanto* reason for action. But, as we shall see, this is not necessary. Under Shapiro's theory of law, the existence of a legal norm is not itself a *pro tanto* reason for a decision. Nevertheless, a participant who refers to a legal norm should, without reasoning according to the realist model, conclude that she has a non-legal *pro tanto* reason (for example, a moral or prudential reason) and act accordingly.[7]

Third, when I say that the norms of morality and prudence are practice-independent, I mean that they bind people and give them reasons for action independent of the social practices in which people participate. That does not mean that the norms are *applicable* to people whether or not they participate in social practices. The moral norm that people's reasonable expectations ought not be frustrated is not applicable to someone who is not in a position to upset anyone's reasonable expectations. What makes that moral norm applicable—what *triggers* it—is a person's factual circumstances, which can include her participation in social practices. But even if the norm never actually gets triggered for a person, it still binds her. It is true for everyone, everywhere, that they ought not frustrate people's reasonable expectations.

---

enacted in 1933). And it will disappear at a particular time (when it is repealed). The same point is true of some moral norms. A particular promissory obligation might be understood to have been created when the promise was made and to end when it is discharged.

[6] Indeed, legal norms might make legally relevant the existence of the participants' legal practices as a whole. An official of the Monarchy, adjudicating facts that arose right around the time that the Monarchy came into being in a revolution, might refer to the existence of the Monarchy's legal practices when justifying her decision, because Rex has limited the scope of his laws to events occurring post-revolution. This is compatible with the Requirement, because the official is not justifying her decision solely according to the realist model. She is justifying her decision through legal norms. It is also unproblematic under the Requirement that participants in legal practices who find that legal norms are indeterminate (in the sense that they do not tell participants how to decide), look beyond such norms to consider how social facts about legal practices, as well as other relevant descriptive facts, implicate moral or prudential norms.

[7] I should also note that although a *pro tanto* reason for a decision is a reason that genuinely speaks in favor of the decision, it need not do so decisively. The overall balance of reasons (including moral reasons) may recommend that one diverge from legal practices.

Fourth, and conversely, when I say that legal norms are practice-dependent, in the sense that they have normative force only for participants, I do not mean that they *apply* only to those participating in legal practices or only as long as the practices exists (Southwood 2011, 765–66). Legal norms might be universal in their scope.[8] What I mean is that, unlike moral norms, which have normative force for everyone, legal norms have normative force for participants only. This is most significant and problematic under theories of law in which legal norms have normative force because the existence of the legal norm is itself a *pro tanto* reason for action. That means that even if the legal norm is *universal* in scope, this universal norm provides reasons for action only for participants. In effect, the practice-dependence of legal norms is a form of normative relativism. Participants in different legal practices inhabit different and incommensurable normative spaces.

The idea that legal norms are practice-dependent is less problematic if, as in Shapiro's theory of law, all that it means to say that legal norms have normative force is that, on the basis of a participant's reference to a legal norm, she should conclude, without engaging in reasoning according to the realist model, that she has a *pro tanto* reason for a decision. Since the *pro tanto* reason she should conclude she has can be practice-independent (in particular, moral or prudential), the practice-dependence of legal norms under Shapiro's theory is compatible with everyone inhabiting the same normative space.

Because legal norms are practice-dependent, there will be a discontinuity of appropriate justification as one moves from one set of legal practices to another (whether spatially, as one moves from one legal system to another existing in a different place, or temporally, when a legal system changes through revolution). Participants in the legal practices of Ancien Régime France should terminate justification of decisions in legal norms that point to the King of France, whereas participants in the legal practices of France in 1791 should terminate justification of decisions in legal norms that point to the National Assembly (or the People of France it represents).

By contrast, under the realist model there should be no justificatory discontinuity as one moves between legal practices. The moral and prudential norms to which participants should appeal will be the same before and after the move. Only the social facts that trigger the moral and prudential norms will have changed. For

---

[8] The notion that a legal norm is practice-dependent also does not mean that participants in legal practices offer their practices as a *justification* for the norm's existence. A legal norm can be practice-dependent even though participants in the relevant practices don't point to anything (even their own practices) as the ground for the norm's existence. Southwood claims that conventional normative judgments (which would include those judgments in which officials justify their decisions by reference to legal norms) are distinguishable from moral judgments because social practices are the non-derivative justifications for conventional normative judgments (Southwood 2011). I do not think his account of the conventional/moral distinction succeeds. It is not essential to conventional normative judgments that practices justify such judgments. Those making conventional normative judgments might insist that no justification can be offered, not even one that looks to their practices.

example, a judge of Ancien Régime France who enforced the King of France's commands because he thought people's reasonable expectations should not be upset would find himself appealing to the same norm in 1791. He would still be trying not to upset people's reasonable expectations (although what their expectations are would have changed dramatically).

2 Three Theories of Law That Satisfy the Requirement

As evidence that the Requirement is commonly accepted by philosophers of law, consider three different theories of law, each of which satisfies it. The first is Scott Shapiro's planning theory.

2.1 *Shapiro's Planning Theory of Law*

The basis of Shapiro's planning theory of law is the normative constraint that planning puts upon our action. In themselves, plans are merely abstract propositional entities—standards for our behavior (Shapiro 2011, 41; Green 2013b, 350–53). But, having established a relationship to a plan by adopting it, the norms of instrumental rationality exercise an important normative force. If I make a plan to cook dinner, these norms rationally obligate me to act according to the plan (Shapiro 2011, 127). I should not reconsider my plan unless there is a compelling reason. In addition, I am rationally obligated to generate subplans at the appropriate time concerning how my plan is to be effectuated (Shapiro 2011, 121). These subplans are *nested*, in the sense that their creation is in the context of, and is rationally constrained by, the plan.

Groups can also adopt plans. When they do, the norms of instrumental rationality constrain the members of the group in much the same way that they constrain individual adopters of plans (Shapiro 2011, 129–30). Members of the group are rationally constrained to not reconsider their shared plan (absent a compelling reason), to create nested subplans, and so on. In addition, members can be rationally required to cooperate with one another, including by adopting subplans created by other members of the group (Shapiro 2011, 134–37).

Having adopted a plan, one has reasons for action that one would not otherwise have had: reasons to act without further deliberation, reasons to create nested subplans, and so on. These reasons for action bind even in the face of contrary desires. If one is not aware of a compelling reason for reconsidering the plan, one ought to stop deliberation at the plan and act, even if one wants to continue deliberating. To be sure, these reasons for action are weak compared to moral reasons for action. Having made a plan to torture a puppy, I have a reason to act accordingly, but this reason should immediately yield to a recognition of the immorality of my project.

The notion of a group plan stands at the heart of Shapiro's theory of law. Laws are a particular type of group plan. The basis of a legal system—the foundational law—is a master plan adopted by the members of a planning organization. This master plan is intended to overcome the fact that the community of which the planning organization is a part faces numerous and serious moral problems whose solutions are complex, contentious, or arbitrary (Shapiro 2011, 170–73).[9] Once the master plan is adopted, the norms of instrumental rationality assert a binding force upon the organization's members. Unless there are compelling reasons for reconsideration, they should act according to the plan. Furthermore, they are rationally obligated to create appropriate subplans and to accept the subplans made by other members. These subplans are the other laws of the legal system.[10]

In understanding Shapiro's planning theory of law, it is crucial to see that although a planning organization adopts a master plan for reasons (because the members think it is a good method to overcome the moral problems the community faces), after adoption instrumental rationality recommends that the reasons for conformity to the plan not be reassessed. The whole point of having a plan is stopping justification at the plan and acting, rather than recapitulating the justification for adopting it.

Shapiro's theory of law satisfies the Requirement. Under Shapiro's theory, the officials in the Community are acting improperly. Since the Monarchy was a legal system, its officials must have created a master plan and subplans. But they are now ignoring these plans and demanding further deliberation about why conformity to legal practices is justified. This violates the norms of instrumental rationality.[11]

Notice that under Shapiro's theory of law the existence of a plan is not a *pro tanto* reason for a decision. Plans are simply abstract objects—standards of conduct. In themselves, they give us no reasons for action. After having adopted a plan, officials have justifying reasons for action (in the sense that they should act according to the plan if a compelling reason for reconsideration does not exist, should create nested subplans, and so on) only because the *practice-independent* norms of instrumental rationality say so. The adoption of a plan is, in effect, a social fact that triggers these practice-independent norms.

But that does not mean that under Shapiro's planning theory of law officials justify their decisions, in realist fashion, by appeal to social facts and practice-independent norms. Instead they abide by the practice-independent norms by ending justification with their plans. Just as it violates the norms of instrumental rationality for a planner to reconsider her reasons for adopting a plan, so it violates those norms for her to

---

[9] This is not to say that the master plan succeeds in this purpose or that those who accept it always do so to effectuate this purpose. I should also note that Shapiro restricts the planning organization in other ways that are irrelevant to our concerns, by demanding that it be self-certifying (Shapiro 2011, 217–24) and compulsory (Shapiro 2011, 211–12).

[10] Technically, some of these laws are not subplans, but are "planlike" norms that are accepted by the master plan because they perform much the same settling function as plans (Shapiro 2011, 225). I ignore this wrinkle.

[11] Indeed, if they keep it up, we can say that they have abandoned their master plan and that the Community has no law.

justify why she ought not reconsider those reasons. Someone who follows a plan only after concluding that she has adopted a plan and that the norms of instrumental rationality recommend that she not reconsider it is also violating the norms of instrumental rationality, for that too is not stopping justification at the plan.

Thus, we can say that plans have normative force of the sort demanded by the Requirement. They play a unique role in practical reasoning—a role that cannot be satisfied by reasoning about social facts about legal practices (as well as other descriptive facts) and the norms of morality and prudence.

Of course, under Shapiro's theory the normative force of a legal norm is very different from the normative force of a moral norm. The existence of the moral norm is itself a reason for action. That's not so of a plan. For plans, the ultimate reasons for action rest in the norms of instrumental rationality. But that is arguably a virtue of Shapiro's theory. By understanding laws as plans, he explains the unique role of legal norms in practical reasoning in a manner that does not assume the existence of a realm of distinctly legal entities that themselves provide participants with reasons for action.

Notice that legal norms have normative force only for participants. Only members of the planning organization have a reason to stop justification at their plans. Shapiro's theory can therefore explain the discontinuity of appropriate justification as one moves from one legal system to another (Green 2013b, 962–63). In 1788, French officials should stop justification of their decisions at a master plan that points to the King of France, whereas in 1791, after the French Revolution, they should stop at a different master plan that points to the National Assembly.

It is worth emphasizing how deftly Shapiro's planning theory of law satisfies the Requirement within a positivist framework. (As a general matter, I think that the virtues of Shapiro's theory have been insufficiently appreciated by philosophers of law (Green 2013b).) Positivist theories of law have a particular difficulty satisfying the Requirement. One essential element of positivism is the *social fact thesis*, according to which the existence and content of the law ultimately depend solely upon social facts, in particular, social facts about official behavior and attitudes (Coleman and Leiter 1996, 241). Given that the positivist thinks that the law essentially consists of social facts, how can it be a problem that officials in the Community, when talking about the law, speak solely about such facts?[12] What could be wrong in legal officials' talking about what the law essentially is?

But Shapiro's theory can explain why officials should not speak about what the law essentially is when justifying their decisions. It is true that for Shapiro the existence and content of the law are ultimately solely determined by social facts (in

[12] Another essential element of positivism is *the separability thesis*, according to which there is no necessary connection between law and morality (but see Green 2008). Under one reading of the thesis, nothing about the existence of law *qua law* gives an official a justified moral reason (even a *pro tanto* reason) for conformity (Coleman 1989, 66). Here too it would appear that the positivist would see nothing in the Community about which to object. Officials are apparently doing precisely what they should do—looking to moral norms to consider whether the law, positivistically understood, gives them a reason for obedience.

particular social facts about officials' adopting plans).[13] But, having adopted a plan, one has a reason to stop justification at the plan—at the non-empirical object—unless there is a compelling reason for reconsideration. In a well-functioning legal system, therefore, officials would have no reason to speak about what the law essentially is when justifying their decisions. Indeed, to speak about the law in terms of social facts about officials' adopting plans would be contrary to the planning function of law.

To sum up, Shapiro's theory of law satisfies the Requirement in the following manner:

1. When participants in legal practices justify decisions that conform to those practices, they should generally do so by reference to their master plan and subplans created in accordance with the master plan. To justify their decisions solely by reference to how social facts about legal practices, combined with other descriptive facts, trigger the practice-independent norms of morality and prudence (that is, according to the realist model) would be contrary to the planning function of law.
2. The master plan and subplans have normative force for participants. Solely on the basis of the participant's reference to these plans, without engaging in reasoning according to the realist model, a participant should conclude that she has a *pro tanto* reason for her decision.
3. The master plan and subplans are non-empirical entities that are not reducible to social facts.
4. The master plan and subplans are practice-dependent, in the sense that they have normative force only for participants. Only participants, who adopt the master plan, should conclude that they have a *pro tanto* reason for a decision when pointing to the master plan or subplans.

2.2 *Dworkin's Interpretive Theory of Law*

Let us now move on to Ronald Dworkin's interpretive theory of law, particularly as presented in *Law's Empire*. Under this theory, the law of a jurisdiction is the set of norms that would be accepted after a process in which "the interpreter settles on some general justification for the main elements of [legal] practice" and then reforms it by "adjust[ing] his sense of what the practice 'really' requires so as better to serve the justification" (Dworkin 1986, 66). In particular, the interpreter attempts to come up with a justifying connection between past political decisions and present coercion (Dworkin 1986, 98). Because law is the set of norms that would result from the best moral interpretation of a jurisdiction's legal practices, it is not

[13] There is a sense in which the law depends upon more than social facts for Shapiro. If there were no abstract propositional objects or no norms of instrumental rationality there would be no law as Shapiro understands it, even if social facts still existed. But law does not depend for its existence upon *moral* facts.

reducible to social facts about those practices. If moral facts were to disappear (say God extinguished them), law would necessarily disappear too, even if social facts remained (Greenberg 2004, 157–58). In this sense, Dworkin's theory of law is anti-positivist.

Does Dworkin's theory of law satisfy the Requirement? Under the Requirement, participants in legal practices must generally justify their decisions by reference to practice-dependent legal norms. They should not justify their decisions solely by reference to how social facts about legal practices, combined with other descriptive facts, trigger the practice-independent norms of morality and prudence. Under one reading, Dworkin's interpretive theory does not satisfy the Requirement. The process of interpretation is simply the determination of how social facts about legal practices trigger or make applicable practice-independent moral norms. A participant's justification of her decision under the interpretive theory conforms to the realist model.

Although I cannot pursue the argument in detail here, I believe that this reading of *Law's Empire* is mistaken (see, e.g., Dworkin 1986, 102). Interpretation does not identify how practice-independent moral norms are triggered by social facts about legal practices. In interpretation, identification of the content of legal norms is constrained (one might say *distorted*) by the particular community's legal practices that are being morally justified. Justification must *fit* those practices (Dworkin 1986, 67–68), and this requirement of fit means that the norms in one legal system can deviate in a fundamental way from those of another—and from the moral norms that exist for all of us, independent of the community within which we find ourselves.

This reading of interpretive legal norms is supported by the role in practical reasoning that Dworkin assigns to them.[14] For Dworkin, interpretive legal norms are the source of, or are, *associative obligations*, which provide reasons for action that participants in a type of community have toward fellow members.[15] Although Dworkin speaks of associative obligations as moral obligations (Dworkin 1986, 196), he does not suggest that we can cash them out in terms of how practice-

[14] The reading is also supported by Dworkin's suggestion that it is only participants in the relevant legal practices who engage in interpretation (Dworkin 1986, 65–66). For example, in *Law's Empire* he says "[i]nterpretation folds back into the practice, altering its shape, and the new shape encourages further reinterpretation" (Dworkin 1986, 48). Legal practices are not merely the object of interpretation; they are also the lens through which one engages in interpretation. By contrast, if interpretation involved determining how social facts about legal practices trigger practice-independent moral norms, non-participants should be capable of determining what a system's interpretive legal norms are, just as someone who has not made a promise can determine another's promissory obligations. The idea that interpretation can be engaged in only by participants suggests that interpretive legal norms exist only for participants.

[15] It is true that associative obligations as Dworkin understands them are not practice-dependent simply because they apply only to and between participants in a practice. As we have seen, practice-dependent norms can have a universal scope and practice-independent norms can be applicable only to participants in a practice. The evidence that associative obligations are practice-dependent is Dworkin's disinclination to reduce such obligations to the way that practices trigger abstract moral duties.

independent moral norms are triggered by participation in a community.[16] Indeed, associative obligations can conflict with practice-independent moral norms (Dworkin 1986, 202–06). Someone with an associative obligation, in effect, inhabits a different normative space than someone who does not. It follows that there is a discontinuity of appropriate justification as one moves from one set of legal practices to another. In 1788, judges in France should justify their decisions by reference to a different set of associative obligations than they should in 1791.[17]

So understood, Dworkin's interpretive theory of law in *Law's Empire* satisfies the Requirement. Under Dworkin's interpretive theory, something has gone wrong when the officials in the Monarchy adopt the realist model. By justifying their decisions solely according to the realist model, they are insensitive to the distinctive role that associative obligations play in their practical reasoning.

To sum up, Dworkin's theory of law satisfies the Requirement in the following manner:

1. When participants in legal practices justify decisions that conform to those practices, they should generally do so by reference to interpretive legal norms. To justify their decisions solely by reference to how social facts about legal prac-

---

[16] Although I believe that Dworkin's interpretive theory of law in *Law's Empire* (and *Justice in Robes* (Dworkin 2006)) satisfies the Requirement, I don't think that is true of Dworkin's theory of law in *Justice for Hedgehogs*, published only 2 years before his death. The main thesis that Dworkin defends in *Hedgehogs* is the unity of value, which includes the unity of law and morality. For Dworkin, law is simply "a branch, or subdivision, of political morality" (Dworkin 2011, 405). Social facts about a community's legal practices make our practice-independent moral obligations more concrete and particular.

The same point appears to be true of the moral impact theory of law recently offered by Mark Greenberg, under which legal norms are simply "the moral impact of the relevant actions of legal institutions" (Greenberg 2014, 1290). To be sure, Greenberg would say that officials in the Community are mistaken about what the law is, because they speak about the law solely in terms of social facts. Nevertheless, they arguably justify their decisions by reference to law as the moral impact theory conceives it, since they justify their decisions by reference to how social facts about legal practices implicate practice-independent moral norms.

In saying that Mark Greenberg's and the later Dworkin's theories of law fail to satisfy the Requirement, I do not mean they should be rejected. Although, so understood, they fail to explain how legal norms play a unique role in practical reasoning, the notion that participants in different practices inhabit different normative spaces, which follows from Dworkin's interpretive theory of law, is deeply problematic. Indeed, one might say that insofar as one can *explain* why participants in different practices are subject to different normative demands, one must do so by reference to how different social facts about those practices trigger practice-independent norms (Enoch 2011). The implausibility of practice-dependent norms is why the realist model, which does away with such norms, poses such an important challenge. It is also a reason why Shapiro's theory of law is attractive. The planning theory satisfies the Requirement by showing why participants in different practices should stop justification at different plans (and so appear to inhabit different normative spaces), while understanding them as ultimately inhabiting the same normative space of practice-independent norms.

[17] Curiously, the legal norms to which participants should justify their decisions under Dworkin's theory do not—or, at least, do not solely—include what would normally be identified as law, that is, statutes, constitutional provisions and the like. Legal norms include a peculiar sort of non-empirical object tied to associative obligations.

tices, combined with other descriptive facts, trigger the practice-independent norms of morality and prudence (that is, according to the realist model) would show insensitivity to their associative obligations.
2. Interpretive legal norms have normative force for participants. The existence of an interpretive legal norm is a *pro tanto* reason for a participant's decision.
3. Interpretive legal norms are non-empirical entities that are not reducible to social facts.
4. Interpretive legal norms are practice-dependent, in the sense that they have normative force only for participants in the interpretive community.

2.3 Kelsen's Pure Theory of Law

My third example of a theory of law that satisfies the Requirement is Hans Kelsen's pure theory. Kelsen's theory of law is pure in the sense that law is independent of morality and social facts (Kelsen 1960, 1). To be sure, social facts, such as the fact that a majority of people in a legislature raised their hands, can be legally relevant (Kelsen 1960, 2). As Kelsen puts it, social facts can have *legal meaning* in the light of legal norms (Kelsen 1960, 4). But neither legal meaning nor legal norms are reducible to social facts. Indeed, Kelsen insists that legal norms stand outside the spatio-temporal order (Kelsen 1934, 12).

For Kelsen, anyone interpreting social facts as having legal meaning is presupposing a fundamental legal norm, the basic norm (Kelsen 1960, 198–205). The basic norm legally authorizes those responsible for the first act in the legal system that created law and legally obligates conformity to that law and all laws created pursuant to it. For example, let us assume that the first enactment of law in the American legal system was the Constitutional Convention's creation of Article VII, which established a method for ratification of the Constitution (Green 2009). If so, the basic norm would legally authorize the Constitutional Convention to create Article VII and would obligate conformity to Article VII and all laws (such as the Constitution) created pursuant to it.

Because of his insistence that legal norms are distinct both from social facts and moral norms, Kelsen would conclude that something has gone wrong when officials in the Monarchy adopt the realist model. As he would put it, these officials, despite scrupulously enforcing what Rex says, are "anarchist[s]," who understand the law's regulation of human relationships "as mere power relations" (Kelsen 1945, 413). They are ignoring an important element of practical reason by failing to take into account legal norms.[18]

[18] In my discussion here, I assume a very common interpretation of Kelsen, according to which legal norms provide practical reasons for action, that is, "a justified demand on practical deliberation" (Marmor 2011, 25). In fact, it is unclear whether Kelsen believes that someone who recognizes a legal norm as existing thereby takes himself to have a reason for action in the sense relevant

Furthermore, unlike both Shapiro and Dworkin, Kelsen's approach to the law is maximally anti-reductive. Although they agree with Kelsen that justifying decisions through legal norms is different from justifying them on the basis of how social facts trigger practice-independent norms, Shapiro and Dworkin both ultimately define legal norms in terms of social facts and practice-independent norms. For Shapiro, a legal norm is the result of a social fact (the act of planning) triggering the practice-independent norms of instrumental rationality. For Dworkin, a legal norm is the result of how social facts about legal practices and moral norms interact in the process of interpretation. For Kelsen, by contrast, legal norms can be understood only legally (Kelsen 1960, 11).

Despite his anti-reductionism, Kelsen also understands legal norms as practice-dependent. For Kelsen, the existence of law is relative to the presupposition of a basic norm (Kelsen 1960, 72).[19] Furthermore, which basic norm is presumed will depend upon the actual legal practices in place. With a successful revolution, the basic norm that is presumed will change (Kelsen 1960, 86). Thus, for Kelsen, there is a discontinuity of appropriate legal justification as one moves between legal systems. The terminus of legal justification will be different before and after a revolution.[20] Indeed, like Dworkin (but unlike Shapiro), for Kelsen a revolution puts people into different normative spaces.

To sum up, Kelsen's theory of law satisfies the Requirement in the following manner:

1. When participants in legal practices justify decisions that conform to those practices, they should generally do so by reference to the basic norm and legal norms created pursuant to the basic norm. To justify their decisions solely by reference to how the existence of their legal practices, combined with other descriptive facts, trigger the practice-independent norms of morality and prudence (that is, according to the realist model) would show insensitivity to the role that legal norms play in practical reasoning.
2. The basic norm and legal norms created pursuant to the basic norm have normative force for participants. The existence of such a legal norm is a *pro tanto* reason for a participant's decision.[21]
3. The basic norm and legal norms created pursuant to it are non-empirical entities that are not reducible to social facts.

for practical reasoning (Paulson 2012; Delacroix 2004, 512–18). I ignore this alternative interpretation here.

[19] This relativity is tied to Kelsen's Neo-Kantianism (Green 2003).

[20] A more nuanced discussion of these matters would require discussion of Kelsen's doctrine of the unity of law and his views about international law (Green 2016).

[21] Kelsen is sometimes described as denying that the reasons for action provided by legal norms are capable of being considered, with moral norms, to come to an all-things-considered decision. They are incompatible normative orders. If so, one could not describe the existence of a legal norm as a *pro tanto* reason for action. But he is better understood as claiming that if legal and moral norms are understood as simultaneously valid, they must be so understood in the light of an overarching normative order that includes them both (Kelsen 1945, 374).

4. The basic norm and legal norms created pursuant to it are practice-dependent, in the sense that they have normative force only for those who presuppose the basic norm.

3 Hart on ILSs: The Puzzle

To repeat, the theories of law offered by Shapiro, Dworkin, and Kelsen all satisfy the Requirement. Each explains why participants in legal practices should justify their decisions by reference to legal norms, rather than solely according to the realist model. What about H.L.A. Hart's theory of law? Does his theory also satisfy the Requirement?

The foundation of Hart's theory of law is the idea of a social rule. A social rule exists when participants do not merely regularly conform to a standard, but also adopt the internal point of view—they respond to deviation from the standard with criticisms (including self-criticisms) and demands for conformity (Hart 1994, 57). These criticisms and demands are expressed in internal statements framed in normative language like "You ought to do this" or "That is wrong." Internal statements *express* acceptance of conformity with the standard (Hart 1994, 102); they do not describe this acceptance. In addition, someone making an internal statement *presupposes*, but does not describe, the existence of the social rule as a social fact (Hart 1994, 102–03).

Under Hart's theory of law, a social rule among officials (judges, legislators, sheriffs, and the like) stands at the foundation of every legal system. This rule, which Hart calls the rule of recognition, identifies which standards officials are obligated to back up with force. Because the rule of recognition is a social rule, it exists (and thus law exists) only if officials make internal legal statements (*ILSs*). They must treat deviation from the standard in the rule of recognition with criticism and demands for conformity made in ILSs. These ILSs express acceptance of conformity with the standard and presuppose the existence of the rule of recognition as a social fact (Hart 1994, 108). In addition, the existence of a legal system requires that it be efficacious, in the sense that standards identified by the rule of recognition are generally, although not necessarily always, obeyed by the citizenry (Hart 1994, 116–17). Hart's theory of law is therefore positivist: the existence and content of the law are ultimately determined solely by the above social facts, which we can call *rule of recognition facts*.

In saying that ILSs *presuppose* rule of recognition facts, Hart must mean that without those facts in place, officials would not accept conformity with the standard in the rule of recognition.[22] Thus, we can say that an ILS does not merely presuppose rule of recognition facts, put also presupposes judgments (for example, moral or

[22] For a revision of Hart's theory, in which acceptance can at times occur even when the factual presupposition does not obtain, see Toh 2011.

prudential judgments) about the appropriateness of conformity to the standard in the rule of recognition given the presence of those facts.

I think it is clear that Hart would describe the Community as lacking law, because its officials no longer make ILSs. It is true that the Community's officials would still respond to deviation from legal practices using normative statements. If one official did not enforce what Rex says, other officials would criticize her. But these criticisms would not presuppose the existence of their legal practices as social facts. Instead, they would describe their practices as social facts (as well as other relevant descriptive facts) and explicitly speak of conformity to the standards in the practices as appropriate in the light of moral or prudential norms.

3.1 Prediction Theories of Law

The conclusion that the Community has no law under Hart's theory of law is supported by his discussion of prediction theories of law (Hart 1994, 136–47). Hart is usually read as criticizing only a highly implausible prediction theory, according to which the law concerning a set of facts is whatever judgment will be issued by the court that gets the case (e.g., Leiter 2007, 17–18). Because this theory reduces the law to concrete decisions of courts, it is better described as a *decision* theory of law rather than a prediction theory. If a court's decision differs from one's prediction of the decision, it is the decision and not one's prediction that is the law.

As Hart notes, the decision theory appears to be motivated by the phenomenon of judicial supremacy—the fact that a court's judgment is binding, unless overturned on appeal, even if the court that issued the judgment misapplied or misinterpreted the law (Hart 1994, 145–46).[23] From judicial supremacy the realists (allegedly) conclude that the law is the court's judgment itself, since that judgment, and not the legal rule the court misapplied, is what officials are bound to enforce.

Understood as a theory of law, that is, an account of what is essential to law in every possible legal system, the decision theory is clearly a failure. First, it is not necessary that a legal system have judicial supremacy.[24] Concerning legal systems without judicial supremacy, the decision theory would apparently have nothing to say. Furthermore, even in those legal systems with judicial supremacy, the theory

[23] More accurately, Hart understands the decision theory to be motivated by *weak* judicial supremacy—the fact that a court's judgment (for example, that Jones is liable to Smith for $10,000) is binding even if the court that issued the judgment misapplied or misinterpreted the relevant law. In legal systems with *strong* judicial supremacy, by contrast, not only is the court's judgment binding, its interpretation of the law is binding on officials beyond the judgment in which the interpretation was issued. For a discussion of the distinction between weak and strong judicial supremacy in the context of the realists' decision theory of law, see Green 2011, 390–91.

[24] Officials might be legally licensed, or obligated, to ignore an otherwise valid judgment because the judge that issued it misapplied the law. Indeed, even in the American legal system it is arguably the case that judgments that involve egregious misapplications of the law are not legally binding even when they have not yet been overturned on appeal (Green 2005b, 402–03).

cannot explain how participants can understand a court's judgment as binding despite being legally in error (Hart 1994, 141–46). If the law is whatever a court decides, its decision cannot be understood as contrary to law. But officials commonly criticize judgments as being legally in error, even if they are binding. Finally, the decision theory cannot explain the law that identifies the items to which the theory seeks to reduce the law, namely the binding judgments of courts (Hart 1994, 136). By reducing the law concerning a set of facts to whatever a court with legal power to issue a judgment says about the facts, the theory lacks the resources to identify a court with legal power to issue a judgment.

I think it is unquestionably true that some realists, particularly Jerome Frank, offer a decision theory, although even Frank came to regret having done so (Green 2011, 408; Green 2005a, 1987–93). But the most philosophically sophisticated of the realists—in particular Felix Cohen and Walter Wheeler Cook—offer another, and much more plausible, prediction theory of law, with which I began this essay. Under this theory, the law is not reduced to the particular judgment that a court would issue concerning a set of facts, but to patterns of behavior and attitudes of officials and the population as a whole (Green 2011, 409–12).[25] It is precisely this prediction theory of law that is employed by officials in the Community.

Notice that without the requirement of the internal point of view, Hart's theory of law would itself be a type of prediction theory. For Hart, the existence and content of the law are ultimately determined solely by social facts about official practice. What is more, it is clear that for Hart it is *current* social facts that are relevant. Past facts—such as members of Congress raising their hands in 1933—can have legal relevance only in light of current official practice. If official practice has changed, even very recently, the existence and content of the law can change. Since what is essential to law is current official practice, anyone making a statement about the law must be relying upon a prediction, on the basis of evidence from the past, about what that practice is like.

Hart nevertheless rejects a prediction theory of law because it fails to account for the internal point of view. For example, at one point in *The Concept of Law* he considers the position that a statement that a rule is legally valid is semantically equivalent to a statement that the rule is part of a legal system that is efficacious, in the sense that the standards identified as the laws of the system are generally obeyed by the citizenry (Hart 1994, 102–05). One reason that Hart would consider such a position to be inadequate is that rule of recognition facts include more than efficacy. Official behavior and attitudes are relevant as well. But Hart's main criticism would

[25] According to Brian Leiter, statements that appear to express a decision or prediction theory are rather "claim[s] about how it is *useful* to think about law for attorneys who must advise clients what to do" (Leiter 2007, 71). American legal realism is essentially only a theory of adjudication. The realists do not purport to offer a theory of law. Those philosophers who have considered Leiter's reading have been skeptical (Moore 2000, 32–33; Tuzet 2013, 58–59), and rightly so. For a detailed criticism, see Green 2011, 400–16. Indeed, by ignoring the prediction theory of law, Leiter misses out on the most challenging and important aspect of legal realism. Note that one can disagree with Leiter on the realists' decision and prediction theories of law while accepting much of what he says about their theory of adjudication (Green 2011, 383–400).

apply even to the position that a statement that a rule is legally valid is semantically equivalent to a statement concerning rule of recognition facts. The reason is that such a position is incompatible with the internal point of view. When justifying their decisions, officials must use ILSs, which presuppose, rather than describe, rule of recognition facts.

3.2 *Hart's Theory Fails to Satisfy the Requirement*

To repeat, Hart would say that the Community does not have law, because officials do not make ILSs. But does Hart's theory satisfy the Requirement?

One might argue that Hart's theory is much like Shapiro's. Legal norms are non-empirical entities that do not create reasons for decisions through their existence (the way they do create such reasons under Dworkin's and Kelsen's theories of law). The standard in the rule of recognition and standards identified as law by that standard are simply abstract objects that give one no reason to do one thing rather than another. They have normative force only because, having pointed to them, a participant should conclude that she has a non-legal *pro tanto* reason (for example a moral or prudential reason) for her decision. For Shapiro this is because legal norms are plans. For Hart it is because when a participant points to the standard in the course of making an ILS, that ILS presupposes a judgment about the appropriateness of conformity to the standard given the existence of rule of recognition facts. So understood, Hart, like Shapiro, explains the normative force of legal norms in a manner that is compatible with everyone inhabiting the same space of practice-independent norms.

Such a reading of Hart is supported by his description of why participants in legal practices accept the standard in the rule of recognition. After noting that they may take themselves to be morally obligated to conform to the standard, Hart adds that acceptance could also be based on prudential concerns:

> [I]t is not … true that those who do accept the system voluntarily, must conceive of themselves as morally bound to do so … their allegiance to the system may be based on many different considerations: calculations of long-term interest; disinterested interest in others; an unreflecting inherited or traditional attitude; or the mere wish to do as others do. There is indeed no reason why those who accept the authority of the system should not examine their conscience and decide that, morally, they ought not to accept it, yet for a variety of reasons continue to do so. (Hart 1994, 203)

These are the varied judgments about the appropriateness of conformity to the standard in the rule of recognition that are presupposed in an ILS.

But there is an important difference between Shapiro's theory of law and Hart's, so understood. Shapiro can explain why a legal norm has normative force for participants in legal practices, because legal norms are plans. The officials in the Community, by deliberating according to the realist model, rather than simply stopping justification at their plans and acting accordingly, are doing something they *should not do*. They are failing to take into account an important factor in their practical reasoning.

But for Hart law is not essentially a planning activity. Hart's theory does not require that officials adopt plans for law to exist. Thus, it is not clear why the shift by the officials in the Monarchy to a realist model is improper. If officials deliberate under the realist model, Hart will say that they do not have law (because they make no ILSs), but there is nothing normatively inclining the Monarchy's officials against such an approach. The presupposition that goes on in ILSs is something that participants in legal practices simply *do*. Hart does not speak of it as something that they *ought to do*. There is no sense in which the officials in the Monarchy, by shifting to a realist model, are missing out on any important factor in their practical reasoning.

One way to solve the problem is to read Hart as implicitly relying on a planning theory of law. Perhaps Hart's talk about presupposition was simply his way of saying that officials, having adopted a *plan* of conformity to the standard in the rule of recognition, should presuppose the appropriateness of conformity to the standard, because reconsideration would be contrary to the norms of instrumental rationality. I think such a conclusion should be resisted, however. There is no evidence in *The Concept of Law* that Hart thought a legal system requires officials to engage in anything like the psychological act of adopting a plan. Indeed, the fact that a legal system can arise without such acts is arguably a reason to prefer Hart's theory over Shapiro's (Gardner and Macklem 2011).

But even if Hart's theory of law is not a planning theory, couldn't one argue that officials in the Community are acting contrary to the norms of instrumental rationality? Isn't the realist model, in which one always determines whether conformity to legal practices is morally or prudentially appropriate, wasteful? Shouldn't participants in legal practices spare themselves deliberative effort by presupposing the appropriateness of conformity to the standard in the rule of recognition?

It may be true that ILSs are recommended by instrumental rationality. But I think reading Hart as relying on this fact should be resisted as well. Nowhere does Hart suggest that legal norms have a normative force based in the wastefulness of recurrent deliberation. Indeed, he never suggests that the presupposition that occurs in ILSs is in any sense normatively recommended.

It follows that Hart's theory of law does not satisfy the Requirement. For Hart, legal norms arise in the context of ILSs, but he offers no explanation of why legal norms, so understood, play a meaningful role in the practical reasoning of participants in legal practices. The way Hart describes it, it would make no practical difference if participants in legal practices justified their decisions according to the realist model.

Because Hart fails to satisfy the Requirement, he leaves it unclear why ILSs should be necessary for law at all. The demand that officials make ILSs for law to exist looks ad hoc. The difference between the Monarchy and the Community is too insignificant to explain why one has law and the other does not.

3.3 *Toh on ILSs*

The puzzle of why Hart thinks law requires ILSs is reinforced by the most well-developed account of ILSs, offered by Kevin Toh. Toh's account primarily focuses on ILSs' expressive character. Hart is attracted to expressivism because of its ability to explain, in a naturalistically respectable manner, the *reason-giving* character of a normative statement—the fact that someone who makes such a statement thereby takes herself to have a reason for action. Under an expressive approach, normative statements do not describe mysterious entities that generate reasons for action. Instead, they express non-cognitive states, such as the speaker's acceptance of a standard.

An ILS is a normative statement, in the sense that an official who makes an ILS thereby takes herself to have a reason for action. Rather than adopting a cognitivist approach, in which someone making an ILS is describing the actual existence of reason-giving entities that stand outside of the causal order, Hart understands ILSs as the expression of the speaker's acceptance of the standard in the rule of recognition (Toh 2005, 81–105).

Notice that under Toh's account of ILSs, the form of acceptance expressed in an ILS can be moral or prudential. To be sure, Toh argues that Hart does not exclude the possibility that a different form of acceptance is expressed in an ILS (Toh 2007, 417–18). But he does not say that Hart thinks ILSs *require* a different form of acceptance. Indeed, such a reading would appear to be precluded by Hart's description of official acceptance of the rule of recognition as based on morality and prudence.

Since the acceptance of the standard in the rule of recognition expressed in ILSs can be moral or prudential, the only element of Hart's account of ILSs that stands in the way of understanding officials in the Community as making ILSs themselves is his insistence that someone making an ILS presupposes rather than describes rule of recognition facts. Although officials in the Community express their moral and prudential acceptance of the standard in the rule of recognition (since they speak normatively of the moral and prudential reasons for following the standard), these expressive statements are not ILSs, because they involve description, rather than presupposition, of rule of recognition facts and they make, rather than presuppose, judgments about the moral or prudential appropriateness of following the standard given those facts.

But nothing about the presupposition in ILSs, as Toh describes it, explains why it should be required for law's existence. There are two prevailing accounts of a linguistic presupposition. According to the *semantic* account, a presupposition concerns the relationship between the truth values of sentences (or propositions): *P* presupposes *Q* if and only if the truth of *Q* is necessitated both by the truth of *P and* by the truth of not-*P* (Strawson 1950; van Fraassen 1968). For example, "The President of the United States is male" semantically presupposes that one and only one President of the United States exists, because it follows from the truth of "The President of the United States is male" and from the truth of "The President of the

United States is not male" that there is one and only one President of the United States.

Under the broader *pragmatic* account, a presupposition is a propositional attitude on the part of *speakers*, rather than a semantic relation between sentences or propositions. Sentence *P* presupposes *Q* if and only if the use of *P* would normally be inappropriate unless it is commonly accepted that *Q*. One presupposes a fact in this sense if he takes it for granted and assumes that others in the context do so as well (Stalnaker 1999, 38).

Semantic presuppositions will also be pragmatic presuppositions. I would not normally say that the President of the United States is male except in a context in which it is taken for granted that one and only one President of the United States exists. But not all pragmatic presuppositions are semantic. For example, it is a pragmatic but not a semantic presupposition of my uttering "My wife is either in the kitchen or the bathroom" that I don't know for certain that she is in the kitchen.

Toh argues that Hart's understanding of a presupposition is pragmatic (Toh 2005, 86–87 n.21; Toh 2014, 719 n. 28). Saying "The President of the United States is male" in circumstances in which there is not one and only one President of the United States is an *error*, because the fact that there is one and only one President is semantically presupposed by the sentence (Toh 2005, 113 n.57). But the statement made in an ILS can be made, without error, in circumstances in which rule of recognition facts are absent. As Hart puts it, "it is normally pointless" (not erroneous) to make such a statement in the absence of the relevant rule of recognition facts (Hart 1994, 104). Furthermore, it is only *normally* pointless: in a course on ancient Roman law, a teacher might speak of certain norms as legally valid, even though the relevant rule of recognition facts are not in place.

But even if officials pragmatically presuppose rule of recognition facts when making ILSs, the question remains why law should vanish when they systematically make their pragmatic presuppositions explicit. We would not consider someone who said "I am not sure whether my wife is in the kitchen or the bathroom; she might be in either" to be in a substantially different psychological state from someone who said "My wife is either in the kitchen or the bathroom," thereby presupposing rather than describing that he did not know where she was. It should not matter—certainly not matter so much that law should *disappear*—that officials in the Community systematically make their beliefs about rule of recognition facts explicit and then make normative statements that conformity with legal practices is morally or prudentially appropriate in the light of those facts. Indeed, Hart himself admits that "[i]f the truth of this presupposition [of rule of recognition facts] were doubted, it could be established by reference to actual practice: to the way in which courts identify what is to count as law, and to the general acceptance of or acquiescence in these identifications" (Hart 1994, 108).

Other discussions of Hart on the internal point of view likewise fail to explain why Hart thinks that the presuppositions in ILSs are necessary for law. Shapiro, for example, argues that Hart understands the internal point of view as a practical attitude of rule acceptance, which can, but need not, be moral acceptance (Shapiro 2006, 1161). Under his reading, it is not even necessary to the internal point of view that rule of recognition facts and judgments about the appropriateness of conformity to legal standards given those facts be presupposed. It would follow that there is no reason not to attribute the internal point of view to the officials in the Community.

Indeed, the main criticism about Hart's doctrine of the internal point of view is not directed at the idea that ILSs involve presuppositions, but at the notion that non-moral (especially prudential) acceptance of the standard in the rule of recognition could explain ILSs that criticize other participants for non-conformity (Holton 1998; Raz 1990, § 2.1). The thrust of these criticisms is precisely the opposite of what I argue here. If the form of acceptance that Hart should attribute to those who make ILSs is moral, then it should be appropriate for someone making an ILS to identify the social facts about legal practices that trigger the relevant moral norms. And yet Hart puzzlingly claims that if such social facts are systematically identified by officials, they no longer inhabit the internal point of view and law no longer exists.[26]

4 Conclusion

To sum up, under the prevailing reading of ILSs we must conclude that Hart's theory of law fails to satisfy the Requirement. He cannot explain why legal norms have normative force and thus cannot explain why officials in the Monarchy are missing out on anything relevant to their practical reasoning by shifting to a realist model. As a result, his theory of law itself looks ad hoc. Because he cannot explain why the shift from the Monarchy to the Community is a problem, he leaves it a mystery why the Community has no law.

I would like to end with another possibility, however. Hart may think that it is essential to an ILS that one expresses an acceptance of conformity with the standard in the rule of recognition that cannot be cashed out in moral or prudential terms. Officials, in stopping justification at the standard, would be manifesting an acceptance of conformity as intrinsically valuable—the acceptance expressed would not be based on rule of recognition facts' triggering the norms of morality or prudence, even though participants might also accept the standard for these reasons.

Consider the following passage in which Hart discusses the form of acceptance that occurs when one adopts the internal point of view:

> [I]f a social rule is to exist some at least must look upon the behavior in question as a general standard to be followed by the group as a whole. A social rule has an 'internal' aspect, in addition to the external aspect that it shares with a social habit.... This internal aspect of rules may be simply illustrated from the rules of a game. Chess players do not merely have

[26] The criticism of Hart's theory that I make here should be distinguished from Kenneth Ehrenberg's (Ehrenberg 2011), who argues that Hart's theory cannot account for the anarchist official—that is, an official who does not believe that the law gives him non-prudential reasons for action. My criticism does not concern the *kind* of official acceptance that is necessary for law. It concerns Hart's claim that law exists only when judgments standing behind such acceptance are presupposed by officials, rather than explicitly stated.

> similar habits of moving the Queen in the same way.... In addition, they have a reflective critical attitude to this pattern of behavior: they regard it as a standard for all who play the game. (Hart 1994, 56–57)

Hart does not make it clear in what sense participants in the practice accept the relevant standard. They might accept it solely because social facts about the practice make conformity to the standard morally or prudentially appropriate. If so, then an adoption of the internal point of view should be compatible with demands for conformity that make these social facts and their relationship to moral or prudential norms explicit. But Hart might be saying that participants consider conformity to the standard to be valuable in itself.

Assume, for example, that I try to move my Queen like a Knight, and my opponent criticizes me using normative language. She might be criticizing me solely because she thinks that social facts about our practice have triggered practice-independent norms. For example, by moving my Queen in that way, I have frustrated her reasonable expectations, and reasonable expectations ought not be frustrated without a compelling reason. If so, she does not accept the standards of chess as valuable in themselves. Under our new reading, therefore, Hart would say that my opponent has not adopted the internal point of view. To adopt the internal point of view, she must treat the rules of chess as themselves appropriate, independently of the moral or prudential reasons one might have to follow them (Green 2013b, 368–69).[27]

Indeed, if the relevant attitude standing behind the internal point of view were merely moral, Hart would not be speaking about an attitude unique to participants. People who have never played chess can think that frustrating chess players' reasonable expectation by failing to follow the rules of the game is morally wrong. They too can have a reflective critical attitude toward deviance. But Hart treats the relevant attitude as one that arises only for participants in the game.

If those adopting the internal point of view in a legal system treat conformity to legal standards as intrinsically valuable, the standards would have normative force for them in the sense demanded by the Requirement. Having pointed to a standard, a participant ought to conclude that she has a *pro tanto* reason for her decision, without considering whether the decision is morally or prudentially justified. In adopting the realist model, the practical reasoning of officials in the Monarchy would have become seriously flawed. As participants in the Monarchy, making ILSs, they must have accepted conformity to the legal standards in the Monarchy as intrinsically valuable. But now they leave justification by appeal to this intrinsic value out of their practical reasoning.

---

[27] Of course, to say that my opponent treats conformity to the rules of chess as intrinsically valuable does not mean that she thinks one should conform in circumstances outside the game of chess. Hart makes it clear that the scope of the accepted standard is limited to participants: "[T]hey regard it as a standard for all who play the game" (Hart 1994, 56). But there is a difference between pointing to the existence of a practice as a social fact because it is relevant to the scope of a practice-dependent norm, and pointing to that social fact because it triggers a practice-independent moral or prudential norm. The former is compatible with the internal point of view as I am now reading it. The latter is not.

Furthermore, these standards would be practice-dependent norms. Although non-participants might accept conformity to the standards for moral or prudential reasons, only participants would treat conformity as intrinsically valuable. Given Hart's expressivism, in which reasons for action exist only within an expressive context, the standards would have normative force only for participants. Hart's theory would be like Dworkin's and Kelsen's in being committed to a form of normative relativism. Participants in different legal practices would, in a sense, inhabit different and incommensurable normative spaces.

Thus, Hart could explain the discontinuity of appropriate legal justification as one moves from one legal system to another. The legal norms that a French judge used to justify his decisions in 1788 and in 1791 would indeed be fundamentally different. In 1788, he should have justified his decisions through normative judgments that expressed acceptance of conformity with what the King of France says as intrinsically valuable. In 1791, he should have justified his decisions through normative judgments that expressed acceptance of conformity with what the National Assembly says as intrinsically valuable. Because his non-cognitive states would have fundamentally changed, he would, in effect, be inhabiting a different normative space.

To sum up, under this interpretation, Hart's theory of law satisfies the Requirement in the following manner:

1. When participants in legal practices justify decisions that conform to those practices, they must generally do so by reference, in an ILS, to the standard in the rule of recognition and standards identified as law by that standard. To justify their decisions solely by reference to how rule of recognition facts, combined with other descriptive facts, trigger the practice-independent norms of morality and prudence (that is, according to the realist model) would ignore what participants consider to be the intrinsic value of conformity to legal standards.
2. The legal standards, when referred to in ILSs, have normative force for participants. Having referred to the standard in an ILS, a participant should conclude that she has a *pro tanto* reason for her decision.
3. The legal standards are non-empirical entities that are not reducible to social facts.
4. The legal standards are practice-dependent, in the sense they have normative force only for those who make ILSs.

Because, under this reading, Hart's theory of law explains why legal norms play a meaningful role in the practical reasoning of participants in legal practices, his demand that participants make ILSs for law to exist no longer appears ad hoc. As we have seen, by shifting to a realist model of justification, officials in the Monarchy are failing to take into account what they consider to be the intrinsic value of conformity with legal standards. What is more, if they keep it up, we would have to conclude that they do not treat conformity to legal standards as having intrinsic value anymore. As far as they are concerned, legal norms don't exist. Only moral and prudential norms do. It makes perfect sense that Hart would conclude that the

Community therefore lacks law, even though Rex's commands are still scrupulously enforced.

Although this reading of ILSs allows us to make sense of why Hart considers them to be necessary for the existence of law, it is not without its own problems. For example, when Hart speaks of why officials accept the standard in the rule of recognition, he fails to mention a form of acceptance in which conformity to the standard is considered intrinsically valuable. Instead, he describes the relevant acceptance as largely moral or prudential (Hart 1994, 203). To be sure, my reading is *compatible* with participants also accepting the standard for moral and prudential reasons. But given that it is acceptance of the standard as intrinsically valuable that is essential to an ILS under my reading, one would have expected Hart to have at least mentioned this form of acceptance as a reason participants conform to legal practices.

But the biggest problem with my reading is that it is unclear why Hart should say that someone making an ILS *presupposes* rule of recognition facts. Let us say that someone is a participant in legal practices and has developed an acceptance of the standard in the rule of recognition as intrinsically valuable. In what sense does she need to presuppose rule of recognition facts to make an ILS? It is true that without the presence of legal practices, she would have never developed the attitude she is expressing. But the causes of one's statements are neither semantic nor pragmatic presuppositions of those statements.

Hart's talk of presuppositions may force us back into the standard reading of ILSs. If that is the case, however, I think my negative conclusions still stand. Hart's theory of ILSs fails to satisfy the Requirement, and his demand that officials make ILSs for the law to exist is ad hoc and unmotivated.

Acknowledgement Thanks to Brian Bix, Scott Shapiro, and the participants in the Workshop on the Normativity of Law at the IVR in Washington DC for helpful suggestions.

References

Cohen, F. S. (1933). *Ethical systems and legal ideals: An essay on the foundations of legal criticism*. Westport: Greenwood Press.

Cohen, F. S. (1935). Transcendental nonsense and the functional approach. *Columbia Law Review, 35*, 809–849.

Coleman, J. L. (1989). On the relationship between law and morality. *Ratio Juris, 2*, 66–78.

Coleman, J. L., & Leiter, B. (1996). Legal positivism. In D. Patterson (Ed.), *A companion to philosophy of law and legal theory* (pp. 241–260). Oxford: Oxford University Press.

Cook, W. W. (1935). Oliver Wendell Holmes: Scientist. *American Bar Association Journal, 21*, 211–213.

Cook, W. W. (1942). *The logical and legal bases of the conflicts of laws*. Cambridge: Harvard University Press.

Delacroix, S. (2004). Hart's and Kelsen's concepts of normativity contrasted. *Ratio Juris, 17*, 501–520.

Dworkin, R. (1986). *Law's empire*. Cambridge: Harvard University Press.

Dworkin, R. (2006). *Justice in Robes*. Cambridge: Harvard University Press.

Dworkin, R. (2011). *Justice for Hedgehogs*. Cambridge: Harvard University Press.
Ehrenberg, K. M. (2011). The anarchist official: A problem for legal positivism. *Australian Journal of Legal Philosophy, 36*, 89–112.
Enoch, D. (2011). Reason-Giving and the law. In L. Green & B. Leiter (Eds.), *Oxford studies in philosophy of law: Volume 1* (pp. 1–38). Oxford: Oxford University Press.
Gardner, J., & Macklem, T. (2011). Review of Shapiro 2011. In G. Gutting (Ed.), *Notre Dame philosophical reviews*, http://ndpr.nd.edu/news/27609-legality/. Accessed 25 Apr 2015.
Green, L. (2008). Positivism and the inseparability of law and morals. *New York University Law Review, 83*, 1035–1058.
Green, M. S. (2003). Hans Kelsen and the logic of legal systems. *Alabama Law Review, 53*, 365–413.
Green, M. S. (2005a). Legal realism as theory of law. *William and Mary Law Review, 46*, 1915–2000.
Green, M. S. (2005b). Legal revolutions: Six mistakes about discontinuity in the legal order. *North Carolina Law Review, 83*, 331–409.
Green, M. S. (2009). Kelsen, quietism, and the rule of recognition. In M. D. Adler & K. E. Himma (Eds.), *The rule of recognition and the United States constitution* (pp. 351–378). Oxford: Oxford University Press.
Green, M. S. (2011). Leiter on the legal realists. *Law and Philosophy, 30*, 381–418.
Green, M. S. (2013a). Felix Cohen on legislation. *The Theory and Practice of Legislation, 1*, 113–128.
Green, M. S. (2013b). On Hart's category mistake. *Legal Theory, 19*, 347–369.
Green, M. S. (2014). Prediction theories of law and the internal point of view. *San Diego Law Review, 51*, 921–938.
Green, M. S. (2016). Marmor's Kelsen. In D. A. Jeremy Telman (Ed.), *Hans Kelsen in America* (pp. 45–84). Dordrecht: Springer.
Greenberg, M. (2004). How facts make law. *Legal Theory, 10*, 157–198.
Greenberg, M. (2014). The moral impact theory of law. *Yale Law Review, 123*, 1288–1342.
Hart, H. L. A. (1994). *The concept of law* (2nd ed.). Oxford: Oxford University Press.
Holton, R. (1998). Positivism and the internal point of view. *Law and Philosophy, 17*, 597–625.
Kelsen, H. (1934). *Introduction to the problems of legal theory. A translation of the first edition of the Reine Rechtslehre or pure theory of law* (Bonnie L. P., & S. L. Paulson, Trans.). 1997, Oxford: Oxford University Press.
Kelsen, H. (1945). *General theory of law and state.* (W. Anders, Trans.). Cambridge, MA: Harvard University Press.
Kelsen, H. (1960). *The pure theory of law* 2nd ed., (M. Knight trans.). 1967, Berkeley: University of California Press.
Leiter, B. (2007). *Naturalizing jurisprudence: Essays on American legal realism and naturalism in legal philosophy*. Oxford: Oxford University Press.
Marmor, A. (2011). *Philosophy of law*. Princeton: Princeton University Press.
Moore, M. S. (2000). *Educating oneself in public: Critical essays in jurisprudence*. Oxford: Oxford University Press.
Paulson, S. L. (2012). A 'Justified Normativity' thesis in Hans Kelsen's pure theory of law? Rejoinders to Robert Alexy and Joseph Raz. In M. Klatt (Ed.), *Institutionalized reason: The jurisprudence of Robert Alexy* (pp. 61–111). Oxford: Oxford University Press.
Raz, J. (1990). *Practical reasons and norms*. Princeton: Princeton University Press.
Shapiro, S. J. (2006). What is the internal point of view? *Fordham Law Review, 75*, 1157–1170.
Shapiro, S. J. (2011). *Legality*. Cambridge, MA: Harvard University Press.
Southwood, N. (2011). The moral/conventional distinction. *Mind, 120*, 761–802.
Stalnaker, R. C. (1999). *Context and content*. Oxford: Oxford University Press.
Strawson, P. F. (1950). On referring. *Mind, 59*, 320–344.
Toh, K. (2005). Hart's expressivism and his benthamite project. *Legal Theory, 11*, 75–123.

Toh, K. (2007). Raz on detachment, acceptance, and describability. *Oxford Journal of Legal Studies, 27*, 403–427.
Toh, K. (2011). Legal judgments as plural acceptances of norms. In L. Green & B. Leiter (Eds.), *Oxford studies in philosophy of law: Volume 1* (pp. 107–137). Oxford: Oxford University Press.
Toh, K. (2014). Four neglected prescriptions of Hartian legal philosophy. *Law and Philosophy, 33*, 689–724.
Tuzet, G. (2013). What is wrong with legal realism? In D. Canale & G. Tuzet (Eds.), *The planning theory of law: A critical reading* (pp. 47–63). Dordrecht: Springer.
van Fraassen, B. C. (1968). Presupposition, implication, and self-reference. *Journal of Philosophy, 65*, 136–152.

Can Metalinguistic Negotiations and 'Conceptual Ethics' rescue legal positivism?

Teresa Marques

Abstract In recent years, David Plunkett and Tim Sundell have published a series of interesting articles that made an original use of resources from linguistics and philosophy of language to reply to arguments for legal antipositivism, the thesis according to which moral or value facts are part of what determines what the law is in a given jurisdiction at a given time. Plunkett and Sundell's strategy for resisting antipositivism appeals to the notion of a metalinguistic negotiation, which incorporates the notion of a metalinguistic or context disagreement. Sundell (Philos Stud 155(2):267–288, 2011) had argued that metalinguistic disagreements are a possible component of disputes about evaluative matters. A further notion deployed is that of conceptual ethics, an essential component of metalinguistic negotiations. This paper approaches a crucial concern about the deployment of both notions against disagreement-based arguments for legal antipositivism. Metalinguistic negotiations displace disagreements from the semantic to the metalinguistic level, but do not eliminate the appeal to moral or other normative reasons from legal disagreements. Conceptual ethics purports to be a normative activity, engaged with prescribing ways one ought to think and talk. On a broad understanding of legal reasoning and practice, metalinguistic negotiations and conceptual ethics are an integral part of it, and hence are consistent with evaluative and normative facts being essential to, and constitutive of, the law. Or so this paper argues.

Keywords Metalinguistic negotiation • Legal positivism • Legal disagreement • Grounding • Constitution

1 Introduction

Legal positivism is the view that facts about the existence and content of the law are determined solely by social facts. Hart 2012 distinguished between internal and external legal statements. Internal legal statements are statements of

T. Marques (✉)
Law Department, Law and Philosophy Group, Universitat Pompeu Fabra, Barcelona, Spain
e-mail: mariateresa.marques@upf.edu

F. Poggi, A. Capone (eds.), *Pragmatics and Law*, Perspectives in Pragmatics, Philosophy & Psychology 10, DOI 10.1007/978-3-319-44601-1_9

law – normative statements made from the point of view of the participants within a legal system. External legal statements are about individual laws or other aspects of legal systems – descriptive statements made from the point of view of an external observer. In so-called 'hard cases' (Shapiro 2011), it is difficult to figure out what the law is solely on the basis of the existing social facts. Where the existing social facts do not determine what the law is, the corresponding internal legal statements are indeterminate. However, participants within a legal system may take themselves to be in disagreement even when the legal statements they disagree about are indeterminate.

Now, legal discourse seems often to rely on moral considerations, as legal actors avow. This casts doubt on the soundness of the legal positivist view. A challenge that originates in Dworkin's disagreement-based argument highlights the importance of normative and evaluative considerations in legal discourse and reasoning (Dworkin 1986, 2011). Dworkin distinguishes between two types of legal dispute about what the law is in a given jurisdiction. In the first type of dispute, the parties agree on the conditions for something being a law but disagree about whether those conditions are met. In the second type of dispute, legal actors have different views about what the law is even though they agree about all the relevant empirical facts, and so the disagreement of this second type is not about these empirical facts. Plunkett and Sundell 2013b call disagreements of the latter kind "bedrock legal disputes" (Dworkin himself called them "theoretical disagreements").

If Dworkin is right, those disagreements are not about external legal statements, but arise from the point of view of the participants in the legal system. These disputes, which are pervasive in the practices of higher courts, represent a challenge to legal positivism. Since the essential positivist claim is that social facts posit the content of the law (see also Gardner 2001), it allows that if and wherever social facts do not decide or determine the content of the law, nothing else does. It is hence possible that in some theoretical or bedrock legal disagreements nothing prior to the dispute has settled what the law is. Some legal statements will simply be undetermined as a result. That is problematic since it seems to preclude the possibility of making sense of apparently very real legal disagreements, depriving legal actors of a common subject matter over which to disagree.

Recently, Moreso 2009 has proposed that these disputes should be treated as faultless disagreements, importing to the legal philosophy debate a notion that has been deployed prolifically in the philosophy of language in the past decade. And, in recent years as well, David Plunkett and Tim Sundell have published a series of articles that make a very original use of further linguistic resources from linguistics and philosophy of language to reply to arguments against legal positivism (Plunkett and Sundell 2013a, b, 2014). They use pragmatic explanations to account for *at least some of those* disputes as metalinguistic negotiations.[1]

[1] It must be highlighted that Plunkett & Sundell *do not* claim that all such disputes are cases of metalinguistic negotiations, but that at least some *may be* and that, at least for those that are indeed metalinguistic negotiations, the objection that legal actors are talking past each other and not really disagreeing cannot be raised. Granting that this is the case, the present paper aims to address the

Metalinguistic negotiations have two components. First, they are disputes or disagreements not directly about the truth of the semantic content literally conveyed by a used sentence (if any), but about other pragmatically conveyed information. Secondly, it is essential to metalinguistic disputes that they involve "conceptual ethics", a normative activity engaged with prescribing ways one ought to think and talk (Burgess and Plunkett 2013a, b).

This displacement of the location of a dispute could successfully rescue a sense in which participants in a dispute who fail to express the same (or any) semantic content by their words may nonetheless genuinely express a conflict. In the legal case, even though the law may be indeterminate at a given moment, legal actors might indeed be engaging in real metalinguistic negotiations about, for instance, what concept should be expressed by a given term in a legal provision.

In the next section, §2, I briefly present the disagreement-based argument against legal positivism, and the notion of an interpretative concept. In §3, I present the notion of a metalinguistic negotiation, and its virtues in accounting for normative disputes in general. After conceding (and agreeing with) the possibility of shifting the *locus* of disagreement to the metalinguistic level, in the second part of this section I draw attention to possible sources of resistance to this proposal that arise from the very wide range of cases that the notion of conceptual ethics is meant to cover.

In §4 I address what is, I think, the core issue in contention. The core issue is not merely whether there is a possible explanation for the existence of persistent disagreements, but whether these disputes essentially involve appeals to normative and evaluative facts (in brief, value facts). On a narrow interpretation of legal reasoning, metalinguistic negotiations may seem to provide some support to legal positivism. On a broader interpretation, however, metalinguistic negotiations do not rescue positivism. Metalinguistic negotiations, and specifically, *conceptual ethics*, may be seen as a notational variant of Dworkin's *conceptual interpretation*. Consequently, bringing metalinguistic negotiations to bear on legal disagreements may not begin to address the core metaphysical contention about *the nature* of the law. Although what the law is in a given jurisdiction may be determined by, i.e., grounded in, social conventions and practices, what the law *is*, it could be argued, is nonetheless *constitutively* normative. I draw an analogy with the philosophical debate about the constitutive norm of assertion to drive the point home.

The main point of the paper is conditional on what *conceptual ethics* means. *If* conceptual ethics is a practice that is guided by moral and normative considerations, then it's not clear that metalinguistic negotiations can be used to defuse the antipositivist argument. But if conceptual ethics is just a term of art applied to the reasoning about how to use words (not necessarily guided by moral considerations), then it can contribute to a defence of legal positivism.

cases in which legal actors are actually engaged in metalinguistic negotiations and to assess the extent to which – if at all – *in those cases* the antipositivist does not have a case against the positivist based on disagreement.

2 The Problem of Disagreement

In this section, I will follow Plunkett and Sundell's terminological use of "legal facts" and "legal reasoning". For now, let "legal facts" stand for what the law is in a given jurisdiction and at a given time, and let "legal reasoning" apply to the reasoning that goes on in legal contexts with the aim of discovering the legal facts. Let us moreover concede, as they do, that legal thought and talk involves "a great deal of moral thought and talk". Their main aim is to show that metalinguistic negotiations may account for some of the relevant legal disputes, and in particular that speakers may often be engaged in other projects besides legal reasoning. Metalinguistic negotiations are processes that aim to settle the interpretation of words whose correct interpretation was unclear or undetermined up to a point. These processes may be sensitive to moral considerations and reasoning, although various concerns may push towards one or another way of making a given word more precise, or of fixing the meaning of a word that was previously undetermined.[2]

Briefly, legal positivism is the view that facts about the existence and content of the law are determined solely by social facts. A natural way to interpret the relevant determination relation is to say that social facts (descriptive facts about people's activities, conventions, mental states, goals, etc.) ground the existence and content of the law.[3] Also briefly, interpretivism is the thesis that the law includes not only the rules enacted by a community, but also "the principles that provide the best moral justification for those enacted rules" (Dworkin 2011, 402). Interpretivism contradicts legal positivism insofar as it allows that the content and existence of the law is not determined solely by social facts. Dworkin claimed that the concept Law, like other concepts (DEMOCRACY, EQUALITY, FREEDOM), is an interpretative concept, and that in bedrock legal disputes participants disagree about the correct application of the concept. The best application of the concept is to be determined by normative and evaluative facts.

> we must recognize at least one more family of concepts—a family that we share in spite of not agreeing about a decisive test. These are our interpretative concepts. We share these concepts, as I said, not because we agree in their application once all other pertinent facts are agreed upon, but rather by manifesting an understanding that their correct application is fixed by the best interpretation of the practices in which they figure. (Dworkin 2011, 160)

---

[2] Plunkett and Sundell are primarily committed to showing that it is not impossible for the legal positivist to "neutralize" the data appealed to in favor of antipositivism (and against legal positivism). The aim is not to show that the analysis in terms of metalinguistic negotiation counts in favor of legal positivism, just that it's possible to reduce or eliminate the "bite" of the data against it. Thanks to Hrafn Asgeirsson for discussion on this point.

[3] From recent communication, it appears that Plunkett is also inclined to read 'determines' as 'grounds', defining legal positivism as a thesis about social facts being the sole ultimate grounds of legal facts. In the last section, I'll argue that on this natural reading, the determination relation is trivially true, but uninteresting for the legal antipositivist, who may still argue that the fact that social facts ground legal facts *is compatible* with a constitutively normative and evaluative account of the nature of the law (Greenberg's (2006) can be interpreted in a way that renders such a constitutively normative account of the Law of this kind).

Now, Dworkin's disagreement-based argument against legal positivism is structurally similar to recurrent arguments against so-called *indexical contextualism*. Indexical contextualism is, roughly, the view according to which the semantic content of particular kinds of expressions varies with, and is determined by, features of the context at which the expression is used. Clear undisputed cases are indexicals like "I", "here" or "now", but it has been argued that other expressions, for instance gradable adjectives like "tall" or "rich", are also context-dependent. Among the most disputed kinds of expressions in the recent literature are predicates of personal taste, knowledge attributions, and epistemic and deontic modals of the form "must φ", "might φ" or "ought to φ".

According to indexical contextualism, sentences with taste predicates express in a context a property relative to, or dependent on, a particular standard of taste. The standard of taste in question is settled at the context where the token of the particular taste predicate is used. It is possible, on this view, for two distinct tokens of the same taste predicate (on different uses) to express different taste properties. Two independent utterances made in different contexts of the apparently inconsistent sentences in (1) below may in fact be both true[4]:

(1)
Ana: Tripe is delicious.
Bea: Tripe is not delicious; it is disgusting.

In general, where contexts of use fail to contribute a relevant standard or parameter to the content, the sentence uttered lacks full semantic content, and is thereby undetermined in truth-value.

Likewise, on a given context of utterance, a use of a deontic modal "might/may φ" expresses what is permissible or possible with respect to a given set of rules or deontic standards. It is possible for two distinct uses of a deontic modal sentence to respectively express a truth – that some course of action is permissible, and in another context to express a falsehood, where that same course of action is forbidden.[5]

(2)
Ana (to her children during school holidays): You may stay up after 9pm.
Ana (to her children on school nights): You can't stay up after 9pm. In fact, you ought to be asleep by 8pm.

Disagreement-based arguments against indexical contextualism are used to show that indexical contextualism about, for instance, taste predicates is unable to explain the appearance of disagreement between two subjects who don't share a standard of taste. Imagine that Ana and Bea are two seasoned, reflective gastronomes, with tastes optimally refined by training, and are engaged in a dispute in which they utter the sentences above in (1) in optimal circumstances for appraisal.

Intuitively, in so judging, Ana and Bea disagree. But it seems that the "contextualism" outlined misses this. On indexical contextualism, there are two possible

---

[4] For a defense of flexible contextualism about taste predicates, see for instance Glanzberg (2007).

[5] For a recent defense of flexible contextualism about deontic modals, see for instance Dowell (2013).

explanations of the dialogue between Ana and Bea. On one option, Ana and Bea each speak from their own perspective, each saying something true (from their perspective). Sundell 2011, and Plunkett and Sundell 2013a; b; 2014 assume the interpretation above: each speaker may speak the truth since each aims at her standard. The contents of their utterances could be paraphrased thus:

(3)
Ana: Tripe is delicious, given Ana's standard.
Bea: Tripe is not delicious, it is disgusting, given Bea's standard.

On the second option, the context of the dialogue between Ana and Bea is infelicitous, since it fails to pick a single shared standard of taste as part of their common ground. On this interpretation of what indexical contextualism predicts, Ana's and Bea's utterances are undetermined and lack a truth-value, because the context failed to pick up a single property to express by means of the predicate "is delicious":

(4)
Ana: Tripe is delicious, given – ? – standard.
Bea: Tripe is not delicious, it is disgusting, given – ? – standard.

Here, the fact that there is no one shared standard in context results in the absence of a standard on which to evaluate tripe as a culinary dish. On either interpretation of the results of there being no shared standard of taste, indexical contextualism appears to lack the resources to explain the impression of disagreement between Ana and Bea that we arguably share.[6]

Now, the disagreement-based argument against indexical contextualism is structurally similar to Dworkin's disagreement-based argument against legal positivism. As Dworkin says,

> If two lawyers are actually following different rules in using the word "law", using different factual criteria to decide when a proposition of law is true or false, then each must mean something different from the other when he says what the law is… So the two judges are not really disagreeing about anything when one denies and the other asserts this proposition. They are only talking past one another. Their arguments are pointless in the most trivial and irritating way, like an argument about banks when one person has in mind savings banks and the other riverbanks. Dworkin 1986, 43–44

Setting aside the fact that here Dworkin does not mean *proposition* to be interpreted in any standard technical sense (for instance, that of a function from possible worlds to truth-values), we can see that his argument echoes arguments from domains where context-sensitivity is presumed to play a role in the determination of the propositions communicated, and in the truth-evaluation of uttered sentences.

[6] This objection has been raised against contextualism by various authors. Among them, Kölbel (2004) argues on this basis for what has been called moderate (truth-)relativism. Other authors that have used disagreement-based arguments against contextualism include Egan (2010), Lasersohn (2005) and MacFarlane (2007; 2014).

3 Metalinguistic Negotiations & Conceptual Ethics

Plunkett and Sundell (2013a, b, 2014) appeal to pragmatic explanations of resilient impressions of disagreement. They purport to account for those disputes as metalinguistic negotiations, thus trying to defend legal positivism from Dworkin's disagreement-based argument. As they present it, legal antipositivism is the thesis according to which moral facts are part of what determines what the law is in a given jurisdiction at a given time. Legal positivism by contrast is, roughly, the thesis that the existence and content of the law in a given jurisdiction and at a given time depends solely on social facts (on some interpretations of what legal positivism is, at least).

3.1 Metapresentation and/or Conceptual Divergence

Metalinguistic disagreements or disputes, as Sundell (2011) had already argued, are a possible component of disputes expressed with uses of aesthetic evaluative predicates. As Plunkett and Sundell put it,

> Two features serve to characterize the class of linguistic disputes that we are interested in—the class of disputes we label 'metalinguistic negotiations'. First, metalinguistic negotiations employ a distinctive communicative mechanism — metalinguistic usage. And, second, they concern a distinctive normative question — how best to use a word relative to a context. (*Idem,* 2013a, 43–44)

The existence of metalinguistic uses is fairly uncontroversial. Here is an illustration of the phenomenon from Volkswagen's commercial campaigns:

(5)
(a) It's not a car. It's a Volkswagen.
(b) For 10 000 euro, you can buy a car or you can buy a Polo.[7]

In (5a) we are not literally denying that the Volkswagen is a car, and in (5b) we are not entailing that you can buy a Polo only if you don't buy a car. In both (5a) and (5b) it only seems to be conveyed that Volkswagens are not cars. But the reader clearly knows that they are, and that Volkswagen is not denying that it makes cars. In (5a) and (5b) the material in the scope of either the negation or the disjunction is not used literally, but is arguably used echoically, or at a metarepresentational level. What is conveyed pragmatically is that cars that are not Volkswagens are found wanting in some respect.

Other words may be used metalinguistically for a variety of purposes, e.g. to correct aspects of others' utterances, or to highlight different aspects of the pronunciation of the same word. For instance, (6) highlights the different ways that 'tomato' can be pronounced, (7) educates someone on socially appropriate expressions co-

[7]This was from a recent campaign for the VW Polo in parts of Europe that took a different metalinguistic take – arguably not as successful as the classic campaign in the previous example.

extensional with inappropriate expressions, and (8) objects to the use of a slur word by echoically using that very same word. (9) again echoes a slur word in order to ascribe a derogatory attitude to someone else who had previously used the same word.

(6) You like tom[eiDouz] and I like tom[a:touz].[8]

(7) Now, Cindy, dear, Grandma would like you to remember that you're a young lady: Phydeaux didn't shit the rug, he soiled/had an accident on the carpet.[9]

(8) I beg your pardon: Lee isn't an uppity nigger/broad/kike/wop— (s)he's a strong, vibrant black/woman/Jew/Italian![10]

(9) The *broad* would appreciate it if you stopped disrupting her lecture. (Says the speaker after overhearing someone in the audience referring to her as a 'broad'.)

These examples are slightly distinct from the ones that Plunkett and Sundell use to make the case for metalinguistic negotiations. But they are nonetheless relevant and common uses that illustrate the range of possible *foci* of metarepresentational disputes.

The second aspect of metalinguistic negotiations "concern(s) a distinctive normative question — how best to use a word relative to a context." Of the cases above, (7) and (8) presumably already fall under the range of disputes about how (if at all) to use a word. Notice that in these examples there is no dispute about which concept is expressed or about the extension of the words as used.[11] Nonetheless, the distinctive normative aspect of metalinguistic negotiations, according to Plunkett and Sundell, is conceptual ethics.

What is conceptual ethics? Whereas conceptual analysis seeks to illuminate and analyse our concepts, conceptual ethics seeks to help establish what our concepts should be, or what concepts we should use.[12] Two parenthetical remarks must be made before we proceed. We should not be misled about what the name 'conceptual ethics' connotes. Plunkett and Sundell (2013a) signal this warning:

> These normative questions about thought and talk — how should we use our words? which concepts should we use? how should we use them? — are questions in what we will call conceptual ethics. Two important points about our use of the term 'ethics' are in order here. First, we use the term 'ethics' in a broad sense, to designate questions about how to live and what to do. Second, we do not mean to indicate that conceptual ethics necessarily concerns practical norms as opposed to broadly theoretical ones. (Plunkett and Sundell 2013a, 3).

Examples (6)–(9) indicate that the source of a dispute may be much less erudite than is suggested by the designation 'conceptual ethics' (as (6) shows). We may however

[8] This example is from Carston (1996), after Cole Porter.

[9] This example is from Horn (2001), p. 371.

[10] This example is from Horn (2001), p. 372.

[11] The examples involving slurs are disputable. On most theories, the extension of the slurring word is the same as that of the non-slur word offered, and Horn seems to assume this. But some authors like Hom (2008) claim that slurs have null extensions. The cases make it clear that normative discussions of this kind need not amount to a substantive ethical disagreement.

[12] See Burgess and Plunkett (2013a) and (2013b) for further development of the notion. I'm ignoring for present purposes the objections to the very possibility of conceptual analysis. See e.g. Williamson (2007).

be worried about the conceptual part of the normative dimension of how words are to be used.

What 'conceptual ethics' denotes includes a very wide, and perhaps too wide, range of phenomena. Some of the phenomena encompassed by the description 'normative issues about how to best use words relative to a context' are barely related to any conceptual issues (however one may use 'concept' – again, see (6), and perhaps (7)). It is one thing to disagree with someone about how to pronounce 'tomato', another to disagree with someone about whether 'shit' is a socially acceptable thing to say by someone of one's social status in specific contexts. Neither of these hinge on any conceptual issue in any sense. And, in turn, (6) and (7) are far removed from Barker's 'context-sharpening uses' that Sundell (2011) used to develop the idea of context-, or metalinguistic, disagreement.

Here is Barker (2002) on context-sharpening uses:

> Normally, (1) will be used in order to add to the common ground new information concerning Feynman's height:
>
> (1) Feynman is tall.
>
> But (1) has another mode of use. Imagine that we are at a party. Perhaps Feynman stands before us a short distance away, drinking punch and thinking about dancing; in any case, the exact degree to which Feynman is tall is common knowledge. You ask me what counts as tall in my country. "Well," I say, "around here, ..." and I continue by uttering (1). This is not a descriptive use in the usual sense. I have not provided any new information about the world, or at least no new information about Feynman's height. In fact, assuming that tall means roughly 'having a maximal degree of height greater than a certain contextually supplied standard', I haven't even provided you with any new information about the truth conditions of the word tall. All I have done is given you guidance concerning what the prevailing relevant standard for tallness happens to be in our community; in particular, that standard must be no greater than Feynman's maximal degree of height. The context update effect of accepting (1) would be to eliminate from further consideration some candidates for the standard of tallness. My purpose in uttering (1) under such circumstances would be nothing more than to communicate something about how to use a certain word appropriately – it would be a metalinguistic use (Barker 2002, 1)

Cases of gradable adjectives like 'tall' presumably have a fixed meaning: 'having a maximal degree of height greater than a certain contextually supplied standard'. This example has some legitimacy as a candidate to disputes in conceptual ethics – although the concept tall is arguably not variable among speakers, it presumably admits of varying precisifications in application, which can be a focus of dispute. There may be disagreements about how to use a gradable adjective, or how to make it more precise, which are expressed by using the adjective itself (rather than explicitly mentioning the term).

Plunkett & Sundell want to further extend the possible range of application of 'conceptual ethics' from these kinds of cases to others where it is under dispute which concept is being used, and even which concept should be used. Now, I assume that we do not want to consider 'conceptual ethics' to describe all cases where people dispute which concept is expressed (or should be expressed) by a given word, on pain of rendering all cases of hermeneutics and exegesis cases of conceptual ethics. To illustrate the new kinds of cases, they mention an example from Ludlow (2008):

> In "Cheap Contextualism", Ludlow describes a heated debate he heard on sports radio. The debate concerned a list of the greatest athletes of the 20th century, and the question of whether that list should include the racehorse Secretariat. Simplifying a bit, we can imagine the following exchange as part of that debate:
>
> (5a) Secretariat is an athlete.
> (5b) No, Secretariat is not an athlete.
>
> Unlike the cases of metalinguistic sharpening involving gradable adjectives, there is little reason to think that the relevant linguistic expression here — 'athlete' — is semantically context-sensitive. But as in those cases, there is also little reason to think that the dispute in (5) concerns straightforward factual matters about the topic at hand. The speakers of (5a) and (5b) mutually know all of the facts about Secretariat's speed, strength, etc., and what races, awards, metals he won, etc[…] The question on the table, then, is this: suppose we want to preserve the intuition that there is a genuine disagreement that is expressed in the exchange that Ludlow overheard. How then should we understand what is going on? (Plunkett and Sundell 2013a, 16)

The fact that speakers employ 'athlete' in different ways (one applies it only to humans, the other speaker applies it to humans and to non-human animals) could be seen as an indication that they mean different things by 'athlete'. As they conclude,

> Thus, their metalinguistic dispute reflects a genuine disagreement about how to use the word 'athlete'. In particular, it is a debate in conceptual ethics about which among a range of competing concepts, and in particular, which of C_1 or C_2, is most appropriate to the conversation and should be expressed by the term 'athlete' (Plunkett and Sundell 2013a, 17)

I personally do not think that what is going on here is a "debate about which of the competing concepts is more appropriate and should be expressed" by a given word. I think that using 'athlete' to refer to a racehorse in this case is just a figure of speech, a metaphor or a metonymy, because of some properties of horses that are also shared by athletes. But it is not a debate about which concepts should be expressed by the term 'athlete' any more than Romeo expresses a distinct concept with 'sun' in "Juliet is the sun", or Mark Antony expresses a distinct concept by 'ears' in "lend me your ears". Hence, I am not convinced that the 'athlete' example successfully serves to include in the range of phenomena designated as 'metalinguistic negotiations' disputes about which concepts we should use, or have.

Some further examples of more complex, and polemical, normative disputes that Plunkett & Sundell claim to count as conceptual ethics are directly concerned with concepts and conceptual variability. For instance, Haslanger (2003, 2006 and 2012) distinguishes three types of conceptual projects one may be engaged with, arguing that a relevant project to effect social and political change in society consists not in finding out what we declare our concepts to be, or what can be revealed about which concepts we have, but in embarking on an ameliorative project of setting the best concept for "our political and social goals" at hand.[13]

Haslanger's concern is essentially normative in a political and moral sense – what best contributes for a just society. However, the linguistic evidence in support

[13] I have doubts that such conceptual manipulation is either necessary or sufficient to effect the social and political changes aimed for, but this is not the focus of the current paper.

of metalinguistic negotiation does not, I think, support the idea that what is going on across the board is a fundamentally *conceptual* activity. The linguistic data available, to a large extent, illustrates independently explainable linguistic phenomena. It does not suffice to establish that what is going on, in general, is a matter of deciding which concept we should be using, let alone a conceptual activity with an essential a moral or normative import.

3.2 *Hurdles and Metahurdles*

What matters for present purposes is to assess how metalinguistic negotiations allow a theorist to defuse disagreement-based arguments of the kind considered in the former section. Can the seeming disagreement between Ana and Bea in (1) above, and the seeming legal disagreements targeted, be accounted for as real metalinguistic disputes?

How would a metalinguistic negotiation explain the resilient sense of disagreement in the dialogue (1) between Ana and Bea?

(1)
Ana: Tripe is delicious.
Bea: Tripe is not delicious; it is disgusting.

Let us assume that we are committed to a context-sensitive account of the semantics of the sentences uttered. Although the utterances of Ana a Bea seem to express contradictory contents, the fact that they don't share a standard of taste would mean that in (1) there is no single standard of taste relative to which it may be true (or false) that tripe is delicious. The content of their respective utterances is undetermined (because it is *not* determined). But Ana and Bea seem to us to disagree, and presumably take themselves to disagree.

Their disagreement can be characterized as a metalinguistic dispute insofar as Ana and Bea are disputing further information that is being conveyed pragmatically through their utterances.

As Sundell argues, if words can be used to convey information at a metalinguistic level, then there may be disagreements about that information. The dispute between Ana and Bea could be seen as a dispute about which standard of taste they should come to adopt (assuming that there was no shared standard in that context prior to the dispute). This does not amount to a *shift* in the meaning or *concept* expressed. It is a dispute about different ways to determine the full semantic content of context-dependent expressions (if one embraces indexical contextualism for taste predicates).

A natural way to import the idea of metalinguistic uses to the case of legal disputes is to say that whenever (or at least some of the times when) the law is indeterminate at a given jurisdiction and legal officials nonetheless disagree, their disagreement may be located at a metalinguistic level, and possibly concern how their words should be made more precise or determinate. I agree that these disputes exist, and that, *prima facie*, they are a way to take the bite from disagreement-based arguments against legal positivism.

However, the proposal is not uncontroversial. The fact that there can be disputes at a metarepresentational level does not mean that all such apparent disputes in the absence of a shared standard (in the example given, of taste) will be automatically disputes at a metalinguistic level. Richard (2004) in fact considers and rejects this metalinguistic account of disagreement. He has three objections.

(i) The parties need not be part of the same conversation.
(ii) The proposal does not capture the phenomenology of speakers, who would not think of themselves to be sharpening indeterminate usage.
(iii) Finally, the proposal does not capture any disagreement in a fundamental sense (on which one party affirms, and the other denies, the semantic content of the utterances). There may be possible replies to Richard's objections.[14]

Yet, even if there are possible replies to Richard's objections in the general case, there is a non-negligible worry that, in the legal case, legal officials are hardly irreflexive speakers whose self-perception can be systematically in error. Moreover, legal officials will often not take themselves as sharpening indeterminate usage, but rather as appealing to normative considerations to ascertain what the law is.

Now, Plunkett & Sundell *do not* argue that legal actors do not in fact appeal to moral considerations in order to discover what the law is in their jurisdiction, *nor* do they argue that legal actors need not appeal to such moral considerations to decide what the law is. Instead, Plunkett & Sundell allow legal practitioners to appeal to moral considerations but not while engaged in legal reasoning *in the narrow sense*. Instead, legal actors *may* appeal to moral considerations while engaged in metalinguistic negotiation. If these moral, normative and evaluative considerations are made only in arguments over which concepts ought to be used in legal contexts, then Plunkett & Sundell may have succeeded in making the point that those normative or moral considerations are not a part of a narrow understanding of legal reasoning. For their argument to proceed, those disputes that are metalinguistic negotiations must not be an integral part of legal reasoning.

What is legal reasoning in a narrow sense?

> Begin with the idea that some reasoning in legal contexts indeed aims at discovering the content of the law in a given jurisdiction (at a given time). It thereby aims at uncovering what we can call the legal facts. (Plunkett and Sundell 2014, 57)

What happens in cases where the law is indeterminate? That is, what happens when the law at a jurisdiction and a given time does not determine (fully) how or whether a concept is to be applied? In this case,

> … [I]t must be that judges—who are often legally obligated to make a decision about a case—will be making new law as well as simply discovering existing law… in many cases where participants think that what they are doing is advancing moral claims in the service of legal reasoning, they are in fact advancing moral claims in the service of something else.

[14] We consider some possible replies in Marques and García-Carpintero (2014). See note 27, p. 15.

> This response grants that legal actors make genuinely moral claims in legal contexts, but holds that those claims are advanced not in the service of legal reasoning, but in the service of some other project, perhaps the project of deciding what the law should be. (Plunkett and Sundell 2014, 57)

How much have Plunkett and Sundell succeeded in establishing? First, and as mentioned earlier, the fact that it is possible that there are disputes at a metarepresentational level does not mean that all such apparent disputes in cases of (seeming) indetermination must be metalinguistic negotiations (as they explicitly concede). Second, the fact that a dispute takes place at a metarepresentational or metalinguistic level does not entail that it concerns an issue about which there is no fact of the matter. But the transition between the first and the second quotes above seems to make this implicit assumption. Without it, the argument is a non-sequitur: it is possible to advance moral claims while engaged in a metalinguistic dispute and engaged in legal reasoning in the narrow sense. We may worry that 'legal reasoning in the narrow sense' is a convenient term of art, devised to exclude by *fiat* metalinguistic disputes. Such exclusion seems to be ungrounded. In either case, it is possible to introduce a term, 'legal reasoning in the wide sense', which can deploy metalinguistic representation and dispute.

4 Determining: Grounding or Constituting?

My further and final aim in this paper is to make another point (in my view, at least, a more crucial one). Assume that we concede that the law is not entirely determinate (as presumably we should), and that sometimes legal officials engage in metalinguistic negotiations that can contribute to make the law more precise (or to determine what the law should be). Assume further that this is one of the various processes through which the law is *grounded* on social facts, one of the various mechanisms that ground what the law is in a jurisdiction. Although I am very sympathetic to the broader project of understanding the effects of metalinguistic disputes in cases of disagreements within normative and evaluative domains, I am concerned that the main metaphysical contention of the antipositivist can be described as a contention about evaluative and normative facts being *constitutive of*, and hence *essential to*, what the law is, and that this is not even touched upon by conceding that social facts ground legal facts.

Before I proceed, I'd like to sketch schematically the diachronic effect of metalinguistic negotiations on the law, if the assumptions we've made in the above paragraph are correct. Imagine that at t_0 two legal actors are engaged in a legal dispute about a legally relevant term, *N*. *N*'s meaning is, on assumption, undetermined at t_0, and the actors at t_0 are engaged in a metalinguistic negotiation about what *N* should mean – presumably even disputing which of various concepts C_1, C_2, C_3, … it should express. In other words, the legal actors are engaged in a project of "conceptual ethics", as described by Plunkett and Sundell. Imagine, moreover, as an inclusive legal positivist could, that projects of conceptual ethics may indeed involve appeals to moral and normative considerations.

Suppose now that some (meta-)agreement is arrived at, because "it must be that judges–who are often legally obligated to make a decision about a case—will be making new law as well as simply discovering existing law". If and where this happens, *N*'s meaning will be settled, partly by an appeal to moral considerations and reasoning. Since *N* is used to phrase the decision arrived at, a dispute at t_0 about what the law should be effectively settles what the law is at t_1. So, what the law is at t_1 is determined partly by moral considerations. The point generalizes. It will be true *for any arbitrarily chosen time* that the law at that time may have been determined partly by appealing to moral considerations and reasoning.

Now, how is 'determine' to be understood? Plunkett and Sundell assume that 'determine' is to be interpreted as "grounds", citing Greenberg (2006), Shapiro (2011) and Rosen (2010). Nonetheless, Rosen (2010) identifies some cases in which metaphysical grounding cannot do all the explanatory work, and Greenberg (2006) identifies two kinds of *determination* relations, only one of which can properly be called 'grounding'.

Rosen (2010) illustrates the kind of relation that grounding is with a variety of examples, one of which is indeed the case of the law:

> If it is against the law to keep a tiger as a pet in Princeton, there must be some constellation of non-legal facts in virtue of which this is so. One of the aims of jurisprudence is to identify in general terms the facts in virtue of which the legal facts are as they are. One distinctive claim of legal positivism is that the grounds of law are wholly social, consisting ultimately in the acts of officials and the social practices in which they are embedded (Hart 1961; Raz 1979). Antipositivists typically maintain that pre-institutional moral facts often play a role in making the law to be as it is. (Rosen 2010, 110)

Yet, an entirely unrelated sort of case – that of pain and c-fibres firing – reveals how saying that some facts ground other facts may still not be explanatorily sufficient:

> Consider a version of non-reductive materialism in the philosophy of mind according to which every fact about phenomenal consciousness is grounded in facts about the material organ of consciousness (in our case, the brain) even though no phenomenal property is reducible to any neurophysiological property or to any functional property that might be realized by a brain state. On this sort of view, I might be in pain in virtue of the fact that my c-fibres are firing, even though my being in pain would not consist in the firing or my c-fibres, nor in any disjunctive state of which c-fibre firing was a disjunct, nor in some existentially general state of which c-fibre firing was an instance. According to this non-reductive materialist, its phenomenal character exhausts the nature of pain; and yet, when my c-fibres are firing, I am always in pain in virtue of this fact in the same sense in which a thing is square in virtue of being an equilateral rectangle. (Rosen 2010, 132)

Now, the practices of a legal system are not like pains – mental states of a (presumably) irreducible phenomenal character. However, the antipositivist about the law need not deny that legal facts are grounded in social descriptive facts, just as the non-reductive materialist does not deny that pains are grounded on facts about c-fibres firing. What the antipositivist does is to offer an explanation of what the law consists in just as the non-reductive materialist offers an explanation of what pains consist in (by appeal to pain's phenomenal character).

What is the distinctive claim that the antipositivist makes? Here is Greenberg's summary of Dworkin's (1986) antipositivism:

> According to Dworkin, a legal proposition is true in a given legal system if it is entailed by the set of principles that best justify the practices of the legal system. Since the notion of justification on which Dworkin relies is a normative notion, a consequence of Dworkin's view is that the content of the law depends on value facts (Greenberg 2006, 158)

Greenberg endorses legal antipositivism, and hence defends the claim that value facts are among the determinants of the content of the law. Greenberg is also aware of ambiguous uses of 'determination' and 'dependence' in discussions over positivism and antipositivism. He distinguishes two kinds of relation: metaphysical, and "epistemic". Although he refers to the metaphysical relation as "constitutive" (Greenberg 2006, 158), I will henceforth consider it as the *grounding* relation, to guarantee the continuity with metaphysical debates elsewhere. I will reserve *constitutive* for the "epistemic" relation, also to preserve continuity with other philosophical debates.

Here is how Greenberg sets up the difficulty of identifying the different metaphysical status of the two sorts of "determination" relations. First, he makes an argument from modal disparity[15] between value facts and descriptive (social) facts:

> Descriptive facts about what people said and did (and thought) in the past are among the more basic facts that determine the content of the law. I claim that the content of the law depends not just on descriptive facts but on value facts as well. Given the plausible assumption that fundamental value facts are necessary rather than contingent, there is, however, a difficulty about expressing my claim in terms of counterfactual theses or theses about metaphysical determination. Even if the value facts are relevant to the content of the law, it is still true that the content of the law could not be different from what it is without the descriptive facts being different (since it is impossible for the value facts, being necessary, to be different from what they are). Necessary truths cannot be a nonredundant element of a supervenience base. Hence both positivists and antipositivists can agree that descriptive facts alone metaphysically determine the content of the law (Greenberg 2006, 159)

What an antipositivist is required to supply, in addition to the grounding of legal facts on descriptive facts, is a way of making it essential to the law that it should require legal officials to reason about value. Greenberg's suggestion appeals to what he calls a rational determination relation. Making an analogy with other evaluative domains, he points to aesthetic properties of paintings, such as elegance, and argues that a similar modal disparity exists here: a description of the underlying configuration of non-aesthetic properties that make a painting what it is does not tell us, as yet, why that painting with that configuration of non-aesthetic properties has the aesthetic property of elegance. But the aesthetic property, elegance, that a painting has depends, i.e., is grounded, on its non-aesthetic properties. In the case of the law, descriptive facts metaphysically ground legal facts, "and the obtaining of the

[15] The designation "Argument from Modal Disparity" is García-Carpintero's (MS). Arguments that appeal to the distinctiveness of two kinds of things on the basis of their modal disparity have been made, for instance, by Boghossian (1997) and Williamson (1996).

[descriptive facts] make intelligible or rationally explain" the legal facts obtaining. (Greenberg 2006, 163)

I do not intend to offer a full discussion of Greenberg's argument, but just to recast the rational determination relation as an essential constitutive norm of the law. This will allow for further theoretical continuity with other on-going philosophical debates. This paper's argument will then be complete if we understand legal reasoning in a broad sense, and metalinguistic negotiations are taken as an integral part of legal reasoning in the broad sense. On this understanding, neither metalinguistic negotiations nor conceptual ethics are an obstacle to a constitutive view of rational justification as essential to what the law is. Even if the existence and content of the law are grounded solely on social facts, it has not been ruled out that value facts are essential to what the law is.

An analogy with disputes over the nature of the speech-act of assertion illustrates the point. In a well-known argument, Williamson 1996 argues against conventional accounts of assertion, and in favour of a constitutively normative theory of the nature of assertion. He says:

> Constitutive rules are not conventions. If it is a convention that one must φ, then it is contingent that one must φ; conventions are arbitrary, and can be replaced by alternative conventions. In contrast, if it is a constitutive rule that one must φ, then it is necessary that one must φ... a rule will count as constitutive of an act only if it is essential to that act: necessarily, the rule governs every performance of the act. (Williamson 1996, 239)

As is well known, Williamson goes on to defend a constitutive knowledge rule of assertion, where

KR One must ((assert *p*) only if one knows *p*).

Much of the ensuing debate in the following years is concerned with whether KR is the constitutive rule of assertion, or whether for instance a justification rule or a truth rule is constitutive:

JR One must ((assert *p*) only if one is justified in believing *p*).
TR One must ((assert *p*) only if *p* is true).

Other authors reject constitutive normative accounts entirely, and favour exclusively descriptive accounts of the practice of assertion.[16] Each of the alternative possible norms unconditionally forbid doing something, if some given condition does not obtain. Each of the three norms individuates distinct forms of assertion: assertion$_K$, assertion$_J$, assertion$_T$. Each norm gives necessary wide-scope requirements. And as argued by García-Carpintero (2015, MS), any possible constitutive rule of assertion is necessary in one sense. But there is another sense in which a rule of assertion is conventional (which García-Carpintero identifies but does not endorse): which of the various possible norms a community of speakers in fact adopts depends on a convention.[17]

[16] For an overview, see Pagin (2015).

[17] See Lewis (1969) and (1975) on conventions and language.

The conventionality of the implementation of a rule is tantamount to the arbitrariness, and hence contingency, of the particular norm that is in fact followed in a community. Hence, arguing for the conventionality of a given norm of assertion is not, as yet, arguing against its essentially normative dimension. The speech-act of assertion, like the law according to Greenberg, may be grounded on actual social practices and conventions, while being essentially normative. An assertion is, on a constitutive normative account, the only speech act that is incorrectly performed when [insert the preferred condition here]. Signalling cases of assertions that fail to conform to the norm does not, moreover, refute normative accounts: if one asserts what one does not know (or what is untrue), one still asserts – i.e., performs an act subject to the norm, albeit asserting incorrectly. Analogously, the existence of unjust laws, for instance, would not refute the antipositivist position in itself.

I am not committing myself to an antipositivist stance. My goal is to draw attention to the fact that distinguishing between representational and metarepresentational levels of legal reasoning does not, in itself, address the core challenge of the antipositivist – that of the essential normative dimension of legal reasoning and practice. Presumably, there are many ways to understand the claim of the essential normativity of the Law, and legal positivist may be happy to agree on several of them. So, let me clarify the analogy between the constitutively normative character of assertion and a possible parallel with constitutively normative claim in the case of the Law, compatible with Greenberg's account summarized above.

In the case of assertion, the constitutively normative claim is that assertion is, essentially, the speech-act that is correctly performed only if one asserts what one knows (if KR is the right norm). This is compatible with a speaker asserting while not knowing: either speakers knowingly violate the norm (by lying, or otherwise deceiving), or speakers try to conform to the norm by asserting what they are justified to believe.

The antipositivist could offer a constitutive norm for the Law similar to the norm of assertion KR. For instance, LR could be (or one of) the constitutive rule of the Law (that characterizes what the Law essentially is):

> LR A legal practitioner ought to settle on the meaning of disputable terms in such a way that it is in accordance with the moral facts (i.e. settle on the morally best meaning; they ought to settle on a meaning M of 'N' only if M is the morally best meaning of 'N').

LR would be compatible with the possibility of legal officials often intentionally not following the norm, and with legal officials trying and failing to follow the norm.

The legal positivist would not accept LR as a constitutive norm of legal practice. If that is the case, then we have good reason to take a careful look at what is being proposed as involved in metalinguistic negotiations: do they, or don't they, require a robust understanding of conceptual ethics?

If metalinguistic negotiations are just a part of normal discourse about what reasons we have to do *x* or *y*, and (as I think is the case with examples like Secretariat, and other cases), it carries no deeper essentially moral considerations. In that case, it can contribute to defuse antipositivist arguments. However, if metalinguistic negotiations have a more robust ethical dimension (which I don't think they do, nor need to, in any case), then it can be argued that they turn out to be notational variants of concept interpretivism, in which case they can't defuse antipositivist arguments.

5 Conclusion

This paper's goal was to assess the prospects of using the pragmatic process of metalinguistic negotiations to defuse the disagreement-based argument against legal positivism. Although I agree with the importance of pragmatic processes of this sort in various domains, including many disagreements in normative and evaluative matters, I have raised doubts about the effectiveness of shifting the *locus* of the debate to a metarepresentational level in order to defend legal positivism. At the end of §3, I suggested that conceptual ethics – an essential component of metalinguistic negotiations as understood by Plunkett and Sundell, does not appear to replace Dworkin's interpretivism. Rather, conceptual ethics seems to be a notational variant of conceptual interpretation. This puts considerable pressure on the claim that metalinguistic negotiations can offer an alternative to interpretivism. In §4, I argued that not only does the shift of the level of the debate not defuse the antipositivist argument, but also it does not touch on the central antipositivist contention about a rational determination relation being an *essential* constitutive norm of the law. And if *conceptual ethics* is just another name for *conceptual interpretation*, the existence of metalinguistic negotiations is indeed compatible with the antipositivist thesis.

Acknowledgments I am very grateful to Hrafn Asgeirsson, Samuele Chilovi, Luís Duarte d'Almeida, Manuel García-Carpintero, Josep Joan Moreso, and Chiara Valentini, for comments and discussion of some of the material in this paper. This work was supported by a Marie Curie intra-European fellowship (622114, under FP7-PEOPLE), by the *Grup Consolidat en Filosofía del Dret* (2014 SGR 626, AGAUR de la Generalitat de Catalunya), project *About Ourselves* (FFI2013-47948-P), and by *Online Companion to Problems of Analytic Philosophy* (PTDC/FIL-FIL/121209/2010).

References

Barker, C. (2002). The dynamics of vagueness. *Linguistics and Philosophy, 25*(1), 1–36.

Boghossian, P. A. (1997). Analyticity. In B. Hale & C. Wright (Eds.), *A companion to the philosophy of language* (pp. 331–368). Oxford: Blackwell.

Burgess, A., & Plunkett, D. (2013a). Conceptual ethics I. *Philosophy Compass, 8*(12), 1091–1101.

Burgess, A., & Plunkett, D. (2013b). Conceptual ethics II. *Philosophy Compass, 8*(12), 1102–1110.

Carston, R. (1996). Metalinguistic negation and echoic use. *Journal of Pragmatics, 25*, 309–330.

Dowell, J. (2013). Flexible contextualism about deontic modals: A puzzle about information-sensitivity. *Inquiry, 56*(2–3), 149–178.

Dworkin, R. (1986). *Law's empire*. Cambridge, MA: Harvard University Press.

Dworkin, R. (2011). *Justice for hedgehogs*. Cambridge, MA: Belknap Press of Harvard University Press.
Egan, A. (2010). Disputing about taste. In T. Warfield & R. Feldman (Eds.), *Disagreement* (pp. 247–286). Oxford: Oxford University Press.
García-Carpintero, M. (2015). Are constitutively normative practices necessarily non-conventional? Manuscript
Gardner, J. (2001). Legal positivism: 5 1/2 myths. *The American Journal of Jurisprudence, 46*(1), 199–227.
Glanzberg, M. (2007). Context, content, and relativism. *Philosophical Studies, 136*(1), 1–29.
Greenberg, M. (2006). How facts make law. In S. Hershovitz (Ed.), *Exploring law's empire: The jurisprudence of Ronald Dworkin* (pp. 157–198). Oxford: Oxford University Press.
Hart, H. L. A. (2012). *The concept of law* (3rd ed.). Oxford: Oxford University Press.
Haslanger, S. (2003). Social construction: The "debunking" project. In F. Schmitt (Ed.), *Socializing metaphysics* (pp. 301–325). Oxford: Rowman and Littlefield.
Haslanger, S. (2006). What good are our intuitions? Philosophical analysis and social kinds. *Aristotelian Society Supplementary Volume, 80*(1), 89–118.
Haslanger, S. (2012). *Resisting reality: Social construction and social critique*. Oxford: Oxford University Press.
Hom, C. (2008). The semantics of racial epithets. *Journal of Philosophy, 105*(8), 416–440.
Horn, L. (2001). *A natural history of negation*. Chicago: CSLI, reissue edition.
Kölbel, M. (2004). Faultless disagreement. *Proceedings of the Aristotelian Society, 104*(1), 53–73.
Lasersohn, P. (2005). Context dependence, disagreement, and predicates of personal taste. *Linguistics and Philosophy, 28*(6), 643–686.
Lewis, D. (1969). *Convention*. Cambridge, MA: Harvard University Press.
Lewis, D. (1975). Languages and language. In K. Gunderson (Ed.), *Minnesota studies in the philosophy of science* (Vol. 7, pp. 3–35). Minneapolis: University of Minnesota Press.
Ludlow, P. (2008). Cheap contextualism. *Philosophical Issues, 18*(1), 104–129.
MacFarlane, J. (2007). Relativism and disagreement. *Philosophical Studies, 132*(1), 17–31.
MacFarlane, J. (2014). *Assessment sensitivity: Relative truth and its applications*. Oxford: Clarendon.
Marques, T., & García-Carpintero, M. (2014). Disagreement about taste: Commonality presuppositions and coordination. *Australasian Journal of Philosophy, 92*(4), 701–723.
Moreso, J. J. (2009). Legal positivism and legal disagreements. *Ratio Juris, 22*(1), 62–73.
Pagin, P. (2015). Assertion. In E. N. Zalta (Ed.), *The Stanford encyclopedia of philosophy*. Stanford: Metaphysics Research Lab – Stanford University, spring 2015 edition.
Plunkett, D., & Sundell, T. (2013a). Disagreement and the semantics of normative and evaluative terms. *Philosophers' Imprint, 13*(23), 1–37.
Plunkett, D., & Sundell, T. (2013b). Dworkin's interpretivism and the pragmatics of legal disputes. *Legal Theory, 19*(3), 242–281.
Plunkett, D., & Sundell, T. (2014). Antipositivist arguments from legal thought and talk: The metalinguistic response. In G. Hubbs & D. Lind (Eds.), *Pragmatism, law, and language* (pp. 56–75). Cambridge: Routledge.
Richard, M. (2004). Contextualism and relativism. *Philosophical Studies, 119*(1–2), 215–242.
Rosen, G. (2010). Metaphysical dependence: Grounding and reduction. In B. Hale & A. Hoffmann (Eds.), *Modality: Metaphysics, logic, and epistemology* (pp. 109–136). Oxford: OUP.
Shapiro, S. (2011). *Legality*. Cambridge, MA: Harvard University Press.
Sundell, T. (2011). Disagreements about taste. *Philosophical Studies, 155*(2), 267–288.
Williamson, T. (1996). Knowing and asserting. *Philosophical Review, 105*(4), 489–523.
Williamson, T. (2007). *The philosophy of philosophy*. Oxford: Blackwell Publishers.

The Dark Side of Imperatives

Alessio Sardo

Abstract In this essay, I provide a general overview on some of the main solutions offered to the never-ending problem of the semantic meaning of imperatives. After a short introduction (Sect. 1), I focus on legal theory, considering both the current trend (Sect. 2), and the prominent accounts developed in the period comprised between the late sixties and the early nineties (the "heydays" of linguistic analysis). I use a similar scheme also for the analysis of some of the main theories developed by philosophers of language (Sects. 3 and 4). Each section contains a few objections to the accounts under consideration: in this way, it will be possible for the reader to get a "balanced assessment" of the theoretical models at stake. The chapter ends with a couple of concluding remarks.

Keywords Imperatives • Directives • Illocutionary force • Norms • Meaning

1 Introduction

In this chapter I try to offer a general survey of some of the prominent accounts that have been defended up to now both in legal theory and in philosophy of language, with respect to the difficult relation between the semantic meaning of an imperative clause and its use. My main concern is with the possibility of offering a semantic analysis of imperative – or "directive", "normative", "prescriptive" – meaning (with rough simplification, I will use these words as synonyms). Apparently, imperatives challenge the idea of a classic truth-conditional approach to semantics, and raise doubts about some of the most entrenched philosophical presumptions: the idea that

I would like to thank Damiano Canale, Alexis Galán, Francesca Poggi and Giovanni Tuzet for their precious comments to a precedent version of this work. I would also like to thank Alejandro D. Calzetta, Mauro Barberis, Alessandro Ferrari, Riccardo Guastini, Andrej Kristan, Nicola Muffato, Stanley L. Paulson and Giovanni Battista Ratti for our long discussions on this topic.

A. Sardo (✉)
Dipartimento di studi giuridici "A. Sraffa", Università Bocconi, Milan, Italy
e-mail: alessio.sardo@unibocconi.it

F. Poggi, A. Capone (eds.), *Pragmatics and Law*, Perspectives in Pragmatics, Philosophy & Psychology 10, DOI 10.1007/978-3-319-44601-1_10

declaratives provide the paradigm for the logical form of every sentence, that every sentence expresses propositions, and that propositions are primitives in semantics.[1] There are many possible responses to this challenge, which are more or less conservative with respect to the idea that semantic meaning corresponds to truth-conditions. Perhaps, the most conservative solution is the one that purports the existence of a common element between imperatives and declaratives (or indicatives), which corresponds to a standard proposition (that is, a proposition defined in terms of truth-values). The least conservative solutions are those views that define the content of imperatives exclusively in terms of actions, intentionality and context-change (what we might call also a definition in terms of "agentive content", if we want to rely on a lexicon introduced by Belnap 1990).

The necessity to bring the analysis of imperatives beyond the boundaries of a (purely) pragmatic analysis of language arises from two facts (or so I argue). First, apparently, imperatives display a peculiar behavior with respect to semantic properties, relations and inferential patterns. Second, it seems plausible both to ground (at least part of) the idea of imperativeness on a semantic level, and to explain the use of an imperative sentence by referring to semantic structures: this is very helpful for predicting how imperatives are used in context and, maybe, offers a better explanation of how certain syntactical forms get associated with determinate uses. Moreover, I think that the decision of getting involved into such a project is also corroborated by the fact that this central issue – which is still the object of a lively, ongoing debate in philosophy of language – has been neglected by legal philosophers in the last three decades. This phenomenon is surprising, especially if we consider that analytic legal philosophers had been always aware of the importance of this issue, since the very beginning of their tradition. Let me give just three examples.

In the XIX Century, Jeremy Bentham (who can be considered as the "father" of analytic legal theory) built up a "rudimental" semantics of norms that takes into consideration not only the representational contents of these utterances, but also features which are somehow connected to *what we do in saying something, i.e.* the illocutionary force, (See Austin 1962) of the utterance. Sure enough, for Bentham, every law is 'an assemblage of signs declarative of a volition', which, on its turn, is composed by two elements: *an act description* (that includes the agent-specification) – which is the object of a wish, or volition – and *the wish or volition* itself. (Raz 1970, 55; Bentham 1945, 88, 178); according to Bentham, once we presuppose the idea of authority, the element of volition establishes a connection between the representational content of a law and the speech act which is normally performed by issuing a norm.

A similar idea (perhaps enriched with a few details) can be found in John Austin, a student of Bentham (not to be confused with the inventor of the speech acts theory, J.L. Austin). Paraphrasing Austin, we can say that a certain utterance *u* is a command *if, and only if*: a certain subject *S* expresses explicitly her desire that another

[1] Nuel Belnap 1990 defined this tendency as "declarative fallacy". On this point see also Mastop 2005 and 2008.

agent S_2 behave as indicated; *S* intends to inflict pain to S_2 if the command is not fulfilled; and, finally, *S* has the actual power to do it (Austin 1954, 14, 17, 19; Raz 1970, 11). In other words, for Austin, a genuine command necessarily requires a relation of subordination between the commander and the addressee (Austin 1954, 24).[2] A command is an "abstract entity" that "is not identical either with the act of issuing a command or with the words used in that act, just as a proposition is not identical either with its assertion or the words used in asserting it.[3]" (Raz 1970, 12) Joseph Raz, has formalized Austin's intuition as follows: a command can be represented by the formula 'x!*AC*', where x is a variable for persons, '!' is the imperative operator, and *A* and C are, respectively, variables for acts and circumstances (Raz 1970, 23).

A whole different approach can be found in the works of Hans Kelsen (another "giant" of the analytic school in legal theory), which contain some interesting ideas on the semantics of legal norms, and, perhaps less explicitly, about the relation between meaning and force. Under the Kelsenian view, norms are conceived as abstract entities, which are "the expression of the idea that something ought to occur, especially that an individual ought to behave in a certain way (Kelsen 1961, 36, 1966, 3, 4, 17)." They come into existence if there is a norm-creating event (that is, a voluntary human act performed with the intention to settle the norm), even if the standard of behavior prescribed is unknown to the normative authority (Kelsen 1961, 10; Kelsen 1966, 22–5). Norms are supported by a peculiar (and very strong) reason for compliance: the prospect of some evil (*i.e.* a sanction) in case of disobedience. For Kelsen every norm has the structure of a conditional sentence; the deontic element belongs to the semantic content of legal norms and, more precisely, to the conditional itself. To put it in a different way, we can say that the idea of "ought" pertains to the relation between the antecedent and the consequent of a normative conditional, which is *not* a relation of *causality* – for normative conditionals are not equivalent either to causal relations or material implications – but a special "connection" of (purely normative) *imputation*. In addition, Kelsen characterizes the typical purpose of a norm almost in terms of *direction of fit*: "The laws of nature formulated by natural science must conform to the facts, but the facts of human action and refrainment ought to conform to the legal norms described by the science of law (Kelsen 1966, 88)".

Now, I hope that a general and broad survey of the different solutions that have been proposed in order to explain the semantics of imperative meanings will help to renew this kind of debate in legal theory. Actually, I think that we need an "integrated approach", which combines the precision and sophistication of the philosopher of language with the expertise of the legal theorist.

Here, briefly, is an overview of this chapter's structure: in Sect. 2 I describe the current trend in legal philosophy (which consists in avoiding the problem); in Sect. 3 I offer a reconstruction of the best theories and arguments proposed by legal phi-

[2] It's definitely worth noting that this assumption is now commonplace in philosophy of language.

[3] To be more specific, for Austin, a command is a psychological entity that can be linguistically expressed.

losophers in the period of time comprised between 1968 and 1981, which represents the "golden age" of linguistic analysis in legal theory; in Sect. 3 I sketch out two classic accounts defended in speech acts theory; in Sect. 4 I offer a minimal overview of some of the current solutions proposed in philosophy of language; Sect. 5 contains my concluding remarks. At the end of each section (or sub-section), I offer also some general objections, in order to provide a balanced assessment, which might help to understand better the advantages and limitations of each theory.

2 Imperative Meaning in Legal Theory: The Current Trend

The current trend in legal theory is to assume, or to presuppose, that "normative" ("directive", "imperative") statements express *propositions*, and that (illocutionary) force has no semantic relevance whatsoever. The semantic content of an imperative sentence can be perfectly understood, or grasped, without taking into account its force (*i.e.* it is force-neutral). Propositions, on their turn, are generally conceived as truth-functional entities. A defender of this view could maintain, for instance, that an assertion such as "Alejandro is in Genova" expresses the proposition 'ALEJANDRO $_{\text{(in Genova)}}$', which is true *if and only if* Alejandro is really in Genova, and that the very same proposition is expressed by the command "Alejandro, go to Genova!", and also by the question "Is Alejandro in Genova?" I think that, among the others, Joseph Raz (1970, 1975), Andrei Marmor[4] and Vittorio Villa (2012) endorse this view.

Only a few authors (the members of the so-called School of Genova, for instance)[5] maintain that illocutionary force is (connected to) a semantic feature that is either attached to, or embedded in, the representational content of a certain normative statement (namely, a prescriptive sentence *S* in a certain context of utterance C), for we cannot fully understand semantic contents without taking into account elements that are connected with their illocutionary force and with the idea of obligation. It seems then much better to distinguish between two kinds of semantic types: meanings can be either (descriptive) propositions, or (directive/imperative) proposition-

[4] Marmor 2011, 84: "At least three levels of content can be conveyed by an occasion of speech: communicative content may consist of *semantic* content, *assertive* content, and some further content that is *implicated* by the speech in the particular context of its utterance. The semantic content consists of the content that is determined by the semantics and syntax of the expression uttered. Normally, this would consist of the literal meaning of the words used and the syntactical structure of the sentence. The assertive content is the content of the truth-evaluable proposition that is conveyed by the speaker in the particular context of the utterance. [...]" Marmor 2011, 85, assumes that laws have (also) an "assertive content" (when he considers that the Gricean notion of conversational implicature can be applied to legal communication). Implicatures are considered as rules that, applied to the relevant speech situation, along with a specific contextual knowledge, enable us to "understand content of expressions beyond their assertive content" (Ross 1968, 89).

[5] See at least Barberis 1988, 1990; Chiassoni 1987; Guastini 1982, 2008; Muffato 2007; Poggi 2012, 2013; Ratti 2012.

like entities/sentences (*i.e.* "norms"). Norms are not supposed to be truth-apt, for they lack any connection with the categories of reality and truth; they belong to a different sphere of thought: the dimension of *ought*. This "minority party" considers, for instance, that an utterance such as "Alejandro, go to Genova!" expresses a normative meaning, which cannot be understood as a description of a portion of reality. I think that this theoretical choice is mainly determined by two convictions, which are generally shared by all these authors: the consideration that *what is done by saying something* has a deep impact on the inferential treatment of *what is said*; a strong distrust toward the idea of giving priority to assertion (and truth) over prescription (and will) and, consequently, to use truth as a conceptual primitive in order to define what prescription is.

The authors that belong to the dominant view have something in common with the authors that belong to the "minority party": nobody provides any argument in order to justify his/her assumptions on the matter, let alone a theoretical model that helps us to capture the details of their respective positions, and to go beyond the level of vague assumptions. If we want to find arguments and theoretical models on imperative meaning we have to go back as far as to the period comprised between the late sixties and the early eighties. In these two decades, the most interesting proposals and arguments were developed by Alf Ross, Giovanni Tarello and by the co-authors Carlos E. Alchourrón & Eugenio Bulygin.

3 Imperative Meaning in Legal Theory: The Heydays of Linguistic Analysis Applied to Legal Discourse

3.1 Alf Ross: Directives and Norms

Alf Ross endorses the thesis that *meaning is entirely derivative from use*. Accordingly, *semantics* (*i.e.* the analysis of linguistic expressions *qua* bearers of meaning) and *syntax* (*i.e.* the logical and grammatical principles that determine the structure of the language) are to be considered as abstractions from *pragmatics* (*i.e.* the use of linguistic tools in human acts). Such abstractions are acceptable *if and only if* they reflect (empirical) facts of linguistic behavior.[6] Let us consider, for instance, the following slogan written at the beginning of his 1968 classic *Directives and Norms*: "It is only through speech that we know language" (Ross 1968, 4). Ross then splits all the *possible uses* of language – or, in J.L. Austin's (1962) lexicon, illocutionary

[6] Ross does not assume that a semiotic theory has to distinguish a full range of different contents – one for each function of our language. If he were to assume the controversial view that every function of language points to a corresponding kind of content, he would expose his theory to the strong objection of "hypostatized-functions", which, armed with Ockham's razor, goes directly to the jugular of an excessively crowded metaphysical constellation. Moreover, Ross analysis is deeply behavioristic. We cannot consider meaning as something that could be fixed by the power of mind alone.

acts – in two broad *categories*, corresponding to different *pragmatic functions*: "indicatives" and "directives".

Indicative meaning is associated with a heterogeneous range of *speech act types* that are all connected with the *ideas of truth and knowledge*. This large group includes acts of saying, assertions, conjectures, and so on. All these different acts have the common *typical* (perhaps *conventional*) *function* of presenting some topic as *real* (for instance: 'Smoking a cigarette by Alejandro – so it is'). By the same token, directive meaning is associated with a second range of heterogeneous *speech act types* that includes: suggestions, requests, orders, supplications, entreaties, invitations, recommendations, warnings, and similar.[7] All these acts have the common *typical function* of presenting a topic as something that *ought to be*: *i.e.*, they express an "action idea", conceived as a "pattern of behavior" ('Smoking a cigarette by Alejandro – so it ought to be'). A directive meaning can realize speech acts such as orders, supplications, requests, etc. in virtue of being a directive; conversely, this kind of meaning is incompatible with all those speech act types that are associated with indicative meaning (Ross 1968, 34).

The content of an indicative speech is a *proposition*, symbolized as 'i(T)', where 'i' stands for the idea of reality ('so it is'); the content of a directive speech, instead, is a *directive*, symbolized as 'd(T)', where 'd' stands for the idea of obligation ('so it ought to be'). Propositions are conceived as representations of a state of affairs and, therefore, they can be treated as truth-bearer sentences. The opposite holds for directives. Directives *qua* meaning-contents are *type-entities*. The *idea of a topic* ('T') is the element that directives and indicatives have in common. Accordingly, the main difference between directives and indicatives is located in the operators, 'i' (the thought of reality), and 'd' (the thought that something ought to be). Under this respect, Ross remains still very close to the Neo-Kantian approach that characterized his early writings: *Sein* and *Sollen* are conceived as sharply separated categories of thought.

Following these premises, legal systems are considered as *sets of heteronomous quasi-commands*, whose authority derives from the legal order, conceived as an impersonal system of norms.[8] The *legal order* is an institutional system. This means that a legal order is not composed only by rules that establish a certain pattern of behavior, but also by many constitutive rules, *i.e.* norms that provide necessary conditions for the existence of legal institutions ("agencies empowered to create or enforce the law"), such as legislative assemblies and courts of justice (Ross 1968, 51). These institutions appear to the individual mind as "public authorities", being part of "the machinery of the law". Every constitutive rule of a certain legal system

[7] On the problem of heterogeneity, see Kaufmann 2012 and Portner 2007.

[8] Ross 1968, 50: These entities (or abstractions) are similar to propositions under the following respects: (i) they are language-dependent; (ii) they shall not be confused with the sentence that expresses them; therefore, (iii) their existence depends on two linguistic facts: formulation and interpretation; (iv) in order to be correctly produced they have to respect syntactic rules; (v) both can be mentioned without making use of them; (vi) both of them can be used in therapeutic speech exercise; (vii) both of them can be considered without being used.

is established by a social convention, which comes into existence through contextualized linguistic interactions (Ross 1968, 54 ff.). Nevertheless, the ultimate ground for a social convention– and its ultimate source of effectiveness – is settled by a subjective moral judgment. Legal norms are thus considered not as illocutionary acts, but as *perlocutionary effects* produced by directive speech acts, issued by normative authorities.

Ross uses (at least) four arguments in support of his main claim – the idea that we have two different kinds of semantic content: directives and indicatives – trying to show that *pragmatic use* has a strong impact on our systems of representation, and on their logic. The first argument focuses on the acceptance of a meaning content, the second relies on the distinction between internal and external negation of a directive, the third is the well-known *Ross's Paradox*, and the fourth is the opposition internal/external consequence:

1. *The Argument from Acceptance.* According to Ross's view, both propositions, and directives have an *adjudicative function*: they are subject to "acceptance" and "rejection", which are attitude-deciding acts. However, the acceptance/rejection of a proposition is radically different from the acceptance/rejection of a directive: the former is a declarative and cognitive attitude-deciding act ('true' and 'false' are assumed to be intrinsic properties of the content); the latter is an act of volition, which has a non-cognitive nature. For this reason, it makes no sense to consider true and false as predicates of a directive. This claim is supported by a quick analysis of the basic features of human action. In Ross's opinion, a directive is a practical content characterized by the dispositional property of being *action-determining*. However, a directive-content is incapable of determining human action on its own, because it necessarily requires the accomplishment of an act of acceptance by the addressee; however, once it is accepted, a directive-content can provide what we might call – departing from Ross's lexicon – a "sufficient reason" for action. Cognitive (or descriptive) contents are completely different: even if we accept a proposition (or a set of propositions), this piece of information about the world is not even potentially capable of being action-determining by itself.[9]

Under normal circumstances, a directive issued by the legislator will be perceived as a valid claim, mainly because it generally comes with the threat of some sort of sanction (Ross 1968, 40). However, feelings of obligation can derive also from different factors: intrinsic respect for the authority of the commander, consistency with personal views on the morals, and so on. This is simply because human minds have different motivational processes: legalistic, conformist, opportunistic, etc. These processes can be either categorical (derived from a pure feeling of obligation), or teleological (derived from a means-ends, interest-based reasoning).

[9] It's worth noting that this is a controversial assumption: on the one hand, it seems plausible to maintain that also indicative contents play an action-determining role, just because they could change the context of practical reasons; on the other, we have to concede the possibility that a normative content might offer only a *pro tanto* reasons for action.

If we analyze this first argument, we can easily realize that the non-cognitivist alternative proposed by Ross is primarily a speech act semantic account of directive discourse. The author suggests that the primary meaning of a directive consists in the speech act performed through the expression of a particular attitude. In other words, he holds that to express a mental state *just is* to perform a speech act of some sort. What it is to think that 'T' does not directly bear upon the question of what 'T' means. The route for grasping what 'T' means must include the previous step of explaining the conditions under which thinking that 'T' *also counts as* doing *S*, where '*S*' is a speech act of some sort.

2. *The Opposition External/Internal Negation.* Alf Ross tries to show that, while in propositional logic internal and external negations are equivalent, the opposite holds in deontic logic. As far as indicative speech is concerned, external negation (symbolized as follows:'– i(T)') expresses the refusal to accept that things stand in the way described by 'i(T)' – negation is thus embedded in a second order proposition. On the opposite, internal negation (symbolized as follows: 'i(-T)') is embedded in a first-order proposition, which states that things in the world are not in a certain way (Ross 1968, 144 ff.). These two propositions are clearly equivalent: external negation '–i(T)' is the rejection of the proposition 'i(T)'; once we have assumed the principle of non-contradiction ("one must not at the same time accept and reject the same proposition"), if a proposition is not accepted, its complement – in this case 'i(T)' – shall be accepted. Therefore, '–i(T) ≡ i(-T)'.

Now, following Ross, directive speech is a whole different story: "to say that *A* is under no obligation to stay at home is not the same as to say that he is under the obligation not to stay at home, that is, to go out" (Ross 1968, 150 f.). If one accepts a certain directive, she must not, at the same tame, reject the same directive. Moreover, if somebody accepts the directive under evaluation, she must also accept its complement. However, this does not hold for rejections: the "rejection of a directive is compatible with rejection as well as acceptance of its complement" (Ross 1968, 152). For instance, from the external negation of the directive "Stay at home!" it doesn't follow the obligation to go out.[10]

3. *The Opposition External/Internal Disjunction and Ross's Paradox.* According to Ross, 'O(*p*) v O(*q*)' is totally different from O(*p* v *q*), even if we are not usually conscious of this distinction in everyday discourse. The former disjunction means that there is an obligation to choose between *p* and *q*, while the latter means either that we have an obligation to perform *p*, without choice, or to perform *q*, again with no choice (Ross 1968, 158 ff.). Moreover, whereas in indicative logic '$p \rightarrow p \vee q$' is valid, in deontic logic O*p* does not imply O(*p* v *q*). Here goes the famous example: the obligation to post a letter does not imply an obligation to whether post it or burn it.

[10] On the negation of conditional norms see Ratti 2013, 81 ff.

4. *The Opposition External/Internal Consequence.* Internal implication is expressed by the formula $O(p \rightarrow q)$, whereas external implication is expressed by the formula $O(p) \rightarrow O(q)$. For the Danish author they are not equivalent, and they shall not be confused (Ross 1968, 166 ff.). The latter states that a certain obligation is tied up with a second obligation (for instance, "if Alejandro is under the obligation of driving safely, he is also under the obligation of respecting the speed limits"); rather, the former states that if someone has made something, then he is also obliged to something else, without implying the obligation of the first action (for instance, "if Alejandro is driving a motorbike, he is under the obligation of wearing a safety-helmet").

Ross's account is not free from pathologies and, most important, the arguments he offered are not sufficient to demonstrate that directive meaning cannot be reduced to indicative meaning: argument (1) works only if we presuppose non-cognitivism and, as we shall see, arguments (2) to (4) do not impede the reduction of imperative semantic contents to modalized propositions. Let's proceed step by step.

First, the semantic role of what Ross calls "the idea of a topic" is far from being clear. If we read the first chapters of *Directives and Norms*, we have the impression that the idea of a topic (T) in the formulas 'i(T)' and 'd(T)' should be considered as a gerundive or a verbal name, whereas the semantic abstraction from the pragmatic use (either "d" or "i") should be understood as a peculiar predicate, which is attached to the verbal name, or gerundive, in order to obtain a well-formed sentence. Accordingly, we shall conclude that, without force-predicate, no inference is possible, for gerundives and verbal names are singular terms, and no inference is possible if we have only a singular term (in effect, from 'the action of smoking' we cannot infer anything at all). However, in some passages taken from the last chapter of the book, Ross's scheme seems to be completely overturned: the cognitive part of a directive clearly becomes a proposition, which – according to the definition proposed by Ross himself – is considered as the object of truth-functional inferences. Moreover – and this is truly surprising – this proposition is not neutral, because it is defined in terms of truth-conditions (as something that 'ought to be truth'). I honestly don't understand why, but even the symbolization changes: for instance, 'd(T)' becomes 'Op' (Ross 1968, 155). I do not see any simplification in this move. What is more, all of this is completely inconsistent, for it goes directly against Ross's fundamental assumptions, and especially against the idea that directives have no connections with reality (Ross 1968, 35). To crown it all, Ross does not even explain whether 'i' and 'd' are connected to '(T)' in the same way, or whether the connection is different; the concept of "content" itself is obscure, and Ross doesn't offer any argument against non-assertive propositions: for instance, if we define a proposition in terms of "compliance" or "satisfaction" conditions, Ross's battle against propositional contents seems to become empty.

Second, Ross should have adduced further arguments in favor of the view that there are two semantic contents at hand (instead of one propositional content, qualified by non-truth-conditionally conveyed elements). Actually, it does not immediately follow that the prescriptive counterpart must be a pragmatically enriched proposition. For instance, it could very well be a descriptive (non-normative) proposition about the creation of a norm, or the issuing of a command (Jørgensen 1937/1938, 293). This thesis can be the result of a cognitivist "paratactic approach" (*infra*).

Third, the Frege-Geach objections to non-cognitivist accounts of directive speech – objections that are connected with the complicated relations between predication and assertion – should also have been rejected (Geach 1960, 1965): once we decide to include force in the semantic content in the way proposed by Ross (i.e. assuming that predication is not force-neutral) we have to explain how, on the one hand, it is possible to have indicative sentences without assertive force and, on the other, it is also possible to have directive sentences without directive force, like in the case of conditionals.

Moreover, there is still a heap of problems pertaining to how we are to explain the inconsistency of speech-acts (or attitudes) that are not reducible to each other: in other words, we have to show how certain attitudes, other than beliefs, are "inconsistencies transmitting". And it is quite easy to see that a non-cognitivist approach gets in serious troubles here: it cannot rely on a traditional explanation of inconsistency, for there is nothing contradictory in expressing two different mental states, or speech acts (Schroeder 2008, 43 ff. has recently developed a possible line of defence).

Now, let's finally come to the main objection. The inferential patterns that Ross considers as peculiar features of imperatives, in arguments from (2) to (4), characterize also modal propositions in indicative speech (Kaufmann 2012, 39, 60 ff.). Therefore, the main arguments adduced by Ross in order to demonstrate the semantic distinctiveness of directive meaning doesn't block its reduction to some sort of modalized or, alternatively, quantified proposition. In this chapter I focus only on argument (3), but similar considerations hold for arguments (2) and (4). First of all, it's worth considering that phenomena that are very close to Ross's Paradox and that are related to implication arise in the domain of indicative modals. For instance, an indicative modal such as "It is possible that Marta is in Paris" does not seem to imply "It is possible that Marta is either in Paris or in Turin", for the disjunction is stronger than the first statement: $\Diamond$ $(\phi \vee \varphi)$ is stronger that $\Diamond$ (ϕ) because, while $\Diamond$ (ϕ) cancels only $- \phi$, $\Diamond$ $(\phi \vee \varphi)$ cancels both $-\phi$ and $-\varphi$ (Yablo 2009). Second, it is possible to avoid Ross's Paradox by using an approach that is more conservative with respect to truth-functional semantics, which considers the paradox in analogy with phenomena related with quantifiers such as "any" or "some" (see Aloni and Ciardelli 2013). Accordingly, it is possible to maintain that an atomic imperative such as "Post this letter!" specifies that all the conducts in which the letter is posted are possible, whereas a disjunctive imperative such as "Post the letter or burn it!" is a choice offering imperative and, therefore, it is analogous to "Take any letter!" where the free-choice seems to be licensed by the presence of the existential quantifier "any". Now, both disjunction and existential quantifiers can be interpreted as tools that introduce sets of propositional alternatives. The disjunctive imperative cannot be implied by the atomic imperative, and this can be demonstrated as follows. The meaning of an imperative such as "Call Alf!" formalized as "!Ca" (where "C" stands for the action of calling and "a" stands for Alf) allows only one possibility $|Ca|$. Instead, an imperative such as "Call Alf or Bea" allows two possibilities: $|Ca \wedge - Cb|$ and $|Cb \wedge -Ca|$; therefore, in order to be satisfied, the following must be satisfied: [1] $s \subseteq |Ca \vee Cb|$ and [2] $s \cap |Ca \wedge - Cb| \neq 0$ & $|Cb \wedge -Ca| \neq 0$. This solution avoids Ross's Paradox: the set of options that satisfy !Ca cannot satisfy also !(Ca ∨ Cb), because the set should contain also a conduct which satisfies Cb ∧ -Ca, and, therefore, does not satisfy !Ca (Aloni and Ciardelli 2013).

3.2 Giovanni Tarello and His "Intrusive" Neustic

In 1974, one of the most famous Italian legal philosophers, Giovanni Tarello, tried to demonstrate that the "semantic reference" (*riferimento semantico*) of a certain sentence *S* changes according to its "pragmatic function". The latter can be prescriptive (*i.e.* action-guiding), or descriptive (*i.e.* it tells something about the real world). Following Tarello, the content of a certain sentence *S*, uttered with a descriptive function, should be considered as an "assertion" (*asserzione*), whereas the content of a certain sentence *S'* uttered with a prescriptive function should be considered as a "prescriptive proposition" (*proposizione prescrittiva*), or "precept" (*precetto*). A prescriptive proposition, in turn, can be defined as a peculiar kind of proposition which puts the addressee into the following set of possibilities: (i) fulfill the prescribed action; (ii) act in a different way; (iii) be undecided on what to do (Tarello 1974, 329). The class of prescriptive propositions includes: propositions that impose duties and obligations; propositions that "contain" (*contengono*) a request, an invitation, or a plea to do or not to do something; propositions that predicate a value which is different from true and false; propositions that qualify an action which is relative to obligations, duties, values, invitations, and similar (Tarello 1974, 330).

According to Tarello, the distinction between assertions and precepts is not determined by "morphological" (namely, syntactic) characteristics that belong to the grammatical surface, for it is rather determined by the "function" that the sentence plays in a certain communicative context (Tarello 1974, 331). Following R. M. Hare (1967), Tarello assumes that the deep logical structure which can be ascribed to a certain sentence *S*, in a context C, is characterized by two elements: a set of symbols that denote an action (corresponding to Hare's "phrastic"), which is the referential part of the content expressed; a symbol that explains its function, assertive or preceptive (corresponding to Hare's "neustic"[11]).

However, in opposition to Hare, Tarello claims that the neustic has a strong impact on the interpretation of the referential part of the statement. The main argu-

[11] On this point, see Muffato 2007.

ment that Tarello puts forward to prove his claim can be summed up as follows: let's take into account a personal, individual and concrete order such as (1) "Close the window!". It goes without saying that this prescription is indeterminate, for interpretive doubts can come up. Let us put (1) in a conversational context where the addressee stands in a room with four windows, two portholes and a door. Tarello considers that, in such a context, there are at least five possible interpretations of the statement: (2) "Close *a* window!", (3) "Close *all* the windows!", (4) "Close *all* the windows *and all the portholes*!", (5) "Close *all* the windows, *all* the portholes, *and the door*!", (6) "Close *only* the window and the porthole *that cause a draft of air*!" In this case, the addressee needs a supplement of information in order to solve the interpretive doubt, and to avoid a mechanical or "wrong" application of the order, which might not be (correctly) fulfilled, especially when the speaker, without precision, uses (1) to mean (5) (Tarello 1974, 337–8).

According to Tarello, the interpretation of descriptive statements is guided by different principles. Let's take, for instance, a descriptive statement such as (1') "You have closed the window", which, apparently, bears the same representational content of (1). Following Tarello, it is hard to see how this statement could be interpreted as (6') "You have closed the window and the porthole that cause a draft of air" – which is similar to (6), namely the best interpretation of (1) – for it would normally be interpreted as (2') "You have closed the window." – which is analogous to (2), a poor interpretation of (1) (Tarello 1974, 339).

Now, Tarello claims that we should consider his argument as a valid and sound demonstration that "What changes, when the function of the statement changes, is the semantic value of the terms used to express the phrastic part of the proposition (Tarello 1974, 340)". In my opinion Tarello is completely wrong: his argument is neither sound, nor valid. In effect, it is easy enough to imagine a context in which the very same interpretive problems that affect (1) arise with respect to an assertion such as (7) "Alejandro has closed the window". If I am sitting in a different room – and I don't know anything about any possible draft of air, I would have to face the very same interpretive doubts that come up when I interpret a command such as (1) "Close the window!", and an option such as (7') "Alejandro has closed the door and the porthole that cause a draft of air" – which is analogous to (6') – cannot be ruled out, just because these doubts arise from a problem of context dependency, and not from a difference of illocutionary "functions".

In addition, it's worth stressing that Tarello's account is affected by several conceptual flaws and terminological confusions: for instance, it does not make any sense to say that a proposition "contains" a request, a plea, etc. It would be wrong as well to say that a proposition "expresses" a request, a plea, and so on, for propositions are abstract entities and, therefore, they cannot express or contain a speech act. It seems also counter-intuitive to include in the class of prescriptions every proposition that expresses a value that is different from true/false: this move extends the class of prescriptions beyond any reasonable limits. Moreover, if we are willing to accept that propositions are to be defined in terms of conditions of satisfaction, instead of truth-conditions, the class of prescriptions will include every proposition whatsoever.

3.3 *Alchourrón and Bulygin:* The Expressive Conception of Norms

A third, remarkable, account of imperative meaning was offered by Alchourrón and Bulygin in a famous article written in 1981 under the title "The Expressive Conception of Norms" (EC). The core of the EC is the conservative thesis that the semantic meaning of an imperative is an ordinary proposition (namely, a proposition defined in terms of truth-conditions, with no modal elements, nor quantifiers). The Authors maintain that law can be understood (also) as a peculiar social phenomenon, where certain normative authorities issue sequences of legal norms *qua* speech acts. Legal norms *qua* speech acts are nothing else than prescriptions (in the sense introduced by Von Wright 1963, 7 ff.), that is, sentences uttered by a certain authority with a normative pragmatic function, and directed to some agent. In other words, prescriptions are the expression of a wish, or a will, directed to the addresse(s) of a norm.

Alchourrón and Bulygin use the signs '⊢' (Assertion), '!' (Command) and '¡' (Rejection) to represent the types of linguistic act performed by a certain speaker *S*. In the EC, an expression such '*!p*' is *not* to be intended as a sentence which *describes* a speech act (like "*A* commands that *p*"), for expressions of this kind "do not express any proposition at all, although they are constructed by the help of the proposition *p*; so they have no truth-value and cannot be negated nor combined by propositional operators" (Alchourrón and Bulygin 1981, 97). Surprisingly, in the very same text, the Authors maintain also – in overt contradiction – that "the content of a norm is the proposition expressed by '*p*'" (Alchourrón and Bulygin 1981, 100). However it might be, the central idea of the EC is that we have two types of prescriptive speech acts: *commands*, which are those speech acts that introduce, by addiction, propositions such as *p, q, r, – p, – q, – r, ...* into a certain set of commands A, which is relative to a certain normative authority Rex; and *rejections*, which are defined as speech acts that remove, by subtraction, propositions such as *p, q, r, – p, – q, – r, ...* from the set of commands A, which is relative to a certain normative authority Rex. As stressed by the Authors, rejection shall not be confused with negation, for rejecting *p* is equivalent to subtracting *p* from the system, whereas negating *p* (which, according to Alchourrón and Bulygin, is an act of assertion) is equivalent to introducing – *p* in the system.

If we consider legal systems, "the act of commanding can be described as the act of *promulgating* a norm"(Alchourrón and Bulygin 1981, 100), which brings instantaneously the norm into a factual existence. Rex commands propositions or sets of propositions. Every time Rex issues a new proposition, we have a change in the commanded set (from A_0 to A_1); a series of different commands issued in the course of a certain time-lapse t_0–t_1 generates a sequence of sets (A_1, A_2, $A_{3, ...}A_n$). Given a certain set of proposition, it is possible to derive implicit commands by making explicit the logical consequences of a certain proposition *p*: for instance, if the professor commands that all her students shall leave the classroom now, she commands (implicitly) that Alejandro – one of her students – shall leave the classroom now.

The EC allows the possibility of contradictions: for instance, Rex can promulgate *p* at a certain time t_0 and, later on, promulgate – *p* at t_1. In this case, the conflict between two acts such as '!*p*, ! – *p*' is entirely determined by the contradiction between the propositions '*p* & – *p*'. Normative conflicts arise also when Rex commands *p* (!*p*) and then rejects *p* (¡*p*): in this case, according to the Authors, we have a *conflict of ambivalence* (a notion introduced by Carnap 1942, 187) between "propositional attitudes": "the same proposition is (directly or indirectly) commanded and rejected by the same authority, or by different authorities, in the same system [...] The two acts are incompatible because they tend to achieve incompatible results" (Alchourrón and Bulygin 1981, 100, 112). Both kinds of normative conflicts can be solved with the introduction of *preference rules* in the system, stipulating that one of the two acts prevails over the other.

According to Alchourrón and Bulygin, endorsing the EC should be considered by no means as a stumbling block to genuine propositions about the existence of a norm. These propositions are conceived as meta-descriptions, which can be equated to purely cognitive contents. To put it in the lexicon used by Alchourrón and Bulygin these meta-descriptions are called "normative propositions". Normative propositions are often formulated using deontic words; nonetheless (*pace* Kelsen) their deep logical structure should be a proposition of the form 'The norm *N* belongs to the normative system NS_X'. For this very reason, we cannot consider the presence of a deontic syntactical element on the "surface" of a certain deontic formulation as a sufficient condition for the conclusion that the content expressed by the formulation at stake is a norm. On the other hand, we should realize that it's clearely possible to express norms even without relying on deontic words. For instance, I can command something using a future indicative tense ("You will not smoke!" said by me to Alejandro, now, in this room should be interpreted as a norm, if we presuppose my authority). In every legal order, there are three different kinds of commands: (i) prohibitions or rejections ("It is prohibited to smoke"); (ii) obligations ("Smoking is obligatory); (iii) permissions ("Smoking is permitted"). To be sure, most of the times, legislators issue conditional norms ("If there is a medical prescription, then smoking marijuana is permitted").

Finally, in the EC, the imperative element is not encoded in the logical form, for it is entirely confined in a pragmatic derivation-process. There are basically three reasons for playing this move. First, it provides a very simple and elegant solution: apparently, it satisfies Ockham's razor – there is only one kind of content, not two or even more, and avoids any confusion between meaning and force. Second, it can be used in order to justify a division of labor between semantics, conceived as the (logical) analysis of truth-functional meanings, and pragmatics, conceived as the study of illocutionary forces. The consequence of this division is a tremendous simplification of the tasks assigned to legal philosophers: these fellows are not obliged to tackle with pragmatics in order to talk about normative (legal) systems. Third, starting from these premises, it is really easy to defend the idea that there is a logic for the normative discourse, which applies only to the contents, without telling us anything at all about the relations between genuine normative components (*i.e.* illocutionary forces): it has to be conceded that it makes no sense to talk about logical relations between norms *qua* speech acts, however, after this quick clarification, it is possible to maintain that propositional logic applies straightforwardly to propositional contents, without any serious concern about the nature of implication, the role of deontic features, and so on. Actually, it is well known that logical connectives have been traditionally defined by means of truth tables.

Now, the EC is a very traditional account: the imperative operator is simply prefixed to a sentence of first-order logic.[12] However, in my view, it seems really a short step to using this quick move in order to deal with the semantic complexity of imperative sentences. First of all, we cannot assume, without further arguments, that the legislator commands, prescribes or uses propositions: the legislator prescribes to realize (or to refrain from) a certain action – or a certain state of affair – which is not necessarily a proposition. Second, if we define propositions in terms of truth-values (and not only in terms of truth-conditions), it is hard to see how could we maintain, at the same time, that norms contain propositions, and that they are not truth-functional abstractions: this would strike any reasonable man as a contradiction. Third, we might ask to Alchourrón and Bulygin how can we attach the so-called "pragmatic indicator" to the truth-functional component, for this is far from being clear. Fourth, I think that it is incorrect to consider "rejection" as a speech act: rejections can occur in different speech acts (directives, assertions, declarations, etc.). Perhaps it would be better to consider *repeal* (a notion that is introduced also in Alchourrón and Bulygin 1981) as a speech act, and rejection as the consequence of an act of repeal. Fifth, there are many arguments in favor of a semantic analysis of the imperative mood or force (Kaufmann 2012, 18 ff.): (i) imperatives are resistant with respect to embedding (e.g. quantifiers take wide scope on imperatives); (ii) imperative forms can cover a variety of other pragmatic functions (suggestion, command, well-wish, etc.); (iii) sometimes, a sentence token can be identified as an imperative "without being associated with any particular speech act type" (Kaufmann 2012, 20); (iv) if it is all a matter of pragmatic derivations, it becomes less clear how the assignment of a pragmatic meaning becomes associated with certain syntactic objects that belong to the form-type.

However, the main problem of this account of normative speech is that it has no resources to deal with a "puzzle" proposed by Ota Weinberger in the early Eighties (Weinberger 1985a, b), and which is related with the semantic problem of normative contradictions. I will use the reformulation that I have developed together with Alejandro Calzetta (Calzetta and Sardo 2014) in order to present this puzzle.[13]

If all speech acts are just pragmatic operations on propositions, lacking any semantic relevance whatsoever, and if propositions have logical priority on their uses, we should want to say that from a *contradiction* between two propositions *p* and – *p* a whole series of *incompatibilities for contraries* between speech acts will obtain. From *p* and –*p* we obtain the following: (a) Assertions ' ⊢*p*'/' ⊢ –*p*'; (b) Commands: '!*p*'/'! – *p*'; (c) Rejections: '¡*p*'/'¡ – *p*'; (d) Positive Permissions:

[12] See Kristan 2015 for a defense of the expressive conception.

[13] Calzetta and Sardo 2014; in our demonstration we assume the validity of conglomeration's principle.

'Per*p*'/'Per –*p*' ('Per' stands for "positive permission"); (e) Questions '*p*?'/–*p*?'. If we want to stick to some *basic assumptions* of the Expressive Conception, we shall conclude that all these speech acts yield *incompatibilities for contraries*. However, it is possible to demonstrated that this is not the case, for *p* and –*p* do not generate incompatibilities in all the speech acts in which they are embedded:

1. The presence of *p* and – *p* does not imply any incompatibility when they are embedded in the act of rejection (c). Let's take, for instance, "Smoking marijuana is rejected." "Not smoking marijuana is rejected." We can issue both of them at the same time and, surprisingly, the result of these two speech acts is not a contradiction but, at best, a normative gap. The rejection of a contradiction is no contradiction at all.
2. The two speech acts 'Per*p*' and 'Per–*p*' are not incompatible. If, for instance, my mother tells me "You are permitted to smoke marijuana" and "You are permitted not to smoke marijuana" or, if you prefer, "You are permitted both to smoke marijuana and not to smoke marijuana", she is basically saying that I can do whatever I want: no contradiction is implied, once again.
3. Finally, the same kind of consideration holds for the questions: '*p*?' and '-*p*?' are not incompatible at all, and they can be answered with the very same question. "Does Alejandro smoke marijuana?" is compatible with "Alejandro smokes marijuana, doesn't he?" Indeed, I can even ask: "Does Alejandro smoke marijuana or not?" And the answer to both questions can be always the same: "Alejandro smokes marijuana."

Now that we have overviewed the fundamental solutions and arguments within legal philosophy, we can move on to some of the main theories that have been developed by philosophers of language. Due to the complexities of these theories, a huge amount of simplification will be required in my presentation.

4 Imperative Meaning in Philosophy of Language: Traditional Approaches

4.1 The Standard View in Speech Acts Theory

The idea that a perspicuous account of language requires to attend, along with sense and reference, the feature of (illocutionary) force is rather old, for it was first stated by Gottlob Frege (1879, 1918). In his *Begriffsschrift* (1879), Frege introduced the judgment-stroke (⊢) as a sign which contributes to the meaning of the sentence, by asserting that the thought expressed is true (Dummett 1973, 315–6). However, the feature of force and its relation with the dimensions of sense and reference has been deeply explored in the field of the *speech acts theory.*

The standard view defended in speech acts theory – which partly differs from the one proposed by J. L. Austin (1962), the founder of this tradition – claims that, *by convention*, certain sentences get to be associated with a certain illocutionary force, through some illocutionary force indicating devices (IFIDs) (Recanati 2013). IFIDs are force-markers that activate a certain illocutionary force; they basically work as (sentential or sub-sentential) operators (or functions) that combine a certain ordinary proposition, sentence, sentence-radical or state description with a certain illocutionary force (or a set of illocutionary forces).[14] Accordingly, the representational part of the sentence (ordinary proposition, sentence-radical, state description, or whatever) is generally considered as a force-invariant feature: in other words, the content of any speech act is always of the same semantic type (Recanati 2013).

The utterance of an imperative such as (1) "Open the window!" both expresses a certain representational content *p* (*e.g.* the action of opening the window by a certain subject *S*), and conveys the wish that the addressee realizes the situation described in the content. If the communication is effective, the utterance of (1) will normally induce the addressee to bring about the content. If this is so, it makes sense to consider, for instance, that the meaning of an imperative utterance is composed by a sentence radical, which provides the representational content – if we take (1), it would be something like: '((you) open the window)' – and by a certain "force", or "mood", which is activated by an IFID that shows the role of the sentence in the language game (Stenius 1967), by specifying the cognitive attitude of desire associated to the representational content – namely, the description a possible state of affairs (Sperber and Wilson 1988). With respect to commands, the force or mood could be represented using symbols such as 'IMP', 'PLEASE', "So it ought to be", "Make it the case that" (McGinn 1977), etc. Accordingly, the complete meaning of an utterance such as (1) consists of the combination of the sentence radical with the imperative mood, or imperative force. In other words, the content of (1) basically corresponds to something like: 'IMP ((you) open the window)'.

Moods (indicative, imperative optative, etc.) can be described as elements *sui generis* that *directly* classify classes of sentences – to make assertions, to give orders, etc. – and *indirectly* classify classes of utterances (Geach 1965, 458; Davidson 1979, 9). As we have already said, the IFID expresses the role that a certain sentence, or sentence-radical, or proposition plays in communication, without modifying its content (See, for instance, Searle 1968, 149). This is thesis that, as we have seen, Tarello tried to refute. Moods and forces are generally conceived as primitives that show all the range of speech acts that are conventionally associated to a certain sentence: given certain contextual assumptions and pragmatic principles, they tell us how a certain utterance should be interpreted (Sperber and Wilson 1988).

[14] Searle 1969; Searle and Vanderveken 1985; Vanderveken 1990. In recent times, several authors have also tried to explain the logical statute of this operator. See, for instance, Han 1998. Please notice that, in order to pursue the virtue of simplicity, I will not distinguish between: *performative analysis*, which treats the imperatives as explicit or implicit performatives; *parametric analysis*, which splits the imperative into a sentence type expression and a sentence-radical; *operator analysis*, which considers non-declaratives as type expressions that scope over a statement. This distinction can be found, for instance, in Mastop 2008.

The standard view leaves room for imperative-logic, and also for the possibility of "mixed" inferences between imperatives and indicatives. For instance, from (1) 'If you have savings, buy a new car' and (2) 'You have savings' it is possible to infer validly (3) 'Buy a new car' (See Searle and Vanderveken 1985).

Before moving any criticism to this position, I will briefly present Donald Davidson's account, which can be considered as a variation of the standard picture. Then, at the end of Sect. 4.2, I shall present an attack strategy that applies to both.

4.2 Donald Davidson's "Paratactic" Approach

Donald Davidson (1979) introduces some changes in the standard view, by attempting to represent mood without crossing the boundaries of a theory of truth. He offers a kind of explicit performative analysis, but he claims also that "it is plausible that if there are conventions linking indicatives and assertions, there are additional conventions linking other moods with assertion (Davidson 1979, 12)." These conventional links are part of the so-called linguistic competence. The solution proposed by Davidson is the following: it is possible to maintain that an imperative sentence such as "Close the door!" can be easily paraphrased using an explicit performative such as "I order you to close the door", where "I order" shall be considered as a description of the speech act that can be subject to a truth-functional analysis. In other words, for Davidson (who stands in strong disagreement with J.L. Austin on this point), an explicit performative has the effect of two different utterances, for "we may think of non-indicative sentences […] as indicative sentences plus an expression that syntactically represents the appropriate transformation; call this expression the *mood-setter*." (Davidson 1979, 18). The Author does not explain what is the logical role of this element: on the contrary, he recognizes that he has "failed to say what the mood-setter means", even though he considers that it cannot be semantically treated as a sentential operator (Davidson 1979, 18).

However, it is clear enough that the mood-setter of an imperative is true "if and only if the utterance of the indicative core is imperative in force" (Davidson 1979, 19). This is a reductionist approach, for it tries to explain use-conditional features of meaning through categories that belong to old school truth-conditional semantics. As Josh Parsons points out, this kind of strategy is now very common among the "Australian Cognitivists".[15]

Now, as demonstrated in a recent work written by Josh Parsons, there are several flaws that affect this sort of cognitivist approach (Parsons 2012, § 3). First of all, there is plenty of room for "unwanted validities", because the theoretical model ends up by transforming arguments that are patently invalid into perfectly valid arguments. Here goes Parson's example. Consider the following argument (S): (S1)

[15] Parsons 2012, 52: "The thesis of cognitivism, then, is that imperatives are equivalent to the corresponding performatives, and the performatives in turn are true iff it is so commanded". An example of "Australian cognitivism" is offered by Jackson and Pettit 1998.

'Attack at dawn!' – Therefore (S2) 'Someone commands something'. According to this kind of cognitivism, this argument can be translated in (S′): (S1′) 'I command that you attack at dawn' – Therefore (S2′) 'Someone commands something'. Considered that the argument S' is valid if cognitivism is true, then also the argument S should be valid. Unfortunately, this is not the case: in (S) the premises and the conclusion have a different subject matter. Second, cognitivism produces also "unwanted consistencies". In this case the demonstration given by Parsons is very close to the one used in our reformulation of Weinberger's puzzle. Let's take an inconsistent set of commands: SET {(1) 'Attack!' (2) 'Do not attack!'}. It's very likely that the cognitivist will offer the following paraphrases: (1′) 'I command that you attack'; (2′) 'I command that you do not attack'. Now, the problem is the following: (1′) and (2′) are not inconsistent, "for it is not inconsistent to report that an inconsistent set of commands has been made'. Actually, I can say (3) "I commanded that you attack and I commanded that you do not attack" without any worry of falling in a contradiction, because I am just "describing" speech acts.

As anticipated at the end of Sect. 3.1, I would like to conclude this paragraph by showing that a whole series of arguments that stand against both what we have called the "standard" approach, and Davidson's "paratactic" strategy have been raised by Baker and Hacker's, in their radical (and Wittgensteinian) criticism to truth-functional semantics and compositionality. The gist of Baker and Hacker's argumentation can be summed up as follows: every attempt to demonstrate that sentences in different moods share a common descriptive content is either "nonsensical" or "vacuous" (Baker and Hacker 1984, 81):

1. We have to consider that *describing* is a language-activity directed to certain objects. A typical description generally requires more than one sentence. Furthermore, "not every sentence which is about something which might be an object of description is itself either a description or necessarily a part of description" (Baker and Hacker 1984, 82). For instance, it is impossible to describe a ceremony of the Catholic Church with a single sentence.
2. If we use "description" in an ordinary sense, then the thesis that all sentences describe (or *partly* describe) something is completely false. Imperatives, optatives, interrogatives and explanations are not commonly used as description units. *Wh-questions* do not describe anything ("What did you do yesterday"?). The same holds for exclamation and ejaculations ("What a day!"), for imperative sentences, ("Give me some alcohol!") and optatives ("If only I could have some alcohol!").
3. If we want to use "description" in a philosophical sense, then the thesis that all sentences "describe" something is empty, because it's based on arbitrary stipulations. It's not a discovery about the nature of sentences, but it is rather a "piece of legislation" that establishes a new way of talking about sentences. Moreover, it is still hard to see how a logical truth ("Nothing can be red or green all over") or a self-contradiction can be understood as a description of something, or as having a descriptive content (Baker and Hacker 1984, 85–6).

4. The demonstration that all the different sentences of a language have a descriptive part in common is based on a "weird" strategy, which is methodologically questionable: choosing two intuitively similar unasserted sentences, and rephrasing them in a way that split their "common cognitive part" and their variable pragmatic part.

For instance, according to a strategy adopted by many authors, the following sentences:

[1] "You smoke marijuana."
[2] "Do you smoke marijuana?"
[3] "Smoke marijuana."

Could be reformulated in the following way:

[1′] "It is the case/that you smoke marijuana."
[2′] "Is it the case/that you smoke marijuana."
[3′] "Make it the case/that you smoke marijuana."

And this shall be considered as a clear demonstration that force and meaning are sharply separated, and that every speech act expresses the same cognitive content. According to Baker and Hacker, these strategies are "pure nonsense". Leaving aside the fact that the objects of these reformulations are not clear at all (are they *type* sentences or *token* sentences?) the apparent uniformity of these sentences is an illusion that masks their logical differences. Moreover, in many cases the paraphrases fail, and this is by no means a merely formal problem (Baker and Hacker 1984, 95–6): the aim of these paraphrases is to represent the deep logical structure that stands behind the grammatical surface of ordinary language sentences. Baker and Hacker's point is that the logical structure of ordinary language sentences cannot be captured by intrinsic paraphrases, for it is entirely dependent from their use. This is easy to demonstrate. Let's take for instance the following cases:

[4] "Everybody smoke a joint."	[4′] Make it the case that everybody smoke a joint.
[5] "Let A be an isosceles triangle!	[5′] Make it the case that A is an isosceles triangle.
[6] "If it rains, smoke a joint."	[6′] Make it the case that, if it rains you smoke a joint.
[7] "Let me smoke!"	[7′] Make it the case that I will smoke.

In each of these cases the result of the paraphrases is a complete failure:

- [4′] and [5′] obscure, or mask, the addressees of the command.
- [6] is a conditional command, while [6′] is a command to make a conditional true.
- [7′] would be equivalent to "Make me go", which is very different from "Let me go!"

The examples could, of course, be multiplied. However Baker and Hacker's arguments do not come for free: the price is the rejection of the idea that compositionality can be used to explain the unity of meaning, and the need to explain what is the "glue" that keep the different part of a sentence together.

5 Meaning and Force in Philosophy of Language Part Two: Current Trends

The solutions that we have sketched in the preceding paragraphs are not the only options and, possibly, they are not even the best – especially if we consider that semanticists have proposed a whole series of different theories in the last decades. First of all, there are good arguments in favor of a reductionist approach, which considers imperatives as modal sentences, and confines their performativity to the pragmatic dimension. Second, there are also new theories that, starting from analogous premises, end up by consider that semantic meanings of imperatives and indicatives sentences or utterances are different: while indicatives are sentences/utterances expressing propositions, imperatives are sentences/utterances expressing properties. Third, there are new theories that have developed an interesting (non-reductionist) analysis of imperatives, using a dynamic-logic. All these three approaches have important implications. The modal analysis is very powerful, both because it explains and predicts the peculiar logical behavior of imperatives – by treating them like necessities or possibilities (recall Ross's Paradox, for instance) – and because it offers a good explanation of the use of an imperative in communication, which could be seen as nothing else than a performative interpretation of a modal proposition (Portner 2004, 2007). The property analysis is also interesting, because it saves the intuition that imperatives express actions, which are ascribed to the addressee. Finally, the dynamic, non-reductionist approach captures very well the role of an imperative content in a communication process, by explaining how an accepted imperative determines a revision of the addressee's plans (in this case, the starting point is the idea that meaning is equivalent to the context-change potential).

David Lewis (1979) was perhaps the first author who developed a full-fledged modal approach, combined with a kind of analysis that belongs to the model-theoretic tradition. Lewis, by means of a thought experiment, proposed to analyze permissions and commands using possible-worlds semantics. With brutal simplification, we can describe Lewis's system as follows: the representational contents expressed by commands ($!\phi$) and permissions ($¡\phi$) are the same (ϕ). There is a first function that assigns to any sentence ϕ, at any pair $\langle t, w\rangle$ – where 't' stands for time, and 'w' represents a suitable world – a value 1 or 0: if the value is 1, then ϕ is true; if the value is 0, then ϕ is false. There is also a second function that assigns to any pair $\langle t, w\rangle$ a set of worlds, which is called "sphere of permissibility" (Lewis 1979, 20); and a third function that assigns to the same pair a set of worlds that are accessible at *t* and *w* (the "sphere of accessibility") (Lewis 1979, 21). A command '!ϕ' is true at *t* at *w if and only if* ϕ is true at every world that is accessible and permissible at *t, w* (Lewis 1979, 21). The same holds for a permission '¡ϕ'. At the beginning of the thought experiment we have a situation where we have a set of all possible worlds; when the authority (Master) starts to issue commands and permissions, the sphere of permissibility of the addressee (Slave) starts to adjust itself in order to make commands/permissions issued by the authority true. In case of an act of command, we have a contraction of the possible (and accessible) worlds; in case of an act of permission, we have an expansion of the possible (and accessible) worlds. Any new command or permission changes the sphere of permissibility in a way that makes the command true: if *P* is the old sphere before the issuance of '!ϕ' at *t*, then we have a new sphere, after *t*, which is the intersection '$P \cap [\phi$ at $t]$', and all the worlds where ϕ is false at *t* must be removed from the set (Lewis 1979, 25). The operation of adjustment is automatic (Lewis 1979, 22); therefore, the sphere of permissibility holds a direct control over the actions of the addressee. This kind of approach is not necessarily reductive,[16] but it still uses assertive propositions as a conceptual primitive: in the artificial language created by Lewis, permissions and commands are composed by a propositional element (ϕ) combined with a force indicator (<!,¡>).

Several linguists and philosophers of language have followed the road opened by Lewis. For instance, Magdalena Kaufmann (2012) has developed an interesting theory that belongs to this tradition. Kaufmann thinks that there is a fundamental difference between imperatives and declaratives, both intended as clause-types that have prototypical functions by virtue of an interaction between their lexical form and their pragmatic function in communication (Kaufmann 2012, 10 ff.): declaratives are more concerned with what the world is like, while imperatives are more concerned with what the world should be like (Kaufmann 2012, 2). Accordingly, she maintains that the meaning of an imperative can be represented as a performative usage of a modal verb, which determines the addition of a modal proposition to the common ground of communication – after all, also performative modal verbs (like "should") seem to lack a truth-value, just as imperatives (Kaufmann 2012, 58 ff.). Nevertheless, modal propositions do have truth-conditions; therefore, there is no need to postulate the existence of different kinds of semantic content. More precisely, modalities (necessity, possibility, or combinations of the two) express quantification over domains that are determined, on the one hand, by a contextual modal base (worlds) and, on the other, by an ordering source that expresses preferences.[17] To be sure, we do normally consider that we cannot treat imperatives as being true

[16] See Lewis 1979, 25: "I have no real dispute, however, with anyone who finds it intolerable to say that an imperative sentence, when used to command, has a truth value. In describing the language game I did not really use any semantic terms as primitives. I could have; but the description I actually gave is related to a description using semantic primitives as the Ramsey sentence of a term-introducing scientific theory is related to the theory itself. For instance, 'truth value' serves only as a mnemonic label for the values of the function introduced [...] by the existential quantification. If you dislike that label – or any other – feel free to substitute the euphemism of your choice."

[17] Kaufmann 2012 endorses a Kratzer-style treatment of modal elements. See Kratzer 1978.

or false; however, according to Kaufmann, this perceived impossibility is entirely dependent on pragmatic (and not semantic) elements; the validity of her claim is proved also by the consideration that, sometimes, imperatives are not used as commands or orders (Kaufmann 2012, 2): an imperative can be used for permissions, invitations, suggestions, instructions, well-wish. The modal element is grounded on the speaker's desire to induce the addressee to perform a certain action.

In details, imperatives express modal necessities that the speaker introduces into the common ground of communication. The idea of obligation is placed in the conversational background: it works as a set of presuppositions that grants performativity to the modal; the connection between the modal element and the background presuppositions is entirely pragmatic:

> [...] in contrast to modal verbs, imperatives can only be used performatively. I suggest that they carry an additional meaning component that confines them to usage in context where the corresponding modalized declarative would be used performatively. In order to establish the content of that additional meaning component, we only have to understand what contextual factors give rise to performative usage of modal verbs [...] I think that the crucial property shared by the respective utterance contexts is that the participant in the conversation agree that the speaker cannot be mistaken about the modality in question. This can be either because it is up to the speaker herself to order, to command, to permit, etc. or because the speaker is considered as an expert on the issue under discussion (Kaufmann 2012, 63)

Under this aspect, Kaufmann's theory is an expansion of Robert Stalnaker's dynamic model of discourse (Stalnaker 1978, 1999), in which the semantic meaning of a sentence is represented as its "context change potential" (Kaufmann 2012, 35). Context is conceived as a quadruple containing a speaker C_S, an addressee C_A, a time C_T and a world C_W, that presupposes, as an additional parameter, the "common ground", which is a set of possible worlds that are compatible with the mutual joint beliefs of the speaker and the hearer (Kaufmann 2012, 21 ff.). A successful imperative determines a change of context. Kaufmann assumes that there is a special, pre-speech act, update function '*J*' "that specifies how semantic objects are integrated in the course of conversation if accepted". This function takes care of every kind of speech act.

As said before, this kind of modal approach is very powerful: the first step consists in establishing a connection between imperatives and deontic modals; the second step is to reduce the deontic modal either to a necessity operator (for orders), or to a possibility operator (for permissions) – and here an imperative becomes a function from worlds to set of propositions. In this way: (A) we can explain in an elegant way the function that an imperative plays in communication, assuming that to order *p* is equivalent to claim that the proposition *p* necessarily must be made true; (B) we can predict most of the semantic relations between imperative sentences, because they behave just like modals (recall Ross's Paradox); (C) we can explain imperative consistency and validity with an adequate formal system.

Despite all these goods, Kaufmann's account presents two fundamental defects: first, it seems to involve circularity, for it presupposes that the speaker is issuing a command but, at the same time, the command itself is presented as a pragmatic effect of uttering a sentence characterized by the presence of an imperative operator;

second, we can legitimately maintain that presuppositions constrain the truth-value assignment, but this does not justify also the claim that an expression which, intuitively, is not consider to bear truth-values becomes a truth-conditions bearing expression (Mastop 2008).

To overcome similar problems, Paul Portner (2004, 2007, 2010, 2011) had recently proposed a model which is still quite close to the one developed by Lewis (1979), but assumes that there is a deeper semantic distinction between imperatives and indicatives: the basic idea is that directive force is associated with a 'To-Do List' function 'T', which, given a certain context C ascribes to a certain addressee x, a set of properties '(T(x))'.[18] Accordingly, the 'To-Do List' is a peculiar discourse parameter, namely: a set of properties that shall be considered as a common ground of communication.[19] Hence, imperative utterances express semantic objects of a non propositional-type: properties that should be added to the addressee's To-Do List. Two are the main differences between Portner and Lewis. First, according to Portner, the force marker of a declarative sentence-type is associated to propositions, while the force marker of a directive sentence-type is associated to potential properties of the addressee. In other words, when a certain speaker *S* issues an imperative, she is asking the addressee to acquire a certain property. For instance: if I issue the imperative "Alejandro, you are obliged to smoke!" I am asking Alejandro to acquire the property of being a smoker. Second, Portner's model contains also an ordering pragmatics for imperatives: "By contributing to the addressee's To-Do List an imperative affects the ordering of worlds, which in turn guides how the addressee's actions will be judged and understood." (Portner 2010, 6).[20] These differences shall not be underrated: if we conceive the meaning of an imperative in terms of properties of the addressee, we end up by endorsing a non-propositional and, ultimately, "agentive" interpretation of the semantic content. According to Portner, propositional contents can be used to describe the semantics of declaratives, but cannot play the same role with respect to imperatives.

From the point of view of legal theory, the main defect of Portner's account is the analysis of permissive norms: to be sure, Portner concedes that permissions are actually "requirement imperatives" – and, therefore, they are genuine commands – but, then, he also claims that "true permission imperatives are characterized by the fact that they contradict something else in the To-Do List." (Portner 2010, 6). This assumption is incorrect, for we can have permissions that allow actions that have not been prohibited before. However, Portner's solution on permission is still better than the one proposed before by Sperber and Wilson for the traditional view, which

[18] To put it in a more formal way: $\langle CG, Q, T\rangle: C + \phi_{imp} = \langle CG, Q, T[\textit{addressee}/T(addressee)\{[\phi_{imp}]\})]\rangle$. See Portner 2010, 5.

[19] A similar idea is defended by Han 1998, even though he uses the locution "Plan set" instead of "To-Do List", considering the "Plan set" as a set of propositions about future actions of the addressee, and not as a set of potential properties of the addressee.

[20] Portner 2010, 6: Ordering worlds: "For any $w_1, w_2 \in \cap CG$ and any participant i, $w_1 <_i w_2$ iff for some $P \in T(i), P(w_1)(i) = 1$ and $P(w_2)(i) = 0$, and for all $Q \in T(i)$ if $Q(w_2)(i) = 1$, then $Q(w_1)(i) = 1$.

can be described as a "paternalistic nonsense": these authors claim that, from a pragmatic point of view, permissions are issued in order to help the addressee in pursuing her own interests when she is reluctant to undertake a certain action which is good for her (Sperber and Wilson 1988). It's worth stressing that, on the other hand, the theoretical model developed by Portner has a special characteristic that makes it very palatable for a legal theorist: in effect, a 'To-Do List' admits inconsistencies (Portner 2011) and, in this case, we are told that the agent has to choose among the incompatible action-properties.[21]

Finally, I would like to bring Rochus Jacobus Mastop (2005) as an outstanding example of the third kind of (non-reductionist) approach, which relies on a dynamic, update logic (Veltman 1996). Mastop's starting point is fundamental idea that directives are primarily requirements by the speaker on the addressee to perform a certain action; therefore, directives provide *instructions*.[22] Instructions, on their turn, are considered as semantic primitives "on a par with propositions" (Mastop 2008). According to Mastop, it is impossible to analyze imperatives using a double-layer semantic, which divides imperatives into separate components, and considers at least one of them as descriptive. On the opposite, the Author considers that we need a special "update" semantics in order to describe imperative meaning, which is based on a dynamic theory.

A dynamic theory assumes that imperative meaning can be considered as an update function of the discourse context. As Berislav Zarnic (2011: 70) explains, "[t]he basic idea of dynamic semantics is that a sentence φ acts upon interlocutor's mental (i.e. intentional) state σ, and changes it into state σ'; φ is "projected" onto σ'. In the typical case φ is "projected" onto $\sigma' = \sigma[\varphi]$ in such a way that it is "accepted" there (σ' is a fixed point): $\sigma[\varphi] = (\sigma[\varphi])[\varphi]$. [...] In the formal sense intentional states can be molded using standard structures, first order and possible worlds structures as the building blocks." Thus, we can say that the meaning of an imperative corresponds to a function that produces a change in the cognitive state of who accepts it.

Dynamic semantics relies also on a "generalized" notion of consequence: "[U]nlike static semantics, in which the semantic notions, like consequence or consistency, are defined by sentence/interpretation relation, in dynamic semantics the sentence/set-of-interpretations relation is used. In the exemplar case of so called 'update', the semantics of an updating sequence is conceptualized as an operation on a given set of interpretations, i.e. on a context (Zarnic 2011: 89)." The discourse context represents preferences/requirements, while the change of context is considered as an effect produced by the introduction of an action (i.e. the *denotatum* of a

[21] Portner 2007 seemed to endorse a different solution: if two incompatible imperatives are uttered in a temporal sequence, the second must be interpreted (necessarily?) as a revision of the first. Kratzer 1981 introduces a ranking or preference structure in order to solve this kind of conflicts: a preference structure relative to a certain doxastic state W can be defined as a pair $\langle P, \leq \rangle$, where $P \subseteq \wp(W)$ is a modal ordering source and $\leq$ is an importance ranking on P; $\langle P, \leq \rangle$ is consistent if and only if for any p, q $\in P$, p < q OR q < p. On this point see Condoravdi and Lauer 2012.

[22] Charlow 2010, 2011 and Starr 2010, 2011 are also dynamic theories of imperatives.

piece of communication) with directive function in the addressee's schedule. Different semantic types (directives/indicatives) produce different context-change effects.

The peculiarity of Mastop's proposal consists in considering imperatives as a primitive semantic types, which is defined in terms of action-plans: for Mastop, a semantics based on truth-condition is incapable of explaining the special properties of imperatives. Following Belnap (1990), Mastop criticizes the 'Declarative Fallacy' – namely, the idea that all sentences express the same content (propositions) as a primitive semantic type: for Mastop, a semantic based on truth-condition is incapable of explaining the special properties of imperatives (Mastop 2005: 5). Under this respect, Mastop is very close to Alf Ross. To be sure, this is not the only similarity between the two authors: Mastop considers that a directive produces an obligation to perform an action *if and only if* it is accepted by the addressee; as we have seen before, the same claim was made by Alf Ross. In fact, the framework of Veltman's update semantics – which offers the base for Mastop's theory – "is a formalization in terms of acceptance" (Mastop 2005, 99): the meaning of a sentence is understood in terms of the changes that it produces in the cognitive state of the person that accepts it. In this framework, the classical idea of truth-assignment is substituted by an update system, which is defined as a triple $\langle L, \Sigma, [.]\rangle$, where L is a language (a set of atomic sentences), Σ represents a state space (a set of states σ, which represent both the information and the commitment for action of the addressee or interpreter or, in other words, the possibilities under consideration) and for each $\varphi \in L$, we have a (recursive) update operation such as $[\varphi]:\Sigma \rightarrow \Sigma$. We say that φ is accepted in a state $\sigma \in \Sigma$ *if and only if* $\sigma[\varphi] = \sigma$ (Mastop 2005, 99–101). Indicatives have TRUE and FALSE as possible values; imperatives, on the other hand, have DO and DON'T as possible "partial" values (Mastop uses '$\wp$' in order to represent a "partial" evaluation, that is, an evaluation which is possibly inconsistent with other evaluations of atomic sentences). We have two kinds of operations: adding a positive fact or commitment ('+'), and adding negative facts or commitments ('–'). In this way it is possible to represent all the updates that we have on a certain system.[23]

Mastop proposal is well suited to explain the non-representational function of imperatives, which are used to influence behavior, and not to explain how the world is. However, I have got at least two perplexities on his work: first, I cannot imagine how it is possible to define an action plan without relying on possible-world semantics and, therefore, reintroducing a cognitivist explanation of imperative meaning; second, the very idea of considering imperative meaning in terms of context-change could blur the distinction between imperatives and declaratives, considered that, under this view, both are defined in terms of action-determining.

[23] The formal system is contained in Mastop 2005, 105 ff.

6 Conclusion

I truly hope that this survey of both new and old solutions to the problem of imperative meaning could be taken as a starting point for the development of an "integrated approach". As we can see very clearly, there are many affinities between the underlying intuitions between the models proposed by legal theorists and the models proposed by philosophers of language: for instance, the analyses put forward by Alf Ross and by Alchourrón and Bulygin are very close to the standard view defended in speech act theory. In virtue of these similarities, legal philosophers could rely on the very sophisticated work made by their colleagues (*i.e.* philosophers of language) in the last decades for a refinement of their lacking theories. Let me make just two examples: Mastop's formalization can be used to restate (or, at least, to update) some parts of Alf Ross's account; analogously, we can integrate Portner's preference-structures in the Expressive Conception. On the other hand, philosophers of language could rely the expertise of legal theorists in order to modify some counter-intuitive assumptions of their accounts: in this case, the misleading analyses of permissions offered by Portner and Sperber and Wilson are good examples. My conviction is that this kind of interdisciplinary work could produce important results.

References

Alchourrón, C. E., & Bulygin, E. (1981). The expressive conception of norms. In R. Hilpinen (Ed.), *New studies in deontic logic* (pp. 95–125). Dordrecht: Holland.

Aloni, M., & Ciardelli, I. (2013). A logical account of free-choice imperatives. In M. Aloni, M. Franke, & F. Roelofsen (Eds.), *The dynamic, inquisitive, and visionary life of ϕ, $?\phi$, and $\Diamond\phi$*. Amsterdam: Onbejend.

Austin, J. (1954). *The province of jurisprudence determined*. New York: The Noonday Press.

Austin, J. L. (1962). *How to do things with words*. Oxford: Claredon Press.

Baker, G. P., & Hacker, P. M. (1984). *Language, sense and nonsense*. Oxford: Basil Blackwell.

Barberis, M. (1988). *Il diritto come comportamento*. Torino: Giappichelli.

Barberis, M. (1990). *Il diritto come discorso e come comportamento*. Torino: Giappichelli.

Belnap, N. (1990). Declaratives are not enough. *Philosophical Studies, 59*(1), 1–30.

Bentham, J. (1945). *The limits of jurisprudence defined*. New York: Columbia University Press.

Calzetta, A. D., & Sardo, A. (2014). Una nueva visita a la concepción expresiva. *Doxa, 37*, 45–63.

Carnap, R. (1942). *Introduction to semantics*. Cambridge: Harvard University Press.

Charlow, N. (2010). Restricting and embedding imperatives. In M. Aloni, H. Bastiaanse, T. de Jager, & K. Schulz (Eds.), *Logic, language and meaning* (pp. 223–233). Berlin/Heidelberg: Springer.

Charlow, N. (2011). *Practical language: Its meaning and use*. Doctoral dissertation, University of Michigan.

Chiassoni, P. (1987). Precetti non logicamente strutturati. In margine alla teoria della norma giuridica di Giovanni Tarello. *Materiali per una storia della cultura giuridica, 17*(2), 403–439.

Condoravdi, C., & Lauer, S. (2012). Imperatives: Meaning and illocutionary force. *Empirical Issues in Syntax and Semantics, 9*, 37–58.

Davidson, D. (1979). Moods and performances. In A. Margalit (Ed.), *Meaning and use* (pp. 9–20). Dordrecht: Reidel.
Dummett, M. (1973). *Frege: Philosophy of language*. London: Gerald Duckworth.
Frege, G. (1879). *Begriffsschrift*. Halle: L. Nebert.
Frege, G. (1918). Der Gedanke. Eine logische Untersuchung. *Beiträge zur Philosophie des deutschen Idealismus, 2*, 58–77.
Geach, P. (1960). Ascriptivism. *The Philosophical Review, 69*, 221–225.
Geach, P. (1965). Assertion. *The Philosophical Review, 74*, 449–465.
Guastini, R. (1982). *Lezioni di teoria analitica del diritto*. Giappichelli: Torino.
Guastini, R. (2008). Teoria del significato e teoria dell'interpretazione. *Materiali per una storia della cultura giuridica, 38*(2), 463–471.
Han, C. H. (1998). *The structure and interpretation of imperatives: Mood and force in universal grammar*. Phd dissertation, University of Pennsylvania.
Hare, R. M. (1967). Some alleged differences between imperatives and indicatives. *Mind, 76*, 309–326.
Jackson, F. C., & Pettit, P. (1998). A problem for expressivism. *Analysis, 58*, 239–251.
Jørgensen, J. (1937/1938). Imperatives and logic. *Erkenntnis 7*, 288–296.
Kaufmann, M. (2012). *Interpreting imperatives*. Berlin/Heidelberg: Springer.
Kelsen, H. (1961). *General theory of law and state*. New York: Russell & Russell.
Kelsen, H. (1966). On the pure theory of law. *Israel Law Review, 1*, 1–7.
Kratzer, A. (1978). *Semantik der Rede*. Königstein: Scriptor.
Kratzer, A. (1981). The notational category of modality. In H. J. Eikmeyer & H. Rieser (Eds.), *Words, wolds, and contexts. New approaches in word semantics* (pp. 38–74). Berlin: de Gruyter.
Kristan, A. (2015). In defense of the expressive conception of norms. *Revus, 22*, 151–172.
Lewis, D. (1979). A problem about permission. In E. Saarinen, R. Hilpinen, I. Niiniluoto, & M. P. Hintikka (Eds.), *Essays in honour of Jaakko Hintikka* (pp. 163–175). Dordrecht: Reidel.
Marmor, A. (2011). Can the law imply more than it says? On some pragmatic aspects of strategic speech. In A. Marmor & S. Soames (Eds.), *Philosophical foundations of language in the law* (pp. 83–104). Oxford: Oxford University Press.
Mastop, R. (2005). *What can you do: Imperative mood in semantic theory.* Doctoral dissertation, University of Amsterdam.
Mastop, R. (2008). Imperatives as semantic primitives. *Linguistics and Philosophy, 34*(4), 305–340.
McGinn, C. (1977). Semantics for nonindicative sentences. *Philosophical Studies, 32*, 301–311.
Muffato, N. (2007). *La semantica delle norme*. Genova: Ecig.
Parsons, J. (2012). Cognitivism about imperatives. *Analysis, 72*, 49–54.
Poggi, F. (2012). Contextualism, but not enough. *Revus, 17*, 55–65.
Poggi, F. (2013). The myth of literal meaning in legal interpretation. *Analisi e Diritto, 2013*, 313–335.
Portner, P. (2004). *The semantics of imperatives within a theory of clause types.* In K. Watanabe & R. B. Young (Eds.) *Proceedings of semantics and linguistic theory* 14 (pp. 235–252). Cornell University Linguistics Department, CLC Publications. URL: http://semanticsarchive.net/Archive/mJIZGQ4N
Portner, P. (2007). Imperatives and modals. *Natural Language Semantics, 15*, 351–383.
Portner, P. (2010). *Permission and choice.* Manuscript available at: www.semanticsarchive.net/Archive/jIiYjMyY/Permission_Choice_Portner.pdf
Portner, P. (2011). Permission and choice in discourse and grammar: From sentence types to lexical categories. In G. Günther & Z. Thomas Ede (Eds.), *Studies in generative grammar*. Berlin: Mouton de Gruyter.
Ratti, G. B. (2012). *Diritto, indeterminatezza, indecidibilità*. Madrid: Marcial Pons.
Ratti, G. B. (2013). *Studi sulla logica del diritto e della scienza giuridica*. Madrid: Marcial Pons.
Raz, J. (1970). *The concept of a legal system*. Oxford: Claredon Press.

Recanati, F. (2013). Content, mood, and force. In E. Barnes (Ed.), *Philosophy compass* (pp. 622–632). Hoboken: Wiley.
Ross, A. (1968). *Directives and norms*. London: Lawbook Exchange, Ltd.
Schroeder, M. (2008). *Being for. Evaluating the semantic program of expressivism*. Oxford: Oxford University Press.
Searle, J. (1968). *Austin on locutionary and illocutionary acts*. Reprinted in I. Berlin (Ed.), *Essays on J.L. Austin* (pp. 141–169). Oxford: Claredon Press.
Searle, J. (1969). *Speech acts*. Cambridge: Cambridge University Press.
Searle, J., & Vanderveken, D. (1985). *Foundations of illocutionary logic*. Cambridge: Cambridge University Press.
Sperber, D. & Wilson, D. (1988). Mood and the analysis of non-declarative sentences. In J. Dancy, J. Maravcsik, & C. Taylor (Eds.), *Human agency: Language, duty and value* (pp. 77–101). Stanford: Stanford University Press.
Stalnaker, R. (1978). Assertion. In P. Cole (Ed.), *Syntax and semantics 9* (pp. 315–332). New York: Academic.
Stalnaker, R. (1999). On the representation of context. In R. Stalnaker (Ed.), *Context and content* (pp. 96–113). Oxford: Oxford University Press.
Starr, W. B. (2010). *Conditionals, meaning and mood.* Doctoral dissertation, Rutgers University.
Starr, W. B. (2011). *A preference semantics for imperatives.* Cornell University: Manuscript. http://williamstarr.net/research/a_preference_semantics_for_imperatives.pdf
Stenius, E. (1967). Mood and language game. *Synthese, 17*, 254–274.
Tarello, G. (1974). *Diritto, enunciati, usi.* Bologna: Il Mulino.
Vanderveken, D. (1990). *Meaning and speech acts. Vol. I: Principles of language use*. Cambridge: Cambridge University Press.
Veltman, F. (1996). Defaults in update semantics. *Journal of Philosophical Logic, 25*, 221–261.
Villa, V. (2012). *Una teoria pragmaticamente orientata dell'interpretazione giuridica.* Torino: Giappichelli.
Von Wright, G. H. (1963). *Norm and action*. London: Routledge & Kegan Paul.
Weinberger, O. (1985a). The expressive conception of norms – An impasse for the logic of norms. *Law and Philosophy, 4*, 165–198.
Weinberger, O. (1985b). On the meaning of norm sentences, normative inconsistency, and normative entailment. A reply to Carlos E. Alchourrón and Eugenio Bulygin. *Law and Philosophy, 4*, 465–475.
Yablo, S. (2009). A problem about permission and possibility. In A. Egan & B. Weatherson (Eds.), *Epistemic modality*. Oxford: Oxford University Press.
Zarnic, B. (2011). Dynamic models in imperative logic. In A. Brozek, J. Jadacki, & B. Zarnic (Eds.), *Theory of imperatives from different points of view* (pp. 60–120). Warszawa: Warsaw University.

Disputable Means: Pragmatic Knowledge Practices in Sovereign Debt Agreements. Reflections on the Argentinian Case

Leticia Barrera

Abstract This essay follows an interest in socio-legal studies in taking on the legal technicalities (e.g., legal instrumentalism, managerialism, procedures) as a subject of inquiry (Riles A, Buffalo Law Rev 53:392–405, 2005, Collateral knowledge. Legal reasoning in global financial markets. University of Chicago Press, Chicago, 2011; Valverde M, PoLAR 26(2):86–108, 2003, Soc Leg Stud 18(2):139–158, 2009). Accordingly, it focuses on the means to end relationship embedded in legal techniques to elaborate on the "pragmatic knowledge practices" (Valverde M, PoLAR 26(2):86–108, 2003) they further. The study draws on a concrete case of sovereign debt litigation in US courts: *NML Capital, Ltd. v. Republic of Argentina* that came out of this country's foreign debt default in 2001 (following a larger economic crisis) and debt restructurings in 2005 and 2010. Rather than focusing on the effects of the court's rulings on the parties in the case, third interested parties (namely payment and clearing institutions), or even on the alleged impacts upon the sovereign debt world (Gelpern A, Houston Law Rev 50 1095–1127, 2013, 2014), the case becomes in this essay a venue to engage in a context-based analysis of the use of some legal formulas or terms which became routinized knowledge practices in foreign debt agreements. Consequently, the study moves beyond the question of judicial interpretation of contractual terms to look at the function that those legal devices are thought to perform in the contexts in which they are placed, represented, appropriated, negotiated, and even anticipated by the agents. In this vein, the piece seeks to assess the political spin of legal technicalities by looking into their constitution as mere vehicles of pragmatism while serving a disputable ideological agenda; and thus, they are means to multiple ends.

Keywords Sovereign debt • Knowledge practices • Means and ends • Argentina

L. Barrera (✉)
CONICET-ISES, Tucumán, Argentina
e-mail: leticiabarrera@conicet.gov.ar

F. Poggi, A. Capone (eds.), *Pragmatics and Law*, Perspectives in Pragmatics, Philosophy & Psychology 10, DOI 10.1007/978-3-319-44601-1_11

1 Introduction

In February 2012, the United States District Court for the Southern District of New York entered an injunction prohibiting the defendant, Argentina, from paying holders of its restructured bonds unless it also, and at the same time, paid the accelerated principal and the interest owed to the holdout bondholders, namely the plaintiff in this case.[1] In November 2012, the same court issued an amended injunction broadening the scope of the latter to reach interested third parties who participate in the payment system (e.g., banks, indenture trustees, and clearing institutions).[2] Both of the court's decisions are part of a judicial saga on Argentinian debt that began in 2005 when *NML Capital Ltd,* a coalition of distressed debt funds and retail investors[3] sued that country before the NY Southern District court. Since then, litigation has developed through different judicial instances in the US, including its Supreme Court of Justice, and other foreign jurisdictions.[4] This case, in turn, can be

[1] See *NML Capital, Ltd. v. Republic of Argentina,* 699 F.3d 246 (2d Cir. 2012). The court held that "Argentina has breached its obligations to the holders of the original bonds under an Equal Treatment Clause, which prevents the debtor from subordinating or otherwise treating unequally similarly positioned creditors, by continuing to pay the exchange bondholders without also paying the holdouts" (Neve 2013:632, note 11). Holdouts creditors (or just holdouts) are the holders of securities eligible for exchange within a scheme a debt restructuring program that refused to participate in such an exchange and pursued litigation to claim the full payment of their defaulted bonds. The holdout litigation saga in the Argentine case, has uncovered another category of holdout creditors: those who did not pursue litigation in NY courts in the beginning but after the ruling that favored the holdouts 'filed a suit before the same court claiming that the ruling extends to their situation too. They are known as the "me too". In June 5 2015, the District Court ruled that they are entitled to the same rights as the holdout litigants.

[2] See, Amended February 23, 2012 Order, NML Capital, Ltd. v. Republic of Argentina, Nos. 08 Civ. 6978 (TPG), 09 Civ. 1707 (TPG), 09 Civ. 1708 (TPG), 2012 WL 5895784 (S.D.N.Y. Nov. 21, 2012 (Order clarifying the scope of the injunction). Litigation came to an end, however, very recently, in early 2016, a few months after this piece was written and submitted for consideration in this edited volume. On December 10th 2015, Mauricio Macri, an opposition party leader became the Nation's President, and decided to settle the conflict with the holdouts. He argued that the settlement would allow the country to get access to international financial markets. The settlement was reached on February 29, 2016. Nonetheless, to become legally effective according to Argentinian Law, it demanded that the Argentine Congress—urged by the Macri Administration and after negotiations between the ruling party and the opposition parties—repealed the laws blocking the payment on defaulted debt. On March 30th 2016, those laws were lifted by Congress. On April 22 Argentina started paying more than $9 billion to creditors who had refused debt restructurings. On the same day, Judge Thomas P. Griesa lifted the Injunction against Argentina in all cases pending before his court. To raise the funds to pay the settlements it had issued sovereign debt bonds for $16.5 billion a few days before, on April 13th 2016. See, "Argentina pays holdouts after 14 years, US judge Griesa lifts injunction", Buenos Aires Herald, April 22, 2016. Available at http://www.buenosairesherald.com/article/213070/argentina-pays-holdouts-after-14-years-us-judge-griesa-lifts-injunction (accessed May 15 2016).

[3] The lead plaintiff, NML is a subsidiary of *Elliot Management Associates* a fund specialized in distress-asset investing.

[4] As Weidemaier and Gelpern recount, NML's collection efforts have included the attempt to seize defaulted bonds tendered in the 2005 debt exchange, central bank funds on deposit at the Federal

placed within a larger political and economic context involving the restructuring of Argentina's sovereign debt and its contingencies—expected or not—such as the creditors'[5] reactions to that political and economic decision.

After the financial breakdown of December 2001, which was followed by a profound economic and political crisis (Goddard 2006; Smulovitz 2006) Argentina defaulted on its obligations to bondholders (see Gelpern 2005, 20).[6] In 2005 this country implemented a dramatic debt restructuring program[7] offering all the owners of the original bonds the opportunity to exchange their defaulted bonds for new debt securities. The swap implied that the creditors would adopt the terms and conditions of the new bonds and relinquish their rights under the old ones. In 2010 a similar proceeding was enacted. Bondholders who opted out of the restructurings, like the plaintiff in this case, had the door opened to pursue litigation to secure full payment of the obligations under the original bonds. The majority of the holdouts, in particular the hedge funds (also known as "vulture funds"[8]) had purchased the bonds in the secondary market at well below face value at the time of or subsequently to the default (Neve 2013, 636; citing NML Capital Ltd., 699 F. 3d, 252–254).

Reserve Bank of New York and the Bank for International Settlements, taxes and revenues owed by French companies to Argentina, the presidential airplane, and a frigate docked in Ghana (2014, 194). Still, there is a more extensive litigation associated with Argentina's 2001 debt default. According to Panizza et al. (2009, 658) by late 2004 almost 140 lawsuits, including class action suits had been filed against Argentina in New York, Italy and Germany by distressed debt investment funds and retail investors.

[5] Arguably, reactions to sovereign debt restructuring by creditors like NML can be framed as unexpected contingencies in light of previous (and "copycat") holdout litigation that challenged other debt restructurings, like those of Peru 2000 and Nicaragua 1999. See the accompanying text. In Roubini's understanding, the practice of "rush to the courthouse" or "grab race" and the free rider (or holdout or rouge creditor) are two different types of externalities to debt restructuring (2002, 322–3).

[6] As I explained elsewhere (Barrera 2012), probably the most salient aspect of the economic breakdown (both the financial crisis and the following debt default) were the restrictions imposed by then President De la Rua's Administration (1992–2001) on cash withdrawals from bank accounts, called *corralito* (the blockade drawn around bank accounts restricting access to savings) and the "pesification", the forced conversion of the previously frozen savings accounts in US dollars into Argentine pesos at unfavorable rates. The image of hundreds of depositors banging pots at banks´ doorsteps epitomized that situation.

[7] The final offer includes a 75 % write-off over the nominal value of a total outstanding debt of $81.200 million in default, but as accrued interest were finally acknowledged, the amount of debt to be restructured was $99.400 million to be capitalized in the same time frame as the new bonds issued (between 30 and 40 years). See, Garcia-Hamilton et al. 2005; Prospectus Supplement (to Prospectus Dated December 27, 2004), available at http://www.mecon.gov.ar/finanzas/download/us_prospectus_and_prospectus_supplement.pdf (accessed June 5th 2015).

[8] "Vulture funds" refers to investment funds that select and purchase sovereign debt securities at deep discount in the secondary market given the risk of nonpayment when the debtor experiences critical financial problems or once the debt has been defaulted. Later through litigation they seek to collect the face value of the bonds In terms of Cohen, distressed-sovereign debt investors "acquire the opportunity to realize profit above the discounted price" (2011, 13). However, in practice, they do not sue to get back the money they invested but an exorbitant profit.

Certainly, the case has attracted much attention in the financial press and elsewhere (Weidemaier and Gelpern 2014). The scope of the remedies granted by the court have raised concerns about their potential impact upon the sovereign debt world (Gelpern 2013, 2014; Neve 2013; Von Bogdandy and Goldmann 2013), and fueled debates about the appropriate approach toward sovereign debt restructuring within international organizations (G 77 plus China, Summit 2014 Declaration; NU General Assembly Resolution, Sept. 9, 2014; G20 Leaders' Communiqué, Brisbane Summit 2014). In addition, reactions to the development of holdout litigation before US courts have merged with long-term scholarly and institutional analyses of sovereign financing and debt restructuring (IMF 2002; UNCTAD Principles 2012; Roubini 2002; Espósito et al. 2013; Gelpern 2013).

This chapter does not present a focused analysis of the legal, economic and political effects of US court's rulings. Nor does it engage in questions of legal reasoning and judicial interpretation to address the rationale of the decisions in question. Rather, it proposes to shift the attention away from the case results and to focus on what remains latent in the background: the technical knowledge embedded in the constitution of legal and financial instruments in the context of sovereign debt agreements. When they are moved from the margins to the center of the debate—and to the analysis along the way -as prompted by this judicial case, legal techniques can be taken on as an object of inquiry in their own right (Riles 2005; Valverde 2009). Moreover, working on this technical dimension of law implies not only turning the actual tools of legal knowledge (e.g., legal instrumentalism, managerialism, procedures, legal technocrats, and the forms of legal doctrines) into analytical objects themselves but also using them as a means to advance one's knowledge. This move replicates, to some extent, what anthropologist Annelise Riles has called the "literalization" of the Realist metaphor; that is, the Realist insight about the instrumental nature of law is, itself, fashioned as an actual instrument (2005, 1009).

This essay takes on the conflict of judicial interpretation of contractual terms such as *pari passu* or the equal treatment clause triggered by this case in particular, and the speculations about the concrete effects that other provisions (namely, the—Rights Upon Future Offers-clause) might cause as manifestations of the central role of legal instruments. To put it differently, legal instruments are not merely *means to- an- end-* relations, marginal to allegedly more substantial economic and political debates on sovereign debt. On the contrary, they can operate as techniques of governance (Riles 2011,15).

Therefore, law cannot be reduced to just a tool, either an auxiliary for changing aspects of social life or maintaining the *status quo.* In this conception, law is interpreted as outside of real life, as an artificial category, when in fact, law is already an integral part of what it regulates (Sarat et al. 2003). In thinking about an idea of law, I favor, instead, an approach to legality more akin to that of scholars who adopt a constitutive perspective and "tend to see the links between law and society at the level of networks of legal practices on the one hand, and clusters of beliefs, on the other" (ibid., 7). Indeed, the idea that the social and the legal operate on separate and different milieus has been challenged by contemporary social theorists like Bruno

Latour, who has given an account of the legal as a way of organizing relations and connections (Latour 2004). In this author's view, the legal process manifests as an assemblage of people, texts, everyday objects and even architecture. Accordingly, "legality is a quality of the network, not of the entity" (Levi and Valverde 2008, 61).

Following Riles's insights on how legal reasoning unfolds and law experts operate in private market transactions (2011) and other recent socio-legal literature on legal technicalities (Valverde 2009; Latorre 2012) I seek in this essay to make technical legal knowledge and legal technicalities,[9] as encountered in the context of Argentinian debt restructuring agreements, accessible ethnographically. In this vein, I pay close attention to the constitution of legal terms such as *pari passu* often deemed as "boilerplate" clauses—that is, "terms conveyed from contract to contract with minimal alteration" (Johns 2008, 259)—in sovereign debt agreements (Gulati and Klee 2001; Gulati and Scott 2013), and the RUFO clause which seemed to be an innovation of Argentina's debt restructuring in 2005 (Gelpern 2005). In doing so, I am aiming at unpacking procedural practices, authoritative expert knowledges, institutional and social relations, and the politics inherent to those legal instruments. Such a constellation, however, is shadowed by the technical character of law and legal instruments (Riles 2011).

The present study draws on archival research, document and media analyses, and on scholarly work about the genealogy of pari passu, as well other academic literature on sovereign financing and debt restructuring. I also conducted semi-structured interviews with researchers of Argentinian sovereign debt, economists, former civil servants, corporate lawyers and sovereign debt experts who either directly or indirectly were involved in the 2005 and 2010 Argentina's sovereign debt restructuring processes. Due to promised confidentiality, the names of my interlocutors remain anonymous.[10]

Finally, is worth noting that this piece also resonates with two recent works on the sophisticated context of sovereign debt legal practice: first, the research carried out by Weidemaier et al. (2013) among sovereign debt lawyers working at prestigious global law firms on the origins of pari passu clause and these experts' actual practices of contract drafting; and second, the research and analysis by Gulati and Scott (2013) on the stickiness of boilerplate contract provisions. The former work contributes to shed light on the disjuncture between the myths about the origins of that contractual term that circulate within the world of sovereign bond lending and how sovereign debt lawyers actually behave. The latter, building upon the effects of

---

[9] For Riles, the technical character of law encompasses subject and practices that include: "(1) certain ideologies —legal instrumentalism and managerialism; (2) certain categories of experts—especially scholars, bureaucrats and practitioners who treat the law as a kind of tool or machine and who see themselves as modest but expertly devoted technicians; (3) a problem-solving paradigm—an orientation toward defining concrete, practical problems and toward crafting solutions; (4) a form of reasoning and argumentation, from eight-part tests to reasoning by analogy, to the production of stock types of policy arguments to practices of statutory interpretation or citation of case law" (Riles 2011, 64–5).

[10] Additionally, given that the field of sovereign debt to which I had access was composed mostly of men, I refer to my respondents as masculine subjects.

Elliot v. Peru (2000) before Belgian tribunals and subsequent holdout litigation asks why the *pari passu* persists and proliferates in sovereign debt instruments (produced by the world's most elite law firms) in spite of the adverse rulings to the sovereign debtor's interests following that case. In other words, what is of Gulati and Scott's most concern is "why sovereign debt instruments post-Elliot have not addressed the risks created (or at least revealed) by that case" (Boyack 2013–2014, 10). Certainly, these two pieces are central to the analysis pursued herein. Nonetheless, in this essay, I seek to move beyond both the *gap* between language and practice pointed out by the former research, and the *failure* of agency in contract-research and design posed by the latter, to emphasize, instead, the instrumentality of legal tools and the pragmatic knowledge that those artifacts expose in the context of my research setting. My interest in law's technical capacity is not just to argue that "means defines the ends and vice versa" (Riles 2011, 229), but to explore how in my field these technical instruments further an inscription of political possibility through a description of economic inevitability.[11] In other words, I would argue that the means are themselves intriguing political possibilities.

2 The Place of Law: The Focus on the Means

According to Riles, American corporate and securities laws—both forms that have successfully extended far beyond the US territory-further "one of the hallmarks of twentieth-century American legal thought"; that is, the concept of legal technicality as "a tool, a technology for doing something, a means to an end" (2011, 68). Indeed, this idea of law was one of the nine programmatic points of departure to pursue a realist study of law, in Karl Llewellyn's account: "The conception of law as a means to social ends and not as an end in itself; so that any part needs constantly to be examined for its purpose, and for its effect, and to be judged in the light of both and of their relation to each other" (Llewellyn 1930–1931, 1236). Such an understanding of law, Riles notes, also builds upon American Pragmatism's insight that knowledge (of all kinds) is "a tool with practical consequences" (ibid): a tool we use to solve problems. Law, therefore, "should be valued by the extent to which it meets its end, not by the beauty of its logical processes or the strictness with which its rules proceed from the dogma it takes for its foundation" (ibid; quoting Pound 1908, 605).

Notably, the legacy of pragmatism within the field of (US) law,[12] social theorist Valverde remarks, can be encountered in habits of governance rather than in a debate of philosophical ideas. And because pragmatist effects are driven by a problem-solving paradigm, they are mainly practical (2003, 86–7). By getting things done "without drawing theoretical attention" is what have enabled actors "to

[11] I thank Guillermo Moro for this observation.

[12] Pragmatism in the legal field was closely linked to the Legal Realism associated with the Progressive Era's faith in social science to judgement.

use pragmatic/pragmatist tools mixed pell-mell with legal tools of very different, even contradictory provenance" (ibid. 87). To put it differently, the "functionalized knowledge" of classical pragmatism (Kellogg 2012, 114) advances the instrumental capacity of law. Accordingly, law (technical law) is an instrument, a way to achieving certain stated objectives.

That law remains instrumental ("collateral" to paraphrase Riles) to more important economic and political decisions is palpable in the appreciation of sovereign debt restructuring as both *procedural* and *substantial* (Garcia-Hamilton et al. 2005; Olivares-Caminal 2009). From this point of view, the procedural dimension of debt restructuring refers to the architecture (the legal framework) whereas the substantial focuses on the actual restructuring of the debt, that is, the rescheduling of amortization schedules, the writing off the debt principal, etc. This view of law as procedural and instrumental is also encountered among the corporate lawyers (sovereign debt experts) that I interviewed. These actors share the understanding of (their) legal work as a side-activity; secondary to what they find lies at the core of debt restructuring proceedings: the financial issue. In the words of a former in-house counsel at an investment bank: "I regret to say that our work is less important than that of others (economists, finance experts, political agents involved in sovereign debt lending)". Moreover, in this person's view, "any corporate lawyer working at an elite law firm involved in market transactions would like to become a bank CEO".

Along the same lines, legal experts tend to frame their workings within the boundaries set by market conditions. Law's capacity to extend the limits depends upon the market's approval. New legal forms—for instance, innovative sovereign debt instruments are subject to their acceptance by the "market", as legal counsels pointed out to me. When explaining law firms' reliance on templates at their drafting of sovereign debt agreements, a counsel mentioned to me his attempt to introduce amendments to the indenture he was currently drafting. According to him, the proposed amendment would heighten the duties and obligations of one of the third parties involved in sovereign lending, namely, the potential trustee. He was not sure, though, whether the trustee-to-be would accept the proposed new conditions given the concrete consequences that holdout litigation on Argentine debt securities carried on the operation of payment agents.[13]

Underlying this counsel's account is the assumption of law as conservative, which is reinforced by another statement he made to me about contract law (civil law) as "backward", as always falling behind market transactions. "Law is a technique, a technical tool; a companion practice of the economy… civil law cannot follow economic changes in society" he assessed. Interestingly, this lawyer's distrust of legal forms as a vehicle for change evokes the realist idea that society moves

[13] See, for instance, "Argentina Warns Citibank It Could Lose Banking License" at http://www.nytimes.com/aponline/2015/03/13/world/americas/ap-lt-argentina-default.html (last accessed April 20, 2015); "Citibank in Argentina to Stop Making Bond Payments" at http://www.nytimes.com/aponline/2015/03/17/world/americas/ap-lt-argentina-debt-standoff.html (last accessed April 20, 2015); "Government sues Citibank", at http://www.buenosairesherald.com/article/186275/government-sues-citibank

faster than the law, and hence, demanding that "law needs reexamination to determine how far it fits the society it purports to serve" (Llewellyn 1930–1931, 1236).

In addition, the idea of law as purely technical is supported by the corporate lawyers' perception of financial law and their workings on the field of financial markets as "objective". One legal practitioner with vast experience on capital market transactions, who unwilling to be interviewed about his participation in sovereign debt deals, reacted to my approaching him that both his work and that of his law firm colleagues was "only technical, and very objective". "When I sense that the (interviewer's) question has ideological motivations, I refuse to answer", he anticipated to any potential question I might want to ask. In so doing, he also sought to cast a self-conscious image of himself as removed from any political consequence that his work might have. Likewise, another counsel challenged my assumption that contractual terms (in his field of expertise) are likely to serve multiple ends: "Law is technical", he stated. "I do not agree with your argument about that clauses like pari passu may be subject to different interpretations". If they (the clauses' text) are open to many interpretations, it means that they were written very poorly", he concluded. Underlying both statements is the assumption that a technical legal question or issue is not political *per se* (Riles 2011, 67).

So far, I have stressed the argument that "the idea of the means to an end is an important element of legal technique "(ibid., 93). Following this understanding of law as just technical, law is represented as objective, "neutral and agnostic to its purpose and applications" (ibid., 67). However, in the context of sovereign debt practice, how do the actors that I encountered in the field imagine or represent the ends that their means (themselves, their work) are called to meet? From the vantage-point of the lawyers that I interviewed, those ends rely on the market's rationality. Noticeably, in the lawyers' discourse, the market is represented as an "entity", in sharp contrast to the complex assemblage of knowledge and social relations (and even face-to-face interactions) suggested by other experts drawn from the field of economics and finance that I also interviewed.

Consequently, the means appeared as pre-determined by the ends: rational, with no political implications. According to a corporate lawyer: "A bond issuer wants his operation to be successful, which means to pay a low interest rate for the notes, to collect as much money as possible through public offering, and yet, that a broad secondary market is created for the securities. The debtor wants all of this, without overlooking some legal aspects of the transaction that might cause him some troubles in the future". Within this ends-oriented framework, law (and legal work alongside) is just a tool among others, furthering a representation of legality as collateral (literally and figuratively) to the market (Riles 2011, 64).

3 Law as a Promise

In this paper, I would argue that the ongoing holdout litigation on Argentinian sovereign debt has succeed in bringing attention to law as a fundamental question in sovereign debt lending, a phenomenon that is often deemed as purely economic, or a policy question. How to deal with holdout litigation in sovereign debt restructurings has been of scholarly and institutional concerns for many years (for instance, Gelpern 2005). However, when addressing the fulfillment of holdouts' claims in previous sovereign debt renegotiations, experts tend to frame the question as economic.[14]

As a central implication of the judicial saga on Argentine bonds, contractual terms such as pari passu and RUFO that will be discussed further, have been put under the spotlight, not only in their textuality and material aggregation to sovereign debt contracts, which has been addressed by a vast law review literature (Mokal 2001; Buchheit and Pam 2004; Varotill 2008–2009; Gulati and Scott 2013; Weidemaier et al. 2013, among others), but as indexical of strategies and forms of expertise.

The promise that the equal treatment protection of a pari passu clause can be made a reality encourages investors to continue to participate in the sovereign debt market... This simple promise of equality is understood by the original investors in the sovereign debt, is understood by today's investors, and is recognized by the courts that have been asked to enforce pari passu's plain language." (Cohen 2011, 14).

According to the above opinion-which by no means can be taken as representative of all the creditors' voices[15]-contractual terms are inscriptions that would realize the conditions envisioned by the parties to enter into business. Thus, law is assumed as neutral, plain, and, in some extent, inevitable. This means-to-an end quintessencialism of the law would preclude any consideration of the context in which law is produced, circulates and is implemented; that is, law as a historical construction. Nonetheless, in this judicial case, the political context in which the clause (and the overall agreement) was enacted arguably has set the basis of the court's understanding of the actual debtor's intension. As Boyack notes, contract law presumes writing "is the best indication of contracting party intend and several key legal doctrines are based on build this assumed primacy of a written document" (2013, 20). But, on the other hand, as Derrida remarks, meaning does not lie just in a text but in the writing and reading of it (Hodder 2000, 704); though, words in context (in a Derridean sense), "are not malleable putty that can mean anything we desire (Yablon 1990, 1352).[16] In the present case, the question about judicial interpretation of contractual terms has moved the analysis beyond the framework of the agreement document to delve into the wider political, legal and economic circumstances at play in a concrete experience of debt restructuring. I will return to this point the next section.

---

[14] An exception is Gulati and Scott's interpretation of Peru's willingness to a quick settlement with Elliot after the court's ruling due to domestic politics issues.

[15] For instance, the bonds eligible for exchange in Argentina's debt restructuring were held by 700,000 creditors with differing interests. Arguably, to coordinate with them was one of the biggest problems facing the restructuring. (Garcia-Hamilton et al. 2005: 257, note 61). See accompanying text.

[16] In his analysis of the materiality of the summons, probably the most routine legal form in civil action in the US, Yablon remarks that this form, understood in the context of production and reading, also becomes "an instrument of power and pain" (1990, 1353).

In addition, since the late 1970s' the world of sovereign debt restructuring has experienced changes in the legal environment that made "much easier for holdout creditors to obtain judgment claims" (Panizza et al. 2009, 659). Accordingly, courts have held the interpretation of contractual terms advanced by the plaintiffs (Gulati and Scott 2013) either it is the" plain meaning" of the text, as in Cohen's understanding (2011); or a historical (original) meaning, as suggested by the judicial decision on the Argentinian case. The dependence on context, as shown by recent litigation on sovereign debt does not imply a need to regard law—more concretely, the law of sovereign debt lending-as the direct expression of (extra-legal) power; nor as its necessary antithesis. Rather, it speaks about how law and politics are intertwined, and the strategical character of such association.

4 Crafting the Law

According to Johns, a deal is not a domain of pure freedom. In fact, there are rules ("background rules" in her words) "by which legal choosers and choices are shaped, circumscribed, and empowered" (2008, 256). In sovereign lending agreements in particular, there are some clauses subject to standardization; that are often referred to as "boilerplate provisions". As I mentioned above, among these terms is the pari passu clause, which, as legal scholars stress, is repeatedly used in sovereign debt documents even in the face of adverse judicial interpretation to the sovereign debtor's interest (Gulati and Scott 2014).

Certainly throughout my research I was puzzled over the inclusion of the pari passu provision in Argentinian sovereign debt restructuring agreements of 2005 and 2010. I could not help but think that Argentina's legal counsels should have known the 2000 Brussels Court of Appeals' ruling in *Elliott Assocs*. I wondered why the pari passu had persisted in the exchange bonds, and why the drafters had chosen one of its most problematic versions (cf. Weidemaier et al. 2014). This commonsensical question that I naively posed to my interlocutors was successfully turned into an object of inquiry by Gulati and Scott (2013), who framed the resilience of the pari passu provision in sovereign debt contracts as a "sticky" boilerplate issue. As I briefly mentioned in the introduction, these authors discussed extensively the problem of "sticky" boilerplate clauses by drawing on empirical data collected from interviews with hundreds of experienced lawyers. After exploring various theories of contract form stickiness as regards as the use of pari passu in sovereign debt practice, these scholars conclude, on the grounds of their findings, that elite law firms fail, for different reasons, to engage in contract research and design (ibid). This "structurally engendered agency failure" (ibid, 105) of law firms means in Boyack's words that they "firms discourage contract evolution, push transactional volume and conformity, and penalize innovation" (2013, 17).

Like Gulati and Scott's respondents, my legal interlocutors in Argentina could not give any cogent explanation of the adoption of the pari passu clause in sovereign debt instruments after the aforementioned decision by the Belgian court of appeals.

They just took the pari passu provision for granted. This is not surprising. Like Gulati and Scott's respondents, my subjects inhabit the very sophisticated world of global financial markets that makes them part of the transnational expert elite. And they hold this symbolic capital with pride. Additionally, their expertise secures them their continuing participation in the kinds of deals and transactions performed in sovereign debt restructurings. "Expertise makes you stay", a counsel on sovereign debt told me, explaining that usually governments and private actors such as banks or corporations do not hire any law firm to perform capital market transactions.

The more standard the contractual terms are, the more likely they will be understood by potential exchange participants, another lawyer asserted, pointing out to me the deferral of contract drafting practices to market decisions as well as the idea that innovation is not allowed in the making of financial instruments, to which I referred above. Underlying this statement is the idea that standardized contractual terms-as opposed to innovative provisions-look more attractive to market agents because "they have been proven already", to quote this lawyer. Noticeably, this reasoning recalls the secondary place that lawyers in my field assign to law in the context of debt restructuring proceedings. As I referred about, legal experts tended to downplay the role of law by highlighting the dense array of political strategies and influences that partake in sovereign lending negotiations.

Concerning the durability of the pari passu in Argentina's debt instruments, a lawyer mentioned to me that that clause was already in an old bond issued in 1994 that was replaced by new securities in the 2005 debt exchange. The terms of new bonds just repeated the wording of the old clause which, in his view, was poorly written. Interestingly, another corporate lawyer indicated that from his point of view, there had not been a definition about the meaning of the pari passu until the New York court's ruling in the holdout litigation against Argentina. Moreover, this lawyer, like other legal experts, had interpreted this clause to have a different meaning than that advanced by the New York court. But even more remarkably, as I anticipated and will discuss further, is my interlocutors' view of this latter case not as a question of interpretation of a written document. For them, what has been at stake here is the broader political context in which this document is inscribed.

Of course, there is a caveat in respondents' accounts. Lawyers, for instance, may not want to reflect the actual "role they or their firms played in producing or maintaining the problematic version of the pari passu" (Weidemaier et al. 2014, 94). In this sense, it was noticeable in my field the lawyers and ex-civil servants' willingness to draw a line between foreign and native law firms while addressing the question of the pari passu in Argentina's debt restructuring agreements. Accordingly, for many of my respondents the version of this clause that appeared in the agreements was introduced by a foreign law firm that "traditionally" has served as Argentina's legal counsel on sovereign debt issuance under NY Law. I would like to reframe this caveat as a question of both individual and collective interests that are encountered in sovereign debt lending, as suggested by another informant, a well-known public finance expert. By recalling examples drawn from the 2005 debt restructuring, he reflected on law as an instrument that also serves professional agendas.

5 The Making of a "Unique" Situation

In addition to contractual terms such as the pari passu discussed above, the choice of foreign law and forum as the applicable law to the contract are often encountered in emerging market bonds deals. For my interviewees, to subject the deal to foreign law (usually the law of New York or England) was something they take for granted too. It is argued, an expert explained to me, that having a foreign law and court governing the deal makes it more "stable" and provides a "neutral" venue for adjudicating potential claims.[17] Underlying this argument, there is an assumption that emergent countries are not reliable enough to fulfill the payments due to their creditors. However, to have a foreign-currency and foreign-law debt stock does not grant necessarily market confidence to an emergent country. On the contrary, sometimes it raises the spreads of its debt to a point that undermines the aimed confidence, as shown by the Argentine situation previous to its 2001 debt default (cf. Gelpern 2005).

Despite the provisions of foreign legal regimes that pervade emerging market debt contracts, the evolution of capital markets debts has made sovereign bonded debt very complex and vast to the extent that a country's debt stock may be governed by multiple legal regimes, including its domestic law. The Argentine debt that was restructured in 2005 was not an exception. In fact, it included 152 bonds held by thousands of creditors. Those securities had been issued in six different currencies and under eight different laws (Chodos 2011). As a result of the exchange, the old securities were replaced by new 11 bonds issued in four currencies under four applicable laws (ibid). According to experts, the large amount of debt to be restructured and the atomistic composition of the bondholders made the situation were unique up to that date. In Gelpern's understanding, Argentina's debt swap marked "a big shift in scale and tone, if not technique" from previous debt restructuring experiences. However, in her view, what was all the most impressive of the Argentine debt exchange, was that "it proceeded against the background of thousands of creditors' lawsuits, mostly in Argentina, but also dozens in New York and over 100 in Europe" (ibid. 21).

Interestingly, in my subjects' descriptions of the context in which the 2005 debt exchange developed, they did not mention any lawsuit filed with either domestic or foreign courts as a potential jeopardy to the restructuring,[18] though a few of them acknowledged that something different might have been done then to solve the

[17] A recent analysis of the judicial saga on Argentinian defaulted bonds pursued by the holdouts postulates that it actually contributes to destabilizing NY's place as a "stable" and "neutral" forum. See, "Where the Argentine Debt Case Stands Now, and Why it Still Matters" available at https://nacla.org/news/2015/04/06/where-argentine-debt-case-stands-now-and-why-it-still-matters (accessed June 29, 2015), I thank Karen Faulk for this reference.

[18] Nonetheless, the action of vulture funds against debt restructuring proceedings was an important issue of political concern at that time. See, for instance, Argentina's President Nestor Kichner's discourse to Congress explaining the results of the 2005 debt restructuring on March 3rd 2005, http://www.casarosada.gob.ar/discursosnk/24701-blank-21716353 (accessed June 9, 2015).

holdout litigation that spawned afterwards. In general terms, my interlocutors accounted for other kinds of impediments that the restructuring process had to overcome. Among them, they found that the market acceptance of the terms and conditions of the debt exchange proposal was the most challenging. To get a favorable reception to the proposed restructuring it was essential?, they said, to convey to the financial world the image of Argentina as a *trustworthy* and *predictable* agent.

Argentina's need to recover from a history of recurring bad political and economic decisions that had triggered the country's stagnation was part of quasi-foundational official rhetoric of change that spawned after the 2001–2002 crisis and intensified after the inauguration of President Nestor Kirchner (2003–2007) in May 2003. In this context, transparency, accountability, and predictability became the buzzwords of a larger discourse of social change aimed at regaining public confidence in Argentina's legal and political institutions, both domestically and internationally. Accordingly, Argentina's need to solve the problem of its excessive indebtedness, or to achieve a sustainable economic growth in order to pay its creditors, or still the willingness to negotiate in *good faith*, among other official statements made by that time, can also be interpreted as part of rhetorical strategy conducive to similar ends. Yet, that strategy needed to be translated into concrete tools that were able to reflect the uniqueness of the Argentine situation,[19] as interpreted by the government actors.

Accordingly, a series of provisions were introduced into the financial instruments issued in the 2005 debt restructuring program.[20] Among them, the new debt issuance (that is, the bonds that would be issued in place of the outstanding debt) would have a value recovery right linked to the country's Gross Domestic Product (GDP) to make the exchange offer more attractive to bondholders.[21] However, from my interlocutors' point of view, the innovation of Argentina's 2005 debt exchange with regard to past sovereign debt restructuring experiences was that this country adopted a clause called RUFO.[22] According to this contractual term, the accepting creditors of the new securities would be entitled to participate in any transaction

[19] More recently, the "uniqueness" of Argentina's situation has been argued in support of the NY court's decisions in *MNL vs. Argentina*. However, as Gelpern notably states, a more useful question is whether "Argentina's courtroom dramas might or might not impact crisis and restructuring going forward" than arguing about its uniqueness. See Anna Gelpern: "Missed Payment Date Musings-Offshore Openings, Free Riding the Free Riders, and Argentina's 'Uniqueness'", *Credit Slips,* available at http://www.creditslips.org/creditslips/2014/06/missed-payment-date-musings.html (accessed November 14th 2014).

[20] See the Prospectus Supplement (to the Prospectus Dated on December 27 2004), available at http://www.mecon.gov.ar/finanzas/download/us_prospectus_and_prospectus_supplement.pdf (accessed May 5 2015). For a good summary of the debt restructuring final proposal presented on January 12 2005, see Garcia-Hamilton et al. (2005).

[21] The Value Recovery Right would annually increase the payments resulting from the new bonds in the event that Argentina's GDP growth during the year exceeded the calculus done by the Argentine government (Garcia-Hamilton et al. 2005: 262).

[22] See the Prospectus Supplement. Or more simply, in Gelpern's words: "It is a promise by Argentina to the restructured bondholders that, should it give holdouts more favorable terms, the restructured bondholders would get the same", See Anna Gelpern, "Argentina: The RUFO Crazy",

(voluntary purchase, exchange, offer to purchase or exchange extended or agreed) with holdout creditors. But they also noted that this "most favored creditor clause" was not written from scratch. Indeed, it draws on the *Most-Favored Nation* (MFN) clause that rules international trading. In fact, the MFN (meaning treating other people equally) is one of the WTO basic principles.[23] Moreover, a few of my respondents recalled that this kind of contractual provision was used in a previous debt restructuring program from another country, though they were very imprecise about the date and the country's name.

Noticeably, the above comments reinforce, on the one hand, the sovereign debt experts' *discourse*[24] about the lack of creation and innovation that permeates sovereign debt agreements. On the other hand, they evoke Weidemaier, Scott and Gulati's representation of the field of sovereign debt lawyering as a venue where legal experts tend to replicate vague stories about the origin of some contractual terms (for instance, the pari passu) which at certain point become like a myth (2013).

However, the descriptions that my subjects gave of the RUFO clause was more in terms of the function that, in their view, this provision was aimed to perform than in terms of its history. They described the Argentine's proposal of debt exchange as an "extreme" situation. It was extreme, a lawyer explained to me, because the issuance of new debt in conditions of debt default is *per se* a very complex phenomenon and, in the Argentinian case in particular, the new bonds established a 75 % write-off over the nominal value of the total outstanding debt. Certainly, such a condition did not make the proposal attractive for bondholders to enter into the exchange. As one informant recalled, it was an economist working as adviser to Argentina, who argued that nobody would "buy" a proposal for exchange with a 75 % cut off, and came across with the conditions that finally made up for the RUFO clause. Other respondents, however, did not remember who the intellectual author of this clause was, but they did remember that it was discussed originally in negotiations between the Argentine government and the banks that provided it with technical support on the debt exchange.

To make a point on the extraordinary context of the 2005 debt restructuring, a lawyer recounted that at the outset of negotiations between government officers and participating banks there was a request that the financial instruments to be offered in exchange of old securities should encompass conditions that would make the exchange financially attractive to the potential bondholders. In contrast to this, in "ordinary conditions', that is, in non-debt default contexts, discussions on debt issuance usually begin by the figures that are translated later in to legal forms.

Accordingly, the RUFO was thought as a political strategy for marketing purposes rather than as a concrete economic incentive offered to bondholders (Garcia-

---

Credit Slips. 2014, available at http://www.creditslips.org/creditslips/2014/07/argentina-the-rufo-crazy.html (accessed November 14th 2014). The RUFO expired on January 1st 2015.

[23] See, Principles of the trading system, https://www.wto.org/english/thewto_e/whatis_e/tif_e/fact2_e.htm#seebox (accessed on June 8, 2015).

[24] As Weidemaier, Gulati and Scott (2013) note, there is a difference between legal counsels' discourse and practice.

Hamilton et al. 2005). Of course, investors must have evaluated the cost of opportunity and financial risk in deciding whether or not to accept Argentina's offer. But beyond any cost analysis, the RUFO was there "to guarantee to the accepting creditors the offer "that no better terms would be offered to other creditors" (ibid., 259). As another respondent, a lawyer, indicated, the provision sought to make investors believe that no other and better opportunity of payment of the defaulted bonds would be offered by the Argentine government. In the words of a legal scholar, "the bondholders were faced with the choice between taking the exchange bonds, ensuring partial return on principal, or retaining the original bonds, which Argentina made clear it had no intention of honoring" (Neve 2013–2014, 635).

After the confirmation of the New York court's ruling that favored the holdouts' position against Argentina, the RUFO clause became subject to different and opposed interpretations.. The Argentinian government stated that, due to the terms of the RUFO clause, to fulfill the holdouts' claim as mandated by the US court, would force it (the government) to take the same step as regards as those creditors who had exchanged their bonds in 2005 and 2010, respectively. And that, the government's representatives argued, would affect the country's finances very dramatically.[25] In contrast to this opinion, some of my interlocutors argued that it was unlikely that the court's ruling would make it mandatory for Argentina to extend future payments to the holdouts to the exchange bondholders. In their opinion, the terms of the RUFO referred to "voluntary" transactions; and hence, a judicial settlement would be excluded from the scope of the norm.[26] No settlement between the parties has been reached yet; and even subsequent rulings by the same court decided new claims brought by other plaintiffs on similar basis to that granted to the holdout litigants.[27]

According to my informants, the drafters of the exchange agreement did not foresee the kind of conflict that the RUFO allegedly triggered. Above all, they explain, the RUFO was aimed to convey the message to the holders of the defaulted debt that they should exchange their old bonds for the new securities because Argentina would not give its creditors any other chance of payment than the 2005 offer.[28] The intended unique and exceptional character of the debt exchange was

[25] See, for instance, El gobierno advirtió que la clausula RUFO podria disparar un pasivo de u$s 500 mil millones, INFOBAE, available at http://www.infobae.com/2014/07/21/1582136-el-gobierno-advirtio-que-la-clausula-rufo-podria-disparar-un-pasivo-us500-mil-millones (accessed June 16, 2015); Rufo y coma, el que lo activa se embroma, Pagina 12, available at http://www.pagina12.com.ar/diario/economia/2-251656-2014-07-27.html (accessed June 16, 2015); El gobierno busca postegar hasta diciembre el pago a los holdouts, La Nación, available at http://www.lanacion.com.ar/1707771-el-gobierno-busca-postergar-hasta-diciembre-el-pago-a-los-holdout (accessed June 16 2015).

[26] For an interesting analysis of the mess about the RUFO clause, see Gelpern, 2014, available at www. "Argentina: The RUFO Crazy" (accessed November 14th 2014).

[27] These creditors are known as the "me too". They are also holders of securities who decided to opt out the 2005 and 2010 exchanges. See *infra* 1.

[28] There was another opportunity to swap old defaulted bonds by new securities in 2010.

reinforced by the passing of Law 26017, known as Lock Law (*Ley Cerrojo*),[29] by Argentinian Congress a few days before the end of the 2005 exchange. The statute was approved by a wide congressional majority and its passing was very quick (Chodos 2011). This norm forbade government officials to reopen the bond exchange offer to allow the creditors of defaulted bonds to swap them for new securities after the deadline. The purpose, it was argued, was to limit the government's capacity of maneuver (ibid., 2011). Overall, the Lock Law was deemed by government officials a key element to strengthen Argentina's credibility and make visible that the government was conducting the debt exchange proceedings in *good faith* (ibid., 2011).[30]

Interestingly though, it was the enactment of Lock Law which, according to my informants, became the issue that set up the grounds of the judicial interpretation of the NY district court that ruled against Argentina, holding that the country had treated differently the exchange bondholders *vis-à-vis* the creditors who decided to opt out the debt restructurings. In their understanding of the judicial decision, what breached the law—namely the equal treatment clause as interpreted by the judge—was not the contractual terms but the political context in which the agreement was performed. That is to say, it was not the contract wording what was under scrutiny, but how its words played out in a concrete context.

6 Conclusion

In this essay, I have proposed to think of the relationship between Law and Pragmatism ethnographically by focusing on means-ends orientation of legal reasoning. The field of financial markets is a very interesting venue to explore the workings of that relationship. Commonplace representations of market transactions advance the idea of an *a priori* distinction between fact and value. Accordingly, law is seen as purely instrumental to a market rationality that builds upon a rational actor model, and policy debates are shadowed by forms and practices that are often associated with private interests and governance. Remarkably, this view is shared in general by the legal experts that I met in the field of sovereign debt in Argentina, who see the law's workings as marginal to the process of making financial debt instruments.

In the midst of the political discussions triggered by the holdouts litigation on Argentina's bond debt, the place of law has remained "collateral", to quote Riles

[29] See Law 26017, Boletin Oficial de la República Argentina 30590, February 11th 2005, 1. The Lock Law was one of the laws lifted by the Argentine Congress on March 31st 2016, thus, paving the way for the Macri Administration´s settlement with the holdouts. See Law 27249, Boletín Oficial de la República Argentina 33348, April 1st 2016, 1. See also *infra* 2.

[30] The effects of Lock Law had been suspended only temporarily by Law 26547 (Boletin Oficial de la República Argentina 31798, December 10th 2009, p. 1) to enable the Executive to launch a new debt exchange in 2010.

again (2011). And yet, when public opinion and the press shifted their attention to legal provisions such as the pari passu and RUFO that judicial scrutiny put under the spotlight, these legal terms were deemed as pieces of a broader economic and political endeavor, that is, the means to achieve a social end.

This essay has aimed to challenge those representations of law by focusing on the means rather than the ends. Accordingly, I have proposed to look at legal forms as sites of knowledge-making and not taken-for-granted instruments. In this vein, knowledge may be manifested in different forms: it can be perceived as a failure of agency (as in Gulati and Scott's work and suggested by my informants); or an overreaction to a contingent political context (as in my subjects' appreciation of the passing of Lock Law). And even, it may be oriented toward multiple ends, as pointed out by one of informant's framing of sovereign debt default through the binary collective-individual interests. By unpacking the pragmatic knowledge practices embedded in the constitution of legal forms, ultimately I have sought to foreground the technical character of law as a site of creation, dispute, validation and circulation of knowledge, as well as the instantiation of relations, subjectivities and power.[31]

References

Barrera, L. (2012). Relocalizing the judicial space: Place, access and mobilization in judicial practice in post-crisis Argentina. *Law, Culture and the Humanities, 8*(2), 350–373.

Boyack, A. J. (2013–2014). Sovereign debt and the three and a half minute transaction: What sticky boilerplate reveals about contract law and practice. *Whittier Law Review, 35*, 1–25.

Buchheit, L. C., & Pam, J. S. (2004). The Pari Passu clause in sovereign debt instruments. *Emory Law Journal, 53*, 869–922.

Chodos, S. (2011). La Experiencia Argentina. *Buenos Aires sovereign debt seminar: The missing link in the International Financial Architecture.* Available at http://www.mecon.gov.ar/finanzas/deuda%20soberana/corrales.pdf. Accessed 6 Mar 2015.

Cohen, R. A. (2011). 'Sometimes a cigar is just a cigar': The simple story of Pari Passu. *Hofstra Law Review, 40*, 11–23.

Espósito, C., Li, Y., & Bohoslavsky, J. P. (2013). *Sovereign financing and international law The UNCTAD principles on responsible*. Oxford: Oxford University Press.

Garcia-Hamilton, J., Olivares-Caminal, R., & Zenarruza, O. (2005). The required threshold to restructure sovereign debt. *Loyola of Los Angeles International and Comparative Law Review, 27*, 249–274.

Gelpern, A. (2005). What bond markets can learn from Argentina. *International Finance Law Review, 2015*(April), 19–24.

Gelpern, A. (2013). A skeptic's case for sovereign bankruptcy. *Houston Law Review, 50*, 1095–1127.

Gelpern, A. (2014). Missed Payment Date Musings-Offshore Openings, Free Riding the Free Riders, and Argentina;s 'Uniqueness", Credit Slips, at http://www.creditslips.org/creditslips/2014/06/missed-paymentdate-musings.html.

[31] I want to express my gratitude to all my interlocutors for sharing their time and knowledge. For careful reading and insightful comments to this piece, I am deeply grateful to Karen Faulk and Sergio Muro. I am also thankful to two anonymous reviewers and book co-editor Francesca Poggi, who provided me with incredible support for the writing of this piece.

Goddard, V. (2006). This is history. Nation and experience in Times of Crisis–Argentina 2001. *History and Anthropology, 17*(3), 267–286.

Gulati, M., & Klee, K. N. (2001). Sovereign piracy. *The Business Lawyer, 56*, 635–651.

Gulati, M., & Scott, R. E. (2013). *The three and a half minute transaction. Boilerplate and the limits of contract design*. Chicago: The University of Chicago Press.

Hodder, I. (2000). The Intepretation of Documents and Material Culture", *Handbook of Qualitative Research*, Second Edition, N. K. Denzin and Y. S. Lincoln ed. Thousands Oaks, CA: Sage Publications, 703–15.

International Monetary Fund (2002). The Design of Sovereign Debt Restructuring Mechanisms–Further considerations, at: https://www.imf.org/external/np/pdr/sdrm/2002/112702.pdf.

Johns, F. (2008). Performing party autonomy. Transdiciplinary conflict of laws. *Law and Contemporary Problems, 71*(3), 243–271.

Kellogg, F. R. (2012). American pragmatism and European social theory: Holmes, Durkheim, Scheler, and the sociology of legal knowledge. *European Journal of Pragmatism and American Philosophy, 4*(1), 107–119.

Latorre, S. (2012). *Legal technicalities in conditions of political conflict: The case of land tenure disputes in Colombia*. J.S.D. dissertation, Cornell University.

Latour, B. (2004). *La fabrique du droit. Une ethnographie du Conseil d'État*. Paris: La Découverte/Poche.

Levi, R., & Valverde, M. (2008). Studying law by association: Bruno Latour goes to the Conseil d'Etat. *Law & Social Inquiry, 33*, 805–825.

Llewellyn, K. (1930–1931). Some realism about realism. Responding to dean pound. *Harvard Law Review, 44*, 1222–1264.

Mokal, R. J. (2001). Priority as pathology: The *Pari Passu* myth. *Cambridge Law Journal, 60*, 581–621.

Neve, B. (2013). *NML* Capital, Ltd. v. Republic of Argentina: An alternative to the inadequate remedies under the Foreign Sovereign Immunities Act. *North Carolina Journal of International Law and Commercial Regulation, 39*, 631–673.

Olivares-Caminal, R. (2009). Understanding the *Pari Passu* clause in sovereign debt instruments: A complex quest. *The International Lawyer, 43*, 1217–1236.

Panizza, U., Sturzenegger, F., & Zettelmeyer, J. (2009). The economics and Law of sovereign debt and default. *Journal of Economic Literature, 47*(3), 651–698.

Pound, R. (1908). Mechanical jurisprudence. *Columbia Law Review, 8*, 605–623.

Riles, A. (2005). A new agenda for the cultural study of law: Taking on the technicalities. *Buffalo Law Review, 53*, 392–405.

Riles, A. (2011). *Collateral knowledge. Legal reasoning in global financial markets*. Chicago: University of Chicago Press.

Roubini, N. (2002). *Do we need a new bankruptcy regime?* Available at www.stern.nyu.edu/sites/default/files/assets/documents/con_039551.pdf. Accessed 18 Mar 2015.

Sarat, A., Douglas, L., & Umphrey, M. M. (2003). Where (Or what) is the place of law? An introduction. In A. Sarat, L. Douglas, & M. Merrill Umphrey (Eds.), *The place of law* (pp. 1–20). Ann Arbor: The University of Michigan Press.

Smulovitz, C. (2006). Protest by other means. Legal mobilization in the Argentinian crisis. In E. Peruzzotti & C. Smulovitz (Eds.), *Enforcing the rule of law. Citizens and the media in Latin America* (pp. 55–74). Pittsburgh: Pittsburgh University Press.

UNCTAD (2012). Principles on Promoting Responsible Sovereing Lending and Borrowing, at http://unctad.org/en/PublicationsLibrary/gdsddf2012misc1_en.pdf.

Valverde, M. (2003). Pragmatist and non-pragmatist knowledge practices in American law, symposium: Ethnography in the realm of the pragmatic: Studying pragmatism in law and politics. *PoLAR: The Political and Legal Anthropology Review, 26*(2), 86–108.

Valverde, M. (2009). Jurisdiction and scale: Legal 'technicalities' as resources for theory. *Social and Legal Studies, 18*(2), 139–158.

Varotill, U. (2008–2009). Sovereign debt documentation: Unraveling the *Pari Passu* mystery. *DePaul Business & Commercial Law Journal, 7*, 119–143.

Von Bogdandy, A., & Goldmann, M. (2013). *Sovereign debt restructurings as exercises of International Public Authority: Towards a decentralized sovereign insolvency law*. Available at http://ssrn.com/abstract=2089480 or http://dx.doi.org/10.2139/ssrn.208948. Accessed 9 Apr 2015.

Weidemaier, M., Scott, R. E., & Gulati, M. (2013). Origin myths, contracts, and the hunt for *Pari Passu*. *Law & Social Inquiry, 38*(1), 72–105.

Weidemaier, W., Mark, C., & Gelpern, A. (2014). Injunctions in sovereign debt litigation. *Yale Journal on Regulation, 31*, 189–218.

Yablon, C. M. (1990). Forms. *Cardozo Law Review, 11*(5), 1349–1353.

The Role of Pragmatics in the Web of Data

Pompeu Casanovas, Víctor Rodríguez-Doncel, and Jorge González-Conejero

Abstract This chapter is an introduction to the Semantic Web, the Web of Data, regulatory models, and the law. It does not take anything for granted. The first part of the chapter describes the languages of the Semantic Web, and shows how the perspective of the Web of Services and Linked Data is related to the conditions under which services can be offered, managed and used. The Web has been massively populated with both data and services. Semantically structured data, the Linked Data Cloud, allows and fosters human-machine interaction. Linked Data aims at creating ecosystems to facilitate the browsing, discovery, exploitation and reuse of datasets for applications. Licensed Linked Data is offered along with information about the rights involved. Rights Expression Languages are able to regulate half-automatically the use and reuse of content.

The second part of the chapter shows that the nature of law is experiencing a deep transformation in the cloud. What links the information flow, social intelligence, rights management, and modelling in the Web of Data is the pragmatic approach —what we call the *pragmatic turn, i*.e. the representation of users' needs and contexts to facilitate the automated interactive and collective management of knowledge. Both ontology building and knowledge acquisition share this perspective. The Web of Data brings about new challenges on agency, knowledge, communication, and the coordination of actions. Institutions can regulate both human and machine behaviours within these new environments. *Licensed Linked Data, Licensed Linguistic Linked Data, Right Expression Languages, Semantic Web*

P. Casanovas (✉)
UAB Institute of Law and Technology (IDT), Autonomous University of Barcelona, Barcelona, Spain

Data to Decisions Cooperative Research Centre, Deakin Law School, Deakin University, Geelong, Australia
e-mail: pompeu.casanovas@uab.cat; p.casanovasromeu@deakin.edu.au

V. Rodríguez-Doncel
Ontology Engineering Group, Universidad Politécnica de Madrid, Madrid, Spain
e-mail: vrodriguez@fi.upm.es

J. González-Conejero
UAB Institute of Law and Technology, Autonomous University of Barcelona, Barcelona, Spain
e-mail: jorge.gonzalez.conejero@uab.cat

F. Poggi, A. Capone (eds.), *Pragmatics and Law*, Perspectives in Pragmatics, Philosophy & Psychology 10, DOI 10.1007/978-3-319-44601-1_12

Regulatory Models, *Electronic Institutions*, *Artificial Socio-cognitive Systems* are examples of regulatory and institutional design (Regulations by Design). Regulatory systems become more complex in the cloud, in order to be simpler.

Keywords Web of Data • Semantic Web • Regulatory model • Linked Data • Licenses

1 Introduction

According to (Kasper and Rose 1999) pragmatics has two roles in socio-linguistic analysis, (i) it acts as a constraint on linguistic forms and their acquisition (representing a type of communicative knowledge); and (ii) on a par with morphosyntax, lexis, and phonology it focuses on learners' knowledge, use, and acquisition of pragmatics in a second language (interlanguage pragmatics).

However, if pragmatics is seen through the prism of human-machine interaction considering the cognitive and computational perspectives, we may go a bit further. Machine-languages (models) are a kind of second language, too. We will use functional and cognitive pragmatics as a part of a broader methodology. In this sense, stemming from technology and law, a third role comes into play, as pragmatics is able to bridge common and expert knowledge into iterative cycles of legal practical analysis and computational modelling.

First, we will focus on the Web of Data, setting the contextual requirements for such an aim —not in vain, the Web is the space where the most relevant human-machine communication acts take place. In particular, we will analyse the Linked Data cloud, as a semantised subset of the Web of Data. Second, we will describe the crucial role of pragmatics to help debugging the so-called "*knowledge acquisition bottleneck*" (Feigenbaum 1984, 1992). It is our contention that such an approach can better define the situated knowledge that is needed to set platforms and build up legal ontologies, functionalities, applications and mash-ups within social ecosystems. This constitutes a particular theoretical trend. Third, we will state that this kind of bridge requires the construction of intermediate institutions —*Semantic Web Regulatory Models* (SWRM)— to anchor the reuse of ontologies, datasets, and general knowledge into specific contextual legal settings. At present, there are coordination and cohesion problems between the regulatory instruments —law, policies, standards, and ethical principles— and the scenarios set forth within the Web of Data. Fourth, we will concentrate on licenses for Linked Data on the Web. The lawful consumption of online datasets across different jurisdictions constitutes a good example of regulatory problem, and the mere idea of having Licensed Linked Data (data semantically described with a machine-readable rights expression) deserves our analysis. Fifth, we will discuss the use of autonomous agents and Electronic Institutions to behave and to perform legal acts in this new environment. In the end, we will introduce some contextual and anchorage problems of Artificial Socio-cognitive Systems (ASCS).

At the implementation level, the reuse of knowledge patterns on a Web of Linked Data needs to be much more specific about design conditions, strategies and guidelines. This is what Hoekstra (2010) has called "*the knowledge reengineering bottleneck*". We think that this chapter will contribute to clarify and partially solve the cost of control in the new scenarios raised by the Web of Data.

2 The Web of Services and Linked Data: A Broad Landscape

The Web is not only the place where the most exciting information lives, but also a scenario where things *happen*. Besides passive information, actions can be triggered, either having a physical effect in the real world or a purely informational effect. The regular provision of these actions is organised through *services*, which are invoked by humans and machine alike. One informational service may offer the current temperature in Barcelona; another service may place a purchase order in the stock market.

In the last few years the Web has been massively populated with both data and services. Data has been offered by public and private organizations, by sensing devices (Internet of Things) and by internet users in social networking users. A small fraction of this Web of Data is the so called *Linked Data cloud*, with special interest for its semantic foundation. The Linked Data cloud is perhaps the most visible result of the Semantic Web (SW) vision, an endeavour aimed at providing structure to the Web so that machines can better understand it. This section analyses the Service Web, the Linked Data cloud and a further fragment of it: the *Licensed* Linked Data (LLD), namely, Linked Data that is offered along with rich semantic rights information.

2.1 The Web of Data

2.1.1 The Semantic Web

The World Wide Web is estimated to contain information in the order of zettabytes, but raw data is still a small share of it: many Web pages are built based on databases which are not directly accessible, and most information is in an unstructured form difficult to parse by computers. The inventor of the World Wide Web, Tim Berners-Lee, conceived the idea of connecting all the data on the Web, establishing relationships between data published by different entities. Information would then build the Giant Global Graph, a unique global database, a *Web of Data*.

For this information to be comparable, data on the Web had to be structured and intelligible for computers. He was thinking of the *Semantic Web*; in his own words:

> The first step is putting data on the Web in a form that machines can naturally understand, or converting it to that form. This creates what I call a Semantic Web – a web of data that can be processed directly or indirectly by machines (Berners-Lee 1999, 191)

This vision would open up vast amounts of data to be mined by Artificial Intelligence processes, enabling a smarter use of the resources, increasing the productivity of the society and improving the understanding of our world. Public institutions, companies and individuals were invited to dump their data in open standard formats, to build the Web of Data as the WWW had been.

These open standard formats would eventually be published by the W3C, the guardian of the WWW essences. One of the grounds of the Semantic Web is RDF (*Resource Description Framework).* RDF is a standard model for data interchange on the Web that organises information as small units called *RDF triples*: one subject, one predicate and one object. Each of the elements in this triple can be related to elements in other triples, weaving a web of relationship –an RDF graph.

By the time RDF appeared, XML was at its peak. XML is a good serialisation format, namely, a good way of encoding information so that two computers can understand it. But these two computers must have agreed on the structure of the XML document. There is no XML format, but many XML formats. Different computer programs use different XML structures and XML merely defines a syntax. Grammars can be defined with other standards in the XML family, like DTD or XML Schema. Semantics are outside the realm of the XML specification. However, semantic interoperability with RDF is much easier. In RDF all objects are independent entities and mapping between two RDF models is a straightforward task. So even if two organizations want to exchange data in different RDF models, aligning the models (either manually or automatically) is a much easier task than with XML.

The way of identifying objects in the Semantic Web is using URIs (Uniform Resource Identifier). While XML grammars never aimed at being universal, RDF willingly accepts that two different modellers referring to the same concept use the same identifier.

Computer scientists like enumerating two alternatives to declaring semantics: *procedural* and *declarative*. In the procedural approach, the meaning of an expression is given by describing the effect that some procedure (e.g. a computer program) will have on it. In the declarative approach, the meaning of an expression is given by describing its properties or the conclusions that can be derived from it. The latter approach (which is the one followed by RDF) is considered to be a more shareable and extensible form of declaring semantics.

Further, the RDF models can be supported by OWL ontologies (Ontology Web Language).[1] OWL facilitates reasoning (a simple deductive reasoning) through sets and properties that model formally concepts, relationships and instances. The result drives to information management and processing as *knowledge —hypertext* links, connection of objects, and information retrieval from the Web using not keywords

[1] For a technical introduction, cfr. Antoniou and van Harmelen (2004, 2012), cfr. also Domingue et al. (2011).

Table 1 Semantic web technologies

	Hypertext technologies
Web 1.0/2.0	IRI [*Internationalised Resource Identifier*], generalization of URI [*Uniform Resource Identifier*], it facilitates the identification of semantic resources to manipulate and handle them.
Web 1.0/2.0	*Unicode* is a codification standard of features of multiple technical and natural languages (including the ancient ones). It drives to uniformity, unicity and universality of their representation.
Web 1.0/2.0	XML [*Extensible Mark-up Language*] is a tag or mark-up language (a meta-language in fact) defining a set of documents in a readable format language, either by humans or by machines.[a]
Web 1.0/2.0	*XML Schema* is a schema language that constraints the structure and content of XML documents, adding more abstraction into it.[b]
Web 1.0/2.0	*XML Namespaces* furnish elements and attributes with a single name to a XML sequence; this sequence may contain element names or attributes coming from a more than one vocabulary. It is used to identify and single out entities to be referred to without any ambiguity.[c]
	Standard Semantic Web Technologies (meaning for structured data)
Web 3.0	*Resource Description Framework* [RDF] is a knowledge representation language to create sentences as triples. It makes their conversion into expressions with the form subject-predicate-property (resource-property/relationship-property/property value-relationship) and facilitates its representation as a graph.[d]
Web 3.0	*Resource Description Framework Schema* [RDFS] extends RDF vocabulary allowing the description of taxonomies of classes and properties. It also sets the domain and range of properties and relates the RDF classes and properties to taxonomies (hierarchies).[e]
Web 3.0	OWL [*Web Ontology Language*] adds more structures to describe the semantics of RDF sentences (cardinality, restrictions of values, transitivity….). It is based on descriptive logics, and provides reasoning capabilities to the SW. It defines sets, properties, instances and operations through the construction of *ontologies.*[f]
Web 3.0	SPARQL [***S** PARQL **P** rotocol **a** nd **R** DF **Q** uery **L** anguage*] allows the search of structured data (in RDF, RDFS and OWL). It is a W3C recommended search language specifically devised to retrieve and manage data stored in RDF, to perform graph queries, and to build up SW applications.[g]

[a]http://www.w3.org/XML/
[b]http://www.w3.org/XML/Schema
[c]http://www.w3schools.com/XML/xml:namespaces.asp
[d]http://www.w3.org/RDF/
[e]http://www.w3.org/TR/rdf-schema/
[f]http://www.w3.org/TR/owl-guide/
[g]http://www.w3.org/TR/rdf-sparql-query/

(terms), but concepts. RDF (hence OWL) can be serialized as XML, but also as Turtle or N3; they are different encodings of the same model.

We have described URIs, XML, RDF and OWL. They are the key components of the Semantic Web technologies.[2] At least, they were in the Semantic Web stack of technologies as initially proposed. Table 1 summarizes these technologies. It distin-

[2] See the last version of the famous SW 'cake' or stake of languages by T. Berners-Lee at http://www.w3.org/2007/03/layerCake.png

guishes between Berners-Lee's hypertext original ones, and those adding structure and meaning to the information, transforming it through *metadata* from "tagged" or "marked" data into a set of linked objects of knowledge. The use of XML and related technologies (XML Schema, XPATH) to publish linked data is declining fast in favour of the simpler JSON (JavaScript Object Notation) structures, but the overall ideas still remain valid several years after the publication of the SW technologies stack.

2.1.2 Linked Data

The Semantic Web ideas have been embraced relatively slowly. More than a decade had elapsed and these technologies did not abandon the academic circles, not being embraced by the crowd —like other technologies like HTML or web programming. However, in recent years the Semantic Web has been incarnated under the form of Linked Data, and RDF is at last being adopted as a data publication model.

Linked Data still represents a negligible fraction of the information in the Web, but it attracts our attention for three reasons: (i) it is highly *semantised* data, (ii) it is growing at a very fast pace, (iii) and it is supported by the W3C recommendations described before and public institutions (institutional data portals).

Linked data might be defined as data published in a structured manner, in such a way that information can be found, gathered, classified, and enriched using SW annotation and query languages. It is almost a commonplace by now to quote the Linked Data principles laid down by Tim Berners-Lee in a famous speech note at W3C in July 2006: (i) Use URIs (Uniform Resource Identifiers) as names for things, (ii) use dereferenceable[3] HTTP URIs, so that people can "look up" those, (iii) when someone looks up a URI, provide useful information, using the web standards like RDF or SPARQL (SPARQL Protocol and RDF Query Language), (iv) include links to other URIs, so that they can discover more things. We will go back in a moment to what these languages mean and how they are related (see Table 2).

It is worthwhile to notice that Linked Data principles are described therefore from a pre-normative point of view, as they consist of a set of *best practices* for publishing and connecting structured data on the Web. We should distinguish the process from the result, but both are embedded into an ongoing and interactive design planning, massively followed by a great plurality of users using a great plurality of distributed and diverse sources:

> In summary, Linked Data is simply about using the Web to create typed links between data from different sources. These may be as diverse as databases maintained by two organisations in different geographical locations, or simply heterogeneous systems within one organisation that, historically, have not easily interoperated at the data level. Technically,

---

[3] "The act of retrieving a representation of a resource identified by a URI is known as *dereferencing* that URI. Applications, such as browsers, render the retrieved representation so that it can be perceived by a user. Most Web users do not distinguish between a resource and the rendered representation they receive by accessing it" (Lewis 2007).

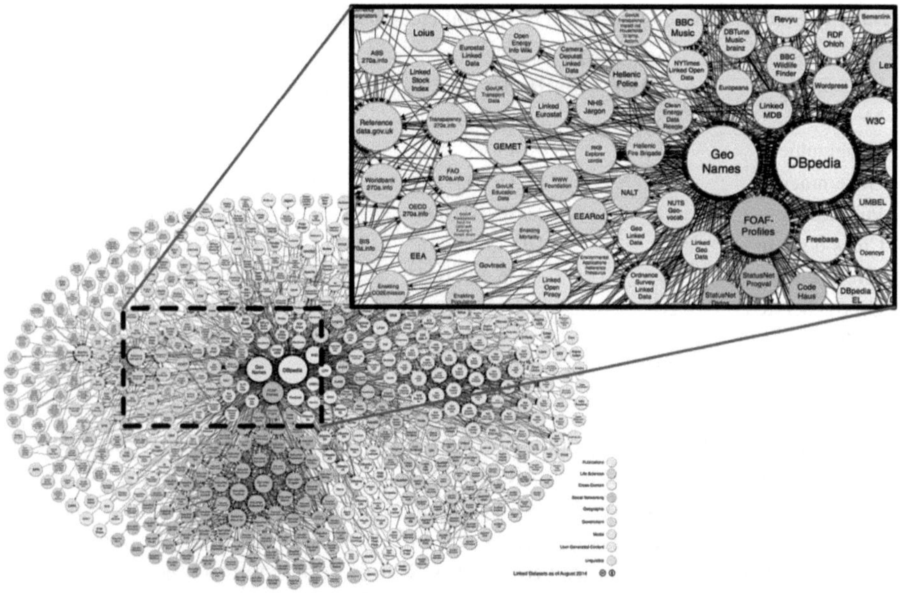

Fig. 1 Linked open data cloud diagram 2014, by M. Schmachtenberg, C. Bizer, A. Jentzsch and R. Cyganiak (Source: http://lod-cloud.net/)

> Linked Data refers to data published on the Web in such a way that it is machine-readable, its meaning is explicitly defined, it is linked to other external data sets, and can in turn be linked to from external data sets (Bizer et al. 2009, 256)

Independent Linked Data producers publish their datasets as collections of RDF. These RDF datasets are mutually interlinked —or at least encouraged to be so. There is an increasing number of linked datasets that are available on the Web, growing very fast. Heterogeneous data publishers participate in this race, including individuals, private and public institutions. If we represent datasets as nodes, and arrows as links between the nodes, we may represent the connectivity between datasets in a graph-like diagram. This diagram changes every day —datasets are not necessarily static, and an analogy has been made calling this diagram the Linked Data Cloud.

Considering the best quality datasets, Jentzsch, Cyganiak, and Bizer used the descriptions of the data sets in this group to generate the Linked Open Data Cloud diagram at regular intervals. The latest of these diagrams[4] was made by Schmachtenberg (Schmachtenberg et al. 2014), and it is shown (slightly modified) in Fig. 1. The size of the circles indicates their valency, the degree or number of edges incident to the vertex. Thick arrows indicate a greater degree of linkage. Bidirectional arrows point at the coexistence of elements.

[4] http://linkeddatacatalog.dws.informatik.uni-mannheim.de/state/LODCloudDiagram.html

Table 2 Source: Jentzsch et al. (2011) http://lod-cloud.net/state/

Domain	Number of datasets	Triples	%	(Out-)Links	%
Media	25	1,841,852,061	5.82	50,440,705	10.01
Geographic	31	6,145,532,484	19.43	35,812,328	7.11
Government	49	13,315,009,400	42.09	19,343,519	3.84
Publications	87	2,950,720,693	9.33	139,925,218	27.76
Cross-domain	41	4,184,635,715	13.23	63,183,065	12.54
Life sciences	41	3,036,336,004	9.60	191,844,090	38.06
User-generated content	20	134,127,413	0.42	3,449,143	0.68
	295	31,634,213,770		503,998,829	

Perhaps one of the most popular projects (at the centre of Fig. 1) is the DBpedia project.[5] Since 2007 onwards, it offers the key information present in the Wikipedia pages as Linked Data by regularly making an automatic extraction. This extraction parses the boxes in the HTML articles and information in the natural language text, and transforms it into structured RDF. This RDF is connected to other datasets, like GeoNames about geographical names (on the left of DBPedia in the figure), which in turn is linked by many others etc.

The topic of the datasets is disparate, and colours in the Fig. 1 represent a vague categorisation: geographic in orange, governmental in green, purple the multimedia etc. In the magnified box of Fig. 1, the relevance of some datasets is captured: Eurostat, UK government data, BBC music, Govtrack (Federal US legislation), etc. Table 2 shows an overview of the amount of triples as well as the amount of RDF links in datasets of the different domains coloured in Fig. 1.

Table 2 shows data from 2011. Five years later, numbers have increased dramatically —85,567,007,302 triples from 3426 datasets.[6] This huge amount of data entails a cultural and organisational shift. This semantic data is a drop of water in the immense ocean of the general Internet. Every second 30,000 gigabytes of data (1 gigabyte = 10^9, 1,000,000,000 bytes) are shed on the web (Marz and Warren 2014, 1). What is happening now? A multiple and converging technological process in which the different fields of big data —data mining, advanced statistics, predictive analytics, data engineering, and visualization— meet the second Web Semantic generation, Natural Language Processing (NLP), and a plurality of theoretical approaches in Robotics and Artificial Intelligence. We have stated elsewhere that this process is not natural or neutral, but deeply political and literally crossed by global strategies and punctual decisions at all levels (Casanovas 2015a, 2015b).

Some of the datasets in Fig. 2 belong to the language domain, or can be useful for the community of linguists (Chiarcos et al. 2012; Francopoulo et al. 2006; Markoff 2006; McCrae et al. 2012). The so called Linguistic Linked Data Cloud is such a

[5] http://dbpedia.org/About

[6] http://stats.lod2.eu/

fragment of the Linked Data Cloud. This subset is of special interest for the purpose of this chapter. First because these datasets are being used in applications facilitating the human-machine communication in natural language, second because these datasets are likely to be traded in commercial exchanges, requiring a closer legal attention.

The need for consuming linked datasets in a lawful manner did not trigger the first requirement of having licensing information. It had happened before, with the wide acceptance of Creative Commons among the Web surfers. Many RDF datasets were also licensed, and as a matter of 'good behaviour', Web users generally give credence to the author and respect the license even if they know that they will not suffer effective prosecution.

2.1.3 Use of Licenses for Linked Data

We have defined in detail Linked Data irrespective of its legal status in the previous pages. Some of the linked datasets have been published as Linked *Open* Data, referring to the fact that they are open —being either in the public domain or licensed under quite liberal terms, e.g. under Creative Commons Share-Alike licenses. Some institutions also publish data with more restrictive licenses or even in a completely closed fashion.

But, how much data is already being licensed? The licenses used in linked datasets have been systematically studied (Rodríguez-Doncel et al. 2013b), finding a notable amount of datasets published with a license. The most recent snapshot of the licenses in the Linked Data Cloud of Fig. 1, finds an even bigger use of licenses if not in absolute numbers at least in terms of important datasets covered. Figure 2 colours the nodes according to the type of license.

But the numerical results of the license analysis, shown in Fig. 3, reveal that a significant number of datasets still had been published without a license or under restrictive terms.

The main idea of Linked Data is to create an ecosystem that facilitates the browsing, discovery and exploitation/reuse of datasets for applications. The issue of whether datasets can be actually used for a specific purpose is thus a crucial one; so that understanding the conditions under which a certain dataset has been licensed is also crucial. Such licensing information should be expressed ideally in a machine-readable fashion to facilitate automated reasoning by end applications on the conditions of use of a dataset.

2.1.4 Rights Expression Languages (REL)

Leaning on the perspective described above, we can identify six challenges for legal services (Breuker et al. 2009; Casanovas et al. 2010, 5–7): (i) the relationship between the Social Web (Web 2.0) and the Web of Data (broadly, Web 3.0); (ii) the

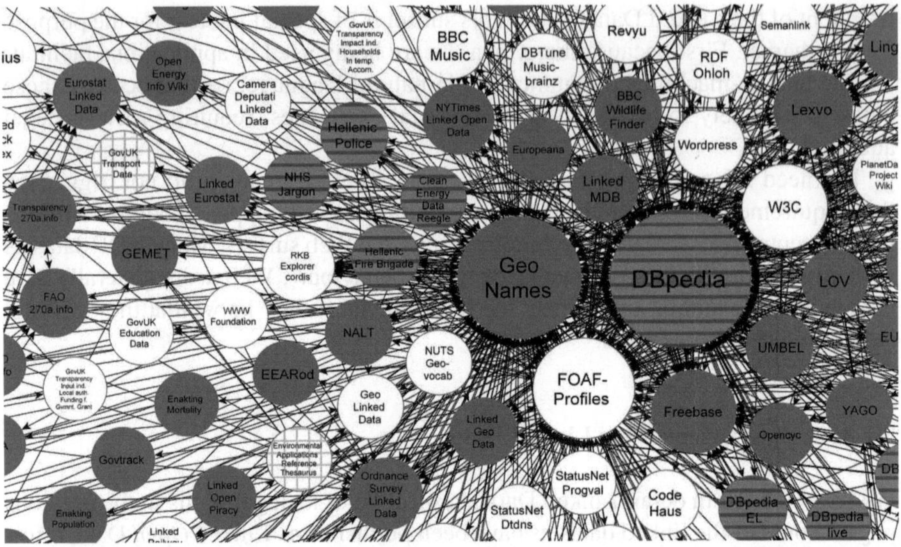

Fig. 2 RDF Datasets with different license types. Those with a “share-alike” license (cc-by-sa, gfdl,odc, odbl, etc.) are represented with *horizontal stripes*; those in the public domain (cc-zero or odc pddl) or with a attribution license (cc-by, odc-by) are *grayed*. Datasets with ‘some restrictions’ like “non-commercial” or “no derivatives” are represented with a *windowpane pattern*. Datasets with unspecified license are represented in *white* (Source: http://lod-cloud.net/)

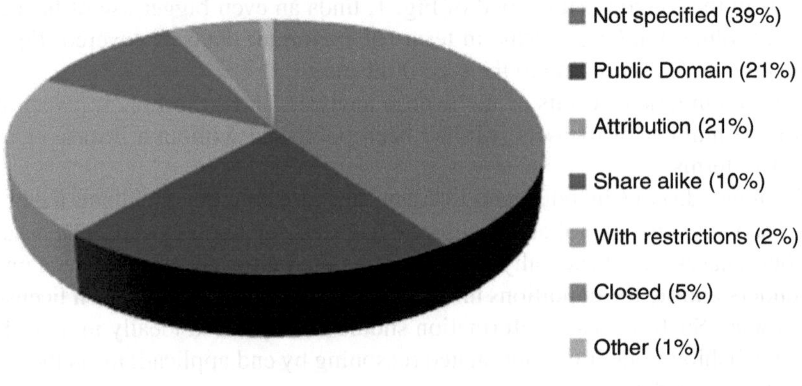

Fig. 3 Kind of licenses used in datasets annotated present in the LOD cloud (Source: Vila-Suero et al. (2014))

construction of evolving and contextual *legal ontologies* (and their relationship with *folksonomies*)[7]; (iii) the construction of Legal Semantic Web Services (LSWS); (iv) the bridge between Information Technology (IT) law (e.g. intellectual property), and IT for lawyers (computational support); (v) the convergence between Web 2.0 and Web 3.0 to grasp the changing and evolving nature of regulations; (vi) the addition of reasoning —e.g. defeasible and non-monotonic logic, among others— to facilitate users' exchanges and legal operations on the Web.

But this is only half of the story. If we open up the objective of the lens to broaden the angle of sight we will realise that Linked Data Best Practices (LDBP) propose that every dataset should provide provenance and licensing information, data-set level metadata, and information about additional access methods (Schmachtenberg et al. 2014). To sum up, each one should provide self-describing metadata. The other way around, everyone should practically use this information in a "pro-sumer" (consumer/producer) way, i.e. creatively, adding, using, and reusing content. The link between Wikipedia and DBpedia is an example of dynamic *social intelligence,*[8] in which *crowdsourcing* —the aggregation of multiple and massive individual behaviour— and the structural framework where actions are carried out by users, bring about a collective output that keep evolving over time and causes the growth of the web. *Personalisation*, user-centred approach, is one of the main trends of the second-generation Semantic Web (d'Aquin et al. 2008). We will come back to this later, after exploring some structural constraints.

As already shown, licensing is crucial for the use and reuse of information in the new Web environment. However, there are some differences between the way licenses are traditionally defined in commercial law treaties and how they are conceived in computer science. Traditionally, licensing is conceived as a specific type of commercial *contract* between a licensor (owner or possessor of rights) and a licensee (who receives them) under certain *conditions* settled by the agreement under a mandatory national or international *law*. In computer science, licensing is "the act of transferring limited *rights* to another party, under certain terms and conditions, for *use and reuse* of *content*" (Iannella 2003). Since the very beginning, then, the scope of the so called Digital Rights Management technologies had a broader focus, which could not be simply adapted to a single jurisdiction or, so to speak, a "legal" conception of the law. As Iannella (ibid.) put it:

> Digital Rights Management (DRM) technologies cover the broad area of intellectual property management by providing secure and trusted services to control the use and distribution of content. DRM technologies consists of a mix of business models, social issues, legal conformance, and technical capabilities. This implies that DRM Technologies are an integral part of the entire end -to - end content management lifecycle, not just a single service that exists in isolation. Hence the key to successful DRM technologies is that it is not to be

---

[7] Folksonomies relate to crowdsourcing. They are usually understood as a system in which users apply public tags to online items. We will define ontologies and come back in the next sections on this particular problem.

[8] http://www.sintelnet.eu/

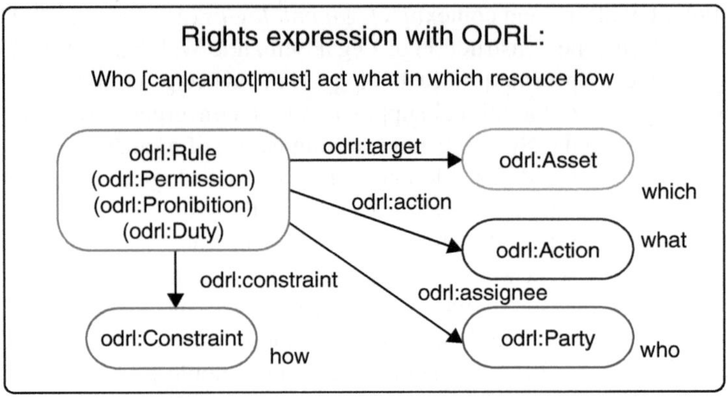

Fig. 4 Main elements in ODRL policies. An ODRL policy is made up of rules. These rules declare which actions are permissible, obligatory or forbidden effected over an asset by a certain party under certain constraints

> seen as a separate 'DRM system', but as part of the overall content management and consumption framework.[9]

DRM is a term with controversial connotations in the Internet community (Casanovas 2015b). But, for the past twenty-five years, *Rights Expression Languages* (REL) have been a key element in these systems. Nowadays, within the new versions of it, there is a shift between law conceived as a set of centralised normative systems, and law conceived as set of enacting rights empowering at the same time stakeholders (such as big companies) and users (consumers, citizens).[10] REL models focus on permissions (usages allowed over the content: play, print, sell…), constraints (limits to permissions, e.g. time-based restrictions), and requirements (obligations needed to exercise the permissions) (Iannella 2015). Figure 4 shows the most important elements in an ODRL policy —although similar schemas are found in other policy languages and rights expression languages.[11]

Open Digital Rights Language (ODRL) supports open publishing, distribution, and consumption of content, applications and services on the Web. This model respects and puts in the users' hands the management of their rights: it requires their explicit permission. Otherwise, moves are forbidden by default. This model sets a common vocabulary to allow reusing by a plurality of communities, and an ontology to allow interoperability built by McRoberts and Rodríguez-Doncel (2015).

[9] http://www.nicta.com.au/pub?doc=764

[10] REL were born in the early nineties, when Mark Stefik developed at Xerox PARC a language that would became the eXtensible Right Markup Language (XrML). Permissions and restrictions can be modelled according to Creative Commons principles (ccREL), Open Digital Rights Language (ODRL), MPEG-21, or national copyright protections. There is no universal Right Expression Language, but many —among the more relevant: ODRL, MPEG-21 REL, XACML, ccREL, MPEG-21, MVCO and WAC (Rodríguez-Doncel et al. 2013a; 2013b).

[11] https://www.w3.org/community/odrl/model/2.1/ See a recollection of models at http://delicias.dia.fi.upm.es/~vrodriguez/pdf/Poster-LicensingPatternsForLinkedData.pdf

Some rules, such as "permission", are introduced and grouped with basic restrictions and conditions.[12]

As example, we should stress the success of half-automated Creative Commons licenses, massively adopted by now.[13] CC licenses make use of REL. They incorporate a three-layer design. The first one is a standard legal description of rights ("legal code"). The second one ("Commons Deed") summarises and explain in plain non-technical language the content of the licence. The third layer is machine-readable, CC *Rights Expression Language* (ccREL): "*a specification describing how license information may be described using RDF and how license information may be attached to works*". People can easily find CC open content using search engines.

2.2 *A Web of Services*

2.2.1 The Service Web

An overview of data on the Web has been given in the above section —particularly addressing *semantic data* on the Web. The present one explores its proactive components, the Services that are offered and consumed within Web technologies.

Electronic communications between companies had happened long before, but the first generation of services in the Web was born around 2000. The term "Web Service" is defined by the W3C as "*a software system designed to support interoperable machine-to-machine interaction over a network*".[14] The technologies on which Web Services are based have several purposes: describing the data model syntax (XML), the transference protocol (SOAP, Simple Object Access Protocol), the available services (WSDL, Web Services Description Language) and the services discoverability through a directory (UDDI, Universal Description, Discovery and Integration). SOAP Web Services gained wide acceptance, but UDDI, which was supposed to be the "yellow pages" of Web Services, never took off. The programmer of a system consuming Web Services (*client*) should know and learn about the Web Service existence before using it.

A few years ago, Semantic Web developers were envisaging that the combination of semantic technologies and Service Oriented Architectures (SOAs) would lead to the creation of a Service Web "*allowing billions of parties to expose and consume billions of services seamlessly and transparently, where all types of stakeholders—from large enterprises to SMEs and singleton end users— engage as peers, consuming and providing services within a network of equals*" (Davies et al. 2009). Semantic Web services would be eventually discoverable and understood by machines, and their consumption automatable.

[12] https://www.w3.org/community/odrl/model/2.1/#section-References

[13] http://creativecommons.org/licenses/

[14] W3C Working Group Note, Web Services Glossary, http://www.w3.org/TR/2004/NOTE-ws-gloss-20040211/#webservice

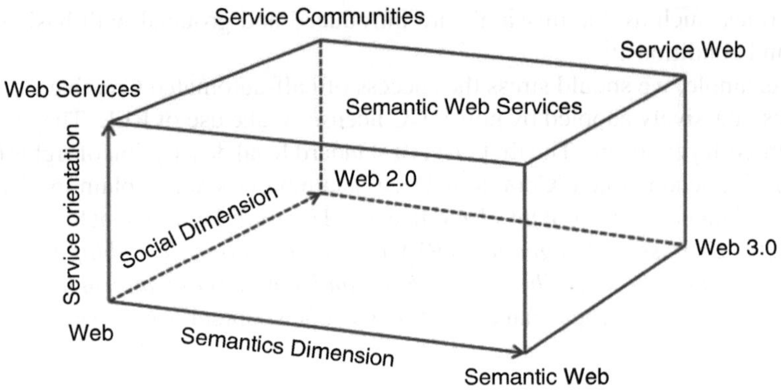

Fig. 5 Service web pillars (2.0/3.0) (Source: Davies et al. (2009))

However, they were also aware that SOAs could not scale without incorporating several regulatory requirements: (i) principles for a worldwide communication infrastructure (already satisfied by the standard Web Services); (ii) significant mechanisation of service lifecycle activities (location, negotiation, adaptation, composition, invocation and monitoring, service interaction requiring data, protocol and process mediation); (iii) and a balanced integration of services provided by humans and machines (Pedrinaci and Domingue 2010; Pedrinaci et al. 2011). Figure 5 summarises this framework, the so called *Service Web*, as drawn by Davies et al. (2009), combining social dimensions, Web 2.0 and semantic technology. The lower layer of the rectangle (the Web) reaches the upper one (the Services) by means of combining semantic technology and Web Services (Semantic Web Services); and by combining Web 2.0 and Web Services, the possibility of creating Service Communities arises.

The Service Web, as figured out by J. Davies, C. Pedrinaci, D. Fensel, and many other players in computer science and industry, is still under development. It has to be fleshed out at many levels of abstraction and operating languages. Syntactic, semantic and pragmatic dimensions are involved in this broad landscape. The problem we are dealing with is how they should be represented and combined to produce effective results in specific settings and different contextual levels.

The Web of Services has experienced an exuberant growth in the last few years, and the service orientation paradigm has been massively adopted under the form of online APIs (Application Programming Interface) using standard protocols (HTTP) in simple stateless REST (Representational State Transfer) services.

As of today, the provision of services is a very lucrative business. Consumers pay for the usage of services under different modalities and this flourishing industry is expected to grow and be supported by the cloud computing paradigm. In fact, the peak of inflated expectations for *cloud computing* has been surpassed. According to Gartner,[15] cloud computing will be found on the plateau of productivity in a couple of years. However, much work has still to be done towards the automatic discovery,

[15] Gartner's 2014 hype for emerging technologies, https://www.gartner.com/doc/3100227

composition and exploitation of services. Not in vain, according to Singh (2002), the automated web services composition lied in the path towards achieving a *pragmatic semantic web*; one of the four open challenges being identified to be the existence of automated compliance and trust mechanisms.

3 The Pragmatic Turn

Some lessons can be drawn from the last section. In the cloud, not only law but the nature of law is experiencing a deep transformation. The difference lies on that which the regulation of data and metadata would require for an effective, secure, and fair functioning. It is our contention that law alone as it is generally defined — the production of legislative and parliamentary documents, administration or court-ruling— is not well-adapted to take into account the dynamicity of social intelligence and big data environments.

The old way of drafting and enacting regulatory models assumed a simple ontology, in which human knowledge could be treated as separated knowledge *about* human behaviour (understood as either inner or outer experiences). However, the structuring of data by means of metadata incardinate action *and* knowledge at the same time in a more complex dynamic flow (action, knowledge, shared knowledge, meta-knowledge) —i.e. it is endowed through an *intelligent* flow. How could this social intelligent flow be described, controlled, monitored, and guided?

The clear-cut line between human norm-regulated external actions and normative legal systems, at least in the usual positivistic way as they are assumed by lawyers and jurisprudence, is becoming blurred in information-processing environments. What kind of connection can be constructed in between? And what does it link agency, agents' behaviour, be they digital or human, with the normative design of regulatory planning?

We are pointing at: (i) the interface between virtual and non-virtual *contexts* (a set of scenarios in social ecosystems); (ii) intentional communicative acts understood as the exercise of rights (e.g. intentional acts of selecting a license); (iii) regulatory performative acts constrained by standards or guidelines embedded into computer design (e.g. Privacy by Design, PbD), (iv) the collaborative coordination between agents' decisions, intentional acts and planning. Summing up:the asymmetric relationship between the exercise of rights and the regulatory power of norms. Self-described data (metadata) are bounded by the general course of agents' behaviour in a specific ecosystem.

3.1 Pragmatics

3.1.1 Some Preliminary Thoughts

Pragmatics is often defined as the study of language as it is used in a social context, including its effect on the interlocutors (utterers and interpreters). Context is placed at the centre, as pragmatics studies the meaning in actual situations assuming an interactional and dynamic notion of context. Equivalently, legal pragmatism emphasizes the need to include a more diverse set of data than the one usually considered from a positivistic view, and again the specific context at hand plays a central role in judicial decision-making. The evaluation of the circumstances on a particular issue is a genuine human task. Machines are fast and accurate when performing specific procedures, but the evaluation of context requires the comprehensive understanding of a human being.

However, the latest technologies might improve the capabilities of machines in this regard, possibly bringing practical tools that include context for decision-making in a near future. These promises are brought by means of a combination of new developments in the fields of Big Data, the Semantic Web and Natural Language Processing (NLP).

Advances in NLP increase machine understanding of natural languages. Disambiguation algorithms are among technologies which have experienced a larger improvement. Disambiguation is the capability of correctly identifying the referred entity when a piece of text (word or words) makes reference to different things without any additional context. Disambiguation is carried out considering the text as a whole, taking into account past experience and the social perception of it. Once this hurdle is falling, machines will be able to safely establish relationships between unrelated pieces of text. Undoubtedly, this task will be accomplished in a smoother manner by using a new breed of resources based on semantic technologies. In what follows, we will link them with the knowledge acquisition process, ontology building, institutional analysis, and other developments in Normative Multi-agents Systems (norMAS).

3.1.2 The Pragmatic Web

Pragmatics always played a role in SW developments. Invoking the metaphor of Polya's inventors paradox —"the more ambitious plan may have more chances of success"— M.P. Singh wrote a seminal paper launching the "Pragmatic Web" in 2002.

> The core mission of the semantic web, namely, to enable information to be shared across the web, faces significant challenges. The challenges come from the difficulty of capturing semantics in a manner that is reusable across applications, the priority of process over data, the importance of interaction, and the critical need for accommodating user context. Overcoming these challenges takes us from the realm of semantics and brings us into the realm of pragmatics, which we view as supervenient upon the semantics. We claim that when the vision of the semantic web is realized, it will be via the pragmatic web. (Singh 2002, 82)

Several conferences have been organised on the topic following this trend.[16] There is an active research community, taking inspiration from semiotics and philosophy of language —C.S. Peirce, C. Morris, P. Grice, J.R. Searle. This perspective has been already applied to several SW fields —multi-agent systems, interaction design, self-organizing communities of practice, and Web Services (Bonacin et al. 2013). Speech-acts theory, illocutionary force, intended meaning, implicatures, and communicative acts and processes have been used as bases for computer design with interesting results.

This approach usually stems from the classical semiotic distinction between syntax, semantics, and pragmatics. E.g., as applied to the Web, de Moor (2005) distinguishes between (i) the *Syntactic Web* (interrelated syntactic information resources linked by HTML references), (ii) the *Semantic Web* (a collection of semantic resources, mainly in the form of ontologies), (iii) and the *Pragmatic Web* (a set of pragmatic contexts of semantic resources). He contends that meaning negotiation can be based on a set of fundamental *pragmatic patterns*, which can be made available in a *meta-ontology*. Pragmatic patterns are defined as "template definitions that can be used as the basis of conceptual definitions used in meaning negotiation and other meaning evolution processes". Communities may use and extend them for a plurality of purposes.

Core pragmatic patterns include (de Moor, ibid.): (i) *Pragmatic context* ("a pattern that defines the speakers, hearers, type of communication, and identifiers of the individual and common contexts of a community"); (ii) *Individual context* ("a pattern that defines an individual community member, individual context parameters and an identifier of the individual context ontology"); (iii) *Common context* ("a pattern that defines the common context parameters and an identifier of the common context ontology of a community"); (iv) *Individual pragmatic pattern* ("a meaning pattern relevant to an individual community member", "an individual context ontology consists of the total set of meaning patterns relevant to that individual"); (vi) *Common pragmatic pattern* ("meaning pattern relevant to the community as a whole").

Paschke et al. (2007) focus on the infrastructure for collaborative human-computer networks. Using RuleML,[17] they aim at extending "the Semantic Web to a rule-based S*emantic-Pragmatic Web* which puts the independent micro-ontologies and domain-specific data into a pragmatic context such as communicative situations, organizational norms, purposes or individual goals and values". Some methodological notions —such as "Elementary Pragmatics" (EP) and Elementary Norms (EN)— have followed, applying LegalRuleML on patent and intellectual property law.[18]

[16] http://www.csw.inf.fu-berlin.de/pragweb/

[17] RuleML is a markup language to express rules in XML for inferential purposes and reasoning. Vid. an introduction to LegalRuleML principles in Athan et al. (2015).

[18] "EPs are considered as disclosures about an 'object' (e.g. patents-norms/ precedents/guidelines) of law, with its pragmatics referring to the context in which such an 'object' is understood and

Following the three semiotic distinctions proposed by Liu (2009) —who groups illocutions into three dimensions: *time*, *invention*, and *mode*— Bonacin et al. (2013) have recently built *CactO*, a communication act ontology that links acts, agents and behaviour patterns. In the same vein, applying Sperber and Wilson's (1995) relevance theory on implicit inferences and contextual inferred meaning, Mazak and Wally (2014) make use of meta-information and weighted graphs for ontology building and aligning.

All these approaches deal with and deepen into contextual constraints, interactive communication and collaborative work. But in the field, semantic web technologies in general and ontologies in particular, play a crucial role —at a different level of depth and granularity. The "Pragmatic Manifesto" addresses particularly ontology-building processes:

> The vision of the Pragmatic Web is thus to augment human collaboration effectively by appropriate technologies, such as systems for ontology negotiations, for ontology-based business interactions, and for pragmatic ontology-building efforts in communities of practice. In this view, the Pragmatic Web complements the Semantic Web by improving the quality and legitimacy of collaborative, goal-oriented discourses in communities. (Schoop et al. 2006)

3.1.3 Ontologies and the Pragmatic Approach

Leaning on the same distinction between the three linguistic dimensions, Cardoso (2006) proposed a gradual understanding of semantics and he placed (formal) ontologies on top of it. He distinguishes four main representations that can be used to model and organize concepts to describe terms: controlled vocabularies, taxonomies, thesaurus, and ontologies (Fig. 6).

In the same way that the Semantic Web is not a separate web, but an extension of the current one, the Pragmatic Web does not entail a different web, but an extension of the Semantic Web.

From a computational point of view, Cardoso (2006) differentiated between three kind of different approaches to bring semantics to Web services: (i) by mapping concepts in a Web service description (Web Semantics Descriptive Language specification) into ontological concepts; (ii) by using OWL-S to describe Web services, mapping OWL-S into WSDL operations; (iii) by using Web Service Modelling Ontology (WSMO). It includes Web services, goals, ontologies and mediator concepts. He proposed to combine the functionalities of WSMO and OWL-S to create SW processes, allowing complex interactions among organisations to be represented in all stages of their lifecycle.

However, each of these three alternatives placed a burden on the shoulders of developers that they were not willing to accept, and Semantic Web Services never took off. The latest efforts in this line have been directed towards describing a sim-

applied by a 'reasonable man'" (Ramakrishna and Paschke 2014: 312). See also Weigand and Paschke (2012), and Paschke (2013).

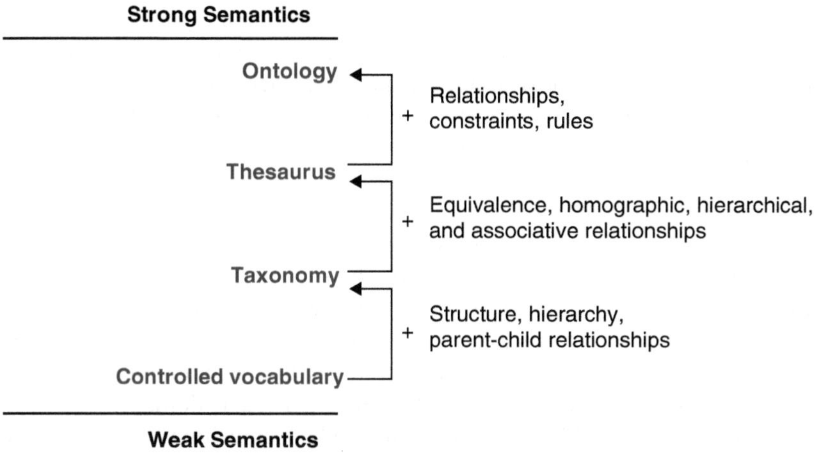

Fig. 6 Levels of semantics (Source: Cardoso (2006, 8))

pler vocabulary to document APIs: the Hydra Core Vocabulary.[19] But even if Hydra fails to succeed, massive adoption of structured API documentation is taking place. Technologies like APIBluePrint or Swagger's describe JSON structures to derive automatic human-readable documentation, but they could also be automatically parsed by semantically enabled tools.

The pragmatic basket is full of phenomena analysed from different theoretical backgrounds —rhetoric, discourse analysis, dialectics, argumentation theory, ethnomethodology, cognitive anthropology, socio-linguistics, and cognitive linguistics, among others. Actually, the pragmatic approach to semantics can be faced also gradually, according to the different operational stages in ontology-building, at the knowledge acquisition level (KA) and at the representation level.

Pragmatism, the attitude to learn and building knowledge in a machine-operable way, has been a *common motto* for SW researchers since the beginning. The common assumption is that there is no clear difference between pragmatic and semantic conceptualisations of meaning. There is a *continuum* between the actual use and the fixed content of language. The difference lies on the specific objectives and weight allocated onto the interactive view (e.g. community-building), or onto the structural one (eg. upper-top, core or domain ontology building). There is a large room for positioning and selection in between. This means that there is a *hybrid* approach. E.g. E. Motta, M. d'Aquin, and A. Gangemi, among many others, differentiate between *conceptual coverage* and *pragmatic sustainability* (d'Aquin and Gangemi 2011), and they apply this distinction to reach a *trade-off design* (Distinto et al. 2016).

This is consistent with Gruber's (1993, 1) original and most quoted definition of what a computational ontology consist of: "An *ontology* is an explicit specification

[19] https://www.w3.org/community/hydra/, spec. published by the W3C Hydra Community Group.

of a conceptualization."[20] In Studer et al. (1998) words: an ontology is "a f*ormal, explicit specification of a shared conceptualization*". Portability, clarity, certain degree of formality, and, most of all, the quality of being *shareable and reusable*, are attributes of computer ontologies. In this sense, they are not dependant on the philosophical usage of the term (Guarino and Giaretta 1995). The term *ontologia* does not possess Greek origins. It was coined at the beginning of 16 c. to express the quality for an object (being) to be *known* (Øhrstrøm et al. 2008).

Gruber (2000) assessed many times the pragmatic understanding of what ontologies are built for: e.g. "Ontologies are not about truth or beauty. They are agreements, made in a social context, to accomplish some objectives. It's important to understand those objectives, and be guided by them". Thus, *ontological commitment* expresses this kind of epistemic agreement within a community —lay people, computer scientists, and experts pertaining to a particular domain of knowledge. This goes back to the problems raised in knowledge acquisition processes, which is something particularly familiar to computer scientists working on expert systems in the eighties and nineties.

3.1.4 The Knowledge Acquisition Perspective: Some Remaining and New Questions

Knowledge Acquisition (KA) is a well-trodden path in computer science. Starting in 1986, several Workshops have been organised over the last thirty years with regular attendees, setting a working group to discuss epistemological, problem-solving and ontological problems. According to Musen (2013, 196), this community achieved remarkable consensus on a number of issues: (1) the rejection of the notion of knowledge as a commodity to be transferred from one locus to another, (2) an acceptance of the situated nature of human expertise, (3) emphasis on knowledge acquisition as the modelling of problem solving, and (4) the pursuit of reusable patterns in problem solving and in domain descriptions that can facilitate both modelling and system implementation.

M. Musen recalls W. Clancey going to the point in a Workshop Keynote in 1997: knowledge acquisition is not hard because it is difficult to get domain experts and knowledge engineers to speak the same language; knowledge acquisition is hard because *the domain experts and the knowledge engineers together must create a*

[20] "For knowledge-based systems, what "exists" is exactly that which can be represented. When the knowledge of a domain is represented in a declarative formalism, the set of objects that can be represented is called the universe of discourse. This set of objects, and the describable relationships among them, are reflected in the representational *vocabulary* with which a knowledge-based program represents knowledge. Thus, we can describe the ontology of a program by defining a set of representational terms. In such an ontology, definitions associate the names of entities in the universe of discourse (e.g., classes, relations, functions, or other objects) with human-readable text describing what the names are meant to denote, and formal axioms that constrain the interpretation and well-formed use of these terms." (Gruber 1993, 1).

language to define a model of professional expertise —a model that never existed previously in any formal sense (Musen, ibid. 197).

The "situated cognition" approach developed by Clancey stated that *experts do not provide knowledge that covers all possible contexts*. He pointed at the level of abstraction of modelling and simulating work processes in organisational settings. Individual work practice, collaboration, communication, 'off-task' behaviours, multi-tasking, interrupted and resumed activities, informal interactions, use of tools and movements were described and integrated in BRAHMS, a programme developed at NASA Ames Research Center. The influential Brahms design was geared towards modelling people's activity behaviour (Clancey et al. 1998; Sierhuis et al. 2007).

After thirty years of research in knowledge acquisition this problem has been addressed in many ways. I.e. Compton (2013, 184) figured out how to bridge problem solving, contextual and data approaches, and situated meaning through "Ripple-down rules". I.e. if people distinguish between different conclusions in different contexts, they do so because they can identify features that distinguish the contexts. This type of case or context differentiation could be readily integrated with a range of knowledge acquisition frameworks. *Ripple-Down Rules* would provide a way to gather a large amount of knowledge for a system, simply identifying such contextual knowledge.

The shift from intensive problem solving approach and the early Semantic Web, to knowledge management and the Web of Data raises many questions and issues. Some of them are related to ontology building, use and reuse, and have had a strong continuity with the early KA issues. As Aussenac-Gilles and Gandon (2013) put it: Which kind of knowledge can be modelled? How important is the distortion between the computer interpretation of an ontology and the human interpretation of the associated knowledge? What kind of intelligent behaviour and tasks can formal representations be useful for? Other issues are new, as the initial problem of having too few sources has shifted towards the problem of too many, big, and diverse sources.

After the experiences of WATSON[21] as iFAQ and SIRI[22] as i-Virtual Personal Assistent, Gruber (2013, 194) asks for an even more radical change:

> As computers get faster and bigger they can look through more data, but they are still being told what to look for. For knowledge acquisition systems, the inductive bias is the endowment from nature that guides how the agent adapts to its nurturing environment. [...] For our field, a fundamental question for knowledge acquisition is this: to learn from collective human knowledge, what kind of structure applied to what kind of knowledge in what form can lead to learning genuinely new knowledge? Will the structure be in the patterns to look for, the relationships among things, the statistical properties of collections, or other inductive biases? Will the golden discoveries be found in the human generated content, structured data, graphical or auditory sources, query streams, or other breadcrumb trails of human experience? What will be the most useful measures of interestingness when learning from everything? The answers to this inquiry will guide us into the next level, which is: can this process be applied recursively to itself? That is, can our machine learners apply what they learn to improve their own learning? [...] Is there an epigenetics of knowledge?

[21] http://www.ibmwatson.com/

[22] http://siri.com

Summing up, there is a possible loop in the self-reflective descriptions provided within and across the Web of Data. The ongoing openness, participation and creative thinking of the many are seen as essential to sustain the Web. Closeness should be avoided. This means that heuristics matters, and the plurality of human languages and human cultures should be taken into account when "shared knowledge" is at stake.

We can distinguish both the formal and the cultural side of social intelligence. On the one side, as stated by Hitzler and van Harmelen (2010), reasoning for the SW "should be understood as *shared inference*, which is not necessarily based on deductive methods".[23] On the other, the work by Breuker (2013) provides some useful examples of the modelling issues stemming from social intelligence and cognitive foundations. Breuker leans on previous pragmatic studies to show some difficult decisions in ontology-building —especially for upper-top or foundational ontologies. E.g. the notions of "space" and "position" are not uniform. Levinson (2003) distinguished three frames of reference for locating objects: absolute, relative, and intrinsic. As summarised by Breuker (2013, 180):

> The intrinsic reference frame locates an object A relative to another object B. For instance, in "the dog is in front of the car", the position of the dog is defined by what is considered the 'front' of the car. In other words, in (many) intrinsic references a property of object B, in particular its 'form', connects here object properties with spatial locations. Spatial reference frames can be viewed as what has recently become an important topic in discussing ontology engineering: (design) patterns or frameworks. Frameworks go beyond concepts as simple building stones, fit for any combination. It restricts far more the semantics than simple lists of properties, but emphasizes essential relationships that can be used for reasoning. For instance, the relative spatial reference frame defines a triple relationship between an observer, object A and object B for which transitivity can be claimed. These frameworks are important because they enable specialized inference.

Therefore, there are cultural shifts and nuances about time, space, distance, positioning… at different levels of knowledge. Cultures differ in which notions can be used, and usually they use more than one. Depending of what the ontology is aiming at, it should reflect these differences and diverse "common knowledge" cultural features (Breuker 2013, 180).

However, the level of abstraction in which the Web of Data operates makes this "grasping tasks" a bit more difficult. Again, trade-offs and intensive exchanges appear to be essential to reach acceptable results.

One of the classical players in the knowledge acquisition field, Gaines (2013, 133) identifies the different tiers for what he calls a *developing symbiosis science*. The first four belonging to computer science, the remaining ones to knowledge sci-

[23] "Model-theoretic semantics (and sound and complete reasoning based on it) functions as a gold standard, but applications dealing with large-scale and noisy data usually cannot afford the required runtimes. Approximate methods, including deductive ones, but also approaches based on entirely different methods like machine learning or nature inspired computing need to be investigated, while quality assurance needs to be done in terms of precision and recall values (as in information retrieval) and not necessarily in terms of soundness and completeness of the underlying algorithms." (Hitzler and van Harmelen 2010, 39).

ence: (i) the underlying digital electronics; its application in computer architectures; (ii) the programming of general-purpose computers through software; (iii) the development of computer–people and computer–computer interactivity; (iv) the representation of human knowledge; (v) the acquisition of additional knowledge from interaction with the world, people and stored knowledge; (vi) the development of goal-directed autonomous knowledge creating processes; (vi) the increasing coupling of knowledge processing entities in social networks; (vii) the development of techniques to facilitate the synergy between human and computer knowledge processes; (viii) the synthesis of both into a unified system.

3.2 *Institutions*

3.2.1 The Institutional Turn

Let's deepen into the subject of a hybrid, symbiotic approach. In this section, we will recover the legal thread we left ready in Sects. 1 and 2.[24] Let's start with Feingebaum's "knowledge acquisition bottleneck". At the acceptance speech for the establishment of the *Feigenbaum Medal* presented at the World Congress on Expert Systems at Orlando in December 1991, he recalled how he invented the dynamically growing decision trees, under Herbert Simon's mentorship. This was an example of what he termed the "performance motive" of Artificial Intelligence —"less theory, more system building"— or learning by practicing. The process of hypothetic induction constituted one of the main problems to be tackled on the Newell and Simon's path. Envisaging the future, he said:

> Knowledge sharing, to these researchers, means more than just the knowledge bases of several expert systems interoperating to solve a problem. Knowledge sharing also means the computer-facilitated cooperation of many people in the building of a large body of codified knowledge. The vision is that hundreds or thousands of knowledge base builders would cooperate.

Well, times are most ripe for such a vision, and perhaps the lesson to be drawn nowadays is that dealing with billions of structured data and metadata would require more attention to cooperative, common processes and single, detailed, performances. In a way, this is what Hoekstra (2010) is pointing at with his reformulation of Feigenbaum's dictum. *The knowledge engineering bottleneck*: Semantic Web content can no longer be assumed to have been produced in a controlled task-independent environment. When reused in a non-controlled task environment, "Semantic Web content needs to be remoulded, refiltered and recurated for a new task". In contrast to Feigenbaum's problem, the knowledge reengineering bottleneck refers "to the general difficulty of the correct and continuous reuse of pre-existing knowledge for a new task". We do believe that this is the new problem we

[24] See the state of the art in law and the semàntic web, summarising fifteen years of research at Casanovas et al. (2016).

are facing now. How are we going to proceed with legal and political tasks and content in the Web of Data?

Certainly one feasible way of doing it is remaining stuck to legal documents and texts. Organising at present huge legal libraries, such as the millions of documents gathered in the EURLex repository, constitutes a real challenge (Francesconi et al. 2015). Structuring legal knowledge is the aim of successful projects on LegalXML interchange formats for legal resources, such as Akoma-Ntoso[25] and CEN MetaLex[26] —the later one due partially to Hoekstra's own work. But this is not solving the raised problem of contextual and *personalised* reuse of such repositories. One of the main problems is that which both approaches are taking for granted —law and legal knowledge are assumed to be contained into documents, liable to be extracted and self-described through metadata and a set of reusable ontologies.

These are useful trends. However, again, this is only half of the story. Dynamic and specific legal acts, performances and knowledge are being produced daily in many global places —e.g. markets; political and public scenarios— through the conflictive and cooperative behaviour of millions of players alike in specific and changing social scenarios. People are using licenses and referring to intellectual property or fundamental rights in a wide range of different contexts in a conflicting world. In a way, *rights are becoming independent from the coded content of legal norms* in this new environment. To bring some order into the social scenarios of the Web of Data, ethical principles, governance and law should be worked out at the same time in regulatory instruments, as stated by several recent EU reports (Schindler et al. 2012).

This constitutes a challenge to be faced in the immediate future, at different levels of abstraction and formalisation, through different kind of regulatory instruments. We will advance in this Section the notion of Semantic Web Regulatory Models (SWRM) to cope with these objectives, compatible with electronic institutions, Multi-agent Systems (MAS), platforms and APIS. They can bridge users' needs, decisions and protections with big lexical repositories and RELs.

3.2.2 Iterative Pragmatic Cycle (IPC)

The aim of field research is to elicit and describe all the processes, interactions, patterns of behaviour, and scenarios in which end users get involved. As a result, the expert knowledge obtained through knowledge acquisition processes is modelled as "situated knowledge" —in Clancey's sense—, allowing an active participation of end users in the ontology-building process. End users are integrated into the process from the beginning to the end. Accordingly, this Section introduces (i) the dynamic knowledge acquisition stage carried out to collecting and transforming knowledge (e.g. into ontologies) (ii) to be integrated into a regulatory model set for specific purposes to be embedded into a particular social ecosystem.

[25] http://www.akomantoso.org/

[26] http://www.metalex.eu/

Our ontology-building methodology finds its theoretical roots and follows the *middle-out approach* —in contrast with top-down and bottom-up ones— advanced by MethOntology, the engineering perspective set by Gómez-Pérez et al. (2004), and refined and updated to adapt it to networked ontologies on the web exploiting the NeON toolkit (Suárez-Figueroa et al. 2012). Building ontologies has become a more complex task now, in which several levels of formality and different engineering groups are involved. As described by Corcho et al. (2015): (i) Upper-level ontology engineers (formal ontologies: DOLCE, BFO, GFO, SUMO); (ii) heavyweight ontology engineers being domain experts (for example, graduates in biology, geography, or law) or computer scientists (OWL-based domain and application ontologies developed by this profile may reuse axioms, properties and concepts from upper-level ontologies); (iii) lightweight ontology engineers (they develop vocabularies to be used in the linked data context, usually written in RDF Schema or in OWL profiles with little expressivity, e.g. OWL Lite); (iv) SKOS [*Simple Knowledge Organization System*] concept scheme developers (who are interested in developing thesauri and other types of classifications forlibrary sciences); (v) Web developers contributing to *Schema.org*[27] or using it to annotate websites from the cluster of Schema.org vocabulary developers (HTML, RDFa and JSON-LD).

What it is worth to notice is that ontology-building can be integrated into a broader institution-building cycle. From our perspective, the process comes to an end only when a regulatory instrument or set of instruments have been built, delivered and put into practice into a specific organisation, setting or community. We call it an *Iterative Pragmatic Cycle* (IPC). The final output can be a judicial iFAQ —such as IURISERVICE (Casanovas et al. 2006; Casellas 2011); a mobile application —such as MEDIAKIDS (Poblet et al. 2015); a platform for Online Dispute Resolution (ODR) —such as CONSUMEDIA (Suquet et al. 2014), or a set of ontologies and ethical and policy principles to monitor and control the information flow of a security platform —such as CAPER (González-Conejero et al. 2014; Casanovas et al. 2014a). Sometimes the lifecycle cannot be completed. Eventually, the regulatory instrument does not reach the implementation stage.

Many different methodologies have been already described to build legal ontologies at different levels (Sartor et al. 2011). Casellas (2011) shows and explains a full array of them. Since ten years now, wikis and collaborative devices have improved the discussion phase (Casanovas et al. 2007), and the levels and accuracy of ontology integration (Casellas et al. 2005). Our starting point is an *Iterative Knowledge Acquisition Process* (IKAP) stemming from a socio-legal approach (Casanovas et al. 2011), using all kind of linguistic and sociological methods (quantitative and qualitative). Hua (2008) discusses different families of techniques that are specifically devised to elicit and analyse knowledge acquired from experts. We propose an IKAP based on five stages: *elicitation, collection, analysis, modelling and validation* (see the schematic description in Fig. 7).

However, linking this bulk of acquired social knowledge with ethical, governance and legal issues constitute a separate problem. Figure 8 draws the filtering

[27] https://schema.org/

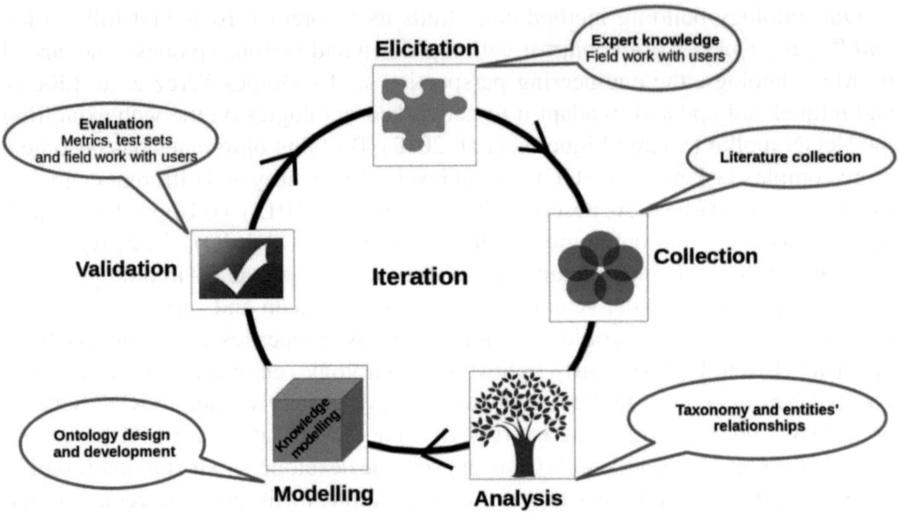

Fig. 7 Iterative Knowledge Acquisition schema (IKAP schema)

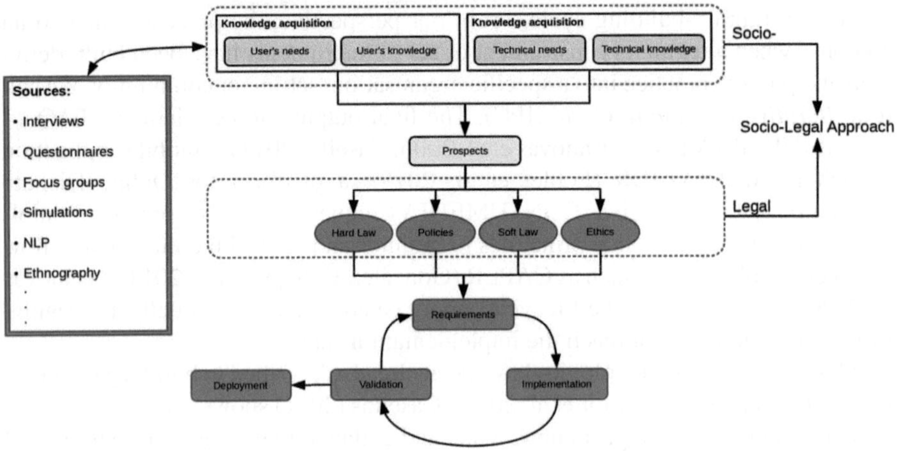

Fig. 8 Pragmatic socio-legal approach

position of regulatory models that set the requirements to be taken into account in a legal modelling process.

3.2.3 Semantic Web Regulatory Models (SWRM)

Regulatory Models (RM) can be defined as a set of values, patterns, rules, norms and principles conceptually represented in a certain natural, half-artificial or artificial language. They can be represented as constraints and conditions for agency and

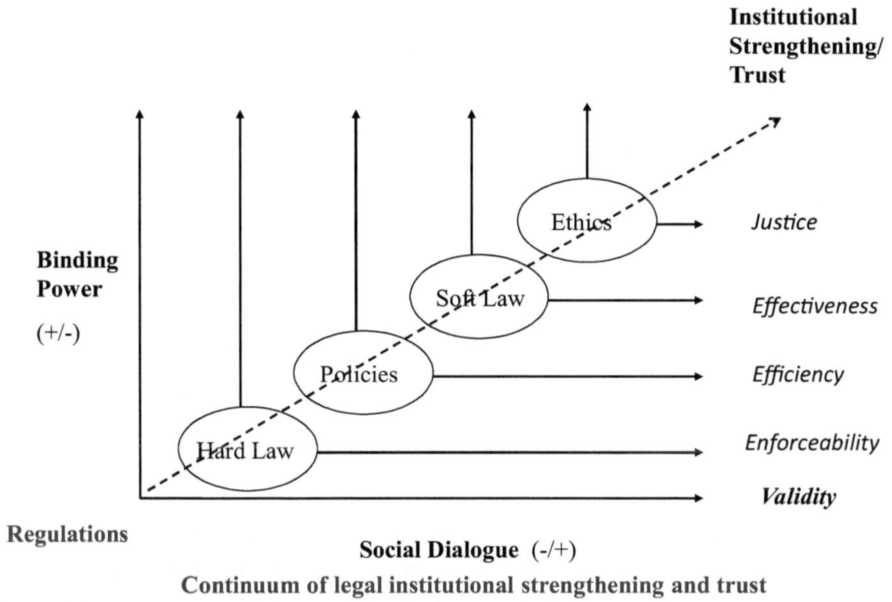

Fig. 9 Meta-model of SWRM (Source: Casanovas (2015a))

the performance of moral, political and legal rights. They can be implemented into the social ecosystem in which Right Expression Languages and Digital Rights Management operate. They can be strategically used to regulate the informational flow on platforms, and to implement Data Protection, security, privacy and compliance by design. Figure 9 draws a simple schema, a general meta-model, in which Ethics (e.g. Fair Information Practices, FIPs) play a regulatory role, along with hard law (national and international acts and court decisions), governance (national and international agency policies), and soft law (transnational standards, professional guidelines, corporate models) (Casanovas et al. 2014b; Casanovas and Zeleznikow 2014; Casanovas 2015a, b).

These regulatory sources are located according to their distance to *binding power* and *social dialogue*, the two converse axes of the rule of law. Legality or validity of a particular regulatory system, as a whole, depends onto the degree of compliance of their components. It is a second-order property. According to a certain threshold for the degree of enforceability, efficiency, effectiveness, and justice, the system becomes stable, and a third axis of trust and institutional strengthening (security) emerges as a result. This is an example of strategic collective rationality, as trust cannot be directly commanded or induced.

When this structure is applied to ODRL policies or to the W3C Core-model for rights and policies governance (Iannella 2015),[28] the result is a *Meta-rule of law*, a set of conditions to be taken into account and restrictions for the possible normative

[28] https://www.w3.org/community/odrl/model/2.1/

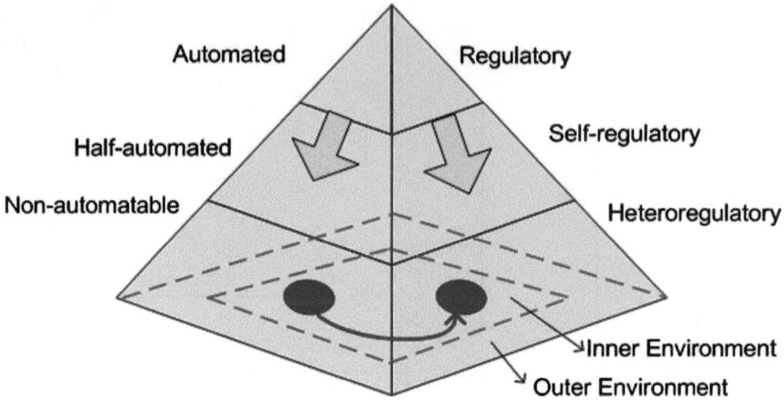

Fig. 10 Layered regulatory automation

inferences drawn from data and meta-data models (Casanovas 2015b). Thus, this is a way to enhance democratic values on the new global environment of the Web of Data, linking micro and macro scenarios to a common understanding of regulations.

SWRM can be applied to a great deal of different legal problems and situations, operating on the web at a transnational level through Semantic Web languages. Different dimensions (the type of regulation) and jurisdictions (related to public powers -e.g. where courts are located) can be distinguished. SWRM are conceived as *intermediate institutions* between the enhanced positive norms of a particular legal system and the actual performances of technological devices (platforms, APIS, mashups…). This is why they are able to be modelled as electronic half- or self-regulated systems, embedded into the design of technological devices, and help fasten decision-making when it is needed (Fig. 10).

SWRM seem also well suited to build the institutional outer context for normative Multi-agent Systems (norMAS) operations. I.e. linking social, legal and governance scenarios with the particular ecosystem that electronic institutions are aiming to produce. Electronic Institutions (EI) are a way to implement interaction conventions for agents —human or software— who might establish commitments on an open environment (within and outside organisations, administrations or companies).[29] The dynamic entrenchment between agreement technologies (Ossowski 2013) and such environment constitute the place in which SWRMs come to play, as they furnish the structured and consistent information that is needed for EI to perform legal acts—such bidding, contracting or mediating.

[29] http://e-institutions.iiia.csic.es/

3.2.4 Artificial Socio-Cognitive Systems (ASCS)

Challenges for Artificial Socio-cognitive Systems (ASCS) (Noriega et al. 2014) are two-fold and can be understood in two directions. The first one goes from the system to the users, as it sets forth the conditions in which the system can be managed, imposing some conditions to users. In the other way around, from the users-to-system perspective, both human and artificial agents are embedded into a broader socio-legal context that must be taken into account for the effective implementation and acceptance of ASCS performances. The "valid" or "legal" acts carried out by ASCS should be effectively legal.

Pragmatics matters at all layers, as open multi-agent systems can be effectively designed and implemented as electronic institutions (d'Inverno et al. 2012). In 1997, Noriega proposed building computational environments —agent-mediated institutions— that allow heterogeneous agents to interact successfully by imposing appropriate restrictions on their behaviour—<*speaker,role; hearer set, role; action; timestamp*>. Moves are represented as illocutionary acts in a dialogical framework, but carrying out complete performative acts (Noriega 1999).[30] The final result of a negotiated process is intended to be a full trade or a settled agreement.[31]

E.g. we can define the framework for an EI for mediation setting a *conceptual model* to describe the institution, a *computational model* that explains how it is enacted, and a *pragmatic model* that establishes how it is implemented. Interactions between agents within EI are speech acts that *count as* actions in the world, repetitive and organised as if they were *scenes in a play*. Again, (i) the dialogical frame specifies which speech acts are admissible; (ii) the performative structure is formed by a network of scenes, understood as conversation protocols or dialogue games (specified as directed graphs were arcs are labelled by speech acts *schemata*, and nodes as *institutional states*). Actions are *illocutions* made by individuals who are playing a given role, constrained by rules of behaviour that establish the normative positions of commitments that arise from agent interactions (Noriega and López del Toro 2009).

ASCS create their own institutional and social context, their specific social ecosystem, as shown by the meta-model drawn in Noriega et al. (2013). However, some interesting aspects still remain to flesh out ASCS full capabilities, mainly related to their social use, implementation and effects. As advanced by Noriega and d'Inverno (2014), electronic institutions might be open to be *anchored* in a specific environment (Fig. 11).

---

[30] tuple DF = <O, L, I, CL, *Time*>, where O stands for Ontology, L stands for language for domain content, I is the set of Illocutionary particles, CL is the agent (communication) language, *Time* is a discrete and partially ordered set of instants.

[31] Cfr. Ossowski (2013) for the state of the art in agreement technologies. An example of electronic institution for mediation purposes can be found at the Annex of the *Catalan White Book on Mediation* (Spanish version), cfr. Noriega and López del Toro (2009), http://www.llibreblancmediacio.com/. For the full study, cfr. Poblet et al. (2010a), and Casanovas et al. (2009).

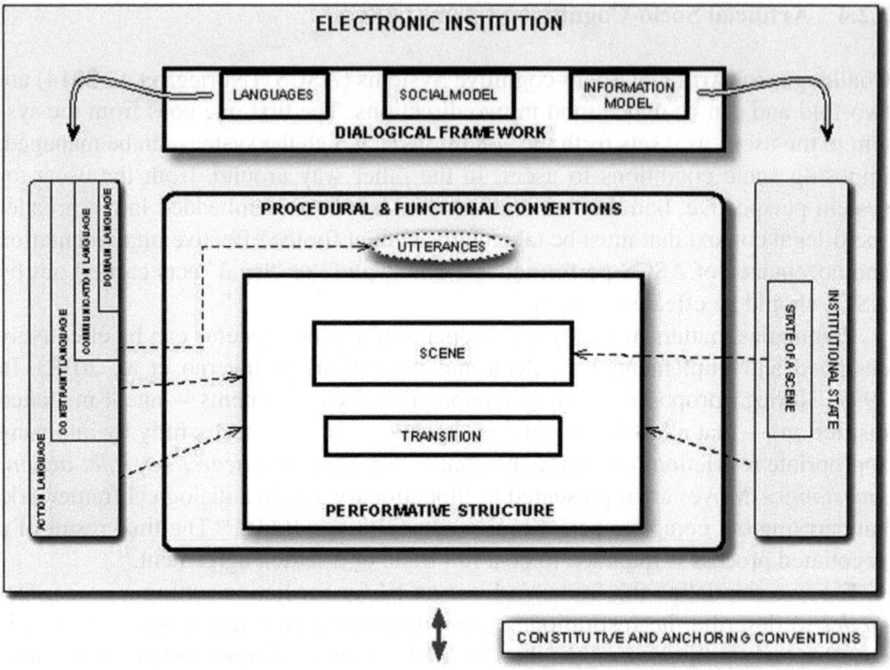

Fig. 11 Conceptual model of electronic institutions (Source: Noriega and d'Inverno (2014))

Thus, they cannot be completely settled in a situated context without selecting and taking into account some salient treats of the outer ecosystem. They should be *accommodated* into a broader social environment. Still, this is a dynamic and two-fold process, as there is a bidirectional flow between the ASCS creation of ecosystems, and the outer ones, which put their own constraints (to be understood, negotiated and eventually balanced). In this sense, it is our contention that ASCS pragmatic cycle could be completed making use of SWRM. Some *metapragmatic awareness* (Verschueren 1999, 196) is needed to trigger the systems. The pragmatic attitude in building ASCS, the representation of interactions as speech acts, and actions (moves) as illocutionary acts —or "utterances" (d'Inverno et al. 2012)— could be completed by filtering the outcomes as full *perlocutionary acts* through SWRM.

The statement assumed so far — "Actions in the computational systems *count as* actions in the real world where they are subject to appropriate regulations" (Noriega et al. 2013, 95) — could be fleshed out more explicitly. What do "appropriate regulations" mean? Things are usually a bit more complex in the real world. We cannot simply assume that EI are "mirroring" regulations. The issue of coupling (and decoupling) the ASCS generated ecosystems with the already existing ones should be carefully addressed, as it seems richer than merely assuming *ex hypothesi* the correspondence between facts and actions in the physical world, and institutional facts and actions in the IE space.[32] What links an EI with the outer (legal, political) contexts in which their outcomes will be re-evaluated and implemented?

Governance and legal implementation of existing statutes and regulations constitute a complex process on its own (Poblet et al. 2014). The norMAS community does not ignore the problem. Researchers have begun collecting and describing specific experiences involving software systems, people, and organizations (Singh et al. 2013), i.e. *hybrid* systems (Noriega and Sensoy 2015).[33]

Let's put an example of the importance of the outer environment to create social ecosystems. In emergencies, crisis, terrorist attacks, and natural disasters (bushfires, floods, hurricanes, earthquakes…), things run very fast. Conveying true and quick information among the population, all volunteers, organizations and authorities is vital. Mobile technologies are massively used (Poblet 2011). Victims, relatives and friends have a common need for information, but they may be located in different countries *under a different metadata and data protection regime*. That is to say, *existing privacy laws and policies can create legal barriers* to the way missing persons organizations collect, use and share information. However, there is a common agreement that anticipation, cooperation, and adjustment can balance all interests involved to achieve a proportional result (Reidenberg et al. 2013).

Up to date, after the many experiences gathered internationally in many of these events (2002 Bali bombing, 2004 Boxing Day tsunamis, 2005 Katrina etc.), governments have started to change *manually* the legislation for these kind of situations. In the 2011 Christchurch earthquake, the New Zealand Privacy Commissioner reacted within 24 h of the emergency declaration and issued a "temporary information sharing code" to assist in the relief effort, granting broader discretion to emergency services and government agencies. However, this kind of general personal data and metadata disclosure may create unintended effects. What about media storing all these information? What about the aggressive behaviour shown by some companies or organizations collecting and using later on this information for commercial or political purposes? What about people with special protection needs (not that uncommon: e.g., the localization of threatened women protected by a residence restraining order)?

---

[32] This is the approach proposed by Searle (1995) —*X counts as Y in context C.* According to Searle, the underlying principles in any society are quite simple: (i) collective intentionality, (ii) the assignment of function, (iii) constitutive or institutional structures: function-status assignments that take the form X counts as Y in context C. "*What is an institution? An institution is any collectively accepted system of rules (procedures, practices) that enable us to create institutional facts*" (Searle 2005). Cfr. Searle (2010) for further developments of the same thesis. This perspective stems from philosophy of language, not from empirical social sciences. Tuomela (2011) contends that the emergence of intentional collective action goes beyond Searle's individualistic account based on speech act theory. Cfr. Bolander et al. (2014).

[33] See especially the example furnished by Singh et al. (2013, 192 and ff.) as part of the NSFfunded Ocean Observatories Initiative (OOI), a thirty-year $400 million project, with thousands of stakeholders (ocean scientists, resource providers, technicians, operators, policy makers, application developers, and the general public). "*OOI provides novel capabilities for data acquisition, distribution, modelling, planning and control of oceanographic experiments, with the main goal of supporting long-term oceanographic and climate research*".

It is our contention that general provisions, exceptions and even conditions for particular cases can be better managed through SWRM and REL, which in addition: (i) have the property to coordinate the agency of different related powers (Legal Enforcement Agencies, DP agencies, supervisory commissions, local and national bodies…), (ii) can facilitate the common interoperability of norms, rights, and concepts —as for this case e.g. the legal concept of *permitted purpose* for the disclosure—, (iii) may offer a general framework to *coordinate* the legal actions to be taken before, during and after the exception. *Visualisation* of law and regulatory systems is one of the main problems in order to induce participation and an easy coordination of collective behaviour (Poblet 2013).

EI, ASCS for crisis and disaster management could help to managing the overall situation in a faster and more efficient way, but they should take into account the experiences and lessons learned.

4 Conclusions and Further Work

The previous example leads to these preliminary conclusions, as the use and reuse of ontologies and big lexical repositories come into play and should be encompassed with the use of ASCS. Enactment, protection and exercise of rights, i.e., the actual *empowerment* of individuals and communities on the Web of Data are the next step. The implementation of Artificial Socio-cognitive Systems, Semantic Web Regulatory Models, Rights Expression Languages, and Linked Licensed Open Data could help to reach this objective.

What is the role of pragmatics in the Web of Data? This chapter brings about the following conclusions: (i) Pragmatics has always been the main perspective in the Semantic Web area; (ii) this approach is maintained in the methodology to be applied, especially in knowledge acquisition processes and in ontology building; (iii) we should look closely at the notions of situational context, environmental context and social ecosystems when creating and implementing institutions; (iv) this pragmatic approach can bridge the gap between legal systems and the kind of computational models which are needed to manage data and metadata; (v) especially hybrid systems, encompassing human and artificial agents, deserve a special attention in the immediate future.

Besides, the application of LD technology to the publication of linguistic data promises to alleviate issues related to the integration and aggregation of datasets stemming from heterogeneous sources and using different vocabularies. This has led to coining the term Linguistic LD for all linguistic datasets that are published following the LD principles (Vila-Suero et al. 2014). Three essential issues need to be addressed for such data to be easily exploitable by language technologies.

First of all, datasets need to be enriched with machine-readable licensing information so that applications can reason about conditions under which it is legitimate to use a particular resource. While in the general case open licenses are preferable and compatible with the Web-style publishing used in LD, some *use cases* and datasets might require more restricted licenses or even datasets to be closed while being at the same time linked. Second, linked linguistic datasets need to have a minimum quality in order to build trust by end applications. Finally, we need shared and agree-upon vocabularies and guidelines to foster standardisation and thus easier exploitation of resources. We have briefly discussed these issues in the first sections of this chapter, and presented some preliminary investigations on the distribution of licenses in the Linguistic LD Cloud.

Different Licensing models can co-exist in Licensed Linguistic LD, from totally open to more restrictive licenses through to completely closed datasets. However, these models and LLLD should be adopted and adapted within the ethical, political, and legal constraints that apply in different countries and legal cultures. This is a big problem. Even CC licenses can be turned down and redefined by Courts in national jurisdictions, as it already happened in Germany.

Therefore, we contend that intermediate institutions such as *Semantic Web Regulatory Models* are needed in order to bridge the different kinds of regulations, and coordinate at different levels the exercise of rights with law and policy compliance. Regulations and rights on and through the Web of Data do not operate in the same way that the law used to do it in a non-virtual world. Regulatory systems need to become more complex, in order to be simpler. This is not a paradox. If we want to introduce some order and solve the "Frankenstein" puzzle (Corcho et al. 2015) in our already legally hyper-regulated global world, we should devote some effort to build up the necessary tools that social ecosystems require to work in favour of everybody. The pragmatic perspective, a hybrid and symbiotic approach, can help to achieve this goal.[34]

References

Antoniou, G., & van Harmelen, F. (2004). *A semantic web premier*. Cambridge: The MIT Press, Third ed., with P. Groth and R. Hoekstra, 2012.

Athan, T., Governatori, G., Palmirani, M., Paschke, A., & Wyner, A. (2015). LegalRuleML: Design principles and foundations. In W. Faber & A. Paschke (Eds.), *Reasoning web. Web logic rules* (pp. 151–188). Dordrecht/Heidelberg: Springer.

Aussenac-Gilles, N., & Gandon, F. (2013). From the knowledge acquisition bottleneck to the knowledge acquisition overflow: A brief French history of knowledge acquisition. *International Journal of Human-Computer Studies, 71*(2), 157–165.

Berners-Lee, T. (1999). *Weaving the web: The past, present, and future of the World Wide Web*. London: Orion Books.

Berners-Lee, T. *Linked Data*, 27 July 2006 (last change 18 June 2009) http://www.w3.org/DesignIssues/LinkedData.html

[34]This work has been carried out under the projects: DER2012-39492-C02-01 CROWDSOURCING, IPT-2012-0968-390000 CROWDCRISISCONTROL and the Australian Project CRC Data2Decisions. We thank Pablo Noriega and Marta Poblet for previous reading and useful comments.

Bizer, C., Heath, T., & Berners-Lee, T. (2009). *Linked data-the story so far.* In Semantic services, interoperability and web applications: Emerging concepts, "IJSWIS", 205–227, http://linked-data.org/docs/ijswis-special-issue

Bolander, T., Casanovas, P., Castefranchi, C., Craven, R., Franssen, M., d'Inverno, M., Herzig, A., Jones, A., McBurney, P., Nash, W., Noriega, P., Osman, N., Padget, J., Pitt, J., Pearce, D., Sierra, C., Tummolini, L., Verhagen, H. (2014). *Issues in social intelligence: Problems and challenges*, SINTELNET FP7-ICT-2009-C Project No. 286380, version: 02.2015 b.

Bonacin, R., Dos Reis, J. C., Hornung, H., & Baranauskas, M. C. (2013). An ontological model for supporting intention-based information sharing on collaborative problem solving. *International Journal of Collaborative Enterprise, 3*(2/3), 130–150.

Breuker, J. (2013). A cognitive science perspective on knowledge acquisition. *International Journal of Human-Computer Studies, 71*, 177–183.

Breuker, J., Casanovas, P., Klein, M. C. A., & Francesconi, E. (Eds.). (2009). *Law, ontologies and the semantic web.* Amsterdam: Ios Press.

Cardoso, J. (2006). Approaches to developing semantic web services. *International Journal of Computer Science, 1*(1), 8–21.

Casanovas, P. (2012). Legal crowsourcing and relational law. What the semantic web can do for legal education. *Journal of Australian Law Teachers Association, 5*(1/2), 159–176. http://www.alta.edu.au/resources/PDFs/JALTA/Full%20Volumes/2012_vol5_no1&2.pdf

Casanovas, P. (2015a). Semantic Web Regulatory Models. Why Ethics Matter? *Philosophy & Technology, 28*(1), 33–55.

Casanovas, P. (2015b). Conceptualisation of rights and meta-rule of law for the web of data. *Democracia Digital e Governo Eletrônico, 1*(12), 18–41. http://buscalegis.ufsc.br/revistas/index.php/observatoriodoegov/article/view/34399, reprinted in *Journal of Governance and Regulation, 4*(4): 118–129.

Casanovas, P., & Zeleznikow, J. (2014). Online dispute resolution and models of relational law and justice: A table of ethical principles. In P. Casanovas et al. (Eds.), *AI approaches to the complexity of legal systems IV–V* (LNAI 8929, pp. 55–69). Dordrecht/Heidelberg: Springer.

Casanovas, P., Poblet, M., Casellas, N., Vallbé, J., Benjamins, V. R., Contreras, J., Peña, R., & Blázquez, M. (2006). Semantic web: A legal case study. In J. Davis, R. Studer, & P. Warren (Eds.), *Semantic web: Trends and research* (pp. 259–280). London: Wiley.

Casanovas, P., Casellas, N., Tempich, C., Vrandečić, D., & Benjamins, R. (2007). OPJK and DILIGENT: Ontology modeling in a distributed environment. *Artificial Intelligence and Law, 15*(2), 171–186.

Casanovas, P., Díaz, L., Magre, J., & Poblet, M. (Eds.). (2009). *Materiales del Llibro Blanco de la Mediación en Cataluña* (La mediación: conceptos, ámbitos, perfiles, indicadores, Vol. I). Barcelona: Generalitat de Catalunya, Departament de Justícia CEJFE.

Casanovas, P., Pagallo, U., Sartor, G., & Ajani, G. (2010). Introduction: Complex systems and six challenges for the development of law and the semantic web. In P. Casanovas et al. (Eds.), *Artificial intelligence and complex legal systems* (LNAI 6237, pp. 1–11). Heidelberg/Berlin: Springer.

Casanovas, P., Casellas, N., & Vallbé, J. J. (2011). Empirically grounded developments of legal ontologies: A socio-legal perspective. In G. Sartor, P. Casanovas, M. A. Biasiotti, & M. Fernández-Barrera (Eds.), *Approaches to legal ontologies: Theories, domains and methodologies* (pp. 49–68). Dordrecht/Heidelberg: Springer.

Casanovas, P., Arraiza, J., Melero, F., González-Conejero, J., Molcho, G., & Cuadros, M. (2014a). Fighting organized crime through open source intelligence: Regulatory strategies of the CAPER project. In R. Hoekstra (Ed.), *Legal knowledge and information systems: JURIX 2014: The twenty-seventh annual conference* (Vol. 271, pp. 189–198). Amsterdam: Ios Press.

Casanovas, P., Pagallo, U., Palmirani, M., & Sartor, G. (Eds.). (2014b). *AI approaches to the complexity of legal systems IV. Social intelligence, models and applications for law and justice systems in the semantic web and legal reasoning* (AICOL IV–V, LNAI 8929). Dordrecht/Heidelberg: Springer.

Casanovas, P., Palmirani, M., Peroni, S., van Engers, T., & Vitali, F. (2016). Special issue on the semantic web for the legal domain guest editors' editorial: The next step. *Semantic Web Journal, 7*(2), 1–13.

Casellas, N. (2011). *Legal ontology engineering: Methodologies, modelling trends, and the ontology of professional judicial knowledge*. Dordrecht/Heidelberg: Springer.

Casellas, N., Blázquez, M., Kiryakov, A., Casanovas, P., Poblet, M., & Benjamins, R. (2005). OPJK into PROTON: Legal domain ontology integration into an upper-level ontology. In Z. Tari (Ed.), *On the move to meaningful internet systems 2005: OTM 2005 workshops* (LNCS 3762, pp. 846–855). Berlin/Heidelrberg: Springer.

Chiarcos, C., Hellmann, S., & Nordhoff, S. (2012). Linking linguistic resources: Examples from the open linguistics working group. In C. Chiarcos, S. Nordhoff, & S. Hellmann (Eds.), *Linked data in linguistics. Representing language data and metadata* (pp. 201–216). Dordrecht/ Heidelberg: Springer.

Clancey, W. J., Sachs, P., Sierhuis, M., & van Hoof, R. (1998). Brahms: Simulating practice for work systems design. *International Journal of Human-Computer Studies, 49*, 831–865.

Compton, P. (2013). Situated cognition and knowledge acquisition research. *International Journal of Human-Computer Studies, 71*, 184–190.

Corcho, O., Poveda-Villalón, M., & Gómez-Pérez, A. (2015). Ontology engineering in the era of linked data. *Bulletin of the American Society for Information Science and Technology, 41*(4), 13–17.

Davies, J., Potter, M., Richardson, M., Stinčić, S., Domingue, J., & González-Cabero, G. (2009). Towards the open service web. *BT Technology Journal, 26*, 2.

d'Aquin, M., & Gangemi, A. (2011). Is there beauty in ontologies? *Applied Ontology, 6*(3), 165–175.

d'Aquin, M., Motta, E., Sabou, M., Angeletou, S., Gridinoc, L., Lopez, V., & Guidi, D. (2008). Towards a new generation of semantic web applications. *IEEE Intelligent Systems, 24*, 20–28.

de Moor, A. (2005). Patterns for the Pragmatic Web. *In Proceedings of the 13th international conference on Conceptual Structures (ICCS'05): Common Semantics for Sharing Knowledge* (LNCS 3596, pp. 1–18). Heidelberg, Berlin: Springer.

d'Inverno, M., Luck, M., Noriega, P., Rodriguez-Aguilar, J. A., & Sierra, C. (2012). Communicating open systems. *Artificial Intelligence, 186*, 38–94.

Distinto, I., d'Aquin, M., & Motta, E. (2016). LOTED2: An ontology of European public procurement notices. *Semantic Web, 7*(3), 267–293.

Domingue, J., Fensel, D., & Hendler, J. A. (Eds.). (2011). *Handbook of web semantics technologies*. Heidelberg/Dordrecht: Springer.

Feigenbaum, E. A. (1984). Knowledge engineering: The applied side of artificial intelligence. *Annals of the New York Academy of Sciences, 426*, 91–107. Original publication in 1980 as Report of the Stanford Department of Computer Science.

Feigenbaum, E. A. (1992). *A personal view of experts systems: Looking back and looking ahead* (Knowledge System Laboratory, Report n. 92–41). Stanford: KSL.

Francesconi, E., Küster, M. W., Gratz, P., & Thelen, S. (2015). The ontology-based approach of the publications office of the EU for document accessibility and open data services. In *Electronic government and the information systems perspective* (pp. 29–39). Dordrecht/Heidelberg: Springer.

Francopoulo, G., Monte, G., Calzolari, N., Monachini, M., Bel, N., Pet, M., & Soria, C. (2006). *Lexical markup framework (LMF)*. In International conference on Language Resources and Evaluation-LREC 2006- LREC 2006, G^enes/Italie, 2006. <inria-00121468 >.

Gaines, B. R. (2013). Knowledge acquisition: Past, present and future. *International Journal of Human-Computer Studies, 71*, 135–156.

Gómez-Pérez, A., Fernández-López, M., & Corcho, O. (2004). *Ontological engineering with examples from the areas of knowledge management, e-commerce and the semantic web*. Dordrecht/Heidelberg: Springer.

González-Conejero, J., Varela-Figueroa, R., Muñoz-Gómez, J., & Teodoro, E. (2014). Organized crime structure modelling for European Law Enforcement Agencies interoperability through ontologies. In P. Casanovas et al. (Eds.), *AI approaches to the complexity of legal systems* (AICOL IV-V, pp. 217–231). Dordrecht/Heidelberg: Springer.

Gruber, T. R. (1993). A translation approach to portable ontology specifications. *Knowledge Acquisition, 5*(2), 199–220.

Gruber, T. R. (2000). *It is what it does: The pragmatics of ontology for knowledge sharing*. Presentation available at https://www.yumpu.com/en/document/view/31975231/it-is-what-it-does-the-pragmatics-of-ontology-as-tom-gruber

Gruber, T. R. (2013). Nature, nurture, and knowledge acquisition. *International Journal of Human-Computer Studies, 71*(2), 191–194.

Guarino, N., & Giaretta, P. (1995). Ontologies and knowledge bases towards a terminological clarification. In J. N. I. Mars (Ed.), *Towards very large knowledge bases: Knowledge building & knowledge sharing* (pp. 25–32). Amsterdam: Ios Press.

Hitzler, P., & van Harmelen, F. (2010). A reasonable semantic web. *Semantic Web Journal, 1*(1), 39–44. http://corescholar.libraries.wright.edu/cse/25

Hoekstra, R. (2010). The knowledge reengineering bottleneck. *Semantic Web Journal, 1*(1/2), 111–115.

Hua, J. (2008). *Study on knowledge acquisition techniques.* In Intelligent Information Technology Application, 2008. IITA'08. Second international symposium IEEE, 1: 181–185.

Iannella, R. (2003). *Digital rights management technology*, Available at NICTA http://www.nicta.com.au/pub?doc=764

Iannella, R. (2015). ODRL Version 2.1 core model final specification: 5 March. https://www.w3.org/community/odrl/model/2.1

Jentzsch, A., Cyganiak, R., & Bizer, C. (2011). State of the LOD Cloud Version 0.3, 09/19/2011. http://lod-cloud.net/state/

Kasper, G., & Rose, K. R. (1999). Pragmatics and SLA. *Annual Review of Applied Linguistics, 19*, 81–104.

Levinson, S. (2003). *Space in language and cognition.* Cambridge: Cambridge University Press.

Lewis, R. (ed.). (2007). *Dereferencing HTTP URIs*, (31 May, 2007), W3C, http://www.w3.org/2001/tag/doc/httpRange-14/2007-05-31/HttpRange-14

Liu, K. (2009). *Pragmatic computing – A semiotic perspective to web services.* In J. Filipe, & M.S. Obaidat (eds.), Communications in computer and information science, 23: 3–15.

Markoff, J. (2006). *Entrepeneurs see a web guided by common sense* (11/12/2006). http://www.nytimes.com/2006/11/12/business/12web.html?_r=1&pagewanted=1&ei=5088&en=254d697964cedc62&ex=1320987600

Marz, N., & Warren, J. (2014). *Big data. Principles and best practices of scalable real time data systems*. Shelter Island: Manning.

Mazak, A., & Wally, B. (2014). *Pragmatic-based ontology design and alignment.* In *Proceedings of the 8th international workshop on Value Modeling and Business Ontology (VMBO 2014).* Available at: http://www.csw.inf.fu-berlin.de/vmbo2014/papers.htm

McCrae, J., Aguado-de-Cea, G., Buitelaar, P., Cimiano, P., Declerck, T., Gómez-Pérez, A., Gracia, J., et al. (2012). Interchanging lexical resources on the semantic web. *Language Resources and Evaluation, 46*(4), 701–719.

McRoberts, M., & Rodríguez-Doncel, V. ODRL Version 2.1 Ontology, W3C, 2015-03-05. http://www.w3.org/ns/odrl/2/ODRL21

Musen, M. A. (2013). The knowledge acquisition workshops: A remarkable convergence of ideas. *International Journal of Human-Computer Studies, 71*, 195–199.

Noriega, P. (1999). *Agent mediated auctions: The fishmarket metaphor*. Barcelona: IIIA.

Noriega, P., Chopra A. K., Fornara, N., Lopes Cardoso, H., & Singh, M. (2013). Regulated MAS: Social perspective. In Andruguetti et al. (Eds.), *Normative multi-agent systems, Schloss Dagstuhl – Leibniz-Zentrum für lnformatik GmbH* (pp. 93–134). Saarbrücken/Wadern: Dagstuhl Publ. http://www.dagstuhl.de/dagpub/ 978-3-939897-51-4

Noriega, P., & d'Inverno, M. (2014). *Crowd-based socio-cognitive systems.* In M. Poblet, P. Noriega, & E. Plaza, *Sintelnet WG5 workshop on crowd intelligence: Foundations, methods and practices,* Barcelona, 1–15. http://ceur-ws.org/Vol-1148/CROWD2014_Full.pdf

Noriega, P., & López del Toro, C., (2009). *Towards a platform for online mediation.* In M. Poblet, U. Schield & J. Zeleznikow (eds.), *Legal and Negotiation Decision Support Systems (LDSS 2009), a Post-conference workshop of the 12th international conference on artificial intelligence and law, proceedings,* Barcellona: IDT Series, 69–76.

Noriega, P., & Lopez del Toro, C. (2010). Annex of the *Catalan White Book on Mediation,* http://www.llibreblancmediacio.com/

Noriega, P., & Sensoy, M., (eds.). (2015). *Agent teams for design problems.* In *The XVIII international workshop on coordination, organizations, institutions and norms in multiagent systems,* Istambul: COIN@ AAMAS 2015.

Noriega, P., Padget, J., Verhagen, H., & d'Inverno, M. (2014). *The challenge of artificial socio-cognitive systems.* In The XIX international workshop on coordination, organizations, institutions and norms in multiagent systems, Paris: COIN@AAMAS2014.

Øhrstrøm, P., Schärfe, H., & Uckelman, S. (2008). Jacob Lorhard's ontology: A 17th century hypertext on the reality and temporality of the World of Intelligibles. In P. Eklund & O. Haemmerlé (Eds.), *ICCS 2008* (LNAI 5113, pp. 74–87). Dordrecht/Heidelberg: Springer.

Ossowski, S. (Ed.). (2013). *Agreement technologies.* Dordrecht/Heidelberg: Springer.

Paschke, A. (2013). *Pragmatic web 4.0. Towards an active and interactive semantic media web,* W3C Aspect of Semantic Technologies, at http://www.slideshare.net/swadpasc/pragmatic-web-paschke

Paschke, A., Boley, A., Kozlenkov, A., Craig, B. (2007). *Rule responder: RuleML-based agents for distributed collaboration on the pragmatic web.* In 2nd international conference on the pragmatic web Oct 22–23, Tilburg/New York: ACM.

Pedrinaci, C., & Domingue, J. (2010). Toward the next wave of services: Linked services for the web of data. *Journal of Universal Computer Science, 16*(3), 1694–1719.

Pedrinaci, C., Domingue, J., & Sheth, A. P. (2011). Semantic web services. In J. Domingue et al. (Eds.), *Handbook of semantic web technologies* (pp. 977–1035). Berlin, Heidelberg: Springer.

Poblet, M. (Ed.). (2011). *Mobile technologies for conflict management: Online dispute resolution, governance, participation.* Dordrecht/Heidelberg: Springer.

Poblet, M., (2013). Visualizing the law: Crisis mapping as an open tool for legal practice. *Journal of Open Access to Law, 1,* 1. https://ojs.law.cornell.edu/index.php/joal/article/view/12

Poblet, M., Noriega, P., Pérez del Toro, C., Suquet, J. & Redorta, J. (2010). *Capítulo 16. Tecnologías para la mediación en línea: estado del arte, usos y propuestas.* In P. Casanovas, J. Magre, & E. Lauroba, (eds.), *Libro Blanco de la Mediación en Cataluña,* Barcelona: Departament de Justícia, Generalitat de Catalunya, Huygens Editorial, 896–1008. http://www.llibreblancmediacio.com/

Poblet, M., Noriega, P., & Plaza, E. (2014). *Sintelnet WG5 workshop on crowd intelligence: Foundations, methods and practices.* http://ceur-ws.org/Vol-1148/CROWD2014_Full.pdf

Poblet, M., Teodoro, E., Gonzalez-Conejero, J., Varela, R., & Casanovas, P. (2015). *A co-regulatory approach to stay safe online: reporting inappropriate content with the MediaKids mobile app.* Journal of Family Studies, http://dx.doi.org/10.1080/13229400.2015.1106337

Ramakrishna, S., & Paschke, A. (2014). A process for knowledge transformation and knowledge representation of patent law. In A. Bikakis et al. (Eds.), *RuleML 2014* (LNCS 8620, pp. 311–328). Dordrecht/Heidelberg: Springer.

Reidenberg, J. R., Gellman, R., Debelak, J., Elewa, A., & Liu, N. (2013). *Privacy and missing persons after natural disasters.* Washington, DC/New York: Center on Law and Information Policy at Fordham Law School and Woodrow Wilson International Center for Scholars.

Rodríguez-Doncel, V., Suárez-Figueroa, M. C., Gómez-Pérez, A., & Poveda M. (2013a). *License linked data resources pattern.* In *Proceedings of the 4th international workshop on ontology patterns,* Sydney. *Proceedings of the 4th workshop on ontology and semantic web patterns.* CEUR-WS n. 1188, http://ceur-ws.org/Vol-1188/

Rodríguez-Doncel, V., Gómez-Pérez, A., & Mihindukulasooriya, N. (2013b). *Rights declaration in Linked Data.* In O. Hartig, et al. (eds.) *Rights declaration in Linked Data*, CEUR 1034. http://ceur-ws.org/Vol-1034/RodriguezDoncelEtAl_COLD2013.pdf

Sartor, G., Casanovas, P., Biasiotti, M. A., & Fernández-Barrera, M. (Eds.). (2011). *Approaches to legal ontologies: Theories, domains and methodologies*. Dordrecht/Heidelberg: Springer.

Schindler, H. R., Cave, J., Robinson, N., Horvath, V., Hackett, P. J., Gunashekar, S., Botterman, M., Forge, S., & Graux, H. (2012). *Europe's policy options for a dynamic and trustworthy development of the internet of things*, RAND Europe. *Prepared for European Commission, DG Communications Networks, Content and Technology (CONNECT)*, RAND Corporation, SMART 2012/0053 http://www.rand.org/content/dam/rand/pubs/research_reports/RR300/RR356/RAND_RR356.pdf

Schmachtenberg, M., Bizer, C., Jentzsch, A., & Cyganiak, R. (2014). *Adoption of the linked data best practices in different topical domains, in the semantic web – ISWC 2014* (LNCS 8796, pp. 245–256). Dordrecht/Heidelberg: Springer.

Schoop, M., de Moor, A., & Dietz, J. L. G. (2006). The pragmatic web: A manifesto. *Communications of the ACM, 49*(5), 75–76.

Searle, J. R. (1995). *The construction of social reality*. New York: Free Press.

Searle, J. R. (2005). What is an institution? *Journal of Institutional Economics, 1*(01), 1–22.

Searle, J. R. (2010). *Making the social world: The structure of human civilization*. Oxford: Oxford University Press.

Sierhuis, M., Clancey, W. J., & Van Hoof, R. J. (2007). Brahms: A multi-agent modelling environment for simulating work processes and practices. *International Journal of Simulation and Process Modelling, 3*(3), 134–152.

Singh, M. P. (2002). *The pragmatic web: Preliminary thoughts.* In A. Sheth, & R. Meersman (eds.), *Proceedings of NSF-OntoWeb W. on database and information systems research for semantic web and enterprises,* Position papers, April 3–5, Georgia: AmicalolaFalls and State Park, 82–90. Available at: https://www.academia.edu/2816888/DB-IS_Research_for_Semantic_Web_and_Enterprises_Brief_History_and_Agenda

Singh, M. P., Arrott, M., Balke, T., Chopra, A., Christiaanse, R., Cranefield, S., Dignum, F., Eynard, D., Farcas, E., Fornara, N., Gandon, F., Governatori, G., Khanh Dam, H., Hulstijn, J., Krueger, I., Lam, H., Meisinger, M., Noriega, P., Savarimuthu, B. T. R., Tadanki, K., Verhagen, H., & Villata, S. (2013). The uses of norms. In G. Andriguetto et al. (Eds.), *Normative multi-agent systems* (pp. 191–229). Saarbrücken/Wadern: Schloss Dagstuhl.

Sperber, D., & Wilson, D. (1995). *Relevance: Communication and cognition* (2nd ed.). Oxford, Cambridge, MA: Blackwell Publishers.

Studer, R., Benjamins, V. R., & Fensel, D. (1998). Knowledge engineering: Principles and methods. *Data and Knowledge Engineering, 25*(1/2), 161–197.

Suárez-Figueroa, M. C., Gómez-Pérez, A., & Fernandez-López, F. (2012). The NeOn methodology for ontology engineering. In M. C. Suárez-Figueroa et al. (Eds.), *Ontology engineering in a networked world* (pp. 9–34). Dordrecht/Heidelberg: Springer.

Suquet, J., Casanovas, P., Binefa, X., Martinez, O., Ruiz, A. & Ceballos, J. (2014). Consumedia. Functionalities, emotion detection and automation of services in a ODR platform. In P. Casanovas et al. (Eds.). *AI approaches to the complexity of legal systems* (LNCS 8929, pp. 247–260). Dordrecht/Heidelberg: Springer.

Tuomela, R. (2011). Searle's new construction of social reality. *Analysis, 71*, 706.

Verschueren, J. (1999). *Understanding pragmatics*. London: Arnold.

Vila-Suero, D., Rodríguez-Doncel, V., Gómez-Pérez, A., Cimiano, P., McCrae, J. P., & Aguado de Cea, G. (2014). *3LD: Towards high quality, industry-ready linguistic Linked Licensed Data.* European Data Forum-2014, 1–29.

Weigand, H., & Paschke, A. (2012). The pragmatic web: Putting rules in context. In A. Bikakis & A. Giurca (Eds.), *Rules on the web: Research and applications* (LNCS 7438, pp. 182–192). Berlin/Heidelberg: Springer.

Part III
Pragmatics and Legal Adjudication

Pragmatics of Adjudication. In the Footsteps of Alf Ross

Mauro Barberis

Precedent is a Jewish mother.
You don't have to do what it tells you, but
it makes you feel terrible about not doing it (S. Sedley)

Abstract Three insights about a pragmatic theory of legal interpretation are enumerated here: on legal sources, judicial precedents, and statutory interpretation, respectively. Firstly, with regards legal sources, a theory of them in terms of legal materials is restated on the basis of Ross 1952, with a slight caveat: legislation seems even more indeterminate than precedents, a mere starting point for such judicial inferential processes as qualification of facts-of-the-case, interpretation, and application. Secondly, common law's precedents and civil law's *jurisprudence* (in French), are different sorts of customary law which are likely to replace statutory law (in common law) or complement it (in civil law) in order to make judicial decisions less unpredictable. Finally, as far as the statutory interpretation is concerned, interpretive skepticism is restated by assuming that it is a trivial starting point for a truly realistic, pragmatic-contextualist and inferentialist theory of such an interpretation. This theory needs to conceive interpretation as the recontextualization of decontextualized statutes, where the ultimate context is provided by precedents or *jurisprudence* itself.

Keywords Legal adjudication • Interpretive scepticism • Legal precedent • Context

1 Introduction

The received view in the theory of law – a mix of legal positivism and legal realism I will call legal creationism, as opposed to legal evolutionism – relies on the wrong paradigm, legislation. After all, legislation is a discourse which is decontextualized

M. Barberis (✉)
Department of Law, Language, Interpretation and Translation (IUSLIT), University of Trieste, Trieste, Italy
e-mail: barberis@units.it

F. Poggi, A. Capone (eds.), *Pragmatics and Law*, Perspectives in Pragmatics, Philosophy & Psychology 10, DOI 10.1007/978-3-319-44601-1_13

enough to discourage one from pragmatic analysis. In order to clarify such a bold statement, the *first* section revisits Alf Ross's realistic theory of *legal sources* as mere legal materials actually used by courts in order to justify their decisions. The *second* section focuses on specifically judicial legal sources, namely common law's precedents and civil law's *jurisprudence constante* (in French), by distinguishing three steps in the history of common law adjudication: "pure" adjudication or mere case-law, non-binding precedents, and binding precedents. Finally, the third section extends such a history to a fourth and seemingly more refined step, namely legislation and statutory interpretation, by providing a first, rough and tentative pragmatic analysis of the latter.

2 Three Types of Legal Materials

After so many recent debates on legal sources, it is amazing to read the third chapter of *On Law and Justice* (1952; 1958) today: the classic formulation of a realistic theory of sources «as a factor in the motivation process of the judicial decision» (Ross 1946, 144). More than 60 years later this theory still seems to be the most sensitive and comprehensive available, just needing to be updated with regards subsequent constitutionalization and internationalization processes and, by the way, to be rephrased in pragmatically more sophisticated terms (but cf. yet Ross 1968, 1972 and Sardo 2015). Ross redefines the sources of law as legal *materials*, picked up by judges by establishing both a *ideology* and a *doctrine* of them, the latter explaining the former, which are in turn described by a realist, value-free *theory* of sources. Before analyzing the three types of materials listed by the author, let us consider the metaphor of materials itself.

According to him, far from dictating a complete regulation of their conduct, law only provides judges with legal materials: different kinds of products from which such a regulation can be inferred.

> Metaphorically speaking, we can perhaps say that legislation delivers a finished product, immediately ready for use, while precedent and custom deliver only semi-finished product, which have to be finished by the judge himself, and "reason" produces only certain raw materials from which the judge himself has to fashion the rule he needs (Ross 1958, 76–77).

Shortly after, Ross replaces this metaphorical notion of materials or products with a different, less metaphorical terminology: «The scheme of classification [of legal sources] will be: (1) the completely objectivated type of source: the authoritative formulations (legislation in the wide sense); (2) the partly objectivated type of sources: custom and precedent; and, (3) the non-objectivated, "free" type of source: "reason"» (Ross 1958, 78). Such "artificialist" metaphors (materials, industrial products), inspired by von Jhering 1857 (cf. Lloredo 2012), replace here the traditional "naturalist" metaphor of sources, making explicit Ross' view of law as an artefact, if not as a sort of object-in-the-world: an idea which is far from the more pragmatic view of law and interpretation then provided by the same author. Now let us see, in reverse order, the three main types of legal materials listed in Ross 1958.

2.1 Surprisingly enough, if one thinks of Ross' meta-ethical emotivism, the *first* type of (mere) materials, i.e. raw materials or non-objectivated sources, is *reason* or, as Ross is quick to point out, *cultural tradition*: the "source" of both ancient and non-Western law. The use of "source", here is, of course, improper: reason, tradition, natural law, classic Greek *dikaion*, Roman *ius* and modern Islamic *shar'ia* too, strictly speaking, do not have sources as modern legislation does, i.e. do not provide anything like a fully-fledged rule-formulation. On the contrary, modern Western codes and legislation are sources-based in the sense they list a set of strictly legal materials, thus distinguishing them from religion, morals, and non-law in general. Herbert Hart also speaks about only modern law as a customary rule of recognition, thus denying that ancient law has such a rule and is sources-based.

Accordingly, in order to build a truly general theory of law which also applies to ancient and non-Western law, the term "sources" needs be replaced by "materials": a repository of maxims, arguments and techniques actually used by jurists. According to Ross, by the way, this replacement of "legal sources" with "legal materials" sheds light on the positivism-realism relationship: «The term"positivism" is ambiguous. It can mean both "which builds on experience" and"what is formally established" [...] A realistic doctrine of the sources builds on experience, but recognises that not all law is positive, in the sense of "formally established"» (Ross 1958, 100–101). Here Ross reminds us, in spite of more recent neo-formalistic attitudes (cf. Barberis 2015b), legal realism by definition recognizes the existence of living law, which is of course different from the formally established one.

2.2 The *second* main type of legal materials, semi-finished products, or partially objectivated legal sources, includes *customs* and *precedents*: two different but strictly intertwined materials. In spite of John Austin's well-known theory, according to which customs are legal sources only insofar as they are applied by courts, an application that would turn them from positive morality into legal precedents, Ross rightly argues customs are legal sources in their own right, *ratione materiae*, when they regulate legal matters. The relationship of customs and precedents, however, is a bit more complex than he believes; in fact, it is not one but triune. *First*, as the so-called classic, declarative theory of the common law claims, English courts applied the immemorial customs of the land, thus turning them into precedents: as was the case with the origins of common law, but which can still occur (cf. Sect. 4.3 *in fine*).

Second, English courts began to follow their decisions on similar cases, first as a mere practice or regularity of behaviour, without the conviction they had to do so, or an explicit doctrine prescribing it. When such a conviction and doctrine prevailed definitively, between the eighteenth and nineteenth century, following precedents became a general judicial custom of the kingdom. *Third*, such a general judicial custom can be opposed to all the more particular judicial customs, namely a chain or line of precedents – in French, a *jurisprudence* – on the same legal question. As we shall see in Sect. 3, in fact, common law's chains of precedents and the very *stare decisis*' doctrine not only have customary origins but also a customary character – they are but judicial customs (cf. Barberis 2015c).

According to Ross, anyway, precedents work as materials suited to find and justify the solutions given by courts to cases: this is what transpires with common law's precedents, but also with civil law's *jurisprudence*. Ross's realist warning – non-formally established law does exist and, what is more important, it is what gives real life to the formally established one – reminds us that the distinction between Anglo-American precedents and European-continental *jurisprudence* is thinner than it is generally believed. In fact, the traditional legal comparatists' dichotomies – "binding" vs. "persuasive" precedents, "formal" or "factual" binding force of them – are increasingly blurred every day, as we shall see in Sect. 3.3: civil law and common law do not come close to one another, as is commonly said, rather it is Western law as a whole which is becoming, or coming back, more and more judicial.

2.3 The *third* main type of legal materials, as (allegedly) finished products or completely objectivated legal sources, is *legislation* widely conceived, including statutes, administrative regulations, and constitutional documents too. The remarks Ross makes on this subject are somewhat trivial: he seems to share here the common idea of legislation as the final result of a political will, decided once and for all. That, in fact, is an idea that Scandinavian realists share with mainstream legal positivists, but which in the case of Ross's chapter on sources is justified mainly by the opposition between legislation and other legal materials. In fact, the core of Ross's realistic stance on the subject is not here, in the third chapter of the book, but later, in the fourth one devoted to statutory interpretation. A critique of these remarks on legislation can be outlined here, however.

From a *legal* perspective, firstly, by opposing legislation to other sources, Ross seems even to adopt the simplistic idea that legislators produce ready-made rule formulations to be merely applied by courts without interpreting them – in contrast to Ross's own theory of interpretation. Such a view, that I have labelled elsewhere *legal creationism* (cf. Barberis 2015c), is close to the distinction drawn by Jeremy Bentham in a manuscript quoted by Postema 1986, 228, between *actual* law (legislation, codes) and *inferential* law (customs, precedents): «Though statute laws are "actual", Common Law rules are "inferential" [norms] as shall appear to be just the expression of judicial practice in like cases». *Common law* «exists not in any certain form of words: the acts it is founded on are acts of authority: but the words in which they are expressed are yours, are mine, are anyone's»: which amounts to the conclusion that, as an abstract norm, common law does not exist.

Secondly, from a *linguistic* perspective, Ross's attitude still relies on an old-fashioned semantic, non-pragmatic view: in fact, a very common one among the legal theorists of the 1950s, still influenced by logical positivism. According to such a view, adjudication could be reduced to statutory construction, conceiving the latter, moreover, as a mere decoding of signs previously encoded. This is a stance which is still very common in European-continental legal realism (cf. Barberis 2015a), especially in the Genoa School's mainstream theory of interpretation: just think of Pierluigi Chiassoni's theory of interpretive codes here (cf. Chiassoni 2007, and below, Sect. 3) Of course, the following chapter of Ross 1958, about statutory construction, and of course Ross 1968, will come closer to a pragmatic and inferentialist approach to law and interpretation as discursive practices: but it does so by using "pragmatics" more in the sense of a teleological or consequentialist approach than in its strictly linguistic sense.

In short, Ross will also get rid of a merely syntactic or semantic approach, and will adopt a truly realistic, pragmatic-contextualist and inferentialist one. First, a truly *realistic* approach does focus from the beginning on the living law, and therefore on adjudication, by conceiving legislation as a mere limit to it (cf. here 2.). Second, a *pragmatic* approach (and also a *pragmatist* one, distinct from the former: cf. Butler 2005), following the current drift in linguistic studies towards the so-called pragmatization of semantics (cf. Peregrin 1999 and below Sect. 3.1). Third, an *inferentialist* approach which assumes, contrary to Ross's metaphor, that legislation is not a finished product, but that it is only the starting point for such inferential practices as legal qualification of the facts-of-the-case, interpretation, and application (cf. Canale and Tuzet 2007: 39, Canale and Tuzet 2009, both inspired by Brandom 1994).

3 Towards a Really Realistic Theory of Adjudication

A pragmatic analysis of legal discourse is unattractive so long as one adopts, as a model of law, the wrong paradigm, legislation, i. e. by far the most decontextualized type of law. Taking this into account, Karl Olivecrona famously remarked that legislation cannot be reduced to commands issued by the sovereign *vis-à-vis* his subjects, therefore dubbing statutes as *independent imperatives* (Olivecrona 1939, 42–49): where "independent" means precisely "decontextualized". Such legal documents as constitutional or international declarations of rights, indeed, are possibly even more decontextualized than domestic statutes: and this despite the fact their use by the courts is growingly accounted for, in the post-modern jargon, as a "conversation", a "talk", or even a "narrative", between so immaterial actors as courts, States, corporations, NGO's, and so forth.

As we have just seen, Ross himself tends to replace legislation with adjudication in the role of pivotal legal activity. Adjudication, however, is virtually reduced by him, and his Genoese followers, to statutory construction, and accounted for as an activity parasitic to legislation, a sort of decoding of previously encoded signs. In contrast, statutory construction is only an overrated part of adjudication, which is, in turn, not just the living law, but the conceptual core of legal phenomena. As Joseph Raz says, «the existence of norm-creating institutions, though characteristic of modern legal systems, is not a necessary feature of all legal systems», whereas «the existence of certain types of norms-applying institutions is» (Raz 1979, 105). As we will see in Sect. 4, moreover, the real heart of adjudication is not textual construction but legal qualification of the-facts-of-the-case with reference to the very legal materials.

A truly realistic, pragmatic and inferentialist theory of law, therefore, needs to be concerned with Anglo-American precedents or European-continental *jurisprudence* in a double sense. In the *first*, traditional sense, such a theory would still focus only on *binding* legal sources, i.e. statutes and precedents in common law, statutes in civil law: although statutes are applied in their interpretation, which in common law *is* precedent *de iure*, in civil law *de facto*. In a *second*, less traditional sense, such a theory focuses on precedents, and *jurisprudence constante* too, not as binding sources or formally established law, but only as legal materials from which the living law is inferred. It is in this second sense that a new realist analysis is needed, a less demystifying and more constructive one: by conceiving precedents or *jurisprudence* as self-restraining devices emerging from the working of adjudication itself, and by distinguishing, in the wake of Ross, "pure" adjudication, non-binding precedent, and binding precedent.

3.1 *Pure adjudication*, as it were, is judicial activity free from the bounds of both precedents and legislation. Pure adjudication, accordingly, could seem a notion as mythological as Weberian *justice of cadi*, if not an ill-formed concept, contrasting with the very definition of "adjudication" as application of a law different from adjudication itself. Yet, historians and comparatists say that in the old good days of the Western legal tradition, during a period of at least 500 years and starting from events such as the rediscovery of the *Corpus iuris* in continental Europe and the Norman conquest in England, "law" denoted little more than judicial decisions, unbound both by legislation and precedents. In fact, this is precisely the paradigm of Western law: adjudication, i.e. «administering justice according to law between the parties» (Cross 1977, 233).

Here, not elsewhere, lies the alleged necessary connection of law and morals: law is, paradigmatically, the situation in which a judge does justice between two parties. Does such a conceptual remark justify natural law theory's central tenet that law and morals need have a logical, necessary or conceptual connection? In a sense, yes: in a first sense of "justice", internal to the law and more common in ordinary language, law is paradigmatically the situation where the judge aims to do justice (Hayek 1982, vol. II). However, in a second sense of "justice", external to the law and perhaps more common only in philosophical usage, law and morals have no necessary relationship whatsoever. Unjust judicial decisions, unjust legislation and an unjust constitution are perfectly conceivable, and in fact not uncommon: *pace* Robert Alexy's argument from injustice and his alleged performative contradiction (Alexy 2002).

Pure adjudication, by definition, is legally unbound, a sort of judgment one could even classify as merely moral, if any separation of law and morals would make sense here, i.e. with reference to ancient or extra-Western cultures, where the law/morals distinction is often not even nominalized. We must reject, accordingly, the temptation to apply to pure adjudication morally-centered approaches such as particularism: the idea of an *ad hoc*, case by case equitable justice (cf. Dancy 2004; Bouvier 2012; Cuono 2013; Muffato 2015). My own opinion, on the contrary, is that it is not morals that are apt to throw light on adjudication, but just the other way around. Paradoxically enough, one understands more of *moral* evaluation by looking at it from the perspective of its old *legal* true archetype, adjudication.

Courts, perhaps, always did justify their decisions *as if* they were application of a law different from their decisions themselves: a justification, however, which cannot be reduced to a mere fiction or ideology, as Bentham believed, depending instead on the very concept of adjudication as a law-applying activity. The most serious candidates to the role of law to be applied, in the Western tradition, have been three: three types of law, adopting John Gardner's (2007, 73–74) definitions. In the ancient world, where legislation was still unknown or underdeveloped, the first candidate was customary law: e.g., the alleged immemorial customs of Englishmen. In more modern times, the second candidate was case-law: the individual judicial decisions or precedents (cf. Sect. 2.2–2.3.). Only after codification and French Revolution, legislation become the third candidate: a so overbearing one, however, to claim to be the law *par excellence*.

3.2 *Non-binding precedents* are past judicial decisions quoted by judges in order to adjudicate: a concept that after the civil law's codifications bifurcates into civil law and common law contexts. In civil law's contexts, where judicial decisions are not deemed binding sources of law, "non-binding precedents" denotes the use by a judge of a line of past judicial decisions or a *jurisprudence constante*. The case, here, must always formally regulated by some piece of legislation: a piece of legislation, however, which is in the long run interpreted according to such a *jurisprudence* no less than common law's statutes are (cf. Wróblewski 2001; Taruffo 2007). In common law contexts, instead, "non-binding precedents" denotes the application of almost an individual precedent *before* the Nineteenth century's adoption by the House of Lords of *stare decisis* doctrine: and this, mind you, either the instant case was devised by common law itself, or by parliamentary statutes.

It is fairly well known that *stare decisis* is a *doctrine* only in the sense of a general statement made by a Court, not by legal dogmatics. Ironically enough, common law theorists say very little about the pragmatic status of such a doctrine (cf. Tiller and Cross 2006; Kozel 2010). If a civil law theorist like me may hazard a definition, "*stare decisis'* doctrine" means: (1) a *judicial* discourse (as opposed to non-judicial one: cf. Gehrardt 2008, 111 ss), (2) *explicitly* or *implicitly formulated* in a Court's opinion, (3) in order to *bind* the same Court (horizontal force) and/or inferior ones (vertical force of precedents) to follow its decision as a precedent. According to this definition, *stare decisis* doctrine is a metalinguistic discourse about other discourses, the former being constitutive of the latter *qua* precedents: a decision *is* a precedent only according to such doctrine.

Non-binding precedents, in this sense, presupposes binding ones; only *after* the *stare decisis* doctrine prevailed previous decisions could termed, retrospectively, non-binding precedents, namely precedents without binding force at the time of their possible application. According to Gardner's definitions quoted above, a precedent is case-law *plus* the doctrine, peculiar to the common law, of following precedents. As already said (see above, Sect. 2.2.), the related concepts of precedent and *stare decisis* are connected in a threefold way with the concept of custom. First, there is a historical connection, as in declarative theory of common law: Courts do declare immemorial customs. Second and third, there is an even more important conceptual connection: both a chain of precedents, and the very doctrine of following them, *are* judicial customs.

As with all human activities, to be sure, it can be difficult to distinguish the mere *practice* and the proper *custom* of following precedent: that is, to repeat, the same practice *plus* the conviction of being obliged to do so. Such a conviction could, but it does not need to be justified by theoretical views about (external) justice as alike treatment of like cases, or even, more simply, by the practical easiness of justifying inferior courts' decisions by referring to superior courts' ones, or both. In fact, invoking non-binding precedents, as it occurs in civil law with *jurisprudence*, is only a legal argument between many others. The most recent civil law theory of argumentation just mentions the appeal to precedents or jurisprudence, admits its frequency and even its persuasiveness, but it seems reluctant to ascribe it the same status of other arguments (cf. Tarello 1980, 375, Alexy 1998, 215–219).

3.3 *Binding precedent* is the distinctive source of common law, its binding force amounting to the somewhat counterintuitive idea that «following precedent obliges judges to make decisions other than the ones they, in their best judgement, would have made absent the precedent» (Schauer 2009, 41; cf. Alexander, Sherwin 2007). In fact, binding precedent and *stare decisis* are two sides of the same coin, emerging only in the eighteenth century, in William Blackstone's treatise and in John Murray's, Earl of Mansfield, even more influential judicial decisions, and prevailed only in the nineteenth century, with the House of Lords' decisions as *Beamish* vs. *Beamish* (1866) and *London Tramways* (1898). In common law as well, at the end of the day, the only criteria in order to distinguish non-binding from binding precedents are the explicit statements of *stare decisis* doctrine.

Judicial binding precedent could be roughly defined as a previous concrete decision adopted by a judge as a justification of subsequent one, according the *stare decisis* doctrine, on a legal issue decisive for the solution of a case. In fact, two specifications are in order here. First, the concrete (non-general) character of the decision: a precedent is the solution of a concrete case, not – as English practice statements or French *arrêts de reglement* – of an abstract (general) one. Second, it is the very decision, not the formulation of its *ratio decidendi*, to form a precedent. Such a formulation, indeed, is not a necessary condition for the very existence of a precedent: the *ratio decidendi* can even be inferred by the decision *plus* the facts-of-the-case, without any obligation to provide a *motivation* (in French). Even when a *ratio decidendi* is effectively formulated, its formulation is not-canonical, i.e. it is qualitatively different from the formulation of a statute.

Formalistic reconstructions of precedents, such as Edward Levi's syllogistic model (Levi 1949, 2), in fact mirror a quasi-legislative view of precedents – the creationistic idea judges could legislate as Parliaments do. This wrong idea, notwithstanding, almost carries a good suggestion. European-continental codifications and legislation, on the one hand, and Anglo-American precedents and *stare decisis* doctrine, on the other, emerged almost simultaneously on either sides of the Channel in order to perform similar functions, to limit arbitrariness by the Courts as well as confer upon judges a contested legitimacy to produce law, *de iure* in the UK and US, *de facto* on the Continent. If precedent and *stare decisis* were really only a judicial form of legislation – as it is often claimed by the mystifying narrative formulated in Hobbes-Austin creationistic terms – then one could say both *Beames* and *London*

Tramways quasi-legislative acts have been by now repealed by the famous Practice statement of 1966, in the following terms.

> Their Lordships regard the use of precedent as an indispensable foundation upon which to decide what is the law and its application to individual cases [...] Their Lordships nevertheless recognise that too rigid adherence to precedent may lead to injustice in a particular case, and also unduly restrict the proper development of the law. They propose therefore to modify their present practice and, while treating former decisions of this House as normally binding, to depart from a previous decision when it appears right to do so.

It would be really naive, however, to conceive their Lordships' statement as an act of judicial legislation, derogating previous ones. In fact, thereafter, the House of Lords and other superior English courts continued to follow their precedents neither less nor more than before (cf. Duxbury 2008, 126–149, esp. 128). The key to solving such a riddle and dissolving the mystery of binding precedents, I believe, is much simpler. The solution is to adopt Gardner's tripartition of types of law (cf. Sect. 3.1; cf. also Stone 1985, 173), and to admit, accordingly, the *stare decisis* doctrine but allowing – the linguistic formulation of – an abstract judicial custom about case-law. This abstract custom shares with all other less abstract judicial customs, namely chain of precedents on a same legal question, three often underestimated hallmarks.

In the *first* place, *stare decisis*' doctrine is as devoid of any authoritative or "canonical" formulation as both precedents and customs are (cf. Cross 1977, 172): adjudication is oriented to facts, to the solution of the case at hand, not to texts, as statutory construction is (cf. 4.). In the *second* place, the core of common law's adjudication is the legal qualification of the facts of a concrete case in terms of an other concrete case, not necessarily in terms of the concrete case's subsumption under an abstract norm: as occurs instead on the Continent because of the existence of an *obligation de motivation* (in French) according a statute. In the *third* place, finally, precedents and *stare decisis* doctrine are not more binding than customs: bindingness – a definitory property of both – ultimately depends only on the practice itself. Following a precedent, after all, is not a more pretentious thing than following a rule. To the question "Is this judicial decision a *binding* precedent?", one can just answer: wait and see.

All these remarks, I think, apply with a few modifications to statutory interpretation too, the subject of the next section. To adopt the dictum about constitutional law by Charles Hughes (Schauer 2009, 143), the law is, ultimately, what judges say it is: a dictum, however, which requires an important qualification. The law is not, to be sure, what *individual* judges say it is: common law lawyers would say this it's just the *evidence* of law, not the law itself. Law is what *all* judges – or a qualified majority of judges, or a final authority representative of all the judges... – say it is. The starting hypothesis of the next, final section is precisely that legislation, adopted in the Western legal tradition in order to remedy the well known defects of judge-made law, cannot perform this function as long as one does not recognize the decisive and pervasive role of adjudication, and in particular of Anglo-American precedents and Continental *jurisprudence*.

4 Statutory Interpretation: An Overrated Part of Adjudication

In the trend outlined above, legislation and statutory interpretation come just as a fourth step: yet not, so to speak, as the beginning of a different story. Legislation was designed to remedy arbitrariness in adjudication; after two centuries, however, the cure proved to be worse than the disease. Today, in fact, statutes are become less a restraint than a tool for judicial interpretation, and the latter, paradoxically enough, is converted into the last remedy to the darkness of legislation. This final section proposes some guidelines for a realist, pragmatic-contextualist and inferentialist theory of statutory interpretation, addressing three issues: (1) the legally relevant sense of "pragmatics", (2) the pragmatic status of statutory interpretation, and, above all, (3) a restatement of the alleged interpretive skepticism, as opposed to a really realistic interpretive realism.

4.1 First of all, some remarks about a legally relevant linguistic pragmatics are in order. Of course, this is not the place to tell the story of pragmatics (for an updated summary, cf. at least Sbisà 2013; on the highly debated semantics/pragmatics distinction, cf. Bach 1999; Peregrin 1999; Turner 1999, Horn and Gregory 2004; Bianchi 2004; for legal applications, cf. Sardo 2015). In order to apply pragmatic tools to legal issues, a shift is needed from the traditional act-oriented pragmatics, typical of founding fathers such as John L. Austin and John Searle, to a context-oriented and an inferentially driven one. Indeed, a *first*, generic view of context, typical of act-oriented pragmatics, refers only to the environment of the speakers' utterance: but legal acts as statutes or judicial decisions are independent imperatives, i.e. decontextualized texts, always needing recontextualization and so much more specific and sophisticated views of context.

The *second*, more specific view, conceives of context as shared knowledge or more exactly *information*: i.e. the possession of any relevant data whatsoever – facts, norms, values… – apt to be further processed in order to become practically relevant. Here context is only a set of more or less deep, and shared, and coherent assumptions which form the background of texts, and provide the necessary information in order to understand and construe them. This second idea, to be sure, is more in keeping with cognitive sciences, and is not necessarily incompatible, *pace* Marmor 2007, 233 ss., with legal issues, as a matter of normative language and strategic behaviour. However, even if adopted by legal theorists in alleged pragmatically oriented theories (e. g. Villa 2012), such a view of context proves desperately generic, i.e. underdetermined with reference to legal issues.

The *third* view of context, nearer to Yehoshua Bar-Hillel's concept of co-text – the set of other texts relevant for the understanding of a text – seems more suited to modern law, conceived as a legal system: namely, as an ordered set of norms – all the ordered sets of norms – inferred from legal texts. This third idea, coherent with a realistic and inferentialist view of statutes as materials bearing an inferential potential, proves more promising for a theory of statutory interpretation: indeed, the more the law is decontextualized, the more the interpretation amounts to its reco(n) textualization, with reference to different co(n)texts, picked out by judges in order to adjudicate. A legal provision can be interpreted with reference to (1) other provisions in the same section of a statute or code, (2) others sections of the same statute or code, (3) other statutes or codes, (4) legal principles (cf. Poggi 2013).

Such an idea of context, nevertheless, proves problematic with reference to common law's precedents and civil law's *jurisprudence constante* too. These legal materials are not sources in the strict sense, as a statute is: they are only evidence of law, whose text is not canonically formulated. Accordingly, the interpretation of judicial decisions focus less on the text(s) than on the decision(s) themselves, and more specifically on the facts-of-the-case. It is with reference to such facts – whose legal qualification is the core of both previous and subsequent judicial decision – that a judge establishes if the precedent is relevant for the case at hand and can be applied to it. This reference to facts-of-the-case also forms the necessary condition of statutory interpretation, and anyway provides the main context of precedents or *jurisprudences* themselves: but a context, here, only in the first, generic sense of "context" mentioned above.

4.2 The pragmatic status of statutory interpretation was not specifically thematised by J. L. Austin's classic act-oriented pragmatics, nor by more updated versions of the context-oriented one. The trouble with such issues, I fear, is that the traditional Cartesian views of interpretation, understanding, explanation and so forth, as so many mental activities, have been strengthened by today's cognitive sciences. In terms of Wittgenstein's well-known rule-following passages, however, statutory interpretation can be conceived of as the linguistic activity of grasping meanings by means of the reformulation of their canonical formulation: i.e., as inference of a formulation from another. Such an inferential activity, however, can be further conceived by a legal theory pragmatically oriented as the recontextualisation of decontextualized legislative texts, with reference to different contexts in the sense considered in the previous sub-section.

Generally speaking, within so many senses of "statutory interpretation" (cf. Barberis 2014, 188–195), one can distinguish a common core of meaning and three more relevant sub-senses. The common core, according to Wittgenstein's insight, is the ascription of meaning to a statute, with its logical form "X means Y": where X denotes a sentence (a legal provision), Y the reformulation of such a sentence (a legal norm) in reference to a given context, and finally "means" suggests an inferential relationship so that Y is the best reformulation of X in relation to such a context. Such a common reference to a context excludes by the beginning that statutory interpretation can be conceived as a mere act of decoding, as in Chiassoni 2007, 78–80. Such an act can be deemed a move within a broader activity or language-game, as in Chiassoni 1999. Such an activity, with reference to *judicial* statutory interpretation, is adjudication: to do justice between parties.

The three more relevant sub-senses of "judicial statutory interpretation" for a pragmatically oriented theory of adjudication are perhaps the following. The *first* sub-sense denotes the individual *act* of ascribing meaning to a legal provision by a judge: an act instrumental to individual *activity* (interpretation in the second sub-sense), namely to adjudicate or to do justice. Such an interpretive act does not fall into one of five illocutionary acts' types distinguished by J. L. Austin (cf. Austin 1962, 150 ss., Ross 1972; Sbisà 1984). In particular, such an act does not fall under the type of *verdictive* act: a type more suited to the final act of the broader individual activity whose interpretive act is only a part, namely adjudication. The act of judicial statutory interpretation is not an autonomous speech act, but only a part of the language-game of adjudication.

The *second* sub-sense of "judicial statutory interpretation" denotes precisely the individual *activity* of adjudication, as opposed both to the individual *act* (first sub-sense) and to *collective* activity (third sub-sense). A judicial individual activity of statutory interpretation, in this second sub-sense, is a set of acts forming a single instance of the language-game of adjudication: a set including the same individual act (first sub-sense), the argumentation or justification of the result of such an act, the legal qualification-of-the-facts-of-the-case in terms of a statute (subsumption) and especially the individual judicial act of adjudication, the very goal of the activity. Indeed, all these acts of judicial statutory interpretation in the second sub-sense are strictly functional to adjudication, that is they do justice between the parties, in the merely legal, internal sense of "justice» (cf. Fuller 1967, in terms of internal and external morality). Legal interpretation and moral evaluation are different language games precisely because the former concerns justice *according the law*.

Finally, the *third* sub-sense of "judicial statutory interpretation" denotes the *collective activity* of adjudication by different judges, which *can* (but not necessarily *must*) produce a *jurisprudence constante*, as unintended effect of all these acts and activities. Just as one cannot follow a rule *privatim*, so one cannot adjudicate this way: even "pure" adjudication, in the long run, approaches to some form of uniformity. This could even be called a condition of felicity (cf. Siltala 2000, 185–187) of both adjudication and interpretation: at this condition, indeed, one can say courts apply the law, not their individual wills. Anyway, only with reference to the individual act and activity (first and second sub-senses), interpretive skepticism can seem trivially true: as a matter of fact, an interpreter can always ascribe the meaning he likes to a text, and adjudicate accordingly. Interpretive skepticism sounds much less plausible, instead, in reference to the *collective* activities (third sub-sense).

4.3 The current theories of legal interpretation are still classified according to the old tripartite scheme drawn by Hart 1961: interpretive formalism, Hartian "mixed" theory, and interpretive skepticism. Sixty years after, however, perhaps the time has come to adopt other, more sophisticated categories. First, interpretive formalism is over, except perhaps for its normative versions provided by Dworkin and Fred Schauer. Second, Hartian mixed theory seems valid only with reference to the facts-of-the-case's legal qualification by courts: the core of common law adjudication. Third, interpretive skepticism proves to be a mere truism with reference to the *individual* act and activity (first and second senses) of statutory interpretation, and especially to the mere *possibility* of different interpretations. It must be relativized and restated, instead, with reference to the *collective* statutory interpretation's activity (third sense), and above all to the *likeness* of their results (cf. Barberis 2013b).

The very label "skepticism", coined by Hart in order to criticize American legal realism, can be safely replaced by "realism" (cf. Guastini 2006 e 2013). With reference to individual act and activity of statutory interpretation, legal realism proves to be a truism. All the interpretations, taken individually (*uti singulae*), are dubious; only if taken collectively (*uti universae*) they can produce a long-term certainty – the only which is necessary to guide human conduct (cf. Leoni 1991, 76–94). With reference to an individual *act* of interpretation, in particular, it is trivially true that the interpretive question "What is the meaning ot this provision?" always admits two or more answers. With reference to interpretive *activities*, however, the true problem – in fact, the only interesting one for lawyers – is another: provided that there are always several *possible* adjudicative answers, which of them are most *likely*?

It is precisely here that precedents and *jurisprudence constante* become crucially important, and the results of a realist and evolutionary theory of interpretation converge with legal practitioners' daily experience. Indeed, common law precedents, as well as civil law's *jurisprudences*, allow practicians and theorists too to distinguish likely interpretations from merely possible ones. And this is true both if the judicial decisions *replaces* legislation, as occurs in common law, and *a fortiori* when they *complement* it, as in civil law. Yet, European-continental legal realists, particularly Genoese ones, still seem to consider precedents, if not *jurisprudence constante*, as a sort of British eccentricity, like fox hunting. The opposite is true, perhaps: legal realism needs a theory of precedents and *jurisprudence*, if it does not want to remain a Genoese eccentricity (cf. Barberis 2013a).

In fact, European-continental legal realists seem reluctant to adopt pragmatic tools precisely because of their propensity to the following triple reduction. They tend to reduce law to legislation, adjudication to statutory interpretation, and statutory interpretation to the decoding of signs out of context, or referring only to the co-text formed by other texts. Judicial statutory interpretation, instead, is an inferential activity which does not occur in a vacuum. As an instance of the language-game of adjudication, it is a radically contextual activity, referring both to texts and facts. To be sure, among the common elements of the context as authors, readers, available languages, encyclopaedias (cf. Lecercle 1999), legal materials as judicial decisions hold pride of place in law, and through them the very facts-of-the-case relevant according them.

From such a radically pragmatic-contextualist point of view, the only qualitative difference between common law and civil law seems the following. An English or American Court can justify its decision just by referring to an individual precedent, whereas a Continental judge cannot to do so even with a chain of precedents (a *jurisprudence*), always needing a statute in order to justify her decision. This is also the very difference between respective ideals: the German *Staatsrecht* and the French *Etat de droit*, on the one hand, and the English *Rule of law* on the other. In both cases, however, the point of adjudication, including statutory interpretation, remains to do justice between the parties: just as in "pure" adjudication. This is the intended effect of the *individual* act of interpretation and adjudication, whereas the *collective* activity of adjudication is always likely to produce unintended effects as precedents or chains of them.

Common law's precedents and civil law's *jurisprudence constante*, shaped and reshaped by the courts over time, always serve purposes their individual authors had neither foreseen nor wanted. Unintended effects of intentional human action are the very engine of the overall evolution of the law. The evolution of both common law and civil law, indeed, depends not only causally, but conceptually, on judicial decisions. It is with reference to such activities that both take their sense of legal phenomena, by definition aiming to do justice between men. But if it is so, then legislation depends on jurisdiction, not only the other way around. This dependency of legislation on precedents is paradigmatically illustrated by the working of common law's statutory interpretation, itself producing precedents, so that here written law feeds the unwritten one.

At the end of the day, law is an evolutionary phenomenon, like language, market, or religion. For the understanding and explanation of such a phenomenon, accordingly, nothing less and nothing more than an evolutionary theory of law is needed (cf. Hayek 1982). E.g., the next application of a statute, or a precedent, or both, always could reverse an adjudicative or interpretive trend: but it can also confirm it. A chain of precedents is a path-dependent process, not likely to be inverted; its evolutionary direction, nevertheless, could be predictable only in the long term: in the short one, it is a matter for probability calculus, or prophecy. Yet, just as for natural evolution, the knowledge of contextual elements and something like a selection-of-the-fittest-hypothesis could allow us to predict – while not single legal decisions – overall judicial trends. *This* is still legal realism, although without interpretive skepticism and legal creationism.

5 Conclusion

From the three sections of this contribution three main insights could be drawn. First, with regards the theory of legal sources or materials, legislation seems, contrary to Ross's wording, even more indeterminate than precedents – a mere starting point for inferential processes concerning legal qualification of the facts, interpretation, application, and so on. Second, as fast as particular judicial sources or materials are concerned, *stare decisis* doctrine and chains of precedents work as judicial customs, likely not only to replace, but also to complement legislation, by making statutory interpretation more predictable. Finally, interpretive skepticism is assumed to be a mere starting point for a really realistic, pragmatic-contextualist and inferentialist theory of interpretation. By such a theory, interpretation needs be conceived as the recontextualization of decontextualized texts, where the basic context is provided by chains of precedents.

Acknowledgement Many thanks to Nicola Muffato, Francesca Poggi, Alessio Sardo, and an anonymous referee for their insightful comments on an earlier version of this paper.

References

Alexander, L., & Sherwin, E. (2007). Judges as rule-makers. In S. E. Edlin (Ed.), *Common law theory*. Cambridge: Cambridge University Press.
Alexy, R. (1998). *Teoria dell'argomentazione giuridica*, it. trad. of *Theorie der juristischen Argumentation* (1978), Giuffrè: Milano.
Alexy, R. (2002). *The argument from injustice. A reply to legal positivism*. Oxford: Oxford University Press.
Austin, J. L. (1962). *How to do things with words* (J. O. Urmson, Ed.). Oxford University Press: Oxford.
Bach, K. (1999). The semantics-pragmatics distinction: What is and why matters. In K. Turner (Ed.), *The semantic-pragmatics interface from different points of view* (pp. 65–84). Oxford: Elsevier.
Barberis, M. (2013a). Genoa school. A guide to perplexed. *Revista brasileira de filosofia, 240*, 13–25. Also in http://www.academia.edu/7321033/Genoa_School
Barberis, M. (2013b). Interpretación-acto y interpretación-actividad. Nueve extensiones de la teoría genovesa. *Revista Brasileira de Filosofia, 400*(2013), 55–69.
Barberis, M. (2014). *Introduzione allo studio del diritto*. Torino: Giappichelli.
Barberis, M. (2015a). *El realismo jurídico Europeo-continental*. http://biblio.juridicas.unam.mx/libros/libro.htm?l=3875
Barberis, M. (2015b). Da che parte sta il formalismo? Fra ermeneutica e realismo giuridico. *Rivista di filosofia del diritto, 4*, 107–117.
Barberis, M. (2015c). Contro il creazionismo giuridico. Il precedente giudiziale fra storia e teoria. *Quaderni fiorentini per la storia del pensiero giuridico modern, 44, 67–101*.
Bianchi, C. (Ed.). (2004). *The semantics/pragmatics distinction*. Stanford: CLI Publications.
Bouvier, H. G. (2012). *Particularismo y derecho. Un abordaje postpositivista en el ámbito práctico*. Barcelona: Marcial Pons.
Brandom, R. B. (1994). *Making it explicit. Reasoning, representing and discursive commitments*. Cambridge, MA: Harvard University Press.
Butler, B. E. (2005). *Legal pragmatism*. In I. E. P.–Internet Encyclopedia of Philosophy. http://www.iep.utm.edu/leglprag/
Canale, D., & Tuzet, G. (2007). On legal inferentialism. Toward a pragmatics of semantic content in legal interpretation? *Ratio Juris, 20*, 32–44.
Canale, D., & Tuzet, G. (Eds.). (2009). *The rules of inference. inferentialism in law and philosophy*. Milano: Egea.
Chiassoni, P. (1999). Interpretive games: Statutory construction through Gricean eyes. *Analisi e diritto, 1999*, 79–99.
Chiassoni, P. (2007). *Tecnica dell'interpretazione giuridica*. Bologna: Il Mulino.
Cross, R. (1977). *Precedent in English law* (first edition 1968). Oxford: Clarendon.
Cuono, M. (2013). *Decidere caso per caso. Figure del potere arbitrario*. Madrid: Marcial Pons.
Dancy, J. (2004). *Ethics without principles*. Oxford: Oxford University Press.
Duxbury, N. (2008). *The nature and authority of precedent*. Cambridge: Cambridge University Press.
Fuller, L. (1967). *The morality of law* (1964). New Haven: Yale University Press.
Gardner, J. (2007). Some types of law. In D. E. Edlin (Ed.), *Common law theory* (pp. 51–77). Cambridge: Cambridge University Press.
Gehrardt, M. J. (2008). *The power of precedent*. Oxford: Oxford University Press.
Guastini, R. (2006). Lo scetticismo interpretativo rivisitato. *Materiali per una storia della cultura giuridica, 36*, 227–236.
Guastini, R. (2013). Il realismo giuridico ridefinito. *Revus, 19*, 97–111, http://revus/revues.org/2400.
Hayek, F.-A. (1982). *Law, legislation and liberty* (3 Vols.). Routledge: London.
Horn, L., & Gregory, W. (Eds.). (2004). *Handbook of pragmatics*. Oxford: Blackwell.

Kozel, R. J. (2010). Stare decisis as judicial doctrine. *Washington and Lee Law Review, 67*, 111–166.
Lecercle, J. J. (1999). *Interpretation as pragmatics*. London: Palgrave Macmillan.
Leoni, B. (1991). *Freedom and the law* (1.st ed. 1961). Indianapolis: Liberty Fund.
Levi, E. H. (1949). *An introduction to legal reasoning*. Chicago: Chicago University Press.
Lloredo, L. M. (2012). *Rudolf von Jhering y el paradigma positivista. Fundamentos ideológicos y filosóficos de su pensamiento jurídico*. Madrid: Dykinson.
Marmor, A. (2007). What does the law say? Semantics and pragmatics in statutory language. *Analisi e diritto, 2007*, 127–140.
Muffato, N. (2015). Sobre la universalidad y la particularidad de razones y normas. In P. Luque (Ed.), *Particulairsmo. Ensayos de filosofía del derecho e de filosofía moral* (pp. 89–132). Madrid: Marcial Pons.
Olivecrona, K. (1939). *Law as fact*. Copenhagen: Munksgaard.
Peregrin, J. (1999). The pragmatization of semantics. In K. Turner (Ed.), *The semantics/pragmatics interface from differents points of view* (pp. 419–442). Oxford: Elsevier.
Poggi, F. (2013). The myth of literal meaning in legal interpretation. *Analisi e diritto, 2013*, 313–335.
Postema, G. J. (1986). *Bentham and the common law tradition*. Oxford: Clarendon.
Raz, J. (1979). *The authority of law*. Oxford: Clarendon.
Ross, A. (1946). *Towards a realistic jurisprudence*. Copenhagen: Munksgaard.
Ross, A. (1958). *On law and justice*. Stevens: London (1.st ed., in Danish, 1952).
Ross, A. (1968). *Directives and norms*. London: Routledge and Kegan Paul.
Ross, A. (1972). The rise and fall of the doctrine of performatives. In R. E. Olson & A. M. Paul (Eds.), *Contemporary philosophy in Scandinavia* (pp. 197–212). Baltimore: John Hopkins University Press.
Sardo, A. (2015). Legal philosophers, meaning, and force. In L. Burazin, D. Gardašević, & A. Sardo (Eds.), *Law and state. Classical paradigms and novel proposals* (pp. 81–98). Berlin/Bern/Bruxelles/Wien: Frankfurt am Main.
Sbisà, M. (1984). On illocutionary types. *Journal of Pragmatics, 8*, 93–112.
Sbisà, M. (2013). Locution, illocution, perlocution. In M. Sbisà & K. Turner (Eds.), *Pragmatics of speech actions* (pp. 25–75). Berlin: Mouton de Gruyter.
Schauer, F. (2009). *Thinking like a lawyer. A new introduction to legal reasoning*. Cambridge, MA: Harvard University Press.
Siltala, R. (2000). *A theory of precedent. From analytical positivism to a post-analytical philosophy of law*. Oxford/Portland: Hart.
Stone, J. (1985). *Precedent and law. Dynamics of common law growth*. Sydney: Butterworth.
Tarello, G. (1980). *L'interpretazione della legge*. Giuffrè: Milan.
Taruffo, M. (2007). *Precedente e giurisprudenza*. Napoli: Editoriale scientifica.
Tiller, E. H., & Cross, F. B. (2006). What is legal doctrine? *Northwestern University Law Review, 100*, 517–533.
Turner, K. (Ed.). (1999). *The semantics/pragmatics interface from different points of view*. Oxford: Elsevier.
Villa, V. (2012). *Una teoria pragmaticamente orientata dell'interpretazione giuridica*. Torino: Giappichelli.
von Jhering, R. (1857). *Unsere Aufgabe*, Es. transl. *Nuestra tarea*. Eunomia, *4*(2013), 234–275.
Wróblewski, J. (2001). *Concepto y función del precedente en sistemas de statutory law*. In: Id., *Sentido y hecho en el derecho*, Fontamara: Mexico (pp. 295–312) (1.st edition, in English, 1974).

Pragmatic Disorders in Forensic Settings

Louise Cummings

Abstract Clients with pragmatic disorders are over-represented in the criminal justice system in comparison to the general population. Many of these disorders occur as part of conditions which are well recognised for their pragmatic impairments, including autism spectrum disorder, intellectual disability and schizophrenia. Others arise as a result of conditions which are somewhat less well known in clinical pragmatics, but in which there is increasing evidence of impairment in the areas of pragmatics and discourse (e.g. non-Alzheimer's dementias). This chapter will examine the pragmatic disorders in these clinical populations. This examination will consider a number of factors that complicate the presentation, assessment and treatment of pragmatic impairments within forensic settings. These factors include the role of co-morbid conditions such as substance use disorders, the involvement of cognitive deficits such as theory of mind impairments in pragmatic disorders and societal prejudice against incarcerated individuals. These factors limit provision of, and reduce compliance with, pragmatic language assessments and interventions.

The chapter will also address some of the implications of pragmatic disorders for the many verbally mediated interactions that defendants and inmates must comply with in the criminal justice system. These interactions include police arrest and interviews, legal examinations in courtrooms and prison rehabilitation programs which aim to reduce rates of re-offending behaviour. The specific pragmatic demands of these interactions will be considered, as will the ability of defendants and inmates with pragmatic disorders to meet these demands. Examples of the types of pragmatic skills which are integral to these interactions will be examined. The chapter concludes by arguing for an improved level of clinical language services with a focus on pragmatic language skills in prisons and other correctional facilities. It is contended that the substantial investment, which would be needed to achieve this improvement, would be offset by significant gains in the rehabilitation outcomes of incarcerated adults and young people.

Keywords Attention deficit hyperactivity disorder • Autism spectrum disorder • Conduct disorder • Courtroom examination • Intellectual disability • Police interview • Pragmatic disorder • Rehabilitation • Schizophrenia • Traumatic brain injury

---

L. Cummings (✉)
School of Arts and Humanities, Nottingham Trent University, Nottingham, UK
e-mail: louise.cummings@ntu.ac.uk

F. Poggi, A. Capone (eds.), *Pragmatics and Law*, Perspectives in Pragmatics, Philosophy & Psychology 10, DOI 10.1007/978-3-319-44601-1_14

1 Introduction

It has long been recognized that adolescents and adults in the criminal justice system have language and communication disorders. But what has less often been acknowledged is the presence of significant pragmatic disorders in this particular population. These disorders have been largely overlooked by clinicians and researchers who have tended to assess and treat clients in more conventional settings (e.g. hospitals, schools). Also, many language and pragmatic disorders among individuals in prison are masked by a range of comorbid conditions such as substance use disorders, making their identification difficult for clinicians. This chapter undertakes a timely examination of the pragmatic disorders of these clients. The discussion will be developed along the following lines. In the next section, we consider a number of clinical conditions which are more prevalent in the prison population than in the general population and in which there are marked pragmatic impairments. These conditions include most prominently autism spectrum disorder, schizophrenia and intellectual disability, although a number of other conditions (e.g. attention deficit hyperactivity disorder) will also be discussed. As part of this examination, a range of cognitive deficits which have implications for pragmatic language skills will also be addressed. The second half of the chapter will then consider the particular challenges posed by pragmatic disorders to adolescents and adults in the criminal justice system. It will be argued that individuals with pragmatic disorders are unable to cope with the pragmatic demands of a range of verbal interactions including courtroom examinations and prison rehabilitation programs. The chapter concludes by arguing the case that greater emphasis on remediating pragmatic language skills in adolescents and adults in prison can achieve significant gains in a range of rehabilitation outcomes.

2 Clinical Disorders in the Prison Population

It should be stated from the outset that investigators do not have figures for the prevalence of pragmatic disorders in the prison population. Notwithstanding this fact, there are strong grounds for claiming that the prevalence of these disorders is likely to exceed that found in the general population. This is because pragmatic disorders tend to be associated with certain clinical conditions, several of which have an increased prevalence in incarcerated individuals. These conditions include autism spectrum disorder, intellectual disability, schizophrenia, attention deficit hyperactivity disorder (ADHD), traumatic brain injury (TBI) and conduct disorder. In this section, the prevalence of each of these conditions in adolescents and adults in prisons and other correctional facilities is examined. Although figures tend to vary with each epidemiological study, the general pattern is one of the increased prevalence of these conditions in prison populations. An examination of the pragmatic impairments associated with each condition is undertaken. Often, these pragmatic impairments occur in the context of specific cognitive deficits. Typically, these deficits involve impairments of theory of mind (Cummings 2013, 2014a). These cognitive deficits will also be briefly examined. The manifestation of pragmatic impairments in these conditions is complicated by the presence of comorbid conditions, among which are included substance use disorders, alcohol dependence and HIV infection. This section concludes with an examination of some of these comorbid conditions and their implications for the pragmatic skills of incarcerated individuals.

2.1 Autism Spectrum Disorder

Autism spectrum disorder (ASD) is a neurodevelopmental disorder in which there are persistent deficits in social communication and social interaction and restricted, repetitive patterns of behaviour, interests or activities (American Psychiatric Association 2013). The disorder adversely affects social and occupational functioning, with many individuals unable to live independently or perform a range of roles (Cummings 2011, 2015). Using DSM-5 diagnostic criteria, the prevalence of ASD per 1,000 for 2008 was estimated to be 10.0 or 1 % (Maenner et al. 2014). (DSM-5 is the fifth edition of the Diagnostic and Statistical Manual of Mental Disorders (American Psychiatric Association 2013), an internationally recognized diagnostic system.) Much higher prevalence rates have been reported in various prison populations. Ginsberg et al. (2010) found ASD in one fourth of a population of male inmates at Norrtälje Prison in Sweden. Anckarsäter et al. (2008) estimated the prevalence of ASD in three populations in forensic psychiatry and special youth care to be at least 13 %. Siponmaa et al. (2001) studied the prevalence of child neuropsychiatric disorders in 126 young offenders who were consecutively referred for presentencing forensic psychiatric investigation in Stockholm, Sweden. A diagnosis of pervasive developmental disorder was recorded in 15 % of cases. This figure included 12 % with pervasive developmental disorder, not otherwise specified and 3 % with Asperger's syndrome. Similarly increased prevalence rates of ASD have been reported in prison populations in the UK. Scragg and Shah (1994) examined the prevalence of Asperger's syndrome in Broodmoor Special Hospital in Berkshire, England. These investigators obtained a prevalence of 1.5 % which increased to 2.3 % when equivocal cases were added.

Verbal and non-verbal communication can be markedly abnormal in individuals with ASD, with as many as 50 % of individuals with autistic disorder never developing functional speech (O'Brien and Pearson 2004). (The reader is referred to Cummings (2005, 2008, 2014b) for a detailed discussion of the language and communication features of this population.) Pragmatic language skills have been extensively studied in this clinical population (Cummings 2012a, 2016a, b). However, one drawback of these studies from our current perspective is that they based exclusively on children and non-incarcerated adults. Children and adults with ASD have been found to have difficulty comprehending irony and metaphor

(Gold et al. 2010; Martin and McDonald 2004), detecting violations of Grice's maxims (Surian et al. 1996), using features of context[1] in utterance interpretation (Loukusa et al. 2007) and synchronising gestures with speech (de Marchena and Eigsti 2010). Conversational and discourse problems are also commonplace. Jones and Schwartz (2009) found that children with autism initiated fewer bids for interactions, commented less often, used fewer conversational turns to continue ongoing interactions and responded less often to communication bids than typically developing children during dinner conversations. Colle et al. (2008) found that adults with high-functioning autism or Asperger syndrome used fewer personal pronouns, temporal expressions and referential expressions than control subjects during narrative production (see section 2.3 in Cummings (2009) and section 2.2.2 in Cummings (2014c) for further discussion of the pragmatic impairments of ASD).

Alongside pragmatic and discourse impairments in ASD is a severe and persistent deficit in theory of mind (ToM). ToM is the ability to attribute mental states such as beliefs and knowledge to one's own mind and to the minds of others. When these mental states concern events in the world, it is described as first-order ToM. When attributed beliefs and knowledge concern the mental states of another person, it is described as second-order ToM. Children and adults with ASD have been found to fail tests of first-order and second-order ToM (Buitelaar et al. 1999) as well as tests of faux pas detection (Baron-Cohen et al. 1999). They have diminished awareness of their own and others' intentions (Williams and Happé 2010), display impaired visual perspective-taking (i.e. knowledge that different people may see the same thing differently at the same time) (Hamilton et al. 2009), and have impaired understanding of the perception-knowledge relationship (Lind and Bowler 2010). Several studies have established correlations between pragmatic language skills and aspects of ToM performance in children and adults with ASD. Martin and McDonald (2004) found that second-order ToM reasoning was significantly associated with the ability of subjects with Asperger's syndrome in their study to interpret non-literal utterances (ironic jokes). Losh et al. (2012) examined ToM and pragmatic language in children with idiopathic autism and children with fragile X syndrome (FXS) with and without autism. Children with FXS and autism performed similarly to children with idiopathic autism, and performed more poorly than typically developing controls, on measures of pragmatic language and ToM. Children with FXS only did not differ from controls on these measures. ToM was related to pragmatic language ability in all groups. We will see in Sect. 3 that poor mentalizing skills are often the target of interventions in incarcerated adults with ASD.

[1]The reader is referred to Cummings (2007, 2012b) for a clinical pragmatic examination of context.

2.2 *Intellectual Disability*

Intellectual disability involves impairments of general mental abilities that have an adverse impact on adaptive functioning in three domains: the conceptual domain (e.g. language skills); the social domain (e.g. the ability to make and retain friendships); and the practical domain (e.g. personal care). Alongside impaired adaptive functioning, a diagnosis of intellectual disability is made when an IQ test score is approximately two standard deviations or more below the population mean. This equals an IQ score of about 70 or below. According to DSM-5, the prevalence of intellectual disability in the general population is approximately 1 % (American Psychiatric Association 2013). A considerably higher prevalence of intellectual disability has been recorded among incarcerated individuals in a number of studies. In a cross-sectional study of 1,279 adult prisoners who were within 6 weeks of release from custody in seven prisons in Queensland, Australia, Dias et al. (2013) reported the prevalence of intellectual disability to be 9 %. Herrington (2009) reported a point prevalence of borderline intellectual disability of 11 % in a British sample of 185 young adult male prisoners aged 18 and 21 years. Søndenaa et al. (2008) reported a prevalence of intellectual disability of 10.8 % in a random sample of 143 inmates from a Norwegian prison. In a systematic review of the literature which included 11,969 prisoners, Fazel et al. (2008) reported intellectual disabilities in 0.5–1.5 % of prisoners, with a range of 0–2.8 % across studies. Notwithstanding the variation in these findings, it is clear that the trend is towards an increased prevalence of intellectual disability in the prison population.

Individuals with intellectual disability form a clinically heterogeneous group. This group includes children and adults with intellectual disability as part of a genetic syndrome (e.g. Down's syndrome), as a result of exposure to teratogens in the pre-natal period (e.g. foetal alcohol syndrome) and as a consequence of infectious disease (e.g. meningitis). Only some of these individuals with intellectual disability are to be found in the prison population. For example, adults with Down's syndrome are typically not detained in adult prisons. Most studies of pragmatic disorders in individuals with intellectual disability have been undertaken in child subjects and subjects with genetic syndromes, both of whom are not typical of the types of incarcerated individuals who have intellectual disability. With this proviso in mind, some of these pragmatic disorders are now described.

Alongside impairments in phonology, syntax and semantics, individuals with intellectual disability can experience significant disruption of expressive and receptive pragmatic language skills. Subjects with fragile X syndrome have been reported to produce tangential language during conversation, engage in topic repetition, and have difficulty signalling non-comprehension of language to a speaker (Abbeduto et al. 2008; Murphy and Abbeduto 2007; Sudhalter and Belser 2001). Subjects with Williams syndrome have been found to have difficulty with the comprehension of irony and metaphor, and display impaired referential communication, the latter in the context of communicating to a speaker that a message is inadequate (Annaz et al. 2009; John et al. 2009; Sullivan et al. 2003). Godbee and Porter (2013) found that the comprehension of non-literal language in subjects with Williams syndrome was significantly below comprehension levels in typically developing chronological age-matched controls, but not significantly different to that of mental age-matched controls. There is evidence that individuals with Down's syndrome have less impaired pragmatic language skills than subjects with other genetic syndromes (Laws and Bishop 2004). However, even in subjects with Down's syndrome, there are problems with referential communication and impaired metaphor and idiom comprehension (Abbeduto et al. 2006; Papagno and Vallar 2001). The reader is referred to section 2.5 in Cummings (2009) and section 2.2.4 in Cummings (2014c) for further discussion of pragmatic disorders in intellectual disability.

There is evidence of ToM or mentalizing deficits in individuals with intellectual disability, although these deficits are not as severe as those found in ASD. Van Herwegen et al. (2013) found that the performance of 30 children with Williams syndrome on three ToM tasks was significantly poorer than the performance of 30 typically developing children on the same tasks. Moreover, the performance of the children with Williams syndrome was not predicted by receptive vocabulary level or grammatical ability scores, but was dependent on the cognitive demands of the tasks. Cornish et al. (2005) reported impaired performance by children with fragile X syndrome on two ToM tasks, the location change false belief task[2] and the appearance-reality task. Even when compared to an intellectual disability control group, boys with fragile X syndrome have been found to have ToM deficits (Grant et al. 2007). Yirmiya et al. (1996) found that individuals with Down's syndrome performed similarly to individuals with autism and individuals with mental retardation of unknown aetiology, but worse than normal children, on false belief and deception tasks. Some studies have attempted to relate ToM deficits to pragmatic language skills in individuals with intellectual disability. John et al. (2009) examined the referential communication skills of 57 children with Williams syndrome who were aged 6–12 years. These children were required to verbalize to a speaker when a message was inadequate, and also to communicate effectively the way in which it was inadequate. ToM contributed significantly to the prediction of variance in overall verbalization of message inadequacy.

[2] False belief tests have become the standard means of testing ToM skills. In a false belief test, a story is enacted through the use of two dolls. (These tests have become known as Sally-Anne experiments on account of the names of the dolls first used in these experiments.) Children observe a scenario in which one doll (Sally) switches the location of an object that is subsequently requested by the other doll (Anne). Importantly, Anne is unaware that this switch has been made and believes that the object is still in the original location where she placed it. The child who appreciates that Anne now has a false belief about the location of the object, a false belief that leads her to search for the object in its original location, is said to have passed the test. This child is aware that other agents (represented here by the doll Anne) can have beliefs that differ from his or her own.

2.3 Schizophrenia

Schizophrenia is a serious mental illness which has adverse implications for an individual's adaptive functioning. The disorder is diagnosed on the basis of positive and negative symptoms which are contained in DSM-5 (American Psychiatric Association 2013). Positive symptoms include thought disorder, delusions and hallucinations (mostly auditory hallucinations). Negative symptoms include affective flattening, poverty of speech (alogia), apathy, avolition and social withdrawal. Schizophrenia has a lifetime prevalence of approximately 0.3–0.7 % (American Psychiatric Association 2013). However, within forensic settings significantly higher prevalence rates are obtained. Falissard et al. (2006) studied 800 men who were incarcerated in French prisons. Each man was interviewed by two clinicians, one of whom was a senior psychiatrist. The prevalence rates for schizophrenia were 3.8 % and 6.2 %, respectively, for a diagnosis given independently by both clinicians and for a consensual diagnosis. In a study of the prevalence rates of mental disorders in prisoners and new prison arrivals, Sarlon et al. (2012) obtained a prevalence rate of schizophrenia of 4.1 %. Baillargeon et al. (2009) obtained an overall prevalence of schizophrenia of 1.4 % in a study of data from 234,031 Texas Department of Criminal Justice inmates who were incarcerated for any duration between September 2006 and September 2007. In an extensive review of Australian epidemiological data, Mullen et al. (2003) estimated that the prevalence of schizophrenia among prisoners was between 2 and 5 %. These figures clearly indicate that schizophrenia is a significant mental disorder in forensic settings.

The pragmatic impairments of adults with schizophrenia are well documented. These impairments are known to compromise the comprehension and recognition of speech acts, maxims and implicatures (Tényi et al. 2002; Mazza et al. 2008). The understanding of non-literal language, including metaphors, irony, proverbs, idioms and humour, is also impaired (Langdon et al. 2002; Tavano et al. 2008; Thoma et al. 2009; Polimeni et al. 2010). Alongside these receptive pragmatic deficits are a number of expressive deficits in the pragmatics of language. Typically, these are characterized in story-telling contexts.[3] Perlini et al. (2012) reported deficits in local and global coherence during a story-telling task in 30 Italian-speaking patients with schizophrenia. During story retellings, patients with schizophrenia have been found to produce irrelevant information and engage in derailments (Marini et al. 2008). Consistent with this finding of derailments in expressive language, Meilijson et al. (2004) reported that topic was a pragmatic parameter on which their subjects with schizophrenia exhibited a high degree of inappropriate abilities. Clients with schizophrenia also display reduced context processing (Schenkel et al. 2005), are impaired in recognizing and repairing communicative failures (Bosco et al. 2012) and have problems with referential communication (Champagne-Lavau et al. 2009).

[3] Storytelling is somewhat restricted in the pragmatic language forms it can elicit from respondents. See Cummings (2016c) for further discussion of this point in relation to reported speech.

Adults with schizophrenia exhibit a range of severe ToM deficits. Schizophrenic clients perform poorly on first- and second-order ToM tasks (Bozikas et al. 2011). Negative symptoms in schizophrenia have been found to be associated with ToM difficulties, while positive symptoms (e.g. delusions) are linked to overmentalizing (Lincoln et al. 2011; Montag et al. 2011). Several studies have found a relationship between ToM deficits and pragmatic impairments in adults with schizophrenia. Brüne and Bodenstein (2005) found that approximately 39 % of the variance of proverb comprehension in schizophrenic patients was predicted by their ToM performance. Mo et al. (2008) studied 29 schizophrenic patients who were in remission. Although these patients had a ToM deficit and were impaired in their comprehension of metaphor and irony, only metaphor comprehension was significantly correlated with second-order false belief understanding. In a study of schizophrenic patients with formal thought disorder, Langdon et al. (2002) reported that poor ToM performance was associated with impaired understanding of irony in these patients, but not with impaired metaphor comprehension. Mazza et al. (2008) examined ToM and pragmatic language skills in 38 patients with schizophrenia. These patients performed significantly worse than healthy controls on ToM tasks and a pragmatics task examining appreciation of Gricean maxims, even after controlling for IQ and executive function scores. Moreover, a significant correlation was found between the number of errors on the Gricean maxim task and ToM performance in these patients.

2.4 Attention Deficit Hyperactivity Disorder

Attention deficit hyperactivity disorder (ADHD) is a neurodevelopmental disorder which affects behaviour in multiple settings (e.g. school, home) and has adverse implications for an individual's social, academic and occupational functioning. The disorder is diagnosed on the basis of two groups of diagnostic criteria in DSM-5 (American Psychiatric Association 2013), one describing symptoms of inattention and the other describing symptoms of hyperactivity and impulsivity.[4] There are presentation specifiers in DSM-5 for a combined form of the disorder, a predominantly inattentive type and a predominantly hyperactive/impulsive type. According to DSM-5, the general population prevalence of ADHD is approximately 5 % for children and 2.5 % for adults. Considerably higher prevalence rates are reported among prison inmates. Ginsberg et al. (2010) estimated the prevalence of adult ADHD among longer-term inmates to be 40 %. Usher et al. (2013) examined 497 federal inmates in Canada, and reported that 16.5 % met the clinical threshold for a diagnosis of ADHD. A further 25.2 % of inmates had sub-threshold symptoms in the moderate range. Cahill et al. (2012) reported the prevalence of ADHD in 3,962 inmates to be 10.5 %. The prevalence rate of ADHD among female inmates (15.1 %) was higher than among male inmates (9.8 %) in this study. The hyperactive-impulsive

[4] It is argued in Cummings (2012c) that many of these diagnostic criteria are pragmatic in nature.

subtype was the most prevalent form of ADHD for both genders. In a study of 11,603 youths committed to Texas juvenile correctional facilities, Harzke et al. (2012) reported the prevalence of ADHD to be 18.3 %. These prevalence rates, which are consistently elevated across studies, demonstrate that ADHD represents a significant challenge to the mental health of prison inmates.

Although DSM-5 recognises ADHD in adults for the first time, most investigations of pragmatic impairments in this disorder are based on child subjects. The applicability of these investigations to adult prison inmates with ADHD is open to question. This said, much is now known about the pragmatic deficits of children with ADHD. Kim and Kaiser (2000) found that children with ADHD produced more inappropriate pragmatic behaviours in conversational interactions than typically developing children, despite having similar pragmatic knowledge. Mathers (2006) reported that children with ADHD used more tangential and unrelated information during spoken texts than control children. Staikova et al. (2013) used parent ratings, standardised tests and a narrative task to measure pragmatic language skills in 28 children with ADHD. Across all measures, these children had poorer pragmatic language skills relative to their peers. Moreover, pragmatic abilities, as measured by parent ratings, mediated the relationship between ADHD and social skills. In a comprehensive review of the literature, Green et al. (2014) found a consistent profile of pragmatic impairments in children with features of ADHD. These impairments were in the areas of excessive talking, poor conversational turn-taking, and lack of coherence and organization in elicited speech. Receptive aspects of pragmatics are also disrupted in ADHD. In this way, Nilsen et al. (2013) reported that children with ADHD were less accurate in their interpretations of referential statements than typically developing children.

There has been little direct investigation of the ToM skills of individuals with ADHD. Those studies which have been conducted have found that children with ADHD display poorer recognition of emotional facial expressions, engage in lower levels of social perspective-taking and exhibit worse performance on second-order ToM tasks than normally developing children (Buitelaar et al. 1999; Marton et al. 2009; Pelc et al. 2006). In a review of literature in the 30-year period between 1979 and 2009, Uekerman et al. (2010) found some evidence of ToM deficits in ADHD. Other social cognitive impairments in ADHD identified in this review included reduced empathy, and difficulty with emotional face and prosody perception. The ToM impairments of children with ADHD, though significant, are not as severe as those found in ASD (Bühler et al. 2011) or in foetal alcohol spectrum disorders (Greenbaum et al. 2009). The relationship between ToM deficits and pragmatic impairments in ADHD has not been extensively examined to date. A study which has addressed this relationship failed to obtain a correlation between these skills. Adachi et al. (2004) studied metaphor comprehension and ToM in 29 children with ADHD. Although these children were as impaired as children with high-functioning pervasive developmental disorder in the comprehension of metaphor, a high correlation was not obtained between performance in a ToM task and metaphor comprehension.

2.5 *Traumatic Brain Injury*

Traumatic brain injury (TBI) is an acquired brain injury in children and adults. It is most often caused by road traffic accidents, although trips and falls (particularly in children and the elderly) and violent assaults are also significant causes of TBI. There are two forms of TBI. In an open or penetrating head injury, the skull is fractured or otherwise breached by a missile. In a closed head injury, the brain is damaged while the skull remains intact. Raised intracranial pressure, haematoma and diffuse axonal injury are among the immediate consequences of TBI. Long-term neurological sequelae, which can include sensory impairment, aphasia and executive dysfunction, are commonplace in TBI (see section 5.4 in Cummings (2014b) for further discussion).

Estimates of the prevalence of TBI in the general population vary with different studies. Recently, Frost et al. (2013) investigated the prevalence of TBI in the adult general population. A total of 15 studies, all of which originated from developed countries, were examined. In a population of 25,134 adults, Frost et al. found that 12 % had a history of TBI. Considerably higher prevalence rates of TBI have been recorded among prison inmates. Davies et al. (2012) examined the prevalence of TBI in 61 incarcerated male juvenile offenders with an average age of 16 years. More than 70 % of these offenders reported at least one head injury at some point in their lives.[5] In a study of 196 adult male offenders in prison, Williams et al. (2010) found that reports consistent with TBI of various severities were given by 65 % of respondents. Of this sample, 16 % experienced moderate-to-severe TBI and 48 % reported mild TBI. In a study of 69 inmates in a county jail population, Slaughter et al. (2003) recorded that 87 % reported TBI over their lifetime, with 36.2 % reporting TBI in the prior year. Shiroma et al. (2010) undertook a wide-ranging review of studies of TBI prevalence published between 1983 and 2009. The prevalence of TBI in the overall offender population was estimated to be 60.25 %. Clearly, TBI poses a significant health burden in the prison population which has implications for the rehabilitation and management of inmates.

The pragmatic impairments of adults with TBI are well characterized. Adults with TBI have been found to exhibit difficulties in the Gricean domains of quantity, relation and manner (Douglas 2010). During casual conversations with friends, adults with severe TBI have been observed to produce tangential language (Bogart et al. 2012). Moreover, these adults were also found to have difficulty identifying communication breakdown, asking questions (a type of speech act) and engaging in conversational joking (jokes and humour in general make extensive use of non-literal language). Rousseaux et al. (2010) examined pragmatic skills in dyadic interaction in 18 patients with severe TBI during rehabilitation (2–12 months post-injury) and at the chronic phase in recovery (2 years post-injury). Patients displayed impaired greeting behaviour. They also exhibited difficulty in responding to open questions, presenting new information and introducing new themes, organizing dis-

[5] Although this prevalence rate is based on prisoner self-report, there is evidence of reliable reporting of TBI by prisoners (Schofield et al. 2011).

course and adapting to interlocutor knowledge. Dardier et al. (2011) reported pragmatic strengths and weaknesses in 11 French-speaking adults with severe TBI. Adults with TBI were able to comprehend a range of requests (direct, conventional indirect, unconventional indirect) as well as controls. However, these adults displayed poorer metapragmatic knowledge than controls in that they were less able to give a relevant explanation of their comprehension of requests. They also produced fewer topic-maintaining speaking turns and more speaking turns containing a digression than controls.

Evidence for ToM impairments in subjects who sustain a TBI is somewhat inconclusive. While subjects with severe TBI have been found to perform as well as control subjects on first-order false belief tasks (Muller et al. 2010), other studies have reported that the recognition of basic emotions and capacity for mental state attribution in subjects with TBI are both significantly reduced relative to controls (Henry et al. 2006). ToM impairments in TBI clients have also been found to remain stable between the time of injury and at 1-year follow-up (Milders et al. 2006). The relationship between ToM and pragmatics in TBI remains relatively unexplored. One study which has addressed this relationship found that pragmatic impairments contribute to the ToM deficits of these clients. Muller et al. (2010) found that patients with TBI performed significantly worse than controls on a task examining the interpretation of direct and indirect speech acts and on a faux pas test (a test of ToM). The interpretation of indirect speech acts was shown to be significantly correlated with performance on the faux pas-related questions of the faux pas test as well as performance on second-order false belief stories. Muller et al. suggested that impairment in these patients' language skills, specifically pragmatic abilities, may at least partially explain their problems with ToM. Adults with TBI also experience significant executive function deficits. For discussion of these deficits, the reader is referred to section 3.4 in Cummings (2014c).

2.6 Conduct Disorder

Conduct disorder involves a repetitive and persistent pattern of behaviour in which the basic rights of others or major age-appropriate societal norms or rules are violated (American Psychiatric Association 2013). Aberrant behaviours include aggression to people and animals, destruction of property and deceitfulness or theft. The behaviour disturbance causes clinically significant impairment in social, academic or occupational functioning. A series of specifiers in DSM-5 are used to indicate the onset of the disorder (childhood onset, adolescent onset or unspecified onset), the current severity of the disorder (mild, moderate or severe), and whether or not an individual exhibits limited prosocial emotions. One-year population prevalence estimates of the disorder range from 2 % to more than 10 %, with a median of 4 % (American Psychiatric Association 2013). Studies have revealed an increased prevalence of conduct disorder in prisons and other correctional facilities. Harzke et al. (2012) obtained a prevalence rate of conduct disorder of 83.2 % in a population of 11,603 youths who were committed to Texas juvenile correctional facilities.

Zhou et al. (2012) examined the prevalence of conduct disorder among violent and non-violent juvenile offenders in the Hunan and Sichuan provinces of China. Among violent offenders, prevalence rates of conduct disorder of 86.6 % (Hunan) and 69.1 % (Sichuan) were obtained. In the Hunan non-violent group, the prevalence rate of conduct disorder was 75 %. In a study of 230 juvenile detainees in Istanbul, Turkey, Copur et al. (2005) found that the rate of conduct disorder was 46.3 % in detainees who were substance abusers, and 25.3 % in other detainees.

Clinicians and researchers have only recently begun to characterize the pragmatic impairments of individuals with conduct disorder. Donno et al. (2010) reported significantly poorer pragmatic language skills in a group of persistently disruptive school children than in a comparison group. Gilmour et al. (2004) found that two thirds of their sample of 55 children with conduct disorder had pragmatic language impairments as measured on the Children's Communication Checklist (Bishop 1998). The pragmatic impairments of these children were similar in nature and degree to those of children with autism. Adams et al. (2002) examined the conversational behaviour of children with conduct disorder and children with Asperger's syndrome. Children with conduct disorder performed similarly to children with Asperger's syndrome in their ability to respond to questions and comments. ToM impairments in individuals with conduct disorder are not a consistent finding. Buitelaar et al. (1999) found that children with conduct disorder performed similarly to normal children on emotion recognition and first- and second-order ToM tasks. However, Happé and Frith (1996) found evidence of impairment in social insight (theory of mind) in a study of 18 children with conduct disorder. The impaired social insight of these children was judged not to be dissimilar to that found in able individuals with autism. To date, the relationship between ToM and pragmatics in conduct disorder has not been examined.

2.7 Comorbid Conditions

Comorbid conditions frequently accompany each of the disorders examined above. These conditions are very wide-ranging in nature and include bipolar disorder, personality disorder, substance use disorders, alcoholism, and HIV infection. Aside from the conditions just listed, two or more of the disorders examined above may co-occur in an incarcerated client, e.g. intellectual disability and autism spectrum disorder. Comorbid conditions are significant in that they can make an independent contribution to a pragmatic disorder. Even in cases where these conditions do not directly contribute to pragmatic disorders, their presence can mask or otherwise complicate the presentation of these disorders. This can have adverse consequences for the identification and characterization of pragmatic disorders in incarcerated individuals. For example, clinicians may dismiss certain pragmatic findings on the assumption that they are temporary disturbances in a client's communication skills which are related to the use of substances. Also, comorbid conditions can reduce an individual's compliance with assessment procedures and willingness to participate in treatment programs. The presence of a comorbid condition should always be recorded both for its independent contribution to a pragmatic disorder and for its capacity to compromise the management of a client.

Studies of incarcerated individuals indicate that psychiatric and other comorbidities are the norm rather than the exception among prison inmates. Kutscher et al. (2009) found high rates of psychiatric comorbidities in patients with schizophrenia in forensic-psychiatric hospitals. Of 531 patients with schizophrenia, 73.9 % had substance use disorders and 17.2 % had personality disorders. Hassiotis et al. (2011) found a higher prevalence of probable psychosis (11.3 % versus 5.7 %) and cannabis use (51.2 % versus 42.1 %) in prisoners with intellectual disabilities than in prisoners without intellectual disabilities. Among 115 prisoners with intellectual disability, Dias et al. (2013) reported the estimated lifetime and current prevalence of co-occurring mental disorders to be 52.5 % and 37.2 %, respectively. These disorders included depression and substance dependence. In a study of 30 prison inmates with ADHD, Ginsberg et al. (2010) reported that all subjects had a lifetime substance use disorder. Half of subjects exhibited mood and anxiety disorders and one fourth had autism spectrum disorder. Psychopathy was present in one tenth of subjects. In a study population of 336,668 inmates in Texas, Baillargeon et al. (2003) found that inmates with HIV infection exhibited elevated rates of major depression, dysthymia, bipolar disorder, schizophrenia, schizoaffective disorder and non-schizophrenic psychotic disorder. These high rates of psychiatric and other comorbidities in incarcerated individuals have considerable implications for the assessment and treatment of pragmatic disorders, and must be considered in the overall management of these clients.

3 Pragmatic Challenges of Forensic Settings

As the previous section has demonstrated, there is a sizeable burden of pragmatic disorder in the prison population. The question which must now be addressed is what implications, if any, this has for those pragmatically impaired individuals who are in the criminal justice system. From the point of arrest to conviction and imprisonment, incarcerated individuals must negotiate a range of verbally mediated interactions. These interactions, it is argued in this section, often exceed the pragmatic language capacities of incarcerated individuals, a point that is seldom recognised by key actors in the criminal justice system. These actors include, most prominently, solicitors and judges, police officers, and prison wardens and governors.[6] In this

[6] Although it is true to say that these actors in the criminal justice system are largely unaware of the communicative challenges of clients with pragmatic and language disorders, there is also evidence of insight into the harmful consequences of these disorders on the part of some of these professionals. Comments made in 2006 by Lord Ramsbotham, the then Chief Inspector of Prisons in the UK, reveal this to be true of at least one prison governor: 'When I went to the young offender establishment at Polmont I was walking with the governor, who told me that if, by some mischance, he had to get rid of all his staff, the last one out of the gate would be his speech and language therapist'.

section, we examine the pragmatic demands of these various interactions. For the most part, they include police interviews, courtroom examinations and prison rehabilitation programs. Specific pragmatic features of these interactions will be considered with a view to substantiating the claim that they pose significant and, in some cases, insurmountable difficulties for clients with pragmatic disorder. These features range from the use of non-literal utterances to types of questions that are likely to challenge individuals with pragmatic impairments. Having demonstrated the pragmatic demands of key aspects of the criminal justice system, the ground will then be laid for the final section in the chapter. In that section, it is argued that a much greater level of priority must be afforded to the assessment and treatment of pragmatic disorders in forensic settings than has been the case to date.

3.1 Police Interviews

The pragmatic features of police interviews have been investigated in several studies. Among other things, these studies have examined the use of silence, the role of questions and questioning and the functions of discourse operators in police interviews. In a study of the use of *okay* by an interviewing police officer, Gaines (2011) showed how this discourse operator can be used to undertake different types of interactive work including task management, solidarity overture and confrontation. Heydon (2011) examined how the contributions of suspects in police interviews are constrained both in terms of allowable turn types and the management of topic initiations. She argued that if these interactionally restricted contributions are interpreted on the basis of assumptions about 'preferred responses' in ordinary conversation, then they may be susceptible to adverse inference when they come to be presented as evidence. Stokoe and Edwards (2008) examined the asking and answering of silly questions (e.g. 'might sound a bit silly, but do you know whose window it is?') in British police interviews. Silly questions were typically found to occur towards the ends of interviews and following police officers' formulations of suspects' testimony, where their role is to attribute criminal intentions to suspects. For further discussion of pragmatic research into police interviews, the reader is referred to Haworth (2010).

Several pragmatic features of police interviews make them especially challenging verbal interactions for suspects in general. In cases where suspects have pragmatic disorders, this challenge is greatly amplified. In demonstration of these difficulties, consider the following utterances which were spoken by a male police officer during the interview of a rape suspect (Haworth 2009).

(1) What had you had to drink? Tell me in total what you had to drink.
(2) Okay so you're saying on to this morning, what happened this morning? We're talking about Saturday the Xth of (month). What's happened?

The first noteworthy feature of these utterances is the police interviewer's use of wh-questions in *What had you had to drink?* and *What happened this morning?*.

These questions carry an existential presupposition to the effect that the suspect *had* been drinking and that *something* did indeed happen that morning. These presuppositions may be warranted based on the wider context of these utterances, e.g. if the suspect had earlier conceded in the interview that he had been drinking. Nevertheless, their presence reflects a style of questioning that may find some suspects, and particularly those with pragmatic disorders, unwittingly conceding points that may prove ultimately to be damaging to their defence. Moreover, the ability of a suspect to challenge the presuppositions of these questions is made more difficult still when, in (1), a wh-question is immediately followed by the speech act of command (*Tell me*...). The combined effect of these two pragmatic devices is to constrain the suspect's options for response. He is effectively compelled to accept the presupposition of the interviewer's question or else violate the conversational expectations which are set in place by these utterances.

The utterances in (2) contain a further pragmatic feature which may be particularly challenging for a suspect with pragmatic disorder. The police interviewer uses the deictic expression *this morning* with the intention of referring to the morning of the day on which the alleged rape occurred. However, in order for a suspect to establish the correct temporal referent of this expression, he must be able to entertain a discourse context other than the one that applies to the current police interview. One can imagine how the type of representational skills that this requires may lie well beyond the competence of a suspect with pragmatic disorder. Such a suspect may take the referent of *this morning* to be the morning of the day on which the interview is taking place. It is only after using this deictic expression twice that the police interviewer attempts to clarify the temporal referent that he has in mind by using an absolute rather than a relative temporal expression, that is, the exact date of the alleged rape. This clarification may well come too late for the suspect with pragmatic disorder who may already be entertaining a mistaken understanding of the referent of *this morning*.

3.2 Courtroom Examinations

The pragmatic features of courtroom discourse have been extensively examined in a number of studies. Investigators have addressed issues such as politeness and face-threatening acts in courtroom exchanges (Berk-Seligson 1988; Lakoff 1989; Penman 1990), the use of mitigation for coping with disagreement and conflict during courtroom examinations (Martinovski 2006), and the function of discourse markers in legal questioning (Hale 1999). The findings of these studies reveal the use of a wide range of pragmatic devices in courtroom settings. For example, mitigation does more than merely modify the illocutionary force of speech acts in the courtroom, but also modifies the discourse plans of participants in the legal process. Although discourse markers such as 'well', 'now' and 'see' are used in a range of contexts, their function is as markers of argumentation and confrontation during legal cross-examination and to maintain control of the flow of information and to mark progression in a story-line during examination-in-chief. The use of interpreters in reproducing (successfully or otherwise) the pragmatic features of witness testimony and other contributions to the court has also been considered. Jacobsen (2008) examined face-work during a prosecutor's interpreter-mediated questioning of a defendant in a criminal trial at a Danish district court. It was found that the interpreter frequently modified both face-threatening and face-protecting utterances with a view to protecting her own face and/or the face of one of the primary participants. The discourse markers examined by Hale (1999) were frequently omitted or mistranslated by court interpreters.

Notwithstanding the breadth of pragmatic research on courtroom discourse, no studies have been conducted to date of the ability of individuals with pragmatic disorders to participate in legal examination. However, given the pragmatic demands of courtroom proceedings, there are reasons to believe that such individuals will struggle to comply with cross-examination and other forensic processes. For example, it was described in Sect. 2 how individuals with pragmatic disorders exhibit impaired recognition of and adherence to Gricean maxims. This pragmatic impairment is likely to be particularly evident during legal cross-examination where the requirement to observe maxims of quality, relation and manner is strongly enforced by counsel for the prosecution. (Of course, this is in addition to the maxims of quality and quantity during the swearing-in of witnesses who are required to tell 'the truth, the whole truth and nothing but the truth'.) The requirement for strict adherence to these maxims is evident in these extracts from Hansen (2008) of the cross-examination of witnesses during the Oklahoma City bombing trial in the United States. Counsel for the prosecution can be seen to challenge witnesses when their testimony fails to comply with the maxims of quantity, relation and manner, respectively:

(3)
Q: Did he tell you he had seen a pickup truck?
A: Yes.
Q: All right. Did he describe the pickup truck to you?
A: Yes. He said it was dark-colored –
Q: Hold it a second. Did he describe it? Yes or no.

(4)
Q: At that time at the restaurant on April 26, did Mr. Wahl report to you at least in general terms a sighting he had made at Geary State Lake?
A: Yes, sir.
Q: Did you attempt to conduct a full interview of him at that time?
A: No. We had been instructed when we obtain a new piece of information like that - -
Mr. Tigar: Excuse me, you [sic]. Not responsive.
The court: Yes. Not what you were instructed, what you did.
The witness: Okay. No, I did not.

(5)
Q: And did you ever have an opportunity to ask Mr. McVeigh again why it was he wanted you to do this driving for him?
A: Yes. I got the same answer again.
Q: What was that?

A: I didn't need to know. Basically, just change the subject.
Q: I'm just confused on whether you're telling us that you didn't need to know, or he told you you don't need to know.
A: He told me I didn't need to know.

In (3), the witness proceeds to describe the colour of the pickup truck when counsel for the prosecution had merely asked if the truck had been described. The witness's overly informative reply is quickly brought to a halt by the use of a follow-up question which forcefully indicates that a 'yes-no' response *only* is required. Clearly, the witness in this particular scenario will have no difficulty in replying at this point that the truck had indeed been described. However, it is less clear that a defendant with a pragmatic disorder would be capable of this same response. In fact, it is unlikely that such an individual will even be able to identify that his original response exceeded the quantity requirement of the prosecutor's question. Similar considerations apply to (4) above. In this case, the witness's reply is judged to be irrelevant ('not responsive') as he proceeds to say what he was *instructed* to do rather that what he *did*. Once again, the defendant readily recognizes his digression from the question when it is brought to his attention and is able to return to the point of the prosecutor's question. It is less clear that a defendant with a pragmatic disorder would be able to do the same. Finally, in (5) the witness is asked to clarify his somewhat ambiguous response – is the witness saying he didn't need to know or reporting that he had been told he did not need to know? In this case, the witness is being challenged on the manner of his reply. It is doubtful that a defendant with a pragmatic disorder would be any better equipped to address the manner requirements of this exchange than he was the quantity and relation requirements of the exchanges before it. The same point holds throughout these examples. A key aspect of pragmatic competence – recognition of and adherence to maxims – is tested in each of these exchanges, and will be found to be wanting in individuals with pragmatic disorders.

3.3 Rehabilitation Programs

The rehabilitation of offenders involves an eclectic set of approaches and techniques. Although pragmatic language skills are seldom emphasized in rehabilitation programs, it is a range of such skills that play a role, directly or indirectly, in these programs. Most rehabilitation programs encourage offenders to acknowledge the impact of their crimes on victims. This is a particularly challenging undertaking as there are well-documented empathy deficits and theory of mind impairments in a range of offenders (Castellino et al. 2011; Elsegood and Duff 2010; Seidel et al. 2013). In order to achieve victim empathy, offenders must overcome these mentalizing deficits. A technique used to this end is letters of apology which are written by offenders to their victims. Letters of apology are used extensively in the rehabilitation of sexual offenders (Webster 2002), and apologies are a common feature of restorative justice (Stubbs 2007).

As any pragmatist knows, apologies are first and foremost speech acts. As such, they can be performed felicitously and infelicitously. In preparation for writing letters of apology to victims, offenders receive guidance in the purpose and structure of such letters. This guidance is, in effect, rehearsal of the felicity conditions that attend this speech act. To constitute an authentic apology, the letter must include an expression of responsibility or blame on the part of the offender, an explanation or account of his or her behaviour, an indication of how the offender is making amends (like reparation work) and a commitment to act better in the future. If this preparatory work is not carefully undertaken, and these felicity conditions are not afforded proper significance, the results can be disastrous. Just how disastrous they can be was demonstrated by a case in Leeds in the UK in November 2011. A 16-year-old burglar, who was part of an Intensive Supervision and Surveillance Programme (ISSP),[7] penned the following letter to the victims of his crime. Although the letter was widely publicised at the time, it was never sent to the victims:

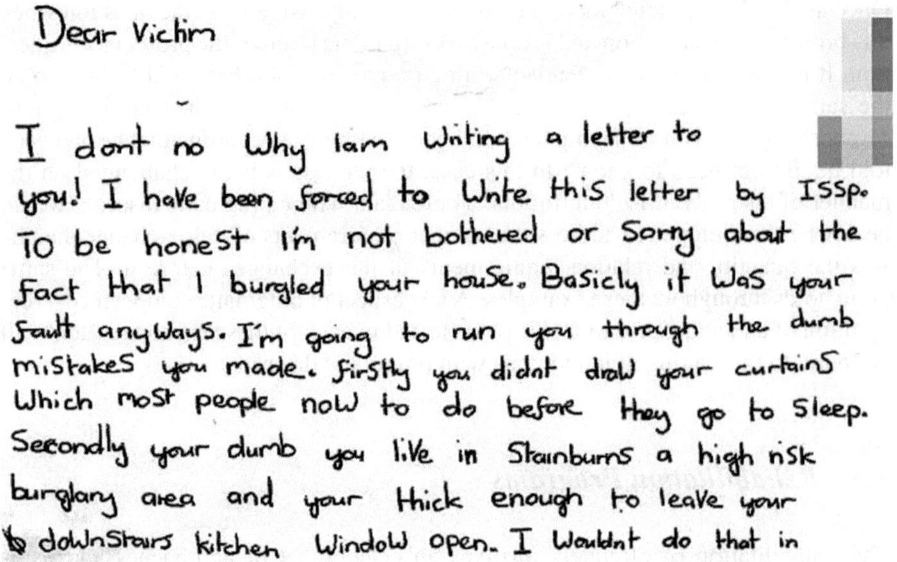
Dear Victim [redacted]

I dont no Why Iam Writing a letter to you! I have been forced to Write this letter by ISSP. TO be honeSt I'm not bothered or Sorry about the Fact that I burgled your houSe. BaSicly it WaS your fault anyWays. I'm going to run you through the dumb miStakeS you made. FirStly you didnt draW your curtainS Which moSt people noW to do before they go to Sleep. Secondly your dumb you liVe in Stainburns a high risk burglary area and your thick enough to leave your ~~to~~ doWnStairs kitchen WindoW open. I Wouldnt do that in a million years. But anyWayS I dont Feel Sorry for you and Im not going to ShoW any Sympath or ~~remose~~ remoies.

yourS Sincerly

[redacted]

from [redacted]

(Reproduced with permission of Ross Parry Agency Ltd.)

[7] ISSP is a community sentence given by the Courts in England and Wales to young people who are classified as persistent and prolific offenders.

Clearly, the offender in this case had no intention of making an authentic apology, as demonstrated by his wilful neglect of this speech act's felicity conditions. As an exercise in developing victim empathy, this letter of apology has certainly failed. But it is equally easy to imagine a situation in which offenders with pragmatic disorders would struggle with the demands of this exercise. For these individuals, the pragmatic knowledge that normally attends the use of speech acts such as apologies may be disrupted or may never have developed along normal lines. It may be far from apparent to these offenders which felicity conditions should be observed in the making of an apology. Even if these offenders do possess knowledge of these conditions, they may not be able to put that knowledge into practice in the context of making a written apology to a victim. The fine-grained judgements which are needed to achieve this are often difficult for language users to make, even when pragmatic language impairments are not a consideration. For example, in the following apology to the female victim of a sexual assault (Bletzer and Koss 2013), the use of the marked expression 'not glad' combined with the admission that the offender initially felt that he had done nothing wrong may be seen to detract from the sincerity of the apology:

(6) "I am not glad that I hurt (name) … Initially, I never felt like I did anything wrong … I never wanted to hurt you, but I did, and for that I am so very sorry …"

Difficult as these judgements evidently are for intact language users, they are more difficult still for offenders with pragmatic disorders. Moreover, the knowledge that underlies the felicitous use of apologies is at some remove from the rather limited advice and guidance which is offered to offenders who are preparing to write a letter of apology.[8] In rehabilitation programs, as elsewhere in the criminal justice system, the lesson is the same: pragmatic demands are likely to exceed the competencies and skills of offenders with pragmatic disorders.

4 Language Services and the Criminal Justice System

The criminal justice system is clearly difficult and challenging territory for suspects and offenders with pragmatic disorders. From the point of police arrest and interview to courtroom examination and prison rehabilitation, this system makes pragmatic demands of many individuals who are inadequately equipped to cope with these demands. The question which must now be addressed is what – if anything – can be done to address this situation. In an age of global austerity the public expenditure that would be required to provide language services to all those individuals in the criminal justice system with communication needs is judged by many governments to be prohibitively expensive. However, it will be argued in this section that

[8] The Ministry of Justice in the UK hosts advice on how to write a letter of apology which has been prepared by Graham Doubleday (2012) of the Wigan Youth Offending Team. It is typical of the advice offered by justice ministries in other developed countries.

language services are particularly cost effective in terms of the improved outcomes that they make possible for prisoners. These outcomes include reduced rates of re-offending behaviour and increased societal re-integration, as measured by the uptake of vocational opportunities and participation in education and training programs. In short, it is contended that investment in language services in prisons and other correctional facilities represents excellent value for money and should be a priority area for funding in future rounds of public spending.

In fairness, it should be pointed out that government committees and bodies with an interest in youth justice and prisoner welfare have very recently made similar claims. In the UK, the Justice Committee (2013) stated in its seventh report: 'We recommend that all youth offending teams and secure institutions should have access to speech and language therapists through a more systematic commissioning process'.[9] When one considers the demonstrable gains that derive from speech and language therapy with offenders, this recommendation would appear to be particularly strongly warranted. In a report commissioned by the Home Office in the UK, Moseley et al. (2006) found that reconviction rates fell sharply in prisoners who participated in oral communication courses. In the first year after release from prison, the reconviction rate among prisoners who had taken courses in oral communication was 21 %. This compares with a national average for all offenders of 44 %. Speech and language therapy enables offenders to access verbally mediated interventions which are aimed at reducing re-offending. Many of these interventions exceed the limited language skills of offenders (Bryan et al. 2007). There were significant improvements on standardized language tests following SLT intervention in a cohort of 72 entrants to an Intensive Supervision and Surveillance Programme (ISSP) studied by Gregory and Bryan (2009). Of these entrants, 65 % had profiles indicating language difficulties, while 20 % scored at the severely delayed level. Although completion and breach rates for young people who had communication plans and SLT intervention were not significantly different from those who did not, these rates were not judged by managers at ISSP to indicate success in the sense of reducing the likelihood of re-offending.

Aside from reduced re-offending, SLT intervention can also enhance the vocational opportunities of offenders and increase their participation in education and training. There are high rates of unemployment among offenders. In the UK, some 67 % of prisoners are unemployed at the time of imprisonment, while 76 % do not have paid employment to go to on release (HM Government 2005). Reduced employment and vocational opportunities are a particularly acute issue among offenders with language impairment, including pragmatic language impairment.

[9] This recommendation followed oral evidence by Professor Karen Bryan to the Committee on 16 October 2012. In her evidence, Professor Bryan reported that of 157 youth offending community services in England and Wales, only 15 had access to speech and language therapy. Only 3 of 11 young offenders institutions have access to a SLT service. The situation is little better in Scotland. In a scoping exercise examining SLT activity in the Scottish criminal justice system during 2010 and up to the end of November 2011, Clark et al. (2012) reported that there was only one dedicated SLT service. This was based at Her Majesty's Young Offender Institution Polmont and Her Majesty's Prison Cornton, and was only for 21 h per week.

Language impairment can have a direct, adverse impact on vocational opportunity in offenders and an indirect effect through its impact on academic achievement (see section 5.5 in Cummings (2014c) for discussion). Language impairment also has a detrimental effect on offender participation in education and training. Snow and Powell (2011) reported that 50 % of a language impaired sub-group of young offenders undertook some form of vocational training since leaving school compared to 68 % of non-language impaired offenders. There is evidence that SLT intervention can lead to increased participation in education and training among offenders. Among 72 entrants to ISSP, Gregory and Bryan (2009) found evidence at an individual level that gains in communication skills through SLT intervention led to wider gains in the young people's engagement with education and training.

The economic case for providing language interventions to offenders could not be more convincing. The cost of crime to the economies of developed countries is enormous. It is estimated that the cost of youth crime alone in Great Britain is £23 million a week or more than £1.2 billion a year (Prince's Trust 2010). In the UK, the cost of literacy failure in terms of involvement in the criminal justice system is £249 million each year (Every Child a Chance Trust 2009). These staggering figures dwarf the sums of money that are spent in total on prison educational programs. In the year to 31 March 2011, the Skills Funding Agency in the UK spent just over £146 million on offender learning in prisons in England and Wales (Skills Funding Agency 2011). On an individual level, the economic case in support of the provision of language intervention to offenders is even more compelling. Based on figures from October 2003, the Audit Commission (2004) in the UK estimated that the cost of two custodial sentences, each of 6 months' duration, for a 15-year-old boy called James was £102, 818. However, a 12-month course of speech and language therapy could have been administered to James when he was 6 years old at a cost of just £392. If James had received interventions such as speech and language therapy at an early age, his cost to statutory agencies by the age of 16 years would have been £42,243. However, his actual cost to these same agencies from his participation in crime up to 16 years of age was £153, 687. These figures can leave little doubt that speech and language therapy is a cost-effective intervention in terms of the criminal justice system.

5 Summary

This chapter has addressed a topic which has been almost entirely overlooked in the literature to date: pragmatic disorders in forensic settings. The neglect of this topic is particularly inexplicable given the increased prevalence of these disorders in various forensic contexts. A number of pathological conditions were examined in which there are marked pragmatic impairments. These conditions, which include autism spectrum disorder and schizophrenia, are more prevalent in prisons and other correctional facilities than in the general population. The chapter considered the pragmatic demands of three aspects of the criminal justice system: police interview;

courtroom examination; and rehabilitation programs. These demands, it was argued, were considerable and were likely to exceed the competence and skills of individuals with pragmatic disorders. Finally, the case was made for greater provision of language services with a focus on pragmatics in prisons and other correctional facilities.

References

Abbeduto, L., Murphy, M. M., Richmond, E. K., Amman, A., Beth, P., Weissman, M. D., Kim, J.-S., Cawthon, S. W., & Karadottir, S. (2006). Collaboration in referential communication: Comparison of youth with down syndrome or fragile X syndrome. *American Journal on Mental Retardation, 111*, 170–183.

Abbeduto, L., Murphy, M. M., Kover, S. T., Giles, N. D., Karadottir, S., Amman, A., Bruno, L., Kim, J.-S., Schroeder, S., Anderson, J. A., & Nollin, K. A. (2008). Signaling noncomprehension of language: A comparison of fragile X syndrome and down syndrome. *American Journal of Mental Retardation, 113*, 214–230.

Adachi, T., Koeda, T., Hirabayashi, S., Maeoka, Y., Shiota, M., Wright, E. C., & Wada, A. (2004). The metaphor and sarcasm scenario test: A new instrument to help differentiate high-functioning pervasive developmental disorder from attention deficit/hyperactivity disorder. *Brain & Development, 26*, 301–306.

Adams, C., Green, J., Gilchrist, A., & Cox, A. (2002). Conversational behaviour of children with asperger syndrome and conduct disorder. *Journal of Child Psychology and Psychiatry, 43*, 679–690.

American Psychiatric Association. (2013). *Diagnostic and statistical manual of mental disorders* (5th ed.). Washington, DC: American Psychiatric Association.

Anckarsäter, H., Nilsson, T., Saury, J. M., Råstam, M., & Gillberg, C. (2008). Autism spectrum disorders in institutionalized subjects. *Nordic Journal of Psychiatry, 62*, 160–167.

Annaz, D., Van Herwegen, J., Thomas, M., Fishman, R., Karmiloff-Smith, A., & Rundblad, G. (2009). Comprehension of metaphor and metonymy in children with Williams syndrome. *International Journal of Language & Communication Disorders, 44*, 962–978.

Audit Commission. (2004). *Youth justice 2004: A review of the reformed youth justice system*. London: Audit Commission.

Baillargeon, J., Ducate, S., Pulvino, J., Bradshaw, P., Murray, O., & Olvera, R. (2003). The association of psychiatric disorders and HIV infection in the correctional setting. *Annals of Epidemiology, 13*, 606–612.

Baillargeon, J., Penn, J. V., Thomas, C. R., Temple, J. R., Baillargeon, G., & Murray, O. J. (2009). Psychiatric disorders and suicide in the Nation's largest state prison system. *Journal of the American Academy of Psychiatry and the Law, 37*, 188–193.

Baron-Cohen, S., O'Riordan, M., Stone, V., Jones, R., & Plaisted, K. (1999). Recognition of faux pas by normally developing children and children with asperger syndrome or high-functioning autism. *Journal of Autism and Developmental Disorders, 29*, 407–418.

Berk-Seligson, S. (1988). The impact of politeness in witness testimony: The influence of the court interpreter. *Multilingua, 7*, 411–439.

Bishop, D. V. M. (1998). Development of the Children's Communication Checklist (CCC): A method for assessing qualitative aspects of communicative impairment in children. *Journal of Child Psychology and Psychiatry, 39*, 879–891.

Bletzer, K. V., & Koss, M. P. (2013). Restorative justice and sexual assault: Outcome appraisal through textual analysis. *The Open Area Studies Journal, 5*, 1–11.

Bogart, E., Togher, L., Power, E., & Docking, K. (2012). Casual conversations between individuals with traumatic brain injury and their friends. *Brain Injury, 26*, 221–233.

Bosco, F. M., Bono, A., & Bara, B. G. (2012). Recognition and repair of communicative failures: The interaction between theory of mind and cognitive complexity in schizophrenic patients. *Journal of Communication Disorders, 45*, 181–197.

Bozikas, V. P., Giannakou, M., Kosmidis, M. H., Kargopoulos, P., Kioseoglou, G., Liolios, D., & Garyfallos, G. (2011). Insights into theory of mind in schizophrenia: The impact of cognitive impairment. *Schizophrenia Research, 130*, 130–136.

Brüne, M., & Bodenstein, L. (2005). Proverb comprehension reconsidered – "Theory of Mind" and the pragmatic use of language in schizophrenia. *Schizophrenia Research, 75*, 233–239.

Bryan, K., Freer, J., & Furlong, C. (2007). Language and communication difficulties in juvenile offenders. *International Journal of Language & Communication Disorders, 42*, 505–520.

Bühler, E., Bachmann, C., Goyert, H., Heinzel-Gutenbrunner, M., & Kamp-Becker, I. (2011). Differential diagnosis of autism spectrum disorder and attention deficit hyperactivity disorder by means of inhibitory control and 'Theory of Mind'. *Journal of Autism and Developmental Disorders, 41*, 1718–1726.

Buitelaar, J. K., van der Wees, M., Swaab-Barneveld, H., & van der Gaag, R. J. (1999). Theory of mind and emotion-recognition functioning in autistic spectrum disorders and in psychiatric control and normal children. *Development and Psychopathology, 11*, 39–58.

Cahill, B. S., Coolidge, F. L., Segal, D. L., Klebe, K. J., Marle, P. D., & Overmann, K. A. (2012). Prevalence of ADHD and its subtypes in male and female adult prison inmates. *Behavioral Sciences & the Law, 30*, 154–166.

Castellino, N., Bosco, F. M., Marshall, W. L., Marshall, L. E., & Veglia, F. (2011). Mindreading abilities in sexual offenders: An analysis of theory of mind processes. *Consciousness and Cognition, 20*, 1612–1624.

Champagne-Lavau, M., Fossard, M., Martel, G., Chapdelaine, C., Blouin, G., Rodriguez, J.-P., & Stip, E. (2009). Do patients with schizophrenia attribute mental states in a referential communication task? *Cognitive Neuropsychiatry, 14*, 217–239.

Clark, A., Barrow, E., & Hartley, K. (2012). Unmet need in Scotland's criminal justice system. *Bulletin, 718*, 20–21.

Colle, L., Baron-Cohen, S., Wheelwright, S., & van der Lely, H. K. J. (2008). Narrative discourse in adults with high-functioning autism or asperger syndrome. *Journal of Autism and Developmental Disorders, 38*, 28–40.

Committee, J. (2013). *Seventh report of session 2012–13: Youth justice*. London: The Stationery Office Limited.

Copur, M., Turkcan, A., & Erdogmus, M. (2005). Substance abuse, conduct disorder and crime: Assessment in a juvenile detention house in Istanbul, Turkey. *Psychiatry and Clinical Neurosciences, 59*, 151–154.

Cornish, K., Burack, J. A., Rahman, A., Munir, F., Russo, N., & Grant, C. (2005). Theory of mind deficits in children with fragile X syndrome. *Journal of Intellectual Disability Research, 49*, 372–378.

Cummings, L. (2005). *Pragmatics: A multidisciplinary perspective*. Edinburgh: Edinburgh University Press.

Cummings, L. (2007). Clinical pragmatics: A field in search of phenomena? *Language & Communication, 27*, 396–432.

Cummings, L. (2008). *Clinical linguistics*. Edinburgh: Edinburgh University Press.

Cummings, L. (2009). *Clinical pragmatics*. Cambridge: Cambridge University Press.

Cummings, L. (2011). Pragmatic disorders and their social impact. *Pragmatics and Society, 2*, 17–36.

Cummings, L. (2012a). Pragmatic disorders. In H.-J. Schmid (Ed.), *Cognitive pragmatics, handbook of pragmatics* (Vol. 4, pp. 291–315). Berlin/Boston: Walter de Gruyter.

Cummings, L. (2012b). Theorising context: The case of clinical pragmatics. In R. Finkbeiner, J. Meibauer, & P. Schumacher (Eds.), *What is context? Theoretical and experimental evidence* (pp. 55–80). Amsterdam: John Benjamins.

Cummings, L. (2012c). Establishing diagnostic criteria: The role of clinical pragmatics. *Lodz Papers in Pragmatics, 8*, 61–84.
Cummings, L. (2013). Clinical pragmatics and theory of mind. In A. Capone, F. Lo Piparo, & M. Carapezza (Eds.), *Perspectives on linguistic pragmatics* (Series: Perspectives in pragmatics, philosophy & psychology, Vol. 2, pp. 23–56). Dordrecht: Springer.
Cummings, L. (2014a). Pragmatic disorders and theory of mind. In L. Cummings (Ed.), *Cambridge handbook of communication disorders* (pp. 559–577). Cambridge: Cambridge University Press.
Cummings, L. (2014b). *Communication disorders*. Basingstoke: Palgrave Macmillan.
Cummings, L. (2014c). *Pragmatic disorders*. Dordrecht: Springer.
Cummings, L. (2015). Pragmatic disorders and social functioning: A lifespan perspective. In J. L. Mey & A. Capone (Eds.), *Interdisciplinary studies in pragmatics, culture and society* (Series: Perspectives in pragmatics, philosophy & psychology, Vol. 4, pp. 179–208). Dordrecht: Springer.
Cummings, L. (2016a). Clinical pragmatics. In Y. Huang (Ed.), *Oxford handbook of pragmatics* (pp. 346–361). Oxford: Oxford University Press.
Cummings, L. (2016b). Clinical pragmatics. In G. Yueguo, A. Burn, & G. Stern (Eds.), *Routledge handbook of pragmatics*. London/New York: Routledge.
Cummings, L. (2016c). Reported speech: A clinical pragmatic perspective. In A. Capone, F. Kiefer, & F. Lo Piparo (Eds.), *Indirect reports* (Series: Perspectives in pragmatics, philosophy & psychology, Vol. 5, pp. 31–55). Dordrecht: Springer.
Dardier, V., Bernicot, J., Delanoë, A., Vanberten, M., Fayada, C., Chevignard, M., Delaye, C., Laurent-Vannier, A., & Dubois, B. (2011). Severe traumatic brain injury, frontal lesions, and social aspects of language use: A study of French-speaking adults. *Journal of Communication Disorders, 44*, 359–378.
Davies, R. C., Williams, W. H., Hinder, D., Burgess, C. N., & Mounce, L. T. (2012). Self-reported traumatic brain injury and postconcussion symptoms in incarcerated youth. *Journal of Head Trauma Rehabilitation, 27*, e21–e27.
de Marchena, A., & Eigsti, I.-M. (2010). Conversational gestures in autism spectrum disorders: Asynchrony but not decreased frequency. *Autism Research, 3*, 311–322.
Dias, S., Ware, R. S., Kinner, S. A., & Lennox, N. G. (2013). Co-occurring mental disorder and intellectual disability in a large sample of Australian prisoners. *Australian and New Zealand Journal of Psychiatry, 47*, 938–944.
Donno, R., Parker, G., Gilmour, J., & Skuse, D. H. (2010). Social communication deficits in disruptive primary-school children. *British Journal of Psychiatry, 196*, 282–289.
Doubleday, G. (2012). *Have you agreed to write a letter of apology?* Online. Available: www.justice.gov.uk/youth-justice/effective-practice-library/letter-of-apology-to-victims. Accessed 11 Feb 2014.
Douglas, J. M. (2010). Relation of executive functioning to pragmatic outcome following severe traumatic brain injury. *Journal of Speech, Language, and Hearing Research, 53*, 365–382.
Elsegood, K. J., & Duff, S. C. (2010). Theory of mind in men who have sexually offended against children: A UK comparison study between child sex offenders and nonoffender controls. *Sexual Abuse, 22*, 112–131.
Every Child a Chance Trust. (2009). *The long term costs of literacy difficulties* (2nd ed.). London: KPMG Foundation.
Falissard, B., Loze, J.-Y., Gasquet, I., Duburc, A., de Beaurepaire, C., Fagnani, F., & Rouillon, F. (2006). Prevalence of mental disorders in French prisons for men. *BMC Psychiatry, 6*, 33.
Fazel, S., Xenitidis, K., & Powell, J. (2008). The prevalence of intellectual disabilities among 12,000 prisoners – A systematic review. *International Journal of Law and Psychiatry, 31*, 369–373.
Frost, R. B., Farrer, T. J., Primosch, M., & Hedges, D. W. (2013). Prevalence of traumatic brain injury in the general adult population: A meta-analysis. *Neuroepidemiology, 40*, 154–159.

Gaines, P. (2011). The multifunctionality of discourse operator okay: Evidence from a police interview. *Journal of Pragmatics, 43*, 3291–3315.
Gilmour, J., Hill, B., Place, M., & Skuse, D. H. (2004). Social communication deficits in conduct disorder: A clinical and community survey. *Journal of Child Psychology and Psychiatry, 45*, 967–978.
Ginsberg, Y., Hirvikoski, T., & Lindefors, N. (2010). Attention deficit hyperactivity disorder (ADHD) among longer-term prison inmates is a prevalent, persistent and disabling disorder. *BMC Psychiatry, 10*, 112.
Godbee, K., & Porter, M. (2013). Comprehension of sarcasm, metaphor and simile in Williams syndrome. *International Journal of Language & Communication Disorders, 48*, 651–665.
Gold, R., Faust, M., & Goldstein, A. (2010). Semantic integration during metaphor comprehension in asperger syndrome. *Brain and Language, 113*, 124–134.
Grant, C. M., Apperly, I., & Oliver, C. (2007). Is theory of mind understanding impaired in males with fragile X syndrome? *Journal of Abnormal Child Psychology, 35*, 17–28.
Green, B. C., Johnson, K. A., & Bretherton, L. (2014). Pragmatic language difficulties in children with hyperactivity and attention problems: An integrated review. *International Journal of Language & Communication Disorders, 49*, 15–29.
Greenbaum, R. L., Stevens, S. A., Nash, K., Koren, G., & Rovet, J. (2009). Social cognitive and emotion processing abilities of children with fetal alcohol spectrum disorders: A comparison with attention deficit hyperactivity disorder. *Alcoholism, Clinical and Experimental Research, 33*, 1656–1670.
Gregory, J., & Bryan, K. (2009). *Evaluation of the leeds speech and language therapy service provision within the intensive supervision and surveillance programme provided by the Leeds Youth Offending Team.* Online. Available: www.leeds.gov.uk/docs/Leeds%20SLT%20report%20Jun%2010.pdf. Accessed 14 Feb 2014.
Hale, S. (1999). Interpreters' treatment of discourse markers in courtroom questions. *Forensic Linguistics, 6*, 57–82.
Hamilton, A. F., Brindley, R., & Frith, U. (2009). Visual perspective taking impairment in children with autistic spectrum disorder. *Cognition, 113*, 37–44.
Hansen, M.-B. M. (2008). On the availability of 'Literal' meaning: Evidence from courtroom interaction. *Journal of Pragmatics, 40*, 1392–1410.
Happé, F., & Frith, U. (1996). Theory of mind and social impairment in children with conduct disorder. *British Journal of Developmental Psychology, 14*, 385–398.
Harzke, A. J., Baillargeon, J., Baillargeon, G., Henry, J., Olvera, R. L., Torrealday, O., Penn, J. V., & Parikh, R. (2012). Prevalence of psychiatric disorders in the Texas Juvenile correctional system. *Journal of Correctional Health Care, 18*, 143–157.
Hassiotis, A., Gazizova, D., Akinlonu, L., Bebbington, P., Meltzer, H., & Strydom, A. (2011). Psychiatric morbidity in prisoners with intellectual disabilities: Analysis of prison survey data for England and Wales. *British Journal of Psychiatry, 199*, 156–157.
Haworth, K. (2009). *An analysis of police interview discourse and its role(s) in the judicial process*, PhD thesis. University of Nottingham.
Haworth, K. (2010). Police-suspect interviews. In L. Cummings (Ed.), *Routledge pragmatics encyclopedia* (pp. 325–327). London/New York: Routledge.
Henry, J. D., Phillips, L. H., Crawford, J. R., Ietswaart, M., & Summers, F. (2006). Theory of mind following traumatic brain injury: The role of emotion recognition and executive dysfunction. *Neuropsychologia, 44*, 1623–1628.
Herrington, V. (2009). Assessing the prevalence of intellectual disability among young male prisoners. *Journal of Intellectual Disability Research, 53*, 397–410.
Heydon, G. (2011). Silence: Civil right or social privilege? A discourse analytic response to a legal problem. *Journal of Pragmatics, 43*, 2308–2316.
HM Government. (2005). *Reducing re-offending through skills and employment.* London: The Stationery Office.

Jacobsen, B. (2008). Interactional pragmatics and court interpreting: An analysis of face. *Interpreting, 10*, 128–158.

John, A. E., Rowe, M. L., & Mervis, C. B. (2009). Referential communication skills of children with Williams syndrome: Understanding when messages are not adequate. *American Journal on Intellectual and Developmental Disabilities, 114*, 85–99.

Jones, C. D., & Schwartz, I. S. (2009). When asking questions is not enough: An observational study of social communication differences in high functioning children with autism. *Journal of Autism and Developmental Disorders, 39*, 432–443.

Kim, O. H., & Kaiser, A. P. (2000). Language characteristics of children with ADHD. *Communication Disorders Quarterly, 21*, 154–165.

Kutscher, S., Schiffer, B., & Seifert, D. (2009). Patients with schizophrenia in forensic-psychiatric hospitals (Section 63 German penal code) in North Rhine-Westphalia. *Fortschritte der Neurologie-Psychiatrie, 77*, 91–96.

Lakoff, R. T. (1989). The limits of politeness: Therapeutic and courtroom discourse. *Multilingua, 8*, 101–129.

Langdon, R., Coltheart, M., Ward, P. B., & Catts, S. V. (2002). Disturbed communication in schizophrenia: The role of poor pragmatics and poor mind-reading. *Psychological Medicine, 32*, 1273–1284.

Laws, G., & Bishop, D. V. M. (2004). Pragmatic language impairment and social deficits in Williams syndrome: A comparison with Down's syndrome and specific language impairment. *International Journal of Language & Communication Disorders, 39*, 45–64.

Lincoln, T. M., Mehl, S., Kesting, M.-L., & Rief, W. (2011). Negative symptoms and social cognition: Identifying targets for psychological interventions. *Schizophrenia Bulletin, 37*, S23–S32.

Lind, S. E., & Bowler, D. M. (2010). Impaired performance on see-know tasks amongst children with autism: Evidence of specific difficulties with theory of mind or domain-general task factors? *Journal of Autism and Developmental Disorders, 40*, 479–484.

Losh, M., Martin, G. E., Klusek, J., Hogan-Brown, A. L., & Sideris, J. (2012). Social communication and theory of mind in boys with autism and fragile X syndrome. *Frontiers in Psychology, 3*, 1–12.

Loukusa, S., Leinonen, E., Kuusikko, S., Jussila, K., Mattila, M.-L., Ryder, N., Ebeling, H., & Moilanen, I. (2007). Use of context in pragmatic language comprehension by children with asperger syndrome or high-functioning autism. *Journal of Autism and Developmental Disorders, 37*, 1049–1059.

Maenner, M. J., Rice, C. E., Arneson, C. L., Cunniff, C., Schieve, L. A., Carpenter, L. A., Van Naarden Braun, K., Kirby, R. S., Bakian, A. V., & Durkin, M. S. (2014). Potential impact of DSM-5 criteria on autism spectrum disorder prevalence estimates. *JAMA Psychiatry, 71*, 292–300.

Marini, A., Spoletini, I., Rubino, I. A., Ciuffa, M., Bria, P., Martinotti, G., Banfi, G., Boccascino, R., Strom, P., Siracusano, A., Caltagirone, C., & Spalletta, G. (2008). The language of schizophrenia: An analysis of micro and macrolinguistic abilities and their neuropsychological correlates. *Schizophrenia Research, 105*, 144–155.

Martin, I., & McDonald, S. (2004). An exploration of causes of non-literal language problems in individuals with asperger syndrome. *Journal of Autism and Developmental Disorders, 34*, 311–328.

Martinovski, B. (2006). A framework for the analysis of mitigation in courts: Toward a theory of mitigation. *Journal of Pragmatics, 38*, 2065–2086.

Marton, I., Wiener, J., Rogers, M., Moore, C., & Tannock, R. (2009). Empathy and social perspective taking in children with attention-deficit/hyperactivity disorder. *Journal of Abnormal Child Psychology, 37*, 107–118.

Mathers, M. E. (2006). Aspects of language in children with ADHD: Applying functional analyses to explore language use. *Journal of Attention Disorders, 9*, 523–533.

Mazza, M., Di Michele, V., Pollice, R., Casacchia, M., & Roncone, R. (2008). Pragmatic language and theory of mind deficits in people with schizophrenia and their relatives. *Psychopathology, 41*, 254–263.

Meilijson, S. R., Kasher, A., & Elizur, A. (2004). Language performance in chronic schizophrenia: A pragmatic approach. *Journal of Speech, Language, and Hearing Research, 47*, 695–713.

Milders, M., Ietswaart, M., Crawford, J. R., & Currie, D. (2006). Impairments in theory of mind shortly after traumatic brain injury and at 1-year follow-up. *Neuropsychology, 20*, 400–408.

Mo, S., Su, Y., Chan, R. C. K., & Liu, J. (2008). Comprehension of metaphor and irony in schizophrenia during remission: The role of theory of mind and IQ. *Psychiatry Research, 157*, 21–29.

Montag, C., Dziobek, I., Richter, I. S., Neuhaus, K., Lehmann, A., Sylla, R., Heekeren, H. R., Heinz, A., & Gallinat, J. (2011). Different aspects of theory of mind in paranoid schizophrenia: Evidence from a video-based assessment. *Psychiatry Research, 186*, 203–209.

Moseley, D., Clark, J., Baumfield, V., Hall, E., Hall, I., Miller, J., Blench, G., Gregson, M., & Spedding, T. (2006). *Developing oral communication and productive thinking skills in HM prisons*. London: Learning & Skills Research Centre.

Mullen, P. E., Holmquist, C. L., & Ogloff, J. R. P. (2003). *National forensic mental health scoping study*. Canberra: Department of Health and Aging.

Muller, F., Simion, A., Reviriego, E., Galera, C., Mazaux, J.-M., Barat, M., & Joseph, P.-A. (2010). Exploring theory of mind after severe traumatic brain injury. *Cortex, 46*, 1088–1099.

Murphy, M. M., & Abbeduto, L. (2007). Gender differences in repetitive language in fragile X syndrome. *Journal of Intellectual Disability Research, 51*, 387–400.

Nilsen, E. S., Mangal, L., & Macdonald, K. (2013). Referential communication in children with ADHD: Challenges in the role of a listener. *Journal of Speech, Language, and Hearing Research, 56*, 590–603.

O'Brien, G., & Pearson, J. (2004). Autism and learning disability. *Autism, 8*, 125–140.

Papagno, C., & Vallar, G. (2001). Understanding metaphors and idioms: A single-case neuropsychological study in a person with down syndrome. *Journal of the International Neuropsychological Society, 7*, 516–528.

Pelc, K., Kornreich, C., Foisy, M.-L., & Dan, B. (2006). Recognition of emotional facial expressions in attention-deficit hyperactivity disorder. *Pediatric Neurology, 35*, 93–97.

Penman, R. (1990). Facework and politeness: Multiple goals in courtroom discourse. *Journal of Language and Social Psychology, 9*, 15–38.

Perlini, C., Marini, A., Garzitto, M., Isola, M., Cerruti, S., Marinelli, V., Rambaldelli, G., Ferro, A., Tomelleri, L., Dusi, N., Bellani, M., Tansella, M., Fabbro, F., & Brambilla, P. (2012). Linguistic production and syntactic comprehension in schizophrenia and bipolar disorder. *Acta Psychiatrica Scandinavica, 126*, 363–376.

Polimeni, J. O., Campbell, D. W., Gill, D., Sawatzky, B. L., & Reiss, J. P. (2010). Diminished humour perception in schizophrenia: Relationship to social and cognitive functioning. *Journal of Psychiatric Research, 44*, 434–440.

Prince's Trust. (2010). *The cost of exclusion: Counting the cost of youth disadvantage in the UK*. London: The Prince's Trust.

Rousseaux, M., Vérigneaux, C., & Kozlowski, O. (2010). An analysis of communication in conversation after severe traumatic brain injury. *European Journal of Neurology, 17*, 922–929.

Sarlon, E., Duburcq, A., Neveu, X., Morvan-Duru, E., Tremblay, R., Rouillon, F., & Falissard, B. (2012). Imprisonment, alcohol dependence and risk of delusional disorder: A cross-sectional study. *Revue d'Épidémiologie et de Santé Publique, 60*, 197–203.

Schenkel, L. S., Spaulding, W. D., & Silverstein, S. M. (2005). Poor premorbid social functioning and theory of mind deficit in schizophrenia: Evidence of reduced context processing? *Journal of Psychiatric Research, 39*, 499–508.

Schofield, P., Butler, T., Hollis, S., & D'Este, C. (2011). Are prisoners reliable survey respondents? A validation of self-reported traumatic brain injury (TBI) against hospital medical records. *Brain Injury, 25*, 74–82.

Scragg, P., & Shah, A. (1994). Prevalence of asperger's syndrome in a secure hospital. *British Journal of Psychiatry, 165*, 679–682.

Seidel, E.-M., Pfabigan, D. M., Keckeis, K., Wucherer, A. M., Jahn, T., Lamm, C., & Derntl, B. (2013). Empathic competencies in violent offenders. *Psychiatry Research, 210*, 1168–1175.

Shiroma, E. J., Ferguson, P. L., & Pickelsimer, E. E. (2010). Prevalence of traumatic brain injury in an offender population: A meta-analysis. *Journal of Correctional Health Care, 16*, 147–159.

Siponmaa, L., Kristiansson, M., Jonson, C., Nyden, A., & Gillberg, C. (2001). Juvenile and young adult mentally disordered offenders: The role of child neuropsychiatric disorders. *Journal of the American Academy of Psychiatry and Law, 29*, 420–426.

Skills Funding Agency. (2011). *Annual report and accounts 2010–11*. London: The Stationery Office.

Slaughter, B., Fann, J. R., & Ehde, D. (2003). Traumatic brain injury in a county jail population: Prevalence, neuropsychological functioning and psychiatric disorders. *Brain Injury, 17*, 731–741.

Snow, P. C., & Powell, M. B. (2011). Oral language competence in incarcerated young offenders: Links with offending severity. *International Journal of Speech-Language Pathology, 13*, 480–489.

Søndenaa, E., Rasmussen, K., Palmstierna, T., & Nøttestad, J. (2008). The prevalence and nature of intellectual disability in Norwegian prisons. *Journal of Intellectual Disability Research, 52*, 1129–1137.

Staikova, E., Gomes, H., Tartter, V., McCabe, A., & Halperin, J. M. (2013). Pragmatic deficits and social impairments in children with ADHD. *Journal of Child Psychology and Psychiatry, 54*, 1275–1283.

Stokoe, E., & Edwards, D. (2008). Did you have permission to smash your neighbour's door? Silly questions and their answers in police-suspect interrogations. *Discourse Studies, 10*, 89–111.

Stubbs, J. (2007). Beyond apology? Domestic violence and critical questions for restorative justice. *Criminology & Criminal Justice, 7*, 169–187.

Sudhalter, V., & Belser, R. C. (2001). Conversational characteristics of children with fragile X syndrome: Tangential language. *American Journal on Mental Retardation, 106*, 389–400.

Sullivan, K., Winner, E., & Tager-Flusberg, H. (2003). Can adolescents with Williams syndrome tell the difference between lies and jokes? *Developmental Neuropsychology, 23*, 85–103.

Surian, L., Baron-Cohen, S., & Van der Lely, H. (1996). Are children with autism deaf to gricean maxims? *Cognitive Neuropsychiatry, 1*, 55–72.

Tavano, A., Sponda, S., Fabbro, F., Perlini, C., Rambaldelli, G., Ferro, A., Cerruti, S., Tansella, M., & Brambilla, P. (2008). Specific linguistic and pragmatic deficits in Italian patients with schizophrenia. *Schizophrenia Research, 102*, 53–62.

Tényi, T., Herold, R., Szili, I. M., & Trixler, M. (2002). Schizophrenics show a failure in the decoding of violations of conversational implicatures. *Psychopathology, 35*, 25–27.

Thoma, P., Hennecke, M., Mandok, T., Wähner, A., Brüne, M., Juckel, G., & Daum, I. (2009). Proverb comprehension impairments in schizophrenia are related to executive dysfunction. *Psychiatry Research, 170*, 132–139.

Uekerman, J., Kraemer, M., Abdel-Hamid, M., Schimmelmann, B. G., Hebebrand, J., Daum, I., Wiltfang, J., & Kis, B. (2010). Social cognition in Attention-Deficit Hyperactivity Disorder (ADHD). *Neuroscience and Biobehavioral Reviews, 34*, 734–743.

Usher, A. M., Stewart, L. A., & Wilton, G. (2013). Attention deficit hyperactivity disorder in a Canadian prison population. *International Journal of Law and Psychiatry, 36*, 311–315.

Van Herwegen, J., Dimitriou, D., & Rundblad, G. (2013). Performance on verbal and low-verbal false belief tasks: Evidence from children with Williams syndrome. *Journal of Communication Disorders, 46*, 440–448.

Webster, S. D. (2002). Assessing victim empathy in sexual offenders using the victim letter task. *Sexual Abuse, 14*, 281–300.

Williams, D., & Happé, F. (2010). Representing intentions in self and other: Studies of autism and typical development. *Developmental Science, 13*, 307–319.
Williams, W. H., Mewse, A. J., Tonks, J., Mills, S., Burgess, C. N., & Cordan, G. (2010). Traumatic brain injury in a prison population: Prevalence and risk for Re-offending. *Brain Injury, 24*, 1184–1188.
Yirmiya, N., Solomonica-Levi, D., Shulman, C., & Pilowsky, T. (1996). Theory of mind abilities in individuals with autism, down syndrome, and mental retardation of unknown etiology: The role of Age and intelligence. *Journal of Child Psychology and Psychiatry, 37*, 1003–1014.
Zhou, J., Cai, W., Chen, C., Wang, H., Zhang, S., Luo, Y., Qiu, C., & Wang, X. (2012). Prevalence of mental disorders in the male juvenile detention centers of Hunan and Sichuan. *Zhong Nan Da Xue Xue Bao. Yi Xue Ban, 37*, 217–221.

The Pragmatics of Stereotypes in Legal Decision-Making

Federico José Arena

Abstract Shared categories are a key element of legal decision-making within the context of interpretation. However, in this domain we often require judges to avoid or contrast the negative effects of a problematic kind of social categorization: stereotypes. Still, it is not easy to specify on which basis a stereotype is legally relevant and, as a consequence, it is not easy to determine the scope of the requirement. The author claims these difficulties arise because the term "stereotype" has heterogenic uses. On the one hand, some stereotypes purport to offer information about the characteristics of a group and of each one of its members (descriptive stereotypes). On the other hand, some stereotypes define and constitute the roles members of a category or social group should assume (normative stereotypes). The author also claims that given this distinction it is necessary to fine-tune the criteria of relevance. In particular, normative stereotypes play a fundamental role in the construction of identities and that is the reason why it is not justified to embrace a thesis rejecting them in general. In this sense the author proposes to distinguish between internally and externally conventional normative stereotypes.

Keywords Stereotypes • Legal adjudication • Identities (construction of)

1 Premise

The practice of legal interpretation is often described as a coordination activity. In fact, part of the reasons why a judge associates a meaning to a text is that other judges have done or will do the same. This structure allows judges to form expectations about their colleagues' behaviour within the context of interpretation. A key element of this coordinative structure is the role played by shared categories, i.e., shared ways in which items are classified into sets. This includes social categories, that is, the classification of people into groups. However, the use of social categories is not free of controversy. We often require judges to avoid or contrast the negative

F.J. Arena (✉)
Center for Legal and Social Research (Córdoba National University), National Scientific and Technical Research Council (Conicet), Córdoba, Argentina
e-mail: fjarena@conicet.gov.ar

F. Poggi, A. Capone (eds.), *Pragmatics and Law*, Perspectives in Pragmatics, Philosophy & Psychology 10, DOI 10.1007/978-3-319-44601-1_15

effects of social categorization. In particular, judges should be aware of a problematic kind of social categorization: stereotypes.[1] Even if we can agree that stereotypes are closely connected with sensible issues, such as individual auto perception, identity construction and discriminatory attitudes, among others; it is not easy to specify on which basis a stereotype is problematic and, as a consequence, it is not easy to determine the scope of the requirement. That is to say, it is not simple to determine if all stereotypes should be avoided or if, instead, there are acceptable or mandatory uses of stereotypes because some of them are inevitable or valuable. It seems to me that these difficulties arise because the term "stereotype" has heterogenic uses.

Generally, by means of a stereotype we attribute a property to a member of a group on the sole basis that she belongs to the group.[2] That is to say, we attribute a property B to every member of a category in virtue of the fact that, as long as they possess the property A, they belong to the category.[3] The property can be positive or negative (e.g. punk fans are violent, Asians are good at mathematics).[4] We stereotype, for example, when we associate some personal characteristics, like Mohawk haircuts, black leather pants and preference for punk music, with some characteristics of behaviour, such as laziness and propensity to violence. Those personal characteristics may or may not indicate in a probabilistic way those characteristics of behaviour, but certainly they do not indicate them inexorably. That is why stereotypes are discussed in terms of generalisations. Stereotypes do not possess a universal basis and they are introduced as assertions about the existence of a statistical correlation between the properties attributed to the members of a group and the fact of belonging to the group.[5]

However, some uses of stereotypes have a different direction of fit. In these cases, the person that uses the stereotype does not purport to describe, but to attribute a duty to another person on the basis that she belongs to a group. For instance, whoever defends the stereotype according to which mothers should be housewives does not assert that the majority of mothers are housewives (or that there is a

[1] Indeed, the obligation to address stereotypes and to avoid their harmful effects has a legal basis in several legal systems. For instance, it is recognized in the U.N. Convention on the Elimination of All Forms of Discrimination Against Women (article 2 and 5) and in many other international documents.

[2] Oakes et al. 1994.

[3] Schauer 2003.

[4] This is one of the traits that would distinguish stereotypes from other critical forms of social categorization, such as prejudices or implicit bias. Prejudices include a negative attitude towards a group and a tendency to judge its members negatively. In contrast, stereotypes do not necessarily include a prejudice in this sense. For instance, to hold a stereotype about a group X does not always lead to a negative attitude toward the group X. This may be due to the fact that the characteristic associated with the group is neutral with respect to other values (Asians are bad drivers) or to the fact that the feature gives rise to feelings of another type (people of colour know how to dance): Blum 2004. An implicit bias consists in the unconscious attribution of a minor moral value to a person or group. It often entails a categorical preference (context-independent) against or in favour of that person or group (Alexander 1992). I will not indulge here in the analysis of these distinctions.

[5] Schauer 2003 and Appiah 2000.

statistical correlation between being a mother and being a housewife), but he claims that mothers should assume that role. This second kind of stereotype use has been pointed out by several authors but my impression is that its analysis is still underdeveloped, and so are the criteria of relevance to which it should be subjected.[6] In this work I intend to take some steps forward in this direction.

I begin by distinguishing more accurately between different uses of stereotypes (Sect. 2). On the one hand, there are stereotypes that purport to provide information about the characteristics of a group and of each one of its members (descriptive stereotypes). On the other hand, there are stereotypes that define and constitute the roles members of a group should assume (normative stereotypes). Then, I briefly refer to descriptive stereotypes, since several considerations concerning them will contribute to the examination of normative stereotypes (Sect. 3). In particular, it will be important to distinguish between a general (the correction of the stereotype regarding the group) and an individual (the correction of the stereotype concerning a member of the group) direction of fit. Next, I propose a conceptual analysis of normative stereotypes based on the notions of convention and constitutivity (Sect. 4). My claim will be that normative stereotypes are social norms (or conventions), and that as long as they define the roles of a category of people, they have a constitutive function. Finally I introduce some criteria of relevance concerning normative stereotypes (Sect. 5). Normative stereotypes have a direction of fit social group to stereotype; therefore it does not make sense to assess if they represent the true properties either of a group or of an individual. In order to identify the criteria of relevance applicable to normative stereotypes we should distinguish an internal and an external sense of conventionality. The stereotype is internally conventional when the people, on whose convergence of behaviour depends the existence of the social norm, are also the addressees of the stereotype. The stereotype is externally conventional when there is no such a coincidence. On this basis, I claim that a normative stereotype is oppressive when it purports to impose on a group an externally conventional stereotype. A stereotype is also oppressive when it purports to impose on a member an internally conventional stereotype. Therefore, normative stereotypes are problematic when they affect the autonomy of an individual or a group. I close with some preliminary conclusions.

2 Stereotypes, Between Categories and Norms

The term "stereotype" has an intense expressive capacity. To say of an assertion that it is a stereotype is enough for the listener to condemn it. This homogeneous expressive effect hampers the analysis of its meaning, since sometimes this term makes reference to different phenomena. The following example may help to illustrate this point.

[6] There is an explicit reference to them in Appiah 2005 and Cook and Cusack 2010.

During 2014 the United Nations Committee on the Elimination of Discrimination against Women had to decide on how the Spanish Judiciary dealt with the case González Carreño. In this case, after a separation motivated mainly by the maltreatment and abuses suffered by the woman, the husband took advantage of visit hours and kidnapped their daughter. Later he murdered the child and committed suicide immediately afterwards. Concerning this case, the Committee considered that

> the authorities responsible for providing protection chose to follow the stereotypical view that even the most abusive should enjoy visitation rights and that it is always better for a child to be raised by its father and mother; thus failing to appreciate the rights of the child and disregarding the fact that she had expressed fear of her father and rejected the contact. The courts took it for granted that it is better to have contact even with a violent father. The circumstances of the case called for the authorities and courts to evaluate whether the visits respected the child's right to life, to live free of violence, and the principle of the best interests of the child. [... The husband] was not sanctioned for his repeated assaults on the author or his non-payment of child support. Despite a request by the author, [her husband] was also not required to engage in therapy with a view to normalizing his relationship with his daughter. The authorities' assessment of the risk to the author and her daughter seems to have been obscured by prejudice and stereotypes that lead to questioning the credibility of women victims of domestic violence.[7]

Now, not all that in this passage is named "stereotype" seems to work in the same way. In particular, I think we should distinguish between two different uses according to their direction of fit.

In uses of the first type, a stereotype purports to offer information about the world, that is to say, pursues to describe a state of affairs. Thus I will call them descriptive stereotypes. Their direction of fit is stereotype to social group, which is simply to say that if the stereotype does not match the world this is a reason to abandon or modify the stereotype.[8] Descriptive stereotypes may be assessed on the basis of their correspondence with the real properties of the group to which they refer. As for instance, the stereotype according to which Italians are good cooks; or, in the quoted text, the stereotype according to which the victims of domestic violence are not credible.[9]

---

[7] Case of González Carreño (Spain), Committee on the Elimination of Discrimination against Women, 58th session, 30 June to 18 July 2014, Report N° 47/2012 (CEDAW/C/58/D/47/2012).

[8] Although it was originally used to distinguish two types of linguistic acts (assertive and directive), the expression "direction of fit" has been extended to distinguish between different kinds of statements (descriptive and prescriptive) and mental states (beliefs and desires). The actual use of the expression has a combined source. On the one hand, it seems that the first author to use the expression was John L. Austin (in Austin 1953), but to draw a distinction between different types of assertive acts. The current use is similar to Austin's usage of the expression "onus of match". On the other hand, the current use is linked to a distinction made by G. Elizabeth M. Anscombe in her work *Intention* (Anscombe 1957, 56), even if she does not use that expression. It has been John R. Searle who in different works has endowed the expression with the content that currently has. In particular, see Searle 1975. See also Humberstone 1992; Smith 1987; Platts 1979, 256–25).

[9] That is why descriptive stereotypes are often associated with doxastic mental states. For instance, they tend to be defined as "a set of beliefs about the personal attributes of a social group" (Ashmore and Del Boca 1981, 21). I rather focus here on the propositional content of such mental states without judging, at least at the time of definition, which kind of mental state it is.

In uses of the second type, what is considered a stereotype has instead a direction of fit social group to stereotype. This simply means that the lack of coincidence between world and stereotype is a reason to modify the world and not a reason to modify the stereotype. In this case there is a normative relation between the behaviour associated with members of the group and the fact that they belong to the group. I will call them normative stereotypes. Therefore, there is no point in asking if the stereotype properly describes a group. On the contrary, they are norms in virtue of which a person with certain characteristics should perform certain tasks or assume a determinate social role. As, in the text quoted, the stereotype that distributes, between separate parents, the role of custody to mothers and the role of visit to fathers.[10]

It is true that as long as all stereotypes give place to expectations it would be possible to claim that all of them are normative. However, only some stereotypes purport to assess, not an expectation about the properties possessed by the members of a group, but about the roles they should perform. Only these last ones are normative in the sense here proposed.

Certainly, the distinction between two uses of stereotypes does not imply that there are no relations between them. On the one hand, it is often the case that a descriptive stereotype is the basis of a normative stereotype. For instance, under the supposition that women possess some capacities and talents that made them more suitable for domestic work, it is require that if they are mothers they should also be housewives. On the other hand, it is likely that the correctness of a descriptive stereotype would be due to the existence of a normative stereotype. For instance, if there is a normative stereotype according to which military professions correspond to men, it is likely that this would drive women not to undertake that career and therefore it would be correct the descriptive stereotype according to which women do not opt by the military career.

3 Brief Excursus on Descriptive Stereotypes

Theorists have focused their attention mainly on descriptive stereotypes (in this section, and except specification, "stereotype/s" means "descriptive stereotype/s"), and it is on their regard that some criteria of relevance have been advanced. As I have

[10]The distinction, to my mind, is also exemplified in the Case Andrle v. Czech Republic (Application no. 6268/08) decided by the ECRH (Judgment 17/02/2011). The Court had to decide if a pension scheme which established a different pensionable age for women caring for children compared to men in the same position was in breach of the Convention. The two kind of stereotypes were at play in that case as can be noted from this words of the Court: "Acknowledging that, in the former Czechoslovakia, the more favourable treatment of women who raised children was originally designed to compensate for the factual inequality and hardship arising out of the combination of the traditional mothering role of women [descriptive] and the social expectation of their involvement in work on a full-time basis [normative], the Court considers that this measure pursued a legitimate aim."

said, by means of stereotypes we attribute properties or characteristics to members of a group by the fact that they belong to it. Grouping makes interaction simpler; on the basis of the group to which others belong, we may rely on certain expectations regarding their behaviour. Maybe this procedure is not altogether evident when we interact with our closest people. In their regard we have individualized information and we are willing to support our expectations on that information rather than on previous categories. However, in complex and massive societies, social categorization is an indispensable mechanism in order to form expectations about the people we interact with and regarding whom we have little information. This implies that it would be excessive to rule out all stereotypes, since some, although not all, of them may properly describe the characteristics of the members of a group. In this sense, it has been proposed to distinguish between stereotypes with and without statistical basis.[11] Stereotypes have statistical basis when they associate to the members of a group a property that in fact they possess.[12] This does not mean that the majority of the members of the group possesses this property; it means that the fact of being member of the group, and not of another, makes the possession of the property more likely.[13] Stereotypes lack statistical basis, and are called "false stereotypes", when they attribute to the members of a group a characteristic that they do not possess.

False stereotypes are less problematic from a theoretical point of view; they must be avoided because they involve a false representation of a group.[14] The theoretical problem arrives with stereotypes with statistical basis, since claiming that all of them are problematic, without further specification, would amount to ruling out other generalisations or categories that are considered acceptable.[15]

Categories are a basic component of the way in which we think, act, perceive and speak. Conceptual systems are organised in terms of categories and a great part of our thought involves using them. In making our way through the world, we categorise people, animals and physical objects. A big part of the categorisation process is automatic and unconscious; we only notice it when we face some problematic cases. We only think about the properties of the category "wine" or "barbeque" when we

[11] Schauer 2003; Appiah 2005, among others.

[12] For the sake of brevity, even if it is inaccurate, from now on by "properties of the group" I will refer elliptically to "properties of the members of the group". It is imprecise because clearly there are properties of the group that are not properties of its members, e.g., "Argentines are divisible by two".

[13] It is inaccurate to assert that stereotypes are "false" when they lack statistical basis. For if by "statistical basis" we mean a way to collect and analyse data, then the falsehood (or truth) of a stereotype is prior to that epistemic activity. That is to say, a stereotype can be true even without statistical base, in the sense that data has not yet been obtained or processed. The truth/falsehood depends on the correct representation of the group; the presence/absence of statistical basis depends on an epistemic activity. I would like to thank Damiano Canale for this observation.

[14] This implies that the stereotype also constitutes a false representation of each of the members of the group. Note that from the fact that the group does not possess a property A, it does not follow that no member of the group possesses the property A. The false representation of each member, even of those who possess the property, is due to the fact that the possession or not of the property is not the result of (it is not linked to) the belonging to the group.

[15] See (Schauer 2003) and (Case 2000).

have to decide whether it is wine the liquid produced from the alcoholic fermentation of pineapple juice or whether it is a barbeque the cooking of vegetables on a grill and over fire.[16]

It is quite common for people to choose a comprehensible or easy noticeable aspect of a phenomenon and to use it to refer to the phenomenon as a whole. In other words, it is common to use a subcategory to make reference to the whole category.[17] In theses cases the subcategory defines expectations about the category, i.e., the expectation of being identical to the subcategory. Categorisation is an adaptive characteristic since it frees our cognitive capacity from part of its load and allows it to carry out other tasks. For instance, even if some tigers can be tame, to categorise an animal that is in front of me as a tiger allows me to take some decisions in order to keep myself safe. Once we include an individual into a category we can associate it to a big quantity of previous information without the need to obtain it in the current case.[18]

Stereotypes work this way. That is to say, when there is a stereotype a subcategory has received the status of representing (standing for) the category as a whole; usually with the purpose of carrying out fast judgments or reasoning about the stereotyped subjects. Generally, the subcategory that plays the role of stereotype is easier to understand, to remember, to recognise and to use in the context.[19] Thanks to this imprecise character a stereotype is able to fulfil a cognitive function. By associating a group membership with a set of characteristics we can save efforts, since we need only to obtain the indispensable information necessary to establish the group membership in order to associate those characteristics to an individual.

If stereotypes with statistical basis have this structure, then not all of them are unacceptable. As Schauer puts it, the reason of their unacceptability cannot be that they are no universal generalisations, because this is a characteristic shared with many other categories.[20]

However, the cognitive function should not be exaggerated. It is true that stereotypes with statistical basis possess cognitive import. They allow us to manage information about a group and about an individual pertaining to the group. But in this last case only if some other information is lacking. In other words, even if the stereotype might be correct concerning the group, it does not make sense to use it regarding an individual that shows not to satisfy it. In face of contrary evidence, it is only exceptionally justified to insist in the attribution of some characteristic to an individual based on her belonging to a group. Only in exceptional circumstances, linked to the low epistemic quality of the current perception, it seems justified to apply the stereotype in the presence of discordant individual information. By contrast, having information that an individual does not satisfy the stereotype puts pressure on

[16] I take the Pineapple-wine example from (Schauer 2015, p. 36).

[17] (Rosch and Lloyd 1978).

[18] (Mervis and Rosch 1981).

[19] (Lakoff 1987).

[20] See (Schauer 2003, pp. 75–78).

discarding the stereotype in the actual occasion. Clearly, this does not necessarily involve abandoning the stereotype altogether.

Therefore, it seems that we can distinguish a general and an individual direction of fit. General direction of fit refers to the correction of the stereotype regarding the group (with and without statistical basis), individual direction of fit refers to the correction of the stereotype concerning a member of the group (possession or not of the characteristic associated with the group). Lack of general fit puts pressure in favour of abandoning the stereotype. Lack of individual fit puts pressure in favour of discarding the stereotype in the particular case, but not necessarily in favour of abandoning it.

Now, in legal contexts, even if the criteria of relevance tend to rely on the cognitive import of the stereotype, this is not always the case. In some cases, in spite of being correct from the general direction of fit, there is pressure to abandon the stereotype. This is linked with egalitarian considerations regarding "suspicious categories",[21] as with the type of attitudes that stereotypes generate in its bearers (those who reason using the stereotype) and in its addressees (the stereotyped subjects).

For instance, the bearer, first, cannot perceive the members of the group as individuals who have their own personal characteristics and, second, he is insensitive to the variety inside the stereotyped group.[22] Furthermore, stereotypes often produce in the addressee a reaction called stereotype threat. Being perceived as the addressee of a stereotype negatively affects behaviour, so that people tend to underperform and to confirm the stereotype.[23] Besides, individual direction of fit produces complex criteria of relevance. On the one hand, it is often argued that when the individual direction of fit fails, clinging to the stereotype affects the principle of equality. It is usually claimed that using a stereotype to make a decision regarding and individual that does not satisfy the stereotype violates the principle of equality because the same solution is applied to a case that is substantially different. This is the case, for instance, when a woman is not admitted as a teacher, even if she has the necessary skills, because she has exceeded the age limit. However, on the other hand, there are cases in which even if the individual direction of fit fails, we agree that the decision should be nevertheless taken. For instance, think of the stereotype according to which a person over a certain age has the political maturity required to vote. We agree that the decision that forbids voting should be taken regarding a person that has not reached that age but nevertheless has the required maturity.[24]

[21] See, for instance, Case 2000.

[22] See Blum 2004.

[23] Steele 2010.

[24] The reason of this acceptance might be the difficulties to obtain individualized information. For instance, this kind of consideration was clearly at point in the Case of Alajos Kiss v. Hungary, Judgment of ECHR the 20/05/2010. Sometimes individual information can be gathered without adding excessive costs. In that case, and regarding the ban on vote for people with disabilities, the applicant "emphasised that there were important distinctions between minors and people with disabilities, the most significant being that, while an individual assessment of the maturity of all minors would be an unreasonable burden on the authorities, the same could not be said about the

As I have said in the introduction, I intend here to focus mainly on normative stereotypes. Thus, having done these considerations, I analyses next the elements and the operation of normative stereotypes. Then, I propose some criteria of relevance.

4 Normative Stereotypes

In order to carry the analysis of normative stereotypes forward I propose to consider an example taken from the Chilean legal system, regarding the criminal prohibition of juvenile masculine homosexuality. The Chilean Constitutional Court had to decide on the constitutionality of the article 365 of the Criminal Code that punishes homosexual relations between men older than 14 years when (at least) one of them (the passive subject) is younger than 18 years.[25] The criticisms that sustained the unconstitutionality of the article pointed out the different treatment given to masculine homosexuality, concerning all other acts of sexual significance with a person younger than 18 years but older than 14 years. That is to say, the "law recognises to the adolescent of masculine gender [a] field of autonomy to undertake all kinds of acts of sexual significance with an individual of feminine gender and to make almost all kinds of acts of sexual significance with an individual of masculine gender, in as much as they do not amount to be the passive subject of sexual intercourse."[26]

On the 4th of January 2011 the Court established the constitutionality of the article, considering, among other things, mandatory to protect the physical and psychic integrity and the sexual indemnity of minors. This decision was highly criticised. One of the criticisms was that judges had relied on stereotypes. For instance, according to Bascuñán, the vote of the majority "endorses an antique and rooted cultural representation, according to which the passive role in the coitus is incompatible with masculinity. However, in this context, it is something very distinct to consider that it is a valid reason for the law to forbid it. It amounts to subordinate the recognition of the human dignity to the satisfaction of a stereotype."[27]

To understand criticisms like Bascuñán's we should remove the ambiguity of the term "stereotype". That is to say, we should determine if the criticism attributes to the court a descriptive or a normative stereotype. In this sense, and in order to elucidate the elements and the structure of normative stereotypes, it seems to me necessary to distinguish the different fields of the legal phenomenon in which they may appear.

---

fitness to vote of adults under guardianship, whose status was in any event determined in individual judicial proceedings".

[25] Tribunal Constitucional, Decisión n° 1683–2010, 4th January 2011. See also Bascuñán Rodriguez et al. 2011.

[26] Bascuñán Rodríguez 2011, 121–122.

[27] Bascuñán Rodríguez 2011, 128–129. Agreeing on the presence of a stereotype: Casas Becerra et al. 2012, 265–271. For a detailed analysis of the constitutionality issue see the "Informe en derecho" (Report of law) prepared by (Bascuñán Rodriguez et al. 2011).

4.1 Normative Stereotypes and Legal Fields

The Chilean case clearly shows that stereotypes' first sphere of influence is normative production. Following Schauer we can distinguish three levels in the structure of general rules: justification, descriptive generalisation and prescription (or rule properly said).[28] In the known example of the prohibition of dogs in the restaurant, these three levels are represented in the following way:

(i) Justification: it is valuable to avoid annoyances to customers.
(ii) Descriptive generalisation: the presence of the property of being a dog makes it more likely that the property of causing annoyances to customers will also be present.[29]
(iii) Prescriptive generalisation (general rule): if dog, then forbidden the entrance to the restaurant.

We can now go back to the case. The structure can be used to analyse the reasoning that the court attributes to the legislator. In effect, according to the court:

> [The] end pursued by the legislator was the protection of the physical and psychic integrity and the sexual indemnity of adolescents, understood as the need to prevent any harm or damage to their psychosocial development, taking into account that by the circumstances of their physical and emotional maturity, they are not in the position of understanding the meaning of these acts, before arriving to the adult stage.[30]

Simplifying, the reasoning could be reconstructed in the following way[31]:

(i) Justification: it is valuable to protect the physical and psychic integrity and the sexual indemnity of adolescents.
(ii) Descriptive generalisation: The practice of (passive) homosexuality in adolescents affects their physical and psychic integrity and sexual indemnity.
(iii) Rule: If adolescent, then it is forbidden to undertake (passive) homosexual behaviours.

Until here the problem would seem to be at the level of the descriptive generalisation. However, the normative stereotype appears when we note that in the argument there is no other harm to the integrity and indemnity than the practise of

---

[28] In Schauer's word: "A rule's factual predicate consists of a generalization perceived to be causally relevant to some goal sought to be achieved or evil sought to be avoided. Prescription of that goal, or proscription of that evil, constitutes the justification which then determines which generalization will constitute the rule's factual predicate" (Schauer 2004, 86).

[29] This formulation of the descriptive generalization follows Schauer's ideas about the causal relationship as a probabilistic relationship. Also, this wording makes clearer the fact that generalizations at play are not universal and that, therefore, the prescriptive generalization will be under and over inclusive. See Schauer 2004.

[30] Paragraph n. 28.

[31] It is worth clarifying that I am not reconstructing here the reasoning of the court, but the hypothetical reasoning of the legislator.

(passive) homosexuality itself. That is to say, if the argument were to claim that A (homosexuality) produces a harmful effect B (on the integrity and indemnity), then it would be a descriptive stereotype whose direction of fit would allow to evaluate its falsity or not. Since the argument does not make reference to a condition B, it follows that homosexuality is in itself the condition, i.e., that there is a negative assessment of homosexuality. This inference is also based on the fact that passive homosexuality is the only act of sexual significance reached by the normative provision.

Therefore, the reasoning should be reconstructed in the following way, the normative stereotype appearing at the level of justification:

(i) Justification: Individuals of masculine gender should practise heterosexuality.
(ii) Descriptive generalisation: The property of being an adolescent makes it more likely that it would also verify the property of being easily influenced about sexual practices.
(iii) Rule: If adolescent, then forbidden (passive) homosexual behaviour.

This normative stereotype seems to match with the one attributed by Bascuñán to the Court. It means that normative stereotypes can also appear in the activity of judges. They can be found in either in the external justification of the normative premise or in the external justification of the factual premise. In the first case, when interpreting, the judge may use a normative stereotype in order to choose a given interpretation. In other words, between two possible interpretations of the same normative provision, the judge will choose the one that is consistent or coherent with the normative stereotype.

If by "interpretation" we understand the activity that consists in identifying the meaning of the legal sources, i.e., of legal texts, then the result of this activity will be (the formulation of) an interpretative statement. An interpretative statement has the form "D means N", where D is the text (the normative provision) and N its meaning (the norm).[32] Often there are several meanings that might be attributed to a normative provision. This plurality of meanings depends less on some objective "character" of language than on other sources such as"(i) the plurality of interpretive methods; (ii) juristic theories ("legal dogmatics"), and (iii) the sense of justice of interpreters, i.e., their ethical and political preferences (be they expressly declared by means of value judgments or not)."[33]

Given this plurality of meanings, it is precisely through interpretation that interpreters decide which meaning should be attributed to the normative provision. Normative stereotypes often constitute an important part of the ethical and political preferences of judges (in the remaining of the paper, and except specification, I will

[32] Guastini 2011, 138–139. I think that the analysis of stereotypes that I am proposing here does not depend on following Guastini on interpretation. But I do think that in so doing the presentation of the problem is much clearer.

[33] Guastini 2011, 148.

use "stereotype/s" to refer to "normative stereotype/s").[34] Therefore, if the judge shares the stereotype regarding masculine sexual practices, then when interpreting the constitutional text and the Criminal Code, she will choose the meaning according to which the prohibition of homosexual acts with adolescents passes the test of constitutionality. She will do this by resorting to a suitable interpretative method.

In the case at hand, for instance, the majority that voted in favour of the constitutionality resorted to an originalistic, or intentionalistic, argument. First, because from the preparatory discussions it arises that the authors of the legal text had in mind the punishment of homosexuality as away of protecting the psico-physical integrity and sexual indemnity of adolescents. Thus, the majority argued, "from all that has been said up to now, we can conclude that the members of parliament did take into account the controversial points regarding sodomy and the discussion was shaped by their worry regarding the protection of adolescents and their sexual indemnity, ending with the approval of the current wording of article 365 of the Criminal Code". Second, because from the preparatory work it is possible to construe a restrictive interpretation of the constitutional meaning of "freedom" that is not incompatible with the Criminal Code. In this sense, the majority argued, "the Constituent of 1980 did not understand the right to personal freedom as comprehensive of the right to the free development of personality nor of the right of sexual self-determination".

In contrast, the minority judges, that seemed to reject the stereotype, employed the systematic argument (broadly understood as coherence) regarding other international decisions. Thus, by resorting to the "international standard" the minority argued that "an examination of comparative law and of international documents on the matter allows us to conclude that, nowadays, the punishment of consented sodomy has been declared unconstitutional in several countries all around the world".[35]

Finally, stereotypes may also play a relevant role regarding evidence. I will not say much about this point. I only note that regarding evidence theorists have focused on descriptive stereotypes.[36] In spite of this, during the evidential procedure, judges could also resort to normative stereotypes in order to support a statement of fact. If it is true that in a community there is a stereotype according to which the members of the community have to do *p*, the judge can resort to the existence of this stereotype in order to have as likely the fact that a member of this community has done *p*. Of course, this depends on the stereotype having the characteristics of a social norm; more on this below.

---

[34] A note on terminology: the expression "normative stereotypes" is often used to make reference to any stereotype reflected in legal norms. This is not the way I use the expression here since, as I will try to show, legal rules may reflect both descriptive and normative stereotypes.

[35] 29th paragraph of the minority vote.

[36] For instance, according to Coloma: "Profiles or stereotypes play an explanatory function regarding how certain events occur or have occurred, thereby saving efforts on the collection of information for the case. It might certainly be profitable as long as some information may not be available or be too expensive (Coloma 2010, 102).

4.2 Elements and Structure of the Normative Stereotypes

From what I have said so far it follows that stereotypes are sometimes used as norms, more or less rigid, about the role of a category of people.[37] Indeed, normative stereotypes are constituted by two elements. First, they include individuals into a category or social group; and second, they specify the roles that apply to this category of people. In so doing normative stereotypes purport to mould the behaviour, plans and life of the members of a group. According to Akerlof and Kranton, the norms that define the way in which members of a category should behave, can be understood as conventions or social norms.

> In the formal language of the social sciences, people divide themselves and others into *social categories*. And social categories and norms are automatically tied together: people in different social categories *should* behave differently. The norms also specify how people of different types –different social categories, in our new vocabulary- should treat each other.[38]

In this sense, being part of a groups is in part constituted by social norms or conventions that defines the behaviour of the members of the group. When this is the case, normative stereotypes are characterised by two traits, to wit, conventionality and constitutivity. I will invest some paragraphs on them.

The meanings of the term "conventional" have different amplitudes. On the one hand, in a wide sense, something is conventional if it depends on human beings, their actions and beliefs, or other attitudes.[39] In this sense, conventional is the opposite of natural and it is synonymous of social. In a more strict sense, only a subclass of the facts that depend on human actions and beliefs are conventions. Thus, only when human actions and attitudes assume a certain configuration we are in front of a convention.

Generally, it is claimed that there is a convention if actions and attitudes of two or more people interlock in such a way as forming an agreement. Thus, a convention to use some notation exists between logics if they have reciprocally promised each other to use it.[40] Nevertheless, there is another type of conventions for whose existence an agreement is not necessary. For instance, according to Hume, certain types of interaction between individuals may "properly enough be called a convention or agreement betwixt us, though without the interposition of a promise; since the actions of each of us have a reference to those of the other, and are performed upon the supposition, that something is to be performed on the other part. Two men, who

[37] About the notion of prescriptive generalization see Schauer 2004.

[38] Akerlof and Kranton 2010, 11. In the same sense Appiah 2005.

[39] This distinction has to be qualified because actions and beliefs are part of human nature and consequently so are conventions. See Arena 2014.

[40] I am following here the standard conception according to which an agreement is an exchange of conditional promises. See Lewis (1969, 34), Gilbert (1993, 627), Raz (1984, 202–203).

pull the oars of a boat, do it by an agreement or convention, though they have never given promises to each other".[41]

There are three conditions for the existence of a convention without agreement.[42] In the first place, some regularity or convergence of behaviour. A regularity of behaviour can be conceived of as "doing A on the occasion O".[43] Since the convergence is not sufficient to distinguish between conventions and mere habits[44] there are further conditions.

The second condition is an attitude of the people involved, named by the literature "condition of dependence".[45] The condition of dependence refers to the reasons that give place to a convention. In these cases, there is a crucial sense in which we say that we conform to the regularity, in part, due to the fact that others do it too. In particular, the reason for conformity is constituted (at least in part) by the fact that there is a common practice.[46]

Finally, the third condition is arbitrariness.[47] Although it has not been easy to flesh out this condition,[48] it will suffice here to conceive of it in the traditional way as the possibility to choose an alternative regularity and nevertheless to satisfy the same purpose. Thus, the convention according to which the parents of the bride should pay the costs of the wedding party could have been different. That is to say, it could have been the case that the parents of the groom were in charge of the costs.[49]

In a nutshell, the conditions for the existence of a non-agreement based convention are convergence of behaviour, condition of dependence and arbitrariness.[50]

---

[41] Hume 2008 [1739–1740], 659.

[42] For brevity sake I will use here a tone that might sound stipulative regarding the concept of convention. However, there are philosophical arguments behind each of them. See Lewis 1969 and Marmor 2009.

[43] A regularity of behaviour exists within a group G, when the members of G do A each time that the occasion O verifies. See Gilbert 2008: 8. The regularity requires O to be present with certain frequency, or at least to have verified once and to be possible that it verifies again (Gilbert 1983, 229).

[44] Hart 1994 [1961], 51–61.

[45] See Celano 2010, 330.

[46] Marmor 2009, 10.

[47] Arbitrariness is not the same as indifference towards the chosen alternative; nor does arbitrariness imply indifference. See Lewis (1969, 76–80) and Marmor (2009, 8–9).

[48] For instance, following Forster it is possible to identify three senses of arbitrariness: (a) As the existence of an alternative. (b) As the absence of justification. (c) As the result of an act of will. See Forster 2004.

[49] For a regularity to be an alternative it must satisfy certain conditions: a. Practicability: the same population should be able to conform to the alternative in the same circumstances. b. Incompatibility: the same population should not be able to conform both to the actual regularity and to the alternative regularity at the same time. c. No loss in purpose or function; that is to say, the conformity to the alternative regularity should not import a significant loss in the social function or purpose that the convention fulfils. See Lewis (1969, 70) and Marmor (2009, 10).

[50] There is a further property that has been considered a condition of conventionality, namely, common knowledge. From my point of view common knowledge is not a condition of conventionality but I will not deal with this discussion here. See Burge 1975, 250, contra Celano 2010.

These three elements work well as an account of some activities. For example, the actors that regularly play on a stage the characters of Arlecchino or Brighella and that mix sentences in dialect and in Italian seem to carry on an activity that satisfies these three characteristics. It does not sound exaggerated to claim that the rules of the *Commedia dell'arte* are conventional.

However, to fine-tune the analysis of these conventions it is worthwhile to turn now to the aforementioned second trait, that is to say, constitutivity. Activities like the *Commedia dell'arte* are governed by a set of rules that have a double function: (i) they constitute the practice and (ii) they regulate behaviour inside it. In other words this set of rules define the practice and how to participate in it.[51] They are what Marmor has called constitutive conventions.[52]

Marmor defines these conventions using the distinction between regulative rules and constitutive rules, generally associated with the works of Searle.[53] As is generally known, regulative rules regulate forms of behaviour that exist independently of, and prior to, the creation of the rule (e.g., "it is mandatory to wear a tie during exams"). Constitutive rules, instead, create or define new forms of behaviour (e.g., "it counts as goal when the ball passes the white line behind the three goalposts"). Thus, in the case of regulative rules, as long as the description does make reference to the rule, it would have been possible to describe the action in the same way even if there were no rule. For instance, it is possible to describe an action as "smoking indoors" even before the existence of the rule "It is forbidden to smoke indoors". On the contrary, in the case of constitutive rules, the behaviour can now be described in terms that could not have been used if there were no rule. Although it is possible to describe an action as "making the ball to pass the white line behind the three goalposts", even before the existence of football rules, it is not possible to describe that same action as "marking a goal" before those rules exist.

This distinction has been the target of several criticisms,[54] but I will not indulge in their analysis here. Perhaps most of the problems arise because constitutive rules are often conceived of as isolated rules; while it is more fruitful to think of them as a system of rules that defines a practice. According to Guastini, it is possible to find

[51] Searle 1969, 33. Besides, these rules (iii) define or constitute, in part, the values associated with the practice at hand and define the evaluative discourse applicable to it. Marmor 2009, 37.

[52] Marmor 2009.

[53] Searle makes reference to constitutive rules early in Searle 1964 and, with further elaboration, in Searle 1969. Searle has not been the only philosopher (or the first one) to use that label to refer to a special type of rules. The first appearance of the distinction seems to be the article of Rawls 1955. It can also be found in Ross 1958; Hart 1983 [1954] and Black 1962. Perhaps Searle's centrality is due to the fact that he used the notion as one of the pillars of a general theory of social reality, see Searle 1995 and more recently, Searle 2010.

[54] It has been argued that all rules regulate and create forms of behaviour. On the one hand, the alleged regulatory rules, e.g., "it is mandatory to drive on the right", are constitutive of the action in agreement or disagreement with them. It is one thing to drive on the left and another thing is to do so in violation of the rule that requires driving on the right. On the other hand, the alleged constitutive rules also regulate the behaviour of addresses. For instance, the rule "a move that ends with the opponent king under attack and unable to escape counts as checkmate in chess", also regulates the behaviour of chess players, as long as it mandates the checkmated player to accept defeat. Raz's criticisms can be seen in Raz 1990 [1975], 108–113. See also Schauer 1991, 7.

in Searle a sense of constitutivity according to which this consists in the capacity of a *set* of rules to create or define new forms of behaviour. Where "forms of behaviour" does not mean isolated actions, but practices or activities.[55]

Normative stereotypes, to the extent that they allow for the raising of new forms of behaviour and award new meaning to the actions of those who belong to a category or social group, can be then understood as constitutive conventions.

Perhaps we can understand in this sense Appiah's claim according to which stereotypes allow the uprising of "kinds of people":

"It follows that what I can do intentionally depends on what concepts I have available to me; and among the concepts that may shape my action is the concept of a certain kind of person and the behaviour appropriate to a person of that kind".[56]

This function of stereotypes is clearly independent of the value we assign to the actions or categories that they define and regulate. That is to say, the rules of football, chess or boxing create new possibilities of behaviour, independently of the value that we assign to each game. In the same way, normative stereotypes that define a family father, or a striptease dancer or a university professor define kinds of people, independently of the value we assign to each one of these identities. Therefore, even stereotypes like man-heterosexual and mother-housewife define categories of people, in virtue of the roles that they attribute to each one of them, independently of the value that we assign to each of those categories.

Stereotypes play a constitutive function of the identity of some groups. Being a member of some social aggregate involves behaving according to norms that define the behaviour of those who participate in the group. Not all stereotypes fulfil this function, but some of them do and therefore constitute the identity of a group.[57]

Social identity is constituted, among other things, by a set of stereotypes that mould the behaviour, plans and life of the members of the group. Although some characteristics like race, ethnicity, nationality, gender, religion or sexuality have greater importance in the definition of identity, they are not the only ones.

According to Appiah, all collective identity has the following structure:

(a) A set of terms that serve to pick out the bearers of the identity like criteria of ascription to the group (that is to say, these terms allow recognizing to some people as members of the group). There are descriptive and normative stereotypes associated to these terms.[58]
(b) Self-identification as a member of the group.[59] Identity has a narrative dimension that consists in intertwining my personal history with some patterns of behaviour and with wider stories.

---

[55] Guastini 1986, 262. See also Guastini 1983: 171. See Marmor (2009, 38) and Schauer (1991, 7, n. 13).

[56] Appiah 2005, 65.

[57] Appiah 2000.

[58] Appiah 2005, 66–67.

[59] Appiah 2005, 68.

(c) Hetero-recognition as a member of the group. It means that there are ways of behaviour that consist in treating a person in a certain way, partly, because she is a member of a group.[60]

Appiah also claims that it is possible to distinguish two types of identities.

(i) (Merely) conventional identities, in which the acquisition of the identity requires simply to assume the roles imposed by the conventions. Thus, in order to be part of some so-called "adolescent tribes" like, for instance, an "emo", it is sufficient to behave according to the norms that define the tribe.
(ii) Identities that are not (merely) conventional, in which the acquisition of the identity requires more than "simply" following the conventions about what can or cannot do a member of the group. When it comes to this type of identities people are not simply "assuming a role" or playing a game. Identities built from the more important collective dimensions are of this type. For instance, the Afro-American identity cannot be acquired simply by following the conventions associated with that social category. It does not seem possible to simply choose this type of identities.

Now, given this relation between stereotypes and identity, which are, if any, their criteria of relevance? The following section is devoted to this issue.

5 On Normative Stereotypes' Criteria of Relevance

At this point it might be worthwhile to make a brief balance. Normative stereotypes have a direction of fit social group to stereotype; therefore it does not make sense neither to assess if they have statistical basis nor to establish if they represent the true properties of an individual. Normative stereotypes do not purport to describe the world, but to tell us how it should be. Likewise, as long as they define the roles of a category of people, these stereotypes have a constitutive function. Besides, being norms regarding which there is a convergence of behaviour, it is possible to claim that they are conventions. This type of stereotypes may be present in the justification of general rules as in the process of interpretation, i.e. the attribution of meaning to normative texts.

Once we have made these considerations, the question about normative stereotypes' criteria of relevance can no longer be the following one: under which conditions judges should avoid normative stereotypes, either by repairing the content of stereotypical general rules or by shunning interpretative methods that involve them? Given the tight relation between normative stereotypes and identity the matter is now more complex. Not only a general rejection of normative stereotypes is unjustified, but also in some cases it seems even justified to demand judges to use them in their decisions. From my point of view, it is necessary to ask the following question:

[60] Appiah 2005, 68.

under which conditions judges have the duty to use or to avoid a normative stereotype?

Normative stereotypes are at the core of the tension between oppression and recognition. Between the imposition of roles to those who refuse them and the lack of recognition of roles that individuals and groups attribute to themselves. For instance, this is the case when it comes to normative stereotypes defining the identities of minority groups. Indeed, in Chilean legal system there have been cases in which a minority group has required judges to recognize their social norms. One of them was about norms that define *werken* or *lonko*'s roles within Mapuche community. The *werken* or *lonko* has several tasks inside his own community; among them he procures the solution of cases of domestic violence seeking the composition of the conflict. The Chilean criminal law, by contrast, forbids reparatory agreements in cases of domestic violence. In this context, the Office for the Protection of Mapuche community has repeatedly demanded acquittal of mapuche defendants when the reparatory agreement has been reached observing the community norms, by application of the articles 9 and 10 of OIT, Agreement n. 169.[61]

Now, even if they are a fundamental part of some groups' identity, how is their content fixed? In principle, given that they are conventions, their content would depend on the convergence of behaviour. However, since the convergence of behaviour does not require the conformity of all members of the group, at least some of them will see their identities fixed, partly, by others (members of the group).

A parallelism with descriptive stereotypes might help to cast light on this point. Normative stereotypes may be also assessed in two ways, i.e. regarding the group and regarding the individual. On the one hand, normative stereotypes may affect the identity of a group. This happens when a normative stereotype assigns a role to a group that either does not assign it to themselves or it is incompatible with the roles that members of the group assign to themselves. For instance, the women-housewives and the men-heterosexual stereotypes. On the other hand, some normative stereotypes, even if constitutive of the identity of a group that accepts it, may affect the identity or autonomy of a particular member of the group that rejects the stereotype. As, for instance, Mapuche women that reject the norm requiring them to solve domestic violence by means of a reparatory agreement with the aggressor.

Therefore, it seems possible to distinguish an internal and an external sense of conventionality regarding normative stereotypes. The stereotype is internally conventional when the people on whose convergence of behaviour depends the existence of the social norm, are also the addressees of the stereotype. The stereotype is externally conventional when there is no such a coincidence. Said it another way, normative stereotypes are internally conventional when the group B follows a constitutive convention Z whose addresses are the members of the same group B. They are

[61] These cases are a bit more complex. The Chilean Office for the Protection of Mapuche Community has argued that the rules allow a settlement of the conflict through a simply domestic reparatory agreement between victim and defendant, while other authors argue that the way to solve these conflicts is the one I have mentioned in the text. For an analysis of the case see Ñanculef 2003.

externally conventional when the group A follows a constitutive convention Y whose addresses are the members of the group B.[62]

On this basis, we can then move to the tension between oppression and recognition. First, there are two senses in which a stereotype is oppressive. A stereotype is oppressive when it purports to impose an externally conventional stereotype on a group. In an internal sense, a stereotype is oppressive when it purports to impose an internally conventional stereotype on an individual member. Therefore, the problem with stereotypes rises when they impose an identitarian choice on an individual or on a group that resist it. In these cases, stereotypes affect the autonomy of individuals that resist the convention and the attribution of roles that it presupposes.

Second, respecting internally conventional stereotypes seems indispensable in order to recognize the identity of the group at hand. As said, stereotypes mould the behaviour of people; some activities would not be described in the same way without the existence of the stereotype. Ignoring these stereotypes deprives some behaviour of the meaning that a group assigns to it. Recognition, instead, requires to understand the meaning that such behaviour has for those whose identity is constituted by the stereotype.

6 Conclusions

According to the results obtained so far, even if quite preliminary, it seems possible to distinguish, so much in the speech of the juridical operators, as from a conceptual point of view, two types of stereotypes. On the one hand, stereotypes purporting to offer information about the characteristics of a group and of each one of its members (descriptive stereotypes). On the other hand, stereotypes defining and constituting the roles members of a category or social group should assume (normative stereotypes).

Normative stereotypes play a fundamental role in the construction of identities and that is the reason why it is not justified to embrace a thesis that rejects them all. It is necessary to fine-tune the criteria of relevance. When normative stereotypes are internally conventional, that is to say, when the conditions of conventionality instantiate inside the group that is also the addressee of the stereotypes, it is not in principle reprehensible to resort to them in order to justify an act of normative production or an interpretative decision. Even more, resorting to them is mandatory in order to recognize the group's identity. Now, this does not solve all the problems. For it is still necessary to determine if it suffices, to render a stereotype acceptable, that it is

[62] External conventionality is possible because constitutivity and conventionality are two independent properties. A rule is constitutive if it satisfies Searlean requirements, while it is conventional if it meets the conditions of conventionality. For instance, the rules of chess are constitutive even if no one has ever played a game of chess. Equally, a normative stereotype is constitutive even when the addressee group does not follow it. In this case, the conventionality depends, not on a convergence within the addressee group (B) –that's why it is external-, but on a convergence within the group A.

followed by a group or by each one of its members. In this sense, Appiah proposes that the acceptability of a normative stereotype hinges on it being an "instruments for the construction of a dignified individuality",[63] that is to say, if they do not create an identity in which the individual is pushed into an inferior position or a lower dignity than those of other individuals. According to this author, normative stereotypes have to be avoided when they affect the dignity of (at least some of) his addressees. The assessment of this last affirmation requires analysing its compatibility with other claims of a particular political theory. But this is a task for another occasion.

References

Akerlof, G. A., & Kranton, R. E. (2010). *Identity economics. How our identities shape our work, wages, and well-being*. Princeton: Princeton University Press.

Alexander, L. (1992). What makes wrongful discrimination wrong? Biases, preferences, stereotypes, and proxies. *University of Pennsylvania Law Review, 141*(1), 149–219.

Anscombe, G. E. M. (1957). *Intention*. Oxford: Basil Blackwell.

Appiah, K. A. (2000). Stereotypes and the shaping of identity. *California Law Review, 88*(1), 41–53.

Appiah, K. A. (2005). *The ethics of identity*. Princeton: Princeton University Press.

Arena, F. J. (2014). *El convencionalismo jurídico. Un recorrido analítico*. Madrid: Marcial Pons.

Ashmore, R. D., & Del Boca, F. K. (1981). Conceptual approaches to setereotypes and stereotyping. In D. L. Hamilton (Ed.), *Cognitive processes in stereotyping and intergroup behavior* (pp. 1–35). Hillsdale: Erlbaum.

Austin, J. L. (1953). How to talk-some simple ways. *Proceedings of the Aristotelian Society, 53*, 227–246.

Bascuñán Rodríguez, A. (2011). La prohibición de la homosexualidad masculina juvenil. *Estudios Públicos, 124*, 113–137.

Bascuñán Rodriguez, A., et al. (2011). La inconstitucionalidad del artículo 365 del Código Penal. Informe en derecho. *Revista de estudios de la justicia, 14*, 73–109.

Black, M. (1962). The analysis of rules. In M. Black (Ed.), *Models and metaphors* (pp. 95–139). Ithaca: Cornell University Press.

Blum, L. (2004). Stereotypes and stereotyping: A moral analysis. *Philosophical Papers, 33*(3), 251–289.

Burge, T. (1975). On knowledge and convention. *The Philosophical Review, 84*(2), 249–255.

Casas Becerra, L., et al. (2012). Estereotipos de género en sentencias del Tribunal Constitucional. *Anuario de derecho público de la Universidad Diego Portales, 2012*, 250–272.

Case, M. A. (2000). "The very stereotype the law condemns": Constitutional sex discrimination. Law as a quest for perfect proxies. *Cornell Law Review, 85*(5), 1447–1491.

Celano, B. (2010). *Fatti istituzionali, consuetudini, convenzioni*. Roma: Aracne.

Coloma, R. (2010). El debate sobre los hechos en los procesos judiciales. ¿Qué inclina la balanza? In D. Accatino (Ed.), *Formación y valoración de la prueba en el proceso penal* (pp. 87–117). Santiago de Chile: Abeledo-Perrot.

Cook, R. J., & Cusack, S. (2010). *Estereotipos de género. Perspectivas legales transnacionales*. Bogotá: Profamilia.

[63] Appiah 2000.

Forster, M. N. (2004). *Wittgenstein on the arbitrariness of grammar*. Princeton: Princeton University Press.
Gilbert, M. (1983). Notes on the concept of a social convention. *New Literary History, 14*(2), 225–251.
Gilbert, M. (1993). Is an agreement an exchange of promises? *The Journal of Philosophy, 90*(12), 627–649.
Gilbert, M. (2008). Social convention revisited. *Topoi, 27*(1/2), 5–16.
Guastini, R. (1983). Cognitivismo ludico e regole costitutive. In U. Scarpelli (Ed.), *La teoria generale del diritto. Problemi e tendenze attuali* (pp. 153–176). Milano: Comunità.
Guastini, R. (1986). Six concepts of constitutive rules. *Rechtstheorie, 10*, 261–269.
Guastini, R. (2011). Rule scepticism restated. In L. Green & B. Leiter (Eds.), *Oxford studies in philosophy of law* (pp. 138–161). Oxford: Oxford University Press.
Hart, H. L. A. (1983 [1954]). Definition and theory in jurisprudence. In Id., *Essays in jurisprudence and philosophy*. Oxford: Clarendon Press.
Hart, H. L. A. (1994 [1961]). *The concept of law*. Oxford: Clarendon Press.
Humberstone, L. (1992). Direction of fit. *Mind, 101*, 59–83.
Hume, D. (2008 [1739–1740]). *Tratado de la naturaleza humana*. Madrid: Tecnos.
Lakoff, G. (1987). *Women, fire, and dangerous things. What categories reveal about the mind*. Chicago/Londres: The University of Chicago Press.
Lewis, D. (1969). *Convention. A philosophical study*. Oxford: Basil Blackwell.
Marmor, A. (2009). *Social conventions. From language to law*. Princeton: Princeton University Press.
Mervis, C., & Rosch, E. (1981). Categorization and natural objects. *Annual Review of Psychology, 32*, 89–115.
Ñanculef, J. (2003). La cosmovisión y la filosofía Mapuche: Un enfoque del Az-Mapu y del Derecho Consuetudinario en la cultura Mapuche. *Revista de Estudios Criminológicos y Penintenciarios, 6*, 38–57.
Oakes, P., et al. (1994). *Stereotyping and social reality*. Oxford: Blackwell.
Platts, M. (1979). *Ways of meaning*. London: Routledge and Kegan Paul.
Rawls, J. (1955). Two concepts of rules. *The Philosophical Review, 64*(1), 3–32.
Raz, J. (1984). On the nature of rights. *Mind, 93*(370), 194–214.
Raz, J. (1990 [1975]). *Practical reason and norms*. Oxford: Oxford University Press.
Rosch, E., & Lloyd, B. B. (Eds.). (1978). *Cognition and categorization*. Hillsdale: Erlbaum.
Ross, A. (1958). *On law and justice*. London: Stevens and Sons.
Schauer, F. (1991). *Playing by the rules: A philosophical examination of rule-based decision-making in law and in life*. Oxford: Clarendon.
Schauer, F. (2003). *Profiles, probabilities and stereotypes*. Cambridge, MA: Harvard University Press.
Schauer, F. (2004). *Las reglas en juego. Un examen filosófico de la toma de decisiones basada en reglas en el derecho y en la vida cotidiana*. Madrid: Marcial Pons.
Schauer, F. (2015). *The force of law*. Cambridge, MA: Harvard University Press.
Searle, J. R. (1964). How to derive "ought" from "is". *The Philosophical Review, 73*(1), 43–58.
Searle, J. R. (1969). *Speech acts. An essay in the philosophy of language*. London: Cambridge University Press.
Searle, J. R. (1975). A taxonomy of illocutionary acts. *Minnesota Studies in the Philosophy of Science, 6*, 334–369.
Searle, J. R. (1995). *The construction of social reality*. New York: Free Press.
Searle, J. R. (2010). *Making the social world. The structure of human civilization*. Oxford/New York: Oxford University Press.
Smith, M. (1987). The humean theory of motivation. *Mind, 96*, 36–61.
Steele, C. M. (2010). *Whistling Vivaldi. How stereotypes affect us and what we can do*. New York: W.W. Norton & Co.

Epistemic Stance in Courtroom Interaction

Sune Sønderberg Mortensen and Janus Mortensen

Abstract The oral examination of defendants and witnesses is a cornerstone in most criminal trials, where the weight and credibility of what is said and the certainty with which testimony is delivered will often be decisive for the ruling of the court. This chapter presents a case study of the linguistic construction of certainty and uncertainty – or epistemic stance taking – in Danish courtroom interaction. Based on transcribed audio recordings from a criminal trial in Denmark in 2014, we examine the ways in which the defendant, the alleged victim and an eyewitness construct epistemic stances during their examinations. The study combines a quantitative and a qualitative approach. In the first part of the chapter we develop a method that allows us to compare the epistemic expressions used by the three trial participants and the frequency with which the expressions are employed. In the second part we build on the quantitative findings by characterising and comparing the contextualised pragmatic functions of typical epistemic stances taken by two of the participants. Based on the analyses we argue that the trial participants may be said to adopt different epistemic stance styles, and we suggest that these styles may be motivated by pragmatic and rhetorical aims related to the individuals' roles in the case.

Keywords Danish courtroom interaction • Epistemic stance • Witness examination • Forensic linguistics

---

This work has received financial support by The Danish Council for Independent Research: project ID DFF – 1321-00180.

S.S. Mortensen (✉)
Department of Communication and Arts, Roskilde University, Roskilde, Denmark
e-mail: sunes@ruc.dk

J. Mortensen
Centre for Internationalisation and Parallel Language Use, Department of English, Germanic and Romance Studies, University of Copenhagen, Copenhagen, Denmark
e-mail: jamo@hum.ku.dk

F. Poggi, A. Capone (eds.), *Pragmatics and Law*, Perspectives in Pragmatics, Philosophy & Psychology 10, DOI 10.1007/978-3-319-44601-1_16

1 Introduction

The linguistic aspects of justice are hard to overlook. Apart from the fact that law itself is text, language use is what constitutes the legal institutions *practicing* law, including, of course, the courtrooms. In most societies trials are predominantly oral affairs (Heritage and Clayman 2010, 173) and witness testimony is typically given live in court, through rule-governed encounters in which professional law practitioners interact with lay members of society who may be experiencing this kind of situation for the first time. Trials are in other words complex interactional events, in which not only what is said determines the verdict, but indeed also *how* it is said.

In this chapter we are concerned with how linguistic expressions of certainty and uncertainty, also known as epistemic stance markers, are used by participants during examinations in a Danish criminal trial. Danish courtroom interaction has received little attention from linguists and scholars interested in language use, and has so far been studied mainly from the perspectives of courtroom interpreting (Jacobsen 2002) and rhetoric (Staffe 2008; Beyer 2013; Kjær et al. 2015). This chapter represents a first step in an attempt to remedy this imbalance. Yet, the purpose of the chapter is not only to bring the internationally well-established research tradition of courtroom interaction (cf. Sect. 2 below) into the Danish context, but also to propose a more generally applicable theoretical and methodological framework for exploring epistemic stance taking in the courtroom context. As we discuss in the following sections, epistemic stance taking in courtroom interaction has so far been less than satisfactorily treated in the literature, although it constitutes an important aspect of this particular judicial practice.

The study we present here is part of an ongoing project that seeks to promote the research field of forensic linguistics, including the study of courtroom interaction, in Denmark. Danish forensic linguistics is in its infancy, since access to forensic texts beyond legal documents, court rulings and case summaries is highly restricted by law or administrative tradition. Therefore, the permission given to us by the Court of Frederiksberg, Copenhagen to use their audio recordings of trial examinations is a unique opportunity to present a study of courtroom interaction based on Danish data, which we hope will be followed up by additional research into this and other aspects of law and language in the Danish context.

The chapter is organised as follows. In the following Sect. 2 we provide a general introduction to the courtroom setting as well as some of the features specifically characterising Danish courtroom interaction. Sect. 3 presents our theoretical framework and discusses previous treatments of epistemic stance taking in the courtroom context. A presentation of our data and the methodology employed is given in Sect. 4, before we turn to quantitative and then qualitative analyses of the data in Sect. 5. In Sect. 6 we offer a discussion of the analysis and some concluding remarks.

2 The Danish Criminal Trial as a Context of Talk

The particular characteristics of courtroom interaction as compared to everyday conversation as well as to other kinds of institutional and professional talk have been studied and documented since the late seventies (Atkinson and Drew 1979; Bennet and Feldman 1981; O'Barr 1982; Harris 1984; Atkinson 1992; Drew 1992; Conley and O'Barr 1998; Cotterill 2003; Gibbons 2003; Coulthard and Johnson 2007, 2010; Heritage and Clayman 2010; Komter 2013; Bednarek 2014). Generally speaking, the criminal trial can be distinguished from other kinds of speech events, institutional and otherwise, by a strong and conflicting goal orientation of participants as well as by formal, pre-given constraints on turn-taking and allowable contributions (Drew and Heritage 1992, 22). Talk produced in a courtroom takes place for the benefit of an overhearing audience, i.e. the judge and the jury (Bülow-Møller 1991; Heritage and Clayman 2010, 175) or, in the Danish context, the presiding, professional judge(s) and a number of lay judges (depending on the severity of the accusation). This trait, however, is obviously not unique to the courtroom as it is also characteristic of many types of broadcast talk, including news interviews. In the Danish legal system, both professional judges and lay judges are part of the deliberation process from the beginning till the end, including the final step where the question of guilt is determined and a verdict is passed. This means that the 'audience' in the courtroom – in contrast to a TV or radio audience – cannot be conceptualised as mere overhearers, without any direct influence on the ongoing interaction. On the contrary, they are very much part of the proceedings as powerful silent partners who will eventually determine the outcome of the case. Apart from the physical and technical evidence that may be presented to them during the trial, their final verdict is based on whose testimony they find the most credible. A constant battle of credibility is therefore at the heart of what goes on in a trial, and it is our assumption that the epistemic stance styles adopted by witnesses may play a central role in establishing – or perhaps undermining – a speaker's credibility in the eyes and ears of an overhearing audience.

The questioning (examination and cross-examination) of defendants and other witnesses may be said to constitute the central part of a criminal trial, both in terms of time spent on the activity (Bednarek 2014, 128) and in terms of its impact on the verdict (Beyer 2013, 75). Studies of witness examinations anchored within the Anglo-American adversarial system of trial[1] apply only partially to the Danish context. For instance, examinations, and cross-examinations in particular, in the adversarial system of trial tend to be described as highly formal, hierarchical and sometimes aggressive events:

[1] Under the adversarial system of trial, the prosecutor and defence lawyer present their respective cases against each other, while the judge acts as an impartial arbiter. The adversarial system may be distinguished from the inquisitorial system, in which the judge is the one leading the trial, including the examination of witnesses (Law and Martin 2014).

> the judicial process can be a bewildering and threatening affair, where the casual conversational rights of generally equal access and free negotiation of turns and turn types are suspended, to be replaced by a hierarchical system of interaction, where control and constraint are the norm (Cotterill 2003, 92).

> 'Discrediting the witness', 'disgracing the witness', 'attacking' the witness's testimony, 'pouncing' if contradictions arise during the witness's testimony [...] are typical aggressive actions characterizing the activity of the cross-examiner (Biscetti 2006, 216–217).

Damaška (1997), on the other hand, points out that things appear to be different in European courts:

> Anglo-American observers of the [Continental] court scene are regularly struck by the rarity and the subdued nature of challenges to the witnesses' credibility. If such a challenge occurs, it [...] seldom escalates into a general attack on his character or reputation for truthfulness. With apparent insouciance, Continental courts freely rely on uninterrupted narrative accounts – the testimonial yield of relatively mild, unpenetrating interrogation (Damaška 1997, 80–81).

Moreover, Danish courtrooms stand out by practicing, on the one hand, an adversarial participation structure similar to that of the Anglo-American courtroom (Anderson 1992, 197), and on the other, an informal and less confrontational mode of interaction, apparently even compared to other Continental systems:

> one of the salient differences [noticed by a group of judges from five European countries visiting a Danish court] is how informal everything is. You don't have to ask for permission to speak or stand up, and there's far more dialogue throughout than any of the visitors are used to from their home countries. It's almost snug ["hyggeligt" in Danish]. [Our translation]. (Kæraa 2011, 25–26)

Similar observations have been made by Adelswärd et al. (1988, 263), concerning Swedish trials, also noting the relative casualness of the interaction compared to the US and the UK. The informal atmosphere of the Danish courtroom (at least in the case of petty trials) involves some reluctance towards overt, especially person-targeted, confrontation:

> The examination-in-chief and the cross-examination (and the reexamination) of witnesses must be conducted for the purpose of eliciting clear and truthful statements. If a party fails to comply with this provision, for example by attempting to discredit a witness, the court may intervene or even take over the questioning (Jacobsen 2002, 40)

This does not imply, however, that the issue of credibility plays less of a role in Danish witness examinations than it does in e.g. American witness examinations. It simply means that the matter may not be addressed with the same degree of directness. In a Danish court, the inferences to be drawn from the stances taken by witnesses are unlikely to be spelled out to the lay judges, while this is not uncommon in the Anglo-American system of trial (e.g. Damaška 1997, 18). The fact that particular epistemic stances are typically not challenged overtly in the Danish courtroom does not mean that they are insignificant for the proceedings, quite on the contrary, we suspect. But the fact that epistemic stances are not oriented to explicitly by participants and made the topic of (meta) talk does mean that it can be harder for the analyst to assess their specific impact on the discourse and the question of credibility, since speakers do not display their understanding of individual stances and their implication through talk. The long-term goal of the research project which this chapter forms part of is to investigate whether there are correlations to be found between different epistemic stance styles and degrees of witness credibility. In this chapter, however, we are only able to take a first step in that process by presenting a case study of how epistemic stance styles can be investigated and described quantitatively and qualitatively on the basis of naturally occurring data from a Danish courtroom.

3 Epistemic Stance Taking and Courtroom Interaction

Du Bois (2007) argues that in taking a stance, speakers perform a triune act by concomitantly *evaluating* an object, *positioning* subjects (themselves and others) 'vis-à-vis' the object, and *aligning* with other subjects. In popular terms, epistemic stance taking is what speakers engage in when they evaluate 'objects' – usually propositions – by specifying their certainty or knowledge with regard to epistemic status of the stance object. In linguistics, this phenomenon has typically been treated under the headings of 'epistemic modality' and 'evidentiality', which, following Boye (2012), may be said to concern, respectively, the specification of epistemic support (the relative strength of the speaker's knowledge) and the specification of epistemic justification (relating to the source of the speaker's knowledge). But while the specification of knowledge (or degree of certainty) may be an important aspect of epistemic and evidential expressions[2] such as modal verbs and modal adverbs, this is not necessarily the *only* function they perform in discourse. Politeness researchers have argued that speakers use epistemic expressions as 'illocutionary force modifiers/pragmatic force modifiers', 'mitigating devices', 'downgraders', 'downtoners', 'hedges' etc. to protect the negative face of their interlocutors, and sometimes also to maintain their own positive face (House and Kasper 1981; Coates 1987; Holmes 1988; Carretero 1992; Kärkkäinen 1992; Nikula 1996; Youmans 2001; Caffi 2007; Adolphs 2008). With reference to Du Bois' stance triangle, we might say that politeness research into epistemic expressions highlights the fact that such expressions do not merely allow speakers to evaluate objects, they also – at the same time – enable speakers to position themselves and others.

Mortensen (2010, 2012) argues that epistemic expressions, as part of their alignment potential, allow speakers to negotiate what White (2003) metaphorically calls the *dialogic space* of discourse and accommodate the presence of multiple, possibly conflicting, views and voices. In using epistemic expressions in 'friendly conversa-

[2] Throughout the chapter we use 'epistemic expressions' as shorthand for 'epistemic and evidential expressions', since we regard epistemic justification as a semantic subdomain within the general domain of epistemic meaning (cf. Boye 2012).

tion' Coates (1990) argues that speakers "… design their contributions to maximise the possibility of other, possibly divergent, opinions emerging" (1990, 61–62). Without 'hedging' through the use of epistemic expressions, speakers may be seen to take up uncompromising positions, potentially disaligning with other speakers. So, when taking an epistemic stance, speakers operate on an epistemic scale of support and/or justification, concomitantly evaluating the 'object' which is in the scope of the epistemic expression and positioning themselves vis-à-vis this object and possibly other interactants in the discourse. In doing so, they also define – whether implicitly or explicitly – their alignment (convergent or divergent) with other relevant speakers in the context.

Epistemic stance taking has been studied in many contexts, and has also received some attention in the study of courtroom interaction, though not necessarily under that particular label (see e.g. Komter 1995; Toska 2012; Dong 2013; Mininni et al. 2014). Still, the interest in epistemic stance taking in the context of courtroom interaction appears to have been rather scant, at least when considering how important epistemic stance taking arguably is in this setting, particularly in witness examinations. Among the exceptions the *Duke University Law and Language Project* (see e.g. Lind and O'Barr 1978; O'Barr 1982) deserves mention. Inspired by Lakoff's (1975) much-debated work on 'women's language' this study exposed university students to pairs of manipulated witness testimonies where one testimony was performed without so-called 'powerless' language features – including expressions that may be seen as epistemic stance devices, specifically 'intensifiers', 'hedges' and 'hesitation forms' (see Gibbons 2003 for an overview) – and the other testimony was acted out with such features incorporated. The experiments showed that speakers who gave testimonies with 'powerless language' features were perceived as less credible, less truthful and less trustworthy than speakers who did not use such features. The Duke project's method and conclusions have been heavily criticised (Thompson 2002) and later studies have produced different results (e.g. Hosman 1989), but the results have nevertheless been widely cited in and beyond the literature on courtroom interaction.

As far as the present chapter is concerned, the Duke project does not get us very far in understanding what epistemic expressions are used for in courtroom interaction, and how speakers may utilise the same epistemic expressions for different purposes. As Gibbons (2003) rightly points out, even though O'Barr might be right in claiming that hedging (which we here, for the sake of the argument, take to constitute a type of epistemic stance taking) in some cases indicates 'lack of power', hedging has also been shown to be useful as a *powerful* tool for witnesses in what Jacquemet (1996) calls the 'smoke screen strategies' of Italian mafiosi where statements are rendered "so vague as to be virtually useless as testimony" (Gibbons 2003, 118) due to extensive hedging.

Another shortcoming of the Duke project, seen from our perspective, is the reliance on experimental data. This method may have been adequate for addressing the research questions of the Duke project, but for the questions we ask, we believe it is necessary to look at contextualised, naturally occurring data. Szczyrbak (2013) comes closer to this ideal. Her study, which focuses on epistemic lexical verbs, especially ‘I think’, is based on data from an actual (UK) court case. Yet, the data is taken from a website, and appears to have been transcribed without due attention to a number of features characteristic of spoken language. While this does not necessarily invalidate the study, it does mean that some aspects of the interaction will be lost in transcription, and hence unavailable to the analyst. It is nevertheless interesting to note that Szczyrbak finds that epistemic lexical verbs are used to communicate moderate certainty rather than uncertainty and doubt, and on that basis argues, with reference to Simon-Vandenbergen and Aijmer (2007), that the expressions are used to perform various “rhetorical functions” including persuasion, manipulation, challenging and confrontation – but also acceptance.

In sum, when looking at the literature, we seem to find somewhat conflicting claims about the function of epistemic stance markers and epistemic stance taking in courtroom interaction. The use of epistemic stance markers may, under certain conditions, be seen as part of a ‘powerless’ style associated with a lack of credibility, while in other cases, their use may be seen to help speakers persuade, manipulate, challenge and confront, which would not typically be seen as pursuits of the powerless. The lesson here seems to be that we cannot assume epistemic expressions to have uniform communicative functions or fixed indexical values (cf. Ochs 1992). We would argue that epistemic expressions form part of styles of talk, and they acquire their meaning and realise their communicative potential through being associated with particular styles. Such styles are not to be seen as the property of individual speakers; they are invariably established in context, through interaction with other speakers. For these reasons, an analysis of epistemic stance style in courtroom interaction should ideally be based on a comprehensive approach that is able to consider the use of epistemic expressions in context. In the following we present our proposal for how that goal can be achieved.

4 Data and Method

4.1 *Case Study:* The Alleged Attack on a Parking Officer

The data examined in this study consist of audio recordings of witness examinations conducted during a criminal trial at the Court of Frederiksberg, Copenhagen, October 2014. The trial concerns a case of physical assault, as the defendant is accused of having attacked a parking officer by punching or pushing (henceforth *punching*) him in his face. The witness examinations amount to approximately 63 min of talk, equalling 14,444 transcribed words, distributed across the examinations of the three individuals involved: the defendant, the complainant/alleged victim (henceforth *the parking officer*) and an eyewitness called by the defence.[3] Other

[3] A final re-examination of the defendant (approx. 670 words) is featured in the trial, but this examination is not included in our data here.

participants in the proceedings include the prosecutor, the defence lawyer, the presiding judge, and two (silent) lay judges.

4.2 *Outline of the Case*

The case is essentially a dispute about who started the incident in which a parking officer allegedly was punched while issuing a parking fee. The parking officer, representing a private parking company, claims that he was suddenly and without warning punched by the defendant following a brief conversation. The defendant, on the other hand, claims that the parking officer was the one who initiated the situation by grabbing the defendant's arm, leading the defendant to jerk his arm free of the grip and thereby inadvertently strike his hand against the officer's face. An eyewitness called by the defence corroborates the defendant's story, and the court ultimately acquits the defendant. According to the case summary, the verdict is not reached in agreement between the judges, but on a majority vote, as the presiding (professional) judge votes for conviction, and the two lay judges vote against it.

4.3 *Overview of the Witness Examinations*

Table 1 presents an overview of the most important topics addressed (I–V) during the witness examinations and the evidence given (a., b., c. …), ordered according to the chronology of the incident. Evidence which we consider disputed is italicised and marked by a single asterisk when representing the prosecution version of the events, and a double asterisk when representing the defence version.

As shown in the overview in Table 1, topics III and IV are the most disputed ones, as more or less the entire evidence relating to these topics represents two completely different stories. Not surprisingly, when looking at the distribution of topics addressed during questioning of the three witnesses, as illustrated in Table 2, these two topics are the ones receiving most attention.

4.4 *Method*

Our analysis of the recordings was conducted in five successive steps: transcription, coding, quantitative analyses of the entire data set, with a particular focus on the three participants giving testimony, and finally qualitative analyses of selected sequences from the examinations of the parking officer and the eyewitness. Due to space constraints we have decided not to present qualitative analyses of the defendant's testimony.

Table 1 Topics addressed and evidence given during examinations

I	**Events leading up to the defendant and the parking officer meeting**	
	a.	The defendant parks his car in the courtyard of a private Iraqi association; enters a building
→	*b.*	*Garbage trucks enter the courtyard, blocking the exit* (**)
	c.	The parking officer enters the courtyard, talks to a local car garage worker, observes defendant's car and issues a parking fee
	d.	Inside the building the defendant 'hears rumours' of the parking officer and hurries out to his car
II	**Initial conversation between defendant and parking officer**	
	a.	The defendant enters discussion with the parking officer to have the parking fee cancelled
	b.	The parking officer maintains that the car is illegitimately parked
→	*c.*	*The parking officer urges the defendant to move his car immediately, although this is impossible due to the garbage trucks blocking the exit* (**)
	d.	The defendant claims to suffer from a prostatic condition forcing him to use the toilet
III		**Physical contact between defendant and parking officer**
→	*a.*	*The defendant prods the parking officer twice with one or two fingers on his chest while speaking, although he has been warned not to touch him* (*)
→	*b.*	*The parking officer grabs the defendant's arm tightly, forcing him along to the 'no parking' sign so that he can see it for himself; the defendant yells that he should let go of his arm and that it hurts* (**)
IV		**The punch**
→	*a.*	*The defendant, without warning, punches the parking officer in his face, with a clenched fist* (*)
→	*b.*	*The defendant jerks his arm free of the parking officer's grip, thereby inadvertently hitting him in his face, with a partially closed hand* (**)
V		**Events following the punch**
	a.	The parking officer falls to the ground
→	*b.*	*The parking officer points out to the defendant that he does not find his behaviour appropriate, and that he will have to call the police; proceeds to calling the police* (*)
→	*c.*	*The parking officer cries "attack, attack"; then calls the police* (**)
	d.	Police and health care personnel become involved, photo documentation is secured and general pre-trial procedures are set in motion

Initially, all examinations were transcribed in CLAN (MacWhinney 2000), using the conventions listed in Appendix 1. CLAN is a type of software known as 'linking software' which allows transcribers to link lines of a transcript (or other units therein) to the corresponding stretch of talk in the audio or video recording which the transcript is a representation or 'second-order entextualisation' of (Haberland and Mortensen 2015, 581–600). Once links have been implemented in the transcript, each line comes to function as an index to the underlying recording (the first-order entextualisation of the data), allowing the analyst to call up any stretch of talk represented in the transcript instantaneously by the click of a mouse. In this way, the analysis of particular interactional sequences, the use of particular words, etc. does not have to rely solely on a partial two-dimensional representation (the transcript)

Table 2 Sequence of topics addressed during examinations

Witness	Examiner	Duration (min.)	Topics addressed	Questioning highlights
Defendant	Prosecutor	5.9	I, II, III, IV, V	*General account; special attention to the nature of the physical contact and the punch*
	Defence lawyer	10.1	III, IV, V	*Posture and motion of defendant's hand during the punch; police's response to defendant's injuries*
	Prosecutor	2.5	IV	*Posture of defendant's hand during the punch*
	Judge	0.5	III	*Defendant's response to arm grip before jerking his arm free*
	Defence lawyer	2.0	IV, V	*Defendant's initial police statements expressing doubt whether to have actually hit the parking officer*
	Prosecutor	0.8	IV	*Inconsistencies in defendant's recollection of whether and how the punch was carried out*
Parking officer	Prosecutor	14.8	I, II, III, IV, V	*General account; special attention to parking officer's profession and background, as well as his experience of the defendant's behaviour and the punch*
	Defence lawyer	6.2	III, IV	*Response to defendant's claim that the parking officer grabbed his arm; inaccuracies in parking officer's initial police statements; posture of defendant's hand during the punch*
	Judge	2.1	II, IV	*Defendant's emotional state; posture of defendant's hand during the punch*
	Defence lawyer	3.1	I, II	*Defendant's emotional state; parking officer's activities at the location before writing the fee; parking officer's history of similar physical encounters*
Eyewitness	Defence lawyer	8.7	I, II, III, IV, V	*General account; the physical contact between defendant and parking officer; the content of their conversation; the parking officer's history of similar physical encounters and inclination to overreacting; the eyewitness' relation to the parking officer*
	Prosecutor	6.3	I, II, III, IV	*Eyewitness' relation to the defendant, to the Iraqi association and to the parking officer; the nature of the conversation, the physical contact and the punch*

of the interaction captured on tape but can be conducted as the analyst is simultaneously looking at the transcript and listening to or watching the data at hand.

Once the transcript had been produced, we proceeded to code it for occurrences of epistemic expressions. For the purposes of this study we decided to include four groups of expressions in Danish that may have epistemic or evidential uses:

- Core modal verbs (CMV)
- Epistemic/evidential adverbials (EEAdv)
- Epistemic/evidential adjectives (EEAdj)
- Epistemic/evidential cognition and perception verbs (EECPV)

Complete lists of the forms investigated are included in Appendix 2. Using the coding feature of CLAN called COMBO, all occurrences of the selected forms were identified automatically and issued with a placeholder code, awaiting manual coding. In the case of the modal verbs, we coded manually for epistemic, deontic or dynamic uses. Many of the forms included in the list of adverbs are highly multifunctional, so here we determined whether each token represented an epistemic/evidential use or not. A similar binary approach was used for the adjectives (the least frequent category), while the coding of cognition and perception verbs did not merely record epistemic and evidential uses, but also whether the form had a first person subject or not. Only tokens with first person subjects were included as epistemic expressions.

In composing the list of epistemic expressions, we have tried to be as comprehensive as possible, but we cannot claim that the lists are exhaustive – quite simply because no exhaustive lists exist. Some readers might consider the selection to be too comprehensive. This perhaps particularly goes for the list of adverbs, where the inclusion of dialogic particles like *altså, da, jo* (see below) and dialogic adverbials like *faktisk* ('actually') and *egentlig* ('actually') represent a considerable broadening of the category of epistemic expressions compared to standard treatments in the literature. However, these forms have been included because their interactional function in many cases resembles that of prototypical epistemic expressions since they manage the expression of epistemic support or justification in interaction by orchestrating points of view and evaluating them against each other.

Altså, *da*, and *jo* are all multifunctional and only acquire their dialogic meaning when used in particular sentence positions (cf. e.g. Jensen 2000; Christensen 2007, 132ff). They have no direct translation equivalents in English, but their meaning can be approximated by providing paraphrases of what might be called their "polyphonic instruction" (cf. Nølke et al. 2004; Therkelsen 2004). This can be exemplified by the case of *jo. Jo* carries an abstract polyphonic instruction which can be formalised as *I hold a specific point of view (p) and you do not hold non-p, and will therefore not contradict me* (following Hansen and Heltoft 2011, 1050 ff). *Jo* will thus often index consensus, but it can also be indicative of the opposite in situations where the speaker is trying to *force* a sense of consensus onto the interlocutor, using *jo* as a 'cajoler' (Edmondson 1981). This sort of meaning may not constitute epistemic modality in a traditional linguistic sense, but it quite clearly represents a case of epistemic stance marking where the speaker evaluates an object, positions subjects and aligns with other speakers.

Once the coding had been completed, we were able to establish what we call quantitative 'epistemic stance profiles' for each of the three participants, based on the frequency with which they employ different types of epistemic expressions (normed to number of occurrences per 100 words, cf. Biber et al. 1998). On the basis of these findings, reported in Sect. 5.1, a number of sequences from the examination of the parking officer and the eyewitness were selected for further qualitative analyses, with a view to investigating the stance style of these speakers in greater detail. These analyses are presented in Sect. 5.2.

5 Analyses

5.1 *Quantitative Analysis*

As a first step in our analysis, we investigated how frequently the participants in the data use epistemic expressions. We were interested to see if it would be possible, simply by looking quantitatively at the data, to find different patterns of epistemic stance taking for the three main participants: the defendant, the parking officer and the eyewitness. For each of these speakers, we calculated how many epistemic expressions they used per 100 words, and how many epistemic expressions were used by the other participants (the prosecutor, the defence lawyer and the judge) in their interaction with them. The results are depicted in Fig. 1.

As shown in Fig. 1, the defendant uses slightly less than two epistemic expressions per 100 words, which is more or less on a par with what we see the prosecutor, defence lawyer and judge do in their interaction with him. The parking officer, on the other hand, uses close to six epistemic expressions per 100 words, showing a marked difference from the frequency with which the prosecutor, defence lawyer and judge use epistemic expressions in their interaction with him. Finally, the eyewitness strikes a middle ground between the defendant and the parking officer with

Fig. 1 Number of epistemic expressions per 100 words

just about three epistemic expressions per 100 words. In this particular instance the judge also scores quite high, but given that he only produces 84 words in this particular part of the trial, this figure should not be given too much weight. Comparing the defendant, the parking officer and the eyewitness side by side, we see that there is in fact a certain difference in terms of the frequency with which they employ epistemic expressions. The graphs do not, however, tell us which epistemic expressions the speakers use and what they use them for. For that purpose, more detailed analyses are needed. In the following, we illustrate this by comparing the eyewitness and the parking officer.

Fig. 2 shows how the epistemic expressions used by the parking officer and the eyewitness are distributed across the types of epistemic expressions we have coded for.

The graphs are based on raw numbers, so they cannot be compared directly. Nevertheless, we do see several noteworthy differences. Arguably, the most salient one is that the parking officer has a very high frequency of epistemic/evidential adverbials, whereas the majority of the expressions used by the eyewitness are more evenly distributed across two categories, adverbials and CP verbs.

If we look in more detail at the individual types of epistemic expressions used by the two speakers, we find additional differences (cf. Tables 3 and 4).

The most salient finding here relates to the category of adverbials, where we see that 73 of the 149 adverbials used by the parking officer are tokens of *jo*. As explained above, *jo* is a dialogic particle which prototypically closes the dialogic space. The same thing can be said of the next three adverbials on the list, *faktisk* ('actually'), *selvfølgelig* ('of course'), and *slet ikke* ('not at all'). What this implies is that the parking officer not only has an epistemic stance style that is characterised by frequent use of epistemic expressions, but in fact has a style that is characterised by a frequent use of epistemic expressions that function to close the dialogic space – at least prototypically.

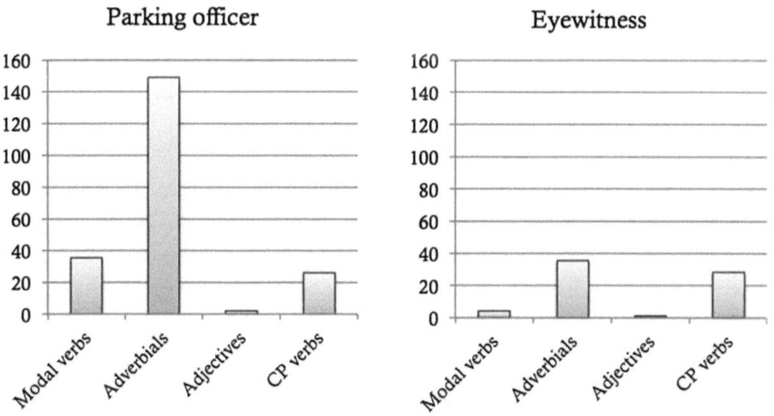

Fig. 2 Distribution of tokens across the four groups of epistemic expressions

Table 3 Epistemic expressions used by the parking officer

EEAdj		EEAdv	
rigtig	1	*jo*	73
klart	1	*faktisk*	13
	2	*selvfølgelig*	10
		slet ikke	6
EECPV		*nok*	6
Tro	9	*måske*	6
huske	7	*i virkeligheden*	6
tænke	3	*egentlig*	6
vide	3	*overhovedet*	4
synes	2	*altså*	4
gå ud fra	1	*reelt*	3
regne med	1	*i hvert fald*	3
	26	*ikke nødvendigvis*	2
		formentlig	2
CMV		*da*	2
kunne	23	*vel*	1
måtte	6	*ikke rigtig*	1
ville	5	*et eller andet sted*	1
skulle	1		**149**
	35		

Table 4 Epistemic expressions used by the eyewitness

EEAdj		EEAdv	
rigtig	1	*jo*	17
	1	*nok*	10
		selvfølgelig	3
EECPV		*i hvert fald*	2
tro	14	*overhovedet*	1
vide	6	*slet ikke*	1
huske	5		**34**
synes	2		
se	1		
	28		
CMV			
ville	2		
kunne	1		
måtte	1		
	4		

The eyewitness also has *jo* as his most frequent adverbial, but it is not nearly as frequent as for the parking officer, and moreover we do not find it in the company of other adverbials that close the dialogic space. On the contrary, the second most frequent adverbial for the eyewitness (which accounts for almost 30 % of the adverbials) is *nok* ('probably'), which is a dialogic adverbial that prototypically opens the dialogic space. This suggests that the eyewitness adopts an epistemic style that tends more towards opening the dialogic space than the style adopted by the parking officer.

As far as the other categories are concerned, it is not as straightforward as in the case of the adverbials to say whether the expressions used function to open or close the dialogic space, since modal verbs, epistemic/evidential verbs and epistemic adjectives are not as clearly coded for this. Their meaning is even more dependent on context than the adverbials, and they therefore require more detailed contextualised analyses, which is what we proceed to in the following section.

5.2 *Qualitative Analysis of Epistemic Stance Styles*

The following analysis of contextualised examples of the parking officer's and the eyewitness' testimonies is based on a series of selected data excerpts that we consider illustrative of the two witnesses' ways of using epistemic expressions. All excerpts are taken from the examinations-in-chief, i.e. the initial examinations by 'same-side' examiners. This enables us to illustrate how each of the witnesses construct their version of the events when speaking under conditions characterised by relative narrative and interactional freedom compared to cross-examinations. It would also be interesting to investigate whether the epistemic stance styles of witnesses differ between the two modes of examination, but this is beyond the scope of the present chapter. Our analysis is guided by the quantitative findings presented above and illustrates, on the one hand, how the predominant epistemic expressions are used, and on the other, how they, in interplay with other relevant linguistic and interactional elements, contribute to the overall epistemic stance styles of the two witnesses.

5.2.1 The Parking Officer

As discussed in Sect. 5.1 above, the parking officer frequently uses epistemic expressions that tend to close the dialogic space. When looking at how he actually deploys these expressions in discourse, this picture seems to be confirmed. In Excerpt 1 we see how the dialogic particle *jo*, his most frequent epistemic expression, is used several times to indicate that the information he presents is to be accepted as 'shared' knowledge.

Excerpt 1
Prosecutor (PRO), Parking officer (PO)

1	PRO:		um but what happens
2			in the afternoon the first of May
3			(0.5)
4			⌈when⌉ you are at work
5	PO:		⌊yes⌋
6			well um:: (.) what happens is:
7		→	I have ***jo*** we have ***jo***
8			a particular round that we go um where we visit various
9			parking lots around the city
10			(0.5)
11		→	and I arrive ***jo*** at this parking lot
12			I (.) call it ↫Name↫
13			it may well physically be located a bit differently
14			but but ⌈but⌉ in ??the?? our language
15	PRO:		⌊mh⌋
16	PO:		it's called ↫Name↫ and I arrive at the parking lot
17			(0.8)
18		→	and um:: (0.4) k- and it and my task is ***jo*** to to (.)
19		→	check um (.) partly it's ***jo*** if there's anyone who
20			needs some service (.)
21		→	we are ***jo*** also service providers
22			regarding ⌈(0.4)⌉ parking and stuff
23	PRO:		⌊mh⌋

The noteworthy point here is that the information which the officer offers in Excerpt 1, e.g. lines 7–9 ('we have a particular round that we go where we visit parking lots around the city') and 18–20 ('my task is to check if there's anyone who needs some service') has *not* been established in previous discourse as shared knowledge amongst the participants in the courtroom. In other words, the postulated sharedness of knowledge relies entirely on the hearers' goodwill to treat the information as somehow obvious or as common knowledge.

The parking officer also uses other epistemic expressions that prototypically close the dialogic space, for example *faktisk* ('actually'), sometimes in the intensified collocation *rent faktisk* ('in fact'). Excerpt 2 illustrates how he uses these to indicate that his testimony counters what one might expect, thereby dismantling potential alternative points of view.

Excerpt 2
Prosecutor (PRO), Parking officer (PO)

PRO:		how um do you perceive his um state of mind
		(0.4)
PO:	→	quite calm **actually**
		(0.3)
PRO:		he ⌈is quite⌉ calm ≈
PO:		⌊the on-⌋
		+≈ yes I ⌈think⌉ so
PRO:		⌊yes⌋
PO:		the only thing I feel: (0.6) that annoys me
	→	that is **in fact** that he prods me in my chest
		(0.5)
PO:		like pushes me a little with two fingers
		(0.5)
PRO:		with two fingers
PO:		yes or one finger that I can't
		but he ⌈prods⌉ me in my chest
PRO:		⌊mh⌋
		(1.0)
PO:		while he's speaking to me but apart from
	→	that I **actually** perceive him as being
		quite calm and:: um:: (0.1) hf: b- but
		he does that thing (0.6) and that makes
		me say to him right away (0.2) that this
		w- (0.3) I won't tolerate
		(0.3)
PRO:		mh ≈
PO:		+≈ I won't tolerate him touching me
		(1.2)
		so that he's being told quite calmly
		(0.7)
	→	and then: I tell him ***jo*** quite calmly that um:
		that that I have written um this fee for him

Note also in lines 9–10 how he *introduces* one of the disputed pieces of evidence, "that he prods me in my chest", by way of presupposition triggered by the factive predicate *irriterer* ('annoys'). This way he indicates that the information is not up for discussion – his use of *rent faktisk* ('in fact') in line 10 does not concern the prodding statement, but merely his being annoyed, leaving the controversial testimony in the background. A similar coercive or cajoling move is made by means of *jo* in line 31, used by the parking officer to purport another disputed piece of evidence as shared knowledge: the claim that he was acting calm.

As shown by the quantitative analysis, the parking officer also – though less frequently – uses epistemic expressions that will prototypically open up the dialogic space. This is illustrated in Excerpt 3.

Excerpt 3
Prosecutor (PRO), Parking officer (PO)

1	PRO:		how long have you been observing it for (.)
2			at this point (0.4) the car
3	PO:		◉before◉ I approach it ≈
4	PRO:		+≈ yes
5	PO:	→	well I have **probably** been at the lot for some minutes
6			(0.5)
7	PRO:		o⌈kay⌉
8	PO:	→	⌊so I⌋ have **probably** been there for five seven minutes
9		→	**I think** (0.1) before I even go over to the car
10			(2.6)
11	PRO:		okay and you've been watching it right from when you
12			ar⌈rive⌉ and then
13	PO:		⌊yes⌋
14	PRO:		yes
15	PO:	→	but the observation time for me starts ***jo*** (0.1)
16		→	**actually** (0.2) also (0.2) at the time when I start
17			writing the parking fee

Here we see how the parking officer employs *vel* ('probably'), *nok* ('probably') and *tror jeg* ('I think') when estimating how long he observed the car before issuing the fee. The epistemic expressions are accompanied by unspecific time indications in lines 5 and 8, also opening up the dialogic space. Immediately after this, however, the parking officer takes a strong epistemic stance in using *jo* (line 15) and *faktisk* ('actually', line 16) when pointing out that the observation time actually starts at a later point. In this way, after initially opening up the dialogic space, he disqualifies the question that lead him to do so, in effect redefining what counts as the relevant question. In doing this, he arguably disaligns with the prosecutor and positions himself in a state of epistemic authority vis-à-vis her.

Following this discussion of observation time, in Excerpt 4 the parking officer is once again asked how long he has been observing the car for.

Excerpt 4
Prosecutor (PRO), Parking officer (PO)

1	PRO:	I just want to (.) um (.) go back
2	PO:	yes
3		(0.3)
4	PRO:	when you um put this in the windshield wiper

5			I assume that's what you do ≈
6	PO:		+≈ yes (.) that's what I end up doing ≈
7	PRO:		+≈ for how long um have you then (0.2)
8			been observing the car
9			(0.2)
10	PO:	→	at that point I have observed the car (0.2)
11			for (0.3) at least three minutes (0.2)
12			from the ⌈time-⌉
13	PRO:		⌊at least⌋ three minutes ≈
14	PO:		+≈ yes

This time he answers the question without epistemic modification, adopting a stance of absolute certainty. Yet once again he changes the perspective of the question, now specifying his *minimum* observation time, viz. three minutes. The absence of explicit epistemic stance marking in this case is possibly related to the distinction the parking officer introduces in Excerpt 3 between observation time in general and observation time as a business-specific technical term relating to the period after the point where the issuing of a fee has commenced. The former seems to be treated as unimportant by the parking officer, whereas the second is treated with great precision and without any epistemic uncertainty, possibly because it has legal consequences.

The example pair in Excerpts 3 and 4 shows that the parking officer is quite adept at varying his epistemic stance style depending on what the situation calls for. In lines 1–14 of Excerpt 3 it is presumably safe to leave the dialogic space open because the question is considered inconsequential. In Excerpt 4, the situation is very different, and the style changes accordingly. To suggest that the use of 'open' epistemic expressions in Excerpt 3 indexes a witness who is uncertain and perhaps somewhat feeble would thus in our view be a mistake. While this does not resemble Jacquemet's smoke screen strategy (cf. Sect. 3), it seems to be part of an attempt to build a persuasive epistemic stance style in which the dialogic space is only left open when it is arguably completely 'safe' to do so.

While the excerpts discussed so far for the most part concern relatively harmless aspects of the case, they give the impression that the parking officer makes the strongest efforts to close the dialogic space when giving the most consequential testimony, e.g. in relation to the issue of chest-prodding in Excerpt 2. Excerpt 5, in which he is confronted with questions addressing the core controversy of the case, and potentially implicating himself, confirms this pattern.

Excerpt 5

Prosecutor (PRO), Parking officer (PO)

1	PRO:	now we'll go back a little
2	PO:	yes we will
3		(1.2)

4	PRO:		do you at any point touch the defendant
5			(0.4)
6	PO:	→	not **at all**
7			(1.1)
8	PRO:		you don't
9			(0.3)
10	PO:		not at any time
11			(0.4)
12	PRO:		you don't touch his arm or (0.2) ⌈any⌉thing
13	PO:		⌊no⌋
14			(0.8)
15	PRO:		not even at the point when you are walking
16			to the sign and: ⌈you know⌉ ≈
17	PO:		⌊no⌋
18			(0.2)
19	PRO:		+≈ please come with me ⌈here⌉
20	PO:		⌊no⌋
21			(1.1)
22	PRO:		not at all
23			(0.1)
24	PO:	→	not ⌈**at all**⌉
25	PRO:		⌊right⌋
26			(0.9)
27			would that um: be
28			um ⌈be normal to do⌉
29	PO:		⌊there would (.) I have to⌋
30		→	tell you that I ***jo*** in my hand ≈
31			(0.4)
32	PRO:		yes
33			(0.4)
34	PO:		+≈ am carrying a camera
35			(0.6)
36	PO:		and a (0.1) fine- (0.1) or a fee protocol
37			(0.7)
38			and maybe also the fee we are:
39			we are dealing with cause I
40			believe it's lying around afterwards (0.5)
41		→	so I have ***jo*** **actually** not **at all** any opportunity
42		→	to touch him **at all**
43			(1.8)
44			and I have no reason to do so either
45			and I don't
46	PRO:		no

When asked whether he touched the defendant, not only does he reject the notion using epistemic and other expressions that close the dialogic space (e.g. lines 6, 10 and 24), he also goes on to account for how he was unable to – and had no reason to – touch the defendant (lines 29–44). Overall, the qualitative analysis of the discourse produced by the parking officer seems to confirm the pattern which we tentatively identified in the quantitative analysis: the parking officer adopts an epistemic stance style that primarily involves closing the dialogic space, even when giving fairly unimportant evidence. In many cases, the epistemic stances he takes up appear coercive as they assume or presuppose the hearers' acceptance, agreement or shared access to the information presented, or they imply and then reject potential alternative points of view.

As a final point in this section, it is worth pointing out that the parking officer's epistemic stance style can be realised by other means than the lexical ones discussed. For example, the excerpts above show how he frequently interrupts or latches with the prosecutor (e.g. Excerpt 5, lines 13, 17, 20 and 29), which is also the case in his interaction with other interlocutors not represented in the excerpts discussed. At times his apparent effort to control the dialogue even leads him to produce utterances that are interpretable as corrective towards the prosecutor, cf. the discussion of Excerpt 3, and as further illustrated in Excerpt 5, lines 29–30. Taken together these interactional practices effectively also lead to a closing of the dialogic space.

5.2.2 The Eyewitness

As discussed in Sect. 5.1, the eyewitness employs notably more epistemic expressions that tend to open up the dialogic space than the parking officer does. Excerpt 6 illustrates how the eyewitness takes a quite open epistemic stance towards details of his own narrative.

Excerpt 6
Defence lawyer (DFL), Eyewitness (EW)

DFL:		will you describe it slo- slowly and calmly
		in chronological order
		(0.6)
EW:		yes I can do that
		(0.2)
DFL:		yes
EW:		the gentleman here (0.1) hrm (0.8)
		had parked his car (0.4) in the courtyard
		(1.4)
		um to go into a um: (.) club (0.4)
	→	which is nearby **I think** he was going there to eat

12 → or whatever he was doing **I don't know**
13 (0.6)
14 he had parked his car
15 (1.0)
16 at that time the parking officer comes along
17 (1.7)
18 in um: his own car
19 (1.0)
20 → **I don't remember** if he was on a moped
21 or in his own car but he used to
22 drive a car you see (.) white car
23 (1.5)
24 um: after that came: (0.4) a big (0.6) van
25 (1.0)
26 and a big garbage truck after that (0.2)
27 to empty the garbage in the courtyard
28 (1.3)
29 and when they come in (0.1) they take up (0.2)
30 then they t- (.) they block the whole area (0.2)
31 around the courtyard (.) cause it's a small courtyard

Epistemic expressions such as *jeg tror nok* ('I think', line 11), *det ved jeg ikke* ('I don't know', line 12) and *jeg kan ikke huske* ('I don't remember', line 20), are here used to frame indeterminate pieces of evidence about the parking officer's possible activities in the club, as well as the vehicle in which he arrived. Curiously, the eyewitness chooses to give these – apparently irrelevant – pieces of evidence without being prompted, even though he is uncertain of them to the extent that he barely gets any information conveyed.

The evidence in Excerpt 6 addresses the fairly uncontroversial Topic I (cf. 4.3), concerning the events leading up to the incriminating incident. Therefore, opening the dialogic space during this sequence may not be problematic for the credibility of the testimony. In Excerpt 7, however, in which highly pertinent details are addressed, the eyewitness also takes weak stances towards the testimony, once again opening the dialogic space, even to the point where he seems to be about to withdraw from it.

Excerpt 7
Defence lawyer (DFL), Eyewitness (EW), Prosecutor (PRO)

1 DFL: before (0.4) um: we get that far (0.7) um:
2 at the beginning when (0.8) that man (0.9) comes out
3 and talks to the parking officer (0.7)
4 do you then notice if there is a (0.5) physical contact
5 xxx you have explained that the parking officer (0.2)
6 grabs hold of the man's arm (0.7)
7 what is it (0.3) do you remember which arm

8			he grabs hold of (0.8) is it the left arm or the right arm
9			(3.0)
10	EW:	→	**I think** it was this one he grabbed (0.3)
11	DFL:		you think it is the right ⌈arm⌉
12	EW:		⌊yes⌋
13		→	**I think** it is the right arm ≈
14	DFL:		+≈ ⌈okay⌉
15	EW:	→	⌊well now **I**⌋ **can't remember** it
16		→	but **I think** it is the ⌈right hand⌉
17	DFL:		⌊well⌋ it's (.) it's hard
18			it's ⌈still xxx⌉
19	EW:	→	⌊it (.) was⌋ back in May ⌈**I can't** um:⌉
20	DFL:		⌊others have also⌋
21			been asked these questions
22	EW:		yes
23	DFL:		there ⌈there is⌉ a (.) there are others ≋
24	PRO:		⌊mh⌋
25	DFL:		+≋ who have stated it is a little hard to ⌈remember⌉
26	EW:		⌊yes⌋

Note how the perceived insufficiency of the testimony is highlighted by the fact that the examiner finds it necessary to provide justification for the uncertainty of the witness by saying that others have also found it is hard to remember details this far back in time (lines 17–25).

As discussed in Sect. 5.1, the eyewitness does in some cases close the dialogic space, seeing that the particle *jo* is his most frequent epistemic expression. However, as Excerpt 8 illustrates, his uses of *jo*, and other expressions that contribute to closing the dialogic space, are often licensed by the context and appear non-coercive.

Excerpt 8

Eyewitness (EW)

1	EW:		the gentleman (0.1)
2			now I don't recall his name (0.3)
3			but he runs out (0.9)
4			from: (0.3) the kitchen (0.3)
5			or the restaurant (0.5)
6			he has s-: f-: (0.4)
7			there has been rumours that there's
8			a parking officer around
9			so he goes out to his own car
10			(0.9)
11		→	and um: wants to move it **of course**
12			(0.9)

13		→	but he is ***jo*** not able to
14			(1.0)
15			because those garbage trucks (0.2)
16			are parked in the middle of the courtyard

In this case the use of *selvfølgelig* ('of course', line 11) does not require much empathy or cognitive processing from the hearers, as anyone would be eager to avoid a parking fee. Also, the use of *jo* is licensed as the eyewitness has already established earlier in his testimony (cf. Excerpt 6, line 30) that garbage trucks blocked the area. For good measure, he even recapitulates this information in lines 15–16.

The excerpts shown so far may imply that the eyewitness provides a somewhat wishy-washy testimony, delivered in a relatively uncertain manner. However, at one central point in the examination, this picture is challenged. This appears towards the end of the testimony where he is questioned about some of the most critical and disputed aspects of the case, here presented as Excerpt 9.

Excerpt 9
Defence lawyer (DFL), Eyewitness (EW)

1	DFL:		does (0.4) ◉that◉ man grab hold of (.) um (0.2)
2			the parking officer or (0.3) or (.) does he have (.)
3			physical contact with the parking officer
4			(0.9)
5	EW:		no he does not grab him at all
6			◉he's◉ the one who starts by grabbing hold of him
7			and it's like he has to push him away or: (0.4)
8	DFL:		okay
9	EW:		and then it (.) then ⌈nothing⌉ more happens there
10	DFL:		⌊okay⌋
11			do you notice if (.) if that man (0.3)
12			for example once prods the parking officer in his chest
13			(0.3)
14	EW:	→	he does not
15			(0.6)
16	DFL:		and also not twice in his chest later
17			(0.2)
18	EW:	→	he does not no ≈
19	DFL:		+≈ he does not

In the end of this excerpt we see that the eyewitness provides a clear answer without resorting to epistemic expressions of any kind, thereby displaying absolute certainty at an important point in the examination.

Overall, the epistemic stance style of the eyewitness is not as straightforward to characterise as that of the parking officer. The eyewitness adopts a style that mostly involves opening the dialogic space, in some cases even when giving important evidence. Moreover, his *manner* of opening the dialogic space is peculiar as he occasionally takes stances that are so weak they nearly disqualify his own statements. Interestingly, this does not seem to be of concern to him. Rather, in some instances he displays an almost nonchalant attitude towards revealing his own uncertainty. He chooses, for instance, on his own initiative to address issues which are basically irrelevant in the context, and which he has nearly no recollection of or even possibility of knowing about, as discussed in relation to Excerpt 6. This *laissez-faire* approach, in turn, may be contrasted to the composed manner in which he *closes* the dialogic space. Thus, in Excerpts 8 and 9 we saw how his use of *jo* is non-coercive, minimizing the risk that he potentially positions others in ways they may not accept, and how he manages to concisely answer a critical and disputed question without the use of epistemic expressions. One possible explanation for this discrepancy is that the eyewitness *strategically* displays the ability to be anything from completely unsure to somewhat uncertain, but also quite certain when the situation calls for it. By utilising a full span of epistemic stances and generally leaning towards *opening* the dialogic space, he may come across as a cautious and self-critical assessor of information, for whom bold statements like the ones in Excerpt 9 are rare and therefore delivered with relatively more weight. In short, the eyewitness could be said to be exploiting various epistemic stance styles, or one complex one, for the purpose of building rhetorical ethos.

6 Discussion and Concluding Remarks

In this chapter, we have illustrated how epistemic stance can be investigated in naturally occurring courtroom interaction by means of a method that combines quantitative and qualitative approaches to the analysis of discourse. Our analyses have clearly shown that two of the witnesses in the case we have investigated, the parking officer and the eyewitness, use epistemic expressions in quite different ways. In fact, we suggest that their use of these expressions amount to quite different epistemic stance styles. The quantitative analysis of the parking officer's discourse showed him to be a frequent user of epistemic expressions that close the dialogic space, and through qualitative analysis of excerpts from his testimony, we were able to unfold how this contributed to his epistemic stance taking in particular key moments of the examination. The eyewitness, on the other hand, generally adopts a more open epistemic stance style. This was quite immediately observable in the quantitative results and further substantiated by excerpts from his testimony. What we also showed, however, was that at a particular key moment in his testimony, the eyewitness adopted a very definite epistemic stance, which represents a stark contrast to his general style. This clearly illustrates that epistemic stance styles are not static products, but dynamic processes that must be studied in context.

It is a common assumption in parts of the literature on courtroom interaction – and perhaps more generally – that there is a link between a witness' ability to testify with confidence and certainty and his or her chances of coming across as a credible witness. However, our analyses suggest that the matter is not as straightforward as that. We do not know what the professional judge and the two lay judges in this particular case thought about the credibility of the two witnesses we have investigated in detail. This is important to make clear. It is, however, interesting to note that the very definitive epistemic stance adopted by the parking officer does not lead the majority of the judges to believe his testimony – at least not enough to decide that the defendant should be convicted. Instead, two out of three judges decide that the defendant should be acquitted, thereby in effect implying that they find the version of events told by the eyewitness to be more credible – despite the fact that we have shown him to adopt a very open epistemic stance, often to the point of apparently not even trusting his own memory. We do not wish to make any definitive conclusions on the basis of the case study we have presented here, but we believe that the method we have presented for the characterisation of epistemic stance styles in courtroom interaction represents a promising first step in designing further empirical studies that may allow us to test how different epistemic stance styles affect judges and juries in their attempt to make up their mind concerning the ever-relevant question of guilt or innocence.

Appendices

Appendix 1: Transcription Conventions

Identifier	PO:
Pause	(0.2)
Overlap markers top	⌈ ⌉
Overlap markers bottom	⌊ ⌋
Latched turns	≈
Turn continues	≋
Unsure	??transcriber unsure??
Inaudible	xxx
Louder	◉this is louder◉
Anonymised item	↫anonymised↫
Analytically significant line(s)	→
Analytically significant expression	**probably**
Untranslated Danish item	*jo*

Appendix 2: Epistemic Expressions Investigated

Core Modal Verbs (CMV)

Any grammatical form of:

- *bør/burde* ('ought')
- *kan/kunne* ('can/could')
- *må/måtte* ('may/might/must')
- *skal/skulle* ('shall/should')
- *vil/ville* ('will/would')

Epistemic/Evidential Adverbials (EEAdv)

afgjort ('definitely')	*garanteret* ('certainly')	*naturligvis* ('naturally')	*sikkert* ('supposedly')
altså ('you know')	*givetvis* ('surely')	*nok* ('probably')	*tilsyneladende* ('apparently')
angivelig ('allegedly')	*helt klart* ('definitely')	*næppe* ('probably not')	*tydeligvis* ('clearly')
antagelig ('presumably')	*i hvert fald* ('definitely')	*nødvendigvis* ('necessarily')	*uden tvivl* ('undoubtedly')
bestemt ('definitely')	*ikke rigtig* ('not really')	*overhovedet* ('at all')	*utvivlsomt* ('undoubtedly')
da ('really')	*i realiteten* ('in reality')	*reelt* ('actually')	*vel* ('I guess')
egentlig ('actually')	*i virkeligheden* ('in reality')	*sagtens* ('very well')	*vist* ('supposedly')
et eller andet sted ('somehow')	*jo* ('as you know')	*sandsynligvis* ('likely')	*øjensynlig* ('apparently')
faktisk ('actually')	*mon* ('I wonder')	*selvfølgelig* ('of course')	*åbenbart* ('evidently')
formentlig ('probably')	*muligvis* ('possibly')	*selvsagt* ('obviously')	*åbenlyst* ('evidently')
formodentlig ('probably')	*måske* ('maybe')	*slet ikke* ('not at all')	

Epistemic/Evidential Adjectives (EEAdj)

Any of the two gender forms (neuter and common gender) of:

diskutabel ('questionable')	*mulig* ('possible')	*tvivlsom* ('doubtful')	*usand* ('untrue')
givet ('obvious')	*plausibel* ('plausible')	*tænkelig* ('conceivable')	*usandsynlig* ('implausible')

(continued)

indiskutabel ('unquestionable')	*rigtig* ('right')	*tydelig* ('evident')	*usikker* ('uncertain')
indlysende ('obvious')	*sand* ('true')	*uklar* ('unclear')	*utvivlsom* ('beyond doubt')
klar ('obvious')	*sandsynlig* ('plausible')	*umulig* ('impossible')	*åbenbar* ('evident')
korrekt ('correct')	*sikker* ('certain')	*uomtvistelig* ('indisputable')	*åbenlys* ('clear')

Epistemic/Evidential Cognition and Perception Verbs (EECPV)

Any grammatical form of:

afvise ('reject')	*fornemme* ('sense')	*håbe* ('hope')	*skønne* ('estimate')
antage ('assume')	*forstå* ('understand')	*mene* ('believe'/'think')	*synes* ('feel'/'think')
bemærke ('notice')	*forvente* ('expect')	*mærke* ('feel')	*tvivle* ('doubt')
betvivle ('question')	*forudse* ('predict')	*nægte* ('reject')	*tro* ('believe'/'think')
bestride ('dispute')	*frygte* ('fear')	*observere* ('observe')	*tænke* ('think')
erindre ('recall')	*føle* ('feel')	*opdage* ('discover')	*undre* ('wonder')
erkende ('realise')	*garantere* ('guarantee')	*opfatte* ('conceive')	*være bange for* ('be afraid')
fastholde ('maintain')	*glemme* ('forget')	*opleve* ('experience')	*vente* ('expect')
finde ('find')	*gå ud fra* ('suppose')	*overveje* ('reflect')	*vide* ('know')
forestille ('imagine')	*huske* ('remember')	*regne med* ('trust'/'suppose')	*vurdere* ('assess')
formode ('suppose')	*høre* ('hear')	*se* ('see')	*ønske* ('wish')

Appendix 3: Transcription Excerpts in Danish

The Parking Officer

Excerpt 1 (Danish)
Prosecutor (PRO), Parking officer (PO)

1	PRO:		øh men hvad er det der sker
2			om eftermiddagen den første maj
3			(0.5)
4			⌈hvor⌉ du er på job
5	PO:		⌊ja⌋
6			ja men øh:: (.) det der sker det er:
7		→	jeg har ***jo*** vi har ***jo***
8			sådan en runde vi kører øh hvor vi besøger forskellige
9			pladser rundt omkring i byen
10			(0.5)
11		→	og jeg kommer ***jo*** til den her plads
12			jeg (.) kalder den ↫Name↫
13			det kan godt være den fysisk ligger et lidt andet sted
14			men men ⌈men⌉ i ??det?? vores sprog
15	PRO:		⌊mh⌋
16	PO:		der hedder den ↫Name↫ og jeg kommer til pladsen
17			(0.8)
18		→	og øh:: (0.4) k- og det og min opgave er ***jo*** at at (.)
19		→	tjekke øh (.) dels er der ***jo*** hvis der er nogen der
20			har brug for noget service (.)
21		→	vi er ***jo*** også servicemedarbejdere
22			omkring ⌈(0.4)⌉ parkering og ting og sager
23	PRO:		⌊mh⌋

Excerpt 2 (Danish)
Prosecutor (PRO), Parking officer (PO)

1	PRO:		hvordan øh opfatter du hans øh sindstilstand
2			(0.4)
3	PO:	→	stille og rolig **faktisk**
4			(0.3)
5	PRO:		han ⌈er stille og⌉ rolig ≈
6	PO:		⌊det enest-⌋
7			+≈ ja det ⌈synes⌉ jeg
8	PRO:		⌊ja⌋
9	PO:		det eneste jeg synes der:: (0.6) der irriterer mig

10		→	det er fa- **rent faktisk** at han prikker mig på brystkassen
11			(0.5)
12	PO:		sådan skubber lidt til mig med to fingre
13			(0.5)
14	PRO:		med to fingre
15	PO:		ja eller en finger det skal jeg ikke kunne
16			men han ⌈prikker⌉ til mig på brystet
17	PRO:		⌊mh⌋
18			(1.0)
19	PO:		mens han taler til mig men ellers så
20		→	opfatter jeg ham **faktisk** som at være
21			stille og rolig og:: øh:: (0.1) hf: m- men
22			han laver den der ting (0.6) og det får mig
23			til at sige til ham som det første (0.2) at det
24			sk- (0.3) vil jeg ikke have
25			(0.3)
26	PRO:		mh ≈
27	PO:		+≈ jeg vil ikke have han rører ved mig
28			(1.2)
29			så det får han at vide stille og roligt
30			(0.7)
31		→	og så: fortæller jeg ham ***jo*** stille og roligt at øh:
32			at at jeg har skrevet øh det her gebyr til ham

Excerpt 3 (Danish)

Prosecutor (PRO), Parking officer (PO)

1	PRO:		hvor længe har du observeret den (.)
2			på det her tidspunkt (0.4) bilen
3	PO:		◉inden◉ jeg går derhen ≈
4	PRO:		+≈ ja
5	PO:	→	ja men jeg har **vel** været på pladsen nogle minutter
6			(0.5)
7	PRO:		o⌈kay⌉
8	PO:	→	⌊så jeg⌋ har **nok** været der en fem syv minutter
9		→	**vil jeg tro** (0.1) inden jeg overhovedet går hen til den der bil
10			(2.6)
11	PRO:		okay og der har du set den lige fra du
12			ankom ⌈mer⌉ og så
13	PO:		⌊ja⌋
14	PRO:		ja
15	PO:	→	men observationstiden for mig starter ***jo*** (0.1)

16		→	**reelt** (0.2) også (0.2) på det tidspunkt hvor jeg
17			begynder at skrive gebyret

Excerpt 4 (Danish)
Prosecutor (PRO), Parking officer (PO)

1	PRO:		jeg skal bare lige (.) øh (.) lige tilbage
2	PO:		ja
3			(0.3)
4	PRO:		da du øh sætter denne her i vinduesviskeren
5			det går jeg ud fra er det du gør ≈
6	PO:		+≈ ja (.) det er det jeg ender med ≈
7	PRO:		+≈ hvor lang tid øh har du så (0.2)
8			observeret bilen
9			(0.2)
10	PO:	→	der har jeg observeret bilen (0.2)
11			i (0.3) mindst tre minutter (0.2)
12			fra ⌈det tidspu-⌉
13	PRO:		⌊mindst tre mi⌋nutter ≈
14	PO:		+≈ ja

Excerpt 5 (Danish)
Prosecutor (PRO), Parking officer (PO)

1	PRO:		nu skal vi lige lidt tilbage
2	PO:		det skal vi
3			(1.2)
4	PRO:		rører du på noget tidspunkt ved tiltalte
5			(0.4)
6	PO:	→	**overhovedet** ikke
7			(1.1)
8	PRO:		det gør du ikke
9			(0.3)
10	PO:		på intet tidspunkt
11			(0.4)
12	PRO:		du rører ikke ved hans arm eller (0.2) ⌈no⌉get
13	PO:		⌊nej⌋
14			(0.8)
15	PRO:		heller ikke i forbindelse med I skal hen
16			til skiltet og: ⌈li⌉ge ≈
17	PO:		⌊nej⌋
18			(0.2)

PRO: +≈ prøv og kom med ⌈her⌉
PO: ⌊nej⌋
(1.1)
PRO: slet ikke
(0.1)
PO: → **overhovedet** ⌈ikke⌉
PRO: ⌊nej⌋
(0.9)
ville det øh: vær-
øh ⌈være normalt at gøre⌉
PO: ⌊det ville der (.) jeg er nødt til at⌋
→ sige til dig at jeg ***jo*** i min hånd ≈
(0.4)
PRO: ja
(0.4)
PO: +≈ bærer et kamera
(0.6)
PO: og en (0.1) bøde- (0.1) eller en gebyrblok
(0.7)
og måske også det der gebyr vi har:
vi har fat i jeg tror nemlig
det ligger og flyder bagefter (0.5)
→ så jeg har ***jo*** **egentlig** ikke **slet** ikke mulighed
→ for **overhovedet** at røre ved ham
(1.8)
og jeg har heller ingen grund til det
og jeg gør det heller ikke
PRO: nej

The Eyewitness

Excerpt 6

Defence lawyer (DFL), Eyewitness (EW)

DFL: vil du beskrive det sti- stille og roligt
i kronologisk orden
(0.6)
EW: jo det kan jeg godt
(0.2)
DFL: ja
EW: herren her (0.1) hrm (0.8)
havde parkeret sin bil (0.4) inde i gården
(1.4)

10 øh for at gå ind i en øh: (.) klub (0.4)
11 → der er tæt på **jeg tror nok** han skulle ind og spise
12 → eller hvad han skulle det **ved jeg ikke**
13 (0.6)
14 han havde parkeret sin bil
15 (1.0)
16 i det kører parkeringsvagten ind
17 (1.7)
18 med øh: hans egen bil
19 (1.0)
20 → **jeg kan ikke huske** om han var på knallert
21 eller i hans egen bil men han plejede
22 at køre i bil nemlig (.) hvid bil
23 (1.5)
24 efter det der kørte der: (0.4) en stor (0.6) kassevogn
25 (1.0)
26 og en stor skraldebil efter det (0.2)
27 for at tømme skraldet ude i gården
28 (1.3)
29 og når de kører ind (0.1) så holder de (0.2)
30 så kan de s- (.) så spærrer de hele området (0.2)
31 ude ved gården (.) for det er en lille gård

Excerpt 7
Defence lawyer (DFL), Eyewitness (EW), Prosecutor (PRO)

1 DFL: inden at (0.4) øh: vi kommer så langt (0.7) øh:
2 lige i starten hvor (0.8) den mand (0.9) kommer ud
3 og taler med parkeringsvagten (0.7)
4 lægger du da mærke til om der er en (0.5) fysisk kontakt
5 xxx du har forklaret at parkeringsvagten (0.2)
6 tager fat i mandens arm (0.7)
7 hvad er det (0.3) kan du huske hvilken arm
8 han tager fat i (0.8) er det den venstre arm eller højre arm
9 (3.0)
10 EW: → **jeg tror** det var den her han tog fat i (0.3)
11 DFL: du tror det er højre ⌈arm⌉
12 EW: ⌊ja⌋
13 → **jeg tror** det er højre arm ≈
14 DFL: +≈ ⌈okay⌉
15 EW: → **jeg ikke huske** det ⌊ja nu **kan**⌋
16 → men **jeg tror** det er ⌈højre hånd⌉
17 DFL: ⌊nej⌋ det (.) det er svært

18 det er ⌈stadig xxx⌉
19 EW: → ⌊det er (.) fra⌋ maj måned så ⌈**jeg kan ikke** øh:⌉
20 DFL: ⌊der er også andre⌋
21 der er blevet hørt i sagen
22 EW: ja
23 DFL: der ⌈der er⌉ en (.) der er andre ≋
24 PRO: ⌊mh⌋
25 DFL: +≋ der har forklaret det er lidt svært at ⌈huske⌉
26 EW: ⌊ja⌋

Excerpt 8
Eyewitness (EW)

1 EW: herren (0.1)
2 nu kan jeg ikke huske hvad han hedder (0.3)
3 men han løber ud (0.9)
4 fra: (0.3) køkkenet af (0.3)
5 eller der i restauranten (0.5)
6 han har så s-: f-: (0.4)
7 der har været rygter om der har
8 været parkeringsvagt
9 så han går ud til hans egen bil
10 (0.9)
11 → og vil øh: **selvfølgelig** flytte den
12 (0.9)
13 → men han kan ***jo*** ikke komme til
14 (1.0)
15 fordi der holder de der skraldebiler (0.2)
16 midt i gården

Excerpt 9
Defence lawyer (DFL), Eyewitness (EW)

1 DFL: tager (0.4) °den° mand fat i (.) øh (0.2)
2 parkeringsvagten eller (0.3) eller (.) har han (.)
3 fysisk kontakt med parkeringsvagten
4 (0.9)
5 EW: nej han tager slet ikke fat ved ham
6 det er °ham° der starter med at tage fat på ham
7 og det er ligesom han skal skubbe ham væk eller: (0.4)
8 DFL: okay
9 EW: og så det (.) så ⌈der sker⌉ ikke mere der
10 DFL: ⌊okay⌋

		lægger du mærke til om (.) om den mand (0.3)
		for eksempel en gang prikker parkeringsvagten i brystet
		(0.3)
EW:	→	det gør han ikke
		(0.6)
DFL:		og heller ikke senere to gange i brystet
		(0.2)
EW:	→	det gør han ikke nej ≈
DFL:		+≈ det gør han ikke

References[4]

Adelswärd, V., Aronsson, K., & Linell, P. (1988). Discourse of blame: Courtroom construction of social identity from the perspective of the defendant. *Semiotica, 71*(3-4), 261–284.

Adolphs, S. (2008). Definitely maybe: Modality clusters and politeness in spoken discourse. In P. Skandera (Ed.), *Phraseology and culture in English* (pp. 257–274). Berlin: Mouton de Gruyter.

Anderson, S. (1992). The transition from inquisitorial to adversarial criminal procedure in Denmark. *Scandinavian Studies, 64*(2), 181–198.

Atkinson, J. M. (1992). Displaying neutrality: Formal aspects of informal court proceedings. In P. Drew & J. Heritage (Eds.), *Talk at work: Interaction in institutional settings* (pp. 199–211). Cambridge: Cambridge University Press.

Atkinson, J. M., & Drew, P. (1979). *Order in court: The organisation of verbal interaction in judicial settings*. London: Macmillan.

Bednarek, G. A. (2014). *Polish vs. American courtroom discourse: Inquisitorial and adversarial procedures of witness examination in criminal trials*. New York: Palgrave Macmillan.

Bennet, W. L., & Feldman, M. S. (1981). *Reconstructing reality in the courtroom*. London: Tavistock.

Beyer, J. (2013). *Retorik i retten*. Copenhagen: Hans Reitzels Forlag.

Biber, D., Conrad, S., & Reppen, R. (1998). *Corpus linguistics: Investigating language structure and use*. Cambridge: Cambridge University Press.

Biscetti, S. (2006). Tag questions in courtroom discourse. In M. Gotti & J. Flowerdew (Eds.), *Studies in specialized discourse* (pp. 209–238). Bern: Peter Lang.

Boye, K. (2012). *Epistemic meaning: A cross-linguistic and functional-cognitive study*. Berlin: De Gruyter Mouton.

Bülow-Møller, A. M. (1991). Trial evidence: Overt and covert communication in court. *International Journal of Applied Linguistics, 1*(1), 38–60.

Caffi, C. (2007). *Mitigation*. Amsterdam: Elsevier.

Carretero, M. (1992). The role of epistemic modality in English politeness strategies. *Miscelánea: A journal of english and american studies, 13*, 17–36.

[4]We would like to express our gratitude to the Court of Frederiksberg for making this project possible. Special thanks are due to judges Jette-Marie Sonne and, especially, Jacob Waage for their invaluable participation, helpfulness and advice. We are also grateful to Hartmut Haberland for providing feedback on an earlier version of this chapter and helping us to clarify the argument in important ways. Any remaining shortcomings should of course be attributed to us.

Christensen, T. K. (2007). *Hyperparadigmer – en undersøgelse af paradigmatiske samspil i danske modussystemer*, PhD thesis, Roskilde: Roskilde University.

Coates, J. (1987). Epistemic modality and spoken discourse. *Transactions of the Philological Society, 85*(1), 110–131.

Coates, J. (1990). Modal meaning: The semantic–pragmatic interface. *Journal of Semantics, 7*(1), 53–63.

Conley, J. M., & O'Barr, W. M. (1998). *Just words: Law, language and power*. Chicago: The University of Chicago.

Cotterill, J. (2003). *Language and power in court : A linguistic analysis of the O. J. Simpson trial*. Basingstoke: Palgrave Macmillan.

Coulthard, M., & Johnson, A. (2007). *An introduction to forensic linguistics: Language in evidence*. London: Routledge.

Coulthard, M., & Johnson, A. (2010). *The Routledge handbook of forensic linguistics*. London: Routledge.

Damaška, M. R. (1997). *Evidence law adrift*. Yale: Yale University Press.

Dong, J. (2013). Interpersonal metaphor in legal discourse: Modality in cross-examinations. *Journal of Language Teaching and Research, 4*(6), 1311–1321.

Drew, P. (1992). Contested evidence in courtroom cross-examination: The case of a trial for rape. In P. Drew & J. Heritage (Eds.), *Talk at work: Interaction in institutional settings* (pp. 470–520). Cambridge: Cambridge University Press.

Drew, P., & Heritage, J. (1992). Analyzing talk at work: An introduction. In P. Drew & J. Heritage (Eds.), *Talk at work: Interaction in institutional settings* (pp. 3–65). Cambridge: Cambridge University Press.

Du Bois, J. W. (2007). The stance triangle. In R. Englebretson (Ed.), *Pragmatics & beyond new series* (Vol. 164, pp. 139–182). Amsterdam: John Benjamins Publishing Company.

Edmondson, W. J. (1981). *Spoken discourse: A model for analysis*. London/New York: Longman Group.

Gibbons, J. (2003). *Forensic linguistics: An introduction to language in the justice system*. Malden/Oxford: Blackwell Publishers.

Haberland, H., & Mortensen, J. (2015). Transcription as second-order entextualization: The challenge of heteroglossia. In A. Capone & J. L. Mey (Eds.), *Interdisciplinary studies in pragmatics, culture and society* (pp. 581–600). Dordrecht: Springer.

Hansen, E., & Heltoft, L. (2011). *Grammatik over det danske sprog*. København/Odense: Det Danske Sprog- og Litteraturselskab/Syddansk Universitetsforlag.

Harris, S. (1984). Questions as a mode of control in magistrates' courts. *International Journal of the Sociology of Language, 49*, 5–28.

Heritage, J., & Clayman, S. (2010). *Talk in action: Interactions, identities, and institutions*. West Sussex: Wiley/Blackwell Publishers.

Holmes, J. (1988). Doubt and certainty in ESL textbooks. *Applied Linguistics, 9*(1), 21–44.

Hosman, L. A. (1989). The evaluative consequences of hedges, hesitations, and intensifies powerful and powerless speech styles. *Human Communication Research, 15*(3), 383–406.

House, J., & Kasper, G. (1981). Politeness markers in English and German. In F. Coulmas (Ed.), *Conversational routine: Explorations in standardized communication situations and prepatterned speech* (pp. 157–185). The Hague: Mouton Publishers.

Jacobsen, B. (2002). *Pragmatic meaning in court interpreting : An empirical study of additions in consecutively interpreted question-answer dialogues*, PhD thesis, Aarhus: Aarhus School of Business, The Faculty of Modern Languages.

Jacquemet, M. (1996). *Credibility in court: Communicative practices in the camorra trials*. Cambridge: Cambridge University Press.

Jensen, E. S. (2000). *Danske sætningsadverbialer og topologi i diakron belysning*, PhD thesis, Copenhagen: University of Copenhagen.

Kæraa, C. (2011). Domstolene på tværs af landegrænser. *Retten Rundt (Domstolsstyrelsen), 8*, 24–27.

Kjær, A. L., Adrian, L., Cederstrøm, C. B., Engberg, J., Gabrielsen, J., Rosenmeier, M., & Schaumburg-Müller, S. (eds.). (2015). *Retten i Sproget: Samspillet mellem ret og sprog i juridisk praksis*. Copenhagen: Jurist- og Økonomiforbundets Forlag.

Kärkkäinen, E. (1992). Modality as a strategy in interaction: Epistemic modality in the language of native and non-native speakers of English. *Pragmatics and Language Learning, 3*, 197–216.

Komter, M. (1995). The distribution of knowledge in courtroom interaction. In P. ten Have & G. Psathas (Eds.), *Situated Order: Studies in the social organization of talk and embodied activities* (pp. 107–128). Washington: University Press of America.

Komter, M. (2013). Conversation analysis in the courtroom. In J. Sidnell & T. Stivers (Eds.), *The handbook of conversation analysis* (pp. 612–629). Chichester: Wiley-Blackwell.

Lakoff, R. T. (1975). *Language and woman's place*. New York: Harper & Row.

Law, J. & Martin, E.A. (2014). *A dictionary of law*, 7 ed. (Online Version), Oxford: Oxford University Press.

Lind, E. A., & O'Barr, W. M. (1978). The social significance of speech in the courtroom. In H. Giles & R. N. S. Clair (Eds.), *Language and social psychology* (pp. 67–87). Oxford: Basil Blackwell.

MacWhinney, B. (2000). *The CHILDES project: Tools for analyzing talk* (3rd ed.). Mahwah: Lawrence Erlbaum Associates.

Mininni, G., Scardigno, R., & Grattagliano, I. (2014). The dialogic construction of certainty in legal contexts. *Language and Dialogue, 4*(1), 112–131.

Mortensen, J. (2010). *Epistemic stance marking in the use of English as a lingua franca*, PhD thesis, Roskilde: Roskilde University.

Mortensen, J. (2012). Epistemisk positionering i dansk talesprog. *NyS, Nydanske Sprogstudier, 42*, 62–91.

Nikula, T. (1996). *Pragmatic force modifiers: A study in interlanguage pragmatics*. Jyväskyla: University of Jyväskyla.

Nølke, H., Fløttum, K., & Norén, C. (2004). *ScaPoLine: La théorie scandinave de la polyphonie linguistique*. Paris: Editions Kimé.

O'Barr, W. M. (1982). *Linguistic evidence: Language, power, and strategy in the courtroom*. New York/London: Academic.

Ochs, E. (1992). Indexing gender. In A. Duranti & C. Goodwin (Eds.), *Rethinking Context: Language as an Interactive Phenomenon* (pp. 335–358). Cambridge: Cambridge University Press.

Simon-Vandenbergen, A. M., & Aijmer, K. (2007). *The semantic field of modal certainty: A corpus-based study of English adverbs*. Berlin: Walter de Gruyter.

Staffe, M. L. (2008). *Retsretorik*. Copenhagen: Thomson Reuters.

Szczyrbak, M. (2013). "I think my own view is that..." On the linguistic construction of evidence in courtroom discourse. *Topics in Linguistics, 12*, 65–74.

Therkelsen, R. (2004). Polyfoni som sproglig begrebsramme og som redskab i tekstanalysen. *Sproglig polyfoni: arbejdspapirer, 1*, 79–109.

Thompson, J. K. (2002). "Powerful/Powerless" language in court: A critical re-evaluation of the Duke language and law programme. *International Journal of Speech Language and the Law, 9*(2), 153–167.

Toska, B. (2012). Epistemic hedges and boosters as stance markers in legal argumentative discourse. *Topics in Linguistics, 10*, 57–62.

White, P. R. R. (2003). Beyond modality and hedging: A dialogic view of the language of intersubjective stance. *Text: Interdisciplinary Journal for the Study of Discourse, 23*(2), 259–284.

Youmans, M. (2001). Cross-cultural differences in polite epistemic modal use in American English. *Journal of Multilingual and Multicultural Development, 22*(1), 57–73.

Assessing Testimony and Other Evidential Sources in Law: An Epistemological Approach

Florencia Rimoldi and Hernán G. Bouvier

Abstract In this paper we seek to address some platitudes surrounding the epistemic weight of testimony in legal domain by taking into account how epistemology explains the different but related phenomenon of forming beliefs based on the words of others. We propose a way of analysing the legal decision-maker in terms of a rational believer without committing ourselves with subjective readings of legal evidential assessments. In light of this, we analyse the pragmatic implications of legal platitudes and the conceptual possibility to hold them together, as well as the singularity of testimony in an institutional domain like the law.

Keywords Testimony • Evidence • Epistemology • Belief • Justification • Law

1 Introduction

Many of our most important beliefs about our surroundings and ourselves were acquired based on what other people tell us. Central beliefs considered as "knowledge" about history -even personal history-, geography, mathematics and so on, stem from testimony broadly conceived. Our dependence on testimony is inevitable and ubiquitous. Nevertheless, there are institutional areas in which the epistemic weight given to it is unstable or controversial. The legal field is one of those areas. Jurists in general share different platitudes about testimony. For example, that expert (i.e. scientific and specialized) testimony has more epistemic weight than other sources of knowledge in legal process. Although in legal field there are several platitudes and shared assumptions around evidence, other common sense assumptions about evidence and testimony are controversial.

F. Rimoldi (✉)
Philosophy Department, Universidad de Buenos Aires/CONICET, Buenos Aires, Argentina
e-mail: rimoldiflorencia@hotmail.com

H.G. Bouvier
Theory of Law, CONICET (National Research Council-Argentina) and University of Cordoba, Argentina, Córdoba, Córdoba, Argentina
e-mail: hernanbouvier@gmail.com

F. Poggi, A. Capone (eds.), *Pragmatics and Law*, Perspectives in Pragmatics, Philosophy & Psychology 10, DOI 10.1007/978-3-319-44601-1_17

Legal debates and disagreements have important coincidences with main discussions in the epistemology of testimony broadly conceived (e.g. reductionism, priority, autonomy of testimony, and the like).[1]

Philosophical discussions on the topic could help, thus, to show the pragmatic implications surrounding some platitudes, which of them could hold together and which should not. Our goal in this paper is to provide the best epistemological support for the legal practice as it stands with respect to some core issues regarding testimony.

Philosophers have given a lot of thought to the question of the epistemic credentials of testimony-based beliefs. Although there is no agreement between epistemologists about how does testimony obtain its epistemic import in the case of human cognisants, we think that some accounts fit better to explain theoretically the legal practice. Which philosophical account fits better legal practice is, however, not so simple to assess. This, we argue, throws some negative consequences on the legal practice as it stands regarding the issues that will be under examination in this paper.

In its turn, a closer look to general assumptions adopted in legal field could also provide a further service in the opposite direction (i.e. from legal field to philosophy). In effect, the philosophical discussions in epistemology of testimony tend to disregard the important influence of social and institutional rules applicable in certain domains. In institutional domains as the law, not every piece of evidence with certain epistemological quality is admissible (for example, victims' testimony cannot be forced if it infringes their dignity). Interestingly enough, there are many ways in which the peculiarity of testimony in an institutional domain as the law becomes useful to the analysis of testimony broadly conceived.

Section 2 is by far the more extensive section of the article. It presents the basic theoretical ground from which to have a useful exchange between epistemology and legal epistemology. We propose a general account of the legal evidential assessment that we hope will prove to be useful in the general application of epistemological results and considerations relevant not only to legal testimony but also to legal epistemology in general. We call "deflationist doxastic approach" to the framework proposed here, since we model the legal evidential process in terms of beliefs without committing ourselves with any subjectivist (nor objectivist) reading of the legal evidential norms. In Sect. 3 we distinguish between two different senses of "testimony", and specify the peculiarity of testimony in legal institutions. We then identify three common assumptions about testimony in the legal field. Section 4 introduces three relevant discussions in the epistemology of testimony that are fundamental for the correct assessment and evaluation of the different platitudes identified in Sect. 3. In Sects. 5 and 6 we draw some conclusions about the profit that could be obtained from the interaction of philosophical and legal remarks on testimony, by showing how the legal testimonial practice can be rationalised.

---

[1] Lackey and Sosa (2006).

2 Defining Legal Evidence Assessment from a Deflationist Doxastic Framework

Evidence is a crucial notion in the legal realm. In a broad sense, it could be characterized as every factor or piece of information that gives reasons to believe in a given proposition. Although the way in which different legal systems characterize evidence vary from place to place, it is possible to identify some common general features on the subject. For our purposes, it is sufficient to identify some features regarding evidence that, if not necessary, at least are typical or persistent in contemporary western legal systems.[2]

We will define those features of legal evidence by using what we call a "deflationist doxastic framework", which applies notions and definitions belonging to the epistemological framework of rational belief to legal evidential assessment. By using the "rational belief talk", we will be able to characterize unambiguously the relevant notion of evidence used in legal systems. This is an approach that distinguishes between a human and a legal cognisant. As will become clear when defining the "legal cognisant", we are not taking sides at any level in the discussion on whether the legal evidential norms have to be interpreted in an objective or subjective way.[3]

Our main goal, in this sense, is to give the best possible rationalization of the practice assuming the terms in which the practice presents itself. Seeking the best rationalization of that practice (according to its proper terms) does not exclude the possibility of empirical research showing that what the practice says about itself is false. We are only seeking the best theoretical explanation of a practice that claims to function in a certain way. We are not assuming that the practice is in fact as it claims to be.

[2] More general accounts of conceptual analysis based in typical, frequent, statiscal features in Margolis and Laurence 1999. About the prospects of conceptual analysis based in "tipical", "prototipical" or "frequent" properties in legal analysis, see Schauer (2015).

[3] That other discussion intends to answer questions like the following: "How are we to interpret the standard of proof norm that says that the defendant is to be found guilty if there is evidence that he is beyond reasonable doubt?". Are we going to appeal to the subjective states of mind of jurors (and their subjective evaluation of evidence)? Or, instead, we must appeal to objective relations between facts? Although the second answer seems to be the right one, it is hard to explain from its perspective how are human jurors and judges going to be able to comply with them ever. See Laudan (2006, ch. 2 & 4) and Goldman and Goldman (2009) for more details on the problem.

2.1 *Human Cognisants, Intellectual Goals and Evidential Assess*

2.1.1 Defining Evidence and Relevance

A human cognisant (HC) is a real person trying to think properly in the sense of forming an adequate view of how things are. A more precise way of saying this is that she intends to form beliefs in accordance with intellectual constraints, related to our epistemic goals: those of having true beliefs and avoiding false ones.[4] At least initially, we can say that her beliefs are going to be adequate, rational or justified as long as they comply with the epistemic principles associated with those two fundamental intellectual commitments and inadequate when they fail to do so. A simple way of explaining further this idea is by appealing to the notion of a doxastic system. A doxastic system (DS) can be seen as the complete system of beliefs of a given person at a given time. At least from her perspective, DS constitutes a global view of how things are, and we might say that when HC intends to comply with her intellectual constraints, she is trying to have the most comprehensive, coherent, and adequate DS as possible.

Suppose John believes the proposition that it is raining, and his belief is based in the fact that he saw his neighbour with a soaking wet umbrella. We would intuitively say that his belief that is raining is adequate since he has good evidence for believing in it. In this sense, what he saw counts as "evidence" of the proposition in question. Notice that, strictly speaking, what functions as "evidence" of the belief that it is about to rain is another belief. It is his belief about what he saw what is relevant as evidence for his belief that it is about to rain. Had he not seen his neighbour, *he wouldn't have evidence* for believing that it is raining. So according to the broad notion of evidence given earlier, as factors that give reasons to believe, there might *be* evidence for believing that it is raining, but if the subject does not have that evidence, then his belief is not adequate. Thus, we can define a narrow notion of evidence, according to which evidence is constituted by *beliefs* that give reasons for believing. Since, from the perspective of a given person, everything she considers to be a fact is therefore believed by her and vice versa, we can see that the narrow definition of evidence is the broad definition of evidence considered from the subject's internal perspective. To say that HC's beliefs are going to be adequate when *she has*

---

[4] William James (1897) was one among the pioneers who noticed that we must not confuse the intellectual commandment to search for the truth with that of avoiding error. Both things are equally important and one does not replace the other. If we should only care about truth, then one easy way of complying with this commitment would be to believe everything we can. In that case, we would be believing lots of truths (and lots of falsities as well, but since we would care only about truth then that would not be a problem for us). On the other hand, if we should care only about the avoidance of error, then the best way of complying with this idea would be to believe nothing at all. That certainly guarantees our success in the avoidance of error. Our epistemic obligations reject credulity as well as skepticism. So we need to be guided by both the need for truth and the avoidance of error. The famous "Truth *and nothing but* the truth" is just another way of putting this last thought.

evidence supporting them, is, therefore, an internalist account of human rationality.[5] So, from now on, we must take expressions as "a belief that p", "a proposition that p", "p", and so forth, as synonymous unless explicitly stated.

In an important sense, thus, "evidence" constitutes a subset of DS related to a certain proposition in terms of relevance and probability.[6] Suppose E stands for an evidential subset related in that way to a proposition p. A basic characterization would be the following

> *E is relevant to p iff the conditional probability of p given E is different from the probability of p.*[7]

This means that E makes p more or less probable: E has to do with the truth or falsity of p. We can use this notion to evaluate the adequacy of beliefs in terms of how well they fit with someone's evidence, taken as relevant beliefs. But first, notice that there are many subsets of beliefs belonging to DS that are going to be relevant to a proposition p in the specified sense. Since the kind of support we can hope to find for empirical beliefs is a non-deductive one, then it is expected that the addition (or subtraction) of a belief to a given evidential subset of DS could radically change the support the belief receives from it. John's belief that it is raining would receive support from his belief that he just saw the neighbour with a soaking wet umbrella, if he also didn't believe that the neighbour is rehearsing for an audition of *Singing in the Rain* in his backyard. For this reason, we need to find the "biggest" subset of DS relevant for p, so that we don't exclude important evidence in relation to p's truth value. Let's call that subset "Doxastic evidential system" (DEs).

In this sense "evidence" is the DEs for stating the (probable) truth or falsity of a certain belief, like when we say "our evidence shows that p is (probably) false". On the other hand, "to have evidence for p" means that our evidence shows that p is (probably) true, like when we say "we have evidence for p".

Given a subject S and a proposition p, we evaluate two different things depending on whether S already believes that p or not. If she already believes that p, then we can evaluate the belief's adequacy or rationality by considering whether her evidence – her DEs- supports her belief that p sufficiently (i.e. whether she has evidence for believing p). If she does not yet have the belief, then we can see if she

[5] An externalist position would claim, instead, that a person's belief is rational when there is evidence supporting it, even if she does not have access to it. Just as in the case of the correct interpretation of legal evidential norms, we are not embracing here an internalist view of human rationality. We choose to define it from the internalist perspective because we believe that this characterization is the best approach for defining evidential assess in the legal realm. But see footnote 9.

[6] Putting things in terms of probabilities simplifies the way of communicating some intuitive ideas about the level of support one proposition gets from another, relevance, and so forth. Thus, we are not thereby defending any positive bayesian theory of rationality or rational belief. Everything we say can be translated into a qualitative language (see Chisholm 1976 for an example of how this can be achieved by means of the relational notion of "more reasonable than").

[7] This is the more common way of defining relevance. See Laudan (2006, *supra* note 2, at 17) for a definition in this vein and Goldman and Goldman (2009, 61) for an alternative (and more complex one). For simplicity, we have chosen the common way.

would be rational or justified in *coming to believe that p* by considering whether the same relation of support obtains. Conversely, believing or coming to believe in p is not adequate when evidence does not support it sufficiently.[8]

2.1.2 Rationality and Truth

We have been equating adequate thinking with epistemic rationality and justification. That is, with the relation between beliefs. If we define this last phenomenon in terms of norms that emerge when considering the two epistemic goals of believing truth and avoiding error, then we can see why a rational belief is going to be adequate in the sense of being supported by evidence. A general principle for epistemic rationality would be something like this: *If you want to get the truth and avoid error, believe in accordance with your evidence*. We will use the notion of adequacy, justification and rationality indistinctively unless explicitly stated.

An important thing to notice is that epistemic rationality, although concerned with truth and error, does not *guarantee* the truth of the belief. Beliefs can be adequate and still be false, since most of our beliefs can only be supported non-deductively.

However, the fundamental concern epistemologists have regarding the relation between rationality and truth does not have to do with the last remark. Instead, it starts with the following question: If the rationality of a belief is going to be stated in terms of the support it receives from other beliefs she already has, what guarantees that those beliefs have the proper epistemic support? This question is still quite local, because we are questioning the epistemic credentials for a subset of DS that constitutes the DEs for a certain belief p.

Suppose then that we try to modify our definition of rationality in this direction. Maybe a belief is rational when it is supported by evidence that is *itself* sufficiently supported. But we can see how the originally local question escalates immediately to the totality of our beliefs as long as we assume (plausibly) that they all share (at least indirectly) some evidential relation of support. It seems that in order to comply with our epistemic goals, we need to show that our complete system is pointing somehow to truth, and this is something that internal support between sets of beliefs cannot by itself guarantee. This problem has two main and well known solutions, and both stress the structure of support within DS.

Fundationalism states that justification is asymmetrical in the sense that if p supports q then we cannot use q as a support for p. This means that if we want to see the structure of a system of well-supported beliefs, then what we see is a pyramidal structure. A belief p is justified by other beliefs r, s, t,…, each one of which get their justification from yet other beliefs, and so forth. What becomes clear now is that

[8] In qualitative characterizations of epistemic rationality the notion of sufficiency is not usually explained further. In terms of probabilities there are no more precisions except for the thought that sufficient is a value sensibly higher than 0.5 but not necessarily as high as 0.9 or more. But see Christensen (2004).

from this perspective, if the belief is going to have more than a conditional justification (something like: *if* the beliefs that support it are supported as well, *then* it would be really justified), the pyramid must have a base. A base constituted by beliefs that can give support to other beliefs but do not get their epistemic import from yet other beliefs. These are called *basic* beliefs, and one account traced to our common sense view is that basic beliefs are those obtained by our basic sources of beliefs, such as perception, memory, reason, introspection, and so forth. Since these sources are taken to be mostly reliable, then the person who ultimately bases her beliefs (with sufficient support) in them is going to have beliefs that globally point to truth.[9]

Coherentists criticise the fundationalist structural approach. They state that justification is not an asymmetrical relation between propositions, but a matter of *coherence* between sets of propositions. Justification is not a property or a status that a belief can pass to another, but a property of sets of beliefs that is directly proportional to the internal coherence of that set. In this sense, there can be co-supporting clusters of beliefs that are not completely independent from each other. No belief, thus, has intrinsic epistemic value, not even those perceptual, memorial, etc. beliefs that fundationalists take as basic.[10]

Besides the question of which position is correct from the normative point of view, it seems that, as a matter of fact, we do take some beliefs as basic. At least in the sense that we do not ask for further support in order to consider ourselves as properly having them. The central issue then, which returns later in this paper, is the following: evaluating the epistemic status of a belief either involves taking a look at the beliefs in which it is sustained, or, if it is not actually sustained by other beliefs, asking about how the belief was originated in the first place.

[9] This characterization of justification and rationality is, after all, not completely internalist, since the consideration of the reliability of basic sources is something that the subject does not need to use as a support for the beliefs obtained by them. As we have already said, we are not assuming at any point of the paper that this is the correct account. We are, nevertheless, convinced that completely externalist accounts of human rationality (accounts that claimed that a person can be rational by believing something to be true in spite of the overwhelming evidence she *has* against it, just because *there is* a much bigger set of overwhelming evidence in favor of it she happens not to be aware of), are not only false, but most importantly, inadequate for modeling legal reasoning (one of the most basic principles of legal justice is that a jury that declares someone guilty in spite of the overwhelming evidence favoring innocence is never correct, adequate or rational).

[10] Things are not so simple, since we do not need to be committed with the thesis that basic beliefs have intrinsic epistemic value for defending that the structure of justification is foundational in the sense that we can legitimately take some beliefs to be basic. Wittgenstein (1972) seems to defend the latter thesis but certainly not the former.

2.2 *Legal Cognisants, Legal Goals and Evidential Assess*

2.2.1 The Relation Between Human and Legal Cognisants

We can now define some features of legal reasoning inside a courtroom by drawing a parallel picture considering a hypothetical subject that we call the legal cognisant (LC). The first difference we can draw between HC and LC is that, while the former is taken as a natural person, the latter is not. It is a *legal* person, in the sense that LC is associated with a particular institutional position regulated by norms of a certain kind.

It is important to keep in mind that whilst LC cannot be *identified* with a specific HC (for it has a different ontological status), it needs to be in certain specific relations with specific HCs (the judge or the group of jurors) in order to properly function. For the sake of simplicity, we will consider the legal subject of *the judge* as the LC under study, and leave apart the more complex entity of *the jury*. From now on, whenever we talk about "the judge" we will be referring to the human counterpart of the LC. We can say that a LC's epistemic life is centred on "making its mind" about a specific matter: the grade of culpability of the defendant. Again for simplicity, let's pretend that the only proposition a LC is interested in, is the proposition "The defendant is guilty". Let's call that proposition "g".[11] We claim, then, that a LC needs to consider whether it has to believe g or not, based on the support g gets from its DEs. If it turns out that it is rational for LC to believe that g, then the judge is ipso facto justified in giving the verdict "The defendant is guilty".

But how are we going to determine the "epistemic life" of a LC? This question calls for a detailed clarification of the relation between the LC's beliefs, estimations of absolute and relative probabilities, and the like, with the judge's ones. We cannot give here such a detailed picture, but we can mention a few clarifications. One thing that is certainly *not* a problem is the question of what sort of things are the LC's beliefs from an ontological point of view (i.e. if they are dispositions, abilities, and so on). We need to remind ourselves, at this point, that talking in terms of beliefs is just a way of simplifying comparisons between the epistemic norms that epistemology studies and the evidential norms belonging to the legal realm. Whenever we say "LC believes that p" there is an alternative reading in terms of a common way of talking in legal context, which usually adopts expressions like "In the context of the trial, p has to be taken as a fact by whoever is legitimately deciding whether q". Another consideration we are explicitly leaving apart is, as we have said, the question of the objective-subjective status of the relevant norms, and because of that, we don't need to tackle here the crucial question of the estimation of probabilities. Once again, the issue at stake here is that of what counts as a fact from the perspective of the decision-maker *qua* LC.[12] In this sense, we claim that LC's doxastic

[11] This is a simplification because juries have to find out the truth of many related propositions (the defendant committed or not the crime, if she did, the circumstances were such and such, she is guilty of this felony but not of this other one, and so forth).

[12] See, again, footnote 9.

system (DS) is not to be equated with the judge's own DS. Although we need to establish a relation between the judge's beliefs and the beliefs of the corresponding LC, it is *not* the case that *if* the judge beliefs that p *then* ipso facto the LC beliefs that p. The judge can believe many things that are not relevant for determining g's truth (for example, her belief that she had eggs for breakfast). Other things that belong to the judge's DS should not be taken into account because some rules forbid it (for example, when the defendant confesses in violation of her rights). And just because of that, it is also not the case that *if* LC believes that p, *then* the judge believes it too. The problem is illustrated thus by asking what exactly is implied when a person (judge) believes that p is false, but as a LC states that p is true.

There are many ways in which specialized literature has dealt with the question regarding the status of LC's beliefs *qua* LC. There are at least two main proposals. According to the first one, the judge has to exclude some of her own beliefs at trial, and has to proceed *as if* some propositions validly proved were true. The second one suggests that the judge *is* LC, and has to *accept* that proposition validly proved. Both proposals could be (and usually are) summarized saying that the proposition based in legal evidence *should be taken as true*. These proposals are unsatisfactory. The statement "as if it were true" is suggestive, but equivocal. In its turn, it is far from clear what "to accept a proposition known to be false" would amount to. This leads to deep philosophical questions regarding the notion of acceptance, and if it does makes sense to "accept/not accept" a proposition, let alone the question regarding if it makes sense at all to state that someone *should* (is obliged) to accept a proposition. "Should be taken" seems to mean in this context that there is an authorization to use certain statements as a premise in her reasoning. What is implied is that there is a norm that authorizes the LC to act according to certain states of affairs verified in the trial. LC is authorized to use a norm if some states of affairs are verified in the process. This, far from denying the idea of truth and true belief, presupposes it.[13] "Should be taken as true" (and equivalents) is an eliptical way to claim that LC is authorized to use some rule when its conditions of application are verified in the process. It is not necessary at all to "accept" as LC the proposition known to be false.

2.2.2 Legal Evidence and Relevance

We have said that we can see a LC as trying to "figure out" whether its DEs supports g or not, in a certain time t. Time t is, of course, the moment when the judge deliberates just before she announces the verdict. This is, *after* the trial, when there is no possibility of adding new beliefs to DS. But how are we going to define DS and DEs in the case of a LC? We will stipulate that DS is the limited set of beliefs that can be traced to the information obtained during the trial, and DEs is a smaller subset of

[13] If the LC does not use the norm she is obliged to use, LC has decided beyond the boundaries of her competence. And she is obliged to use it only when certain states of affairs have been verified in the process.

relevant beliefs for g.[14] It is important to notice that this stipulation is innocent, since the real problem rests, of course, in defining an adequate notion of relevance.

There are several differences between a HC and a LC regarding evidence and evidential procedures. In the legal realm, the search and evaluation of evidence is much more limited and restricted, and, as we will see, the conditions for becoming a "belief" of the LC (this is, a part of its DS) are much stricter than in the case of HC. This difference includes at least two considerations: procedural and evidential.

Procedural Considerations In opposition to a HC, a LC has a limited time for "making up its mind" about the specific question of investigation, and the investigation itself is limited through specific time-rules. Once reached a point, the accumulation of evidence is normative closed by a legal authority. A limitless investigation is forbidden from the beginning.[15] A HC does not have this sort of normatively pre-established limitations (although she certainly has empirical limitations and practical reasons for not spending an indefinite amount of time making up her mind about a subject matter). Secondly, given that legal procedures deal with individual cases, experimentation becomes either conceptually impossible or irrelevant. It is not always possible to play the world over several times, setting aside the fact that it is conceptually impossible to reproduce an individual case. Although during the trial new evidence can come along, it cannot be gained from experimentation. More importantly, experimentation is normally prohibited because it could violate several rights of the alleged victim or defendant, among them her/his dignity. This leads us to a different question.

Evidential Considerations Many legal systems restrict the investigation through a complex set of rules that regulate admission, evaluation and elimination of evidence. No matter its hypothetical relevance to the establishment of the truth, if obtaining evidence infringes rights or rules that regulate the proper functioning of the administration, it must be rejected, not evaluated, eliminated from the process. In criminal procedures and constitutions this rules are usually related with what the

---

[14] One might wonder whether the chosen definition of DS makes room for a real distinction between DS and DEs. Is it not true that things that should be taken as true for the purposes of the trial (i.e. LC's beliefs) are all relevant for determining g? Well, it is certainly true that the majority of DS will also be in DEs. But the distinction between both sets is still existent. First, because there are things that happen during the trial that do not seem to be prima facie relevant for establishing g (for example, a witness asserts that she likes the color blue), and still could be taken as true without violating any legal evidential principles. Second, because during the process things that do not seem at first to be relevant then turn to be so. If we wanted to explain the way LC's beliefs change during the trial (a different concern than ours right now) then we would need to appeal to the difference between DS and DEs.

[15] Even more, the (excessive) time extension of a given process, though within the boundaries of legal term, far from being a virtue, is considered a vice. Rules of USA (FRE) and UK allow to deduce some Principles (sometimes explicit ones) regarding "*simplicity and...elimination of unjustifiable expense and delay, and* [enforcing…] *speedy determination*". Twining, Schum, Anderson, Chapter 3.

doctrine labels as "exclusionary rules". That is, rules that oblige not to take into account some evidence in favour of a given proposition. In this sense, legal systems of the kind we are considering are in some way related to procedural imperfect justice. They distribute, adjudicate, recognize burdens, benefits, rights and duties in certain manner. Some criteria of distribution/adjudication/recognition are not always satisfied, because it is impossible or undesirable according to the legal system itself.

How are we going to define relevance in light of these considerations?

We have seen that during the trial, many pieces of information considered to be relevant for the truth of g can be left out of the relevance set DEs if they don't comply with certain norms that govern the evidential practice within the trial (the so called "exclusionary rules"). This would imply that, unlike HC, LC has other goals other than obtaining truth and avoiding error. Those goals would explain the validity of the non-epistemic norms that govern the evidential practice.

Laudan (2006) relates these norms with two kinds of non-epistemic goals.[16] First, *error distribution*, which states that, given that the decision makers are not infallible, when mistakes are made, it is better to acquit guilty defendants than to convict innocent ones. Second, *nonepistemic policy values*, which are practical (they have to do with the efficient use of resources) and moral in spirit (for instance, protecting the rights of defendants and witnesses). His position is that criminal justice systems are flawed in the sense that non-epistemic values vitiate the system's search for "truth and nothing but the truth".

We believe that whether he has a point or not depends on how we evaluate the notion of relevance and rationality. Such a system (which excludes some true propositions) is irrational only by assuming that "rational" necessarily means acting according to truth. We have to leave aside Laudan's criticism because the question regarding if and in what sense a legal system is irrational cannot be tackled here. For this reason, we are going to interpret the non-epistemic legal procedures as determining what should or should not be part of DS, and thus, they determine what is part of DEs only in a derivative way. In other words, it *cannot* be the case that if p is part of DS and has to do with g's truth or falsity, then it is not part of DEs. The resulting definition of relevance is, as stated for HCs, a pure epistemic one[17]:

---

[16] Actually, Laudan takes distribution of error as an epistemic goal. We believe that this is a mistake, since our aversion for convicting innocent people is not (obviously) an epistemic trace.

[17] We believe, however, that an answer to Laudan's criticism can be given in the following vein. His view would be that certain relevant propositions that belong to DS cannot belong to DEs given the non-epistemic legal goals, and this would be indeed a very flawed way of proceeding. We believe that this view is unnecessarily severe, since there is an alternative way of interpreting the practice. We can think that when some piece of information obtained during trial violates the non-epistemic norms, it is suppressed not only from DEs but also from LC's DS. This would restate the notion of relevance as one that is only concerned with the truth or falsity of a proposition. Of course, this only changes the perspective. Non-epistemic values are still governing the evidence in the sense that what a LC believes or stops believing depends (partially) on not epistemic matters. But is this so different from what a HC does? Isn't it the case that sometimes we prevent ourselves from forming beliefs because of its moral status, even if somehow we would be epistemically

E is relevant to p iff the conditional probability of p given E is different from the probability of p.

Finally, regarding any proposition, we can see that while for HCs there are three possible propositional attitudes, this is different for the case of LCs. A HC can believe that p, disbelieve that p (this is, believe that not-p) and suspend judgment whether p or not p (because evidence is not enough to believe or disbelieve it). A LC must always make up its mind on whether g. It must, at the end of the trial, be in a position to claim that the defendant is guilty, or that she is not. For this reason, while in order to disbelieve p a HC would need positive support for not p (DEs should support p sufficiently), in order to disbelieve g a LC needs something weaker. It needs that there be *insufficient* evidence supporting g. If DEs supports g insufficiently, then LC has to state that not-g. Given the legal non-epistemic goal of *error distribution*, its standard of sufficiency – i.e. the standard of proof- will be very high.

Our last consideration has to do with the structure of the relation of support exhibited in the legal practice. Are there basic beliefs, just as it seems to be the case with HCs? At first sight, we might think that there are not, since LCs do not have basic sources of beliefs such as perception, memory, reason and such. But this is wrong, since the faculties of the judge play a role in how the LC obtains its beliefs.[18] If the judge hears the defendant say that she killed the victim, and she thinks that that should be taken as true for the purposes of the trial, then LC believes that the defendant said that she killed the victim. Just as perceptual beliefs are taken to have an epistemic weight in the case of HCs, so it seems to be the case for LCs. There are also other sources that seem to be basic, such as DNA tests and in general other sort of lab results, and expert testimony.[19]

So far then we have explored what seems to be involved in the notion of evidence in terms of relevance and probability, the differences and similarities between HC

"rational" in forming it? Sometimes, we prevent ourselves from believing because of a general perspective of what kind of a person we want to be, and this is not so different from the non-epistemic values defined by Laudan. Of course, it can be said, whether or not we act intentionally neglecting certain facts is a factual question which does not exclude that in those cases we are irrational. The answer seems plausible, but only at first glance. Take the case of experimentation in natural sciences. Natural sciences are, allegedly, the paradigmatic case of searching for the truth. One important value encourage in that activity is neutrality. In order to seek neutrality about experiments and results, it is necessary to improve impartiality. But if impartiality is a necessary condition to neutrality, and impartiality implies not taking into account some facts, it follows that there is no way to honor your "objective" and "neutral" task without setting aside certain beliefs and states of affairs (about your past beliefs, preconceptions on the matter, preferences, tastes, desired results, and so on). This is close to admit that in order to honor impartiality and neutrality some beliefs of your doxastic system must be set aside in order to fulfill the scientific task properly.

[18] This is the fact that compromises the unqualified objectivist reading of legal evidential norms: even though evidence should *really* support g beyond doubt, the cognitive faculties that will evaluate evidence and the support it gives to g are those belonging to the real people involved in the process (judge or jurors). This is a fact of the legal practice that cannot be ignored in an appropriate explanation of how evidential norms have real impact and thus can be obeyed.

[19] Although see Amaya (2013) for a defence of coherentism in this issue.

and LC, and the main differences regarding time, experimentation and exclusionary rules.

What we intend to explore deeper in the next sections is the epistemic status of testimony in the legal practice, and how these considerations impact on this broad characterization of the structure of justification we just have sketched. We hope, though, that the framework we have just sketched will prove to be helpful for studying other evidential aspects of the legal practice. In the following section, we will give more precise characteristics of testimony within the legal domain.

3 Two Senses of Testimony and Some Specific Features of Legal Testimony

3.1 Two Senses of Testimony

In every day language we refer to various phenomena that resemble the so-called legal testimony, but we do not use the word "testimony" for them. What is common between legal testimony and those other phenomena is that they both seem to refer to cases in which we assume to have acquired information, belief or knowledge because someone says so. When something out of the Courts resembles legal testimony (for example, some story we heard about) we don't actually use expressions like "I've heard a testimony". We simply refer to that phenomenon as "I've heard that" "John told me that" and the like. There are several discussions surrounding the proper way to define that phenomenon. Whether we call it testimony or not, acquiring information, belief or knowledge through the words of others in every day language has its own points of disagreement. The philosophical literature dedicates a huge amount of considerations to capture the phenomenon related to believing or knowing something through the words of others. In general those considerations are tackled under the label of "testimony from the philosophical point of view" (also "non formal testimony"). Although there is some sort of agreement about the core case (someone with words allows another one to gain information), there is no unanimity about its further elements. It is under dispute whether information given by the speaker without the proper intention may qualify as a proper testimony. For example, I hear you by chance thinking in a loud voice about your plans for tomorrow (*I will travel to Bologna*). Although you do not intend it, I have acquired instantly a piece of information. This is in some way different to the case in which you talk or write to me making me know your plans (*tomorrow I will travel to Bologna*). Both cases imply reference about your plans, just one of them implies intention to transmit information.

Suppose further that when you express your plans or something else your voice sounds weird, probably because of a flu. Although you do not intend it, I have acquired another piece of information (probably about your health). Words point to one state of affairs, your voice expresses another. What is involved in a case like this is in some way different to the case in which you say or write to me *I have a flu.* Of course, nothing prevents you to convey the information that you are ill, with an ill-like voice.

In order to assess the concept of testimony, many theoretical conceptions disagree about the proper weight of these and other variables. Is it meaningful to talk about testimony when the speaker fails to have intention to convey information? (Is a diary a piece of testimony?) What is exactly transmitted through testimony? Information, knowledge, both, none? Is the speaker assuming a kind of responsibility or commitment? Complex discussions depend on these and other variables.[20] We tackle some of these discussions in Sect. 4. For the moment, it is sufficient for our purposes to assume a broad characterization.

It is easy to verify that in everyday language the phenomenon related with testimony that interests philosophy has, at least, the following, characteristics. First, it conveys information through verbal language or other speech act (gestures). Second, the speech act is intentional (although not necessary with the intention to convey information). Third, the hearer can acquire some new piece of evidence or confirm one she already has. Under this characterization, expressions like "I've heard that…", "somebody told me", "I heard exactly the same thing", indicates the existence of a testimony in the relevant sense. In specialized literature, there are different labels referring to these kinds of phenomena ("natural testimony", "ordinary testimony", and so on). For the moment, we will use "non-institutional testimony" (NIT) for every phenomenon satisfying only the three characteristics specified above.[21]

In opposition to NIT, "testimony" also refers to a much regulated speech act within normative institutions. We will focus in testimony in contemporary legal systems and use the label "Legal Testimony" (LT) to refer to it. Naturally, testimony in contemporary legal systems relates to the general subject of evidence.

3.2 Some Peculiarities of Legal Testimony

Legal testimony (LT) has always been considered the most common and frequent means of proof. At the same time is one that requires more attention and generates a considerable amount of suspicion. After all, history has long demonstrated how deceitful human beings can be with words.

[20] See Lackey (2008, 33).

[21] The label "natural testimony" like "natural language", although widespread, is misleading. Either "natural" indicates a particular philosophical perspective (related with the so called post-quinean "Naturalism", a perspective that is not assumed by every theorist), or it does not. If it is the first case sounds like question begging for non-Naturalists theorists in language, mind and action. If it is the second case, "natural" together with "language" sounds awkward. Language, at least the language that is here at stake, is a human artifact, and artifacts are in an intuitive sense non-natural. "Natural" in this context, either begs the question, or introduces a counterintuitive label.

There is a long tradition studying the ways in which a witness can be deceitful. Experiments and experience have shown how bias, prejudice, memory, and sense distortions could interfere with the possibility of getting things right.[22] Jurisprudence and theory have developed well known criteria to assess if a testimony or other piece of evidence has relevance, credibility and probative weight. Instead of concentrating on those criteria we will focus on some conceptual assumptions implicated when testimony is at stake. Our main concerns are single testimony, technical or expert testimony, and direct (eye) witness in criminal process.

The relevance of single testimony in legal process has become increasingly important in recent years. There is some sort of social and institutional concern regarding cases in which the available evidence amounts to one and only one witness (this is, DEs is constituted only by propositions related to the sayings of a single witness).[23] In this respect, both in common and civil law traditions it is possible to find at least two conceptions: the numerical and the qualitative.[24] Needless to say, it is difficult to find them pure in practice.

Under the (pure) numerical conception, more witnesses referring to a proposition p increase proportionally the probability of p. At the same time, if for a proposition p there is just one single testimony, then that testimony has an impact of zero on the probability of p. The idea according to which a single witness has no value at all in order to prove a proposition has a long tradition traceable to the roots of our culture (for example, the Bible, Deuteronomy 19:15). Well known is also the Roman law standard according to which *Testimonium unius non valet* or *unus testis nullus testis.*

Under the (pure) qualitative system, the epistemological weight of testimony depends on its merits regarding creditworthiness, truthfulness, accuracy, and so on. One qualitative test often used in assessing the creditworthiness of a testimony is (among others) its coherence. Whatever the merits of the qualitative conception, it can be used to dismiss the strict criterion attached to the numerical conception. Thus, a single testimony could be sufficient to prove the truth of a proposition (or so the argument goes).

The case of expert testimony is partly connected with the previous topic. Actually, expert testimony regarding, for example, the condition of a victim or a witness as "reliable" is often seen as necessary to evaluate the quality of testimony when the latter is the only piece of evidence available at trial.

Although connected with the question of single testimony, expert testimony has also an independent nature. Contrary to lay testimony, expert or technical testimony can be characterized as the one in which the speaker has specialized knowledge relevant to the matter of interest. Her knowledge purportedly helps to understand or make sense of other evidence. In order to differentiate it in a relevant sense from the

[22] For those sympathetic with naturalism, experimentation and any kind of experiment opposite to "thought experiments" it is interesting to revisit Gorphe (1927).

[23] Paradigmatic in this regard the social and institutional attention towards domestic violence and sexual abuse.

[24] We borrow the terminology from Wigmore (1901) adding some specifications of our own.

other kinds of testimony (e.g. "eye witness") we need to add a further feature. In the expert testimony in question the speaker is someone who has *generic* knowledge about the kind of facts under investigation, but no direct knowledge about the individual case in question. She was subpoenaed because she can illuminate us, for example, about the generic causes of an explosion, or the behaviour of certain chemical elements, but not about who set the fire or caused the specific explosion at trial. Every jurist accepts that in nowadays common cases under trial, like those regarding environmental pollution, money laundry, or epidemiology, it is almost impossible to decide without this kind of assistance.[25]

The third case we are interested in is the case of the so called "eye witness". It counts as such witness everyone who actually saw or perceived some act, occurrence, or thing and can give a first-hand account of it. It is often assumed that the eye witness has some priority over other kinds of witnesses who actually did not see or perceived the fact in question. Moreover, there are systems that state (defeasible) rules regarding the necessity that the witness has some personal knowledge on the matter under investigation.[26] Hearsay, rumour and second hand information (*X told me that p*) has lower value than "personal" or "first-hand" perceptions.

The idea according to which, in normal circumstances, eye witness has some epistemological priority over second hand witnesses has also a long tradition, based on the well known Roman distinction between testimony given by *propiis sensibus* vs. *ex audito alieno*. Its primacy has to do with the idea that only someone who knows something in certain way can transmit knowledge. Whatever the "eye" witness had, he or she had a privileged access to some facts and only someone who has knowledge can give rise to knowledge on another person.

It is more or less simple to identify some assumptions surrounding the question of single, expert and eye witness.

Those defending the numerical conception, coupled with the idea that one testimony is never sufficient *(unus testis nullus testis),* assume that testimony alone and for its own sake is not a reliable source of indefeasible knowledge. In terms of the LC defined in the previous section, LC is not justified in believing that p (p cannot be part of DS) merely on the basis of a speaker's testimony that p.

In the case of expert testimony, it is assumed that its importance lies in the ability and capacity of the knower to illuminate some aspects of reality not accessible for lay man (including jurors or judges). This seems to have as grounding reason the idea that we gain information because others have qualifications we can rely on. More important, that we can gain knowledge even if we cannot by ourselves alone test whether the proposition in question is true or not.

Finally, underlying the primacy of direct or eye-witness over other kinds of testimony is the basic idea that only someone who has some privileged knowledge can transmit it.

---

[25] Paradigmatic in this regard the Daubert case, concerning epidemiology. An exhaustive analysis of questions raised by expert testimony since Daubert, in Jurs (2012).

[26] See, FRE, Rule 602.

We are interested in showing what are the epistemological and pragmatic consequences involved in such assumptions and in which sense all these platitudes and assumptions can be hold together. In order to demonstrate a possible case in which holding them together is incoherent, we have to move forward to considerations stemming from philosophy and epistemology of testimony.

4 Three Debates from the Epistemology of Testimony

It is time to introduce some philosophical insights regarding testimony. As we will see in the next section, they will help to assess the prospects of the platitudes identified above.

Non-institutional testimony (NIT), as defined broadly in the last section is evaluated epistemologically in its different aspects. We will consider three interrelated debates that give place to three different epistemological dimensions. These dimensions will prove useful for the epistemological evaluation of legal testimonial practices.

4.1 Reductionists and Anti-reductionists

The first and most important debate begins by asking if testimony is as a source of justified belief. As we have seen, evaluating the epistemic status of a belief involves taking a look at the beliefs in which it is sustained, or, if it is not actually sustained by other beliefs, asking about how the belief was originated in the first place. If Susan believes that her neighbour is killing his cat Tom because she hears Tom's meow and she has a severe obsession that leads her to thinking that massive assassination of cats is some imminent event, then Susan's belief lacks epistemic credentials because at least one of the beliefs that support it can be traced to a mental pathology. On the other hand, if she believes just that because she is seeing with her own eyes that the neighbour is killing the cat, then the belief has the correct epistemic credentials because it can be traced to perception, which we take to be a reliable source of beliefs. Perception is taken to be not only a reliable source of beliefs (i.e. a source of knowledge or justified beliefs), but also a *basic* one. Thermometers are a reliable source of beliefs in the sense that they are reliable indicators of temperature and thus beliefs obtained by looking at thermometers usually have good epistemic credentials. Still, thermometers are not a *basic* source, because beliefs obtained by looking at them do not stand by themselves as justified: we need to know, for instance, that thermometers are usually reliable. We ask for the subject, in order to have a justified belief that the temperature measured by the thermometer is 97°, that she has some additional beliefs about thermometers that would give support to her belief. Thus, beliefs obtained by means of looking at thermometers are not taken to be basic.

Beliefs obtained by means of perception, memory, reasoning, introspection, and so forth are, on the other hand, taken to be prima facie justified just because of their origin.[27]

But what does it mean to say that beliefs obtained by means of basic sources are *prima facie* justified? It means that, *unless* we have positive reasons for doubting them in a specific occasion (for instance, John sees an elephant but then remembers that he just took a hallucinating drug), we take their belief products to be justified. To put this last thought in a more technical way, we can define positive reasons for doubting in terms of defeaters:

S has positive reasons for doubting p iff there are undefeated defeaters *for p*

A *defeater* for p is a belief (or a doubt or an experience) that S actually has or should have, that needs to be answered if the acceptance of p is going to be taken as rational or adequate. There are two sorts of defeaters. *Rebutting* defeaters for p indicate that p is false. *Undercutting* defeaters for p indicate that p has been unreliably obtained.[28] Each one of them alone is sufficient for undermining the intended justification. *Undefeated defeaters* are beliefs (or doubts or experiences) that are not themselves undermined as such by yet another belief.

Thus we can explain in these terms why John would not be justified in believing that there is an elephant in the room. The belief has an undercutting undefeated defeater: his belief that he has taken a hallucinatory drug. Although John had prima facie justification for believing it, that justification was undercut by the presence of an undefeated defeater.[29] But in the absence of it, the belief would have been adequate or rational.

The reductionism-anti-reductionism debate focuses on the basic (or not basic) character of testimony as a source of justified belief. It might be helpful to remind at this point that, as a matter of fact, we broadly trust testimony as a source of beliefs in the sense that we usually trust the word of other people, and virtually every piece of substantial knowledge we have is dependent on testimony (think of our knowledge of facts about our personal history such as where and when we were born and things we did as infants, our geographical, physical, medical knowledge, and so forth). Our broad dependence on testimony is a fact about our epistemic lives. The debate takes this for granted, but focuses on the normative question: Are those beliefs adequate? And if so, where do they get their adequacy from?

Reductionists claim that testimony is not a basic source of knowledge, but a *derived* one.[30] This means that if we are going to have justified beliefs based on

[27] This is a normative way of characterizing basic sources of beliefs, according to which a basic source gives origin to *epistemically* basic beliefs (beliefs that do not need further justification in order to stand with good epistemic credentials). See Audi (2003, 6–7) for an alternative *descriptive* characterization.

[28] See Pollock (1986).

[29] The belief that he took a hallucinating drug would be defeated (as a defeater of the belief that there is an elephant in the room) if he also knew that the drug didn't kick in because it only works on females.

[30] See Hume (1978), Adler (1994, 2002), Lipton (1998), Van Cleve (2006).

testimony, then we need to be able to have justification for believing in its reliability, just as we need justification for believing in the reliability of thermometers. In other words, reductionists claim that there is not a testimonial epistemic principle of the form

> *(TEP) If a belief p is obtained from testimony, then it is prima facie rational or justified.*

Rational believers must have some sort of justification for believing in a proposition like *testimony is generally reliable*, which would give appropriate support for our testimonial beliefs. They would need, thus, a derived epistemic principle of the form:

> *(DEP) If a belief p is obtained from testimony, then it is presumptively rational or justified.*

Since, as we have seen, justification cannot continue indefinitely, eventually the propositions that will give support to the general claim about the reliability of testimony must be traced to basic sources of belief such as perception, memory and so forth. In this sense, the epistemic import of testimony is *reduced* to basic epistemic sources.

The motivation for defending reductionism is based on an intuitive difference between perception, memory, reason, introspection, etc., on the one hand, and testimony on the other. For reductionists, only the former are really *our* sources, and the trust we put in them is clearly bigger than the trust we give to the latter. This difference, according to reductionists, is explained by the fact that the former are basic sources of knowledge and the latter is a derived one. In this sense, testimony has a diminished epistemological status (that implies that someone who intends to rely only on testimony will need some further general reasons to take the content of testimony as it stands).

Anti-reductionists claim, on the other hand, that testimony is a basic source of knowledge and justification.[31] This means that, unless there are positive reasons for doubting a belief based on testimony, its acceptance is adequate or rational. So, according to them, there is an epistemic principle such as (TEP), that makes the existence of basic testimonial beliefs possible. There are two main arguments favouring anti-reductionism. First, there seems to be no way of reducing testimony to other sources of belief in a non-circular manner. Recall that reductionists claim that that sort of reduction has to be made by every HC if they are really going to have well supported beliefs. Our dependence on testimony is so ubiquitous, that in order to give support to a general proposition about testimony such as (DEP), we would certainly need to appeal to facts we happen to know at least partially in a testimonial way. So if we really want to make room in our theory of rational thought to the great amount of beliefs based on testimony, then we better conceive it as a

---

[31] See Reid (1993), Coady (1992), Dummett (1994), McDowell (1994), Goldman (1999), Kusch (2002).

basic source of rational belief.[32] The second motivation is based on a criticism of the individualist conception of human knowledge inherited by the Cartesian philosophical framework. According to this view, the only legitimate cognisant is an autonomous one, who takes in only first hand evidence in order to really have knowledge. This approach to knowledge is not only historically contingent but, most importantly, it is mistaken (See Coady 1992, 4 ff.). So whilst reductionists think they are explaining an intuitive a priori distinction between perception and testimony, they are actually reproducing an old-fashioned, out-dated theoretical view.

This leads us to our second distinction.

4.2 Universalists and Egoists

As we have seen, the disagreement between reductionists and non reductionists centres around the epistemological status of testimony. That explains why reductionism claims that unless we have the support of ulterior beliefs formed by means of true basic sources, the information acquired by testimony lacks epistemic import. We are in need of further justification to take the information as it stands (recall the analogy with thermometers). Metaphorically speaking, reductionism and antireductionism disagree about the epistemological credits of testimony and the justification to take what is conveyed by testimony in good faith. Reductionism tends to assume that testimony has a diminished citizenship as a source of beliefs, and that we are not justified to take the information we received from it as it stands in good faith. We need something more to take in good faith the proposition spelled out in testimony and for that purpose testimony alone is not sufficient.

But suppose we can set this issue aside. An important question is already waiting to be answered. Whether one assumes that testimony alone (without positive defeaters) or testimony plus other considerations allows to hold the justified belief that p, it is possible to disagree about the proper credentials and competence that have to be verified in the speaker in order to move from "S asserted that p" to "p" (or the justified belief that p). Assuming that testimony is a (basic or not basic) source of justified belief, the question here is if, and in what sense, we are justified in believing a proposition without information about who is talking and her qualifications on the matter.

---

[32] However, among reductionism there is a distinction between local and global reductionism. And only global reductionism is subject to the first criticism. The distinction hinges on what kind of further considerations are required to take a piece of testimony as part of our beliefs. Local reductionism states that we do not need to show that testimony is reliable *in general*, but instead that we need specific considerations about the particular testifier in order to take her word. While global reductionism claims that we need to show the reliability of testimony as a generic source, local reductionism claims instead that we need to account for the reliability of specific sources (particular testifiers). We will consider Fricker's local reductionism below.

Richard Foley (2004, cap. 4) explores the subject by distinguishing two positions regarding testimony. He presents us with an imaginary situation to illustrate the point:

> A convenient way of fixing upon these issues is to suppose that I have found a partial inventory of what some other person believes. Call this person Anonymous. Although the inventory is extensive, many of Anonymous's beliefs are not listed, and suppose that among the omitted ones are those from which I could extract information about who Anonymous is. As a result, I know little or nothing about his or her background, training, abilities, and circumstances. Moreover, I have no knowledge about Anonymous from any other source. Under these conditions, how, if at all, should I adjust my opinions in the light of Anonymous's opinions? (Foley 2004, 84)

The fact that in the situation we have a direct access to Anonymous's beliefs permits us to isolate the question of the reliability of others from the question of their sincerity. On the other hand, the fact that the other person in question is anonymous allows us to evaluate in a more straightforward way our intuitions about the reliability of others in general, since in everyday cases we usually have additional information about a specific person's epistemic credentials. *Universalism* claims that it is always reasonable to give authority to other people's opinions, so, unless we had rebutting defeaters for Anonymous's beliefs, we would be rationally authorized in trusting them.[33]

Egoism is a more demanding position. It claims that universalism is false, since every instance of testimonially-based belief must be "specialized" in order to be legitimate. This means that we can only grant epistemic authority to testimony when we have personally evaluated the epistemic credentials of the testifier regarding the attested proposition, and we have concluded that they are adequate (they are experts on the subject matter, they are sufficiently intelligent, they do not possess visual, hearing or memorial limitations, and so forth). This position would claim, thus, that we are never in a position to trust Anonymous's beliefs.

Fricker's conception (1994, 1995, 2006), which she calls *local* reductionism, seems to capture the egoist insights. According to her view, we always need positive reasons for having a specific testimonially-based belief. General principles like (TEP and DEP) are "an epistemic charter for the gullible and undiscriminating" (1994, 126). This position focuses, thus, on the particular testifier instead of testimony in general. We need to have at least good reasons for moving from "S asserted that p" to "p", and those reasons will have to do with S's *trustworthiness*. The property of trustworthiness has to do not only with S's competence but also with her sincerity. Fricker states (*contra* Foley) that since assertion is an intentional act, the sort of property someone needs to look for in S in order to be rational in trusting S's opinion must include not only reliability but also sincerity. Otherwise, she argues, we would be unable to distinguish people from barometers (or thermometers, as we

---

[33] Given the imaginary situation, we could not have undercutting defeaters, since we lack any specific knowledge of the circumstances and reliability of Anonymous. Defined in this broad sense, it is compatible with both anti-reductionism and reductionism, as long as global reductionist claims that we can have a justification for believing in the general reliability of testimony. See footnote 32.

have been doing). According to Fricker, we can evaluate how trustworthy a person is regarding a proposition by applying a common sense psychological theory to the person in question, for sincerity and competence are supposed to be both traceable to the person's psychology. The recognition of the intentional character of testimony leads us to the last relevant debate among epistemologists.

4.3 Evidentialist and Interpersonal Views

This last debate focuses on the specific epistemic import of testimony. Previous debates may be understood as discussing whether testimony is more alike to perception than to a thermometer, or vice versa. *Interpersonal views of testimony* (see Lackey 2008, ch. 8) criticize this way of approaching the phenomenon of testimony, since it completely misses the substantial differences between those other sources of beliefs and testimony. Fricker's and many other epistemologists' recognition of the intentionality of assertion in terms of sincerity is not enough, *as long* as we look for *evidence* in favor of the sincerity of the testifier (basing my belief on S's trustworthiness in applying a psychological theory to S is an evidential procedure). They are still dealing with people as they deal with thermometers.

Instead, interpersonal views claim that what confers epistemic value to acquired testimonial beliefs is (at least partially) an interpersonal phenomenon, in the sense that a second-person phenomenon is essential for it to obtain. Moran (2006) and Ross (1986) explain this features in terms of personal assurance. They claim that when a speaker attests that p to a hearer, she is not only transmitting a piece of information, or letting the hearer know that she happens to believe that p. She is also (and fundamentally) *giving her word* to the hearer, putting herself as a guarantor of p, asking the hearer to believe p because he believes *in* her word. This gives the hearer an additional reason to believe, besides the evidence he could get from finding out that she believes that p is the case.

The idea behind these positions is that since the speaker is performing an intentional act (that of attesting p), she assumes voluntarily the responsibility for the truth of p. Reducing the phenomenon of testimony to that of informing another person about one's beliefs is therefore misconceived and misses its specific epistemic import.

5 Legal Testimony from a Philosophical and Conceptual Point View

It is time to return to the assumptions present in legal practice regarding single, expert and eye witness. For the moment we will concentrate on epistemological considerations, leaving remarks on the relation between testimony and legal rules for the next section.

Before using the categories introduced in Sect. 4, let's take a look at some obvious tensions that arise from a legal practice that accepts the common assumptions regarding single, expert and eye witness coupled with the basic distinction "numerical vs. qualitative".

As we saw, there are conceptions that reject the validity of single testimony. If, on epistemological grounds, it is assumed that it is never sufficient to believe p, just by relying on the words of others, we have to reject not only a "single witness" as a piece of evidence, but every phenomenon that instantiated the property of "relying just on the words of others". This, unfortunately, should lead to the rejection of several institutional acts. In effect, the legal process is plenty of statements stemming from officials. Their content, from the substantial point of view, is just the words (written or verbal) of only one person stating that p or q was the case. For example, that the lawyer did not come to the audience, that the case record was submitted to this or that office, and so on. That is, exactly the same phenomenon that draw the attention to "testimony" as a source of belief in philosophy.

Under the basic idea that "the words of one person alone does not give enough elements to belief in proposition p", all those acts should be declared unreliable or not trustworthy. The same "numerical" argument that dismisses, on epistemological grounds, the weight of words in the case of single testimony should reject on the same basis every act of similar kind. Including the well-known police reports regarding the failure to cooperate of a given person, when they are taken (as it usually happens) as sufficient evidence for a proposition. But that it is not certainly what it is assumed in legal process. The legal practice, far from denying for all cases that "one single testimony is sufficient to form a justified belief", presupposes it. That is evident not only in cases that resemble single testimony (like reports, minutes, certificates, court records and other documents) but also in the case of expert legal testimony.

In effect, what would be the justification to admit the content of a deposition made by an expert if not the idea that in some circumstances it is not possible to form justified beliefs without relying on others' words? Whatever the reasons to trust the words of experts, it has to be assumed that in some circumstances it is not only advisable or sensible but also necessary to rely on the words of others. That is, it is impossible to know everything on a personal and direct manner. Confidence in the words of experts does not prove that what we acquire is some kind of justified belief or knowledge. Rather, it shows that we *assume* that is the case.[34]

[34] Some problems arise regarding the scope given to these assumptions in the legal field. Specially in cases regarding "sexual predators" and "domestic violence". Whatever the sense attached to "knowledge", it is clear that an expert could have more knowledge in general about some discipline or range of phenomenon under the scope of her science. But her general knowledge does not guarantee by itself the truth of the proposition spelled in her testimony. Technicians are fallible. There are very good reasons to take her words as conveying truth, but it is not necessarly so. Besides the question of their fallibility, there remains the question of its scope. Experts have more knowledge (if they have it) about some general and abstract things which do not warrant the knowledge of what happened in the case under trial. This is specially compelling (and sometimes intriguing) in matters regarding the capacity, tendency, and the like of a certain object or person to

Armed with this last remark about expert testimony some could think that the "qualitative" conception of testimony has more plausibility. The epistemological ground for rejecting the value of a single witness in certain cases would be its quality and not its "single" status. The answer, however, is not so simple.

A closer look to some of the statements regarding the *sufficiency* of single testimony seems not to take seriously the extreme case. This would be the case where the only available evidence at trial is just one witness. In terms of our deflationist framework, nothing but a testimony would be part of DEs.

For example, Californian Criminal Jury Instructions state that

> *Except in certain cases, the testimony of only one witness can prove any fact. Before a jury concludes that the testimony of one witness proves a fact, it should carefully review all the evidence*

It is clear that this suggestion means single testimony but not single evidence. It rejects thus the extreme situation, implying that DEs has to be more robust. Let's suppose that this and similar rules refer to a case in which there is only one witness and the rest of the evidence amounts just to expert testimony assessing if the testimony is trustworthy.[35] This would be a case where there is only one proposition in DEs that points directly to g (that the defendant is guilty), the proposition that states that the witness asserted that p (which implies that g). However, in DEs there are other propositions, r, s, t…that assess the reliability of the witness report. (Recall that they would serve as defeaters of possible *undercutting defeaters* of p that could arise during the trial, or as undercutting defeaters when the assessment of the reliability of the witness that they provide turns to be negative)

In such a case, a problem arises for those who think that the numerical conception is out of place.

Resorting to technical testimony in order to prove the quality of a single testimony, far from rejecting the numerical conception, presupposes it at least in one sense. Assuming that for the proposition g there is just one single witness, and assuming that a technical witness cannot replace the judgement of the jury or judge, it has to be assumed that expert testimony is complementary. However, the obvious

---

generate certain states of affairs. The problem is pervasive and relevant whether to ascertain if the defendant is capable of doing p, or the witness is reliable about q. The capacity to bring about certain states of affairs (commit a crime, saying the truth), whether referring to the possibility, probability or ability to cause or generate something, is not sufficient to conclude what took place in this or that case under analysis. It is not permitted, without further premises, to deduce an actuality from a possibility. Actual implies possible, not the other way around. This obvious remark is at place because in the complex procedure of proving, through expert testimony, if the alleged author did commit this or that action, normally there is some weight attached to the conclusion that "his/her character is compatible with the fact under analysis". The same goes for witnesses and their capacity to tell the truth or get the things right, when this capacity is scrutinized by expert testimony. We want to propose the label "fallacy of scope" to refer to this move which based on expert testimony goes from a possibility to an actuality. Federal Rules of Evidence (USA) forbid, with exceptions, evidence regarding capacity, character, tendency or predisposition of a given defendant or witness. FRE, 412, 608.

[35] Actually, it is normally so regarding victim's testimony in cases of domestic violence.

question that arises is, complementary of what? One possible argument would be to answer that the credibility of the proposition g has increased because there is some coincidence between technical witness and what the judge or jury have seen/heard/felt (they give their own "intuitive" assessment of the witness credibility). If that were the case (as usually is), a defender of the numerical conception might argue that that's pretty close to saying that the proposition g has more credibility because more than one person has supported it. That it is *prima facie* contradictory with the assertion that "one testimony alone" could be sufficient to believe in the truth of a proposition. What is at stake here is that the credibility of the single witness has more evidence in its favour because there is more than one person ready to admit it. Under this assumption, numbers perhaps do not decide, but certainly count.[36]

But there is an obvious way to turn things back to a qualitative conception. The argument may have the following structure.[37] What would be at stake here is always one single testimony, whose creditworthiness and quality is supported for several persons ready to state (i.e. to declare) in that way. The numerical factor has its relevance at a different level, and in any case, the number is not sufficient. At that further level -the argument continues- technical testimony and jurors or judges are in a special position regarding the testimony under analysis. That is so because they could perceive and evaluate in first person the testimony as experts. What they are ready to state has a special quality: first hand, direct perception over the fact under evaluation. It is not the number, but the quality of its assessment, which transmits to the quality of their statements. There are not only many, but also good reports of what happen.

Such an argument resembles in an important way the assumption surrounding the priority of "eye-witness" over other potential witnesses. Moreover, it could constitute a continuation of the same conception. What explains our confidence in the testimony of eyewitness about what happened is always the same factor all the way down. We assume we gain relevant information (knowledge, belief) from those who in some way or another are qualified (as experts, as first person witnesses, or both).

However, the idea according to which someone has more credibility if she had a direct, first hand perception, can automatically jeopardize the assumption that underlies the relevance of expert testimony. Unless qualified, the priority of direct, firsthand knowledge undermines the epistemological value attached to the propositions r, s, t… that belong to DEs and refer to the expert testimony about the credibility of the witness. This is so because the judge (and therefore LC) lacks any means to ascertain specifically if the expert's assertion is true or not. The common ways to surmount this problem, and evade what otherwise would be a leap of faith, is evaluating witness' credibility (in this case, expert's credibility). A witness lacks credibility if her deposition is contradictory, unbelievable, erratic, twisting. These criteria

[36] There is another possibility at stake, and it is strictly normative: we should be ready to take as true what a certain *qualified* majority has decided. The argument is also numerical, but with a different justification. We tackle that possibility below.

[37] The following remarks are closely related with problems surrounding the question about dependent/independent reasons to trust a given speaker. See, Lackey 2008, Chapter 8, specially 248.

are certainly unstable because experiments and experience in courts have demonstrated, for example, that extreme precision in a witness, far from supporting its credibility, undermines it. Normally we do not remember so accurate the details. The same goes for coherence and lack of contradictions. A given speech can be "sound" in this sense, and false all the way down (that's what good novelists do every time when they write a fiction). A given set of statements can be coherent but one or all of them false. Finally yet importantly, contradiction in statements is not sufficient to dismiss as false all the propositions stated by a given speaker.

Given as it is, we face an obvious dilemma. Either first hand information has preeminence in the sense that a belief is justified when it stems from some sort of firsthand information. That would explain why what comes from "eye witnesses" and what jurors saw in trial has some sort of epistemological plus, but in that case, expert testimony cannot add too much to jurors' convictions because they get not firsthand information (about their quality as experts). On the other hand, we can accept that firsthand information is one among many sources of equal epistemological import, but that would lead to revise the reluctance against single witnessing and hearsay.

So far, given the assumptions, and the numerical and qualitative distinction, the picture is the following. Sometimes one testimony alone is not sufficient because we are not entitled to trust just the words of others, except for expert testimony and several phenomena that are not called "testimony" but are similar in all aspects to single testimony (police reports, documents where only one official states that p was the case, and so on). On the other side, whoever assumes that some cases of "single testimony" could be sufficient if the single testimony were coupled with expert testimony (about the trustworthiness of the single testimony) has to assume that the expert testimony functions in a relevant sense as an "ulterior single witness". Either you just have to rely on his words, or his words and perceptions of the witness under evaluation are complementary with what judge and jurors perceived about the single witness. It seems to be that in an important sense, the belief formed by judges, with the complement of the expert testimony, about the single witness, gains its justification for the same reasons that it is assumed that "eye witness" has its reliability. A kind of first-hand primacy. Just as the "eye witness" has an epistemological plus because she faced the facts in question, jurors' and judges' assessment of the creditworthiness of a given single testimony has a plus in terms of justification because there was some kind of firsthand information perceived at trial. If that it is not a puzzle, it is a kind of labyrinth. This is so because in legal field there are conflicting theoretical assumptions regarding if and in what sense it is justified to believe in the words of others. Testimony broadly conceived (a speaker intends to transmit information to an audience) receives different and contradictory groundings. It is perfectly legitimate, for example, to say that single witness is never sufficient, but that it is inimical with accepting that some phenomena that resembles "single witness" do give justified reasons to believe in a proposition (full stop). It is not possible to have it both and all ways.

Assuming that the practice, on the one hand, rejects the epistemic value of just pure single witness but, on the other, gives some justification to beliefs based in cases that either resemble or instantiate single witnesses, expert testimony, and eye witness, it is legitimate to question if there is an available theory that could save those assumptions maintaining a decent epistemological equilibrium.

At first sight, we might think that the best way of describing the legal practice we have just sketched is by assuming that the epistemological assumptions behind it respond to some sort of egoistic account. As we have seen in Sect. 4, egoism assumes a certain priority of first hand knowledge, and thus claims that in order to take in the word of others, we always need first hand reasons in favor of their reliability. Fricker's local reductionism might explain, for instance, our legitimate trust in certain witnesses and expert witnesses, as long as the LC can justifiably form a belief about the witness trustworthiness. However, at least this version of egoism leaves unexplained an important part of the practice, precisely that part that seems to permit trusting the word of others without having the possibility of evaluating the others trustworthiness, when the judge (and the LC) take for granted whatever stems from official's reports. Local reductionism, thus, cannot adequately surmount the first horn of the dilemma.

On the other hand, universalism seems to explain perfectly well why we do trust officials, but seems to be faced with the second horn of the dilemma. If testimony has always a positive epistemic status, why do we reject single testimony as a source of justified belief? To answer this question, we need to make some clarifications.

First, recall the reductionist-anti reductionist assumptions. We can see that there is an enormous difference between (a) accepting the general positive import of testimony; and (b) forming a belief based purely on the word of others. In the case in study, to get something like (a), being a global reductionist or an anti-reductionist makes no difference as long as there is some principle like TEP or DEP. In the case of (b), reductionists will claim that it is always needed that something like DEP is part of DEs. Otherwise, if p comes to be part of DEs just because in DS there is a proposition like "it is stated in the records that p", and there is no such thing as TEP, then p would pertain to DEs (and to DS) in an illegitimate way. Anti-reductionism does not claim that. If we assume that TEP is never an explicit part of LC's DS/DEs, then we might want to favor an anti-reductionist interpretation of the practice.

Second, we must remember that (a) does not always imply (b). We are only justified in forming a belief that p based only on the sayings of others, *when there are no undefeated defeaters present*, in this case, in DS. If there were, then we would, before coming to believe that p, need to positively defeat those defeaters. We can, thus, interpret LC's trust in officials by claiming that there are not undefeated defeaters present in DS. And explain LC's reluctance to believe that p based on single testimony by stating that in certain cases there is a presumption of dishonesty that would constitute an *undefeated undercutting defeater* that needs to be defeated (by, for instance, expert testimony or the judge's own psychological evaluation of the testifier's character). This presumption of dishonesty might stem from our principle of presumptive innocence conjoined with the content of the testimony (in an extreme case, when someone testifies that g). We would have here a case where non-epistemic considerations have influence in the content of DS. In other cases, the undefeated defeater would stem from the content of the testimony, or from its contradiction with other pieces of evidence (a case of an *undefeated rebutting defeater*).

Third, and in relation with the last consideration, we can explain our trust in some expert testimony without having any positive reasons for doing so by appealing to the absence of *undefeated defeaters* of any kind.

For these reasons, we believe that an anti-reductionist approach explains most of the platitudes pertaining to the legal practice, successfully explaining why the dilemma is misconstrued.

There is, though, one last consideration regarding the distinction between NIT and legal testimony presented in Sect. 3. According to the universalist interpretation of the practice, there would be no interesting difference between some saying that p and someone asserting that p in the witness stand. This could be seen as a problem, since we do want to say that there is actually a difference between both phenomena. Our response to this possible objection is that, in order to explain that difference in an epistemological way, we should be able to accept an interpersonal reading of legal testimony, which gives epistemic import to the witness personal assurance that p. Placing a hand in the bible is paradigmatic of this feature. However, this reading would imply an evidential practice that is in the opposite road of the actual one. It would imply accepting the word of single witnesses, just because they put themselves as guarantors of the truth of their testimony.

We claim, thus, that whilst there is a difference between NIT and legal testimony, that difference cannot be traced to the epistemology behind our current legal practice. We need to look at other institutional features. Contrary to what is often assumed in the legal field, we cannot appeal only to epistemological considerations to hold together all the assumptions. That leads to our final point, regarding normative considerations.

6 Conclusion: Legal Testimony, Exclusionary Rules and Epistemology

We have seen in Sect. 3 what would be the best theoretical reconstruction of LC's doxastic system DS. Among the reasons that (derivatively) limited the doxastic evidential system of LC are not only epistemological reasons, but also normative ones. This means that it is possible to infer from a legal system a group of rules that authorizes to use certain propositions based on evidence and prohibits using others. According to these normative considerations, even if on epistemological grounds we are entitled to entertain a belief as justified, the LC is not entitled in that way qua LC. The opposite is true as well. Even if on epistemological grounds we are not entitled to entertain some beliefs, the normative considerations allows LC to use it in certain context. The authorization or prohibition to use certain norms and evidence varies within the legal system depending on which branch of law LC is in. What can be part of DS (and therefore of DEs) is not the same in labour law, tort law and criminal law. Depending on the branch in question, one and the same piece of evidence could belong to DS in one case, and be excluded in the other. If a system excludes from DS the declaration of a relative or family member's in divorce process, but allows it in tort or criminal process, that cannot be explained resorting to any epistemological consideration regarding the relevance, importance, weight of single or no single testimony. The question hinges on normative considerations in terms of goals, risks and benefits that, allegedly, the legal systems are ready to afford in that given context. Another issue that remains unexplained within epistemological considerations is the difference between NIT and legal testimony, and the institutional importance of the latter. However, we could shed some light to the puzzle or labyrinth pointed out in Sect. 5 regarding the harmonization of assumptions about single, expert and eye witness, by applying some epistemological considerations to the legal practice.

Somc important legal norms and practices are better explained resorting to epistemological considerations, but not all are better explained in that way. Epistemology, even epistemology of testimony, cannot explain all the aspects involved in legal evidence, because of the simple reason that in legal context, it is not only relevant what epistemological support receives from testimony a given proposition, but also if that support is relevant to the goals and purposes of the practice itself. In this sense, legal evidence has to do with belief, justification and evidence, but cannot be reduced to them. That should be, at this point, by itself, *evident*.

References

Adler, J. E. (1994). Testimony, trust, knowing. *The Journal of Philosophy, 91*, 264–275.

Adler, J. E. (2002). *Belief's own ethics*. Cambridge, MA: The MIT Press.

Amaya, A. (2013). Coherence, evidence, and legal proof. *Legal Theory, 19*, 1–43.

Audi, R. (2003). *Epistemology: A contemporary introduction to the theory of knowledge* (2nd ed.). London: Routledge.

Chisholm, R. M. (1976). *Theory of knowledge*. Englewood Cliffs: Prentice Hall.

Christensen, D. (2004). *Putting logic in its place: Formal constraints on rational belief*. Oxford: Oxford University Press.

Coady, C. A. J. (1992). *Testimony: A philosophical study*. Oxford: Clarendon.

Dummett, M. (1994). Testimony and memory. In B. Krishna Matilal & A. Chakrabarti (Eds.), *Knowing from words* (pp. 251–272). Dordrecht: Kluwer Academic Publishers.

Foley, R. (2004). *Intellectual trust in oneself and others*. Cambridge: Cambridge University Press.

Fricker, E. (1994). Against gullibility. In B. Krishna Matilal & A. Chakrabarti (Eds.), *Knowing from words* (pp. 125–161). Dordrecht: Kluwer Academic Publishers.

Fricker, E. (1995). Telling and trusting: Reductionism and anti-reductionism in the epistemology of testimony. *Mind, 104*, 393–411.

Fricker, E. (2006). Testimony and epistemic autonomy. In J. Lackey & E. Sosa (Eds.), *The epistemology of testimony* (pp. 225–250). Oxford: Oxford University Press.

Goldman, A. I. (1999). *Knowledge in a social world*. Oxford: Clarendon.

Goldman, R., & Goldman, A. (2009). Review of truth, error, and criminal law. An essay in legal epistemology, by Larry Laudan. *Legal Theory, 15*, 55–66.

Gorphe, F. (1927). *La Critique Du Temoignage*. París: Dalloz.

Hume, D. (1978). *A treatise on human nature*. Oxford: Oxford University Press.
James, W. (1897). *The will to believe and others essays in popular philosophy* (Reprinted 1907), New York: Longmans.
Jurs, A. W. (2012). Balancing legal process with scientific expertise: Expert witness methodology in five nations and suggestions for reform of Post-Daubert U.S. reliability determinations. *Marquette Law Review, 95*, 1329–1415.
Kusch, M. (2002). *Knowledge by agreement: The programme of communitarian epistemology*. Oxford: Oxford University Press.
Lackey, J. (2008). *Learning form words. Testimony as a source of knowledge*. Oxford: Oxford University Press.
Lackey, J., & Sosa, E. (Eds.). (2006). *The epistemology of testimony*. Oxford: Oxford University Press.
Laudan, L. (2006). *Truth, error, and criminal law: An essay in legal epistemology*. New York: Cambridge University Press.
Lipton, P. (1998). The epistemology of testimony. *Studies in History and Philosophy of Science, 29*, 1–31.
Margolis, E., & Laurence, S. (1999). *Concepts: Core readings*. Cambridge, MA: MIT Press.
McDowell, J. (1994). Knowledge by hearsay. In B. Krishna Matilal & A. Chakrabarti (Eds.), *Knowing from words* (pp. 195–224). Dordrecht: Kluwer Academic Publishers.
Moran, R. (2006). Getting told and being believed. In J. Lackey & E. Sosa (Eds.), *The epistemology of testimony* (pp. 272–306). Oxford: Oxford University Press.
Pollock, J. (1986). *Contemporary theories of knowledge*. Totowa: Rowman & Littlefield.
Reid, T. (1993). *The works of Thomas Reid*, Sir W. Hamilton (Ed.), Charlottesville: Lincoln-Rembrandt Publishing.
Ross, A. (1986). Why do we believe what we are told? *Ratio, 28*, 69–88.
Schauer, F. (2015). *The force of law*. Cambridge, MA: Harvard University Press.
Twining, W., Schum, D., & Anderson, T. (2005). *Analysis of evidence*. Cambridge: Cambridge University Press.
Van Cleve, J. (2006). Reid on the credit of human testimony. In J. Lackey & E. Sosa (Eds.), *The epistemology of testimony* (pp. 50–74). Oxford: Oxford University Press.
Wigmore, J. (1901). Required numbers of witnesses; A brief history of the numerical system in England. *Harvard Law Review, 15*(2), 1901.
Wittgenstein, L. (1972). *On certainty*. New York: Harper Torchbook.

ERRATUM

Pragmatics and Law

Practical and Theoretical Perspectives

Francesca Poggi and Alessandro Capone

F. Poggi, A. Capone (eds.), *Pragmatics and Law*, Perspectives in Pragmatics, Philosophy & Psychology 10, DOI 10.1007/978-3-319-44601-1

DOI 10.1007/978-3-319-44601-1_18

In chapter 1 titled "Slippery Meaning and Accountability", the text font and punctuation is updated.

In chapter 3 titled "What Inferentialism Tells Us About Combinatory Vagueness in Law", text has been deleted.

In chapter 11 titled "Disputable Means: Pragmatic Knowledge Practices in Sovereign Debt Agreements. Reflections on the Argentinian Case", the text font and punctuation is updated.

In chapter 12 titled "The Role of Pragmatics in the Web of Data", corrections are made in text throughout the chapter.

In chapter 13 titled "Pragmatics of Adjudication. In the Footsteps of Alf Ross", punctuation is updated throughout in the text.

In chapter 16 titled "Epistemic Stance in Courtroom Interaction", font size updated throughout the text.

The updated original online version for this book can be found at DOI 10.1007/978-3-319-44601-1

F. Poggi, A. Capone (eds.), *Pragmatics and Law*, Perspectives in Pragmatics, Philosophy & Psychology 10, DOI 10.1007/978-3-319-44601-1_18

About the Authors

Federico José Arena is currently Researcher at the National Research Council of Argentina (Conicet). Among his recent publications: *El convencionalismo jurídico. Un recorrido analítico*, Marcial Pons (2014); "Una alternativa para el escepticismo interpretativo: convenciones y cuasirrealismo en la interpretación jurídica", *Doxa*, 2013; "Persiguiendo la tesis convencionalista", *Eunomía*, 2013; "Which Kind of Discretion in Constitutional Adjudication?", *German Law Review*, 2013; "Antirrealismo moral vs. positivismo jurídico", *Revista de Filosofía del derecho – Infojus*, 2012; "On other participants' cooperative attitude in legal context", *Phenomenology and Mind*, 2012; "Marmor on the Arbitrariness of Constitutive Conventions", *Jurisprudence*, 2011; "Normas sociales y expectativas bajo El imperio de la ley", *Analisi e diritto*, 2011.

E-mail: fjarena@gmail.com

Hrafn Asgeirsson is Senior Lecturer in Philosophy and Law at the School of Law, University of Surrey Guildford, UK. His main publications are: "On the Instrumental Value of Vagueness in the Law," forthcoming in *Ethics*; "Textualism, Pragmatic Enrichment, and Objective Communicative Content," forthcoming in *Inquiry*, special issue on law and language; "Vagueness and Power-Delegation in Law: A Reply to Sorensen," in eds. M. Freeman and F. Smith, *Current Legal Issues: Law and Language* (Oxford University Press, 2013); "Vagueness, Comparative Value, and the "Lawmakers' Challenge", *Archiv für Rechts- & Sozialphilosophie* 98:3 (2012); "From the Nature of Things to Nature Itself: The Philosophy of Ólafur Páll Jónsson," forthcoming in eds. G. Malenfant and J. Dagsson, Heimspeki – *For the Wisdom of the World: Inquiring into Contemporary Icelandic Philosophy* (University of Iceland Press).

E-mail: h.asgeirsson@surrey.ac.uk

Mauro Barberis is currently full professor of Jurisprudence at the University of Trieste; he taught at the universities of Genoa and Bologna and he is co-editor of the

F. Poggi, A. Capone (eds.), *Pragmatics and Law*, Perspectives in Pragmatics, Philosophy & Psychology 10, DOI 10.1007/978-3-319-44601-1

journals “Ragion pratica”, “Materiali per una storia della cultura giuridica” and “Il mulino”. Among his 30 books in Italian and Spanish: *L’evoluzione nel diritto* (*Evolution in Law*, Giappichelli, 1988), *Europa del diritto* (*Europe and Law*, Mulino, 2008); *Libertad* (Nueva Vision, 2002); *La eterogeneidad del bien* (Fontamara, 2005); *Etica para Juristas* (Trotta, 2008); *Introduccion al estudio del derecho*; (Palestra, 2014) and *Juristas y filosofos. Una historia de la filosofia del derecho* (Communitas, 2015).

E-mail: barberis@units.it

Leticia Barrera is currently a permanent researcher from CONICET, Argentina’s National Research Council, at Instituto Superior de Estudios Sociales (ISES). She holds an LLB from Universidad Nacional de Tucumán, Argentina, a Master in Economic Development in Latin America from Universidad Internacional de Andalucía at La Rábida, Spain, a Master of Laws, and a Doctorate in Law from Cornell University. Her scholarly work draws at the intersection of different areas of socio-legal concern, like legal anthropology, law and society, science and technology studies, and contemporary social thought. Her research interest focuses on the production and circulation of knowledge among legal experts, in particular within the judicial institution, on which she has published a book (Siglo XXI Editores, 2012) and several journal articles and book chapters.

E-mail: leticiabarrera@yahoo.com

Hernán G. Bouvier is Researcher at National Research Council (CONICET-Argentina), professor of Philosophy of Law at Universidad Nacional de Córdoba, Argentina, professor of Criminal procedure at Universidad Nacional de Córdoba, Argentina and Editor in Chief, *Discusiones* Review (Review on legal philosophy, political philosophy and criminal law). Topics he has written on include: Particularism in Ethics and Philosophy of Law, with special emphasis in the discussion around Dancy’s and McDowell’s works and the possibility to apply that discussion in the field of legal philosophy – in that topic he has published *“Particularismo y Derecho: un abordaje postpositivista en el ámbito práctico/Particularism and law: a post-positivist approach”* (Spain, Marcial Pons, 2012); Philosophy of language and legal philosophy, in particular the rule following problem (Wittgenstein); Criminal law and philosophy of criminal law.

E-mail: hernanbouvier@gmail.com

Damiano Canale is head of the Department of Legal Studies “A. Sraffa” and full Professor of Philosophy of Law at Bocconi University (Milan, Italy). He has published two monographic volumes: *Forme del limite nell’interpretazione giudiziale*, CEDAM (2003); *La costituzione delle differenze. Giusnaturalismo e codificazione del diritto civile nella Prussia del ‘700,* Giappichelli (2000). He is co-editor with G. Tuzet of the volume *The Planning Theory of Law. A Critical Reading*, Springer (2013), and he edited with P. Grossi and H. Hofmann the volume *A History of the Philosophy of Law in the Civil Law World, 1600–1900*, Springer (2009). He wrote a number of essays, among them: “Looking for the Nature of Law: On Shapiro’s

Challenge", *Law & Philosophy*, 31 (2012); "Consequences of Pragmatic Conceptualism", *Ratio Juris*, 22 (2009).

E-mail: damiano.canale@unibocconi.it

Alessandro Capone is associate professor in general linguistics at the Department of Cognitive Science at the University of Messina. He has two Ph.D.s from Oxford and the University of Palermo. He is chief editor of the Springer series Perspectives in pragmatics, Philosophy, psychology; he is launching the journal Pragmatics and Philosophy for Mouton De Gruyter, together with Istvan kecskes; he is in the editorial board of the Journal of Pragmatics, Intercultural Pragmatics, etc. He has published several papers in international journals such as Pragmatics and Cognition, Intercultural Pragmatics, Journal of Pragmatics, Pragmatics and Society, Australian Journal of Linguistics, La Linguistique, RASK: International journal of language and communication, International journal of language Studies, etc. He has published four monographs, including The pragmatics of indirect reports (pp. 320) for Springer. He edited several books for CSLI, JP, Springer, Lincom. He coedited Interdisciplinary Studies in pragmatics, culture and society with JL Mey. he has two habilitations as full professor in: general linguistics; philosophy of language.

Pompeu Casanovas is Director of Advanced Research, Professor of Philosophy and Sociology of Law at the UAB Law School, and founder and Head of the UAB Institute of Law and Technology (IDT-UAB). He served as Principal Investigator in over 50 national, European, and international projects. He has published over 10 books and more than 200 scientific articles in the areas of legal philosophy, legal sociology, intellectual history, and AI & Law. He is General Co-Editor of the *Law, Governance and Technology Series* (LGTS) at Springer Verlag, the *Journal of Open Access to Law* (JOAL) at the University of Cornell, and the *Journal of Catalan Intellectual History*, at de Gruyter. He belongs to the Scientific Board of Directors of the Erasmus Mundus Joint Doctorate in Law, Science and Technology (2012–2017). Dr. Pompeu Casanovas holds a Degree in Law and a Doctorate in Philosophy at the UAB, and he has carried out post-doctoral research as Visiting Scholar (VS) at the Universities of Bari (and Rome, 1987), UCSD (California, 1990–1991), and Stanford (California, 2000–2001). He has been VS at the University of Bologna (CIRSFID, 2006) and CNR (IRSIG, 2006), and Visiting Professor at Victoria University (Melbourne, 2012–2013). In March 2014 he was appointed Adjunct Professor at the Royal Melbourne Institute of Technology. Since March 2016 he is Professorial Research Fellow at Deakin University (Victoria, Australia), working at the CRC D2D programme.

E-mail: pompeu.casanovas@uab.cat, p.casanovasromeu@deakin.edu.au

Pierluigi Chiassoni is Professor of Jurisprudence, at TILPH – Tarello Institute for Legal Philosophy, Department of Law, University of Genoa. He is president of the Master Programme "Global Rule of Law and Constitutional Democracy". Among his numerous articles: *Bentham on Legal Order*, in G. Tusseau (ed.), *The Legal Philosophy and Influence of Jeremy Bentham*, Routledge (2014); *A grande evasão:*

técnica e cultura na jurisprudencia sobre o casamento homossexual, in F. Dutra Asensi, D. Giotti de Paula (eds.), *Tratado de Direito Constitucional. Constitução no século XXI*, Vol. 2, Elsevier/Camous Juridico, 2014. Among his numerous books: *Diritti umani, sentenze elusive, clausole* ineffabili, Aracne (2011); *Desencantos para abogados realistas*, Universidad Externado de Colombia (2012); *El análisis económico del derecho*, Lima (2013).

E-mail: pierluigi.chiassoni@unige.it

Louise Cummings is professor in Linguistics at the School of Arts and Humanities, Nottingham Trent University. She is former assessor for English Language and Linguistics on the Academic Awards Committee of the British Federation of Women Graduates; Referee for the Italian Ministry for Education, University and Research; Member of: Higher Education Academy; Royal College of Speech and Language Therapists; Health Professions Council. Among her books: (ed.) (2014) *Cambridge Handbook of Communication Disorders*, Cambridge University Press; (2014) *Pragmatic Disorders*, Springer; (2014) *Communication Disorders*, Palgrave Macmillan; (2014) *Communication Disorders Workbook*, Cambridge University Press. Among her recent essays: (2014a) 'Informal fallacies as cognitive heuristics in public health reasoning', *Informal Logic*; (2014b) 'The 'trust' heuristic: Arguments from authority in public health', *Health Communication*; (2014c) 'Circles and analogies in public health reasoning', *Inquiry*.

E-mail: louise.cummings@ntu.ac.uk

Ekkehard Felder is Dean of the faculty of Modern Languages (from 2011); he is Co-Founder (in 2010) and Director of the *European Centre for Linguistics* (with Prof. Dr. Dr. h.c. Ludwig M. Eichinger, Institute of the German Language, Mannheim, and Prof. Dr. Jörg Riecke, University of Heidelberg), and founder and coordinator of the research network *Language and Knowledge*. From 2006 he is Full Professor (Linguistics), at German Department, University of Heidelberg. Among his numerous publications: Editor of the series *Sprache und Wissen* (*Language and Knowledge*). Berlin/New York: de Gruyter and Editorial Board of the eJournal "Language and Law"; 2012: (Editor with M. Müller, F. Vogel): Korpuspragmatik. Thematische Korpora als Basis diskurslinguistischer Analysen. Berlin/New York: de Gruyter (LIT Bd. 44).

E-mail: ekkehard.felder@gs.uni-heidelberg.de

Jorge González-Conejero graduated in Computer Science at the UAB (2003). He holds a PhD in Computer Science entitled "Coding Techniques Addressed To Images Containing No-Data Regions Within JPEG2000 Framework". He is currently vice director at the IDT-UAB. His research interests are focused on Image and Video Processing, Knowledge acquisition and representation, and Data Protection. He has authored and coauthored 18 contributions to international conferences and 3 on international journals. He has participated in large European consortiums such as CAPER- Collaborative information, Acquisition, Processing, Exploitation and Reporting for the prevention of organised crime (261712-FP7-

SEC-2010-1), SAVASA- Standards based approach to video archive, search and analysis (285621-FP7- SEC-2011-1) and Building Interoperability for European Civil Proceedings Online (JLS/2009/JCIV/AG/0035).

E-mail: jorge.gonzalez.conejero@uab.cat

Michael S. Green is Dudley W. Woodbridge Professor of Law at College of William & Mary since 2012. Among his numerous honours and awards: (2014–2015) Plumeri Award for Faculty Excellence, College of William and Mary; (2012) Chair, AALS Section on Conflict of Laws (Chair-Elect 2011); (2011–2012) Plumeri Award for Faculty Excellence, College of William and Mary; (2010–2012) Robert E. and Elizabeth S. Scott Research Professor, William and Mary Law School; (2009–2010) Blackstone Lecturer, William and Mary Law School; (Since 2009) Contributing Editor Jurisprudence Section of Jotwell; (2001–2002) Visiting Research Fellow, University of London, King's College School of Law. He published numerous articles and the book *Nietzsche and the Transcendental Tradition* (University of Illinois Press, 2002).

E-mail: msgre2@wm.edu

Kasia M. Jaszczolt is Professor of Linguistics and Philosophy of Language at the University of Cambridge and Professorial Fellow of Newnham College, Cambridge. One of her current project concerns *Expressing the Self: Cultural Diversity and Cognitive Universals*; the other is a monograph *The Semantics of Linguistic Interaction* (forthcoming from OUP in 2015). Her authored books include *Representing Time* (2009, OUP), *Default Semantics* (2005, OUP), *Semantics and Pragmatics* (2002, Longman) and *Discourse, Beliefs and Intentions* (1999, Elsevier). She is General Editor of a book series *Oxford Studies of Time in Language and Thought*. She authored over 80 research articles and edited 11 volumes including *The Cambridge Handbook of Pragmatics* (2012, CUP). In 2012 she was elected member of Academia Europaea.

E-mail: kmj21@cam.ac.uk

Teresa Marques is currently a *Marie Curie* Intra-European research fellow with the Philosophy of Law Research Group at the Universitat Pompeu Fabra in Barcelona. She is the editor of the open-access journal of philosophy *Disputatio*, and the PI of the project *Contextualism, Relativism and Practical Conflicts and Disagreement*, part of the collaborative European research project *Communication in Context (CCCOM)*, one of the three EuroUnderstanding projects under the EUROCORES scheme of the European Science Foundation. She has recently been selected for an *Ikerbasque* Research Fellowship 2014, and also been elected as a member of the new steering committee of the European Society for Analytic Philosophy. Among her recent publications: (with Manuel García-Carpintero) 2014, "Disagreement about taste: commonality presuppositions and coordination", *Australasian Journal of Philosophy*, 2014; "Relative correctness", *Philosophical Studies* 167 (2014); Doxastic Disagreement, *Erkenntnis*, 79 (2014).

E-mail: mariateresa.marques@upf.edu

Janus Mortensen is Associate Professor at the Centre for Internationalisation and Parallel Language Use at the University of Copenhagen, Denmark. He has studied functional linguistics, pragmatics and sociolinguistics at Roskilde University and Cardiff University, and received his PhD in linguistic studies in 2011 from Roskilde University based on a thesis on epistemic stance marking in the use of English as a lingua franca. His current research interests include forensic linguistics with particular focus on courtroom interaction, sociolinguistic perspectives on the use of lingua francas, language ideology and language choice in multilingual settings, as well as sociolinguistic aspects of university internationalization.

E-mail: jamo@hum.ku.dk

Sune Sønderberg Mortensen is an Assistant Professor of Danish language at the department of Culture and Identity at Roskilde University. After receiving a PhD degree in Danish functional grammar in 2013, his main focus of research has been forensic linguistics, including the study of courtroom interaction and the general establishment of forensic linguistics as a field of research in Denmark. His general research interests revolve around structural-functional syntax, semantics and pragmatics, in Danish, English and cross-linguistically, and his publications include a number of studies in the structures and functions of subordinators and subordinate clauses, as well as the semantic, interactional and discursive features of certain interjections and other lexical units.

E-mail: sunes@ruc.dk.

Nicola Muffato is lecturer in Legal Philosophy at the I.U.S.L.I.T. Department of the University of Trieste. He has been visiting professor at the University of Girona (2009–2012) and at the University “Pompeu Fabra” of Barcelona (2012), where he teached Legal Philosophy and General Theory of Law, and teaching assistant in Legal Argumentation at the “Bocconi” University of Milan (2010). He has written three books and several articles on the semantics and pragmatics of normative language. Amongst his main research interests are the “nature” of normativity, ethical particularism, the structure of legal justification, the limits of judicial discretion in statutory construction and the interpretation of law, and the method of social sciences.

E-mail: nicola.muffato@gmail.com

Francesca Poggi is associate professor at the Department “Cesare Beccaria”, University of Milan, where she teaches *General Jurisprudence*, *Law and Bioethics* and *Gender Legal Studies*. She is member of the Ethical Committee of the University of Milan. She has published a book on permissive norms – *Norme Permissive*, Giappichelli, 2004 – and a collection of lectures on general legal concepts – *Concetti teorici fondamentali*, ETS, 2013 – as well as a number of essays in Italian, English and Spanish. Among them: *Significado literal: una noción problemática* [*Literal Meaning: a Troublesome Concept*], “Doxa”, 30, 2008; *A Commitment to Naturalism. Bentham and the Legal Realists*, with F. Ferraro, in G. Tusseau (ed.), *The Legal Philosophy and Influence of Jeremy Bentham*, Routledge (2014). She edited a collection of essays on law and bioethics – *Diritto e bioetica*, Carocci (2013).

E-mail: francesca.poggi@unimi.it

Florencia Rimoldi is teaching assistant at the Philosophy Department of the University of Buenos Aires, where she teaches on theory of knowledge. Her areas of interest include epistemology, social epistemology and philosophy of mind. In her doctoral dissertation "Knowledge as a Social Value" she offers a novel account of knowledge as independent from justification and closely related to the nature of testimony and its social practice thereof. She has published papers on theory of knowledge, particularly arguing against the idea that knowledge is a natural class. She is currently working in an interdisciplinary project between epistemology and cognitive psychology to determine the psychological requirements for knowledge.
E-mail: rimoldiflorencia@hotmail.com

Víctor Rodríguez-Doncel is a postdoc research fellow at Universidad Politécnica de Madrid (Spain) interested in copyright and data protection in the Semantic Web. He received his PhD in 2010 from Universitat Politècnica de Catalunya after having done research in the industry (GMV, Barcelona Digital) and the academia (Aristotle Univ. of Thessaloniki in Greece, Univ. Pompeu Fabra) on different topics of Artificial Intelligence. Since 2012 he is with the Ontology Engineering Group. He is editor of the ISO/IEC21000-19 international standard, the Media Value Chain Ontology for representing the intellectual property along the multimedia value chain. He is also author of two books, ten JCR indexed journal papers and has participated in several European research projects. He is also partner at the startup company Mirubee.
E-mail: vrodriguez@fi.upm.es

Alessio Sardo is Post-Doctoral Researcher at Bocconi University (Milan, Italy) and Member of the Tarello Institute (Genoa, Italy). His main publications are: *Autonomia e interpretazione: l'ideale di Francisco Laporta* [*Autonomy and Interpretation: Francisco Laporta's Ideal*], in "Analisi e Diritto", 2011; *Three Theories of Balancing: A Comparison*, in "Dignitas", 2012; *In the Mood for meaning: Considerazioni sulla teoria pragmaticamente orientate dell'interpretazione giuridica*, in "Diritto e Questioni Pubbliche", Vol. 2013; *Alexy, sorazmernost in zatrjevanje pravilnosti* [*Alexy, proportionality and the claim to correctness*], in "Revus" vol. 2014.
E-mail: alessio.sardo@unibocconi.it

Marina Sbisà is full professor of Philosophy of Language at the Philosophy Department of Trieste University, which she has also directed for several years. She has worked in the fields of philosophy of language and semiotics, with particular attention to pragmatic issues. Her main research interests include ordinary language philosophy, speech act theory and discourse analysis. She collaborated with J.O. Urmson (Oxford) on the revised edition of J.L. Austin, *How to Do Things with Words* (1975). Among her more recent publications: *Detto non detto: le forme della comunicazione implicita* [*Said Not Said: the forms of the implicit communication*] (Laterza, 2007); *How to Read Austin* in "Pragmatics" 9 (2007); *Uptake and Conventionality in Illocution* in "Lodz Papers in Pragmatics" 1 (2009); *Austin on*

Meaning and Use in "Lodz Papers in Pragmatics" 1 (2012); *Evidentiality and Illocution* in "Intercultural Pragmatics" 9 (2014). Recently she also edited, with Ken Turner, the book *Pragmatics of Speech Actions* (De Gruyter Mouton, 2013)

E-mail: sbisama@units.it

MIX
Papier aus verantwortungsvollen Quellen
Paper from responsible sources
FSC® C105338

If you have any concerns about our products,
you can contact us on
ProductSafety@springernature.com

In case Publisher is established outside the EU,
the EU authorized representative is:
Springer Nature Customer Service Center GmbH
Europaplatz 3, 69115 Heidelberg, Germany

Printed by Libri Plureos GmbH
in Hamburg, Germany